A Charlton Standard Catalogue

Canadian Coins

Volume One: Numismatic Issues

69th EDITION, 2015

W. K. Cross

TORONTO, O

TRADEMARK NOTICE

The terms **Charlton, Charlton's, The Charlton Press, the Charlton Cataloguing System, Charlton Numbers** and abbreviations thereof, are trademarks of **Charlton International Inc.** and shall not be used without written consent from Charlton International Inc.

DISCLAIMER

While every care has been taken to ensure accuracy in the compilation of the data in this catalogue, the publisher cannot accept responsibility for typographical errors.

Library and Archives Canada Cataloguing in Publication

Canadian coins (Charlton Press)
Canadian coins : a Charlton standard catalogue

Annual
59th ed. (2005) -
Continues: Charlton standard catalogue of Canadian coins, ISSN 0706-0424
ISSN 1716-0782
ISBN 978-0-88968-366-2 (69th edition)

1. Coins, Canadian--Catalogs. 2. Coins, Canadian--Prices--Periodicals. and collecting. I. Title

CJ18610.S82 59- 2005- 737.4971'029 C2005-902187-X

Printed in Canada
in the Province of Quebec

EDITORIAL

Editor	W. K. Cross
Assistant Editor	R. J. Graham
Editorial Assistant	Jean Dale
Graphic Technician	Davina Rowan
Photography	Scott Cornwell
Cover illustration	Phil Arnold

SPECIAL MENTION

A special thanks must go to Mike Marshall of Trenton, Ontario, for his work on the Chinese counterfeit problem that is facing Canadian coin collectors.

CONTRIBUTORS TO THE 69TH EDITION

We would like to thank the following for their contributions to the 69th edition: **Randy Ash**, Alberta; **Sandy Campbell**, Nova Scotia; **Brian Cornwell**, Ontario; **Ray De Posdesta**, Ontario; **Mark Drake**, Toronto; **Jaime Flamenbaum,** Ontario; **Brian Grant-Duff**, British Columbia; **J. Hazeleger**, British Columbia; **Tim Henderson**, New Brunswick; **Jerry Himelfarb**, Ontario; **Michael Joffre**, Quebec; **Roger Kerr**, Ontario; **Roger Paulen**, Ontario; **James Thomas**, Arizona **Rudolph Viehl**, Ontario

CORRECTIONS

The Publisher welcomes information for future editions from interested collectors and dealers concerning any aspect of the listings in this book.

The Charlton Press

Editorial Office
P.O. Box 69509
5845 Yonge Street
Willowdale, Ontario M2M 4K3
Tel.: (416) 488-1418 Fax: (416) 488-4656
Tel.: (800) 442-6042 Fax.: (800) 442-1542
www.charltonpress.com email: chpress@charltonpress.com

GEORGE V 1936 DOT 10 CENTS
PCGS SPECIMEN-68
SOLD BY HERITAGE AUCTIONS
2010 JANUARY SIGNATURE WORLD COIN AUCTION, $184,000.

FOREWORD TO VOLUME ONE: NUMISMATIC ISSUES

The 69th edition of *Canadian Coins, Volume One, Numismatic Issues* was published September 2014. The precious metals' market had stabilized, rising very slightly and improving the tone of the coin market. The dealers, no longer facing a falling metals market, have a renewed outlook on coins resulting in a slight upward basis to prices.

PRICING

Several years ago we at the Charlton Press instituted a line in our pricing tables which was based on the *Population Reports* of third party grading companies. We used these reports to keep the collector informed on what we considered listings that made little sense to price. Populations of two, three, four, or even up to a total of ten coin examples, made little sense for us to try and arrive at a suggested market value. The potential volatility was just too great. If you have only five coins of one specific date spread over ten grades, what is the market price for an EF coin when there is only one in the available five.

It is flattering to see that the "only" line has been adopted by "Trends".

NO, OR MISSING CHROME FIVE-CENT ERROR COINS OF 1944 TO 1954

In 1944 the Mint found that chrome plating the dies increased the life of the die. Their next reasoning was "let's chrome plate the blanks" which they did for the five-cent steel and nickel blanks of 1944 to 1954. Of course, as with all processes, a few of the blanks missed or received only partial chrome plating. The error blank when struck is now an error coin with no chrome or missing chrome. Collectors being collectors, start to collect these error coins. Collectors then turned to third party graders to grade and certify the "missing chrome" error coins. The editors of "Trends" now list these error coins. The circle is complete. Enter a chemical reaction where a little muriatic acid is added to a water bath and a 1953 NSF five-cent coin is placed in the bath – after a short period of time the chrome dissolves. The result is a coin that is extremely difficult to differentiate from an error coin made at the Mint. At the Charlton Press we have avoided listing these errors, and we suggest, when you cannot tell the good from the bad, you do the same.

PRICING OF MODERN HIGH GRADE COINS, 1968 TO 2014

Fifty Cents 1982, Large and Small Bead Varieties

TYPE LARGE BEAD	MS-63	MS-64	MS-65	MS-66
Price - 68th edition	$7.	$15.	$30.	$70.
Pop. Report 2013	#14	#27	#41	#12
Price 69th edition	$7.	$15.	$30.	$75.
Pop. Report 2014	#15	28	#48	#16

TYPE SMALL BEAD	MS-63	MS-64	MS-65	MS-66
Price - 68th edition	$60.	$75.	$200.	$400.
Pop. Report 2013	#292	#352	#119	#4
Price 69th edition	$35.	$75.	$200.	$300.
Pop. Report 2014	#440	#496	#165	#10

This table is a mirror image of all the years and denominational listings for modern Canadian coins. Now what does this table tell us?

- A coin increases in value as the certified population decreases across the grades. Understandably, since the certified population is a measure of scarcity.
- There is little incentive for a collector to incur grading costs for common coins unless they are seeking highest grade placement.
- There is a large incentive for a collector to incur a certification cost if they can confirm a high grade and variety for their coin.
- As time passes the number of certified examples increases while the price decreases. This holds true when the collector population is moving sideways to down. We have not seen a growing collector population since the early 1960s.
- A high catalogue price is a magnet for increased certification supply.
- As the supply increases the price falls because currently there is no increase in collector base. The increase in supply, which is dealer driven, is immediately sold. Mainly in online auctions in which the price falls faster than in land auctions.

THIRD PARY GRADING

It has been 28 years since myself, Brian Cornwell and Ingrid Smith founded ICCS. A lot of water has passed under the bridge, but none so glaring as the recognition that maybe some coin varieties do not exist. As a result we are proposing to remove the following varieties from our listings, all of which have zero population numbers:

Canada:	1892 5¢ Portrait 5; 1872H 25¢ Portrait 1; 1890H 50¢ Portrait 3.
Newfoundland:	1865 5¢ Portrait 2; 1870 5¢ Portrait 2; 1885 10¢ Portrait 3.

If you disagree, please write with confirmation of your claim.

W. K. Cross

HOW TO USE THIS CATALOGUE

Pricing Tables: Their Use and Meaning

Five basic pricing tables are found within the circulation section of the 68th edition. Like all tables in all coin catalogues they are based on finish, and then the grade within that finish. The cohesive factor in the five tables is that while the finish may vary, the design is that of the coin in circulation. Please refer to page xxii for an explanation on finishes. This is a **must read** section.

TABLE ONE: 1858 to 1952
Two finishes are priced: Circulation and Specimen.
The example below is from page 150.

Twenty-Five Cents, Crowned Portrait, 22 Leaves, Short Bough Ends, 1870-1880.

DATE / MINT / PORTRAIT/VAR.	MINTAGE (thous.)	G-4	VG-8	F-12	VF-20	EF-40	AU-50	AU-55	MS-60	MS-63	MS-65	SP-63	SP-65
1870 Q1	900	25.	40.	55.	150.	300.	550.	700.	1,350.	3,000.	—	4,000.	15,000.
1870 Q1 (PE)	Incl.	*	*	*	*	*	*	*	*	*	*	4,000.	15,000.
1870 Q2	Incl.	ONLY FOUR CERTIFIED										*	*
1871 Q1	400	75.	175.	350.	600.	1,200.	2,000.	—	—	—	—	8,000.	20,000.

Line One: 1870 Portrait Q1. Mintage in thousands. Prices in nine grades from G-4 to MS-63. A dash appears in the MS-65 column which means that no Canadian grading company has certified this coin in that grade. The last two columns are for specimen coins which are priced in two grades, SP-63 and SP-65.

Line Two: Again, a 1870 Portrait Q1, but now with a plain edge (PE). The "stars" in columns G-4 to MS-65 indicate that no circulating coins of this type exist, but they do in specimen condition, and those are priced in two grades.

Line Three: A listing of an extremely rare 1870 Portrait Q2 twenty-five cent coin. When a value is not present but rarity is given in words, it means there is no market data available. In such cases the price is a matter between a buyer and seller, when an example becomes available.

Line Four: 1871 Portrait Q1. Prices are given for the grades G-4 to AU-50, and dashes appear in the AU-55 to MS-65 pricing columns, indicating that none or only one example of this date has been graded by a Canadian Grading Service to 2013. Coins with a specimen finish are priced in two grades, SP-63 and SP-65.

TABLE TWO: 1953-1967
Three finishes are priced: Circulation, Proof-like and Specimen.
This pricing table has two columns devoted to proof-like singles which are derived from uncirculated sets (an RCM term) issued by the Royal Canadian Mint. The column PL-65 is considered the average grade in which coins from these sets are found. Naturally, grades higher and lower will be found and prices will move on both sides of the average. PL-65 HC is for similar coins but now with a heavy cameo finish on the relief of the design. The example shown below is from page 157.

Twenty-Five Cents, Laureate Portrait, Caribou Design, 1953-1964.

DATE / VARIETY	MINTAGE	AU-55	MS-60	MS-63	MS-64	MS-65	MS-66	PL-65	PL-65 HC	SP-65	SP-67
1953 NSF LD	10,456,769	10.	15.	20.	35.	125.	1,000.	—	—	300.	600.
1953 SF SD	Included	12.	20.	25.	65.	425.	—	275.	400.	300.	600.
1954	2,318,891	20.	25.	45.	130.	500.	—	100.	175.	*	*

Line One: 1953 NSF LD. Circulation grades from AU-55 to MS-66 are priced. Dashes in columns PL-65 and PL-65 HC show that no proof-like coins of this variety have been graded. As the specimen columns contain prices, we cannot dismiss the possibility of proof-like examples existing.

Line Two: 1953 SF SD. Prices in all columns shows that coins may be found in all three finishes and grades, signifying all finish varieties are possible.

Line Three: 1954. Prices in columns AU-55 to MS-65, and PL-65 and PL-65 HC. A full allotment of circulation and proof-like finishes, however, stars in the specimen columns signify this date was not produced with that finish.

TABLE THREE: 1968-1980, 1992, 1996-2010

Three finishes are priced: Circulating (CLT), Non-circulating (NCLT), and Specimen.

This is the first pricing head that combines the two conflicting circulating finishes, but the finishes on the two types are distinguishable. However, now it takes more knowledge and more care on everyones part, especially that of the grading services. The example shown below is from page 158.

Twenty-Five Cents, Tiara Portrait, Caribou Design, 1968-1972

DATE	MINTAGE	MS-63 C	MS-64 C	MS-65 C	MS-66 C	MS-65 NC	MS-66 NC	MS-67 NC	SP-66	SP-67
1968	88,686,931	5.	10.	35.	100.	20.	45.	—	—	—
1969	133,037,929	5.	10.	40.	100.	10.	50.	100.	50.	100.

TABLE FOUR: 1981-1995

Four finishes are priced: Circulating (CLT), Non-circulating (NCLT), and Specimen and Proof.

The example below is from page 160.

Twenty-Five Cents, Modified Tiara Portrait, Caribou Design, Nickel, 1981-1986.

In 1981 the Royal Canadian Mint revised their product line, adding a proof finish to their offerings. The proof coins were struck on standard nickel planchets.

DATE	MINTAGE	MS-63 C	MS-64 C	MS-65 C	MS-66 C	MS-65 NC	MS-66 NC	MS-67 NC	SP-66	SP-67	PR-67	PR-68
1981	131,583,900	5.	15.	75.	—	5.	15.	50.	10.	20.	10.	25.
1982	171,926,000	5.	15.	60.	—	5.	15.	50.	10.	20.	10.	20.

TABLE FIVE: 2011-2013

Two finishes are priced: Circulating (CLT) and Specimen.

The example below is from page 171.

Twenty-Five Cents, Uncrowned Portrait, Caribou Design, Multi-Ply Plated Steel, 2011-2014.

DATE	DESCRIPTION	MINTAGE	MS-64 C	MS-65 C	MS-66 C	MS-67 C	SP-66	SP-67
2011		187,520,000	10.	15.	20.	50.	10.	25.
2012		153,450,000	10.	20.	35.	75.	10.	25.
2013		68,480,000	10.	20.	35.	55.	10.	35.
2014		N/A	10.	20.	35.	60.	10.	35.

NOTE ON TABLE THREE

The use of "circulation finish" has long been divided by the Royal Canadian Mint into two categories: (1) A circulation finish for coins (business strikes) used in the economy, and (2) a circulation finish for collector coins which are distributed by the marketing department of the Royal Canadian Mint, mainly in the sale of sets.

The steps in manufacture of both these coins are very close. Business strike coins are now produced at the Winnipeg mint, while coins produced for uncirculated sets are struck at the Ottawa mint. The dies are identical with the exception that those used to produce uncirculated coins for sets are polished, the planchets are of a higher quality, the rate of striking is slower, and finally, the coins are removed from the press by hand.

For circulating coinage it is a production process, all operations move at a rapid pace, right to the end of the line where the coins fall into bins, awaiting bulk packaging either in bags or rolls. Hundreds of thousands of coins are produced in this manner.

For Uncirculated Business Strikes (C) it is easy to visualise the difficulty a collector will experience in obtaining high grade examples from a production process, while high grade examples from Uncirculated Sets (NC, non-circulating) is just a snip of the pliofilm packaging away.

Great care must be exercised when buying and selling high grade circulation coins and uncirculated coins from sets for there is a difference in scarcity level between the two. Care must be exercised to see that the correct classification has been applied to the coin before it was priced. The number of MS-65 NC or higher coins is only limited by the total number of sets broken open or, could be broken open and graded.

GEORGE V 5 CENTS 1921
PCGS MS-67, PRINCE OF CANADIAN COINAGE
SOLD BY HERITAGE AUCTIONS
SIGNATURE WORLD COIN AUCTION, 2010 JANUARY, $115,000.

TABLE OF CONTENTS

INTRODUCTION

Canadian Coins is an illustrated, descriptive price catalogue for the principal types of commercial and commemorative coins used in Canada over the years, including pre-Confederation coinages. As a Standard Catalogue it provides an accurate overview and introduction to Canadian numismatics and current market values. Each major variety of all issues of Canadian coins is listed, illustrated and priced. Several minor varieties that have a wide appeal to collectors, such as Arnprior dollars, are also included. Historical introductions provide important background information for each series, and relevant technical information is provided wherever available. A summary of the principal foreign coins used during the French and British regimes is included, as well as local, pre-decimal issues. The decimal series is complete for the provinces of British North America and Canada from its inception to the present, and also includes patterns, essais and test tokens.

The new reader should find in this catalogue all the basic information needed to identify and evaluate individual coins as he or she embarks upon an old and widely enjoyed hobby.

This edition is just the latest in our continuing efforts to bring readers the best possible reference book for one of Canada's most popular and profitable pastimes. Welcome, then, to this new edition of the *Canadian Coins* and to the exciting field of Canadian numismatics.

THE COLLECTING OF CANADIAN DECIMAL COINS PAST AND PRESENT

Today, the majority of those collecting Canadian numismatic material specialize in the decimal coin series. The collecting popularity of decimal coins is a relatively recent phenomenon, however. When Canada's first coin club was formed in Montreal in 1862, there was little interest in either coins or paper money. Eighty years later this was still the case. Most collectors specialized in Canadian tokens, the private coppers that served for so long as a medium of exchange in the absence of official coins. Decimal coins were mostly collected by type. One or two examples of each design were sufficient, and there was little concern regarding the relative scarcity of the various dates and varieties.

The current preoccupation with collecting decimal coins by date and variety arose in the 1940's, under the influence of U.S. dealer Wayte Raymond. Shortly after World War II and on into the 1950's, Canadian pioneers J. Douglas Ferguson, Fred Bowman, Sheldon Carroll and Leslie Hill attempted to establish the relative rarities of the decimal coins issued up to that time.

In 1950 collectors in the Ottawa area joined with scattered groups and individuals to form the Canadian Numismatic Association. Its official publication, and annual conventions beginning in 1954, served to bridge the miles and facilitate the exchange of information and ideas.

Two years after the C.N.A. was formed, the Charlton Standard Catalogue made its appearance. Early editions were modest paperback pamphlets with line drawings, but they were a serious attempts to list and price Canadian coins, tokens, paper money and some medals. The first hard-cover edition of 128 pages appeared in 1960. By 1971 it had grown to 200 pages, and by 1978 so much additional numismatic information was available that it was decided the needs of collectors could best be met by splitting the catalogue into separate, specialized works.

The 27th (1979) Edition became the '*Standard Catalogue of Canadian Coins*,' now issued yearly. This was followed by the annual edition of the *Charlton Standard Catalogue* of *Canadian Government Paper Money,* the *Standard Catalogue of Canadian Colonial Tokens*, and the *Charlton Standard Catalogue of Canadian Bank Notes,* A new series, Canadian Historical Medals, is under development. Now available are Volume One: *Canadian Exhibition, Fair and Carnival Medals* and Volume Two: *Canadian Association, Society and Commercial Medals*.

BUILDING A COLLECTION

Decimal coin collections can be formed in a variety of ways. Coins may come from pocket change, family hoards, the bank, the mint or from other collectors. In general, older coins no longer circulate and the excitement of searching through change for missing dates has been diminished by the withdrawal of silver coins from circulation.

Collecting is a matter of individual taste. Some people collect by design type, others concentrate on one or two denominations or monarchs, while some brave souls try to collect the entire decimal series. Regardless of which path you choose, there is a variety of coin boards, envelopes and other supplies available to help house and organize your collection. For reasons of security many collectors keep their best coins in a bank vault.

Another decision that must be made when building a collection is the minimum state of preservation one will accept when buying coins. As a general rule, it is advisable to buy the best condition coins one can afford.

AGE - RARITY - DEMAND - CONDITION - VALUE

The value of a coin on the numismatic market is dictated by a complex mixture of factors. One feature that those unfamiliar with coins often mistakenly believe to be of great importance is age. That age is a minor contributor to value is illustrated by the fact that the 1969 Large Date variety 10 cents is worth far more than the 1870 10-cent piece, a coin nearly 100 years older!

Basically, a coin's value is determined by a combination of supply and demand. The 1870 50-cent piece does not command as high a premium as the 1921 coin of the same denomination because there are many more 1870s than 1921s available.

Finally, the state of preservation of a coin markedly influences its value. It is not unusual for an uncirculated (brand new) George V silver coin, for example, to sell for 100 times what a coin of the same date and denomination would bring in well-worn condition.

FINISHES

Introduction: A coin finish simply means the surface quality imparted to a blank during the striking process. At the striking stage the main facts influencing the quality of the finish are: (1) The quality of the blanks, (2) the finish of the dies, (3) the speed and pressure of the press, and (4) the number of times the blank is struck.

Circulation Finish: *Brilliant Relief Against a Satin Background*. This is the most common finish found on all business strikes, from the one cent to the two dollar coins. These are production coins struck at the rate of 700 to 800 per minute. They are allowed to tumble into waiting hoppers, then put through counting and wrapping machines before being sent to the banks.

Uncirculated Finish: *Brilliant Relief Against a Satin Background*. This process is very similar to the circulation finish above with common dies being used, but with slower striking speeds and definitely more care in the loading and unloading of the press. There are few less handling marks than the circulation variety, but still marks may be found. The Uncirculated finish is used by the Numismatic Department of the Mint on singles and sets offered to collectors, or sold into the gift market.

Proof-Like Finish: *Frosted to Semi-Mirror Relief Against a Semi-Mirror Background.* These coins, are produced on a slow moving press with reasonably high pressure. The planchets and dies are polished with each coin being removed from the press individually. Large coins may be struck more than once.

The following die states are found on proof-like coins:

(1) **Ultra Heavy Cameo:** Full frosting across the relief of the coin, both effigy and legend, when viewed from all directions under full lighting conditions.

(2) **Heavy Cameo:** The frosting is neither full nor evenly applied across the relief of the coin. In fact, some areas may appear bright when viewed under full lighting conditions.

(3) **Cameo (C):** Touches of frosting may appear on the relief of the coin. There will be bright areas when the coin is viewed under full lighting conditions.

(4) **No Cameo**. No frosting, all relief areas will appear bright. There is no difference in contrast between the bright field and a bright relief. The majority of coins are from this die state.

Nickel has a hardness higher than silver making the striking of coins more difficult. In 1968 with the change from silver to nickel coinage came the need for a new finish on numismatic items. That finish is:

Brilliant Uncirculated Finish: *Brilliant Design, Legends and Dates Against a Brilliant Background.* Coins are struck by a slow moving press using high pressure, and polished dies. Blanks are inserted, and coins removed by hand. This finish was used on all packaged singles and sets offered by the Mint from 1968 to 2004. In 2004 production of sets was divided between Uncirculated and Brilliant Uncirculated.

Specimen Finish: From 1858 to 2012 there have been five different modifications used by the Mint on specimen coinage.

1858-1901: **A Brilliant Relief against a Brilliant Background**
1902-1938: **A Frosted Relief against a Frosted Background**
1937-1995: **A Brilliant Relief against a Brilliant Background**
1996-2009: **A Brilliant Relief, Frosted Legends and Date against a Line Background**
2010-2012: **A Brilliant Relief, Frosted Legends and Date against a Laser Lined Background**

Proof Finish: *Frosted Relief Against a Mirror Field.* This is the highest quality finish used by the Royal Canadian Mint on Canadian coinage. By definition all coins with this finish are designated Ultra Heavy Cameo (UHC). They are identified in the pricing tables by PR.

Reverse Proof Finish: *Mirror Relief Against a Frosted Background.* This type of finish is at times called "satin matte" because of the background texture. All elements of the design that are in relief have a highly reflective finish.

Bullion Finish: *Brilliant Relief Against a Parallel Lined Background.* This finish was first used in 1979 on gold maple leafs for the bullion program. The finish is found on gold, platinum, palladium and silver maples. As this finish is the standard used on the maple leaf issues the grading designation is Mint State (MS).

Bullion-Specimen (Reverse Proof): *Brilliant Relief Against a Satin Background.* A finish not often used, it can be found on special edition bullion singles and sets.

Bullion-Proof: *Frosted Relief Against a Mirror Background.* This finish is the same as that found on all numismatic proof issues.

VICTORIA GRADING GUIDE

OBVERSE DESCRIPTIONS FOR VARIOUS SERIES

Victoria Laureate Portrait 1858

L. C. Wyon's laurel wreath portrait. This is L. C. Wyon's version of the Young Head portrait designed earlier by his father, W. Wyon The long hair styles of the Victorian era played an important part in this braided design.

High points of obverse portrait design.

- The starting strands of the braid over the top of the ear.
- Central leaves of the laurel wreath.
- Two twists making up the back knot supporting the short curls
- Eyebrow.

MS-65 No traces of wear. Nearly perfect. May have minor hairlines or handling contact marks in secondary areas. Full original lustre must be present.

MS-64 No traces of wear. Very minor contact marks and only in the field areas. A full strike, with original lustre.

MS-63 No trace of wear. Will have minor contact marks and blemishes. Typical strike with original mint lustre.

MS-60 No traces of wear. Contact or handling marks are present. May be on all parts of the design. Lustre may be disturbed, but is present to high degree. The strike may be weak.

AU-55 Very slight traces of wear will show on the highest points. Lustre is still strong and present over most of the coin. Again, it will be disturbed only at the highest points.

AU-50 Slight traces of wear now appear on all high points. 60 to 70% lustre is present. Mint lustre has now been disturbed in the fields around the design.

EF-40 Hair on the first strand of the braid has lost detail, but the braid itself is generally sharp and clear. The eyebrow and the two twists of the top knot show loss of detail.

VF-20 The braid, top knot and eyebrow show loss of detail. The design while present is losing sharpness. The braid from the start to down around the ear is beginning to blur.

F-12 The braid, along with the top knot design have lost sharpness. Braiding has begun to run together. The two twists of the top knot are merging. The central leaves of the laurel wreath show wear.

VG-8 No detail in braid around ear.

G-4 The braid, laurel wreath, top knot and facial features are worn through. Basically what is left of the portrait design is a silhouette.

Victoria Diadem Portrait 1870-1901

L. C. Wyon's diadem portrait of Queen Victoria illustrates the use of long hair that was fashionable during her teenage years, 1830-1837, when she was crowned Queen. The hair style produces the highest points of the design. Victoria's hairstyle, which started with a combed parting in the middle, and hair down both sides was crowned with the diadem. The resulting side lengths of hair were swept back over the diadem and twisted to form a knot at the back of the head, all held in place by an ornamental band.

The hair being drawn back over the diadem and twisted to form the back knot results in the highest points of the design.

High points of obverse portrait design.

- The swept back hair covering the ears and the back of the diadem. The twist designs in the back knot.
- Eyebrow and cheek bone
- Top row of jewels in the diadem
- Ribbon end overlapping neck.

MS-65 No traces or wear. Full original mint lustre. May have a few very minor blemishes and contact marks. Overall eye appeal very pleasing.

MS-64 No traces of wear. Full strike with full mint lustre. Minor contact marks in the field areas. Good eye appeal.

MS-63 No traces of wear. Original mint lustre. May have minor contact marks and a few hairline scratches. Overall an attractive coin.

MS-60 No traces of wear. Mint lustre is dull and may have been disturbed. Contact marks are heavy and numerous. Hairline scratches are present. Eye appeal is poor.

AU-58 Very minor signs of wear on the drawn back strands of hair over the ear and diadem. Minor disturbance of the mint lustre is evident on highest points.

AU-55 Minor signs of wear shown on highest points. Lustre is still strong over all parts of the coin except the high points. Over 75% of original mint lustre is still present.

AU-50 Traces of wear now visible on all high points. Mint lustre is now down to 50% of original. The halo effect around the portrait is clearly evident.

EF-40 Traces of wear have now moved down to the eyebrow, the back knot, the top jewels and the ribbon ends. 25% of lustre remain around the letters of the legend.

VF-20 The sharpness of the design is lost. The hair covering the ear and diadem, the back knot, top jewels and the ribbon ends overlapping the neck are clear but have lost detail. Original mint lustre has disappeared. Eyebrow and facial features show wear.

F-12 The hair over the ear and diadem are worn. The diadem is clear but top jewels are worn. The lower twist of back knot is worn, with strands beginning to merge. The overlapping neck ribbon is worn through. Eyebrow and cheek bone are worn.

VG-8 The hair covering the ear and diadem, and moving to the back knot have no detail: they are worn away. The diadem itself shows considerable wear with vague outlines of the top jewels. Eyebrow and facial features worn.

G-4 We are now down to a silhouette with the only detail showing that of the head band on the very back of the neck used to hold the diadem in place.

EDWARD VII
GRADING GUIDE

Edward VII 1902-1910
Imperial State Crown Portrait

G. W. DeSaulles' coronation portrait of Edward VII. Edward is shown in his coronation robes, wearing the Imperial State Crown and the Order of the Garter. The Order is secured at the shoulder with a ribbon bow. In grading the bands, the pearls and the jewels within the bands are important parts of the crown.

These coins were struck with a concave or convex die radius which will greatly influence the wear on the respective coin.

High points of obverse portrait design.

- The bands, pearls and jewels within the crown all have rounded surfaces.
- Moustache and beard of the right of the ear.
- Eyebrow, ear and nose.
- Order of the Garter ribbon bow

MS-65 No traces of wear. A nearly perfect coin with very minor hairline scratches and contact marks only in secondary areas. Must have full original mint lustre with good eye appeal.

MS-64 No traces of wear. Full mint lustre. Full strike with minor contact marks in the field areas. Good eye appeal.

MS-63 No traces of wear. Will have minor hairline scratches, contact marks and blemishes. Will have original mint lustre.

MS-60 No traces of wear. Hairlines, contact marks and blemishes are present on all parts of the design. Lustre may be disturbed but is present to high degree.

AU-55 Very slight traces of wear will appear on the high points. Mint lustre is still strong but showing signs of losing its freshness.

AU-50 Slight traces of wear on all high points. 60 to 70% of original mint lustre still remains. The halo effect is found in the fields around the design.

EF-40 The bands and jewels of the crown have lost their round contours. They are flattened. The eyebrow, tip of the moustache and ribbon bow are worn. Lustre is no longer present.

VF-20 The central bands, jewels and pearls are worn away. The ear, beard to the right of the ear, moustache, eyebrow and ribbon bow all show wear and loss of detail.

F-12 Detail on all the highest points have lost considerable detail. The central crown bands, with jewels and pearls of the crown are 50% worn. Again, all high points show considerable wear.

VG-8 Over 75% of crown bands and jewels are worn away. The hairline, beard, and moustache all blend together. The ermine collar of the coronation robes has lost all detail.

G-4 Only a silhouette of Edward remains. All portrait detail is worn away.

GEORGE V
GRADING GUIDE

George V 1911-1936
Imperial State Crown Portrait

Sir E. B. Mackennal's coronation portrait of George V. This portrait illustrates George V wearing the coronation robes used by Edward VII. Two obverse legend varieties exist. The portrait now faces left, and the design has greater relief. The high points are the same as for the Edward VII coinage, but more so.

The die radius was not varied on this design. The relief of the portrait of George V corrected for the shallow portrait of Edward VII.

High points of obverse portrait design.

- The bands, pearls and jewels of the crown have rounded surfaces.
- Moustache and beard to the right of the ear.
- Eyebrow, ear and nose.
- Order of the Garter ribbon bow

MS-65 No traces of wear. A nearly perfect coin with very minor hairline scratches and contact marks only in secondary areas. Must have full original mint lustre.

MS-64 No traces of wear. Full mint lustre will be present. Minor contact marks in the field areas. Good eye appeal.

MS-63 No traces of wear. Will have minor hairline scratches, contact marks and blemishes. Will have original mint lustre.

MS-60 No traces of wear. Hairlines, contact marks and blemishes are present on all parts of the design. Lustre may be disturbed but is present to high degree.

AU-55 Very slight traces of wear will appear on the high points. Mint lustre is still strong but showing signs of losing its freshness.

AU-50 Slight traces of wear on all high points. 60 to 70% of original mint lustre still remains. The halo effect is found in the fields around the design.

EF-40 The bands and jewels of the crown have lost their round contours. They are flattened. The eyebrow, tip of the moustache and ribbon bow are worn. Lustre is no longer present.

VF-20 The central bands, jewels and pearls are worn away. The ear, beard in front of the ear, moustache, eyebrow and ribbon bow all show wear, with loss of detail

F-12 The highest points of the design have lost considerable detail. The central crown bands, with jewels and pearls are 50% worn away. Again, all high points show considerable wear.

VG-8 Over 75% of crown bands and jewels are worn away. The hairline, beard, and moustache all blend together. The ermine collar of the coronation robes has lost all detail.

G-4 Only a silhouette of George remains. All portrait detail is worn away

GEORGE VI
GRADING GUIDE

George VI 1937-1952
Uncrowned Portrait

T. H. Paget's portrait of George VI was designed for use on the coins of Great Britain and was the first British domestic coinage portrait approved for use on the coinage of most Commonwealth countries. At this time the master tools for Canadian coinage were still being produced by the Royal Mint, London, England. Up until 1949-1950 any modifications to the die tools which were necessary were done in London. After that date all major tool production was transferred to the Ottawa Mint, which had acquired duplicating equipment in 1948-1949 What has this to do with grading question It is simple: two and possibly three obverse portraits are used on the George VI coinage between 1937 and 1952. The first is the rather shallow design features, especially in the hair, of 1937 to 1944. The second is the strengthened portrait design used on the silver dollar of 1945, showing more and deeper detail. The five and twenty-five cents portrait modifications of 1951 and 1952, again with the lowering of the relief, add difficulty in assigning grades to these coins.

Since we are only dealing with portrait designs and their characteristic wear in these thumbnail outline, the collector should be aware of the relief variations on George VI coinage that will affect the grade.

The forties also saw the grading description change because of the disappearance of the satin lustre that was familiar for so long on Canadian coinage, to be replaced with shiny fields resulting from the chrome plating of the dies used to prolong die life.

High points of obverse portrait design.

- The wear on the hair above the ear and that forming the left side of the parting.
- The eyebrow and the pinna and lobe section of the ear.

MS-66	No traces of wear. Above average strike and eye appeal, full mint lustre. Very minor contact marks.
MS-65	No traces of wear. A nearly perfect coin with very minor hairline scratches and contact marks only in secondary areas. Must have full original mint lustre.
MS-64	No traces of wear. Full mint lustre. Minor contact marks in only the field areas. Must have a full strike. A coin with good eye appeal.
MS-63	No traces of wear. Will have minor hairline scratches, contact marks and blemishes. Will have original mint lustre.
MS-60	No traces of wear. Hairlines, contact marks and blemishes are present on all parts of the design. Lustre may be disturbed but is present to high degree.
AU-55	The highest points begin to show very slight wear, the hair above the ear, the eyebrow, and ear lobe all exhibit minor wear. The lustre, or shiny fields show slight disturbance. 75% of the mint bloom is still present.
AU-50	Slight wear on all high points. Only 50% of the mint finish remains.
EF-40	The eyebrow, the pinna and lobe of the ear, the wave of hair above the ear and the top part all show wear. The only mint finish will appear between the letters of the legend.
VF-20	The eyebrow is worn away. The ear and hair wave above the ear have lost detail and are starting to flatten. There is wear on the cheek bone. No mint lustre is present.
F-12	The eyebrow and cheek bone are worn away. A bald effect is starting, with very little detail of hair remaining. The outline or the ear has flattened.
VG-8	Only the outline of hair and ear remains. The eyebrow is worn away.
G-4	The portrait is reduced to a silhouette.

ELIZABETH II
GRADING GUIDE

Elizabeth II Laureate Portrait 1953-1964

Mary Gillick's portrait of Elizabeth II was issued in two varieties: No Shoulder Fold and Shoulder Fold. The weak patterns appear almost identical. However as in the George VI series there are examples minted with dies with a positive die radius such as the issues of 1959 and 1962. These convex coins will show a faster rate of wear on the obverse portrait.

High points of obverse portrait design.

- Eyebrow.
- The hair is swept back over the ear and folds under the laurel wreath.
- The laurel wreath starting slightly over the midpoint down to the ribbon ends.

MS-66 No traces of wear. Above average strike and eye appeal, full mint lustre. Very minor contact marks.

MS-65 No traces of wear. A nearly perfect coin with very minor hairline scratches and contact marks only in secondary areas. Must have full original mint lustre.

MS-64 No traces of wear, with a full strike. Must have full mint lustre with only minor contact marks in the field areas. Must have good eye appeal.

MS-63 No traces of wear. Will have minor hairline scratches, contact marks and blemishes. Will have original mint lustre.

MS-60 No traces of wear. Hairlines, contact marks and blemishes are present on all parts of the design. Lustre may be disturbed but is present to high degree.

AU-55 Very slight wear on the eyebrow and other high points. The mint shine has been disturbed and now forms a distinct halo around the portrait.

AU-50 Slight wear on the highest points. Over 50% of the mint shine is lost.

EF-40 There is now slight wear on the swept back hair and the laurel wreath. The eyebrow is worn. The dress folds are distinct. Mint shine has all but disappeared.

VF-20 The hairline from above the eye down to the nape of the neck shows wear. The four central leaves of the laurel wreath are worn. The dress folds are clear.

F-12 The four central laurel leaves and the top next leaves are almost worn through. The hair detail above and below the ear has disappeared. Dress folds are worn.

VG-8 All detail of the laurel leaves and hair have been worn away. The shoulder folds of the dress are also worn flat.

Elizabeth II Tiara Portrait 1965-1989

Arnold Machin's portrait of Elizabeth II. We must deal with three different metal compositions in this series: 80% fine silver, 1965 to part of 1967; 50% fine silver 1967 to 1968, and 100% nickel from 1968 to 1989. Each of these compositions will wear at a different rate. This, of course, does not affect the degree of wear. A forty year old silver coin will show more wear than a nickel coin of the same age. Other, more important factors are the different design modifications that are found in this series.

For the one cent through to the twenty-five cents, the Machin portrait moved without change through the changing metal compositions until 1976. In 1977 the detail on the portrait was modified. In 1978 the portrait reverted to that used between 1965-1976. In 1981 the portrait was again modified to a low relief version.

The silver coins are long removed from circulation so the wear patterns may never be known. Nickel coinage will last years and it is much too early for wear patterns to have developed

At present the only grades in this series with which the collector should be concerned are Mint State: MS-60 and higher.

Elizabeth II Diadem Portrait 1990-2003

Dora de Pédery-Hunt's portrait of Elizabeth II. There is only one obverse variety for this series. However, the composition which began as 100% nickel changed in the 1999-2000 period to the new multi-ply plated steel, which is 93.25% steel, 4.75% copper and 2.00% nickel. This metal combination will prove interesting over time, when the wear on the outer nickel layer will expose the copper layer on the high points. At present only mint state graded coins are of importance.

Elizabeth II Mature Portrait 2003 to Date

Susanna Blunt's portrait of Elizabeth II. Currently only one variety is in use. Again, only the mint state grades are important in the circulation issues.

Currently there is only one obverse variety, the uncrowned version. As with the previous portrait only the mint state grades command any collector premium in the circulation issues.

Specimen and proof coins are issued by the Royal Canadian Mint in newly defined finished complementary to their names. These are collector issues produced and packaged under special conditions. They normally come enclosed in their protective capsule, thus wear as we know it in the circulation issues does not exist, Instead, the quality of the strike and the care and handling play an important part in their condition.

In the previous pages only the obverse of the coin was discussed with points of wear and loss of mint lustre used to determine the grade.

However, a coins does have three sides, obverse, reverse and edge, and all three sides must be assessed before an overall grade may be established.

FRATERNAL AFFILIATION

Over the years, coin clubs have sprung up in many Canadian communities. In addition, both Canada and the United States have national organizations which hold annual conventions.

Coin clubs constitute one of the most attractive features of present-day collecting. They offer beginning collectors the opportunity for good fellowship and the encouragement and knowledge of more experienced collectors. The larger groups maintain lending libraries and publish a journal or newsletter on a regular basis. Memberships and other information can be obtained from:

Canadian Numismatic Association
5694 Highway #7 East, Suite 432
Markham, Ontario
Canada L3P 1B4
Tel.: (647) 401-4014 Fax: (905) 472-9645
Email: info@rca.ca

Ontario Numismatic Association
P.O. Box 40033, Waterloo Sq. P.O.
75 King Street South
Waterloo, Ontario
Canada N2J 4V1
www.ontario-numismatic.org/index.html

The American Numismatic Association
818 N. Cascade Avenue
Colorado Springs, Colorado
U.S.A. 80903-3279
www.money.org

COIN CERTIFICATION SERVICES

In recent years there has been an increase in the number of North American companies that offer third party professional coin grading services. Another service offered is that of rendering an opinion whether a particular coin is genuine or counterfeit. Most of these companies operate along similar lines, that is, a coin is submitted by its owner for an independent grading and/or authentification assessment, an opinion is offered along with a certificate and a fee is charged on a per coin basis. These services are widely used by collectors and investors who recognize their grading skills are not at an expert's level. Most dealers also make use of such services because their clients often demand that the coins they buy have an official certificate with them. To date the most popular U.S. coin grading services appear to be Professional Coin Grading Service (PCGS), Numismatic Guaranty Corporation (NGC) and ANACS (American Numismatic Association Certification Service). These three services specialize in U.S. coinage. In Canada two services are currently grading coins, International Coin Certification Service (ICCS) and Canadian Coin Certification Service (CCCS).

CANADA

Canadian Coin Certification Service (CCCS)
Box 1051
Ste-Basile-Le-Grand
Quebec J3N 1M5 Canada
Tel.: (450) 723-1204
www.canadiancoincertification.com

International Coin Certification Service (ICCS)
2010 Yonge Street, Suite 202
Toronto, Ontario, M4S 1Z9. Canada
Tel.: (416) 488-8620 Fax: (416) 488-6371

UNITED STATES

Numismatic Guaranty Corporation of America (NGC)
P.O. Box 4776, Sarasota
Florida 34320, U.S.A.
Tel.: (941) 360-3990 Fax: (941) 360-2553
www.ngccoin.com

Professional Coin Grading Service (PCGS)
P.O. Box 9458, Newport Beach
California 92658, U.S.A.
Tel.: (800) 447-8848 or (949) 833-0600
www.pcgs.com

FOREIGN COINS IN CANADA

Strictly speaking, Canada (rather, the areas that now form Canada) did not have a coinage struck for its specific use until the mid-19th century. After 1820, some provincial governments issued their own coppers, but this was without imperial government sanction until the 1850s. Thus, for some two centuries Canada relied on foreign coins to provide the lifeblood for her commerce.

The importance of foreign coins in our currency history has not been given the emphasis it deserves in Canadian catalogues. Certainly it is difficult to deal with this subject. None of the foreign coins that were once so important here can strictly be called Canadian. This includes the coins of the French regime, some of which have been listed in past catalogues. To simply list some French issues is both misleading and illogical. The Spanish-American dollar, for example, was a more important coin in our overall currency history than any French (or British) coin ever was. A more realistic listing must include coins of France, Great Britain, Spain and Spanish-America, Portugal and the United States.

It has been decided to attempt to list the most important foreign coins that circulated in Canada, regardless of their country of origin. In order to qualify for listing a coin must have circulated in colonial Canada in reasonable quantity. The many coins that filtered into North America in small quantities through trade cannot be listed.

NOTE: The prices listed below for broad types of coins, which may encompass several separate types and a span of many years, are for the most commonly encountered form of the coin only. Readers are advised to see specialized foreign catalogues for specific varieties, dates and prices.

COINS OF THE FRENCH REGIME

During the French regime (c.1600-1760), French imperial coins were intermittently shipped to New France by the king or were imported by local merchants. Occasionally these were supplemented by general colonial coinages not intended for circulation in France. But, as New France was just one of the recipients of the colonial issues, they cannot be considered to have been minted specifically for Canada. French coins became less important in Canada after 1760. The silver ecus and ½ ecus, however, remained in commercial use well into the next century.

Between 1680 and the early 1720's, French coins were subject to considerable variation in the rates at which they were to be officially current. We will not attempt to detail these changes or "reformations" for each coin. A single example is sufficient to make the point. One of the few French coins with its original value actually stated on it is the "mousquetaire" or 30-denier piece minted between 1710 and 1713. Its initial rate of 30 deniers was lowered to 27 deniers in 1714 and to 22 deniers the next year. It remained at that level until the wild inflation of John Law (1720-1721), when it soared to 60 deniers and quickly fell back to 45 deniers. In 1724 its rate was returned to 27 deniers and in 1732 it was lowered to 24 deniers. It continued at that level in New France until the Conquest.

By 1726 the French government realized the folly of frequent changes in the value of coins and generally the currency was stabilized.

MINT MARKS ON FRENCH COINS.

Numerous mints produced French coins. Only for issues produced by a small number of mints will the listings by mint be separated. The following mint marks were employed on coins that circulated in quantity in New France and British Canada:

A - Paris	K - Bordeaux	S - Reims	& - Aix
B - Rouen	L - Bayonne	T - Nantes	AA - Metz
C - Caen	M - Toulouse	V - Troyes	BB - Strasbourg
D - Lyon	N - Montpellier	W - Lille	)(- Besancon
E - Tours	O - Riom	X - Amiens	a cow - Pau
G - Poitiers	P - Dijon	Y - Bourges	
H - LaRochelle	Q - Perpignan	Z - Grenoble	
I - Limoges	R - Orleans	9 - Rennes	

COPPER COINS

DENIER TOURNOIS.

Along with the copper double and liard, the denier was one of the predominant coins in circulation in New France up to the early 1660's. The denier, although rated at 1 denier in France, circulated as a 2-denier piece in New France. The merchants saw a chance for a quick profit and imported these coins in large quantities. This resulted in an oversupply prompting the government at Quebec to ban the denier altogether in 1664.

DATE / TYPE	VG	F	VF	EF
1589-1649				
Henri IV	40.	60.	150.	350.
Louis XIII	50.	75.	175.	400.
Louis XIV	35.	50.	125.	275.

DOUBLE TOURNOIS.

In 1664 the Order of the Sovereign Council which demonetized the denier allowed the double to remain in circulation but reduced its value to 1 denier to curb its excessive importation. It had formerly circulated at 4 deniers in New France.

DATE / TYPE	VG	F	VF	EF
1589-1647				
Henri IV	40.	60.	150.	350.
Louis XIII	45.	70.	150.	400.
Louis XIV	180.	300.	450.	750.

LIARD.

Until the Order of Sovereign Council of 1664, the liard passed in New France as a 6-denier piece. After 1664 its value was reduced to 2 deniers to discourage its excessive importation.

DATE / TYPE	VG	F	VF	EF
1643-1774, (13 types)				
Louis XIV	25.	50.	125.	300.
Louis XV	25.	50.	125.	300.

COPPER COINAGE OF 1710-1712.

The first coinage of this denomination in copper took place in 1710-1712. When first issued the ½ sol was rated at 6 deniers.

DATE / TYPE	VG	F	VF	EF
1710-1712 ½ Sol				
Louis XIV	50.	100.	200.	500.

COPPER COINAGE OF 1719-1724.

This coinage consisted of a liard, a ½ sol and a sol. The middle denomination (the half sol) was shipped to New France in large amounts in 1720.

½ Sols

1 Sols

DATE / TYPE	VG	F	VF	EF
1719-1724				
½ Sol	50.	100.	200.	400.
Sol	50.	125.	300.	600.

Note: These prices are for "type" coins only. Certain dates, and mints are rarer than others, and will command higher prices. The prices listed are for the least expensive date/mint.

COLONIAL 6 AND 12 DENIERS, COINAGE OF 1717.

The Perpignan mint was to issue 1.5 million 12 deniers, and three million 6 deniers, struck specifically for the French colonies. The copper that was used was too brassy and of poor quality, and the production was stopped. Known examples of this issue usually have cracked flans, and may have pits on the surface.

6 Deniers

12 Deniers

DATE / TYPE	VG	F	VF	EF
1717				
6 Deniers	Extremely Rare			
12 Deniers	Extremely Rare			

COLONIAL 9 DENIER COINAGE OF 1721-1722.

This was a special colonial issue imported by a private trading company, the Company of the Indies. Following difficulties in circulating their new coins, the company attempted to have them transferred to the government of New France. This was not successful, so most of the coinage was returned to France in 1726 with only 8,000 plus pieces put into circulation in New France. These coins were also sent to other French colonies.

DATE / TYPE	VG	F	VF	EF
1721B	500.	900.	3,500.	10,000.
1721H	175.	350.	800.	2,400.
1722H, Normal Date	150.	300.	700.	2,000.
1722H, 2 over 1	175.	350.	1,000.	3,000.
1722H, Brass	Extremely Rare			

BILLON SOLS MARQUES COINAGES

The most important coinages in circulation during the French regime were a group of billon (low grade silver) pieces collectively called sols (or sous) marques. They often constituted the smallest denomination coins because copper was generally unpopular with the colonists. There were no fewer than six coinages of sols marques; the coinages of 1709-1713 and 1738-1764 also had double sol denominations.

During the Middle Ages a new French coin called a gros tournois made its appearance. It was about the size of a 25-cent piece and made of good silver. By the first part of the 17th century this coin had become a billon piece called a douzain. The douzain or sol was rated at 12 deniers.

In 1640 the French government called in all douzains and counterstamped them with a small fleur-de-lis in an oval to change their rating to 15 deniers. The term sol marque (marked sol) came from the fact that these coins were counterstamped. It later came to apply to all sols.

COINAGE OF 1640

DATE / TYPE	VG	F	VF	EF
1640 Counterstamped Douzain	100.	150.	300.	—

COINAGE OF 1641.

The next billon coin in the series was a new design dated 1641. It was initially rated at 15 deniers and supplemented the douzains counterstamped the year before. Its relation to these coins is clearly shown by its design (both obverse and reverse) containing a fleur-de-lis in an oval, in imitation of the counterstamp on the earlier issue.

DATE / TYPE	VG	F	VF	EF
1641, 15 Deniers	Rare			

COINAGE OF 1658.

The douzain of 1658 was rated at 12 deniers in France but was given a rating of 20 deniers when it made its first appearance in New France in 1662. A 6-denier piece was also struck, but there is no reason to believe that denomination circulated in quantity in the colony.

DATE / TYPE	VG	F	VF	EF
1658 Douzain		Rare		

COINAGE OF 1692-1698.

Beginning in 1692 and continuing through 1698, a new issue of sols marques was made. The designs were new, but instead of being struck on fresh blanks, many were struck over previous issues of sols. It is sometimes possible to detect parts of the undertypes on the overstruck coins. The new issue was rated at 15 deniers when it first came out.

DATE / TYPE	VG	F	VF	EF
1692-1698, 15 Deniers, Billion, (4 types)	40.	60.	120.	225.

"MOUSQUETAIRE" ISSUES OF 1709-1713.

This issue consisted of a 15-denier piece and a 30-denier piece. The name mousquetaire is believed to have come from the cross on the reverse of the coins, which resembled the crosses on the cloaks of the legendary musketeers.

15 Deniers

30 Deniers

DATE / TYPE	VG	F	VF	EF
1710-1713, 15 Deniers	175.	300.	600.	1,100.
1709-1713, 30 Deniers	100.	200.	350.	800.

COINAGE OF 1738-1756.

The final billon coinage used in New France was that of 1738-1756, consisting of a sol and a double sol. The double sol has often been mistakenly referred to as "the" sol marque. First, there is no single sol marque; some six coinages are involved. Second, the sol or sou was by 1738 a coin about the size of our present small cent. The larger coin so often called a sou marque is in fact a double sol.

SOL (SOU) 1739-1748.

This coin was rated at 12 deniers in both France and New France.

DATE / TYPE	VG	F	VF	EF
1739-1748 (14 mint marks)	100.	175.	300.	700.

DOUBLE SOL (2 SOUS) 1738-1756.

Although this type was struck until 1764, large shipments to Quebec and Cape Breton ended in 1756. It is unlikely that any dated later than 1756 circulated extensively in New France. This coin was rated at 24 deniers.

Large quantities of contemporary counterfeits were made of the double sol, particularly of the dates 1740, 1741, 1742, 1750, 1751, 1755 and 1760. Differences in the rendition of the crown are the easiest way to tell the genuine from the counterfeit.

Original

Typical Counterfeit

DATE / TYPE	VG	F	VF	EF
1738-1756, (29 mint marks)	75.	125.	175.	500.
1740-1756, Counterfeit	40.	60.	100.	150.

Note: These prices are for "type" coins only. Certain dates, and mints are rarer than others, and will command higher prices. The prices listed are for the least expensive date/mint.

SILVER COINS

½ ECU (30 Sols).

The half ecu was not routinely imported into French America; nevertheless, it did circulate in considerable quantity. It is assumed that these coins came primarily from issues of Louis XIV and XV. The ecu, a large silver coin about the size of the Canadian silver dollar, was imported into French America in significant quantities. Most types of ecu minted between 1640 and the 1750's probably circulated in Canada. The ecu and its half continued in use after the fall of New France, when they became known as the French crown and half crown.

Heavily worn old French crowns and half crowns were legally overvalued in Lower Canada, where bank notes were often redeemed in such coin, depreciating the notes outside the colony. Corrective action could not be delayed after the Act of Union, and in 1842 the old French silver was finally demonetized.

DATE / TYPE	VG	F	VF	EF
1641-1643 Louis XIII	300.	600.	1,200.	2,000.
1645-1715, Louis XIV	65.	100.	225.	500.
1715-1774, Louis XV	40.	60.	150.	350.

ECU (60 Sols).

The ecu, a large silver coin about the size of the Canadian silver dollar, was imported into French America in significant quantities. The ecu (60 sols) continued in use after the fall of New France, when it was called the French crown. Most types of ecu minted between 1640 and the 1750s probably circulated in Canada.

DATE / TYPE	VG	F	VF	EF
1641-1643, Louis XIII	500.	1,000.	2,000.	4,000.
1643-1715, Louis XIV (4 major bust varieties)	100.	200.	400.	900.
1715-1774, Louis XV (7 major bust varieties)	65.	100.	150.	350.

COLONIAL COINAGE OF 1670

In 1670 a special coinage of silver 5-sol and 15-sol pieces was produced for circulation in the French colonies in the New World. On the reverse was "GLORIAM REGNI TVI DICENT" meaning "They shall speak of the glory of Thy kingdom" and taken from the 145th Psalm of the Bible. Despite their fame, these coins barely qualify as "Canadian." Period documents suggest that they probably were intended for the West Indies rather than New France. Authorities in the West Indies were anxious to obtain a subsidiary silver coinage for payment of day labourers and artisans, who were being paid in goods. In New France these coins were not particularly wanted because they could not be used for buying goods in France; they were not legal tender there. In any case it is quite clear that these coins had a very limited circulation in French America.

5 Sols

15 Sols

DATE / TYPE	VG	F	VF	EF
1670A, Double Sol	Extremely Rare			
1670A, 5 Sols	2,500.	3,500.	6,000.	10,000.
1670A, 15 Sols	25,000.	40,000.	75,000.	150,000.

Note: A 1670A, 5 Sols (PCGS-AU58), from the Ford Collection, sold at Stack's ANA Auction, August 2011, for $37,385. US dollars.

REDUCED SILVER COINAGES OF 1674 - 1709

In the late 17th and early 18th centuries the French government was in a rather precarious financial condition. As a money-raising scheme it struck seven coinages with reduced silver content (approximately .800 fine) at the same time as the regular .917 fine silver types were being produced. Most of the reduced fineness types were sent to New France in quantity.

4 SOLS ISSUES OF 1674-1677

By 1679 there were so many of these coins in circulation in New France that they were being used in payment by the bagful. An ordinance passed in that year lowered their value to 3 sols 6 deniers and placed strict limits on the quantity that could be used for any one payment.

DATE	VG	F	VF	EF
1674-1677	25.	50.	100.	250.

4 SOLS ISSUES OF 1691-1700.

This coin was the successor to the previous reduced silver 4-sol piece and was struck over it.

DATE	VG	F	VF	EF
1691-1700	35.	60.	120.	250.

5 SOLS, 1702-1704.

The next reduced silver coinage used in New France was a piece of approximately the same weight as the old 4-sol pieces, but which was called a 5-sol piece instead.

DATE / TYPE	VG	F	VF	EF
1702-1704, (27 mint marks)	25.	50.	80.	225.

10 SOLS, 1703-1708.

This 10-sol piece is from the same series as the 5-sols.

DATE / TYPE	VG	F	VF	EF
1703 to 1708, (17 mint marks)	30.	60.	125.	300.

20 SOLS DE NAVARRE, 1719-1720.

Twenty sols silver coins with the denomination shown as XX S were struck during an inflationary period, but were reduced to 18 sols by later edicts. They are the first of three coin types recognized by British authorities after the fall of New France as "French Ninepenny pieces". They circulated in Quebec and Nova Scotia.

DATE / TYPE	VG	F	VF	EF
1719-1720, (29 mint marks)	50.	100.	200.	400.

LIVRE OF 1720.

In 1720, during the wild inflation brought about by the schemes of John Law, a special coin was produced in pure silver and issued at the over-valued rating of one livre. The Company of the Indies imported a quantity of these coins into French America in 1722. This is the second of three coin types known as the "French Ninepenny piece".

DATE	VG	F	VF	EF
1720A	150.	300.	700.	1,200.

SIXTH ECU DE FRANCE, 1720-1723.

These coins were struck over the XX sols de Navarre of 1719-1720, and many show portions of the undertype. Their rating eventually settled at 18 sols, and they are the third of three types known collectively as "French Ninepenny pieces."

DATE / TYPE	VG	F	VF	EF
1720-1723, (27 mint marks)	50.	100.	225.	450.

SMALL SILVER LOUIS OF 1720.

In 1720 a new coin called a small silver louis (petit louis d'argent) was brought into Canada. Its initial rating was 60 sols, but this was soon reduced to 40 sols.

DATE	F	VF	EF	AU
1720	200.	300.	450.	700.

Type of 1680

Type of 1723-1725

GOLD COINS

THE GOLD LOUIS.

The only French gold coin to see significant circulation in French North America was the gold Louis (Louis d'or). Louis d'or were regularly sent over and saw use even after the Conquest. Any of the types struck between the 1640s and the 1750s potentially circulated here in quantity.

DATE / TYPE	F	VF	EF	UNC
1643-1715, Louis XIV	650.	1,000.	1,600.	2.500.
1723-1725, Louis XV "Mirlitons" (26 mint marks)	800.	1,200.	2,000.	3,000.
1726-1739 "Lunettes" (30 mint marks)	500.	700.	1,000.	1,500.

COINS OF GREAT BRITAIN

For most of the British colonial period (1760-1870) the British government was hardly better than the French government had been at supplying Imperial coins for use in Canada. British coinage was struck infrequently during the last half of the 18th century, and England and her colonies alike suffered from the lack of coin.

A major alteration took place in the British coinage in 1816. The silver coinage was reduced to a subsidiary status (along with the coppers) by lowering the amount of silver it contained to bring the bullion value of the coins below the face value. This left gold as the sole standard coinage and marks the beginning of the British gold standard. The coinage of silver was begun on a large scale and British coins gradually became more available.

In 1825-1826 a serious attempt was made to establish Imperial coins as the principal coinage of the colonies and to drive out the Spanish-American coins. This attempt largely failed in British North America. Nevertheless, at various times some British coins did achieve a significant circulation here, particularly in Nova Scotia. That province came the closest to adopting sterling coinage: when it was decided to institute a decimal currency in 1859, the dollar was rated so as to allow the continued circulation of British coins. The 2-shilling piece (florin) became a 50-cent piece, the shilling became a 25-cent piece and so on. The halfpenny and shilling also saw much use in Upper and Lower Canada and later in the united Province of Canada.

COPPER COINS

GEORGE II ISSUES.

These coins, along with the George III halfpenny listed next, formed the most important part of the British North American copper currency until the War of 1812. After that time they were supplemented by the tokens issued by local merchants and others. Until the first bank tokens were issued, they formed the only copper currency sanctioned by the British government.

Halfpennies of the United Kingdom have a seated Britannia reverse, while Irish halfpennies have a harp reverse.

U.K. Halfpenny

DATE / TYPE	VG	F	VF	EF	AU	UNC
George II						
1740-1754, U.K. ½d	10.	15.	35.	120.	200.	500.
1736-1760, Irish ½d	10.	20.	35.	150.	250.	600.

GEORGE III ISSUES.

The majority of the coins of this issue that circulated in both Great Britain and North America were contemporary counterfeits. Halfpennies issued during later reigns circulated to a lesser extent in British North America.

Genuine Issue

Typical Counterfeit

DATE / TYPE	VG	F	VF	EF	AU	UNC
George III						
U.K. Genuine, 1770-75	5.	10.	30.	100.	200.	400.
U.K. Counterfeit, 1770-75	10.	25.	75.	250.	—	—
Irish, 1766-82	8.	12.	35.	100.	150.	500.
Machin's Mills, 1747-78	150.	300.	900.	2,000.	—	—

WILLIAM IV ISSUES.

A special shipment of copper coins dated 1831 was sent to Canada in 1832. These could only be circulated at local currency rates, and consequently most were promptly returned to Britain at a profit. The penny was not at that time a frequently used denomination in British North America. Farthings of this issue were also struck for Canada (despite absence of demand for this denomination) but lost en route, together with part of the halfpence.

Penny

DATE / TYPE	VG	F	VF	EF	AU	UNC
William IV, 1831						
Halfpenny	6.	15.	30.	75.	150.	400.
Penny	10.	20.	60.	200.	400.	1,100.

SILVER COINS

British silver coins became more important in circulation in some parts of British North America after about 1830. The intermediate denominations were the most common.

Six Pence

DATE / TYPE	VG	F	VF	EF	AU	UNC
William IV, 1831-1837	5.	15.	50.	125.	200.	400.
Victoria (Young Head), 1838-1866	5.	10.	25.	75.	150.	300.

Shilling

DATE / TYPE	VG	F	VF	EF	AU	UNC
William IV, 1831-1837	8.	15.	40.	150.	300.	600.
Victoria (Young Head) 1838-1863	5.	12.	35.	125.	200.	350.

Florin

This denomination probably saw use in Nova Scotia during the 1850s and 1860s. In 1861 the florin, shilling and sixpence were imported into British Columbia.

DATE / TYPE	VG	F	VF	EF	AU	UNC
Victoria (Gothic Head) 1851-1887*	15.	30.	75.	200.	300.	500.

*On these coins the date is on the obverse in the form of Roman numerals.

Note: These prices are for "type" coins only. Certain dates, and mints are rarer than others, and will command higher prices. The prices listed are for the least expensive date/mint.

Halfcrown

DATE / TYPE	VG	F	VF	EF	AU	UNC
George IV (3 types)	20.	30.	75.	300.	650.	1,000.
William IV	20.	35.	100.	450.	900.	1,200.
Victoria (Young Head) 1839-1850	15.	20.	75.	200.	700.	1,300.

BANK OF ENGLAND SILVER TOKENS

The Bank of England issued captured Spanish-American dollars, restruck as five shilling/dollar pieces over the period 1804 to 1811 although all are dated 1804. The Bank also issued two types of three shilling and one shilling sixpence tokens. The Bank tokens were deficient in silver content in relation to sterling coin, and fell to their bullion value after a recall period. They continued to provide a substantial portion of the silver currency of Prince Edward Island, at enhanced ratings, until the 1840's.

DATE / TYPE	VG	F	VF	EF	AU	UNC
George III						
5 shillings/dollar, 1804	70.	200.	325.	700.	1,000.	1,500.
3 shillings bank token 1811-1816	15.	40.	100.	150.	250.	375.
1s 6d. Bank Token, 1811-1816	12.	25.	65.	100.	200.	375.

GOLD COINS

GEORGE III HALF GUINEA.

The half guinea was usually rated at 10 shillings 6 pence in Great Britain.

DATE / TYPE	VG	F	VF	EF	AU	UNC
1787-1800	BV	225.	300.	450.	600.	1,000.

GEORGE III GUINEA, 1761-1813.

The guinea or 21-shilling piece was one of the principal gold coins to circulate in British North America.

Type of 1765-1773

TYPE	VG	F	VF	EF	AU	UNC
Guinea	BV	BV	400.	600.	900.	1,300.

HALF SOVEREIGN.

The half sovereign was the successor to the ½ guinea and probably saw enough circulation in British North America and the Dominion of Canada to warrant its inclusion in this listing.

TYPE	F	VF	EF	AU	UNC
George III	BV	175.	450.	650.	1,100.
George IV	BV	250.	500.	800.	1,200.
William IV	BV	300.	650.	1,100.	1,600.
Victoria (Young Head)	BV	BV	250.	300.	500.

SOVEREIGN.

The sovereign was perhaps the most widely used gold coin in Canada. It was used extensively by banks and the government for redeeming paper money right up to the 20th century.

TYPE	F	VF	EF	AU	UNC
George III	BV	400.	675.	1,050.	2,750.
George IV	BV	400.	900.	1,250.	2,200.
William IV	BV	400.	900.	1,600.	2,750.
Victoria (Shield)	BV	BV	BV	300.	400.

COINS OF PORTUGAL

During the 18th and early 19th centuries, several types of gold coins issued by Portugal found their way into British North America and were used extensively here.

MOIDORE.

This coin had a denomination of 4,000 reis in Portugal and bore on its reverse the Cross of Jerusalem. It was struck from the reign of Alfonso VI (1656-1683) to the reign of John V (1706-1750).

TYPE	VG	F	VF	EF
Alfonso VI to John V	350.	450.	600.	1,000.

6,400 REIS (½ JOE).

This coin, with a formal denomination of 6,400 reis, was introduced in the 1720's, along with a 12,800 reis coin of similar design. The king of Portugal at the time was John (Joao) V and from his name on the coins, Johannes V, came the nickname "Joe" for the 12,800 reis coin and "½ Joe" for the 6,400 reis coin. The "½ Joe" was also applied to the 6,400 reis coins issued in subsequent reigns. The larger coin was not issued in later reigns and "Joe" was eventually used for the 6,400 reis denomination.

DATE / TYPE	VG	F	VF	EF
John V to John VI, 1706-1826	500.	600.	800.	1,200.

12,800 REIS (JOE).

This was a coin of 12,800 reis issued during the reign of John V (see above).

DATE / TYPE	VG	F	VF	EF
John V, "Joe" 1724 - 1732	1,300.	2,500.	5,000.	7,000.

COINS OF SPAIN, SPANISH AMERICA AND FORMER SPANISH COLONIES

This group of coins was more important in the currency history of what is now Canada for a longer period of time than any other foreign coinage. It was the Spanish-American dollar that served as the basis for the United States dollar, upon which in turn was based the decimal dollar of the Province of Canada in 1858.

COINS OF SPAIN

The Spanish metropolitan coinage is relatively unimportant compared with that of her New World colonies, excepting only the pistareen and, to a lesser extent, the half pistareen. These were nicknames given the reduced standard 2- and 1-real pieces minted only in Spain and which enjoyed wide circulation in British North America in the first half of the 19th century.

DATE / TYPE	VG	F	VF	EF	AU
18th Century					
Half Pistareen	20.	40.	60.	100.	200.
Pistareen	20.	40.	60.	100.	200.

Note: These prices are for "type" coins only. Certain dates, and mints are rarer than others, and will command higher prices. The prices listed are for the least expensive date/mint.

COINS OF SPANISH AMERICA

The coinage of Spain's colonies emanated from the following principal mints: Potosi in Bolivia, Santiago in Chile, Sante Fe do Bogota and Popayan in Colombia (Nueva Granada), Guatemala in Guatemala, Mexico City in Mexico and Lima and Cuzco in Peru. Minting of Spanish-American coins began in the early 16th century with the coins being of conventional round appearance. These were replaced about 1580 by the "cob" series: crude-appearing coins hand-struck on irregular blanks hewn from bars of refined bullion.

The cob series was finally superseded by round coins in 1732. The round gold issues bore the portrait of the reigning Spanish monarch from the first; however, the silver did not carry portraits until 1772. In the intervening 40 years the reverses featured the "two world" or "pillar" design, consisting of two crowned hemispheres between the crowned pillars of Hercules.

The Spanish-American series came to an end in the 1820's as Spain's colonies successfully revolted and became independent. Nevertheless, the Spanish-American coins had been minted in such great quantities that they continued to exert an important influence for decades. Probably the most important coinages for Canada are those struck under the rulers Charles III (1760-1788), Charles IV (1788-1808) and Ferdinand VII (1808-1821).

SILVER COINS

1 REAL

TYPE	VG	F	VF	EF	AU
Philip V to Charles III, Pillar Type	12.	25.	60.	125.	275.
Charles III to Ferdinand VII, Bust Type	10.	18.	30.	100.	175.

2 REALES

TYPE	VG	F	VF	EF	AU
Philip V to Charles III, Pillar Type	20.	50.	80.	175.	300.
Charles III to Ferdinand VII, Bust Type	15.	25.	50.	150.	250.

4 REALES

TYPE	VG	F	VF	EF
Philip V to Charles III, Pillar Type	100.	200.	400.	700.
Charles III to Ferdinand VII, Bust Type	30.	50.	75.	125.

8 REALES.

This is by far the most important foreign coin to circulate in Canada. It was known and appreciated all over the civilized world and was the principal end product of the vast amounts of silver mined in the New World. The 8-real piece had the nickname dollar (even though it was not a decimal coin) due to its similarity in size to the European thalers and daalders. It is the famous "piece-of-eight" of pirate lore. The first 8-real pieces were produced in 1556 at the Mexico City mint.

TYPE	VG	F	VF	EF
Philip V to Charles III, Pillar Type	100.	150.	200.	500.
Charles III to Ferdinand VII, Bust Type	40.	80.	125.	250.

GOLD COINS

2 ESCUDOS (DOUBLOON).

This gold coin popularly known as the Spanish Doubloon was the most widely used Spanish-American gold coin in Canada.

TYPE	VG	F	VF	EF
Charles III to Ferdinand VII	300.	500.	800.	1,500.

4 ESCUDOS

TYPE	VG	F	VF	EF
Charles III to Ferdinand VII	600.	750.	1,100.	2,000.

8 ESCUDOS.

The most important gold coin in Canada was the 8-escudo piece. It circulated widely, but was especially popular in the Atlantic provinces. After the Spanish colonies gained their independence, these coins were called "Royal" doubloons (as opposed to "Patriot" doubloons discussed below).

TYPE	VG	F	VF	EF
Charles III to Ferdinand VII	1,200.	1,350.	1,500.	2,000.

Note: These prices are for "type" coins only. Certain dates, and mints are rarer than others, and will command higher prices. The prices listed are for the least expensive date/mint.

COINS OF FORMER SPANISH COLONIES

By 1826 Spain had lost all her colonies in the New World. This ushered in new coinages on the existing standards by each of the former colonies. They were accepted and circulated alongside the coins of the Spanish-American series. Probably only two denominations are necessary in this listing — the silver dollar and the gold doubloon.

SILVER COINS

8 REALES (DOLLAR).

The most important dollars of former Spanish colonies to circulate in Canada are undoubtedly those of Mexico.

DATE / TYPE	VG	F	VF	EF	AU	UNC
1820s to 1840s, Mexican	BV	30.	50.	90.	150.	200.

GOLD COINS

8 ESCUDOS (DOUBLOON).

In the case of the doubloon it is more difficult to single out any one former colony's coinage as being the most important for Canada. Therefore a general listing is given. Contemporary sources refer to such doubloons as "Patriot" doubloons to distinguish them for the "Royal" doubloons of the Spanish-American series. It is known that "Patriot" doubloons were specifically imported into such provinces as Nova Scotia.

Typical "Patriot" Doubloon from Chile

DATE / TYPE	VG	F	VF	EF	AU	UNC
1817- 1830s "Patriot"	BV	BV	1,200.	1,350.	2,200.	—

COINS OF THE UNITED STATES OF AMERICA

It is to the United States coinage that we owe our present decimal currency system. By the 1850s trade links between British North America and the U.S. were so strong and her coinage so commonplace here that the proponents of a currency akin to that of the U.S. instead of Great Britain prevailed.

The U.S. coinage on a decimal basis began in the 1790s and it has circulated here to varying degrees ever since. A great influx of U.S. silver coins took place during the 1850s and 1860s, after the proportion of silver contained in the 5-, 10-, 25- and 50-cent pieces was reduced. Previous to that time, U.S. large cents came across the border in quantity and large numbers of half dollars were imported to help pay for work on such projects as the Rideau Canal. The larger denominations of U.S. gold coins were important in Canada well into the twentieth century because they were widely imported by banks and the government for use in backing and redeeming paper money.

COPPER COINS

ONE CENT

Many varieties exist in the size of letters, placement of letters, and the size of date and number of stars.

TYPE / DATE	VG	F	VF	EF	AU	UNC
Coronet Head, 1816-1836	24.	32.	70.	140.	250.	400.
Braided Hair, 1837-1857	22.	25.	35.	60.	125.	200.

SILVER COINS

HALF DIME – CAPPED BUST

DATE	VG	F	VF	EF	AU	UNC
1829-1837	75.	80.	110.	165.	250.	375.

HALF DIME – SEATED LIBERTY

DATE / TYPE	VG	F	VF	EF	AU	UNC
1837-1838, No stars on obv.	55.	80.	145.	235.	500.	750.
1838-1859, Stars on obv.	20.	30.	40.	60.	125.	200.
1853-1855, Arrows at date	22.	25.	35.	65.	140.	300.
1860-1873, Legend on obv.	20.	25.	30.	50.	100.	175.

DIME – CAPPED BUST

DATE	VG	F	VF	EF	AU	UNC
1809-1837	40.	45.	80.	300.	450.	1,000

DIME – SEATED LIBERTY

DATE / TYPE	VG	F	VF	EF	AU	UNC
1837-1838, No stars on obv.	75.	100.	300.	500.	700.	1,200.
1838-1853, Stars on obv.	25.	30.	40.	60.	125.	400.
1853-1855, Arrows at date	18.	20.	30.	50.	150.	300.
1856-1860, Stars on obv.	20.	22.	30.	50.	125.	300.
1860-1873, Legend on obv.	20.	25.	30.	40.	100.	200.

QUARTER DOLLAR – CAPPED BUST

DATE / TYPE	VG	F	VF	EF	AU	UNC
1815-1828, Motto	150.	200.	425.	1,200.	2,000.	3,250.
1831-1838	100.	125.	150.	400.	750.	1,250.

QUARTER DOLLAR – SEATED LIBERTY

DATE / TYPE	VG	F	VF	EF	AU	UNC
1838-1853	30.	40.	50.	75.	175.	600.
1853, Rays	30.	35.	60.	200.	300.	1,000.
1854-1855, No Rays	30.	40.	50.	90.	250.	500.
1856-1865, No Motto	30.	40.	50.	75.	180.	375.
1866-1873, Motto	40.	60.	125.	175.	240.	600.

HALF DOLLAR – CAPPED BUST

DATE / TYPE	VG	F	VF	EF	AU	UNC
1807-1836	70.	85.	120.	200.	400.	1,000.
1836-1837, "50 CENTS"	70.	100.	125.	200.	425.	1,300.
1838-1839, "HALF DOL."	80.	100.	125.	225.	400.	1,250.

HALF DOLLAR – SEATED LIBERTY

DATE / TYPE	VG	F	VF	EF	AU	UNC
1839-1853, No motto	50.	60.	80.	150.	275.	600.
1853, Rays	40.	60.	115.	300.	600.	1,500.
1854-1855, No rays	40.	60.	80.	125.	350.	700.
1856-1866, No motto	60.	75.	90.	150.	275.	675.
1866-1873, Motto	50.	65.	85.	125.	225.	500.

GOLD COINS

FIVE DOLLARS – HALF EAGLE

DATE / TYPE	F	VF	EF	AU	UNC
1834-1838, Classic Head	450.	650.	1,000.	1,400.	5,000.
1839-1866, Coronet Head	400.	500.	600.	750.	1,600.
1866-1908	BV	500.	525.	575.	850.

TEN DOLLARS – EAGLE

DATE / TYPE	F	VF	EF	AU	UNC
1838-1865, Coronet Head, 2 Varieties	750.	975.	1,000.	1,100.	3,500.
1866-1907	BV	BV	950.	975.	1,100.

TWENTY DOLLARS – DOUBLE EAGLE

DATE / TYPE	F	VF	EF	AU	UNC
1849-1866, Coronet Head, 3 Varieties	1,500.	1,950.	2,100.	2,600.	7,000.
1866-1876	1,500.	1,875.	1,900.	1,950.	2,750.
1877-1907	BV	BV	BV	1,900.	2,000.

Note: These prices are for "type" coins only. Certain dates, and mints are rarer than others, and will command higher prices. The prices listed are for the least expensive date/mint.

LOCAL PRE-DECIMAL COINS

Although it is sometimes stated that the first coins produced for local use in Canada were the 1858-1859 decimal coins for the Province of Canada, this is not the case. A small but important group of local coinages was produced prior to the adoption of decimal currency. These coinages were at first specially modified Spanish-American silver coins, but coppers were added to this group in the 1850s.

NEW FRANCE (FRENCH REGIME)

COUNTERSTAMPED SPANISH-AMERICAN COINS

During the last part of the 17th century, the quantity of Spanish-American silver coins in circulation in New France increased. This increase was due primarily to the illegal trade in furs which the colonists were carrying on with the Dutch and English. At that time such coins circulated at a value that depended upon their weight; the more worn the coin was, the lower it was valued compared to unworn pieces. Since many Spanish-American coins in New France had varying amounts of wear, their use in commerce was difficult. Colonial authorities were not anxious to see these coins used in preference to French coins, but the latter were so scarce that they relented. In the early 1680s treasury officials weighed a quantity of these coins and counterstamped each with a fleur-de-lis. Underweight coins also received a Roman numeral counterstamp (from I to IV) to indicate the amount by which the weight was deficient. The coins could then be compared to a table to determine the exact value at which they were current.

Unfortunately for collectors, no surviving examples of this interesting local issue are known.

NOVA SCOTIA, NEW BRUNSWICK, PRINCE EDWARD ISLAND

For the pre-decimal coinage of Colonial New Brunswick, Nova Scotia and Prince Edward Island, see the *Charlton Standard Catalogue of Canadian Colonial Tokens*.

HISTORY OF CANADIAN DECIMAL COINS

The decimal coins which we take so much for granted today have a history that stretches back into the last century and beyond. During the 1700s, the single most important coin in North America was the Spanish-American dollar, a large silver coin produced in great quantities by mints in Mexico, Peru and other parts of the New World. The Spanish- American dollar was not a decimal coin; its formal denomination was 8 reales. It was nicknamed dollar in deference to its resemblance in size to German thalers and other large European coins of similar name. This Spanish-American coin was so important in the United States that when the U.S. adopted a decimal system of dollars and cents in the 1790s, their silver dollar was made with the same amount of silver as the Spanish-American dollar.

In British North America in the first half of the 19th century each colony used a system of accounting which consisted of pounds, shillings and pence. However, the coins actually in circulation were mostly Spanish-American and U.S. As trade with the United States increased in the 1840s and 1850s, the British North American colonies (provinces) were naturally drawn toward the adoption of a currency system more like that of the U.S. than Great Britain.

All through the 1850s British North America struggled with the problem of currency standards. The Province of Canada, under Francis Hincks, took the lead in fighting for a decimal system. Acts passed in 1851 and 1853 stipulated that public accounts be kept in dollars and cents, but no coins were issued under their provisions. An 1857 act provided a broader base for a decimal currency system. It directed that both government and private accounts be kept in dollars, cents and mills. A decimal coinage followed in 1858-1859, based upon a dollar equal to the U.S. gold dollar.

Other British North American provinces soon followed the Province of Canada's lead. New Brunswick and Nova Scotia adopted decimal systems in 1859-1860, Newfoundland followed suit in 1864 and Prince Edward Island went decimal in 1871. Thus, even before Confederation the use of decimal coins was firmly established.

DIE AXIS

The obverse design is considered the primary side of the coin. The die axis is the relationship of the reverse design to the obverse design. Consider the obverse die, usually the anvil die in a press, stationary and when installed is the point of reference. The reverse die (moving hammer die) may be turned or set at any of 360 degrees in relation to the set obverse die.

If the obverse die is identified by an upright arrow (↑) then the reverse die may be represented by a second arrow (↑). These arrows now form a relationship to one another. Illustrated below are two common die positions:

Coinage Axes: ↑↓
Obverse die: ↑
Reverse die is set 180 degrees opposite: ↓

Medal Axes: ↑↑
Obverse die: ↑
Reverse die is set in the matching direction: ↑

Two meaningful variations: ↑→, ↑←, as shown on page 161 in the 125th Anniversary of Confederation twenty-five cents coins of 1992, and on page 163 in the Millennium Design twenty-five cent coins of 1999.

NOVA SCOTIA

In the years immediately preceding the adoption of a decimal currency system in Nova Scotia in 1859, British coins formed an important part of the circulating currency, much more so than in the other British North American provinces. Consequently, the Nova Scotia government chose a decimal dollar equal to one-fifth of a pound sterling (i.e. \$5 = £1), allowing British silver coins to conveniently fit into the new system and continue circulating. The British 2-shilling piece (florin) became a 50-cent piece, the shilling became a 25-cent piece and the sixpence became a 12 1/2-cent piece. The only coins the province needed to have specially produced were a cent, and to make change for the sixpence and half crown, a half cent.

HALF CENT and ONE CENT
VICTORIA 1861 - 1864

The half cent was coined with the same diameter as the British farthing and utilized the same obverse. Pattern pieces incorporated the royal crown and a wreath of roses (see NS-1 to NS-3 and NS-5 in the chapter on Patterns). However, a local campaign in favour of the provincial flower, the mayflower, resulted in the adoption of a design using the royal crown surrounded by a wreath of both roses and mayflowers.

The cent was minted with the same diameter as the British halfpenny and used the same obverse. The reverse designs are similar to those used for the half cent, including pattern pieces with a wreath of roses (see NS-4 and NS-6 in the chapter on Patterns).

The circulation issues of this denomination have two distinct reverses. The first (1861) has much detail in the crown and a large rosebud at the lower right part of the wreath. On the second reverse (1861-1864) the crown has a narrower headband and generally less detail, the rosebud at the lower right is smaller, and the rosebud and certain other parts of the design come closer to the lettering and the raised line just inside the rim denticles.

The mintage figures of 800,000 for 1861 and 1,000,000 for 1862 have puzzled collectors for many years since the 1862-dated coins are scarcer. The probable explanation is that some, perhaps most, cents struck in 1862 were from dies dated 1861. Therefore, the mintages for the two years have been combined. Most of the cents issued in 1862 were dated 1861.

Half Cent

One Cent

Designer and Engraver:
Obv.: Leonard C. Wyon
Rev.: Leonard C. Wyon from a model by C. Hill
Composition: .95 copper, .04 tin, .01 zinc
Weight: ½ cent 2.84 grams
1 cent 5.67 grams
Diameter: ½ cent 20.65 mm
1 cent 25.53 mm
Edge: Plain
Die Axes: ↑↑

Large Rosebud (LR)

Small Rosebud (SR)

DATE / DENOM./VAR.	MINTAGE (thous.)	G-4	VG-8	F-12	VF-20	EF-40	AU-50	AU-55	MS-60 Br	MS-63 Red	MS-65 Red	SP-63 Rd/Br	SP-65 Rd/Br
1861 ½¢	400	4.	7.	10.	15.	20.	60.	95.	150.	500.	3,000.	2,000.	4,500.
1864 ½¢	400	4.	7.	10.	15.	25.	50.	75.	100.	375.	3,000.	*	*
1861 1¢ LR	1,800	3.	6.	8.	15.	25.	60.	75.	150.	700.	4,000.	2,000.	4,000.
1861 1¢ SR	Included	6.	10.	15.	30.	50.	125.	175.	250.	750.	3,000.	*	*
1862 1¢	Included	45.	80.	135.	225.	475.	975.	1,500.	—	—	—	*	*
1864 1¢	800	3.	5.	7.	12.	25.	65.	100.	200.	750.	—	—	—

NEW BRUNSWICK

When New Brunswick adopted a decimal dollar in 1860, it chose the same rating for its dollar and ordered the same denominations as the Province of Canada: cents in bronze and 5-, 10- and 20-cent pieces in silver. The effective date for the decimal currency act was November 1, 1860 but, like Nova Scotia, New Brunswick had to wait until early 1862 before the first coins arrived from England. In the meantime, the government introduced other decimal coins as a temporary expedient. Thus, in late 1861 and early 1862 some 500,000 Province of Canada cents and a quantity of United States small denomination silver coins were put into circulation in the province.

HALF CENT and ONE CENT VICTORIA 1861 - 1864

The half cent denomination was not required by the province since its dollar and hence British coins went at a different rating than in the sister province of Nova Scotia. Nevertheless, the Royal Mint became confused and struck a half cent for New Brunswick. Over 200,000 of these coins came off the presses before the error was discovered. Most of the mintage was returned to the melting pot. The circulation strikes that survived are thought to have become mixed with the Nova Scotia half cents and sent to Halifax.

The obverse is that of the British farthing and the reverse is a royal crown and a rose/mayflower wreath very similar to that used for Nova Scotia.

The New Brunswick 1-cent pieces have the British halfpenny obverse and a reverse similar to that used for the Nova Scotia cent.

For the 1864 issue two styles of 6 were used in the date: a figure with a round centre in its loop and a short top, and a figure with a more oval centre and a longer top.

Half Cent

One Cent

Designer and Engraver:
Obv.: Leonard C. Wyon
Rev.: Leonard C. Wyon from a model by C. Hill
Composition: .95 copper, .04 tin, .01 zinc
Weight: ½ cent 2.84 grams
1 cent 5.67 grams
Diameter: ½ cent 20.65 mm
1 cent 25.53 mm
Edge: Plain
Die Axes: ↑↑

Short 6 (S6)

Tall 6 (T6)

DATE / DENOM./VAR.	MINTAGE	G-4	VG-8	F-12	VF-20	EF-40	AU-50	AU-55	MS-60 Br	MS-63 Red	MS-65 Red	SP-63 Rd./Br.	SP-65 Rd./Br.
1861 ½¢	222,800	125.	175.	250.	325.	375.	500.	650.	850.	1,500.	—	2,000.	4,000.
1861 1¢	1,000,000	3.	6.	9.	18.	30.	65.	90.	175.	500.	3,000.	2,000.	4,000.
1862 1¢	Included	*	*	*	*	*	*	*	*	*	*	4,000.	7,500.
1864 1¢ S6	1,000,000	5.	8.	12.	20.	40.	85.	150.	225.	600.	2,000.	*	*
1864 1¢ T6	Included	5.	10.	15.	25.	45.	100.	150.	300.	600.	—	*	*

FIVE, TEN and TWENTY CENTS VICTORIA 1862 - 1864

The production of New Brunswick's first silver decimal coinage had to await the completion of the bronze coinage. Consequently, it could not commence until 1862. The 5-cent piece designs were basically those of the Province of Canada with an appropriately modified obverse legend. Two styles of 6 were employed in dating the 1864 issue: a small 6 and a large 6.

The designs for the New Brunswick 10-cent piece were adapted from existing Province of Canada designs. The reverse was used without modification and the obverse involved changing the legend only. The 1862 issue is usually collected as two varieties. One has a normal date and the other has an obviously double-punched 2.

The New Brunswick 20-cent piece has an unusual reverse design once rejected for the Province of Canada (see PC-4 in the chapter on Patterns). The reverse adopted by the Province of Canada differs in style from that chosen by New Brunswick, while using the same elements. This stylistic difference, plus the fact a die for the New Brunswick 20-cent piece of 1862 was used to strike one side of George W. Wyon's obituary medalet, suggests that it was George Wyon and not Leonard Wyon who engraved this reverse. The obverse utilizes the Province of Canada 20 cents portrait with a special legend for New Brunswick.

Five Cents

Ten Cents

Twenty Cents

Designer and Engraver: Obv.: Leonard C. Wyon
Rev.: Twenty cents - Possibly Geo. W. Wyon
Composition: .925 silver, .075 copper
Weight: 5 cents 1.16 grams
10 cents 2.32 grams
20 cents 4.65 grams
Diameter: 5 cents 15.49 mm
10 cents 17.91 mm
20 cents 23.27 mm
Edge: Reeded
Die Axes: ↑↓

5 Cents, Small 6 (S6)

5 Cents, Large 6 (L6)

10 Cents, Normal Date

10 Cents, Double-punched 2 (2/2)

DATE / DENOM./VAR.	MINTAGE (thous.)	G-4	VG-8	F-12	VF-20	EF-40	AU-50	AU-55	MS-60	MS-63	MS-65	SP-63	SP-65
1862 5¢	100	50.	125.	175.	325.	725.	1,500.	2,250.	3,500.	—	—	6,000.	12,500.
1862 5¢ SP (PE)	Incl.	*	*	*	*	*	*	*	*	*	*	6,000.	12,500.
1864 5¢ S6	100	50.	100.	175.	325.	600.	1,200.	2,500.	—	—	—	*	*
1864 5¢ L6	Incl.	75.	150.	200.	425.	1,000.	1,500.	2,500.	—	—	—	*	*
1862 10¢	150	60.	125.	200.	375.	850.	1,750.	2,000.	3,000.	6,000.	—	*	*
1862 10¢ SP (PE)	Incl.	*	*	*	*	*	*	*	*	*	*	6,500.	17,500.
1862 10¢ 2/2	Incl.	100.	150.	300.	550.	1,200.	—	—	—	—	—	*	*
1864 10¢	150	75.	125.	200.	375.	725.	2,000.	2,500.	—	—	—	*	*
1864 10¢ SP (PE)	Incl.	*	*	*	*	*	*	*	*	*	*	9,000.	18,000.
1862 20¢	150	25.	50.	75.	175.	450.	875.	1,200.	2,500.	—	—	6,500.	18,000.
1862 20¢ SP (PE)	Incl.	*	*	*	*	*	*	*	*	*	*	6,500.	18,000.
1864 20¢	150	25.	50.	75.	150.	300.	550.	900.	2,250.	—	—	*	*

PRINCE EDWARD ISLAND

ONE CENT
VICTORIA 1871

Prince Edward Island adopted a decimal currency system in 1871. Its dollar was given the same rating as those of the provinces of Canada and New Brunswick. The only coinage in the new system was bronze cents in 1871. The island entered Confederation two years later. The provincial government experienced considerable difficulty placing its cents in circulation. It took almost ten years to deplete the stock and the last of it was sold at a 10 percent discount.

The reverse was prepared specifically for the Prince Edward Island government, incorporating the seal of the island and a Latin phrase, "PARVA SUB INGENTI," meaning "The small beneath the great." The seal shows a large oak tree, representing England, sheltering three young oak trees, representing the three counties on the island.

Because of pressure to produce domestic coin, the Royal Mint in London made arrangements with Heaton's Mint in Birmingham to strike P.E.I. cents. For some unknown reason Heaton's familiar "H" mint mark is absent from the coins.

Designer and Engraver:
Obv.: Leonard C. Wyon, from a portrait model by Wm. Theed
Rev.: Leonard C. Wyon
Composition: .95 copper, .04 tin, .01 zinc
Weight: 5.67 grams
Diameter: 25.40 mm
Edge: Plain
Die Axis: ↑↑, ↑↓

DATE / AXIS	MINTAGE (thous.)	G-4	VG-8	F-12	VF-20	EF-40	AU-50	AU-55	MS-60 Br	MS-63 Red	MS-65 Red	SP-63 Rd/Br	SP-65 Rd/Br
1871 ↑↑	2,000	3.	5.	6.	15.	30.	60.	95.	135.	250.	700.	1,200.	3,500.
1871 ↑↓	Included	12.	15.	30.	60.	90.	150.	225.	325.	650.	—	1,500.	4.000.

Note: Br = Brown; Rd/Br = Red/Brown

NEWFOUNDLAND

Since Newfoundland remained separate from Canada until 1949, it has a much larger decimal coin series than the other pre-Confederation British colonies. Newfoundland adopted decimal currency in 1863, hoping to have coins on the new standard in circulation in 1864. The most important coin in Newfoundland had been the Spanish-American dollar or 8-real piece, so the government set its dollar equal in value to this coin. This made the new decimal cent equal to the British halfpenny and $4.80 equal to £1 sterling.

ONE CENT
VICTORIA 1864 - 1896

Beginning in 1864, several designs were considered for the Newfoundland cent. The first tendency was to use the same designs as New Brunswick. Pattern dies are known for an 1864 Newfoundland cent with the royal crown, rose/mayflower design (see NF-1 in the chapter on Patterns). This design was rejected in favour of a royal crown and wreath of pitcher plant (the provincial flower) and oak, with unusual broad, bold lettering and date. The obverse incorporated the British halfpenny portrait with the legend "VICTORIA QUEEN," also in the same bold type (see NF-6 in the chapter on Patterns). However, it was decided that this legend was inappropriate and the cents struck for circulation in 1865 used the obverse legend "VICTORIA D:G:REG:."

An interesting variation in die axes occurs on this denomination. For all dates except 1872 the dies are in the medal arrangement (↑↑) but on the 1872s they are coinage arrangement (↑↓). The most reasonable explanation for this difference is that Ralph Heaton and Sons, who struck the 1872 cents, did not receive specific instructions regarding which die arrangement to use and chose the same arrangement as for the silver. The error was corrected in 1876 when Heaton's next coined cents for Newfoundland.

Three date varieties exist for 1880. The first has a narrow 0 in the date, while the second and third have a wide 0, in different positions.

Designers:
Obv.: Leonard C. Wyon
Rev.: Horace Morehen

Engraver:
Rev.: Thomas J. Minton

Composition: .95 copper, .04 tin, .01 zinc
Weight: 5.67 grams
Diameter: 25.53 mm
Edge: Plain
Die Axes: 1865, 1873-1896: ↑↑
1872H: ↑↓

"H" Mint Mark
Ralph Heaton and Sons issues have an "H" mint mark at the bottom of the wreath (1872, 1876). Royal Mint strikings have no mint mark.

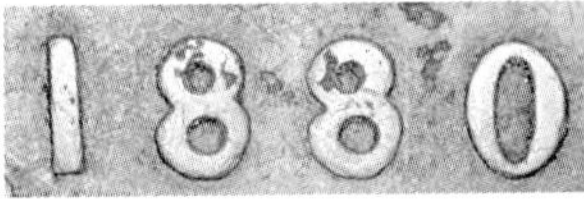

1880 Narrow 0 (NO)

1880 Wide 0 (WO)

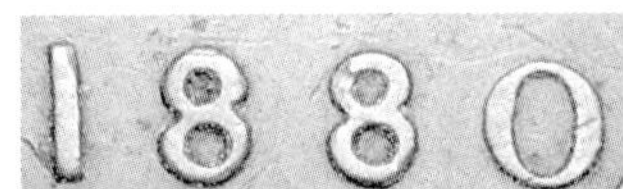
1880 Wide Low 0 (WLO)

DATE / MINT / VARIETY	MINTAGE (thous.)	G-4	VG-8	F-12	VF-20	EF-40	AU-50	AU-55	MS-60 Br	MS-63 Red	MS-65 Red	SP-63 Rd/Br	SP-65 Rd/Br
1864	N/A	—	—	—	—	—	—	—	—	—	—	3,500.	8,500.
1865	240	3.	6.	9.	20.	50.	125.	175.	275.	1,500.	3,000.	*	*
1872H	200	3.	5.	8.	15.	40.	85.	110.	150.	400.	900.	400.	1,200.
1873	200	4.	8.	10.	30.	90.	250.	350.	550.	2,500.	—	2,000.	10,000.
1876H	200	4.	6.	10.	30.	85.	250.	375.	625.	2,000.	—	*	*
1880 NO	400	150.	250.	375.	675.	1,000.	1,800.	2,400.	3,000.	—	—	2,500.	15,000.
1880 WO	Incl.	3.	6.	10.	20.	50.	100.	150.	200.	800.	3,500.	*	*
1880 WLO	Incl.	10.	20.	50.	100.	200.	400.	—	—	—	—	*	*
1885	40	30.	50.	80.	100.	200.	475.	650.	1,000.	3,500.	6,000.	2,000.	10,000.
1888	50	30.	45.	85.	150.	300.	675.	1,000.	2,000.	7,000.	—	*	*
1890	200	3.	5.	9.	25.	70.	150.	175.	350.	1,500.	—	*	*
1894	200	3.	6.	10.	20.	55.	150.	200.	275.	1,300.	—	1,000.	5,000.
1896	200	3.	5.	8.	20.	35.	95.	135.	175.	500.	4,000.	1,000.	5,000.

Note: The 1864 reverse matrix was repunched with a "5" and used to produce the 1865 issue of cents.

ONE CENT
EDWARD VII 1904 - 1909

The reverse design is a modification of the Victorian reverse, substituting the Imperial State crown for the St. Edward's crown. The obverses of most Edward VII denominations were those of the corresponding Dominion of Canada coinage; however, the Newfoundland cent has a distinctive design. The bust is very large and the letter size in the legend correspondingly small.

Designer and Engraver:
Obv.: G. W. DeSaulles
Engraver:
Rev.: W. H. J. Blakemore modifying existing coinage tools
Composition: .95 copper, .04 tin, .01 zinc
Weight: 5.67 grams
Diameter: 25.53 mm
Edge: Plain
Die Axes: ↑↑

"H" Mint Mark
The Mint Birmingham Ltd. issue (1904 only) has an "H" mint mark at the bottom of the wreath. Royal Mint strikings have no mint mark.

DATE / MINT MARK	MINTAGE (thous.)	VG-8	F-12	VF-20	EF-40	AU-50	AU-55	MS-60 Br	MS-63 Red	MS-64 Red	MS-65 Red	SP-63 Rd/Br	SP-65 Rd/Br
1904H	100	12.	20.	40.	75.	175.	300.	500.	1,200.	1,500.	—	4,000.	7,500.
1907	200	4.	7.	15.	45.	125.	150.	225.	1,000.	1,500.	4,500.	*	*
1909	200	4.	7.	10.	30.	75.	100.	125.	275.	425.	700.	*	*

ONE CENT
GEORGE V 1913 - 1936

The reverse for the cents of this reign is that established for the Edward VII series and the obverse is that of the Dominion of Canada cents.

Designer and Engraver:
Obv.: Sir E. B. MacKennal
Composition:
1913-1920: .95 copper, .04 tin, .01 zinc
1929-1936: .955 copper, .030 tin, .015 zinc
Weight: 5.67 grams
Diameter:
1913,1929-1936: 25.53 mm
1917-1920: 25.40 mm
Edge: Plain
Die Axes: ↑↑

"C" Mint Mark
Ottawa Branch Mint issues (1917-1920) have a "C" mint mark at the bottom of the wreath, Royal Mint strikings have no mint mark.

DATE / MINT MARK	MINTAGE	VG-8	F-12	VF-20	EF-40	AU-50	AU-55	MS-60 Br	MS-63 Red	MS-64 Red	MS-65 Red	SP-63 Rd/Br	SP-65 Rd/Br
1913	400,000	3.	5.	7.	12.	40.	50.	90.	150.	200.	450.	*	*
1917C	702,350	3.	5.	7.	12.	40.	60.	125.	300.	800.	1,800.	1,000.	2,500.
1919C	300,000	3.	5.	8.	18.	65.	90.	250.	675.	900.	4,000.	1,000.	5,000.
1920C	302,184	3.	5.	8.	30.	125.	200.	350.	1,800.	—	—	2,500.	12,000.
1929	300,000	3.	5.	7.	15.	35.	55.	95.	200.	325.	1,000.	1,000.	6,000.
1936	300,000	3.	5.	7.	10.	20.	35.	50.	150.	225.	550.	1,000.	7,000.

ONE CENT
GEORGE VI 1938 - 1947

In 1937 the Newfoundland government reviewed the question of converting to a small cent, similar to those used in Canada and the United States. The smaller coin was less expensive to produce and Newfoundlanders objected to the reverse design of the large cent, in which their provincial flower was forced into an unnatural configuration.

The reverse design adopted for the new coins was a very lifelike rendition of the pitcher plant in bloom. The plant is native to Newfoundland, and is one of the insectivores of the plant kingdom. The large leaves are pitcher-like receptacles, the inner surfaces being covered with downward-sloping bristles. Insects are attracted onto their leaves by a sweet sticky syrup at the bottom and the bristles help prevent their escape. The digestible portions of the insects are then absorbed by the plant.

During World War II, Newfoundland cents were coined at Ottawa rather than in England to avoid the risks of transatlantic shipping. In 1940 and 1942 the "C" mint mark was omitted in error.

Designer and Engraver:
Obv.: Percy Metcalfe
Rev.: Walter J. Newman
Composition: .955 copper, .030 tin, .015 zinc
Weight: 3.24 grams
Diameter: 19.05 mm
Edge: Plain
Die Axes: ↑↑

"C" Mint Mark

Royal Canadian Mint issues (1940-47) have a "C" mint mark to the right of CENT on the reverse (except for the 1940 and 1942 issues, which have none). The Royal Mint strikings (1938) have no mint mark.

DATE / MINT/ VARIETY	MINTAGE	VG-8	F-12	VF-20	EF-40	AU-50	AU-55	MS-60 Br	MS-63 Red	MS-64 Red	MS-65 Red	SP-63 Rd/Br	SP-65 Rd/Br
1938	500,000	3.	5.	7.	8.	15.	25.	40.	90.	175.	325.	1,000.	4,000.
1940	300,000	3.	5.	7.	18.	40.	50.	75.	275.	1,000.	2,500.	1,000.	5,000.
1940 RE	Included	30.	45.	100.	200	300.	400.	600.	—	—	—	*	*
1941C	827,662	3.	4.	8.	10.	15.	20.	30.	125.	450.	2,000.	*	*
1941C DD	Included	15.	25.	50.	100.	200.	300.	500.	—	—	—	*	*
1942	1,996,889	3.	4.	8.	12.	20.	25.	40.	150.	450.	—	*	*
1943C	1,239,732	3.	4.	10.	15.	20.	25.	40.	100.	275.	—	*	*
1944C	1,328,776	3.	4.	15.	35.	100.	150.	250.	1,250.	—	—	*	*
1947C	313,772	3.	5.	10.	20.	45.	60.	100.	325.	—	—	1,250.	5,000.

SYMBOLS USED IN PRICING TABLES

—	**No two coins have been assigned this grade by a Canadian grading company.**
*	**Not issued in that finish.**
BV	**Bullion value.**
C	**Circulating coins, coins which are purchased from banks, or found in change.**
FV	**Face value.**
NC	**Noncirculating coins identical in design to the circulating issue, but sold in sets or special packaging by the Royal Canadian Mint.**
N.I.I.	**Not issued individually, but included in a set of some nature.**
P.E.	**Plain edge**

FIVE CENTS
VICTORIA 1865 - 1896

Work on the coinage tools for the silver began later than for the cent, so there are no legend wording varieties for this denomination. The first pattern is a bronze striking of the adopted obverse (derived from the New Brunswick obverse by substitution of "NEWFOUNDLAND" for "NEW BRUNSWICK") and the Canada/New Brunswick reverse with a maple wreath and royal crown (see NF-2 in the chapter on Patterns). A later pattern, in silver, has an arabesque design similar to the adopted design, except the arches are thinner (see NF-8 in the chapter on Patterns). Ralph Heaton and Sons issues have an "H" mint mark under the bust (1872-1876) Royal Mint strikings have no mint mark.

"H" Mint Mark

Designer and Engraver:
Obv.: Leonard C. Wyon
Rev.: Leonard C. Wyon
Composition: .925 silver, .075 copper
Weight: 1.18 grams
Diameter: 15.49 mm
Edge: Reeded
Die Axes: ↑↓

VICTORIA OBVERSE PORTRAIT VARIETIES

The portraits of Victoria for the Newfoundland coinage are easily identifiable by the use of the 'periods' before and after 'Newfoundland' in the obverse legend.

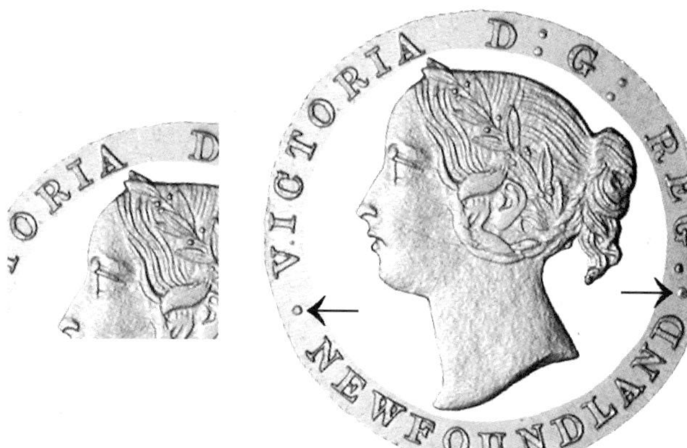

PORTRAIT: NF1
Two well defined strands of hair at top of brow, below top leaf of laurel crown. **Dot before and after NEWFOUNDLAND.** NF1 will be found on the following dates: 1865; 1870; 1873

PORTRAIT: NF2
Two weakly defined strands of hair at top of brow, below top leaf of laurel crown. **No dot before and after NEWFOUNDLAND.** NF2 will be found on the following dates: 1865; 1870; 1872H; 1873; 1873H; 1876H; 1880; 1881; 1885; 1888

PORTRAIT: NF3

Three well defined strands of hair at top of brow, below top leaf of laurel crown. **Dot after NEWFOUNDLAND.** NF3 will be found on the following dates: 1882H; 1888; 1890; 1894; 1896

VICTORIA OBVERSE DOUBLED DIE

1880 (DD) Doubled Eyelids, Nose and Lips Doubled Die

VICTORIA REVERSE VARIETIES

There are currently no major reverse varieties for the five cent silver coins. There is however a variation in the punch numbers used between 1865 and the balance of the issue: 1865 has a Roman numeral "I" in the date, while 1870 to 1896 have an Arabic "I" in the date.

Ralph Heaton and Sons issues have an "H" mint mark on the reverse under the date (1882). Royal Mint strikings have no mint mark.

DATE / MINT PORTRAIT	MINTAGE (thous.)	G-4	VG-8	F-12	VF-20	EF-40	AU-50	AU-55	MS-60	MS-63	MS-65	SP-63	SP-65
1865 NF1	80	25.	50.	100.	175.	450.	—	—	—	—	—	*	*
1865 NF1 (PE)	Incl.	*	*	*	*	*	*	*	*	*	*	3,000.	12,000.
1865 NF2	Incl.	NONE KNOWN TO EXIST										*	*
1870 NF1	40	75.	150.	300.	500.	750.	—	—	—	—	—	—	—
1870 NF1 (PE)	Incl.	*	*	*	*	*	*	*	*	*	*	2,000.	7,500.
1870 NF2	Incl.	NONE KNOWN TO EXIST										*	*
1872H NF2	40	35.	75.	125.	225.	450.	850.	1,800.	—	—	5,000.	*	*
1873 NF1	40	500.	1,000.	—	—	—	—	—	—	—	—	—	—
1873 NF2	Incl.	175.	350.	500.	1,200.	2,500.	—	—	—	—	—	*	*
1873H NF2	Incl.	800.	1,500.	2,500.	3,500.	—	—	—	—	—	—	*	*
1876H NF2	20	150.	325.	500.	800.	1,250.	—	—	—	—	—	*	*
1880 NF2	40	50.	85.	125.	250.	400.	700.	1,000.	—	—	—	2,000.	7,500.
1880 NF2 DD	Incl.	75.	100.	150.	350.	500.	1,500.	—	—	—	—	*	*
1881 NF2	40	30.	70.	100.	250.	500.	1,200.	1,800.	2,500.	—	—	3,00.	10,000.
1882H NF3	60	25.	50.	90.	175.	400.	800.	1,200.	2,000.	3,500.	—	2,000.	4,500.
1885 NF2	16	175.	300.	450.	775.	1,500.	3,000.	—	—	—	—	—	—
1888 NF2	40	750.	1,000.	2,000.	3,500.	—	—	—	—	—	—	3,000.	10,000.
1888 NF3	Incl.	45.	90.	175.	350.	900.	2,000.	—	—	—	—	*	*
1890 NF3	160	10.	15.	30.	70.	175.	750.	1,000.	2,000.	—	—	—	—
1894 NF3	160	10.	20.	35.	125.	250.	—	—	—	—	—	2,000.	8,000.
1896 NF3	400	5.	15.	30.	40.	150.	450.	950.	1,800.	3,500.	—	2,000.	8,000.

FIVE CENTS
EDWARD VII 1903 - 1908

The obverse for this denomination is that of the Dominion of Canada issues. The reverse, a new design by George W. DeSaulles, is one of the last coinage designs he engraved before his death. The Mint Birmingham Ltd. issue of 1904 has an "H" mint mark below the oval at the bottom on the reverse. Royal Mint strikings have no mint mark.

"H" Mint Mark

Designer and Engraver: George W. DeSaulles
Composition: .925 silver, .075 copper
Weight: 1.18 grams
Diameter: 15.49 mm
Edge: Reeded
Die Axes: 1903, 1904 ↑↓
1909 ↑↑

DATE / MINT MARK	MINTAGE	VG-8	F-12	VF-20	EF-40	AU-50	AU-55	MS-60	MS-63	MS-64	MS-65	SP-63	SP-65
1903	100,000	10.	20.	35.	70.	175.	300.	500.	1,500.	2,000.	3,500.	—	—
1904H	100,000	6.	8.	20.	55.	125.	150.	225.	400.	600.	800.	—	3,500.
1908	400,000	8.	10.	20.	50.	125.	175.	325.	925.	1,500.	—	*	*

FIVE CENTS
GEORGE V 1912 - 1929

The obverse is the same as for the Dominion of Canada issue and the reverse is the same as the Newfoundland Edward VII issue. The Ottawa Mint issues (1917-1919) have a "C" mint mark below the oval at the bottom on the reverse. Royal Mint strikings have no mint mark.

"C" Mint Mark

Designer and Engraver:
Obv.: Sir E. B. MacKennal
Rev.: George W. DeSaulles
Composition: .925 silver, .075 copper
Weight:
1912: 1.18 grams
1917-1929: 1.17 grams
Diameter:
1912-1919: 15.49 mm
1929: 15.69 mm
Edge: Reeded
Die Axes: ↑↑

DATE / MINT MARK	MINTAGE	VG-8	F-12	VF-20	EF-40	AU-50	AU-55	MS-60	MS-63	MS-64	MS-65	SP-63	SP-65
1912	300,000	4.	6.	10.	20.	65.	125.	150.	250.	375.	750.	1,500.	—
1917C	300,319	5.	6.	15.	30.	125.	200.	400.	1,400.	2,500.	—	2,000.	—
1919C	100,844	6.	10.	25.	135.	550.	900.	1,500.	3,000.	6,000.	9,000.	2,000.	—
1929	300,000	5.	8.	10.	15.	100.	135.	175.	425.	675.	1,200.	*	*

PRICING

The Charlton Press pricing tables are based on market prices for **Canadian certified coins.** Currently there are two coin grading companies located in Canada. Our prices are gathered from prices realized at land auctions, internet auctions, and dealer fixed price lists and their internet listings. It is important to realize that coin certification incurs a cost, and on low value coins it will be a significant factor in their listed value. The cost for certification per coin averages between $7-$10 for standard service.

FIVE CENTS
GEORGE VI 1938 - 1947

While considering the replacement of the large cent, the Newfoundland government also contemplated dropping its "fish scale" silver 5-cent piece in favour of a nickel coin similar to Canada's. At that time, because of a strong conservative element, it was decided to change only the cent. The reverse design was continued from the previous reign and the obverse used the standard portrait for British colonial coinages.

The 1946C issue is an anomaly. Published official mint reports, as well as unpublished mint accounting records, do not indicate any mintage of this denomination during 1946. It appears that this scarce issue was actually coined during 1947. The mintage figures given for the years 1946 and 1947 must be considered unofficial although they are believed to have come from a mint officer many years ago. Royal Canadian Mint issues (1940-47) have a "C" mint mark below the oval at the bottom on the reverse. The Royal Mint issue (1938) has no mint mark.

"C" Mint Mark

Designer and Engraver:
Obv.: Percy Metcalfe
Rev.: George W. DeSaulles

Composition:
1938-1944: .925 silver, .075 copper
1945-1947: .800 silver, .200 copper

Weight: 1.17 grams

Diameter:
1938: 15.69 mm
1940-1947: 15.49 mm

Edge: Reeded

Die Axes: ↑↑

DATE / MINT MARK	MINTAGE	VG-8	F-12	VF-20	EF-40	AU-50	AU-55	MS-60	MS-63	MS-64	MS-65	SP-63	SP-65
1938	100,000	5.	8.	10.	15.	30.	75.	125.	275.	450.	1,500.	1,500.	5,000.
1940C	200,000	5.	10.	12.	15.	40.	60.	100.	300.	600.	2,000.	1,500.	5,000.
1941C	612,641	5.	6.	8.	10.	15.	20.	25.	40.	110.	400.	*	*
1942C	298,348	5.	6.	8.	10.	15.	25.	35.	75.	110.	425.	*	*
1943C	351,666	5.	6.	8.	10.	12.	20.	30.	55.	100.	400.	*	*
1944C	286,504	5.	6.	8.	10.	20.	25.	65.	100.	275.	1,000.	*	*
1945C	203,828	5.	6.	8.	10.	20.	25.	30.	60.	125.	300.	*	*
1946C	2,041	400.	700.	1,000.	1,400.	1,800.	2,500.	3,000.	3,500.	4,500.	5,500.	*	*
1947C	38,400	5.	6.	8.	25.	50.	80.	110.	250.	350.	500.	*	*

TEN CENTS
VICTORIA 1865 - 1896

Like the 5 cents, the 10 cents exists as a bronze pattern with the adopted obverse (derived from the New Brunswick obverse by substituting "NEWFOUNDLAND" for "NEW BRUNSWICK") and the Canada/New Brunswick reverse (see NF-3 in the chapter on Patterns). As well there is a silver pattern with very thin arches in the arabesque design on the reverse (see NF-9 in the chapter on Patterns). Ralph Heaton and Sons issues have an "H" mint mark under the bust for the years 1872 and 1876. Ralph Heaton and Sons strikings have an "H" mint mark on the reverse under the date for 1882. Royal Mint strikings have no mint mark.

"H" Mint Marks

Designer and Engraver:
Obv.: Leonard C. Wyon
Rev.: Leonard C. Wyon
Composition: .925 silver, .075 copper
Weight: 2.36 grams
Diameter: 17.98 mm
Edge: Reeded
Die Axes: ↑↓

VICTORIA OBVERSE PORTRAIT VARIETIES

The portraits of Victoria for the Newfoundland coinage are easily identifiable by the use of the 'periods' before and after 'Newfoundland' in the obverse legend.

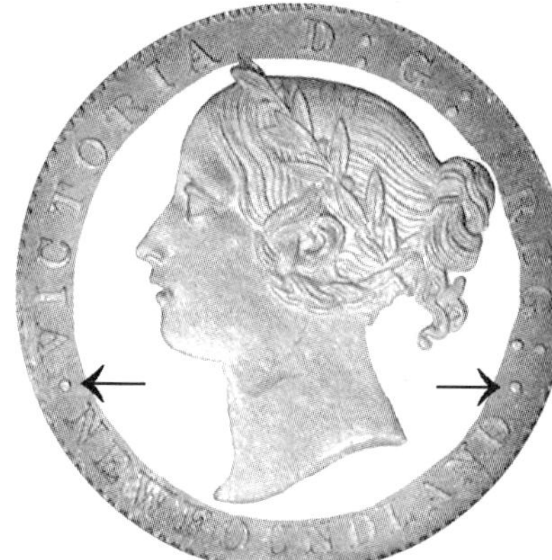

PORTRAIT: ND1
Two leaves at top of laurel crown; uppermost rising into legend band. **Dot before and after NEWFOUNDLAND.** ND1 will be found on the following dates: 1865; 1870; 1873

PORTRAIT: ND2
Three leaves at top of laurel crown; upper-most leaf well into legend band. **Dot before but not after NEWFOUNDLAND.** ND2 will be found on the following dates: 1870; 1872H; 1873; 1876H; 1880; 1885; 1894

VICTORIA OBVERSE PORTRAIT VARIETIES (cont.)

PORTRAIT: ND3

Two leaves at top of laurel crown. Top leaf barely touches legend band. **Dot before and after NEWFOUNDLAND.** ND3 will be found on the following dates: 1882H; 1885; 1888; 1890; 1894; 1896

VICTORIA REVERSE VARIETIES

As with the silver five cents, there are no major reverse die varieties. Again, the Roman numeral 'I' appears on two dates, 1865 and 1870, and the Arabic '1' on 1872 to 1896.

A rare variety exists because an 1871H Dominion of Canada reverse die was muled, apparently accidentally, with an "H" Newfoundland obverse die. All known examples are in well-worn condition. All examples of the 1880 issue are from dies in which the second 8 of the date is punched over a 7.

1871H Newfoundland/Canada Mule

1880 Second 8 over 7

DATE / MINT / PORTRAIT	MINTAGE (thous.)	G-4	VG-8	F-12	VF-20	EF-40	AU-50	AU-55	MS-60	MS-63	MS-65	SP-63	SP-65
1865 ND1	80	30.	50.	90.	150.	375.	750.	1,250.	2,000.	4,000.	7,500.	*	*
1865 ND1 (PE)	Incl.	*	*	*	*	*	*	*	*	*	*	5,000.	15,000.
1870 ND1	30	150.	300.	600.	1,250.	—	—	—	—	—	—	5,000.	10,000.
1870 ND1 (PE)	Incl.	*	*	*	*	*	*	*	*	*	*	10,000.	30,000.
1870 ND2	Incl.	200.	300.	425.	675.	—	—	—	—	—	—	*	*
1871H Mule	Unknown				EXTREMELY RARE							*	*
1872H ND2	40	20.	40.	55.	110.	225.	600.	900.	1,500.	2,000.	4,000.	*	*
1873 ND1	20				ONLY TWO CERTIFIED							—	—
1873 ND2	Incl.	45.	100.	200.	350.	1,150.	—	—	—	—	—	*	*
1876H ND2	10	50.	100.	175.	450.	800.	1,500.	2,000.	3,000.	6,000.	10,000.	*	*
1880 ND2	10	50.	110.	175.	350.	675.	—	—	—	—	—	7,000.	15,000.
1882H ND3	20	35.	75.	95.	200.	500.	—	—	—	—	—	2,000.	6,000.
1885 ND2	8	125.	200.	325.	575.	1,300.	—	—	—	—	—	5,000.	15,000.
1885 ND3	Incl.				NOT KNOWN TO EXIST							*	*
1888 ND3	30	50.	70.	85.	225.	1,500.	3,500.	—	—	—	—	—	—
1890 ND3	100	10.	15.	30.	40.	275.	1,200.	2,500.	—	—	—	5,000.	12,000.
1894 ND2	100				ONLY THREE CERTIFIED							—	—
1894 ND3	Incl.	8.	15.	25.	50.	175.	625.	1,250.	—	—	—	5,000.	12,000.
1896 ND3	230	10.	15.	20.	50.	150.	425.	900.	2,000.	—	—	5,000.	12,000.

TEN CENTS
EDWARD VII 1903 - 1904

The obverse is that used for the Dominion of Canada issues. The reverse is a new design by George W. DeSaulles. The Mint Birmingham Ltd. issue of 1904 has an "H" mint mark below the oval at the bottom on the reverse. The Royal Mint issue (1903) has no mint mark.

"H" Mint Mark

Designer and Engraver: George W. DeSaulles
Composition: .925 silver, .075 copper
Weight: 2.36 grams
Diameter: 17.96 mm
Edge: Reeded
Die Axes: ↑↓

DATE / MINT MARK	MINTAGE	VG-8	F-12	VF-20	EF-40	AU-50	AU-55	MS-60	MS-63	MS-64	MS-65	SP-63	SP-65
1903	100,000	15.	35.	75.	200.	650.	1,200.	—	—	—	—	—	—
1904H	100,000	7.	15.	45.	115.	200.	300.	375.	600.	1,200.	3,000.	1,500.	3,500.

TEN CENTS
GEORGE V 1912 - 1919

The obverse is the same as for the Dominion of Canada issues. The reverse is a continuation of the Newfoundland Edward VII designs. Ottawa Mint issues of 1917-1919 have a "C" mint mark below the oval at the bottom on the reverse. The Royal Mint issue (1912) has no mint mark.

"C" Mint Mark

Designer and Engraver:
Obv.: Sir E. B. MacKennal
Rev.: George W. DeSaulles
Composition: .925 silver, .075 copper
Weight:
1912-1917: 2.36 grams
1919: 2.33 grams
Diameter:
1912: 17.96 mm
1917-1919: 18.03 mm
Edge: Reeded
Die Axes: ↑↑

DATE / MINT MARK	MINTAGE	VG-8	F-12	VF-20	EF-40	AU-50	AU-55	MS-60	MS-63	MS-64	MS-65	SP-63	SP-65
1912	150,000	5.	7.	15.	60.	175.	225.	275.	400.	500.	850.	1,500.	5,000.
1917C	250,805	5.	10.	20.	50.	200.	300.	475.	1,250.	2,000.	—	2,000.	7,500.
1919C	54,342	5.	10.	25.	90.	200.	250.	300.	400.	600.	1,800.	2,000.	7,500.

TEN CENTS
GEORGE VI 1938-1947

The obverse for this denomination used Percy Metcalfe's standard portrait of George VI for British colonial coinages and the existing Edward VII/George V reverse. The 1946C issue was probably coined in 1947 (see preceding comments on the 1946C 5 cents); the mintage figures for 1946 and 1947 must be considered unofficial.

Royal Canadian Mint strikings of 1941-1947 have a "C" mint mark below the oval at the bottom on the reverse. The Royal Mint issue of 1938 and the Royal Canadian Mint issue of 1940 have no mint mark.

"C" Mint Mark

Designer and Engraver:
Obv.: Percy Metcalfe
Rev.: George W. DeSaulles

Composition:
1938-1944: .925 silver, .075 copper
1945-1947: .800 silver, .200 copper

Weight: 2.33 grams
Diameter: 18.03 mm
Edge: Reeded
Die Axes: ↑↑

DATE / MINT MARK	MINTAGE	VG-8	F-12	VF-20	EF-40	AU-50	AU-55	MS-60	MS-63	MS-64	MS-65	SP-63	SP-65
1938	100,000	5.	6.	8.	15.	65.	150.	250.	600.	1,500.	—	1,500.	5,000.
1940	100,000	5.	6.	8.	15.	45.	60.	100.	400.	1,200.	—	1,500.	5,000.
1941C	483,630	5.	6.	8.	10.	20.	25.	40.	125.	175.	500.	*	*
1942C	292,736	5.	6.	8.	15.	25.	45.	60.	200.	500.	—	*	*
1943C	104,706	5.	6.	10.	15.	35.	150.	250.	1,000.	2,500.	—	*	*
1944C	151,471	5.	10.	15.	30.	50.	100.	250.	1,000.	2,500.	—	*	*
1945C	175,833	5.	8.	15.	40.	55.	75.	125.	325.	475.	—	*	*
1946C	38,400	5.	8.	15.	40.	55.	100.	125.	325.	475.	—	—	—
1947C	61,988	5.	7.	15.	35.	65.	80.	125.	350.	650.	1,200.	—	—

TWENTY CENTS
VICTORIA 1865 - 1900

The first pattern known for the Newfoundland 20-cent piece is a bronze striking with the adopted obverse (derived from the New Brunswick obverse) and a reverse from a die for the 1864 New Brunswick 20 cents (see NF-4 in the chapter on Patterns). Later patterns in silver have an arabesque design similar to that finally adopted. The first (see NF-10 in the chapter on Patterns) has very thin arches and corresponds to similar 5-cent and 10-cent patterns. The second stands alone and has arches more like the adopted design and a raised line just inside the denticles (see NF-13 in the chapter on Patterns).

This denomination proved popular with Newfoundlanders and was minted on a regular basis throughout the remainder of Victoria's reign. With the passing years, however, it became increasingly unpopular with Canadians (because of its similarity to their 25-cent piece) and was replaced with a 25-cent coin during World War I.

Obverse "H" Mint Mark

Reverse "H" Mint Mark

Designer:
Obv.: Leonard C. Wyon
Rev.: Horace Morehen
Engraver:
Obv.: Leonard C. Wyon
Rev.: Leonard C. Wyon
Composition: .925 silver, .075 copper
Weight: 4.71 grams
Diameter: 23.19 mm
Edge: Reeded
Die Axes: ↑↓

Ralph Heaton and Sons strikings have an "H" mint mark on the obverse under the bust (1872 to 1876), or on the reverse under the date (1882). Royal Mint strikings have no mint mark.

VICTORIA OBVERSE PORTRAIT VARIETIES

PORTRAIT: NT1
Two leaves at top of laurel crown, with the rear leaf being very thin. Knot of hair at the back of the head touches the legend band. Prominent upper lip.
Dot before and after NEWFOUNDLAND.
NT1 will be found on the following dates: 1865; 1870; 1872H; 1873; 1876H; 1880; 1881; 1885; 1894; 1896 L96, S96

PORTRAIT: NT2
Two leaves at top of laurel crown; both distinctive and well into legend band. Knot of hair at the back of the head enters legend band. Repressed upper lip.
Dot before and after NEWFOUNDLAND.
NT2 will be found on the following dates: 1882H; 1888; 1890; 1894; 1896 (all varieties); 1899 (all varieties); 1900

VICTORIA REVERSE VARIETIES

As with previous denominations there are no major reverse varieties. Use of the Roman numeral 'I' in the date was extended from 1865 to 1880. The Arabic '1' appears in dates from 1881 to 1900.

1896
Small 96 (S96)

1896
Large 96 (L96)

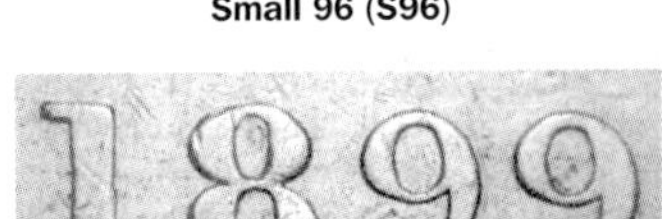

1899
Hooked 99 (H99)

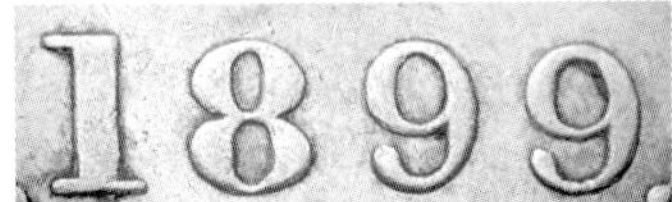

1899
Large 99 (L99)

DATE / MINT / PORTRAIT/VAR.	MINTAGE (thous.)	G-4	VG-8	F-12	VF-20	EF-40	AU-50	AU-55	MS-60	MS-63	MS-65	SP-63	SP-65
1865 NT1	100	15.	25.	50.	100.	350.	750.	1,000.	2,000.	4,000.	—	6,500.	20,000.
1865 NT1 (PE)	Incl.	*	*	*	*	*	*	*	*	*	*	5,000.	15,000.
1870 NT1	50	15.	35.	75.	150.	550.	1,000.	1,500.	2,500.	3,500.	8,000.	5,000.	15,000.
1870 NT1 (PE)	Incl.	*	*	*	*	*	*	*	*	*	*	5,000.	15,000.
1872H NT1	90	10.	20.	35.	65.	275.	1,000.	2,500.	—	—	—	*	*
1873 NT1	40	25.	45.	125.	225.	875.	2,500.	—	—	—	—	8,000.	25,000.
1876H NT1	50	20.	40.	65.	150.	500.	1,000.	2,500.	—	—	—	*	*
1880 NT1	30	20.	50.	90.	200.	750.	—	—	—	—	—	6,000.	16,000.
1881 NT1	60	15.	25.	40.	125.	475.	—	—	—	—	—	6,000.	16,000.
1882H NT2	100	15.	20.	30.	65.	325.	900.	1,500.	—	—	—	3,000.	7,500.
1885 NT1	40	20.	35.	65.	150.	650.	1,800.	—	—	—	—	8,000.	25,000.
1888 NT2	75	15.	25.	45.	90.	425.	1,000.	2,000.	4,000.	8,000.	—	7,500.	22,500.
1890 NT2	100	15.	20.	35.	75.	325.	—	—	—	—	—	5,000.	13,500.
1894 NT1	100	15.	20.	35.	45.	275.	—	—	—	—	—	5,000.	13,500.
1894 NT2	Incl.	15.	25.	60.	100.	250.	—	—	—	—	—	*	*
1896 NT1 L96	125	15.	20.	35.	40.	225.	1,000.	—	—	—	—	5,000.	13,500.
1896 NT1 S96	Incl.	15.	20.	35.	70.	250.	1,000.	—	—	—	—	*	*
1896 NT2 L96	Incl.	15.	20.	35.	70.	250.	1,000.	—	—	—	—	*	*
1896 NT2 S96	Incl.	15.	20.	45.	60.	300.	1,000.	1,500.	—	—	—	*	*
1899 NT2 H99	125	30.	45.	95.	175.	450.	2,000.	—	—	—	—	*	*
1899 NT2 L99	Incl.	10.	15.	25.	40.	175.	750.	1,000.	—	—	—	*	*
1900-NT2	125	10.	15.	25.	50.	175.	500.	1,000.	2,000.	3,000.	8,000.	5,000.	13,500.

SYMBOLS USED IN PRICING TABLES

—	**No two coins have been assigned this grade by a Canadian grading company.**
*	**Not issued in that finish.**
BV	**Bullion value.**
C	**Circulating coins, coins which are purchased from banks, or found in change.**
FV	**Face value.**
NC	**Noncirculating coins identical in design to the circulating issue, but sold in sets or special packaging by the Royal Canadian Mint.**
N.I.I.	**Not issued individually, but included in a set of some nature.**
P.E.	**Plain edge**

TWENTY CENTS EDWARD VII 1904

Coins of this denomination were required on only one occasion during Edward's short reign, making the 1904 issue a one-year type. This issue was coined by The Mint Birmingham Ltd. and bears an "H" mint mark below the oval at the bottom on the reverse.

'H' Mintmark

Designer and Engraver:
Obv.: George W. DeSaulles
Rev.: W. H. J. Blakemore, copying DeSaulles' design for the reverse of 5¢ and 10¢ pieces
Composition: .925 silver, .075 copper
Weight: 4.71 grams
Diameter: 23.19 mm
Edge: Reeded
Die Axes: ↑↑

DATE / MINT MARK	MINTAGE (thous.)	VG-8	F-12	VF-20	EF-40	AU-50	AU-55	MS-60	MS-63	MS-64	MS-65	SP-63	SP-65
1904H	75	25.	45.	80.	175.	700.	1,200.	—	—	—	—	1,500.	5,000.

TWENTY CENTS GEORGE V 1912

Like its Edwardian predecessor, the George V 20 cents is a one-year type. The reverse established for the previous reign was continued.

Designer and Engraver:
Obv.: Sir E. B. MacKennal
Rev.: W. H. J. Blakemore
Composition: .925 silver, .075 copper
Weight: 4.71 grams
Diameter: 23.19 mm
Edge: Reeded
Die Axes: ↑↑

DATE/ MINT MARK	MINTAGE (thous.)	VG-8	F-12	VF-20	EF-40	AU-50	AU-55	MS-60	MS-63	MS-64	MS-65	SP-63	SP-65
1912	350	10.	15.	25.	85.	175.	275.	375.	750.	1,000.	1,500.	2,000.	6,500.

TWENTY-FIVE CENTS GEORGE V 1917 - 1919

The second time 20-cent pieces were required during George V's reign was toward the end of World War I. By that time, however, arrangements had been made for the Ottawa Mint to produce Newfoundland's coins. Canada took a dim view of the 20 cents because it circulated in Canada as well, and was confused with the Canadian 25 cents. The Canadian government convinced the Newfoundland government to drop the 20 cents and adopt a 25 cents, struck on the same standard as the corresponding Canadian coin. Indeed, the obverse of the new coin was identical to that for the Canadian 25 cents. This denomination was coined by the Ottawa Mint and bears a "C" mint mark below the oval at the bottom on the reverse.

'C' Mintmark

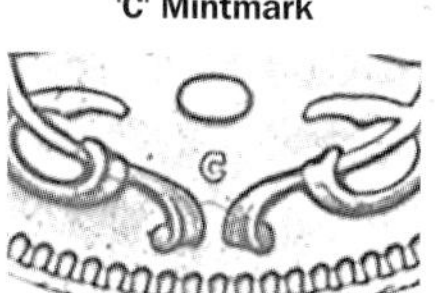

Designer and Engraver:
Obv.: Sir E. B. MacKennal
Engraver:
Rev.: W. H. J. Blakemore, modifying the 20¢ reverse
Composition: .925 silver, .075 copper
Weight: 5.83 grams
Diameter: 23.62 mm
Edge: Reeded
Die Axes: ↑↑

DATE / MINT MARK	MINTAGE	VG-8	F-12	VF-20	EF-40	AU-50	AU-55	MS-60	MS-63	MS-64	MS-65	SP-63	SP-65
1917C	464,779	10.	15.	20.	30.	70.	125.	200.	300.	550.	—	1,600.	6,500.
1919C	163,939	10.	15.	25.	35.	150.	175.	250.	1,000.	2,000.	—	1,600.	6,500.

FIFTY CENTS
VICTORIA 1870 -1900

The 50-cent piece was the last denomination to be added to the Victorian coinage, coming in 1870. Its laureate portrait is stylistically unlike anything used for the rest of the British North America. This denomination became popular on the island and assumed even greater importance after the failure of the Commercial and Union Banks of Newfoundland during the financial crisis of 1894.

Obverse

Reverse

Designer and Engraver: Leonard C. Wyon
Composition: .925 silver, .075 copper
Weight: 11.78 grams
Diameter: 29.85 mm
Edge: Reeded
Die Axes: ↑↓

MINT MARKS

Ralph Heaton and Sons strikings have an "H" mint mark either on the obverse under the bust (1872-1876) or on the reverse under the date (1882). Royal Mint strikings have no mint mark.

OBVERSE LEGEND VARIETIES

As seen on 1896 and 1898

Small W

Large W over Small W

VICTORIA OBVERSE PORTRAIT VARIETIES

PORTRAIT: NH1
Four leaves at top of laurel crown; the upper-most leaf enters the legend band between the 'E' and 'I' in DEI. Prominent upper lip. **No dot before or after NEWFOUNDLAND.** NH1 will be found on the following dates: 1870; 1872H; 1873; 1874; 1876H; 1880; 1881; 1885; 1888; 1894; 1896; 1898

VICTORIA OBVERSE VARIETIES (cont.)

PORTRAIT: NH2
Four leaves at top of laurel crown, with none entering the legend band. Repressed upper lip. **No dot before or after NEWFOUNDLAND**. NH2 will be found on the following dates: 1882H; 1896; 1898; 1899; 1900

VICTORIA REVERSE VARIETIES

1880

All examples of the 1880 issue are from dies in which the second 8 of the date is punched over a 7.

1899

Narrow 9s with thick sides and oval centres (N9)

1899

Wide 9s with thin sides and round centres (W9)

No major reverse die varieties exist for the Newfoundland fifty cent coins. However, in 1880 or 1881 the reverse die was modified with the design being rendered more delicate. The 1865 to 1880 fifty cent coins have wide thick loops, and 1881 to 1898 have thin loops.

DATE / MINT PORTRAIT/ VAR.	MINTAGE	G-4	VG-8	F-12	VF-20	EF-40	AU-50	AU-55	MS-60	MS-63	MS-65	SP-63	SP-65
1870 NH1	50,000	30.	50.	85.	225.	900.	—	—	—	—	—	10,000.	40,000.
1870 NH1 (PE)	Included	*	*	*	*	*	*	*	*	*	*	30,000.	40,000.
1872H NH1	48,000	25.	35.	55.	150.	625.	1,200.	—	—	—	—	*	*
1873 NH1	32,000	45.	100.	175.	350.	1,200.	2,500.	—	—	—	—	—	—
1874 NH1	80,000	25.	50.	75.	175.	750.	—	—	—	—	—	—	—
1876H NH1	28,000	35.	70.	100.	300.	1,000.	—	—	—	—	—	*	*
1880 NH1	24,000	40.	75.	200	425.	1,500.	—	—	—	—	—	25,000.	—
1881 NH1	50,000	25.	40.	65.	225.	825.	1,800.	2,750.	5,000.	—	—	—	—
1882H NH2	100,000	20.	35.	45.	150.	625.	1,100.	2,000.	3,500.	6,000.	—	5,000.	20,000.
1885 NH1	40,000	30.	60.	100.	300.	950.	1,500.	—	—	—	—	10,000.	30,000.
1888 NH1	20,000	30.	60.	175.	325.	750.	5,000.	—	—	—	—	25,000.	—
1894 NH1	40,000	20.	25.	30.	125.	500.	—	—	—	—	—	8,000.	30,000.
1896 NH1 LW/SW	60,000	20.	25.	30.	125.	450.	—	—	—	—	—	8,000.	30,000.
1896 NH2 SW	Included	20.	25.	35.	100.	750.	1,800.	3,500.	—	—	—	*	*
1898 NH1 LW	79,607	20.	25.	35.	85.	225.	1,500.	2,500.	—	—	—	*	*
1898 NH1 SW	Included	30.	50.	100.	500.	1,500.	—	—	—	—	—	*	*
1898 NH2 LW/SW	Included	20.	25.	35.	85.	275.	3,000.	—	—	—	—	*	*
1899 NH2 N9	150,000	20.	25.	35.	75.	250.	1,000.	1,800.	—	—	—	*	*
1899 NH2 W9	Included	20.	25.	30.	110.	375.	1,250.	1,500.	—	—	—	*	*
1900 NH2	150,000	20.	25.	30.	60.	200.	750.	1,500.	3,000.	—	—	*	*

Note: The 1874 fifty-cent coin is found in Specimen-68 condition. Only two are known to exist.

FIFTY CENTS
EDWARD VII 1904 - 1909

The obverse for this denomination is that of the Dominion of Canada issues. The Mint Birmingham Ltd. issue (1904) has an "H" mint mark below the oval at the bottom on the reverse. Royal Mint issues have no mint mark.

"H" Mint Mark

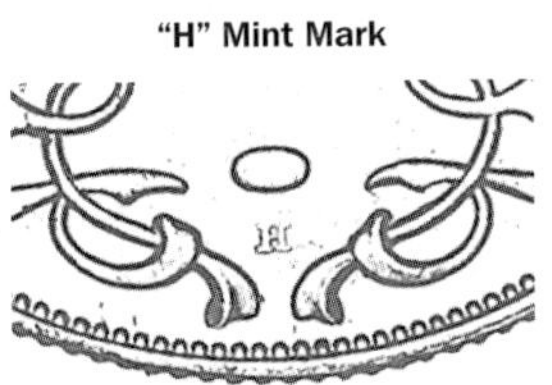

Designer and Engraver:
Obv.: George W. DeSaulles
Rev.: W. H. J. Blakemore, copying DeSaulles' design for 5¢ and 10¢ pieces
Composition: .
.925 silver, .075 copper
Weight: 11.78 grams
Diameter: 29.85 mm
Edge: Reeded
Die Axes: ↑↑

DATE / MINT MARK	MINTAGE	VG-8	F-12	VF-20	EF-40	AU-50	AU-55	MS-60	MS-63	MS-64	MS-65	SP-63	SP-65
1904H	140,000	20.	25.	30.	85.	175.	275.	425.	1,000.	2,000.	3,500.	6,000.	—
1907	100,000	20.	25.	35.	85.	225.	275.	450.	1,250.	4,000.	—	—	—
1908	160,000	20.	25.	30.	85.	135.	175.	375.	900.	1,800.	3,000.	—	—
1909	200,000	20.	25.	35.	100.	150.	225.	375.	1,000.	2,500.	—	—	—

Note: The finish on the 1904H fifty cents specimen is matte.

FIFTY CENTS
GEORGE V 1911 - 1919

The obverse for the Newfoundland 50-cent piece is the same as that for the 1912-1936 Dominion of Canada coins. That legend contains "DEI GRA" (see Dominion of Canada George V one-cent section) indicating that the modification of the Canadian obverses was made during 1911, prior to commencing the production of the Newfoundland issue for the year. The reverse continued the Edwardian design.

In 1917-1919 nearly 1,000,000 50 cents were struck and many were used to replace the discontinued government "cash notes" for making relief payments to the poor. The need for silver for this purpose diminished in 1920, when a new issue of government paper money was made. Ottawa Branch Mint strikings (1917-1919) have a "C" mint mark below the oval at the bottom on the reverse. The Royal Mint issue has no mint mark.

"C" Mint Mark

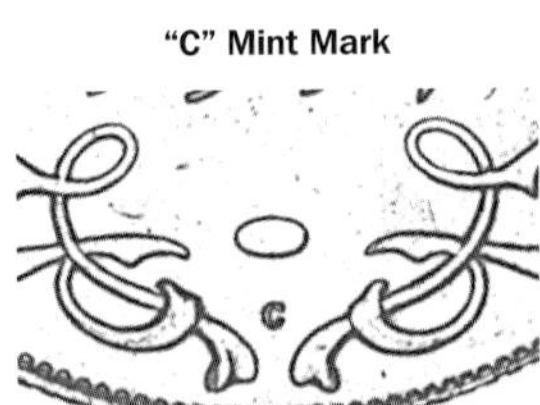

Designer:
Obv.: Sir E. B. MacKennal
Composition:
.925 silver, .075 copper
Weight:
1911: 11.78 grams
1917-1919: 11.66 grams
Diameter:
1911: 29.85 mm
1917-1919: 29.72 mm
Edge: Reeded
Die Axes: ↑↑

DATE / MINT MARK	MINTAGE	VG-8	F-12	VF-20	EF-40	AU-50	AU-55	MS-60	MS-63	MS-64	MS-65	SP-63	SP-65
1911	200,000	20.	25.	35.	60.	120.	175.	325.	675.	1,800.	3,500.	—	—
1917C	375,560	20.	25.	30.	35.	80.	125.	175.	550.	1,000.	2,000.	5,000.	—
1918C	294,824	20.	25.	30.	40.	80.	115.	225.	575.	1,200.	3,000.	—	—
1919C	306,267	20.	25.	35.	45.	115.	200.	475.	1,200.	2,000.	—	5,000.	—

TWO DOLLARS
VICTORIA 1865 - 1888

In the original planning for the Newfoundland coinage a gold dollar was considered. However, it was decided that such a coin would be so small it could be easily lost by the fishermen, so a 2-dollar denomination was chosen instead. The initial bronze pattern combines the adopted obverse (derived from the New Brunswick 10 cents obverse and identical to the Newfoundland 10 cents obverse) with the crown and maple wreath of the Canada/New Brunswick 10 cents reverse (see NF-5 in the chapter on Patterns). The adopted reverse has more conventional letters and the unusual feature of expressing the denomination three ways: 2 dollars, 200 cents, 100 pence, the last being the equivalent value in sterling (British money). Newfoundland was the only British colony with its own gold issue.

The Ralph Heaton and Sons issue of 1882 has an "H" mint mark below the date on the reverse. London Mint strikings have no mint mark.

"H" Mint Mark

Designer and Engraver:
Obv.: Leonard C. Wyon
Rev.: Leonard C. Wyon
Composition:
.917 gold, .083 copper
Weight: 3.33 grams
Diameter: 17.98 mm
Edge: Reeded
Die Axes: ↑↓

VICTORIA OBVERSE PORTRAIT VARIETIES

PORTRAIT: NTD1
Young head portrait. **Dot before and after NEWFOUNDLAND.** NTD1 will be found on the following dates: 1865; 1870

PORTRAIT: NTD2
Mature head portrait. **Dot before NEWFOUNDLAND.** NTD2 will be found on the following dates: 1870; 1872; 1880; 1881; 1885; 1888

VICTORIA OBVERSE PORTRAIT VARIETIES (cont.)

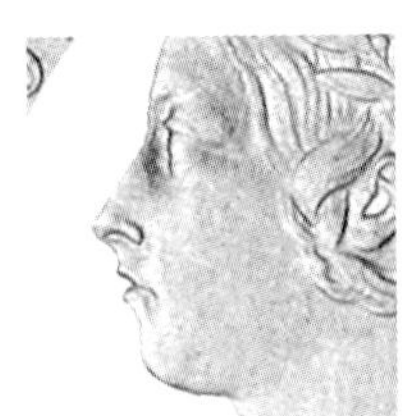

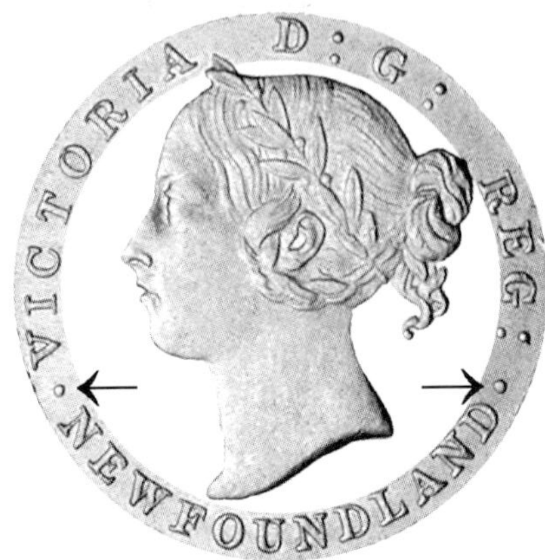

PORTRAIT: P3
Older portrait. **Dot before and after NEWFOUNDLAND.** P3 will be found on the following dates: 1882H; 1888

VICTORIA REVERSE VARIETIES

No major reverse die varieties have been identified for the Newfoundland two dollar coins.

DATE / MINT / PORTRAIT	MINTAGE	F-12	VF-20	EF-40	AU-50	AU-55	MS-60	MS-63	MS-64	MS-65	SP-63	SP-64	SP-65
1865 NTD1	10,000	300.	400.	600.	750.	1,000.	2,000.	12,500.	—	—	*	*	*
1865 NTD1 (PE)	Included	*	*	*	*	*	*	*	*	*	25,000.	50,000.	80,000.
1870 NTD1	10,000	300.	375.	500.	1,500.	1,800.	3,000.	—	—	—	30,000.	50,000.	100,000.
1870 NTD2	Included	275.	350.	500.	1,100.	1,500.	3,000.	10,000.	—	—	*	*	*
1872 NTD2	6,000	400.	500.	800.	1,500.	2,000.	3,000.	12,500.	—	—	25,000.	40,000.	65,000.
1880 NTD2	2,500	1,500.	1,800.	2,500.	3,500.	5,000.	7,500.	20,000.	—	—	75,000.	100,000.	125,000.
1881 NTD2	10,000	250.	350.	550.	675.	1,200.	2,000.	—	—	—	*	*	*
1882H NTD3	25,000	250.	300.	375.	525.	675.	900.	2,250.	3,500.	5,000.	30,000.	50,000.	70,000.
1885 NTD2	10,000	250.	300.	375.	600.	700.	900.	3,000.	7,000.	10,000.	—	—	—
1888 NTD2	25,000	ONLY FOUR CERTIFIED									*	*	*
1888 NTD3	Included	250.	325.	450.	550.	650.	800.	2,500.	6,000.	—	*	*	*

Note: The 1885 two dollar coin is known in Specimen-67 condition. Only one known.

PRICING

The Charlton Press pricing tables are based on market prices for **Canadian certified coins.** Currently there are two coin grading companies located in Canada. Our prices are gathered from prices realized at land auctions, internet auctions, and dealer fixed price lists and their internet listings. It is important to realize that coin certification incurs a cost, and on low value coins it will be a significant factor in their listed value. The cost for certification per coin averages between $7- $10 for standard service.

NEWFOUNDLAND SPECIMEN SETS 1865 - 1940

DATE AND MINT MARK	DESCRIPTION	AVERAGE GRADE	PRICE INDICATION
1865 Double Set	10 Coins, w/box, 1¢ - $2	SP-65	275,000.
1870	5 Coins, n/box, 5¢ - $2	SP-65	200,000.
1880	6 Coins, n/box, 1¢ - $2	SP-65	235,000.
1882H	5 Coins, n/box, 5¢ - $2	SP-65	110,000.
1885	6 Coins, n/box, 1¢ - $2	SP-65	235,000.
1888	4 Coins, n/box, 5¢ - 50¢	SP-65	100,000.
1896	5 Coins, n/box, 1¢ - 50¢	SP-65	70,000.
1904H	5 Coins, n/box, 1¢ - 50¢	SP-65	32,500.
1912	3 Coins, n/box, 5¢ - 20¢	SP-65	17,000.
1917C	5 Coins, n/box, 1¢ - 50¢	SP-65	32,500.
1919C	5 Coins, n/box, 1¢ - 50¢	SP-65	32,500.
1938C	3 Coins, n/box, 1¢ - 10¢	SP-65	15,000.
1940C	3 Coins, n/box, 1¢ - 10¢	SP-65	15,000.

NOTES ON DIE AXIS

The obverse design is considered the primary side of the coin. The die axis is the relationship of the reverse design to the obverse design. Consider the obverse die, usually the anvil die in a press, stationary and when installed is the point of reference. The reverse die (moving hammer die) may be turned or set at any of 360 degrees in relation to the set obverse die.

If the obverse die is identified by an upright arrow (↑) then the reverse die may be represented by a second arrow (↑). These arrows now form a relationship to one another. Illustrated below are two common die positions:

Coinage Axes: ↑↓
Obverse die: ↑
Reverse die is set 180 degrees opposite: ↓

Medal Axes: ↑↑
Obverse die: ↑
Reverse die is set in the matching direction: ↑

Two meaningful variations: ↑→, ↑←, as shown on page 161 in the 125th Anniversary of Confederation twenty-five cents coins of 1992, and on page 163 in the Millennium Design twenty-five cent coins of 1999.

PROVINCE OF CANADA

LARGE CENTS
VICTORIA 1858 - 1859

After the decision to adopt decimal coins was approved, a number of designs, sizes and compositions were considered for the cent. The first trials used a reverse design consisting of 19 maple leaves placed side by side, radiating from the centre (see PC-1 to PC-3 in the chapter on Patterns). However, a serpentine motif of 16 maple leaves was adopted and trial pieces were struck in a cupro-nickel alloy. Later, it was decided the new cents would be bronze.

The adopted obverse design shows a youthful, idealized bust of the queen wearing a laurel wreath in her hair. In fact, by the late 1850s the Queen was quite pudgy and decidedly older looking than the coinage portraits suggested.

The government optimistically ordered approximately 10 million 1-cent pieces, which proved to be much more than the province could absorb. At the time both Canada East and Canada West were inundated with the copper tokens issued by banks and individuals. The cents weighed 1/100lb avoirdupois and were much lighter than the bank tokens they were to replace. This slowed their public acceptance. The majority of the mintage remained unissued in the original boxes. In 1861 part of it was sent to the New Brunswick government to provide a temporary supply of decimal coins while the province awaited the arrival of its own issues, but the bulk of the stock went to the Bank of Upper Canada, the governments's bank. Until 1866, when it closed its doors, the Bank of Upper Canada experienced considerable difficulty in reducing its stock of cents, even when it offered to sell them at 20 percent below face value.

A stock of several million Province of Canada cents was inherited by the Dominion of Canada government in 1867 and it proceeded to issue them as Dominion currency.

Designer and Engraver: Leonard C. Wyon
Composition:
.95 copper, .04 tin, .01 zinc
(except for the rare brass)
Weight: 4.54 grams
Diameter: 25.4 mm
Edge: Plain
Die Axes: ↑↑, ↑↓

TWO MAJOR 1858 REVERSE VARIETIES

Full Vine and Stem Variety (FV)

Most 1858 and all 1859 working dies had a broken vine inside Leaf #13, and several broken leaf stems. Only the first three working dies sunk in 1858 had a completely intact vine and sixteen unbroken leaf stems.

Broken Stem to Leaf 9 Variety (BS)

The stem to Leaf #9 broke during the sinking of this fourth working die sunk in 1858. Only this single die had a completely intact vine, fifteen unbroken leaf stems, and one broken stem. The vine inside Leaf #13 and other stems broke during the sinking of the fifth working die, making this the last working die with an intact vine.

Please see page 51 for an image illustrating the maple leaf numbering system.

For further reading see Turner's *The 1858 Cents of Provincial Canada, Volume I and II.*

Original intact vine Inside Leaf #13

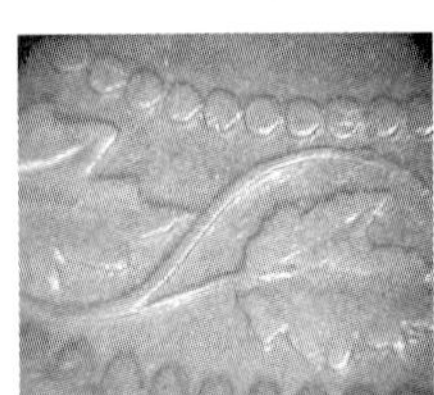

Original intact stem to Leaf #9

Original intact vine Inside Leaf #13

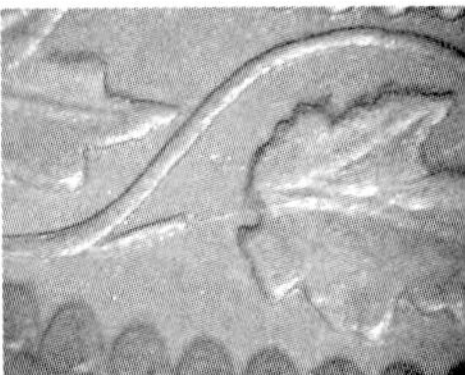

Broken Stem to Leaf #9

DATE / VARIETY	MINTAGE (thous.)	G-4	VG-8	F-12	VF-20	EF-40	AU-50	AU-55	MS-60 Br	MS-63 Red	MS-65 Red	SP-63 Rd/Br	SP-65 Rd/Br
1858 ↑↑	1,540	45.	75.	100.	150.	250.	325.	450.	700.	2,300.	8,000.	1,500.	3,500.
1858 ↑↓	Incl.	ONLY TWO CERTIFIED										*	*
1858 FV ↑↑	Incl.	80.	160.	250.	350.	550.	750.	1,100.	1,500.	—	—	*	*
1858 BS ↑↑	Incl.	100.	200.	350.	450.	675.	1,125.	1,650.	2,250.	—	—	*	*

1859 WIDE 9/8 VARIETIES: Since the coining of cents did not begin until the latter part of 1858, production continued throughout most of 1859, with most coins bearing a 1859 date. The first 1859s were undoubtedly overdates, on which a special wide 9 punch was employed to alter the second 8 on the 1858 reverse die. Below is one variety of the overdating on a 1858 reverse die.

1859 Wide 9/8

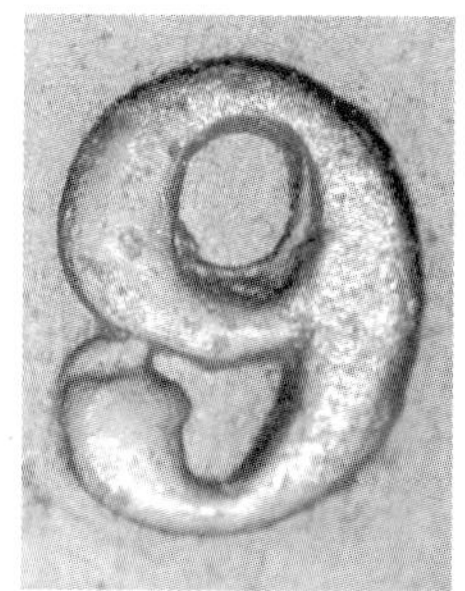

DATE / VARIETY / AXIS	MINTAGE (thous.)	G-4	VG-8	F-12	VF-20	EF-40	AU-50	AU-55	MS-60 Br	MS-63 Red	MS-65 Red	SP-63 Rd/Br	SP-65 Rd/Br
1859 W9/8 ↑↑	8,150	20.	45.	65.	95.	125.	225.	325.	450.	2,000.	12,500.	*	*
1859 W9/8 ↑↓	Incl.	250.	500.	900.	—	—	—	—	—	—	—	2,000.	4,000.

1859 VARIETIES: The majority of the 1859 dies were not overdates: they were dated with a narrow 9 punch. Over 400 dies were made and numerous re-punched varieties exist. Only seven are listed here.

A very rare error variety of the plain, narrow 9 exists in brass, which can be identified by its distinctive yellow colour.

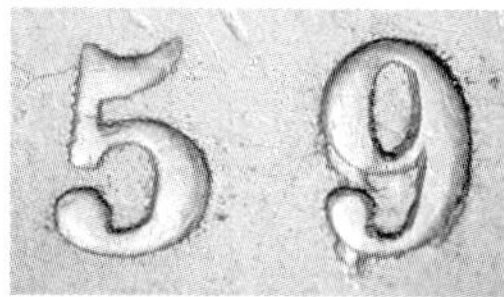

1859 N9 DPI

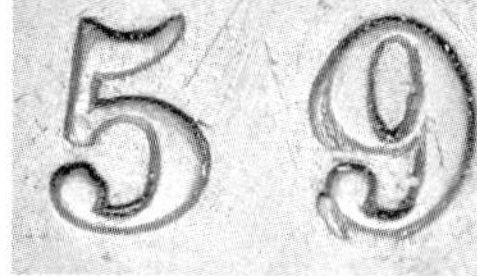

1859 N9 DP2

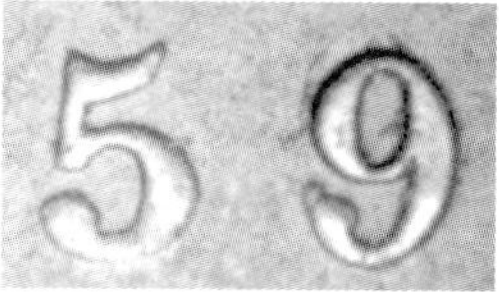

1859 N9 DP3

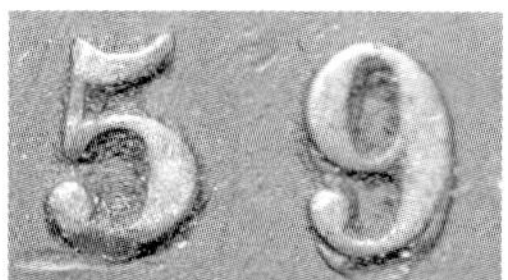

1859 N9 DP4

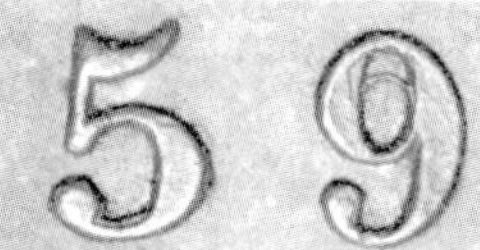

1859 N9 DP5

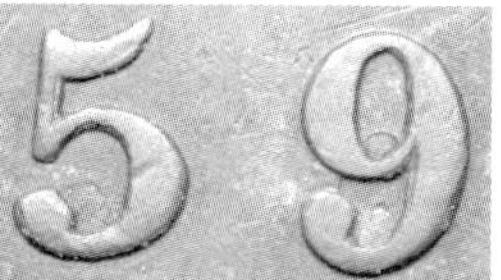

1859 N9/Inverted 9

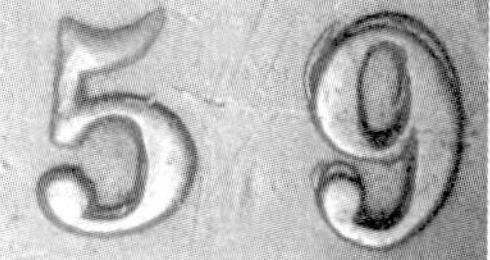

1859 N9 TP1

DATE / VARIETY / AXIS	MINTAGE (thous.)	G-4	VG-8	F-12	VF-20	EF-40	AU-50	AU-55	MS-60 Br	MS-63 Red	MS-65 Red	SP-63 Rd/Br	SP-65 Rd/Br
1859 N9 Bronze	Incl.	5.	10.	12.	15.	20.	40.	50.	150.	275.	2,000.	2,000.	4,000.
1859 N9 Brass	Incl.	15,000.	20,000.	25,000.	—	—	—	—	—	—	—	*	*
1859 N9 DP1	Incl.	200.	325.	400.	500.	800.	1,500.	1,850.	2,250.	—	—	2,000.	4,000.
1859 N9 DP2	Incl.	40.	80.	125.	200.	300.	550.	750.	1,100.	2,500.	—	*	*
1859 N9 DP3	Incl.	50.	100.	150.	225.	325.	900.	1,100.	1,500.	—	—	*	*
1859 N9 DP4	Incl.	50.	100.	150.	250.	375.	600.	900.	1,200.	—	—	*	*
1859 N9 DP5	Incl.	150.	300.	375.	500.	800.	2,000.	—	—	—	—	*	*
1859 N9/Inv 9	Incl.	200.	400.	500.	600.	1,200.	3.000.	—	—	—	—	*	*
1859 N9 TP1	Incl.	250.	300.	400.	600.	1,000.	2,500.	—	—	—	—	*	*

FIVE CENTS
VICTORIA 1858

The 5-cent piece chosen by the Province of Canada was a small silver coin, half the weight of the 10-cent piece and similar to the United States half dime. The obverse depicts an idealized, youthful laureated Victoria and the reverse features a maple wreath of 21 leaves surmounted by the Imperial State or St. Edward's crown.

There was only one matrix which was fully dated with small numerical fonts. The dies, therefore, were also identically dated. The number of punches is unknown. Later strikings carried larger digits punched over the small digits of the die with a four digit logotype punch. Three overpunched dies are known.

Designer and Engraver: Leonard C. Wyon
Composition: .925 silver, .075 copper
Weight: 1.16 grams
Diameter: 15.5 mm
Edge: Reeded
Die Axes: ↑↓

LARGE DENOMINATION 5 OVER SMALL 5

1855 Large 5 over Small 5 (5/5)

LARGE DATE VARIETIES

1858 Large Date (RP1)
Last 8: Primary 8 north of secondary 8

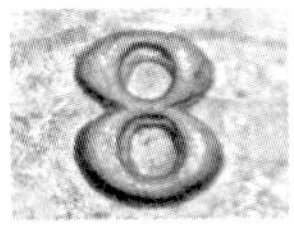

Primary 8 north of secondary 8

1858 Large Date (RP2)
Last 8: Primary 8 east of secondary 8

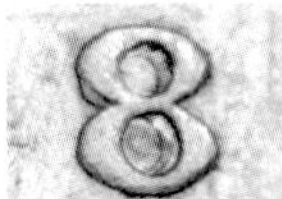

Primary 8 east of secondary 8

1858 Large Date (RP3)
Last 8: Primary 8 west of secondary 8

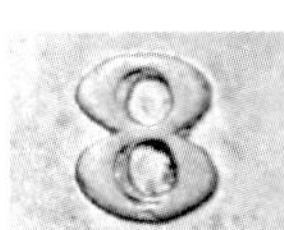

Primary 8 west of secondary 8

DATE / VARIETY	MINTAGE	G-4	VG-8	F-12	VF-20	EF-40	AU-50	AU-55	MS-60	MS-63	MS-65	SP-63	SP-65
1858 SD	1,460,389	15.	30.	45.	70.	125.	225.	300.	400.	800.	4,000.	1,000.	4,000.
1858 SD (PE)	Included	*	*	*	*	*	*	*	*	*	*	1,500.	4,000.
1858 SD 5/5	Included	125.	250.	350.	600.	1,000.	—	—	—	—	—	*	*
1858 LD	Included	100.	200.	300.	500.	900.	1,250.	1,650.	2,250.	4,500.	—	3,500.	8,000.
1858 LD (PE)	Included	*	*	*	*	*	*	*	*	*	*	2,500.	7,500.
1858 LD RP1	Included	100.	200.	300.	550.	950.	1,500.	—	—	—	—	*	*
1858 LD RP2	Included	100.	200.	300.	550.	950.	1,500.	2,000.	2,500.	3,500.	—	*	*
1858 LD RP3	Included	100.	200.	300.	550.	950.	1,500.	—	—	—	—	*	*

TEN CENTS
VICTORIA 1858

In design, the Province of Canada 10-cent pieces resemble the 5-cent pieces. An interesting variety occurred through a dating blunder in which a "5" punch was used to repair a defective first "8". The top of the "5" can be seen rising above the first "8", as these numbers were punched simultaneously.

Designer and Engraver: Leonard C. Wyon
Composition: .925 silver, .075 copper
Weight: 2.32 grams
Diameter: 18.0 mm
Edge: Reeded
Die Axes: ↑↓

Obverse DEI with position marker

Usually identified as a blundered "I" this position marker does not have the correct shape to fit the description of a blundered "I".

Obverse: Repunched "D/D" in DEI and "A/A" in CANADA

The 1858 "First 8 over 5" is interesting in the fact that both the obverse and reverse are varieties.

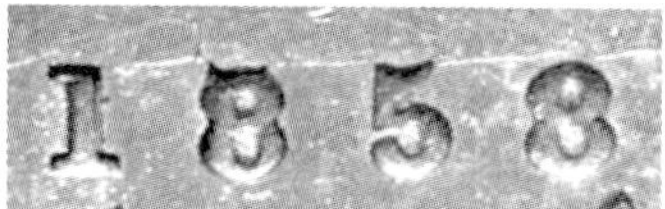

Reverse: 1 8/5 58

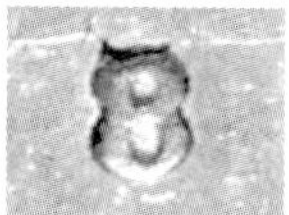

First 8 is an 8/5

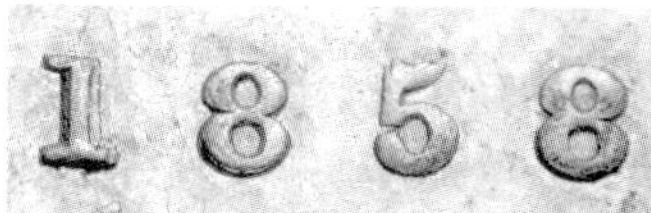

Reverse: 18 5/5 8

5/5

DATE VARIETY	MINTAGE	G-4	VG-8	F-12	VF-20	EF-40	AU-50	AU-55	MS-60	MS-63	MS-65	SP-63	SP-65
1858	1,216,402	20.	40.	65.	125.	175.	250.	325.	500.	1,500.	6,000.	2,500.	7,000.
1858 (PE)	Included	*	*	*	*	*	*	*	*	*	*	2,000.	6,000.
1858 Marker	Incl.	30.	45.	135.	225.	400.	600.	800.	—	—	—	*	*
1858 5/5	Included	30.	50.	100.	150.	275.	425.	—	—	—	—	*	*
1858 8/5	Included	700.	1,250.	1,800.	3,000.	5,000.	7,000.	—	—	—	—	*	*

TWENTY CENTS
VICTORIA 1858

This unusual denomination was chosen as a bridge between two currency systems. It apparently deferred to the pounds, shillings, pence basis of the Halifax currency system while naming the new issue in the dollar, cents, mills system. The relationship between the two systems meant 20 cents was equivalent to a shilling in Halifax currency, and it was assumed that consequently the new coin would be found useful. This assumption proved unfounded because there had been no coin representing a shilling in the old system; the British shilling coin was worth just over 20 percent more than a shilling in Halifax currency. Furthermore, the size and weight of the 20-cent piece led to confusion with both British shillings and U.S. 25-cent pieces. As one would expect, the government had difficulty introducing the 20-cent piece and by 1860 it was decided to replace it with a 25-cent coin as the opportunity arose.

The replacement of the 20-cent piece with a 25-cent coin came after Confederation. The Dominion government actively withdrew the 20-cent pieces and at various times from 1885 onward sent them back to the Royal Mint in London for melting and recoining as 25-cent pieces.

Designer and Engraver: Leonard C. Wyon
Composition: .925 silver, .075 copper
Weight: 4.65 grams
Diameter: 23.3 mm
Edge: Reeded
Die Axes: ↑↓

OBVERSE VARIETIES

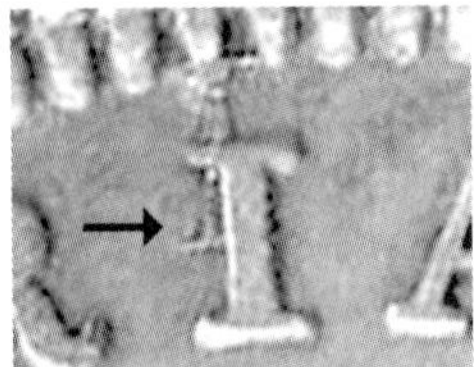

Blundered "I" in VICTORIA

Blundered "I" in GRATIA

Blundered "I" in DEI

REVERSE VARIETIES

1858 Plain 5

Plain 5

1858 Re-engraved 5

Re-engraved 5

DATE VARIETY	MINTAGE	G-4	VG-8	F-12	VF-20	EF-40	AU-50	AU-55	MS-60	MS-63	MS-65	SP-63	SP-65
1858 ↑↓	730,392	65.	95.	125.	175.	350.	625.	850.	1,200.	3,000.	10,000.	2,500.	6.000.
1858 ↑↑	Included	200.	350.	600.	900.	1,500.	—	—	—	—	—	*	*
1858 (PE)	Included	*	*	*	*	*	*	*	*	*	*	1,000.	5,000.
1858 RE 5	Included	65.	100.	150.	200.	425.	700.	900.	1,250.	—	—	*	*
1858 BL-I VIC	Included	85.	110.	150.	200.	425.	700.	900.	—	—	—	*	*
1858 BL-I GRA	Included	85.	110.	150.	200.	425.	700.	900.	—	—	—	*	*
1858 BI-I DEI	Included	85.	110.	150.	200.	425.	700.	900.	—	—	—	*	*
1871 Reeded	Included	*	*	*	*	*	*	*	*	*	*	10,000.	20,000.
1871 (PE)	Included	*	*	*	*	*	*	*	*	*	*	10,000.	20,000.

CANADA

VICTORIA ONE CENT MAJOR OBVERSE VARIETIES

Victoria Obverse Variety OC1 – OPEN “C” IN LEGEND, SMALL SERIF ON CENTRE BAR “E” IN LEGEND

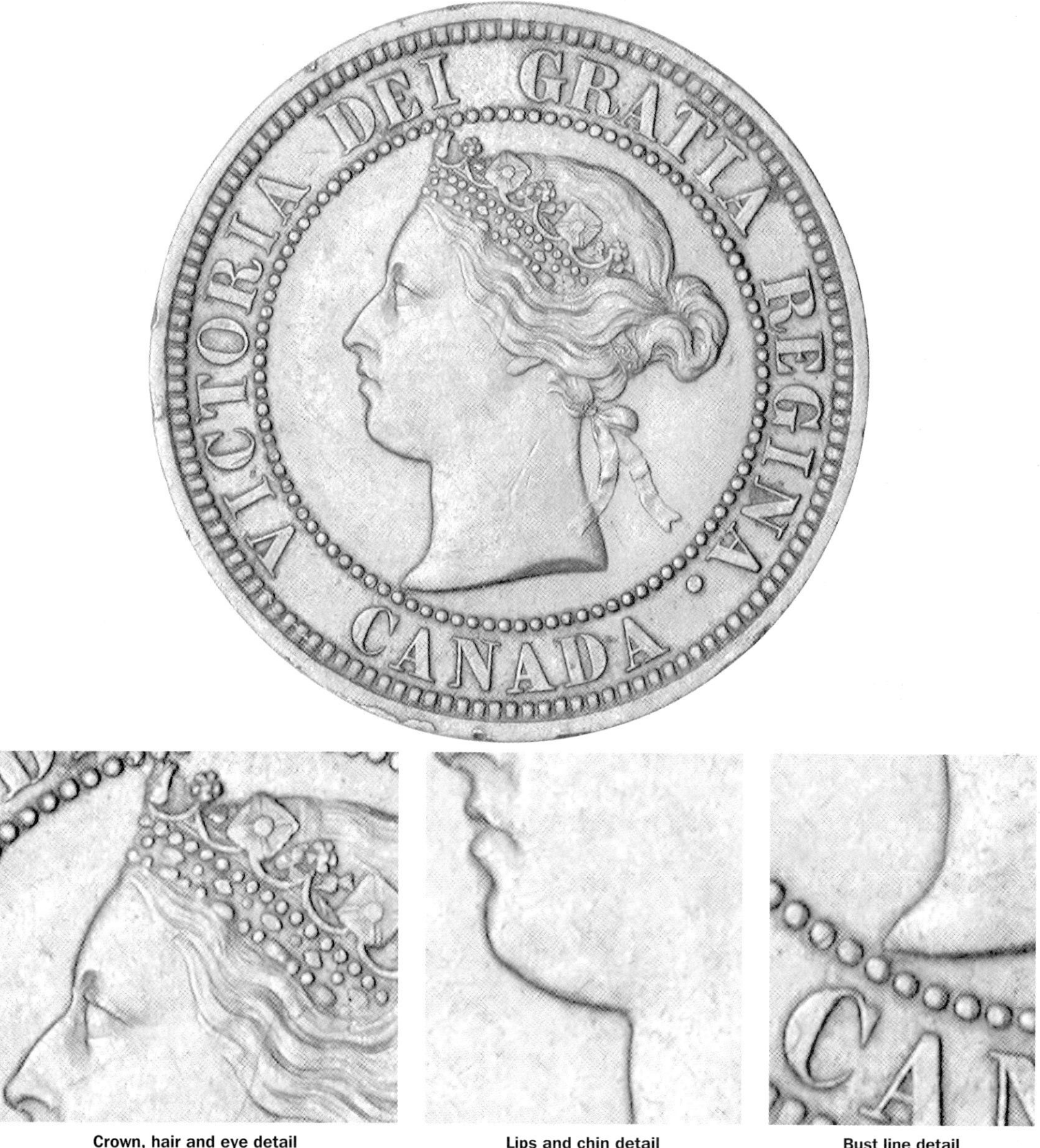

Crown, hair and eye detail

Lips and chin detail

Bust line detail
Open “C” in Legend

OC1 Crown, hair and eye detail: There are three thin strands of hair between the brow and the crown. The upper eyelid is thin and does not meet the lower lid at the corner of the eye.

Lips and chin detail: A small well defined upper lip curves outward. A full lower lip flows into a full round chin, with no doubling.

Bust line detail: The bust line is pointed and very close to the bead directly above the “C” in CANADA.

Dates: Portrait OC1 is currently known on the following dates: 1876H, 1881H, 1882H and 1884.

Victoria Obverse Variety OC1a

OPEN "C" IN LEGEND, SMALL SERIF ON CENTRE BAR "E" IN LEGEND

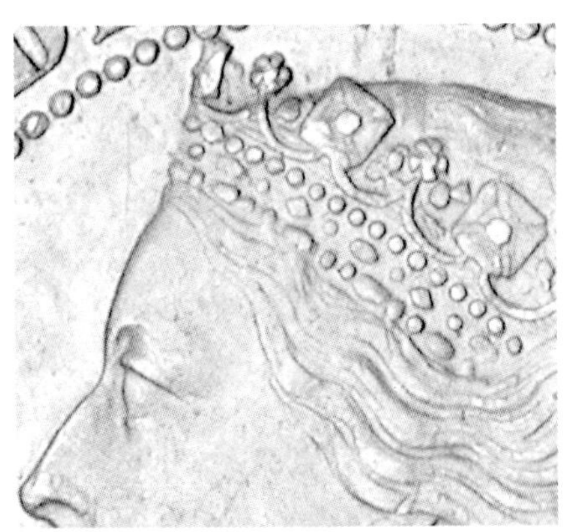

Crown, hair and eye detail

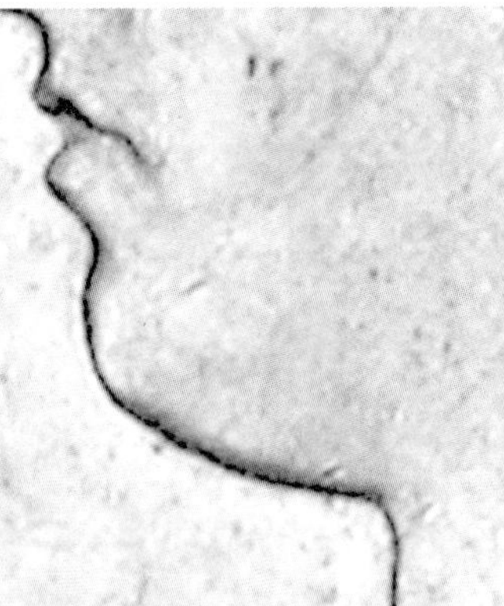

Lips and chin detail

Bust line detail
Open "C" in Legend

OC1a Crown, hair and eye detail: There are three thick strands of hair between the brow and the crown. The upper eyelid is thin and does not meet the lower lid at the corner of the eye (as in OC1).

Lips and chin detail: A small well defined upper lip curves outward. A full lower lip flows into a full round chin, with no doubling. (as in OC1)

Bust line detail: The bust line is rounded but far from the bead above the "C" in CANADA.

Dates: Portrait OC1a is currently known on the following dates: 1881H, 1882H and 1886.

Victoria Obverse Variety OC2

OPEN "C" IN LEGEND, SMALL SERIF ON CENTRE BAR "E" IN LEGEND

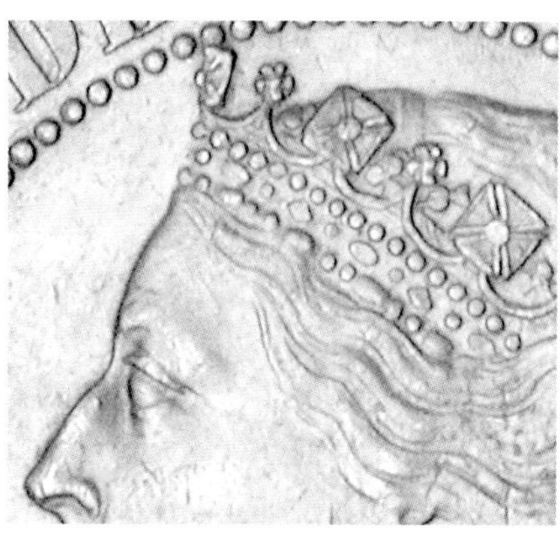
Crown, hair and eye detail

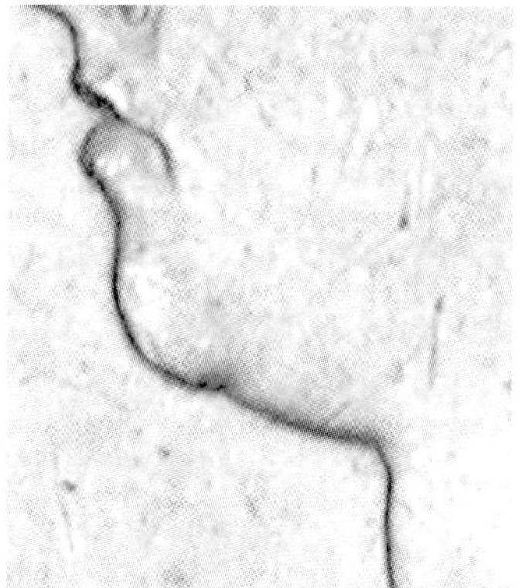
Lips and chin detail

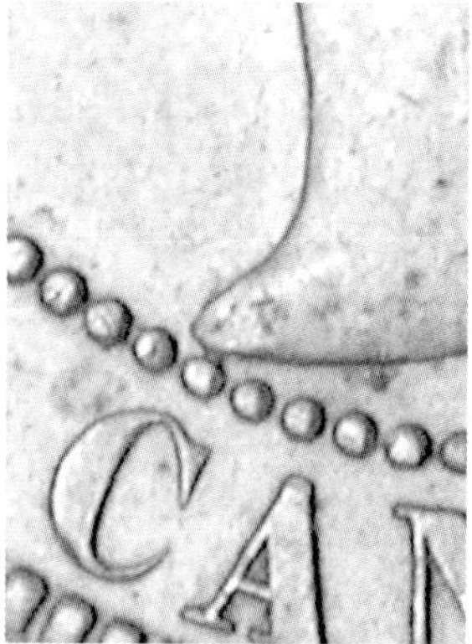
Bust line detail
Open "C" in Legend

OC2 **Crown, hair and eye detail:** There are two medium strands of hair between the brow and the crown. The upper eyelid is triangular, with an open space at the corner of the eye.

Lips and chin detail: A thin upper lip rises almost straight to the nostril. A full lower lip. The chin is doubled on the line to the neck.

Bust line detail: A rounded bust almost touches the bead above the "C" in CANADA, and points to the next bead on the left.

Dates: Portrait OC2 is currently known on the following dates: 1882H, 1884, 1886, 1887, 1888, 1891 and 1892.

Victoria Obverse Variety OC3

OPEN “C” IN LEGEND, SMALL SERIF ON CENTRE BAR “E” IN LEGEND

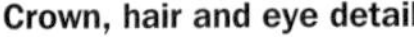

Crown, hair and eye detail

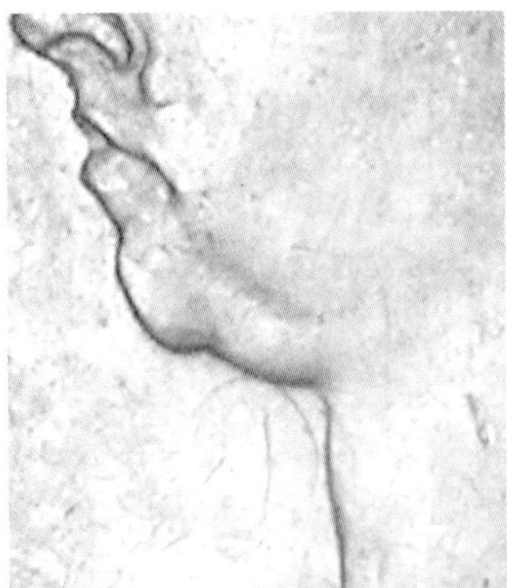

Lips and chin detail

Bust line detail
Open “C” in Legend

OC3 **Crown, hair and eye detail:** There is only one strand of hair between the brow and the crown. The upper eyelid is doubled. There is a gap between the upper and lower lids at the corner of the eye.

Lips and chin detail: The line from the nostril to the upper lip is straight. The upper lip is thin. A thin lower lip falls to a receding double chin.

Bust line detail: A rounded bust line rests on the bead above the open “C” of CANADA and is close to the bead on the right, while pointing to the bead on the left.

Dates: Portrait OC3 is currently known on the following date: 1890H.

Victoria Obverse Variety OC3a

CLOSED "C" IN LEGEND, LARGE SERIF ON CENTRE BAR "E" IN LEGEND

Crown, hair and eye detail

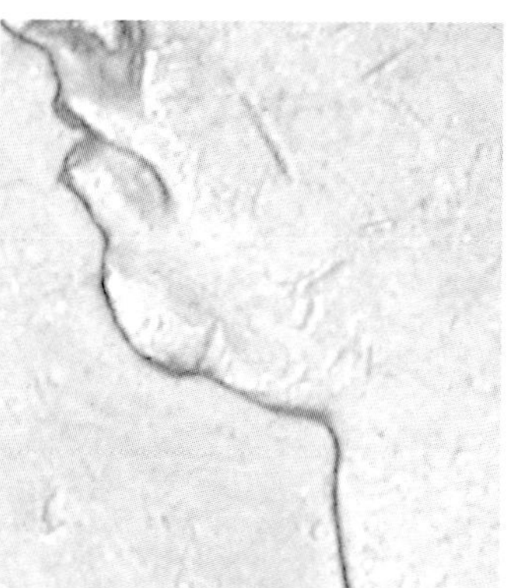

Lips and chin detail

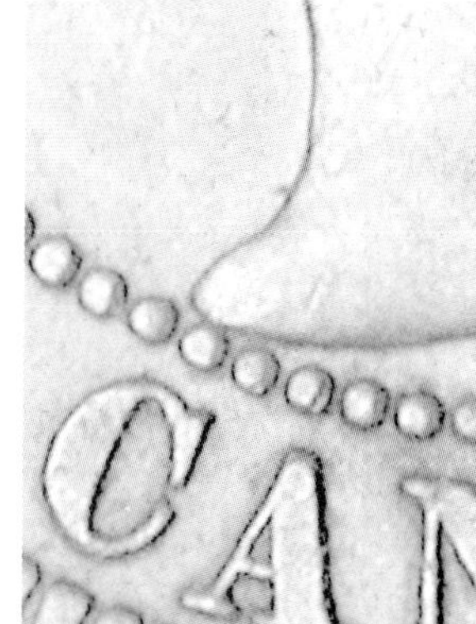

Bust line detail
Closed "C" in Legend

OC3 Crown, hair and eye detail: There is only one strand of hair between the brow and the crown. The upper eyelid is doubled. There is a gap between the upper and lower lids at the corner of the eye.

Lips and chin detail: The line from the nostril to the upper lip is straight. The upper lip is thin. A thin lower lip falls to a receding double chin.

Bust line detail: A rounded bust line rests on the bead above the closed "C" of CANADA and is close to the bead on the right, while pointing to the bead on the left.

Dates: Portrait OC3a is currently known on the following dates: 1891 and 1892.

Victoria Obverse Variety OC4

OPEN "C" IN LEGEND, SMALL SERIF ON CENTRE BAR "E" IN LEGEND

Crown, hair and eye detail

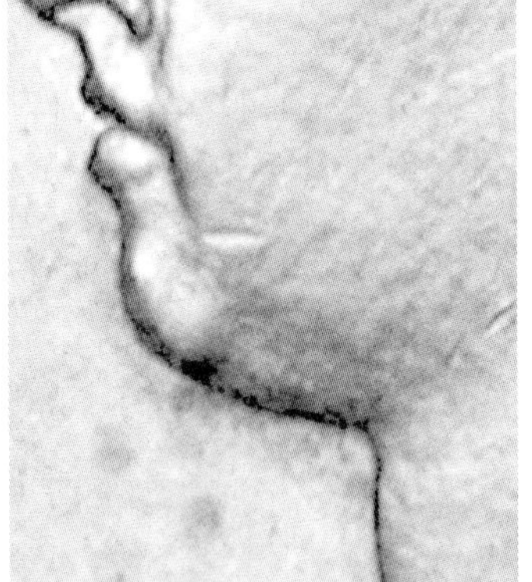

Lips and chin detail

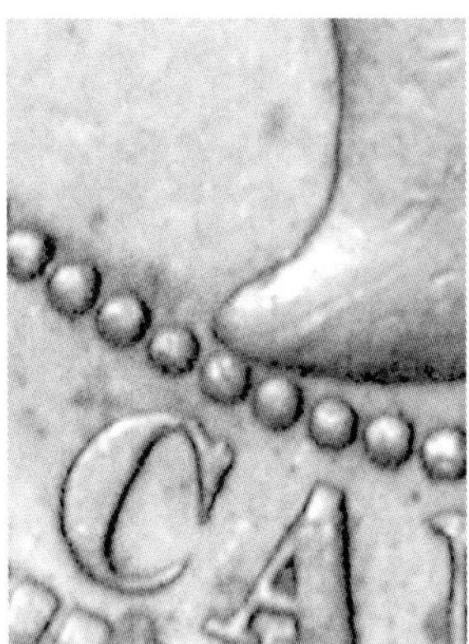

Bust line detail
Open "C" in Legend

OC4 Crown, hair and eye detail: There is a thick strand of hair between the brow and the crown. The upper eyelid is curved and extends well beyond the corner of the eye.

Lips and chin detail: The upper lip falls straight from the nostril, but with a slight curl. The full lower lip falls to a full double chin.

Bust line detail: A rounded bust line rests on the bead directly above the "C" in CANADA. The bead to the right just touches the bust line.

Dates: Portrait OC4 is currently known on the following dates: 1892, 1893, 1894, 1895, 1896, 1897, 1898H, 1899, 1900, 1900H, 1901.

VICTORIA ONE CENT MAJOR REVERSE VARIETIES

Victoria Reverse Variety RC1

Provincial maple leaf detail

RC1 **Leaf detail:** Provincial leaves. Sixteen medium size maple leaves linked to a vine. The leaf numbering system is from Turner's *The 1858 Cents of Provincial Canada*.

Dates: Reverse RC1 is currently known on the following dates: 1858, 1859, 1876H, 1881H and 1882H.

Victoria Reverse Variety RC2

Large maple leaf detail

RC2 **Leaf detail:** Large leaves. Sixteen large maple leaves linked to a vine.
Dates: Reverse RC2 is currently known on the following dates: 1884, 1886, 1887,1888, 1890H and 1891.

Victoria Reverse Variety RC3

Small maple leaf detail

RC3 **Leaf detail:** Small leaves. Sixteen small maple leaves linked to a vine.
Dates: Reverse RC3 is currently known on the following dates: 1891, 1892, 1893, 1894, 1895, 1896, 1897, 1898H, 1899, 1900, 1900H and 1901.

ONE CENT: Victoria 1876 - 1901

The large cents produced in 1858-1859 for the Province of Canada were inherited by the Dominion of Canada government at the time of Confederation. It was decided to issue them as Dominion cents. Nearly ten years were required to use up the stock; the first cents struck for the Dominion came out in 1876. An 1876 pattern cent (see DC-1 in the chapter on Patterns) with the laureate obverse of 1858-1859 suggests that initially it was intended the Dominion cents be the same design as those of the Province of Canada. However, the obverse of the pieces actually issued bore a diademed head adapted from that used for the Jamaica halfpenny and the Prince Edward Island cent. The government also took the opportunity to increase the weight to 1/80th of an avoirdupois pound, the same as the British halfpenny. Heaton Mint strikings of 1876-1882 and The Mint Birmingham Ltd. strikings of 1890, 1898 and 1900 have an "H" mint mark on the reverse under the date. Royal Mint strikings have no mint mark.

"H" Mint Mark

Designer and Engraver:
Obv.: Leonard C. Wyon
Rev.: Provincial Leaves - L. C. Wyon
Large Leaves – Leonard C. Wyon
Small Leaves – G. W. DeSaulles
Composition: .95 copper, .04 tin, .01 zinc
Weight: 5.67 grams
Diameter: 25.4 mm
Edge: Plain
Die Axes: ↑↑, ↑↓

1876 OBVERSE VARIETY, REPUNCHED T and A.

Three dies used in 1876 had the repunched "T" in VICTORIA. Only one of those dies had a repunched "A" in CANADA. (RP T&A).

1876H Repunched "T" in VICTORIA (RP T)

and Repunched second "A" in CANADA (RP A)

1881H OBVERSE VARIETY, SINGLE SERIF N"

Unlike the other obverse working dies used in 1881, this die had both the "N" in CANADA and the "N" in REGINA left with the original single serifs (SS N), identical to those found on 1876H cents..

1881H Single Serif "N" in CANADA (SS N)

and Single Serif "N" in REGINA (SS N)

DIADEMED PORTRAIT, PROVINCIAL LEAVES DESIGN, 1876-1882.

DATE / MINT / PORTRAIT/VARIETY	MINTAGE (thous.)	G-4	VG-8	F-12	VF-20	EF-40	AU-50	AU-55	MS-60 Br	MS-63 Red	MS-65 Red	SP-63 Rd/Br	SP-65 Rd/Br
1876 C1 SP	4,000	*	*	*	*	*	*	*	*	*	*	3,000.	5,000.
1876H C1 (NI)	Incl.	*	*	*	*	*	*	*	*	*	*	3,500.	7,000.
1876H C1	Incl.	3.	7.	8.	10.	15.	30.	45.	80.	225.	1,750.	2,000.	6,000.
1876H C1 RP T&A	Incl.	12.	20.	30.	35.	60.	160.	225.	325.	—	—	—	—
1881H C1	2,000	3.	7.	10	18.	30.	50.	65.	125.	500.	3,500.	2,000.	4,000.
1881H C1 SS N	Incl.	200.	425.	600.	1,200.	1,800.	—	—	—	—	—	*	*

1881H OBVERSE, ROUND THE CLOCK DOUBLED DIE VARIETY

The punch doubling on this 1881 working die affected every letter in the obverse legend, though the degree of offset between original and repunched letter varies. Only three examples of the double legend letters are illustrated below.

1881H OBVERSE PORTRAIT PUNCH OC1a over OC1 VARIETY

Doubled second "A" in GRATIA

Doubled "R" in REGINA

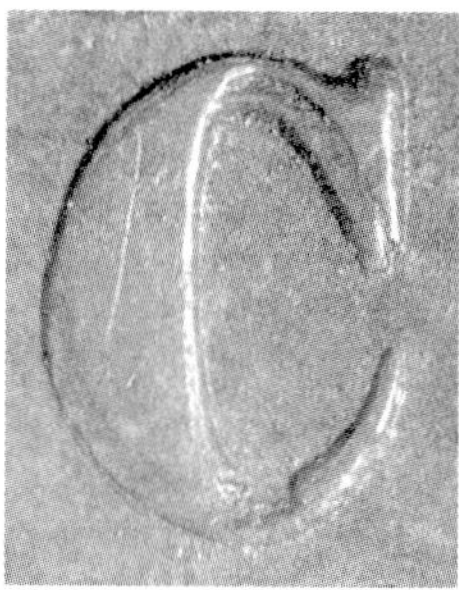

Doubled "C" in VICTORIA

Many working dies used in 1881 were sunk using both an OC-1a punch and an OC-1 punch. These dies show both the OC-1a details (white arrows) and OC-1 details (black arrows) at the bottom left tip of the effigy.

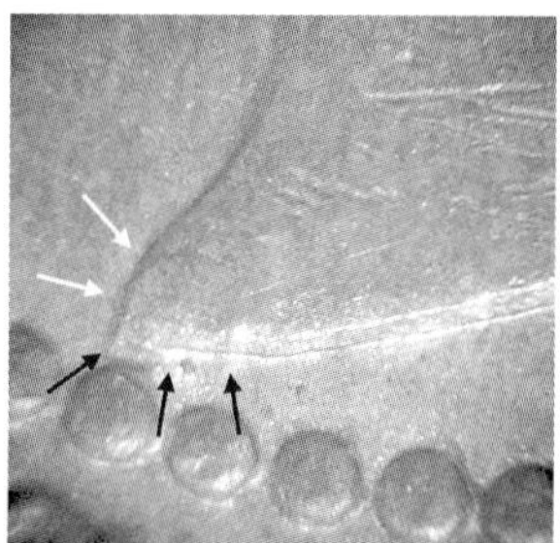

Truncation showing OC-1a over OC-1 details

DATE / MINT / PORTRAIT/VARIETY	MINTAGE (thous.)	G-4	VG-8	F-12	VF-20	EF-40	AU-50	AU-55	MS-60 Br	MS-63 Red	MS-65 Red	SP-63 Rd/Br	SP-65 Rd/Br
1881H C1 DD	Incl.	35.	70.	100.	200.	300.	500.	750.	1,000.	—	—	*	*
1881H C1a	Incl.	3.	7.	10.	20.	30.	50.	75.	100.	600.	4,500.	*	*
1881H C1a/C1	Incl.	5.	10.	15.	25.	35.	60.	85.	125.	450.	4,000.	*	*

NOTE ON PRICING

Certain low grade large cents are plentiful, making coin certification of little importance. Low grade price listings for common cents are for raw, or certified coins.

1882H OBVERSE PORTRAIT PUNCH OC1a OVER OC1 VARIETY

Again in 1882 several working dies were sunk using both an OC-1a punch and an OC-1 punch. In the illustration shown the white arrows point to the OC-1a details and the black arrows to the OC-1 details.

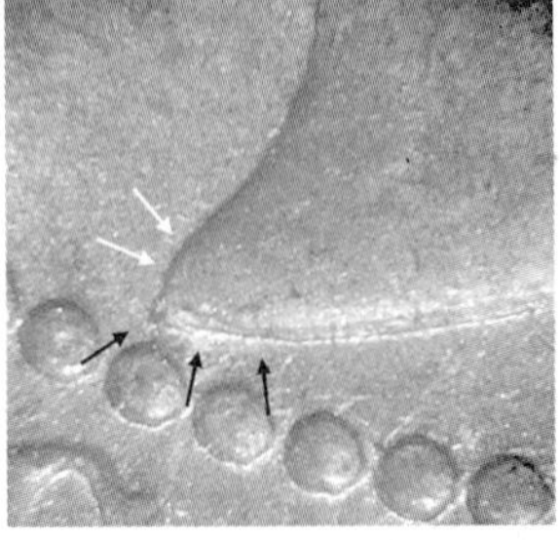

Truncation showing OC-1a over OC-1 details

1882H OC2 PUNCH OVER OC1 PUNCH VARIETY

A few working dies used in 1882 were sunk using both an OC-2 punch and an OC-1 punch. These dies show the typical OC-2 details at the top of the crown and at the bottom left tip of the effigy. They also display the smooth, rounded chin of OC-1

Top of crown detail indicative of OC-2

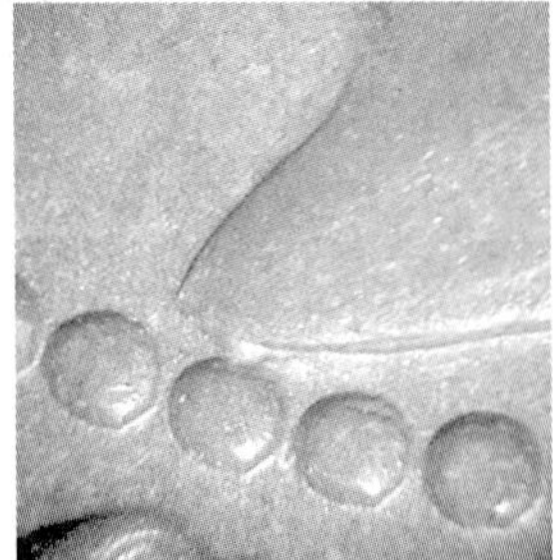

Truncation detail indicative of OC-2

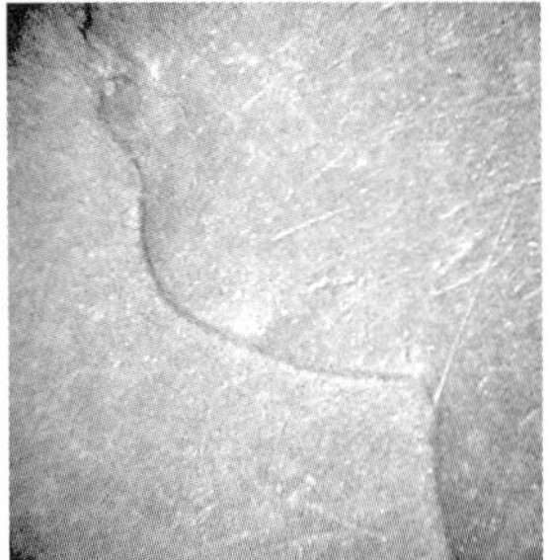

Smooth, rounded chin indicative of OC-1

1882H OC2 PUNCH OVER OC1 PUNCH, DOUBLED DIE VARIETY

This working die shows evidence of heavy punch doubling in the legends CANADA and REGINA. The other obverse legends are doubled to a lesser extent. In addition this working die was sunk with both an OC-2 punch and an OC-1 punch. Other OC2 over OC1 working dies have portions of the obverse legend doubled to a lesser extent.

Doubled letters in CANADA

Doubled letters in REGINA

DATE / MINT / PORTRAIT/VARIETY	MINTAGE (thous.)	G-4	VG-8	F-12	VF-20	EF-40	AU-50	AU-55	MS-60 Br	MS-63 Red	MS-65 Red	SP-63 Rd/Br	SP-65 Rd/Br
1882H C1	4,000	3.	7.	10.	15.	25.	40.	60.	90.	175.	3,000.	*	*
1882H C1a	Incl.	6.	15.	20.	30.	50.	75.	125.	200.	350.	—	*	*
1882H C1a/C1	Incl.	5.	10.	15.	30.	45.	65.	100.	275.	—	—	*	*
1882H C2	Incl.	3.	6.	7.	10.	15.	30.	50.	70.	200.	3,000.	3,000.	5,000.
1882H C2/C1	Incl.	10.	20.	25.	40.	75.	125.	175.	300.	—	—	*	*
1882H C2/C1 DD	Incl.	300.	400.	600.	1,200.	2,000.	—	—	—	—	—	*	*

DIADEMED PORTRAIT, LARGE LEAVES DESIGN, 1884-1891.

VARIETIES OF 1891.

Three major varieties of the 1891 cent are known. The first two have the Large Leaves reverse. The broad, flat leaves have very little detail and the bottom leaf runs into the rim denticles. The third variety has the Small Leaves reverse, which has slightly smaller leaves with much more detail. Leaf #9 ends well short of the rim denticles. The first variety has a large date; the second and third varieties have a small date.

Large Leaves, Large Date
Leaves close to beads and vine. Note broad figure "9."

Large Leaves, Small Date
Leaves close to beads and vine. Note narrow figure "9."

DATE / MINT / PORTRAIT/VARIETY	MINTAGE (thous.)	G-4	VG-8	F-12	VF-20	EF-40	AU-50	AU-55	MS-60 Br	MS-63 Red	MS-65 Red	SP-63 Rd/Br	SP-65 Rd/Br
1884 C1	2,500	75.	150.	200.	300.	650.	1,200.	1,750.	2,500.	—	—	*	*
1884 C2	Incl.	3.	6.	10.	15.	20.	45.	60.	100.	250.	1,750.	*	*
1886 C1a	Incl.	15.	25.	40.	125.	200.	300.	400.	600.	1,000.	—	*	*
1886 C2	Incl.	3.	8.	15.	30.	45.	70.	100.	150.	550.	6,500.	*	*
1887 C2	1,500	3.	6.	10.	20.	30.	65.	80.	100.	250.	1,500.	*	*
1888 C2	4,000	3.	6.	8.	10.	20.	30.	45.	70.	200.	1,000.	*	*
1890H C3	1,000	5.	15.	20.	25.	40.	80.	95.	150.	375.	2,000.	*	*
1891 C2 LL LD	1,453	5.	12.	18.	30.	50.	90.	125.	200.	525.	3,500.	*	*
1891 C2 LL SD	Incl.	60.	100.	150.	200.	300.	525.	800.	1,200.	5,500.	—	*	*
1891 C3 LL LD	Incl.	5.	12.	20.	35.	70.	100.	150.	200.	500.	2,500.	*	*
1891 C3 LL SD	Incl.	60.	90.	125.	200.	350.	600.	800.	1,200.	4,000.	—	*	*

DIADEMED PORTRAIT, SMALL LEAVES DESIGN, 1891-1901

VARIETIES OF 1891

Small Leaves, Small Date:
Leaves far from beads and vine. Note narrow figure "9."

OBVERSE OC3
REPUNCHED T IN GRATIA (RPT)

On this obverse working die the engravers repunched the letter "T" in GRATIA with a "T" having unusually long serifs. This was the same letter "T" punch used to make the obverse dies for the PEI cent of 1871.

DATE / MINT / PORTRAIT/VARIETY	MINTAGE (thous.)	G-4	VG-8	F-12	VF-20	EF-40	AU-50	AU-55	MS-60 Br	MS-63 Red	MS-65 Red	SP-63 Rd/Br	SP-65 Rd/Br
1891 C2 SL SD	Incl.	40.	95.	150.	225.	350.	500.	800.	1,100.	2,250.	—	*	*
1891 C3 SL SD	Incl.	30.	60.	90.	135.	200.	300.	400.	500.	1,450.	6,000.	*	*
1891 C3 SL SD RPT	Incl.	60.	115.	150.	200.	300.	500.	600.	750.	—	—	*	*

DIADEMED PORTRAIT, SMALL LEAVES DESIGN, 1891-1901

1893 REVERSE VARIETY TRIPLED PUNCH 9

The engraver triple punched the "9" into this reverse working die. Remnants of the underlying digit show below and to the left of the final "9". Other 1893 cents exhibited a repunched "9", but all to a lesser degree than those from this die.

1893 Triple punched "9"

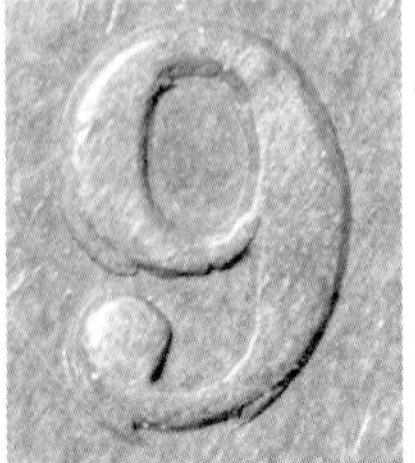

1893 Triple punched "9"

1894 REVERSE VARIETY

Most 1894 reverse working dies had a delicate numeral "4" punched into the date. The engraver punched a much thicker "4" into this reverse working die.

1894 Thick 4

1894 Thicker numeral "4" in the date

1894 Thin 4

1899 REVERSE VARIETY

The engraver repunched the "9" into this reverse working die, probably more than once. Evidence of the underlying "9" shows at the bottom of the final digit. Two other repunched last 9 varieties are known.

1899 Repunched "9"

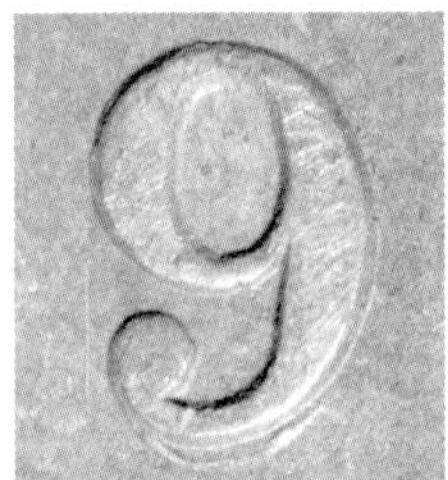

1899 Repunched "9" (RP9-1)

DATE / MINT / PORTRAIT/VARIETY	MINTAGE (thous.)	G-4	VG-8	F-12	VF-20	EF-40	AU-50	AU-55	MS-60 Br	MS-63 Red	MS-65 Red	SP-63 Rd/Br	SP-65 Rd/Br
1892 C2	1,200	6.	20.	35.	60.	95.	150.	200.	300.	900.	—	*	*
1892 C3	Incl.	5.	10.	15.	20.	30.	50.	75.	100.	325.	2,500.	*	*
1892 C4	Incl.	4.	10.	15.	20.	30.	50.	75.	110.	325.	1,750.	*	*
1893 C4	2,000	3.	6.	8.	10.	18.	30.	40.	75.	250.	1,500.	*	*
1893 C4 TP9	Incl.	60.	125.	225.	300.	450.	975.	—	—	—	—	*	*
1894 C4 Thin 4	1,000	8.	16.	25.	30.	50.	85.	110.	150.	450.	1,750.	*	*
1894 C4 Thick 4	Incl.	15.	40.	50.	65.	85.	125.	175.	300.	800.	—	*	*
1895 C4	1,200	3.	8.	15.	20.	30.	55.	75.	110.	225.	1,200.	*	*
1896 C4	2,000	4.	8.	10.	20.	25.	30.	45.	75.	250.	1,200.	*	*
1897 C4	1,500	3.	5.	8.	12.	20.	35.	50.	75.	200.	1,500.	*	*
1898H C4	1,000	5.	10.	15.	25.	30.	65.	90.	150.	375.	3,500.	2,000.	4,000.
1899 C4	2,400	4.	6.	7.	8.	15.	25.	45.	65.	175.	1,100.	*	*
1899 C4 RP9-1	Incl.	15.	25.	50.	75.	100.	150.	200.	300.	600.	2,000.	*	*
1900 C4	1,000	5.	10.	15.	25.	45.	75.	100.	150.	400.	5,500.	*	*
1900H C4	2,600	3.	5.	7.	9.	15.	25.	35.	60.	125.	550.	*	*
1901 C4	4,100	2.	5.	6.	8.	15.	25.	35.	50.	120.	850.	*	*

ONE CENT EDWARD VII 1902-1910

IMPERIAL STATE CROWNED PORTRAIT, SMALL LEAVES DESIGN, 1902-1910. The Victorian small leaves reverse design was carried forward into the Edward VII coinage. The Mint Birmingham Ltd. striking of 1907 has an "H" mint mark on the reverse above the wreath, below the date. London Mint strikings (1902-1907) and Ottawa Mint strikings (1908-1910) have no mint mark.

"H" Mint Mark

Designer and Engraver:
Obv. and Rev.: George W. DeSaulles
Composition: .95 copper, .04 tin, .01 zinc
Weight: 5.67 grams
Diameter: 25.4 mm
Edge: Plain
Die Axes: ↑↑

DATE / MINT	MINTAGE	VG-8	F-12	VF-20	EF-40	AU-50	AU-55	MS-60 Br	MS-63 Red	MS-64 Red	MS-65 Red	SP-63 Rd/Br	SP-65 Rd/Br
1902	3,000,000	3.	4.	5.	12.	18.	25.	35.	85.	175.	400.	*	*
1903	4,000,000	3.	4.	5.	12.	25.	35.	45.	110.	200.	600.	*	*
1904	2,500,000	4.	5.	10.	15.	25.	35.	50.	150.	300.	850.	*	*
1905	2,000,000	6.	8.	10.	18.	35.	45.	75.	175.	275.	800.	*	*
1906	4,100,000	4.	5.	7.	12.	25.	35.	50.	175.	375.	1,200.	*	*
1907 ↑↑	2,400,000	3.	5.	7.	12.	25.	40.	50.	135.	400.	1,250.	*	*
1907 ↑↓	Included	ONLY ONE CERTIFIED											
1907H	800,000	20.	30.	35.	70.	90.	150.	185.	600.	1,600.	10,000.	*	*
1908	2,401,506	4.	5.	7.	15.	25.	30.	55.	100.	275.	775.	200.	800.
1909	3,973,339	3.	4.	5.	10.	20.	25.	40.	85.	300.	1,000.	*	*
1910	5,146,487	3.	4.	5.	8.	15.	25.	40.	85.	275.	1,250.	*	*

ONE CENT - LARGE, GEORGE V 1911 - 1920

IMPERIAL STATE CROWNED PORTRAIT, SMALL LEAVES DESIGN, 1911. The obverse introduced in 1911 broke a tradition set by the coins of the previous two reigns in which the Latin phrase "DEI GRATIA" (or an abbreviation for it) was included in the monarch's titles. Omission of the phrase aroused public criticism during which the coins were labelled "Godless." The coinage tools were modified during the year 1911, and cents with "DEI GRA:" in the legend appeared in 1912. The reverse also marked a departure from the previous reigns with the inclusion of "CANADA" in the legend. It had formerly been part of the obverse legend on this denomination.

Without DEI GRATIA

With DEI GRATIA

Designer and Engraver:
Obv.: Sir E. B. MacKennal
Rev.: W. H. J. Blakemore
Composition:
1911-1919: .95 copper, .04 tin, .01 zinc
1919-1920: .955 copper, .030 tin, .015 zinc
Weight: 5.67 grams
Diameter: 25.4 mm
Edge: Plain
Die Axes: ↑↑

DATE	MINTAGE	VG-8	F-12	VF-20	EF-40	AU-50	AU-55	MS-60 Br	MS-63 Red	MS-64 Red	MS-65 Red	SP-63 Rd/Br	SP-65 Rd/Br
1911	4,663,486	3.	4.	5.	8.	15.	20.	40.	70.	150.	350.	300.	1,000.
1912	5,107,642	3.	4.	5.	8.	15.	25.	35.	85.	175.	700.	*	*
1913	5,735,405	3.	4.	5.	8.	15.	25.	40.	100.	150.	1,000.	*	*
1914	3,405,958	3.	4.	5.	8.	25.	35.	45.	110.	200.	750.	*	*
1915	4,932,134	3.	4.	5.	10.	18.	35.	40.	65.	200.	750.	*	*
1916	11,022,367	3.	4.	5.	7.	10.	15.	20.	80.	125.	475.	*	*
1917	11,899,254	3.	4.	5.	7.	10.	15.	20.	60.	150.	550.	*	*
1918	12,970,798	3.	4.	5.	7.	10.	15.	20.	60.	150.	425.	*	*
1919	11,279,634	3.	4.	5.	7.	10.	15.	20.	60.	125.	475.	*	*
1920	6,762,247	3.	4.	5.	7.	10.	20.	30.	110.	250.	1,100.	*	*

ONE CENT - SMALL
GEORGE V 1920 - 1936

As a matter of economy the Canadian government introduced in 1920 a small cent similar in size and composition to the United States cents. The large cents were not immediately withdrawn, but were allowed to circulate until the late 1930s. The small coins lacked rim denticles, the first instance of this in the Canadian decimal series. The obverse design was retained while a new reverse design, featuring two maple leaves, was used.

IMPERIAL STATE CROWNED PORTRAIT, TWO MAPLE LEAVES DESIGN, 1920-1936.

1929 Standard 9

1929 High 9

Designer: Obv.: Sir E. B. MacKennal
Rev.: Fred Lewis
Engraver: Obv.: Sir E. B. MacKennal
Rev.: W. H. J. Blakemore
Composition: .955 copper, .030 tin, .015 zinc
Weight: 3.24 grams **Edge:** Plain
Diameter: 19.05 mm **Die Axes:** ↑↑

COINAGE USING GEORGE V DIES 1936.

1936 with raised dot below date struck in 1937

In December, 1936, the reigning King, Edward VIII, abdicated in favour of his brother, who became George VI. This placed a great strain upon the Royal Mint in London. It was well along in the preparation of the tools for the British Commonwealth coinage obverses, including those for Canada. All this work had to be scrapped and new obverse tools made for George VI.

In 1937, during the delay involved in the preparation of new obverses in London, the Royal Canadian Mint was forced to strike from 1936 dies quantities of all denominations, except the 5-cent and 50-cent piece. The dies for the 1, 10, and 25 cent pieces are said to have been marked with a tiny dot on the reverse. This was to indicate that the coins were struck in a year different from that borne on the dies and with the bust of the late King.

The 1936 dot cent is an extreme rarity; only three, all in specimen condition, are known. Numerous circulated examples of this rarity have come to light over the years; however, not one has been satisfactorily authenticated. It seems unlikely that any genuine 1936 dot cents ever circulated, despite the supposedly official mintage of almost 700,000 pieces.

DATE / VARIETY	MINTAGE	VG-8	F-12	VF-20	EF-40	AU-50	AU-55	MS-60 Br	MS-63 Red	MS-64 Red	MS-65 Red	SP-63 Rd/Br	SP-65 Rd/Br
1920	15,483,923	3.	4.	5.	7.	10.	15.	20.	65.	175.	700.	2,000.	10,000.
1921	7,601,627	3.	4.	6.	10.	15.	55.	65.	275.	1,250.	5,000.	2,000.	4,000.
1922	1,243,635	20.	30.	40.	65.	110.	175.	275.	1,300.	4,500.	15,000.	2,000.	6,000.
1923	1,019,022	40.	50.	65.	100.	175.	250.	350.	4,000.	6,000.	—	2,000.	4,000.
1924	1,593,195	10.	12.	18.	25.	75.	110.	175.	925.	3,250.	10,000.	2,000.	4,000.
1925	1,000,622	40.	45.	50.	70.	125.	175.	225.	1,250.	3,500.	6,000.	2,000.	3,500.
1926	2,143,372	5.	8.	12.	20.	60.	85.	100.	675.	2,500.	7,000.	2,000.	4,000.
1927	3,553,928	3.	5.	8.	12.	25.	40.	55.	225.	850.	4,500.	2,000.	4,000.
1928	9,144,860	2.	3.	5.	7.	15.	20.	30.	125.	575.	2,750.	1,500.	3,500.
1929	12,159,840	2.	3.	5.	7.	10.	15.	30.	100.	375.	1,725.	1,500.	3,000.
1929 High 9	Included	20.	35.	50.	75.	100.	150.	200.	—	—	—	*	*
1930	2,538,613	2.	3.	5.	15.	30.	50.	75.	250.	800.	5,000.	2,000.	6,000.
1931	3,842,776	2.	3.	5.	8.	25.	35.	65.	225.	700.	3,000.	2,000.	6,000.
1932	21,316,190	2.	3.	5.	7.	8.	15.	25.	80.	225.	1,250.	—	—
1933	12,079,310	2.	3.	5.	7.	8.	15.	20.	70.	125.	650.	*	*
1934	7,042,358	2.	3.	5.	6.	8.	20.	30.	65.	225.	775.	4,000.	10,000.
1935	7,526,400	2.	3.	5.	6.	10.	20.	30.	80.	225.	700.	*	*
1936	8,768,769	2.	3.	5.	6.	10.	15.	20.	65.	125.	375.	*	*
1936 Dot	Included		SOLD JANUARY 2010, HERITAGE AUCTIONS CANADIANA SALE, PCGS SP-66, $402,500.										

ONE CENT
GEORGE VI 1937 - 1952

In the early part of 1937 the Royal Mint in London decided to speed up the production of the new coinage tools for Canadian coinages by having some of the work done by the Paris Mint. Included in this work was the reverse for the cent. The model was sent to Paris for conversion into master coinage tools. The reverse of the new cent continued the trend toward modernization of the Canadian coinage designs begun in 1935 with the voyageur silver dollar.

UNCROWNED PORTRAIT, "ET IND:IMP:" OBVERSE LEGEND, MAPLE TWIG DESIGN, 1937-1947.

The initial obverse (1937-1947) bore a legend containing the Latin abbreviation "ET IND:IMP:," indicating the king was the Emperor of India.

The granting of independence to India resulted in a dilemma for the Royal Canadian Mint in the early part of 1948. New obverse coinage tools with "ET IND: IMP:" omitted would not arrive for several months, yet there was a pressing need for all denominations of coins. The mint satisfied this demand by striking coins dated 1947 and bearing an obverse with outmoded titles. To differentiate this issue from the regular strikings of 1947, a tiny maple leaf was placed after the date.

Blunt 7, Near Maple Leaf (ML Bl 7)

Pointed 7, Near Maple Leaf (ML Pt 7)

Designer and Engraver:
Obv.: T. H. Paget
Rev.: G. E. Kruger-Gray
Composition:
1937-1942: .955 copper, .030 tin, .015 zinc
1942-1952: .980 copper, .005 tin, .015 zinc
Weight: 3.24 grams
Diameter: 19.05 mm
Edge: Plain
Die Axes: ↑↑

DATE / VARIETY	MINTAGE	AU-50	AU-55	MS-60 Br	MS-62 Rd/Br	MS-63 Red	MS-64 Red	MS-65 Red	MS-66 Red	SP-63 Rd/Br	SP-65 Rd/Br	SP-65 Red
1937	10,090,231	5.	7.	8.	10.	18.	30.	70.	200.	100.	200.	300.
1937 Matte	Included	*	*	*	*	*	*	*	*	30.	150.	300.
1938	18,365,608	5.	7.	8.	10.	16.	30.	60.	2,500.	1,000.	4,000.	7,000.
1939	21,600,319	5.	7.	8.	10.	15.	20.	35.	125.	*	*	*
1940	85,740,532	5.	7.	8.	10.	15.	20.	45.	575.	*	*	*
1941	56,336,011	5.	7.	10.	18.	50.	95.	625.	—	*	*	*
1942	76,113,708	5.	7.	10.	18.	50.	95.	575.	—	*	*	*
1943	89,111,969	5.	7.	10.	12.	20.	50.	225.	—	*	*	*
1944 ↑↑	44,131,216	5.	8.	12.	25.	65.	175.	2,500.	—	2,000.	4,000.	7,000.
1944 ↑↓	Included	ONLY ONE CERTIFIED										
1945	77,268,591	5.	7.	10.	12.	25.	50.	325.	—	450.	950.	2,500.
1946	56,662,071	5.	7.	10.	12.	15.	25.	85.	1,500.	100.	200.	300.
1947 Bl 7	31,093,901	5.	7.	10.	12.	15.	20.	60.	1,200.	125.	275.	1,500.
1947 ML Bl 7	43,855,448	5.	7.	10.	12.	30.	60.	275.	1,500.	100.	250.	350.
1947 ML Pt 7	Included	5.	7.	10.	12.	20.	30.	125.	—	100.	200.	300.

UNCROWNED PORTRAIT, MODIFIED OBVERSE LEGEND, MAPLE TWIG DESIGN, 1948-1952.

Following the arrival of the master tools with the new obverse legend lacking "ET IND: IMP:" in 1948, the 1947 Maple Leaf coinage was terminated. For the remainder of the year coins were produced with the new obverse and the true date, 1948. This obverse was employed for the rest of the reign.

OBVERSE VARIETIES OF 1948 AND 1949.

Three different matrices or punches resulted in five varieties for the years 1948 and 1949.

In 1948 three obverse varieties are found:

1. The last "A" in GRATIA points to a small denticle. Reverse has 129 denticles.
2. The last "A" in GRATIA points to a large denticle. Reverse has 129 denticles.
3. The last "A" in GRATIA points between two large denticles. Reverse has 128 denticles.

In 1949 two obverse varieties are found:

1. The last A in GRATIA points to a large denticle. Reverse has 129 denticles.
2. The last A in GRATIA points between two large denticles. Reverse has 128 denticles.

ONE CENT

"A" Points to a small denticle (SDe)

"A" Points to a large denticle (LDe)

"A" Points between large denticles (LDe)

DATE / VARIETY	MINTAGE	AU-50	AU-55	MS-60 Br	MS-62 Rd/Br	MS-63 Red	MS-64 Red	MS-65 Red	MS-66 Red	SP-63 Rd/Br	SP-65 Rd/Br	SP-65 Red
1948 'A' points to SDe	25,767,779	30.	45.	70.	125.	200.	500.	800.	—	*	*	*
1948 'A' points to LDe	Included	5.	7.	10.	15.	35.	90.	450.	—	*	*	*
1948 'A' between LDe	Included	5.	7.	10.	20.	35.	100.	550.	—	100.	150.	350.
1949 'A' points to LDe	33,128,933	40.	55.	70.	110.	200.	600.	2,750.	—	*	*	*
1949 'A' between LDe	Included	5.	7.	8.	10.	12.	20.	55.	1,100.	125.	200.	500.
1950	60,444,992	5.	6.	7.	8.	15.	20.	55.	—	75.	125.	200.
1951	80,430,379	5.	6.	7.	8.	15.	30.	125.	1,000.	75.	200.	1,000.
1952	67,631,736	5.	6.	8.	10.	12.	20.	55.	900.	100.	200.	350.

ONE CENT
ELIZABETH II 1953 TO DATE

The portrait model for the new Queen Elizabeth coinages was prepared in England by sculptress Mrs. Mary Gillick. The relief of this model was too high, with the result that the centre portion containing two lines on the shoulder (representing a fold in the Queen's gown) did not strike up well on the coins. This first obverse variety has been commonly termed the "no shoulder strap" variety by many collectors. Later in 1953, Royal Canadian Mint authorities decided to correct the defects in the obverse design. Thomas Shingles, the Mint's Chief Engraver, lowered the relief of the model, and strengthened the shoulder and hair detail. This modified obverse (often called the "shoulder strap" variety due to the resemblance of the lines to a strap) was introduced before the end of the year and became the standard obverse. By mistake the No Shoulder Fold obverse was used to produce some of the 1954 cents for the Proof-like sets and a small quantity of 1955 cents for circulation. Many collectors have difficulty differentiating the two varieties on slightly worn cents. The best way is to note that the "I's" on the No Shoulder Fold variety are flared at the ends and that an imaginary line drawn up through the centre of the "I" in "DEI" goes between two rim denticles. On the Shoulder Fold variety the "I's" are nearly straight sided and a line drawn up through the "I" of "DEI" runs into a rim denticle. The reverse was a continuation of the George VI reverse.

LAUREATE PORTRAIT, MAPLE TWIG DESIGN, 1953-1964.

Designer and Engraver:
Obv: Mary Gillick
Rev.: G. E. Kruger-Gray
Engraver: Thomas Shingles

Composition: .980 copper, .005 tin, .015 zinc
Weight: 3.24 grams
Diameter: 19.05 mm
Edge: Plain
Die Axes: ↑↑

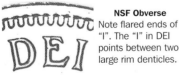

NSF Obverse
Note flared ends of "I". The "I" in DEI points between two large rim denticles.

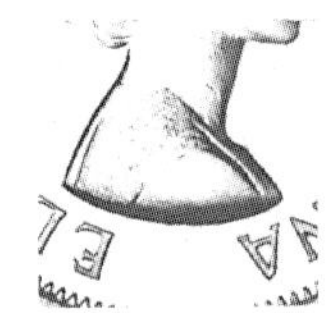

SF Obverse
Note straight-sided "I". The "I" in DEI points to a small rim denticle.

DATE / VARIETY	MINTAGE	AU-55	MS-60 Br	MS-63 Red	MS-64 Red	MS-65 Red	MS-66 Red	PL-65	PL65 HC	SP-63 Rd/Br	SP-65 Rd/Br	SP-65 Red
1953 NSF	67,806,016	5.	6.	10.	15.	45.	300.	—	—	125.	300.	1,500.
1953 SF	Included	15.	20.	70.	300.	1,500.	—	350.	750.	125.	250.	500.
1954 SF	22,181,760	4.	7.	15.	25.	150.	—	85.	200.	*	*	*
1954 NSF	Included	*	*	*	*	*	*	1,500.	2,000.	*	*	*
1955 SF SDe	56,403,193	5.	6.	10.	15.	40.	325.	*	*	*	*	*
1955 SF LDe	Included	4.	6.	10.	18.	45.	—	35.	100.	*	*	*
1955 NSF	Included	600.	800.	2,750.	6,500.	—	—	2,000.	—	*	*	*
1956	78,685,535	4.	5.	8.	12.	40.	500.	25.	60.	*	*	*
1957	100,601,792	4.	6.	8.	12.	25.	250.	15.	80.	*	*	*
1958	59,385,679	4.	5.	8.	12.	25.	150.	15.	80.	*	*	*
1959	83,615,343	4.	5.	8.	10.	20.	175.	10.	25.	*	*	*
1960	75,772,775	4.	5.	8.	10.	20.	200.	10.	15.	*	*	*
1961	139,598,404	4.	5.	8.	15.	20.	200.	10.	25.	*	*	*
1962	227,244,069	4.	5.	8.	15.	20.	175.	10.	15.	*	*	*
1963	279,076,334	4.	5.	10.	12.	20.	100.	10.	15.	*	*	*
1964	484,655,322	4.	5.	10.	12.	20.	50.	10.	15.	50.	100.	200.

Note: **1.** The 1954 NSF variety was struck only with proof-like dies. While most were used in sets, some may be found in circulation, but will still have proof-like characteristics keeping it from the business strike category.
2. SDe - Small Denticles; LDe - Large Denticles, see page 62 for illustration.

TIARA PORTRAIT, MAPLE TWIG DESIGN, 1965-1966.

In 1964 the British government decided to introduce a more mature portrait of Queen Elizabeth for domestic and Commonwealth coinages. The new portrait model, by Arnold Machin, features the Queen wearing a tiara instead of a laurel wreath. A copy of the model was forwarded to Canada and was incorporated into the obverses for 1965.

Designer and Engraver:
Obv.: Arnold Machin
Rev.: G. E. Kruger-Gray
Composition: .980 copper, .005 tin, .015 zinc
Weight: 3.24 grams
Diameter: 19.05 mm
Thickness: 1.55 mm
Edge: Plain
Die Axes: ↑↑

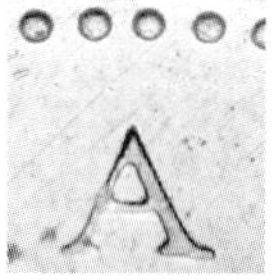

Small Beads Obverse A of REGINA points between beads

Large Beads Obverse A of REGINA points at bead

VARIETIES OF 1965.

1965 OBVERSE VARIETIES

During 1965, difficulties were encountered in striking the cents, resulting in the introduction of a second obverse variety. The first variety has small beads at the rim and a flat field; the second variety has large rim beads and a field that slopes up at the rim. Another way to distinguish the two obverses is by the location of the "A" in "REGINA" relative to the rim beads: on the small beads obverse it points between two beads, whereas on the large beads obverse it points at a bead.

Pointed 5 Top right of 5 comes to a point

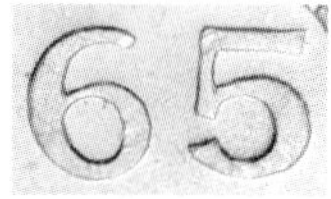

Blunt 5 Top right of 5 is nearly square

1965 REVERSE VARIETIES

In addition, two reverses differing in the style of 5 in the date were used in 1965. The obverses and reverses were employed in all possible combinations, creating four varieties for the year.

DATE / VARIETY	MINTAGE	MS-60 Br	MS-62 Rd/Br	MS-63 Red	MS-64 Red	MS-65 Red	MS-66 Red	PL-65	PL-65 HC	SP-63 Rd/Br	SP-65 Rd/Br	SP-65 Red
1965 Variety 1 (SB P5)	304,441,082	8.	9.	15.	25.	75.	600.	50.	100.	25.	50.	100.
1965 Variety 2 (SB B5)	Included	5.	6.	15.	12.	20.	175.	10.	15.	25.	50.	100.
1965 Variety 3 (LB B5)	Included	5.	6.	8.	10.	20.	90.	95.	—	*	*	*
1965 Variety 4 (LB P5)	Included	30.	40.	75.	120.	375.	1,500.	—	—	*	*	*
1966	183,644,388	5.	6.	10.	12.	20.	65.	8.	10.	*	*	*

TIARA PORTRAIT, CENTENNIAL DESIGN, 1967.

Alex Colville's design of a rock dove was selected for the 1967 cent reverse, struck in commemoration of Canada's centennial of Confederation. The event was marked by a special design for each denomination coined for circulation, plus a special $20 gold piece issued in a set of seven coins for collectors only. The obverse of the cent is the same as that for the 1966 issue.

1967 Obverse Doubled Die Doubled Legend

Designers and Engravers:
Obv.: Arnold Machin
Rev.: Alex Colville
Specifications:
Same as 1965 issue

DATE	MINTAGE	MS-60 Br	MS-62 Rd/Br	MS-63 Red	MS-64 Red	MS-65 Red	MS-66 Red	PL-65	PL-65 HC	SP-63 Rd/Br	SP-65 Rd/Br	SP-65 Red
1967 Confederation	345,140,645	5.	6.	8.	10.	20.	65.	8.	10.	5.	10.	25.
1967 Confed. DD	Included	25.	30.	40.	50.	100.	—	*	*	*	*	*

TIARA PORTRAIT, MAPLE TWIG DESIGN RESUMED, 1968-1978

Designers, Engravers, and Specifications:
Same as 1965 issue.

DATE	MINTAGE	MS-64 Red/C	MS-65 Red/C	MS-66 Red/C	MS-65 Red/NC	MS-66 Red/NC	MS-67 Red/NC	SP-66	SP-67
1968	329,695,772	10.	15.	100.	15.	65.	150.	300.	—
1969	335,240,929	15.	20.	100.	15.	60.	150.	300.	—
1970	344,145,010	15.	20.	80.	15.	60.	—	100.	200.
1971	298,228,936	10.	20.	75.	15.	60.	—	100.	200.
1972	451,304,591	8.	15.	85.	15.	60.	—	15.	25.
1973	457,059,852	8.	15.	90.	15.	60.	—	15.	25.
1974	692,058,489	8.	15.	90.	15.	100	—	15.	20.
1975	642,618,000	8.	15.	90.	20.	70.	—	15.	20.
1976	701,122,890	8.	15.	90.	15.	60.	—	15.	20.
1977	453,050,666	8.	15.	65.	15.	50.	250.	15.	20.
1978	911,170,647	20.	25.	50.	15.	60.	—	10.	15.

MODIFIED TIARA PORTRAIT, MAPLE TWIG DESIGN, 1979.

In 1977 the Mint struck test tokens (TT-1.2) with a considerably reduced weight and a diameter of 16 mm. The change was prompted by the rising price of copper which had resulted in the 1-cent piece being coined at a loss. Unfortunately, the diameter of the token was the same as that for the tokens used by the Toronto Transit Commission. The conflict resulted in the cancellation of the reduced diameter cent.

As part of a general standardization of the coinage, the portrait of the Queen was made smaller beginning with the 1979 coinage. The purpose was to make the size of the portrait proportional to the diameter of the coin, regardless of the denomination.

Designers, Engravers and Specifications:
Same as 1965 issue.

DATE	MINTAGE	MS-64 Red/C	MS-65 Red/C	MS-66 Red/C	MS-65 Red/NC	MS-66 Red/NC	MS-67 Red/NC	SP-66	SP-67
1979	753,942,953	20.	25.	50.	15.	60.	—	10.	15.

MODIFIED TIARA PORTRAIT, MAPLE TWIG DESIGN, REDUCED WEIGHT, BRONZE, 1980.

In 1979 further tests were conducted on reduced weight cents, but this time on a slightly reduced diameter and reduced thickness. In 1980 the mint introduced a coin of the same design as before, but with a decreased diameter and thickness resulting in a diminished weight.

Designer and Engraver:
Obv.: Arnold Machin
Rev.: G. E. Kruger-Gray
Composition: .980 copper, .005 tin, .015 zinc
Weight: 2.8 grams
Diameter: 19.00 mm
Thickness: 1.38 mm
Edge: Plain
Die Axes: ↑↑

DATE	MINTAGE	MS-64 Red/C	MS-65 Red/C	MS-66 Red/C	MS-65 Red/NC	MS-66 Red/NC	MS-67 Red/NC	SP-66	SP-67
1980	911,800,000	10.	25.	150.	15.	70.	—	10.	20.

MODIFIED TIARA PORTRAIT, MAPLE TWIG DESIGN, REDUCED WEIGHT, BRONZE, 1981.

In 1981 the Royal Canadian Mint revised their product line, adding a proof finish to their offerings. The proof coins were struck on standard bronze planchets.

DATE	MINTAGE	MS-64 Red/C	MS-65 Red/C	MS-66 Red/C	MS-65 Red/NC	MS-66 Red/NC	MS-67 Red/NC	SP-66	SP-67	PR-67	PR-68
1981	1,209,468,500	10.	25.	150.	15.	70.	—	10.	20.	15.	40.

MODIFIED TIARA PORTRAIT, MAPLE TWIG DESIGN, 12-SIDED DESIGN, BRONZE, 1982-1989.

In December of 1981 the Ministry of Supplies and Services announced that the Royal Canadian Mint would be modifying Canada's one-cent coin. The design was changed from a round to a twelve-sided piece. Also the rim denticles were removed and replaced with beads on both the obverse and reverse..

Designers and Engravers:
Obv.: Arnold Machin
Rev.: G. E. Kruger-Gray
Composition: .980 copper, .005 tin, .015 zinc
Weight: 2.5 grams
12-sided: 19.1 mm
Thickness: 1.45 mm
Edge: Plain
Die Axes: ↑↑

OBVERSE VARIETIES

1983 Near Beads

1983 Far Beads

REVERSE VARIETIES

1985 Blunt Five

1985 Pointed Five

DATE / VARIETY	MINTAGE	MS-64 Red/C	MS-65 Red/C	MS-66 Red/C	MS-65 Red/NC	MS-66 Red/NC	MS-67 Red/NC	SP-66	SP-67	PR-67	PR-68
1982	876,036,898	10.	20.	75.	15.	50.	—	10.	20.	15.	40.
1983 Near Beads	975,510,000	25.	35.	150.	30.	100.	175.	20.	30.	15.	40.
1983 Far Beads	Included	10.	20.	65.	15.	50.	—	10.	20.	15.	40.
1984	838,225,000	10.	15.	65.	15.	50.	—	10.	20.	15.	40.
1985 BL5	771,772,500	10.	60.	225.	30.	60.	—	10.	25.	15.	40.
1985 PT5	Included	50.	75.	300.	*	*	*	*	*	*	*
1986	788,285,000	10.	35.	60.	20.	30.	—	8.	15.	15.	25.
1987	774,549,000	10.	35.	60.	20.	50.	—	8.	15.	15.	25.
1988	482,676,752	10.	35.	200.	20.	50.	—	8.	15.	15.	25.
1989	1,066,628,200	10.	35.	50.	20.	50.	—	8.	15.	15.	25.

DIADEMED PORTRAIT, MAPLE TWIG DESIGN, 12-SIDED, BRONZE, 1990-1996.

In line with changes in Great Britain and other Commonwealth countries, Canada in 1990 introduced a new portrait for Canadian coins. This crowned portrait of Queen Elizabeth II is the first effigy of the Queen designed by a Canadian, Dora de Pédery-Hunt. The diamond crown is completely circular, decorated with symbolic roses, shamrocks and thistles. It was made for George IV and worn by Queen Victoria for many of her formal portraits. Today it is worn by Queen Elizabeth for her opening of Parliament. In 1992 the reverse design was modified to include the bracket dates 1867-1992 for the 125th birthday of Canada.

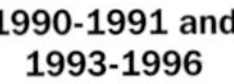

1990-1991 and 1993-1996

1867-1992

Designers and Engravers:
Obv.: Dora de Pédery-Hunt, Ago Aarand
Rev.: G. E. Kruger-Gray

Specifications:
Same as 1982 issue

DATE	MINTAGE	MS-64 Red/C	MS-65 Red/C	MS-66 Red/C	MS-65 Red/NC	MS-66 Red/NC	MS-67 Red/NC	SP-66	SP-67	PR-67	PR-68
1990	218,035,000	10.	35.	75.	15.	50.	—	8.	15.	15.	25.
1991	831,001,000	10.	25.	60.	15.	50.	—	8.	15.	15.	25.
1992 (1867-)	673,512,000	10.	25.	50.	15.	50.	—	8.	15.	15.	25.
1993	808,585,000	10.	25.	75.	15.	50.	—	8.	15.	15.	25.
1994	639,516,000	10.	25.	75.	15.	50.	325.	8.	15.	15.	25.
1995	624,983,000	10.	25.	75.	15.	50.	350.	8.	15.	15.	25.
1996	445,746,000	10.	25.	70.	15.	50.	—	8.	15.	15.	35.

COPPER PLATED ZINC (NON-MAGNETIC) CENTS

In 1997 a decision was made to change the composition of the one cent coin from bronze to copper plated zinc. The twelve -sided design was not conducive to copper plating, which resulted in the restoration of the round shape.

In 2002, in celebration of the Golden Jubilee of Elizabeth II's ascension to the throne, double dates, 1952-2002, were added to the obverse.

DIADEMED PORTRAIT, MAPLE TWIG DESIGN, COPPER PLATED ZINC, 1997-2003.

1997 to 2001 and 2003

Golden Jubilee of Queen Elizabeth II's Ascension to the Throne 1952 2002

Designers and Engravers:
Obv.: Dora de Pédery-Hunt, Ago Aarand
Rev.: G. E. Kruger-Gray
Composition: Copper plated zinc
Weight: 2.25 grams
Diameter: 19.05 mm, round
Thickness: 1.45 mm
Edge: Plain
Die Axes: ↑↑, ↑↓

DATE	COMP.	MINTAGE	MS-64 Red/C	MS-65 Red/C	MS-66 Red/C	MS-65 Red/NC	MS-66 Red/NC	MS-67 Red/NC	SP-66	SP-67
1997 ↑↑	CPZ	549,868,000	10.	25.	35.	15.	25.	60.	8.	15.
1997 ↑↓	CPZ	Incl. above	ONLY ONE CERTIFIED							
1997 ↑→	CPZ	Incl. above	ONLY FOUR CERTIFIED							
1998	CPZ	999,578,000	10.	15.	45.	20.	30.	200.	8.	15.
1998W	CPZ	N.I.I.	*	*	*	10.	20.	50.	*	*
1999	CPZ	1,089,625,000	10.	30.	40.	15.	30.	—	8.	15.
2000	CPZ	771,908,206	10.	30.	40.	15.	30.	75.	8.	15.
2000W	CPZ	N.I.I.	*	*	*	10.	25.	—	*	*
2001	CPZ	919,358,000	10.	20.	30.	*	*	*	*	*
2002	CPZ	716,367,000	10.	20.	40.	*	*	*	*	*
2003	CPZ	92,219,775	10.	20.	40.	*	*	*	*	*

UNCROWNED PORTRAIT, MAPLE TWIG DESIGN, COPPER PLATED ZINC, 2003-2006.

In celebration of the Jubilee of the coronation of Queen Elizabeth II in 2003, a new portrait was introduced for Canadian coins.

In 2006, for some reason, copper plated zinc planchettes (non-magnetic) found their way into a hopper used to feed a press with dies striking copper plated steel (P) cents, thus producing non-magnetic 2006P cents.

Designers and Engravers:
Obv.: Susanna Blunt, Susan Taylor
Rev.: G. E. Kruger-Gray
Specifications: Same as 1997 issue

DATE	COMP.	MINTAGE	MS-64 Red/C	MS-65 Red/C	MS-66 Red/C	MS-65 Red/NC	MS-66 Red/NC	MS-67 Red/NC	SP-66	SP-67
2003	CPZ	56,877,144	10.	20.	40.	*	*	*	*	*
2004	CPZ	653,317,000	10.	15.	35.	*	*	*	*	*
2005	CPZ	759,658,000	10.	15.	30.	*	*	*	*	*
2005P	CPZ	Incl. above	ONLY FOUR CERTIFIED, FOUND IN UNCIRCULATED SETS							
2006	CPZ	886,275,000	10.	20.	30.	*	*	*	*	*
2006P	CPZ	N/A	350.	450.	650.	*	*	*	*	*

COPPER PLATED ZINC (NON-MAGNETIC) CENTS (cont.)

UNCROWNED PORTRAIT, MAPLE TWIG DESIGN, COPPER PLATED ZINC, RCM LOGO, 2006-2010.

Obv.: RCM Logo

Designers and Engravers:
Obv.: Susanna Blunt, Susan Taylor
Rev.: G. E. Kruger-Gray
Specifications: Same as 1997 issue

DATE/ MINT LOGO	COMP.	MINTAGE	MS-64 Red/C	MS-65 Red/C	MS-66 Red/C	MS-65 Red/NC	MS-66 Red/NC	MS-67 Red/NC	SP-66	SP-67
2006	CPZ	176,000,000	10.	20.	30.	*	*	*	*	*
2007	CPZ	9,625,000	10.	25.	50.	*	*	*	*	*
2008	CPZ	Not issued				NOT ISSUED				
2009	CPZ	36,575,000	10.	20.	30.	*	*	*	*	*
2010	CPZ	486,200,000	10.	20.	30.	*	*	*	*	*

UNCROWNED PORTRAIT, MAPLE TWIG DESIGN, COPPER PLATED ZINC, RCM LOGO, 2011-2012.

Currently, no copper zinc (CPZ) cents are found in uncirculated, specimen or proofs sets. The last one cent coin was struck on May 4th, 2012.

Obv.: RCM Logo

Designers and Engravers:
Obv.: Susanna Blunt, Susan Taylor
Rev.: G. E. Kruger-Gray
Specifications: Same as 1997 issue

DATE/ MINT LOGO	COMP.	MINTAGE	MS-64 Red/C	MS-65 Red/C	MS-66 Red/C	MS-67 Red/C	SP-66	SP-67
2011	CPZ	301,400,000	10.	20.	50.	100.	*	*
2012	CPZ	87,972,000	10.	20.	40.	100.	*	*

NOTE ON ONE CENT LISTINGS

1. Up until 2003 the one cent coins contained in the proof sets each year were struck on bronze planchets. Starting in 2004 the composition of the planchets varied between copper and bronze. For a listing of the proof cents see *Canadian Coins, Volume Two, Collector and Maple Leaf Issues*.
2. When the pricing table lists Specimen finishes (SP-66 and SP-67) the prices are for those coins which have been removed from Specimen Sets and certified by a Canadian grading company.
3. The MS-65-NC (non-circulating) and higher grades are listings for coins removed from Brilliant Uncirculated Sets and certified by a Canadian grading company.
4. All RCM Rolls, First, and First/Last Day issues have been transferred to Volume Two.
5. Mintage numbers listed in the pricing tables are for circulation coinage (MS-64 to MS-66-C Business Strikes). The mintage figures for Brilliant Uncirculated (MS-65 to MS-67-NC), Specimen (SP-66 to SP-67), and Proof (PR-67 to PR-68) must be obtained from *Canadian Coins, Volume Two, Collector and Maple Leaf Issues*.

MULTI-PLY PLATED STEEL (MAGNETIC) CENTS

To reduce costs, the Royal Canadian Mint developed a new multi-ply plated steel process which allows for the production of plated steel blanks. The acid based process electroplates a thin coating of nickel, then copper, onto a steel core. Sets of new multi-ply plated steel coinage, from one cent through fifty cents, were provided to the vending industry in early 1999 for testing purposes, in response to their requests for actual coins rather than test tokens. Naturally, samples found their way into collectors' hands resulting in a brisk trade. So that the demand would not get out of hand, resulting in failure of the testing procedures, the Mint issued sets of "P" coins for collectors. The new composition coins are marked with the letter "P" (plated) for identification purposes. The "P' is considered a composition mark, and not a mint mark.

DIADEMED PORTRAIT, MAPLE TWIG DESIGN, MULTI-PLY PLATED STEEL, 1999-2003.

"P" Composition Mark

Designers and Engravers:
Obv.: Dora de Pédery-Hunt, Ago Aarand
Rev.: G. E. Kruger-Gray
Composition: .940 steel, .045 copper, .015 nickel
Weight: 2.35 grams
Diameter: 19.05
Thickness: 1.45 mm
Edge: Plain
Die Axes: ↑↑

DATE / COMP. MARK	COMP.	MINTAGE	MS-64 Red/C	MS-65 Red/C	MS-66 Red/C	MS-65 Red/NC	MS-66 Red/NC	MS-67 Red/NC	SP-66	SP-67
1999P	CPS	Issued for testing	*	*	*	25.	50.	100.	*	*
2000P	CPS	Issued for testing	ONLY EIGHT CERTIFIED. ALL IN MINT STATE.							
2001P	CPS	N.I.I.	*	*	*	10.	40.	—	15.	25.
2002P (1952-)	CPS	114,212,000	10.	20.	30.	10.	25.	40.	15.	25.
2003P	CPS	235,936,799	10.	20.	30.	10.	25.	40.	15.	25.

UNCROWNED PORTRAIT, MAPLE TWIG DESIGN, MULTI-PLY PLATED STEEL, 2003-2006.

In 2006, for some reason, multi-ply plated steel planchettes (magnetic) found their way into the production line for striking 2006 copper plated zinc cents (non-magnetic). The obverse dies used in this line do not carry the "P" composition mark. Thus, the multi-ply plated steel planchettes were struck without the obverse "P" composition mark. This variety is listed below as 2006 (magnetic), signifying multi-ply plated steel, but with no composition mark.

Designers and Engravers:
Obv.: Susanna Blunt, Susan Taylor
Rev.: G. E. Kruger-Gray
Specifications:
Same as 1999 issue

DATE / COMP. MARK	COMP.	MINTAGE	MS-64 Red/C	MS-65 Red/C	MS-66 Red/C	MS-65 Red/NC	MS-66 Red/NC	MS-67 Red/NC	SP-66	SP-67
2003P	CPS	591,257,000	10.	20.	35.	10.	20.	50.	15.	20.
2003WP	CPS	N.I.I.	*	*	*	10.	20.	50.	*	*
2004P	CPS	134,906,000	10.	20.	35.	10.	20.	50.	15.	30.
2005P	CPS	30,525,000	10.	20.	30.	10.	20.	40.	15.	30.
2006P	CPS	233,000	10.	20.	40.	15.	35.	75.	15.	30.
2006	CPS	(222)	150.	200.	225.	*	*	*	*	*

MULTI-PLY PLATED STEEL (MAGNETIC) CENTS (cont.)

UNCROWNED PORTRAIT, MAPLE TWIG DESIGN, MULTI-PLY PLATED STEEL, RCM LOGO, 2006-2010.

Obv.: RCM Logo

Designers and Engravers:
Obv.: Susanna Blunt, Susan Taylor
Rev.: G. E. Kruger-Gray
Specifications:
Same as 1999 issue

DATE / LOGO	COMP.	MINTAGE	MS-64 Red/C	MS-65 Red/C	MS-66 Red/C	MS-65 Red/NC	MS-66 Red/NC	MS-67 Red/NC	SP-66	SP-67
2006	CPS	137,500,000	10.	20.	45.	10.	25.	60.	*	*
2007	CPS	938,270,000	10.	15.	25.	10.	20.	60.	10.	20.
2008	CPS	820,350,000	10.	15.	30.	10.	20.	40.	10.	20.
2009	CPS	419,105,000	10.	20.	30.	10.	20.	40.	10.	15.
2010	CPS	Struck for sets	*	*	*	10.	20.	40.	10.	25.

UNCROWNED PORTRAIT, MAPLE TWIG DESIGN, MULTI-PLY PLATED STEEL, RCM LOGO, 2011-2012.

In 2011 the Brilliant Uncirculated Set was discontinued and replaced by the Uncirculated Set. Thus, the finish Brilliant Uncirculated (MS-65 NC and higher) was also discontinued making it necessary to remove that finish from the pricing table.

The last one cent coin was struck on May 4th, 2012.

Obv.: RCM Logo

Designers and Engravers:
Obv.: Susanna Blunt, Susan Taylor
Rev.: G. E. Kruger-Gray
Specifications:
Same as 1999 issue

DATE / LOGO	COMP.	MINTAGE	MS-64 Red/C	MS-65 Red/C	MS-66 Red/C	MS-67 Red/C	SP-66	SP-67
2011	CPS	361,350,000	10.	15.	30.	50.	10.	15.
2012	CPS	111,375,000	10.	20.	50.	70.	10.	30.

A Note on Catalogue Listings

1. This catalogue is based on circulating legal tender coinage used as a medium of exchange in Canada. Each denomination has a long standing reverse design; for example, the one cent coin carries the twin maple leaves. This design was introduced in 1937 and continued to 2012. Apart from the one-year commemorative design of 1967, the only varieties are the obverse portraits and the specifications such as size, composition, marks, mint marks, and finishes. For an explanation of the pricing tables please refer to pages xiv and xv in the introduction.
2. No CPS (copper plated steel) cents were formally issued for circulation in 2010. However, CPS cents were included in all Uncirculated Sets produced at the Winnipeg Mint for that year. A small quantity of overruns were placed in circulation, discovered by collectors and certified by Canadian grading companies.
4. Mintage numbers listed in the pricing tables are for circulation coinage (MS-64 to MS-66-C Business Strikes). The mintage figures for Brilliant Uncirculated (MS-65 to MS-67-NC), Specimen (SP-66 to SP-67), and Proof (PR-67 to PR-68) must be obtained from *Canadian Coins, Volume Two, Collector and Maple Leaf Issues*.

VICTORIA FIVE CENT MAJOR OBVERSE VARIETIES

Victoria Obverse Variety OF1

Hair and eye detail

Lips and chin detail

OF1 **Strand of hair detail:** Just to the right of the Queen's eye is a thick, truncated strand with two very thin strands rising to the brow.

Eye detail: The upper eyelid is thin with little definition towards the corner of the eye. The lower lid loses definition approaching the corner.

Lips and chin detail: Protruding upper lip with a pronounced curl. The chin is round and smooth to the neck.

Dates: Portrait OF1 is currently known on the following dates: 1858 and 1870W.

Victoria Obverse Variety OF2

Hair and eye detail

Lips and chin detail

OF2 **Strand of hair detail:** The starting point of the first strand is just above the temple, quickly forming a thick slanted curve to the braid.

Eye detail: The upper eyelid is thin, but with greater definition. The lower lid is weak. Both lids meet at the corner of the eye.

Lips and chin detail: The upper lip is thin with an outward curve. The chin is smooth and rounded into the neck.

Dates: Portrait OF2 is currently known on the following dates: 1870N, 1871, 1872H, 1874H, 1875H, 1880H, 1891, 1892, 1893, 1894, 1896, 1897, 1898, 1899, 1900 and 1901.

Victoria Obverse Variety OF3

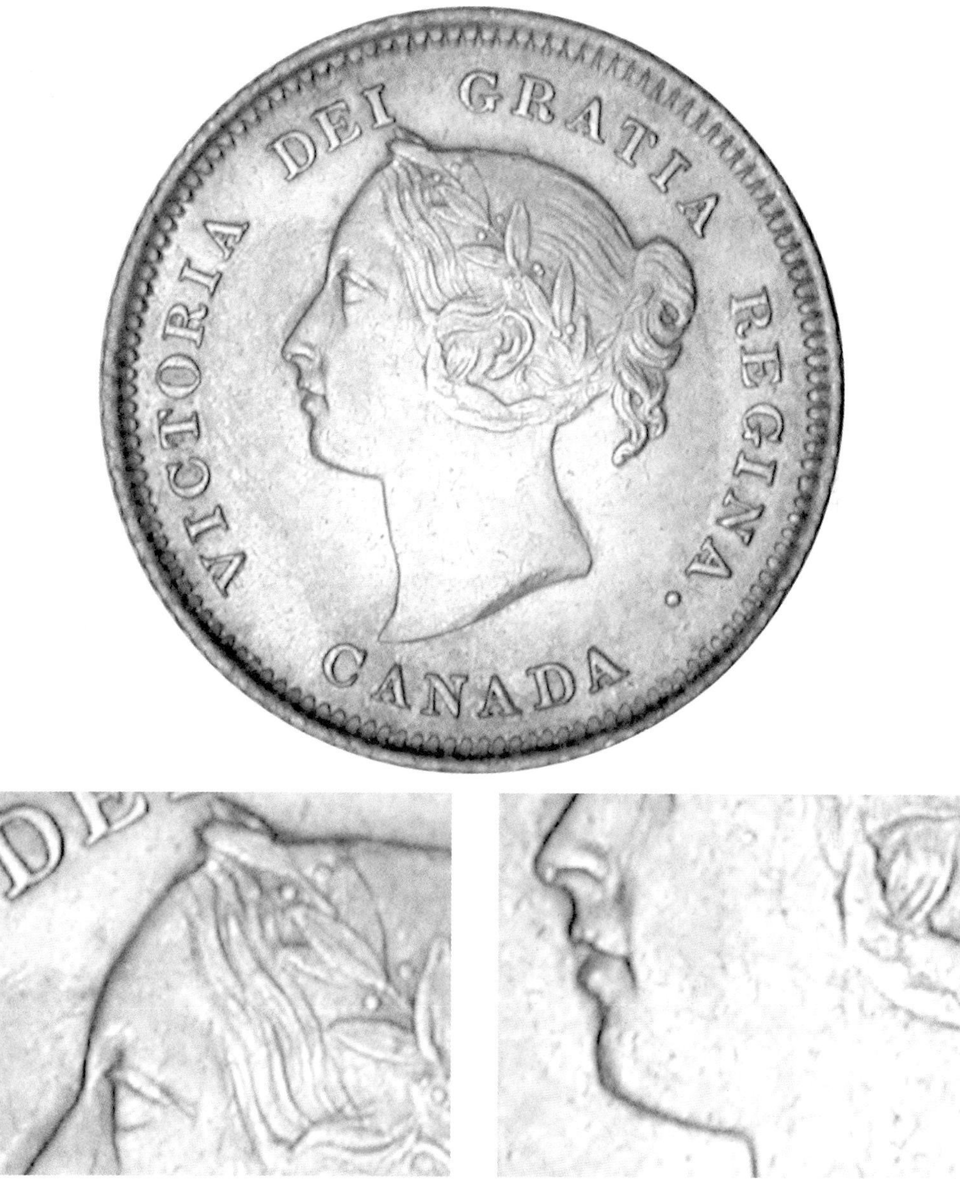

Hair and eye detail

Lips and chin detail

OF3 Strand of hair detail: At the temple the first strand is thin, but thickens rapidly as it falls straight to the braid.

Eye detail: The upper eyelid is thick and drooping to the corner of the eye. The lower lid is partially formed and does not extend to the corner of the eye.

Lips and chin detail: The upper lip curves slightly upwards to the nostril. Age lines appear at the cheek and chin.

Dates: Portrait OF3 is currently known on the following dates: 1880H and 1881H.

Victoria Obverse Variety OF4

Hair and eye detail

Lips and chin detail

OF4 **Strand of hair detail:** Two separate strands start at the Queen's temple and fall to the braid. The next three strands start on the brow, but stop halfway down and continue as two strands.

Eye detail: The eyebrow is bold. The upper eyelid is thick and well formed. The lower lid meets the upper at the corner of the eye

Lips and chin detail: The upper lip falls straight from the nostril to a curled lip. The age lines are softened.

Dates: Portrait OF4 is currently known on the following dates: 1882H and 1883H.

Victoria Obverse Variety OF5

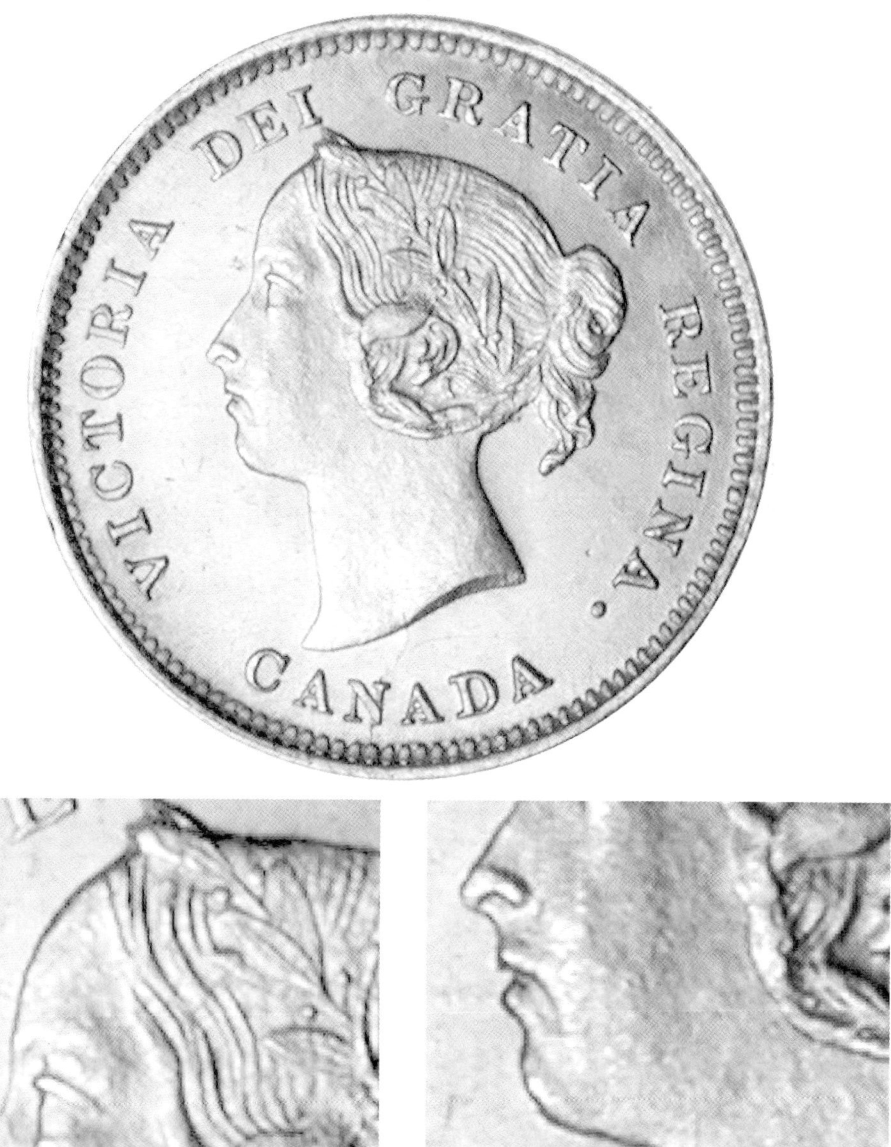

Hair and Eye Detail

Lips and Chin Detail

OF5 **Strand of hair detail:** The thick first strand starts at the temple. The next three strands, starting at the brow, fall into two and then into the braid.

Eye detail: A thick eyebrow. The upper eyelid is also thick. The lower lid is weakly formed. The corner of the eye is open as the lids do not meet.

Lips and chin detail: The upper lip is straight and thin, accented by a drooping depression from the corner of the mouth.

Dates: Portrait OF5 is currently known on the following dates: 1883H, 1884, 1885, 1886, 1887, 1888, 1889, 1890H, 1891 and 1892.

VICTORIA FIVE CENT MAJOR REVERSE VARIETIES

WREATH WITH 21 LEAVES

Reverse Maple Leaf Wreath Design

The wreath has 21 leaves: the left bough has 11 leaves and the right has 10 leaves. The leaves are counted by the order in which they are attached to the bough and are numbered L-1 to L-11 and R-1 to R-10. This numbering will aid in identification of the reverse varieties.

Left Bough **Right Bough**

WREATH WITH 22 LEAVES

Reverse Maple Leaf Wreath Design

The wreath has 22 leaves with both the left and right boughs having 11 leaves. The leaves are counted by the order in which they are attached to the bough, and are numbered L-1 to L-11 and R-1 to R-11. The "22 Leaves" wreath design has an interruption in the sequencing order of leaves 3 and 4.

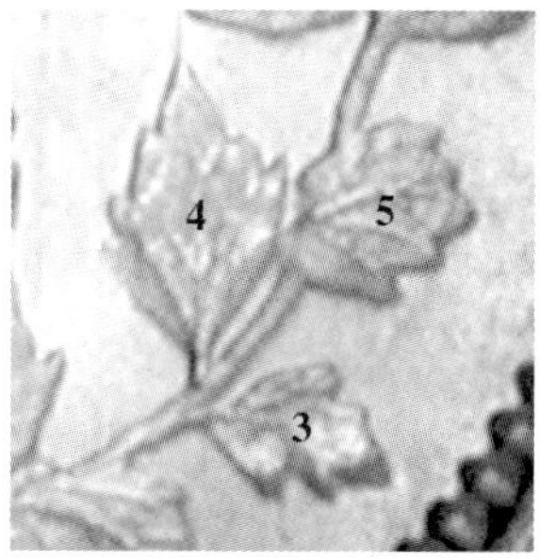

On coins dated 1882 Right Leaf 3 (R-3) appears on the right side of the bough and lower than Right Leaf 4 (R-4).

Left Bough **Right Bough**

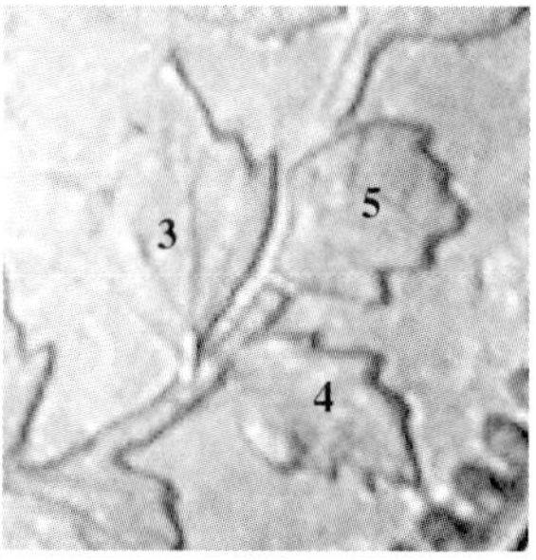

On coins dated 1883 to 1889 Right Leaf 3 (R-3) is on the left side of the bough and higher than Right Leaf 4 (R-4).

Victoria Reverse Variety RF1

Left bough detail | Bough and ribbon detail | Right bough detail

RF1 Crown and 5 detail: Flared crown, closed thin top 5.
Left bough detail: 11 leaves. L-1 is well formed. L-3 touches the bough.
Bough and ribbon detail: The left bough end and ribbon are notched. The right ribbon has a square end.
Right bough detail: 10 leaves. The right bough has three breaks.
Dates: Reverse RF1 is currently known on the following dates: 1858 and 1870.

Victoria Reverse Variety RF2

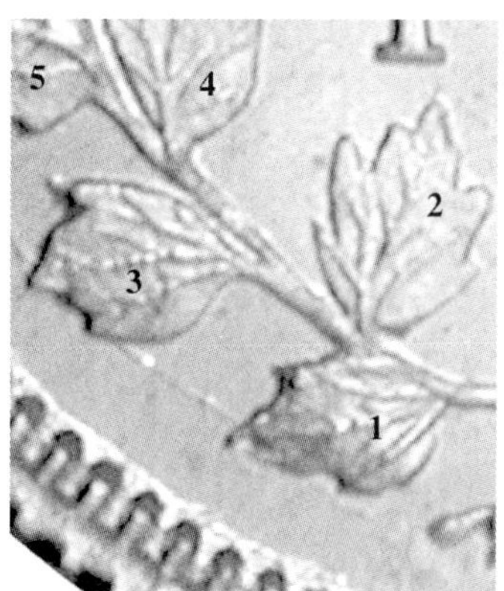

Left bough detail

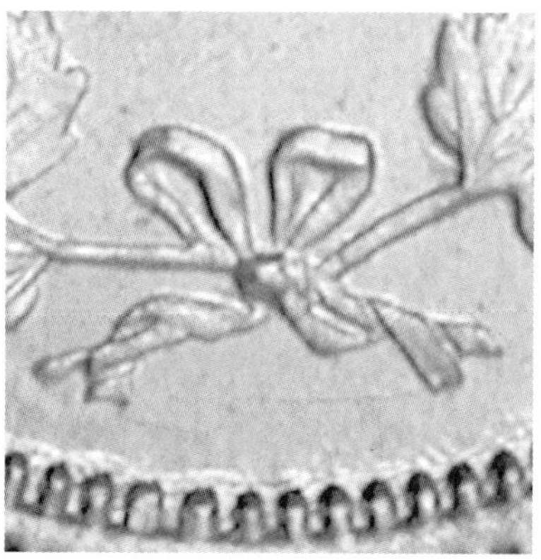

Bough and ribbon detail

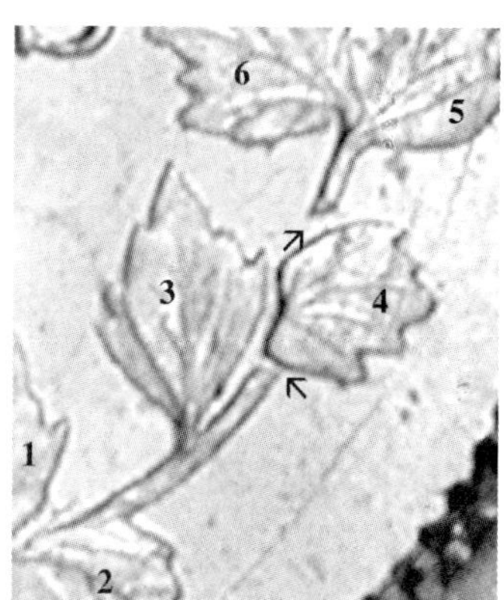

Right bough detail

RF2 **Crown and 5 detail:** Straight crown, closed thin top 5.
Left bough detail: 11 leaves. The tip of L-1 has lost detail. L-3 does not touch the bough.
Bough and ribbon detail: The left bough end and ribbon are notched. The right ribbon has a ragged end.
Right bough detail: 10 leaves. The right bough has two breaks, before and after R-4.
Dates: Reverse RF2 is currently known on the following dates: 1870N, 1871, 1872H, 1874H, 1875H, 1881H.

Victoria Reverse Variety RF3

Left bough detail | Bough and ribbon detail | Right bough detail

RF3 **Crown and 5 detail:** Straight crown, closed thin top 5.
Left bough detail: 11 leaves. The formation of L-1 is well detailed. L-3 is very close to the bough, attached by a thin stem.
Bough and ribbon detail: Both bough ends are pointed and both ribbon ends are notched.
Right bough detail: 10 leaves. The right bough has two breaks, before and after R-4.
Dates: Reverse RF3 is currently known on the following date: 1880H.

Victoria Reverse Variety RF4

Left bough detail | Bough and ribbon detail | Right bough detail

RF4 Crown and 5 detail: Straight crown, closed thin top 5.

Left bough detail: 11 leaves. L-1 is well formed, similar in detail to RF1. L-3 does not touch the bough, and has a thick stem.

Bough and ribbon detail: The bough ends are round. The ribbon ends are faintly notched.

Right bough detail: 11 leaves. The right bough has no breaks. In this variation the extra leaf is in position 3. The stem of R-4 joins the bough above that of R-3. Leaf R-5 is locked in place.

Dates: Reverse RF4 is currently known on the following date: 1882H.

Victoria Reverse Variety RF5

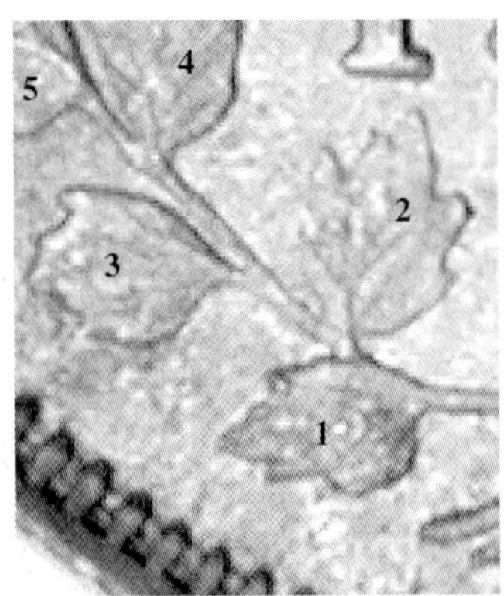

Left bough detail

Bough and ribbon detail

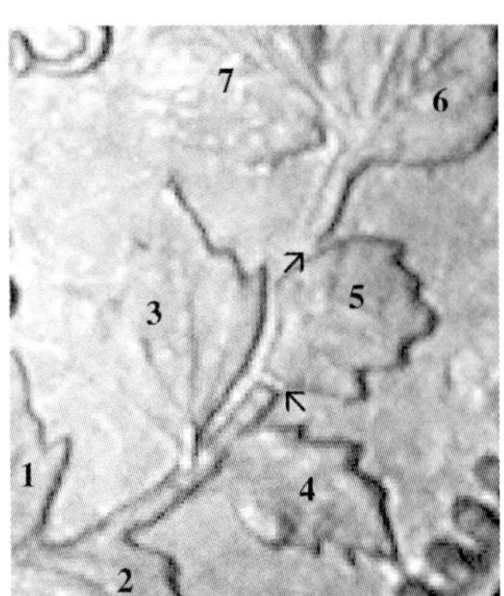

Right bough detail

RF5 **Crown and 5 detail:** Straight crown. Closed thick top 5.

Left bough detail: 11 leaves. L-1 is misshapen by a re-engraved bulge on the lower side. L-3 is close to the bough.

Bough and ribbon detail: The left bough end is round, while the right bough end is pointed. The ribbon ends are well notched.

Right bough detail: 11 leaves. The right bough has two breaks, before and after R-5. In this variation, while R-3 appears higher, the stem is below that of R-4. The extra leaf is now R-4.

Dates: Reverse RF5 is currently known on the following dates: 1883H, 1884, 1885, 1886, 1887, 1888 and 1889.

Victoria Reverse Variety RF6

Left bough detail

Bough and ribbon detail

Right bough detail

RF6 **Crown and 5 detail:** Straight crown. Large 5.

Left bough detail: 11 leaves. L-1 has lost detail and the re-engraved bulge is now outlined. L-3 does not touch the bough.

Bough and ribbon detail: The left bough end is round, while the right bough end is pointed. The ribbon ends are faintly notched.

Right bough detail: 10 Leaves. The right bough has two breaks, before and after R-4.

Dates: Reverse RF6 is currently known on the following date: 1890H.

Victoria Reverse Variety RF2

Left bough detail **Bough and ribbon detail** **Right bough detail**

The RF2 reverse was reintroduced in 1892, with slight modifications.

RF2 **Crown and 5 detail:** Straight crown. Open or closed thin top 5.
Left bough detail: 11 leaves. L-1 is re-engraved with added veins, and a bough that forms part of the leaf. L-3 does not touch the bough.
Bough and ribbon detail: The left bough end and ribbon are notched. The right bough end is pointed, and the ribbon end is ragged.
Right bough detail: 10 leaves. The right bough has two breaks, before and after L-4.
Dates: Reverse RF2 is currently known on the following date: 1891, 1892, 1893, 1894, 1896, 1897, 1898, 1899 and 1900.

Victoria Reverse Variety RF7

Left bough detail

Bough and ribbon detail

Right bough detail

RF7 Crown and 5 detail: Straight crown. Closed thin top 5.

Left bough detail: 11 leaves. L-1 is re-engraved with added veins, and a bough that forms part of the leaf. L-3 does not touch the bough. (Similar to RF2)

Bough and ribbon detail: The left bough end and ribbon are notched. The right bough end is pointed, and the ribbon end is ragged. (Similar to RF2)

Right bough detail: 10 leaves. The right bough has been re-engraved resulting in no breaks. The bough extends into R-4 at the lower section of the leaf.

Dates: Reverse RF7 is currently known on the following dates: 1899 and 1901.

Victoria Reverse Variety RF8

Left bough detail   Bough and ribbon detail   Right bough detail

RF8 Crown and 5 detail: Straight crown. Closed thin top 5.

Left bough detail: 11 leaves. L-1 is re-engraved with added veins, and a bough that forms part of the leaf. L-3 does not touch the bough. (Similar to RF2)

Bough and ribbon detail: The left bough end and ribbon are notched. The right bough end is pointed, and the ribbon end is ragged. (Similar to RF2)

Right bough detail: 10 leaves. The right bough has one break which is below R-4.

Dates: Reverse RF8 is currently known on the following dates: 1899, 1900 Oval 0 and 1901.

FIVE CENTS: Victoria 1870 - 1901

The first 5-cent pieces for the Dominion of Canada were introduced in 1870. The initial designs were identical to those used for the Province of Canada in 1858. During the reign of Queen Victoria, five obverse varieties, differing primarily in the facial features were employed.

The Ralph Heaton & Sons strikings of 1872 to 1883 have an "H" mint mark on the reverse under the wreath. Royal Mint strikings have no mint mark.

"H" Mint Mark

Designer and Engraver:
Leonard C. Wyon
Composition: .925 silver, .075 copper
Weight: 1.16 grams
Diameter: 15.50 mm
Edge: Reeded
Die Axes: ↑↓

21 LEAVES REVERSE, 1870-1881.

1870 Wide Flat Rims (W)

1870 Narrow Raised Rims (N)

Before the coinage of 1870 was complete new master tools for the 5-cent piece were introduced with the result that two varieties were created for that year. The first has wide rims (including unusually long rim denticles) on the obverse and reverse, and the second has more conventional narrow rims.

1870 F1 W 1/1

1/1

1870 F2 N 7/7

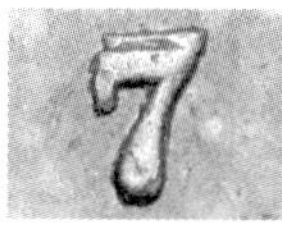

7/7

1871 F2 7/7

7/7

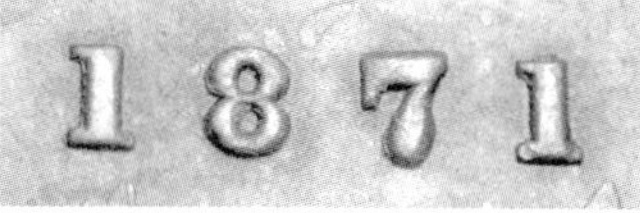

1871 F2 1/1

1/1

1872H F2 7/7

7/7

1872H F2 2/2

2/2

DATE / PORTRAIT/ VAR.	MINTAGE (thous.)	G-4	VG-8	F-12	VF-20	EF-40	AU-50	AU-55	MS-60	MS-63	MS-65	SP-63	SP-65
1870 F1 W	2,800	12.	20.	40.	70.	120.	200.	275.	425.	1,200.	3,500.	2,000.	6,500.
1870 F1 W (PE)	Incl.	*	*	*	*	*	*	*	*	*	*	2,000.	6,500.
1870 F1 W 1/1	Incl.	20.	35.	50.	85.	150.	225.	300.	475.	—	—	*	*
1870 F2 N	Incl.	15.	25.	50.	75.	135.	225.	275.	400.	1,200.	3,500.	2,000.	6,500.
1870 F2 N (PE)	Incl.	*	*	*	*	*	*	*	*	*	*	2,000.	6,000.
1871 F2	1,400	15.	25.	45.	75.	150.	225.	300.	450.	950.	3,000.	*	*
1871 F2 7/7	Incl.	15.	25.	45.	75.	175.	250.	350.	450.	—	—	*	*
1871 F2 1/1	Incl.	15.	25.	45.	75.	175.	250.	350.	450.	—	—	*	*
1872H F2	2,000	15.	25.	40.	70.	150.	250.	400.	550.	1,700.	—	3,250.	8,000.
1872 F2 7/7	Incl.	25.	50.	100.	150.	325.	500.	750.	1,000.	—	—	*	*
1872 F2 2/2	Incl.	25.	50.	100.	150.	325.	500.	750.	1,000.	—	—	*	*

21 LEAVES REVERSE, 1870-1881 (cont.).

In 1874 and 1875 two sizes of digits were used for dating the dies. In addition to date sizes, the style of the 4 and 5 differ in their respective dates. The four of 1874 has either a plain 4 or a crosslet 4, while the five of 1875 has either a short top 5 or a long top 5.

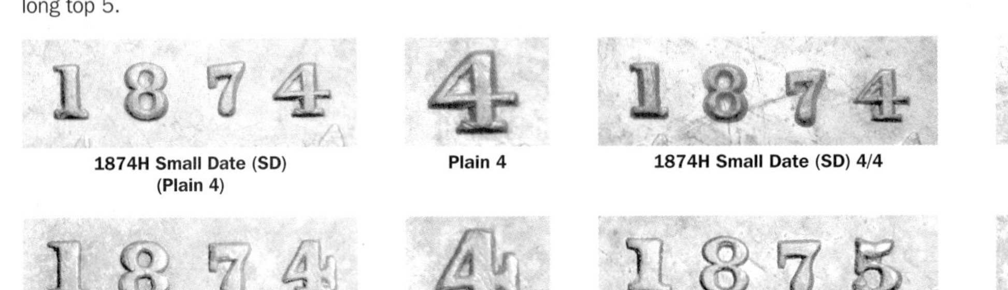

1874H Small Date (SD) (Plain 4)

Plain 4

1874H Small Date (SD) 4/4

4/4

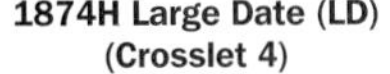

1874H Large Date (LD) (Crosslet 4)

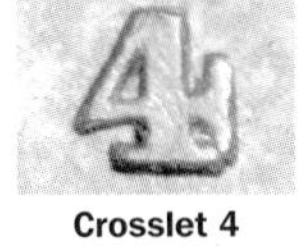

Crosslet 4

1875H Large Date (LD) Large 5

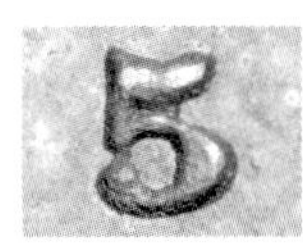

Large 5

1875H Small Date (SD) Small 5

Small 5

1875H Small Date (SD) 7/7, Small 5/5

Small 5/5

DATE / PORTRAIT/ VAR.	MINTAGE (thous.)	G-4	VG-8	F-12	VF-20	EF-40	AU-50	AU-55	MS-60	MS-63	MS-65	SP-63	SP-65
1874H F2 SD	800	20.	40.	85.	175.	250.	375.	450.	700.	1,800.	3,500.	*	*
1874H F2 SD 4/4	Incl.	30.	50.	100.	200.	300.	400.	500.	—	—	—	*	*
1874H F2 LD	Incl.	20.	30.	75.	125.	275.	500.	650.	900.	1,800.	4,500.	2,500.	12,000.
1875H F2 LD	1,000	350.	500.	675.	1,100.	2,000.	4,500.	5,500.	—	—	—	8,000.	25,000.
1875H F2 LD 5/5	Incl.	400.	550.	725.	1,200.	2,200.	5,000.	6,000.	—	—	—	*	*
1875H F2 SD	Incl.	125.	250.	325.	650.	1,000.	1,800.	2,300.	3,500.	9,000.	—	8,000.	25,000.
1875H F2 SD 5/5	Incl.	150.	300.	375.	750.	1,200.	2,000.	—	—	—	—	*	*
1880H F2	3,000	25.	50.	100.	200.	350.	900.	1,250.	1,500.	—	—	*	*
1880H F3	Incl.	10.	15.	20.	40.	100.	200.	275.	450.	950.	4,000.	2,500.	8,000.
1881H F2	1,500	10.	20.	30.	50.	100.	275.	375.	500.	1,200.	4,000.	2,500.	8,000.

22 LEAVES REVERSE, 1882-1889.

In 1884 we find a spacing difference between the 8 and the 4. Besides the digit punch spacing, the cross ends of the fours differ — a pointed end and a blunt end.

During the year 1885, two markedly different styles of 5 were used in the date. One is the small 5 carried forward from the 1875H issue; the other is the larger 5 used in the denomination "5 CENTS." There are also repunched 5 over 5s. Coins of 1886 occur with either a small 6 or a large 6 for the final digit of the date. The uppermost part of the inner portion of the small 6 comes to a point, whereas that area on the large 6 is almost square.

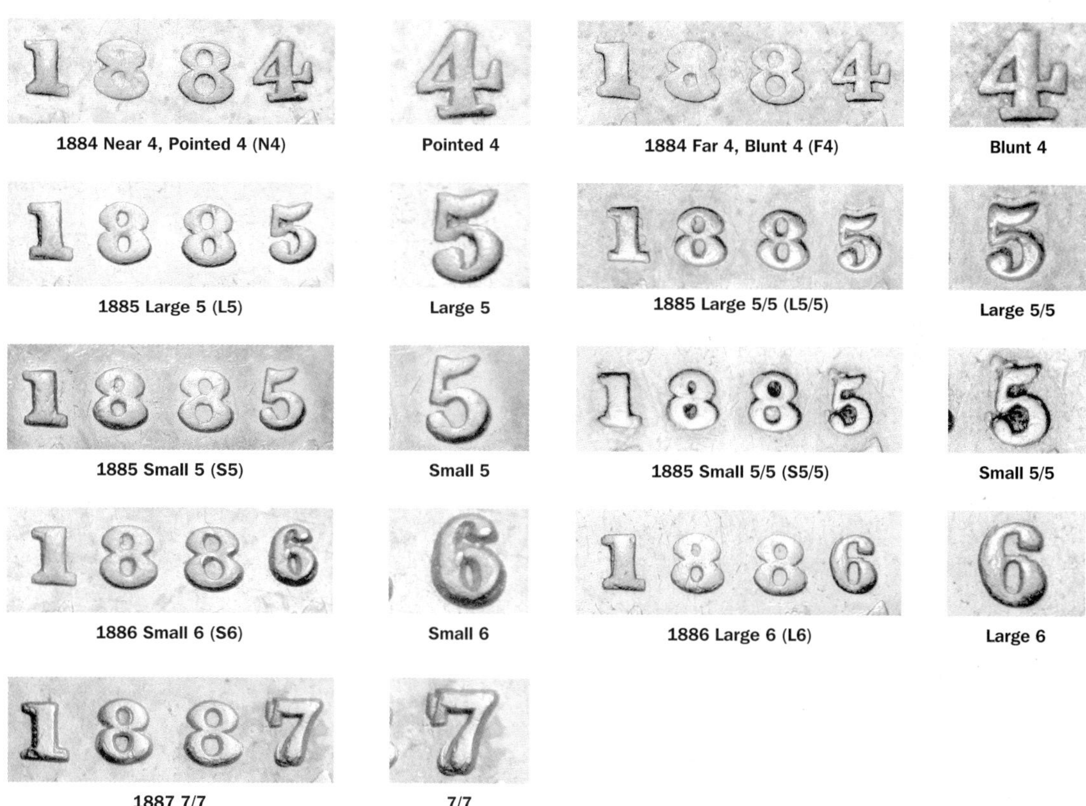

1884 Near 4, Pointed 4 (N4) — **Pointed 4** — **1884 Far 4, Blunt 4 (F4)** — **Blunt 4**

1885 Large 5 (L5) — **Large 5** — **1885 Large 5/5 (L5/5)** — **Large 5/5**

1885 Small 5 (S5) — **Small 5** — **1885 Small 5/5 (S5/5)** — **Small 5/5**

1886 Small 6 (S6) — **Small 6** — **1886 Large 6 (L6)** — **Large 6**

1887 7/7 — **7/7**

DATE / MINT/ PORTRAIT/VAR.	MINTAGE (thous.)	G-4	VG-8	F-12	VF-20	EF-40	AU-50	AU-55	MS-60	MS-63	MS-65	SP-63	SP-65
1882H F4	1,000	10.	20.	30.	75.	150.	250.	350.	500.	1,200.	4,000.	3,250.	8,000.
1883H F4	600	250.	500.	750.	1,000.	—	—	—	—	—	—	*	*
1883H F5	Incl.	20.	40.	75.	125.	325.	700.	1,000.	1,250.	2,500.	—	*	*
1884 F5 N4	200	100.	200.	300.	525.	1,200.	2,250.	—	—	—	—	10,000.	40,000.
1884 F5 F4	Incl.	100.	200.	300.	500.	1,500.	2,750.	—	—	—	—	*	*
1885 F5 S5	1,000	15.	30.	45.	100.	175.	550.	800.	1,250.	3,500.	—	*	*
1885 F5 S5/5	Incl.	60.	120.	175.	225.	300.	1,850.	2,350.	2,700.	—	—	*	*
1885 F5 L5	Incl.	20.	30.	50.	100.	225.	550.	800.	1,600.	4,000.	—	6,500.	12,000.
1885 F5 L5/5	Incl.	30.	60.	110.	175.	300.	700.	1,000.	2,000.	5,000.	—	*	*
1886 F5 S6	1,700	15.	20.	30.	50.	115.	225.	400.	650.	1,650.	3,000.	6,500.	12,000.
1886 F5 L6	Incl.	15.	30.	40.	60.	125.	300.	450.	650.	1,800.	—	*	*
1887 F5	500	15.	30.	50.	90.	225.	375.	550.	750.	1,800.	4,000.	*	*
1887 F5 7/7	Incl.	25.	40.	75.	150.	350.	550.	800.	—	—	—	*	*
1888 F5	1,000	10.	15.	25.	35.	100.	150.	225.	300.	725.	1,500.	*	*
1889 F5	1,200	25.	50.	80.	125.	325.	450.	600.	850.	1,500.	—	*	*

21 LEAVES REVERSE RESUMED, 1890-1901.

Two sizes of the date are seen on the 1900 issue. The large date has been referred to most often as the Round 0s variety and the small date as the Oval 0s variety, but there is a greater difference in the 9s. The large date has a Wide 9 as on the 1898 issue and the small date has a Narrow 9 as on the 1899 and 1901 issues.

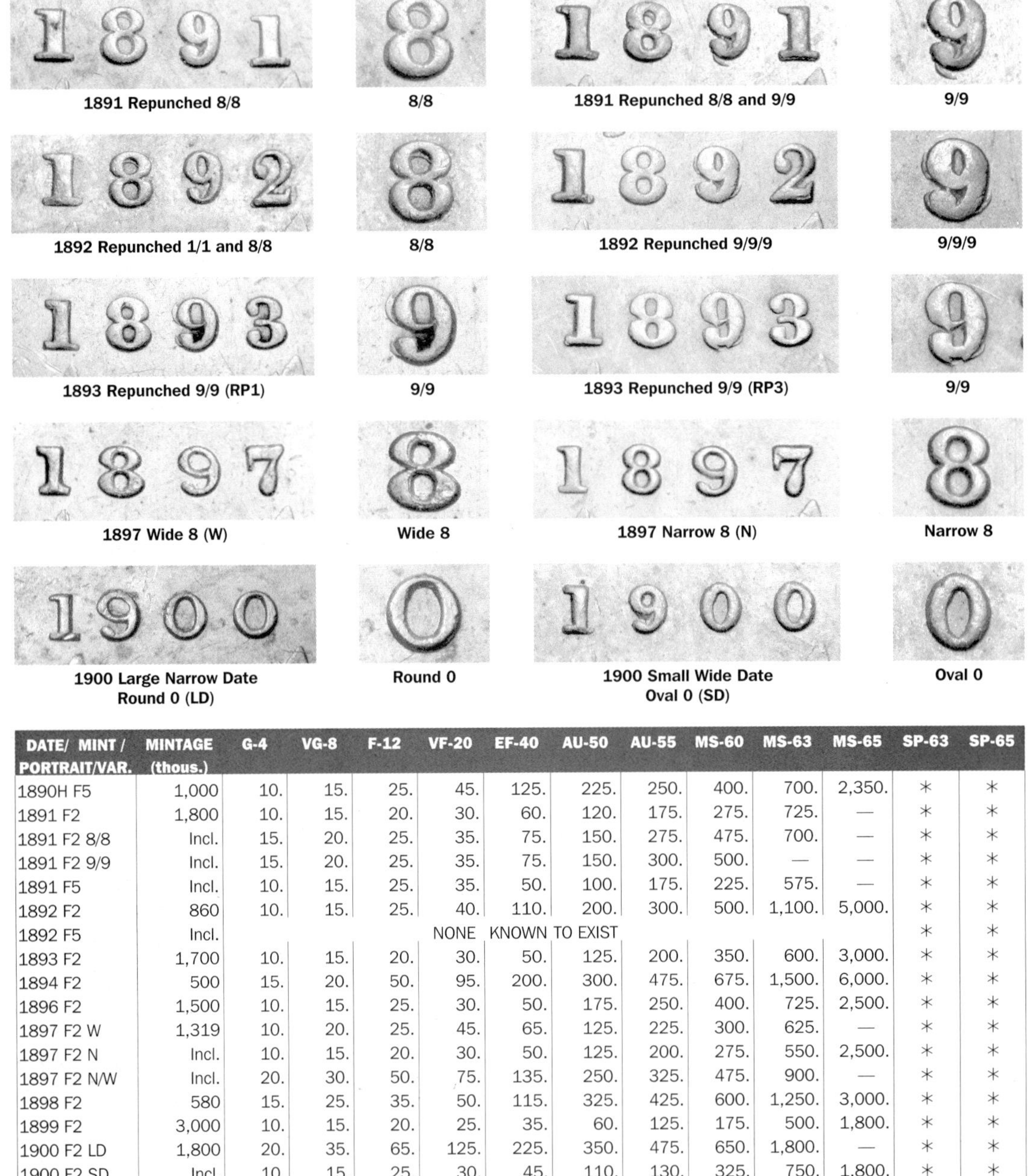

1891 Repunched 8/8 — 8/8 — 1891 Repunched 8/8 and 9/9 — 9/9

1892 Repunched 1/1 and 8/8 — 8/8 — 1892 Repunched 9/9/9 — 9/9/9

1893 Repunched 9/9 (RP1) — 9/9 — 1893 Repunched 9/9 (RP3) — 9/9

1897 Wide 8 (W) — Wide 8 — 1897 Narrow 8 (N) — Narrow 8

1900 Large Narrow Date Round 0 (LD) — Round 0 — 1900 Small Wide Date Oval 0 (SD) — Oval 0

DATE/ MINT / PORTRAIT/VAR.	MINTAGE (thous.)	G-4	VG-8	F-12	VF-20	EF-40	AU-50	AU-55	MS-60	MS-63	MS-65	SP-63	SP-65
1890H F5	1,000	10.	15.	25.	45.	125.	225.	250.	400.	700.	2,350.	*	*
1891 F2	1,800	10.	15.	20.	30.	60.	120.	175.	275.	725.	—	*	*
1891 F2 8/8	Incl.	15.	20.	25.	35.	75.	150.	275.	475.	700.	—	*	*
1891 F2 9/9	Incl.	15.	20.	25.	35.	75.	150.	300.	500.	—	—	*	*
1891 F5	Incl.	10.	15.	25.	35.	50.	100.	175.	225.	575.	—	*	*
1892 F2	860	10.	15.	25.	40.	110.	200.	300.	500.	1,100.	5,000.	*	*
1892 F5	Incl.				NONE	KNOWN TO EXIST						*	*
1893 F2	1,700	10.	15.	20.	30.	50.	125.	200.	350.	600.	3,000.	*	*
1894 F2	500	15.	20.	50.	95.	200.	300.	475.	675.	1,500.	6,000.	*	*
1896 F2	1,500	10.	15.	25.	30.	50.	175.	250.	400.	725.	2,500.	*	*
1897 F2 W	1,319	10.	20.	25.	45.	65.	125.	225.	300.	625.	—	*	*
1897 F2 N	Incl.	10.	15.	20.	30.	50.	125.	200.	275.	550.	2,500.	*	*
1897 F2 N/W	Incl.	20.	30.	50.	75.	135.	250.	325.	475.	900.	—	*	*
1898 F2	580	15.	25.	35.	50.	115.	325.	425.	600.	1,250.	3,000.	*	*
1899 F2	3,000	10.	15.	20.	25.	35.	60.	125.	175.	500.	1,800.	*	*
1900 F2 LD	1,800	20.	35.	65.	125.	225.	350.	475.	650.	1,800.	—	*	*
1900 F2 SD	Incl.	10.	15.	25.	30.	45.	110.	130.	325.	750.	1,800.	*	*
1901 F2	2,000	10.	15.	25.	30.	45.	100.	125.	200.	500.	2,000.	*	*

Note on 1897 N/W Variety

The previously recorded 1897 N/W variety is not an overdate, it is not a narrow 8 over a large 8. It is simply die deterioration around the small 8, and therefore no premium should be attached to it.

FIVE CENTS
EDWARD VII 1902 - 1910

For the coronation in 1902, Edward VII commissioned a new design for his crown. The Imperial State Crown (St. Edward's Crown) in use for nearly 300 years and used for 63 years by Queen Victoria, became known as the Queen's Crown. The finial on the Imperial State Crown is a jewelled Maltese Cross.

The new Imperial or Tudor Crown, which Edward helped design, was in use until 1952. This became known as the King's Crown. The finial on this crown is a stylized gold Maltese Cross, in keeping with the Art Nouveau period in which it was designed.

In 1902 the word CANADA was transferred from the obverse to the reverse legend and new lettering and numerical fonts were used. The wreath design and the Imperial State or St. Edward's Crown were the same as used for the Victoria five cents.

IMPERIAL CROWNED PORTRAIT, ST. EDWARD'S CROWN REVERSE, 21 LEAVES DESIGN, 1902

Obverse: Imperial Crown with stylized gold Maltese Cross finial

Reverse: Imperial State Crown with jewelled Maltese Cross finial

Designer and Engraver: George W. DeSaulles
Composition: .925 silver, .075 copper
Weight: 1.16 grams
Diameter: 15.50 mm
Edge: Reeded
Die Axes: ↑↓

Varieties: The matrix for the 1902 coinage was fully dated with the mint mark being added to the individual dies. The dies were prepared in the Royal Mint and sent to The Mint Birmingham Ltd. for striking. Two different font sizes were used to produce the "H" mint mark on the dies at the Royal Mint.

1902 Large H (LH)

1902 Large H/Small H (LH/SH)

1902 Small H (SH)

DATE / MINT VARIETY	MINTAGE (thous.)	VG-8	F-12	VF-20	EF-40	AU-50	AU-55	MS-60	MS-63	MS-64	MS-65	SP-63	SP-65
1902	2,120	7.	8.	10.	15.	30.	45.	55.	85.	130.	250.	*	*
1902H LH	2,200	7.	8.	10.	20.	30.	45.	60.	80.	175.	375.	3,500.	5,000.
1902H LH/SH	Incl.	15.	25.	40.	75.	100.	135.	175.	275.	1,000.	3.000.	*	*
1902H SH	Incl.	15.	25.	40.	75.	110.	125.	150.	250.	425.	750.	*	*

IMPERIAL CROWNED PORTRAIT, IMPERIAL CROWN REVERSE, 21 LEAVES DESIGN, 1903.

Five cent production continued at The Mint Birmingham Ltd. in the early part of 1903. The changes to the reverse design which began in 1902 were completed. The Imperial State Crown was removed and replaced by the new Imperial or Tudor Crown.

1903H
Imperial Crown with Stylized Maltese Cross Finial

1903 to 1910
Imperial Crown with Maltese Cross Finial

1908 to 1910
Imperial Crown with Cross over Maltese Cross Finial

Designer and Engraver:
Probably George W. DeSaulles

Specifications:
Same as 1902 issue.

Mint Mark Varieties

1903 Large H (LH)

1903 Small H (SH)

1903 Small H over Small (SH/H)

DATE / MINT / VARIETY	MINTAGE (thous.)	VG-8	F-12	VF-20	EF-40	AU-50	AU-55	MS-60	MS-63	MS-64	MS-65	SP-63	SP-65
1903H LH	2,640	25.	35.	60.	125.	200.	275.	450.	1,200.	2,000.	6,000.	*	*
1903H SH	Incl.	7.	8.	15.	35.	70.	90.	150.	450.	1,000.	3,000.	*	*
1903H SH/SH	Incl.	15.	30.	45.	90.	150.	225.	300.	675.	1,000.	—	*	*

IMPERIAL CROWNED PORTRAIT, IMPERIAL CROWN REVERSE, 22 LEAVES DESIGN, 1903-1910.

Mid-year 1903 saw the production of Canadian five cent coins returned from The Birmingham Mint Ltd. to London's Royal Mint. A new reverse matrix was designed, one which carried a wreath of 22 maple leaves, and a smaller Imperial Crown which supported a Maltese Cross as the finial. This new matrix was fully dated.

Being fully dated the matrix of 1903 produced no date spacing varieties. Also, no date spacing varieties have currently been found for the 1904 issues. From 1905 to 1907 the last digit of the date was added to the dies.

In 1907, for the opening of the Branch Mint, Ottawa in 1908, the Royal Mint supplied the production tools a little ahead of the opening date.

In 1909 the reverse design was again modified, altering the rounded maple leaves to more pointed leaves which resembled holly leaves. Thus two reverse designs are found in 1909 and 1910.

Designer and Engraver:
Obv.: George W. De Saulles
Rev.: W. H. J. Blakemore
Composition: .925 silver, .075 copper
Weight: 1903-1910: 1.16 grams
1910: 1.17 grams
Diameter: 15.50 mm
Edge: Reeded
Die Axes: 1903-1907: ↑↓
1908-1910: ↑↑

VARIETIES 1905 TO 1907.

1905 Narrow Date (ND) 5/5-2

1905 Narrow Date Repunched 5/5-1

1905 Narrow Date Repunched 5/5-2

1905 Wide Date (WD)

1906 Narrow Date (ND)

1907 Narrow Date (ND)

1906 Narrow Date Low 6 (ND)

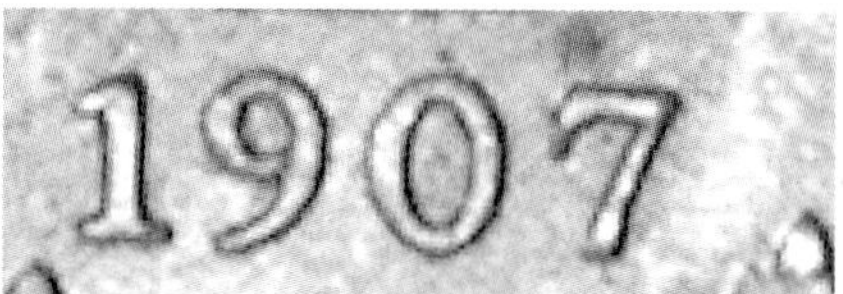

1907 Narrow Date Low 7 (ND)

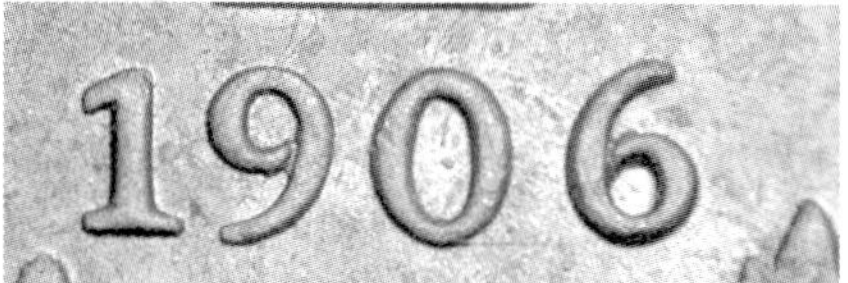

1906 Wide Date (WD)

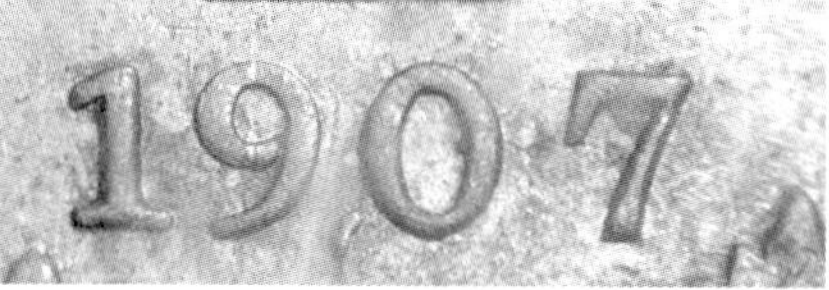

1907 Wide Date (WD)

VARIETIES OF 1908 TO 1910.

The Maltese Cross finial on the Imperial Crown depicted on the reverse design underwent three different style changes. On the 1903H dies it was a stylized Maltese Cross, similar to the finial on the obverse crown. From 1903 to 1910 the classic Maltese Cross was used, but due to space restrictions it resembled a bow tie more than a Maltese Cross. On dies used in 1908, an engraver trying to correct the deformed appearance engraved a straight arm cross over the Maltese Cross.

1908 Large 8 (L8)
The Large 8 is currently known with the 1908 Bow Tie

Large 8

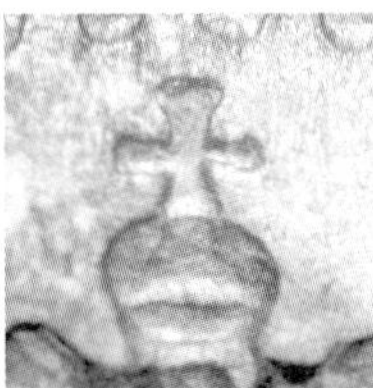

Maltese Cross 1903H

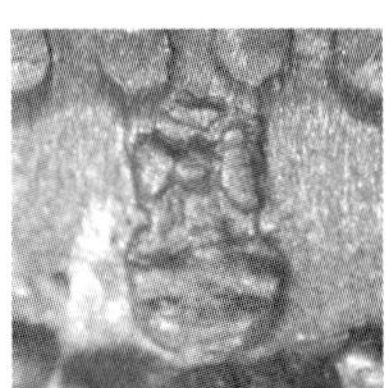

Bow Tie 1903-1910 (Bow)

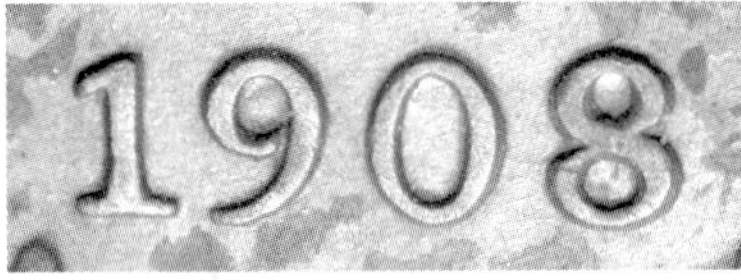

1908 Small 8 (S8)
The Small 8 is currently known with the 1908 Cross / Bow Tie

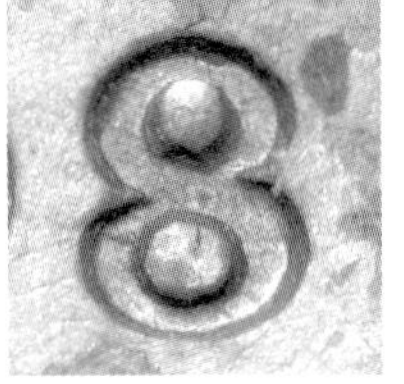

Small 8

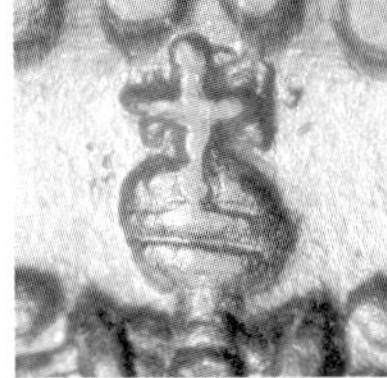

Cross / Bow Tie 1908 (C/B)

Cross / Bow Tie 1909 (C/B)

Maple or Round Leaves (ML)

Holly or Pointed Leaves (HL)

DATE / VARIETY	MINTAGE (thous.)	VG-8	F-12	VF-20	EF-40	AU-50	AU-55	MS-60	MS-63	MS-64	MS-65	SP-63	SP-65
1903	1,000	10.	12.	15.	75.	125.	175.	300.	675.	950.	1,500.	*	*
1904	2,400	8.	10.	15.	35.	100.	150.	275.	675.	1,250.	3,500.	*	*
1905 ND	2,600	7.	10.	15.	25.	45.	90.	135.	400.	600.	1,450.	2,000.	5,000.
1905 ND 5/5-1	Incl.	10.	15.	25.	45.	55.	110.	175.	550.	—	—	*	*
1905 ND 5/5-2	Incl.	10.	15.	25.	35.	55.	110.	175.	550.	—	—	*	*
1905 WD	Incl.	7.	10.	15.	30.	85.	110.	130.	400.	675.	1,200.	—	—
1906 ND	3,100	7.	8.	12.	25.	45.	65.	100.	375.	650.	1,200.	*	*
1906 ND Low 6	Incl.	8.	10.	15.	30.	60.	75.	125.	450.	—	—	*	*
1906 WD	Incl.	7.	8.	12.	25.	45.	65.	100.	450.	725.	—	*	*
1907 ND	5,200	7.	8.	12.	15.	40.	50.	80.	200.	350.	875.	*	*
1907 ND Low 7	Incl.	10.	12.	15.	25.	50.	75.	100.	250.	—	—	*	*
1907 WD	Incl.	7.	8.	12.	15.	40.	50.	80.	175.	325.	775.	*	*
1908 ML Bow L8	1,198	55.	100.	150.	300.	475.	600.	750.	1,250.	2,000.	4,000.	150.	750.
1908 ML C/B S8	Incl.	15.	20.	40.	65.	100.	125.	175.	275.	400.	1,250.	150.	750.
1909 ML Bow	1,891	8.	15.	20.	45.	125.	200.	325.	900.	1,400.	1,750.	*	*
1909 ML C/B	Incl.	250.	475.	750.	1,000.	1,500.	—	—	—	—	—	*	*
1909 HL C/B	Incl.	20.	35.	65.	175.	275.	450.	750.	2,000.	3,500.	—	*	*
1910 ML Bow	5,580	25.	35.	70.	150.	300.	475.	600.	2,000.	3,500.	—	*	*
1910 HL C/B	Incl.	10.	12.	15.	25.	35.	55.	85.	125.	275.	625.	*	*

FIVE CENTS - SILVER
GEORGE V 1911 - 1921

IMPERIAL CROWNED PORTRAIT, 22 LEAVES DESIGN, 1911-1921.

The new obverse introduced in 1911 was criticized by the public because the Latin phrase "DEI GRATIA" (or an abbreviation for it), indicating that the King ruled by the grace of God, was omitted. The coinage tools were modified during the year and a new obverse with "DEI GRA:" included in the legend appeared on the 1912 issue. The Maple Leaves design reverse was that of the previous reign.

During 1920-1921 plans moved forward for the replacement of the small silver 5-cent piece with a larger coin of pure nickel, the same size as the U.S. nickel. The enabling legislation was passed in May 1921 and thereafter no more circulating 5-cent pieces were coined in silver. The mint melted some 3,022,665 coins of this denomination. The presumed composition of this melt was almost all the 1921 mintage and a portion of the 1920 mintage, thus explaining the rarity of the 1921 date today. Only about 400 1921s are believed to have survived. A few are Specimen coins, issued to collectors in sets and the rest are thought to be circulation strikes sold to visitors to the Mint in the early months of 1921. Almost all 1921 5¢ are believed to have remained unissued and were returned to the melting pot in 1922.

1911
Without
DEI GRATIA

1912-1921
With
DEI GRATIA

Designer and Engraver:
Obv.: Sir E. B. MacKennal
Rev.: W. H. J. Blakemore
Composition:
1911-1919: .925 silver, .075 copper
1920-1921: .800 silver, .200 copper
Weight: 1.17 grams
Diameter: 15.50 mm
Edge: Reeded
Die Axes: 1911-1921: ↑↑; 1919: ↑↓

DATE	MINTAGE	VG-8	F-12	VF-20	EF-40	AU-50	AU-55	MS-60	MS-63	MS-64	MS-65	SP-63	SP-65
1911	3,692,350	7.	10	15.	18.	40.	75.	100.	150.	250.	600.	500.	1,000.
1912	5,863,170	10.	12.	15.	20.	45.	60.	110.	225.	475.	1,275.	*	*
1913	5,588,048	8.	10.	12.	15.	25.	35.	40.	100.	150.	350.	*	*
1914	4,202,179	8.	10.	12.	15.	25.	60.	75.	200.	425.	750.	*	*
1915	1,172,258	20.	25.	40.	85.	175.	275.	550.	1,000.	1,500.	3,000.	*	*
1916	2,481,675	7.	15.	18.	35.	65.	95.	225.	350.	625.	2,000.	*	*
1917	5,521,373	5.	15.	18.	20.	25.	40.	65.	110.	175.	500.	*	*
1918	6,052,289	5.	15	18.	20.	25.	30.	40.	100.	200.	525.	*	*
1919 ↑↑	7,835,400	5.	15.	18.	20.	25.	35.	50.	100.	200.	500.	*	*
1919 ↑↓	Included	ONLY ONE CERTIFIED											
1920	10,649,851	5.	15.	18.	20.	25.	30.	35.	85.	150.	400.	*	*
1921	2,582,495	5,500.	7,000.	9,000.	13,000.	17,000.	21,000.	26,000.	35,000.	45,000.	60,000.	40,000.	75,000.

A Note on Catalogue Listings

This catalogue is based on circulating legal tender coinage used as a medium of exchange in Canada. Each denomination has a long standing design feature; for example, the one cent coin bears the twin maple leaves. This design was introduced in 1937 and continue to 2012. Apart from the one-year commemorative design of 1967, the only variables are in the specifications such as size, composition and mint marks, or finishes. (For Notes on Finishes see page xxii.)

For an explanation of the pricing tables please refer to pages xiv and xv in the introduction.

FIVE CENTS - NICKEL
GEORGE V 1922 - 1936

IMPERIAL CROWNED, 'DEI GRATIA', TWO MAPLE LEAVES DESIGN, 1922-1936.

With the introduction of a new design for the five cent coin which was to be struck on nickel blanks came the problems of strike and die wear. Nickel is a hard metal to work with: striking requires far more pressure than when dealing with the silver blanks of the past. The striking problem was showcased in the poor portrait reproduction on the obverse, and a similarly poor rendition of the maple leaves on the reverse. Weak strikes are notorious with this issue.

Flat fields running square to the rim was the common design feature of the time. However, during the period 1922 to 1936 the Mint experimented with basining, a polishing operation on the die, curving the field upward towards the rim reducing die wear, and at the same time allowing more metal to move, filling the portrait design.

Fully dated matrices were used for each date, except for 1926 and 1932 when two were sunk.

Designer and Engraver:
Obv.: Sir E. B. MacKennal
Rev.: W. H. J. Blakemore

Composition: 1.00 nickel
Weight: 4.54 grams
Diameter: 21.21 mm
Edge: Plain
Die Axes: ↑↑

Concave Field
"S" near to rim

Flat Field
"S" far from rim

1926 Near 6
The 6 almost touches the maple leaf

1926 Far 6
The 6 is farther from the maple leaf

1932 Near 2
"2" Near Leaf

1932 Far 2
"2" Far from Leaf

DATE / VARIETY	MINTAGE	VG-8	F-12	VF-20	EF-40	AU-50	AU-55	MS-60	MS-63	MS-64	MS-65	SP-63	SP-65
1922 Near S	4,763,186	5.	15.	18.	20.	35.	45.	60.	150.	250.	1,250.	600.	1,200.
1922 Far S	Included	5.	15.	18.	20.	40.	60.	125.	200.	275.	1,000.	600.	1,200.
1923	2,475,201	5.	15.	18.	20.	65.	125.	175.	350.	850.	2,500.	4,000.	8,000.
1924	3,066,658	5.	15.	18.	20.	35.	55.	150.	300.	550.	2,500.	1,500.	4,000.
1925	200,050	85.	125.	175.	450.	775.	1,350.	2,250.	5,500.	7,500.	—	3,500.	8,000.
1926 Near 6	933,577	10.	15.	30.	70.	250.	350.	600.	1,600.	6,000.	—	3,000.	7,500.
1926 Far 6	Included	175.	225.	275.	800.	1,250.	1,850.	2,500.	6,250.	10,000.	—	*	*
1927	5,285,627	5.	15.	18.	20.	45.	65.	90.	175.	375.	2,500.	2,000.	8,000.
1928	4,588,725	5.	15.	18.	20.	45.	60.	75.	125.	250.	1,000.	2,500.	5,000.
1929 Near S	5,562,262	5.	7.	10.	20.	35.	50.	110.	175.	500.	2,200.	1,000.	4,000.
1929 Far S	Included	5.	7.	10.	20.	35.	50.	110.	175.	500.	2,000.	1,000.	4,000.
1930	3,685,991	5.	10.	15.	20.	50.	65.	125.	325.	800.	3,500.	2,500.	5,000.
1931	5,100,830	5.	10.	15.	25.	70.	135.	450.	875.	2,000.	—	2,500.	5,000.
1932 Near S, Near 2	3,198,566	5.	10.	15.	25.	65.	150.	225.	825.	2,500.	—	8,000.	15,000.
1932 Near S, Far 2	Included	400.	500.	800.	—	—	—	—	—	—	—	8,000.	15,000.
1932 Far S	Included	5.	10.	15.	25.	65.	150.	225.	825.	2,500.	—	8,000.	15,000.
1933	2,597,867	5.	10.	15.	30.	100.	200.	300.	1,100.	2,200.	—	*	*
1934 Near S	3,827,304	5.	10.	15.	25.	60.	100.	200.	850.	1,500.	—	2,500.	5,000.
1934 Far S	Included	5.	10.	15.	25.	50.	100.	200.	850.	1,500.	—	2,500.	5,000.
1935	3,900,000	5.	10.	15.	20.	60.	90.	135.	500.	1,100.	2,500.	*	*
1936 Near S	4,400,450	5.	10.	15.	20.	40.	50.	65.	175.	350.	1,450.	*	*
1936 Far S	Included	5.	10.	15.	20.	40.	50.	65.	175.	350.	1,450.	3,000.	7,500.

FIVE CENTS
GEORGE VI 1937 - 1952

UNCROWNED PORTRAIT, BEAVER DESIGN, ROUND, NICKEL, 1937-1942. In 1937 Canada introduced new coinage designs for the lower denominations, in keeping with a trend towards modernization begun in 1935 with the silver dollar. The reverse of the 5-cent piece depicts a beaver on a rock-studded mound of earth rising out of the water. At the left is a log on which the beaver has been chewing. The master tools for this reverse were produced at the Paris Mint because the Royal Mint in London was pressed for time.

Designer and Engraver:
Obv.: T. H. Paget
Rev.: G. E. Kruger-Gray
Composition: 1.00 nickel
Weight: 4.54 grams
Diameter: 21.21 mm
Edge: Plain
Die Axes: ↑↑

DATE / FINISH	MINTAGE	EF-40	AU-50	AU-55	MS-60	MS-63	MS-64	MS-65	MS-66	SP-63	SP-65
1937 Dot	4,593,263	7.	10.	12.	15.	30.	50.	275.	3,000.	75.	200.
1937 Dot Matte	Included	*	*	*	*	*	*	*	*	50.	150.
1938	3,898,974	20.	40.	65.	90.	200.	925.	7,500.	—	7,500.	20,000.
1939	5,661,123	15.	25.	50.	65.	110.	225.	575.	3,000.	*	*
1940	13,820,197	10.	12.	25.	40.	55.	125.	850.	—	*	*
1941	8,681,785	10.	15.	25.	40.	70.	300.	2,000.	—	*	*
1942	6,847,544	6.	10.	15.	30.	60.	80.	550.	—	6,000.	20,000.

UNCROWNED PORTRAIT, BEAVER DESIGN, 12-SIDED, TOMBAC, 1942.

Nickel is an important component of stainless steel and other alloys needed for producing war materials, so World War II put a great strain upon Canada's nickel producers. By 1942 it was decided that nickel would have to be suspended as a coinage material for the duration of the war and experiments were initiated to find a substitute metal for the 5-cent piece. This led to the adoption of a 12-sided coin made of tombac, a kind of brass. The idea had come from the British 3-penny piece first issued in 1937. The tombac 5-cent coin was given its shape so that when tarnished it would still not be confused with 1-cent pieces.

Designers and Engravers:
Obv.: T. H. Paget, Thomas Shingles
Rev.: G. E. Kruger-Gray, Thomas Shingles
Composition: .88 copper, .12 zinc
Weight: 4.54 grams
12-sided:
21.3 mm (opposite corners)
20.0 mm (opposite sides)
Edge: Plain
Die Axes: ↑↑

DATE / VARIETY	MINTAGE	EF-40	AU-50	AU-55	MS-60	MS-63	MS-64	MS-65	MS-66	SP-63	SP-65
1942 Tombac	3,396,234	6.	10.	12.	20.	25.	35.	150.	3,000.	500.	1,500.

PRICING

The Charlton Press pricing tables are based on market prices for **Canadian certified coins.** Currently there are two coin grading companies located in Canada. Our prices are gathered from prices realized at land auctions, internet auctions, and dealer fixed price lists and their internet listings. It is important to realize that coin certification incurs a cost, and on low value coins it will be a significant factor in their listed value. The cost for certification per coin averages between $7-$10 for standard service.

UNCROWNED PORTRAIT, VICTORY DESIGN, 12-SIDED, TOMBAC, 1943-1944.

In 1943 a new reverse design came into use for this denomination. Its purpose was to help promote the war effort. The idea for the design came from Churchill's famous "V" sign and the V denomination mark on the U.S. 5-cent pieces of 1883-1912. A novel feature was the use of an International Code message meaning, "We Win When We Work Willingly." It was placed along the rim on the reverse instead of denticles. The original master matrix was engraved entirely by hand by Royal Canadian Mint Chief Engraver Thomas Shingles. The obverse was the same as that for 1942, except rim denticles were added.

The Royal Canadian Mint Report for 1944 lists $400. face value, or 8,000 pieces of five cent Tombac coins being issued in Ottawa during that year. The report also states that no tombac composition coins were produced in 1944, but a reconciliation of mintages for the years 1943 and 1944 leaves 7,744 pieces not struck in 1943. Were the coins struck in 1944, and did they carry the 1944 date.

Designer and Engraver:
Obv.: T. H. Paget, Thomas Shingles
Rev.: Thomas Shingles

Specifications:
Same as 1942 Tombac issue

DATE	MINTAGE	EF-40	AU-50	AU-55	MS-60	MS-63	MS-64	MS-65	MS-66	SP-63	SP-65
1943	24,760,256	6.	10.	12.	15.	20.	35.	150.	1,400.	200.	800.
1944	8,000					ONLY ONE CERTIFIED					

UNCROWNED PORTRAIT, VICTORY DESIGN, 12-SIDED, STEEL, 1944-1945.

War demands for copper and zinc forced a suspension in the use of tombac for the 5-cent piece and the institution of plated steel. The steel was plated with nickel and then returned to the plating tank for a very thin plating of chromium. The chromium was hard and helped retard wear. Unfortunately it was necessary to plate the strips prior to the blanks being punched out. This resulted in the edges of the blanks (and hence the coins) being unplated and vulnerable to rusting.

Some collectors have noted steel 5-cent pieces which have a dull gray colour instead of the normal bluish-white colour. This is the result of some of the strips being plated with nickel only and missing the chromium plating. Such coins are error coins and thus not listed here.

Composition:
Steel with .0127 mm plating of nickel and .0003 mm plating of chromium
Weight: 4.54 grams
12-sided: 21.3 mm (opposite corners)
20.9 mm (opposite sides)
Edge: Plain
Die Axes: ↑↑

DATE	MINTAGE	EF-40	AU-50	AU-55	MS-60	MS-63	MS-64	MS-65	MS-66	SP-63	SP-65
1944	11,532,784	6.	10.	12.	15.	20.	25.	50.	200.	300.	600.
1945	18,893,216	6.	10.	12.	15.	20.	25.	75.	275.	500.	2,500.

A Note on Catalogue Listings

This catalogue is based on circulating legal tender coinage used as a medium of exchange in Canada. Each denomination has a long standing design feature; for example, the one cent coin bears the twin maple leaves. This design was introduced in 1937 and continued to 2012. Apart from the one-year commemorative design of 1967, the only variables are in the specifications such as size, composition and mint marks, or finishes. (For Notes on Finishes see page xx.)

For an explanation of the pricing tables please refer to pages xii and xiii in the introduction.

UNCROWNED PORTRAIT, "ET IND:IMP:", BEAVER DESIGN RESUMED, 12-SIDED, NICKEL, 1946-1947.

After the end of World War II, the Mint returned to the issue of nickel 5-cent pieces of the beaver design. However, it was decided to retain the 12-sided shape, because it had become popular. The obverse was a continuation of that of 1943-1945.

The granting of independence to India created a dilemma for the Royal Canadian Mint in the early part of 1948. The new obverse coinage tools (with "ET IND: IMP:" omitted) would not arrive for several months, yet there was a great need for all denominations of coins. Therefore, the Mint struck coins dated 1947 and bearing the obverse with the outmoded titles. To differentiate this issue from the regular strikings of 1948, a tiny maple leaf was placed after the date.

Designer and Engraver:
Obv.: T. H. Paget, Thomas Shingles
Rev.: G. E. Kruger-Gray, Thomas Shingles
Composition: 1.00 nickel
Weight: 4.54 grams
12-sided:
21.3 mm (opposite corners)
20.9 mm (opposite sides)
Edge: Plain
Die Axes: ↑↑

1947 Dot

1947 Maple Leaf

DATE / VARIETY	MINTAGE	EF-40	AU-50	AU-55	MS-60	MS-63	MS-64	MS-65	MS-66	SP-63	SP-65
1946	6,952,684	10.	12.	15.	20.	50.	95.	1,100.	—	150.	450.
1947	7,603,724	6.	10.	12.	15.	45.	65.	850.	—	200.	500.
1947 ML	9,595,124	6.	10.	12.	18.	25.	70	250.	5,000.	150.	275.
1947 Dot	Included	100.	200.	275.	325.	500.	1,000.	2,500.	4,000.	*	*

UNCROWNED PORTRAIT, "DEI GRATIA", BEAVER DESIGN, 12-SIDED, NICKEL, 1948-1950.

Following the arrival of the master tools with the new obverse legend lacking "ET IND: IMP:" in 1948, production of the 1947 Maple Leaf coinage ceased. For the remainder of the year coins were produced with the new obverse and the true date, 1948.

Designer and Engraver:
Obv.: T. H. Paget, Thomas Shingles
Rev.: G. E. Kruger-Gray, Thomas Shingles
Specifications:
Same as 1946-1947 issues

DATE	MINTAGE	EF-40	AU-50	AU-55	MS-60	MS-63	MS-64	MS-65	MS-66	SP-63	SP-65
1948	1,810,789	10.	15.	20.	25.	45.	75.	250.	5,000.	200.	500.
1949	13,736,276	5.	10.	12.	15.	25.	50.	150.	6,000.	150.	325.
1950	11,950,520	5.	10.	12.	15.	25.	70.	250.	—	85.	150.

UNCROWNED PORTRAIT, COMMEMORATIVE DESIGN, 12-SIDED, NICKEL, 1951.

In 1950 plans were made to strike a coin to commemorate the isolation and naming of the element nickel by the Swedish chemist A. F. Cronstedt in 1751. The three Canadian commemorative coins issued up to that time had been silver dollars, but the 5-cent piece was selected for use in 1951 because it was the only denomination struck in nickel. The design was chosen from entries submitted to the Mint in an open competition, the first time in Canada for a coinage that was actually issued. The winning design depicts a nickel refinery, with low buildings flanking a smoke stack in the centre. The obverse is the same as that for the 1948-1950 issues.

Some members of the public became confused and believed that the dates 1751-1951 should have read 1851-1951. This caused hoarding of these coins in the mistaken belief that they would become extremely valuable.

Designer and Engraver:
Obv.: T. H. Paget, Thomas Shingles
Rev.: Stephan Trenka
Specifications:
Same as 1946 issue

DATE	MINTAGE	EF-40	AU-50	AU-55	MS-60	MS-63	MS-64	MS-65	MS-66	SP-63	SP-65
1951 Comm.	8,329,321	5.	10.	12.	15.	20.	25.	125.	—	85.	275.

UNCROWNED PORTRAIT, BEAVER DESIGN RESUMED, 12-SIDED, STEEL, 1951-1952.

The Korean War placed strong demand on nickel, forcing termination of production of the commemorative nickel 5-cent piece before the end of 1951. In its place steel coins of the beaver design were struck. It was found during trials that the beaver design was not as easy to strike in steel as in nickel, so new, lower relief coinage tools were prepared for both obverse and reverse. By mistake, a High Relief obverse die was used to strike a small proportion of the 1951 steel coinage, resulting in two varieties for the year. Aside from the difference in relief, the High and Low Relief obverses differ in the position of the last A of "GRATIA" relative to the rim denticles. On the High Relief variety the "A" points to a rim denticle; on the Low Relief variety it points between denticles. The entire 1952 issue was coined with the Low Relief obverse.

Designer and Engraver:
Obv.: T. H. Paget, Thomas Shingles
Rev.: G. E. Kruger-Gray, Thomas Shingles
Composition: Steel plated with .0127 mm nickel and .0003 mm of chromium
Weight: 4.54 grams
12-sided:
21.3 mm (opposite corners)
20.9 mm (opposite sides)
Edge: Plain
Die Axes: ↑↑

1951 High Relief Obverse A in GRATIA points to a rim denticle

1951 Low Relief Obverse A in GRATIA points between rim denticles

DATE / VARIETY	MINTAGE	F-12	VF-20	EF-40	AU-50	AU-55	MS-60	MS-63	MS-64	MS-65	MS-66	SP-63	SP-65
1951 HR	4,313,410	600.	850.	2,000.	2,500.	3,000.	—	—	—	—	—	2,000.	4,500.
1951 LR	Included	3.	4.	5.	6.	8.	10.	15.	25.	150.	—	*	*
1952	10,891,148	3.	4.	5.	6.	8.	10.	15.	20.	85.	2,500.	200.	750.

FIVE CENTS: ELIZABETH II 1953 TO DATE

LAUREATE BUST, BEAVER DESIGN, 12-SIDED, STEEL, 1953-1954.

Two obverse varieties, termed the No Shoulder Fold and Shoulder Fold obverses, saw use during 1953 (see 1-cent Elizabeth II, 1953 to date, for full explanation). On the 5-cent piece these varieties are best distinguished on worn coins by observing the styles of the letters in the obverse legends: they are more flared (particularly the E and I of "DEI") on the No Shoulder Fold variety. The Reverse was also modified in 1953 resulting in Far and Near Maple Leaf varieties.

Designer and Engraver:
Obv.: Mary Gillick, Thomas Shingles
Rev.: G. E. Kruger-Gray, Thomas Shingles
Composition: Steel with .0127 mm plating of nickel and .0003 mm plating of chromium
Weight: 4.54 grams
12-sided:
21.3 mm (opposite corners)
20.9 mm (opposite sides)
Thickness: 1.90 mm
Edge: Plain
Die Axes: ↑↑

OBVERSE VARIETIES

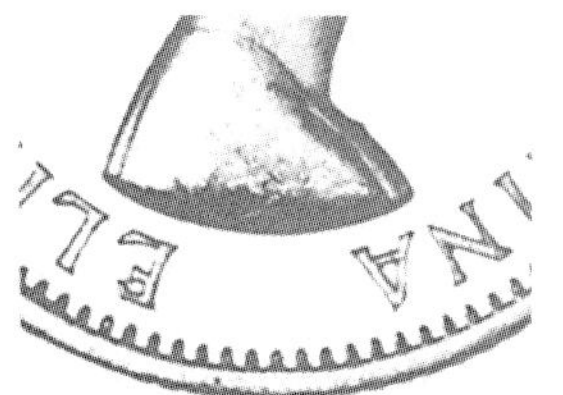

No Shoulder Fold Obverse note flared ends of "I"s

No Shoulder Fold Obverse note flared end of "I"s

Shoulder Fold Obverse note straight-sided "I"s

Shoulder Fold Obverse note straight-sided "I"s

REVERSE VARIETIES

Far Maple Leaf

Near Maple Leaf

DATE / VARIETY	MINTAGE	EF-40	AU-50	AU-55	MS-60	MS-63	MS-64	MS-65	MS-66	PL-65	PL-65 HC	SP-65	SP-67
1953 NSF Far	16,635,552	5.	6.	7.	8.	10.	20.	60.	250.	—	—	300.	1,000.
1953 NSF Near	Included	1,100.	1,500.	1,750.	2,000.	4,000.	5,000.	—	—	—	—	—	—
1953 SF Near	Included	5.	6.	8.	10.	15.	20.	80.	300.	150.	250.	450.	750.
1953 SF Far	Included	600.	800.	1,000.	1,800.	4,000.	—	—	—	—	—	*	*
1954 SF	6,998,662	4.	5.	8.	12.	20.	25.	85.	700.	40.	60.	*	*
1954 NSF	Included	ONLY FOUR CERTIFIED										*	*

PRICING

The Charlton Press pricing tables are based on market prices for **Canadian certified coins.** Currently there are two coin grading companies located in Canada. Our prices are gathered from prices realized at land auctions, internet auctions, and dealer fixed price lists and their internet listings. It is important to realize that coin certification incurs a cost, and on low value coins it will be a significant factor in their listed value. The cost for certification per coin averages between $7-$10 for standard service.

LAUREATE BUST, 12-SIDED, BEAVER DESIGN, NICKEL, 1955-1962.

The mint returned to production in nickel for the 5-cent piece in 1955. The obverse and reverse designs were continued from the previous year.

Designers and Engravers: Same as 1953 issues
Composition: 1.00 nickel
Weight: 4.54 grams
Diameter: 21.21 mm
Edge: Plain
Thickness: 1.75 mm
Die Axes: ↑↑

DATE	MINTAGE	AU-50	AU-55	MS-60	MS-63	MS-64	MS-65	MS-66	PL-65	PL-65 HC	SP-65	SP-67
1955	5,355,028	5.	6.	8.	12.	20.	100.	700.	30.	35.	*	*
1956	9,399,854	5.	6.	8.	12.	20.	65.	300.	25.	35.	*	*
1957	7,387,703	5.	6.	8.	10.	20.	45.	300.	20.	25.	*	*
1958	7,607,521	5.	6.	8.	10.	30.	40.	350.	20.	30.	*	*
1959	11,552,523	4.	5.	6.	10.	15.	45.	350.	20.	25.	*	*
1960	37,157,433	4.	5.	6.	10.	15.	50.	225.	15.	20.	*	*
1961	47,889,051	4.	5.	6.	10.	15.	50.	200.	15.	20.	*	*
1962	46,307,305	4.	5.	10.	20.	25.	60.	600.	10.	20.	*	*

LAUREATE BUST, ROUND, BEAVER DESIGN, NICKEL, 1963-1964.

For strictly economic reasons the production of round 5-cent pieces was resumed in 1963, for the first time since 1942. It was cheaper to make round coins because the collars for the coining presses lasted longer.

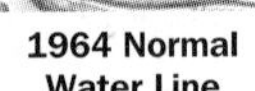
1964 Normal Water Line

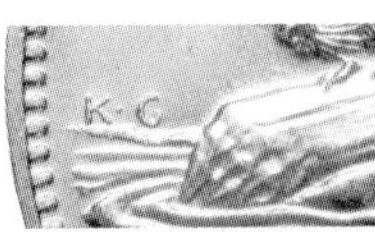
1964 Extra Water Line

Designers and Engravers: Same as 1953 issue
Specifications: Same as 1955 issue

DATE / VARIETY	MINTAGE	AU-50	AU-55	MS-60	MS-63	MS-64	MS-65	MS-66	PL-65	PL-65 HC	SP-65	SP-67
1963 ↑↑	43,970,320	4.	5.	10.	20.	25.	100.	600.	10.	20.	500.	1,000.
1963 ↑↓	Included	400.	500.	600.	—	—	—	—	*	*	*	*
1964 ↑↑	78,075,068	4.	5.	6.	10.	15.	90.	—	5.	20.	200.	400.
1964 ↑↓	Included	400.	500.	600.	—	—	—	—	*	*	*	*
1964 XWL	Included	35.	40.	50.	125.	600.	7,000.	—	*	*	*	*

TIARA PORTRAIT, ROUND, BEAVER DESIGN, NICKEL, 1965-1966.

A new obverse with the Queen showing more mature facial features and wearing a tiara was introduced on all denominations in 1965. Two obverse matrices were used in 1965, one having 138 beads around the rim, the other 119 beads. To complicate matters further the variety with 138 beads is the scarce large bead variety, which in turn comes in two die states, one in which the rear jewel is lightly attached and a second die state where the jewel is detached.

Designers and Engravers:
Obv.: Arnold Machin, R.C.M. Staff
Rev.: G. E. Kruger-Gray, T. Shingles
Specifications:
Same as 1955 issue

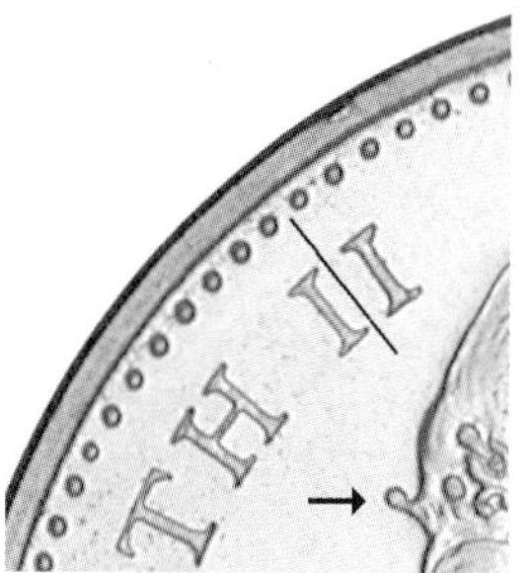

119 Small Beads
Attached Jewel (SB)

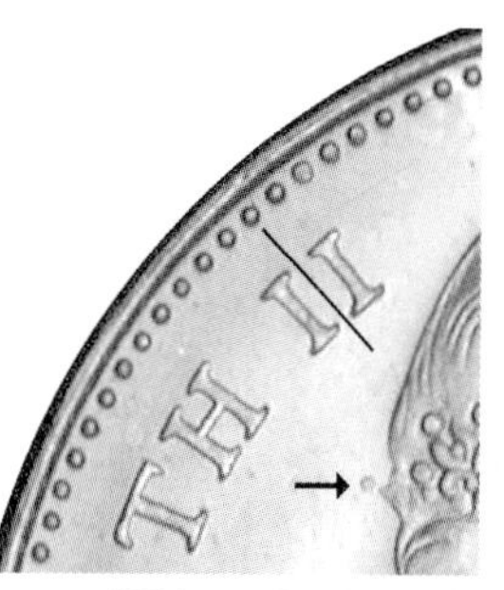

138 Large Beads
Lightly Attached / Detached Jewel (LB)

DATE	MINTAGE	EF-40	AU-50	AU-55	MS-60	MS-63	MS-64	MS-65	MS-66	PL-65	PL-65 HC	SP-65	SP-67
1965 SB	84,876,018	FV	4.	5.	6.	10.	18.	90.	—	10.	15.	175.	500.
1965 LB	Included	1,000.	1,500.	2,000.	2,500.	3,750.	5,000.	—	—	*	*	*	*
1966	27,976,648	4.	5.	6.	7.	10.	20.	250.	—	10.	25.	*	*

TIARA PORTRAIT, ROUND, CENTENNIAL DESIGN, NICKEL, 1967.

A reverse design showing a hopping rabbit was selected for the 1967 5-cent piece. It was by Alex Colville, who also designed the reverses of the other Confederation commemoratives issued for circulation. The obverse was a continuation of the 1965-1966 design.

Designers and Engravers:
Obv.: Arnold Machin, R.C.M. Staff
Rev.: Alex Colville, Myron Cook
Specifications:
Same as 1955 issue
Die Axis: ↑↑, ↑↓

DATE	MINTAGE	AU-50	AU-55	MS-60	MS-63	MS-64	MS-65	MS-66	PL-65	PL-65 HC	SP-65	SP-67
1967 ↑↑	36,876,574	4.	5.	6.	10.	12.	125.	—	10.	20.	20.	150.
1967 ↑↓	Included	ONLY ONE CERTIFIED										

TIARA PORTRAIT, ROUND, BEAVER DESIGN RESUMED, NICKEL, 1968-1980.

During 1977 a change in the matrix resulted in new punches and thus new dies creating a variety in the seven's for that year. The seven's vary in distance from Canada, and are also different in type size.

Beginning with the 1979 coinage and as part of a general standardization of the coinage, the portrait of the Queen was made smaller. The purpose was to make the size of the portrait proportional to the diameter of the coin, regardless of the denomination.

Designers and Engravers:
Obv.: Arnold Machin, R.C.M. Staff
Rev.: G. E. Kruger-Gray, Thomas Shingles
Specifications:
Same as 1955 issue

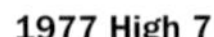
1977 High 7

1977 Low 7

DATE / VARIETY	MINTAGE	MS-63 C	MS-64 C	MS-65 C	MS-66 C	MS-65 NC	MS-66 NC	MS-67 NC	SP-66	SP-67
1968	99,253,330	10.	15.	25.	—	15.	30.	75.	200.	—
1969	27,830,229	10.	15.	60.	—	20.	30.	75.	200.	—
1970	5,726,010	5.	10.	25.	225.	20.	30.	75.	100.	—
1971	27,312,609	5.	15.	35.	250.	20.	30.	70.	10.	25.
1972	62,417,387	8.	15.	35.	250.	15.	25.	55.	10.	25.
1973	53,507,435	5.	10.	25.	225.	10.	20.	30.	10.	25.
1974	94,704,645	5.	15.	45.	250.	5.	15.	30.	10.	20.
1975	138,882,000	5.	15.	30.	150.	5.	15.	35.	15.	20.
1976	55,140,213	5.	15.	40.	250.	5.	15.	35.	15.	20.
1977 High	89,120,791	5.	20.	40.	250.	20.	40.	75.	15.	20.
1977 Low	Included	20.	40.	110.	250.	*	*	*	*	*
1978	137,079,273	5.	10.	25.	225.	5.	15.	35.	15.	25.
1979	186,295,825	8.	10.	25.	200.	10.	15.	35.	15.	25.
1980	134,878,000	8.	10.	80.	300.	10.	15.	25.	5.	20.

TIARA PORTRAIT, ROUND, BEAVER DESIGN, NICKEL, 1981.

The reorganisation of numismatic products in 1980 saw the inclusion of proof coins in sets offered by the Royal Canadian Mint.

DATE / VARIETY	MINTAGE	MS-63 C	MS-64 C	MS-65 C	MS-66 C	MS-65 NC	MS-66 NC	MS-67 NC	SP-66	SP-67	PR-67	PR-68
1981	99,107,900	10.	15.	200.	—	10.	15.	25.	5.	20.	10.	30.

MODIFIED TIARA PORTRAIT, ROUND, BEAVER DESIGN, CUPRO-NICKEL, 1982-1989.

In 1982 the composition of the 5 cent piece was changed because of the increased cost of nickel. The coin was now struck in the less expensive cupro-nickel.

Designers and Engravers:
Obv.: Arnold Machin, Walter Ott
Rev.: G. E. Kruger-Gray, Thomas Shingles
Composition:
1979-1981: 1.00 nickel
1982-1989: .75 copper, .25 nickel
Weight: 4.54 grams
Diameter: 21.2 mm
Thickness: 1.75 mm
Edge: Plain
Die Axes: ↑↑

DATE	MINTAGE	MS-64 C	MS-65 C	MS-66 C	MS-65 NC	MS-66 NC	MS-67 NC	SP-66	SP-67	PR-67	PR-68
1982	105,539,898	10.	115.	—	10.	15.	25.	5.	20.	10.	30.
1983	72,596,000	15.	185.	300.	10.	15.	25.	5.	20.	10.	30.
1984	84,088,000	10.	80.	200.	10.	20.	25.	5.	30.	10.	30.
1985	126,618,000	15.	150.	300.	5.	15.	25.	5.	20.	10.	30.
1986	156,104,000	20.	150.	300.	5.	15.	25.	5.	20.	10.	30.
1987	106,299,000	20.	55.	250.	5.	15.	25.	5.	20.	10.	20.
1988	75,025,000	20.	150.	300.	5.	15.	25.	5.	20.	10.	20.
1989	141,435,538	15.	55.	325.	5.	15.	25.	5.	20.	15.	20.

DIADEMED PORTRAIT, ROUND, BEAVER DESIGN, CUPRO-NICKEL, 1990-1992.

A new obverse portrait of the Queen wearing a diamond diadem and jewellery was introduced on all denominations in 1990. The reverse design was modified to include the bracket dates 1867-1992 for the 125th birthday of Canada in 1992.

1990-1991

Double date 1867-1992

Designers and Engravers:
Obv.: Dora de Pédery-Hunt, Ago Aarand
Rev.: G. E. Kruger-Gray, Thomas Shingles
Composition: .75 copper, .25 nickel
Weight: 4.6 grams
Diameter: 21.2 mm
Thickness: 1.76 mm
Edge: Plain
Die Axes: ↑↑

1990 Standard Beaver

1990 "Bare Belly" Beaver (BB)

DATE	MINTAGE	MS-64 C	MS-65 C	MS-66 C	MS-65 NC	MS-66 NC	MS-67 NC	SP-66	SP-67	PR-67	PR-68
1990	42,537,000	15.	50.	250.	5.	10.	20.	5.	20.	10.	20.
1990 BB	Included	150.	450.	—	*	*	*	*	*	*	*
1991	10,931,000	15.	25.	125.	5.	15.	30.	5.	20.	10.	20.
1992 (1867-)	53,732,000	15.	25.	75.	5.	15.	30.	5.	20.	10.	20.

Note: There is more than one variety of the 1990 "Bare Belly" Beaver, due to die polishing.

DIADEMED PORTRAIT, ROUND, BEAVER DESIGN, CUPRO-NICKEL, 1993-1995.

In 1993 the practice of using a single date was resumed. The transition from rim denticles on the reverse to beads, which began in 1982 on the one cent piece, was carried out on the five cent piece in 1993.

The Winnipeg Mint Mark (W) is found only on coins from the "Oh Canada!" and "Tiny Treasures" sets issued by the Numismatic Department of the Mint. These uncirculated sets are listed in *Canadian Coins, Volume Two: Collector and Maple Leaf Issues*.

Designers, Engravers and Specifications:
Same as 1990 issue

VARIETIES OF 1996.

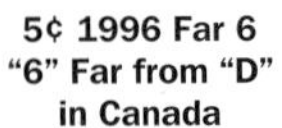

5¢ 1996 Far 6
"6" Far from "D"
in Canada

5¢ 1996 Near 6
"6" Near "D"
in Canada

DATE/ VARIETY	MINTAGE	MS-64 C	MS-65 C	MS-66 C	MS-65 NC	MS-66 NC	MS-67 NC	SP-66	SP-67	PR-67	PR-68
1993	86,877,000	10.	35.	75.	5.	15.	30.	5.	15.	10.	20.
1994	99,352,000	10.	25.	150.	5.	15.	30.	5.	15.	10.	20.
1995	78,780,000	10.	65.	175.	5.	15.	30.	5.	15.	10.	20.

DIADEMED PORTRAIT, ROUND, BEAVER DESIGN, CUPRO-NICKEL, 1996-2001.

Starting in 1996 proof coins issued by the Royal Canadian Mint were struck on (non-standard) sterling silver planchets. For proof coins 1996 to 2011 see *Canadian Coins, Volume Two, Collector and Maple leaf Issues*.

DATE/ VARIETY	MINTAGE	MS-64 C	MS-65 C	MS-66 C	MS-65 NC	MS-66 NC	MS-67 NC	SP-66	SP-67
1996 Far 6	36,686,000	30.	250.	650.	*	*	*	*	*
1996 Near 6	Included	15.	60.	125.	5.	15.	30.	5.	15.
1997	27,354,000	10.	25.	75.	5.	15.	30.	5.	15.
1998	156,873,000	10.	20.	150.	5.	10.	30.	5.	15.
1998W	N.I.I.	*	*	*	10.	25.	30.	*	*
1999	124,861,000	10.	20.	60.	10.	15.	25.	5.	15.
2000	105,868,000	10.	25.	95.	5.	15.	20.	5.	15.
2000W	N.I.I.	*	*	*	10.	35.	60.	*	*
2001	30,035,000	15.	100.	200.	*	*	*	*	*

UNCROWNED PORTRAIT, ROUND, BEAVER DESIGN, CUPRO NICKEL, 2006.

Designers and Engravers:
Obv.: Susanna Blunt, Susan Taylor
Rev.: G. E. Kruger-Gray, Thomas Shingles

Specifications:
Same as 1990 issue

DATE / MINT LOGO	MINTAGE	MS-64 C	MS-65 C	MS-66 C	MS-65 NC	MS-66 NC	MS-67 NC	SP-66	SP-67
2006	43,008,000	10.	20.	75.	*	*	*	*	*

DIADEMED PORTRAIT, ROUND, BEAVER DESIGN, MULTI-PLY PLATED STEEL, 1999-2003.

In 2000 the Royal Canadian Mint began issuing circulating five-cent coins struck on their new multi-ply plated steel blanks. The process is acid based and electroplates a thin coating of nickel, then copper, then nickel again to a steel core.

1999P to 2001P and 2003P

Double dates 1952 2002P

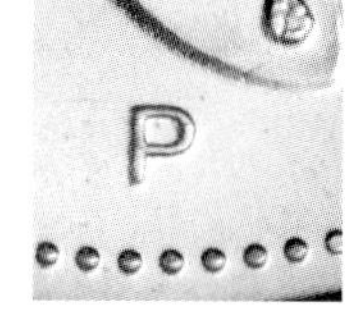

Composition Mark

Designers and Engravers:
Obv.: Dora de Pédery-Hunt, Ago Aarand
Rev.: G. E. Kruger-Gray, Thomas Shingles
Composition:
.945 steel, .035 copper, .02 nickel
Weight: 3.95 grams
Diameter: 21.10 mm
Thickness: 1.76 mm
Edge: Plain
Die Axes: ↑↑

DATE / COMP. MARK	MINTAGE	MS-64 C	MS-65 C	MS-66 C	MS-65 NC	MS-66 NC	MS-67 NC	SP-66	SP-67
1999P	Issued for testing	*	*	*	20.	45.	100.	*	*
2000P	4,899,000	10.	30.	150.	*	*	*	*	*
2001P	136,656,000	10.	20.	80.	5.	15.	30.	10.	20.
2002P (1952-)	135,960,000	10.	20.	50.	5.	15.	30.	10.	20.
2003P	32,986,921	10.	25.	70.	5.	15.	30.	10.	15.

UNCROWNED PORTRAIT, ROUND, BEAVER DESIGN, MULTI-PLY PLATED STEEL, 2003-2006.

Designers and Engravers:
Obv.: Susanna Blunt, Susan Taylor
Rev.: G. E. Kruger-Gray, Thomas Shingles
Specifications:
Same as 1999P issue

DATE / COMP. MARK	MINTAGE	MS-64 C	MS-65 C	MS-66 C	MS-65 NC	MS-66 NC	MS-67 NC	SP-66	SP-67
2003P	61,392,180	10.	45.	70.	5.	15.	30.	10.	15.
2003WP	N.I.I.	*	*	*	10.	20.	40.	*	*
2004P	132,097,000	10.	20.	60.	5.	10.	35.	10.	15.
2005P	89,664,000	10.	20.	25.	5.	10.	30.	10.	15.
2006P	94,226,000	10.	15.	35.	10.	15.	30.	10.	15.

NOTE FOR COLLECTORS

In 1996 the composition of the 5-, 10-, 25- and 50-cent coins used in proof sets was changed from multi-ply plated steel (standard) planchets to sterling silver planchets. This modification, of course, altered the standard or circulating make-up of these four coins making them no longer eligible for standard listings. The listings for these coins have been removed from the pricing tables of *Volume One* and are now listed in *Canadian Coins, Volume Two, Collector and Maple Leaf Issues*.

COMMEMORATIVE VICTORY DESIGN, MULTI-PLY PLATED STEEL, 1945-2005.

In 2005 the Royal Canadian Mint issued a five cent coin to commemorate the 60th anniversary of the Victory in Europe.

Designers and Engravers:
Obv.: Susanna Blunt, Susan Taylor
Rev.: Thomas Shingles
Specifications: Same as 1999P issue

DATE / COMP. MARK	DESCRIPTION	MINTAGE	MS-64 C	MS-65 C	MS-66 C	MS-65 NC	MS-66 NC	MS-67 NC	SP-66	SP-67
2005P (1945-)	V-E Day	59,258,000	10.	15.	30.	5.	15.	25.	*	*

UNCROWNED PORTRAIT, ROUND, BEAVER DESIGN, MULTI-PLY PLATED STEEL, RCM LOGO, 2006-2010.

Obv.: RCM LOGO

Designers and Engravers:
Obv.: Susanna Blunt, Susan Taylor
Rev.: G. E. Kruger-Gray, Thomas Shingles
Specifications:
Same as 1999P issue

DATE / MINT LOGO	DESCRIPTION	MINTAGE	MS-64 C	MS-65 C	MS-66 C	MS-65 NC	MS-66 NC	MS-67 NC	SP-66	SP-67
2006		45,082,000	10.	20.	75.	5.	15.	25.	*	*
2007		221,472,000	10.	15.	20.	5.	15.	25.	5.	15.
2008		278,530,000	10.	15.	20.	5.	15.	25.	5.	15.
2009		266,448,000	10.	15.	30.	5.	15.	25.	5.	15.
2010		126,840,000	10.	15.	30.	5.	15.	25.	5.	15.

UNCROWNED PORTRAIT, ROUND, BEAVER DESIGN, MULTI-PLY PLATED STEEL, RCM LOGO, 2011-2014.

With the cessation in 2011 of the brilliant uncirculated finish (MS-65-NC) on coins contained in the uncirculated sets, it was necessary to remove that block of grades from the pricing tables.

Designers and Engravers:
Obv.: Susanna Blunt, Susan Taylor
Rev.: G. E. Kruger-Gray, Thomas Shingles
Specifications:
Same as 1999P issue

DATE / MINT LOGO	DESCRIPTION	MINTAGE	MS-64 C	MS-65 C	MS-66 C	MS-67 C	SP-66	SP-67
2011		230,328,000	10.	20.	40.	300.	5.	15.
2012		202,944,000	10.	25.	45.	150.	5.	15.
2013		78,120,000	10.	25.	45.	150.	5.	15.
2014		N/A	10.	25.	45.	150.	5.	15.

NOTES ON FIVE CENT LISTINGS

1. When the pricing table lists a Specimen finish the prices are for those coins which have been removed from Specimen Sets and certified by a Canadian grading company.
2. The MS-65 NC (non-circulating) and higher grades are listings for coins removed from Uncirculated Sets and graded by a Canadian grading company.
3. Raw coin prices — Coins which are not certified. As a general rule of thumb third party grading companies offer a standard fee for grading individual coins that ranges between $7 and $10 per coin. If the collector were to subtract half of the lower end of the range from the catalogue price they would obtain an indication of the retail price for a raw coin. For coins of $100 or more in catalogue value it makes little sense to go through this exercise.
4. Mintage numbers listed in the pricing tables are for circulation coinage (MS-64 to MS-66-C Business Strikes). The mintage figures for Brilliant Uncirculated (MS-65 to MS-67-NC), Specimen (SP-66 to SP-67), and Proof (PR-67 to PR-68) must be obtained from *Canadian Coins, Volume Two, Collector and Maple Leaf Issues*.

VICTORIA TEN CENT MAJOR OBVERSE VARIETIES

Victoria Obverse Variety OT1

Hair and Eye Detail

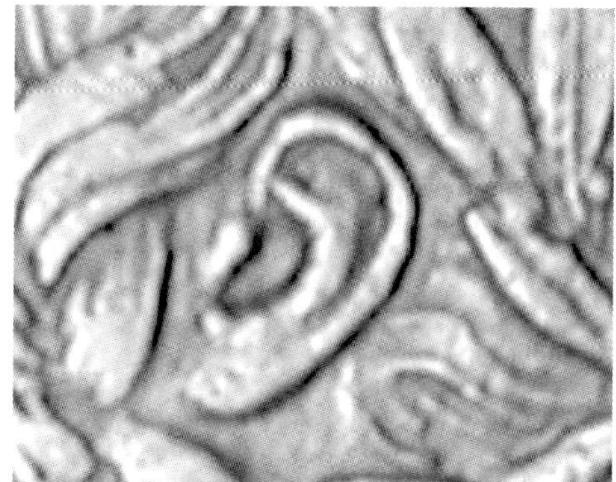

Outer Ear Detail

OT1 Hair detail: The first two strands curve and break at the temple. The next three strands join to make one thick strand.
Eyelid detail: Upper eyelid is completely formed but does not join the lower lid at the corner of the eye.
Outer ear detail: The opening to the ear is completely enclosed by the outer ridges.
Dates: Portrait OT1 is currently known on the following dates: 1858, 1870, 1871, 1871H, 1872H, 1874H, 1875H, 1880H and 1881H.

Note: The outer ear cavity has a distinctive shape for each portrait making it an easy identification point.

Victoria Obverse Variety OT2

Hair and Eye Detail

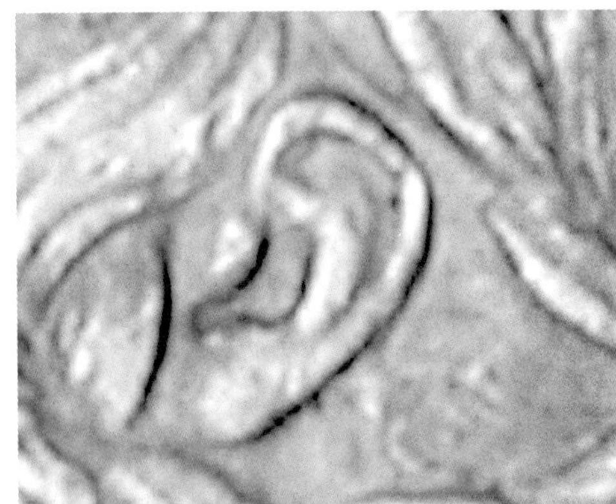

Outer Ear Detail

OT2 **Hair detail:** The first thick strand starts at the temple. The next two strands start at the brow and fall behind the first.
Eyelid detail: An arched tapering upper lid trails off into the corner of the eye. The lower lid does not join the upper lid at the corner of the eye.
Outer ear detail: The outer ear is open at two locations.
Dates: Portrait OT2 is currently known on the following dates: 1880H and 1881H.

Victoria Obverse Variety OT3

Hair and Eye Detail

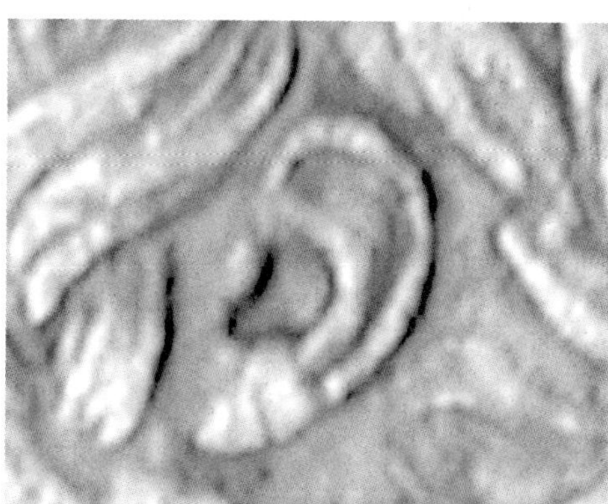
Outer Ear Detail

OT3 **Hair detail:** The first two strands of hair start at the brow and join at the temple. This thick strand forms the beginning of the braid.

Eyelid detail: Both upper and lower lids are well formed, joining at the corner of the eye.

Outer ear detail: The outer ear is open only at the top of the ear canal.

Dates: Portrait OT3 is currently known on the following dates: 1882H and 1883H.

Victoria Obverse Variety OT4

Hair and Eye Detail

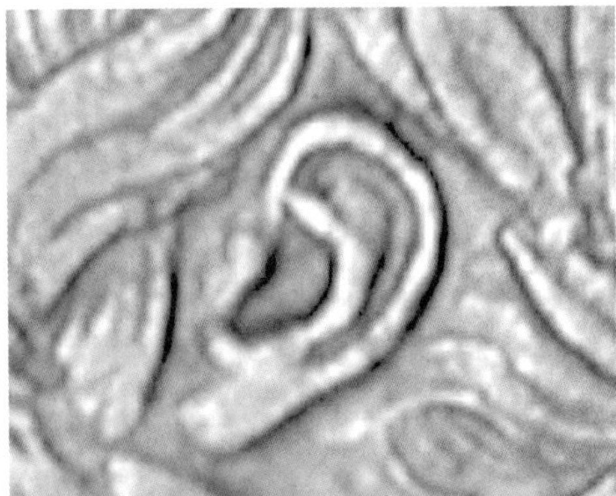
Outer Ear Detail

OT4 **Hair detail:** The first strand of hair folds into the second at the temple forming one thick strand.
Eyelid detail: The upper eyelid is triangular in shape, trailing off to a point at the corner of the eye. The lower lid is poorly formed and does not meet the upper eyelid at the corner of the eye.
Outer ear detail: Two weak openings to the inner ear. The outer ear is 'D' shaped.
Dates: Portrait OT4 is currently known on the following dates: 1884, 1885 and 1886.

Victoria Obverse Variety OT5

Hair and Eye Detail

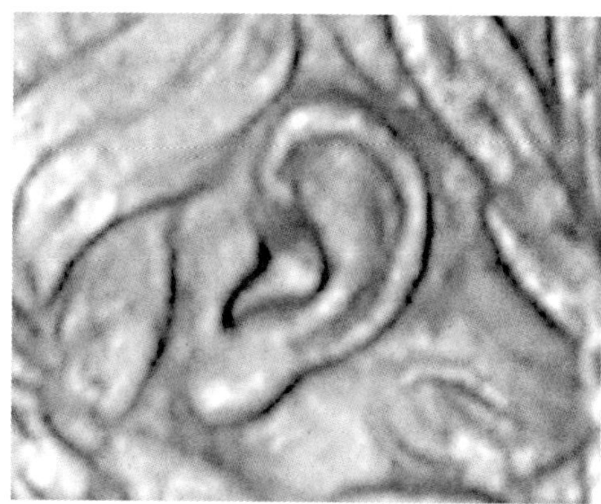

Outer Ear Detail

OT5 Hair detail: Three large strands, lacking detail and design, join at the temple.
Eyelid detail: The upper eyelid curves back and overshoots the corner of the eye. The lower lid is full, and joins the upper lid at the corner of the eye.
Outer ear detail: One opening to the inner ear. Circular outer ear.
Dates: Portrait OT5 is currently known on the following dates: 1885, 1886, 1887, 1888, 1889, 1890H, 1891, 1892, 1893, 1894, 1896 and 1898.

Victoria Obverse Variety OT6

Hair and Eye Detail

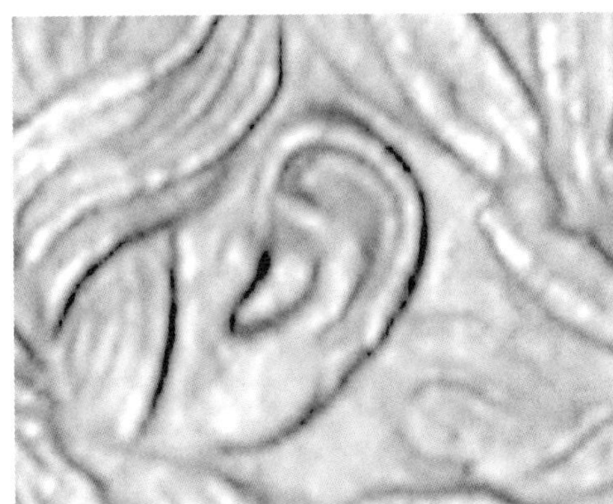

Outer Ear Detail

OT6 **Hair detail:** The first strand of hair joins the second at the temple. The next three strands lack detail at the temple and fall into two strands before the braid.

Eyelid detail: The upper eyelid is straight to the corner of the eye, with the lower lid disappearing before the corner of the eye.

Outer ear detail: One opening to the ear, with a 'D' shaped outer ear.

Dates: Portrait OT6 is currently known on the following dates: 1892, 1893, 1894, 1896, 1898, 1899, 1900 and 1901.

VICTORIA TEN CENT MAJOR REVERSE VARIETIES

WREATH WITH 21 LEAVES

Reverse Maple Leaf Wreath Design

The wreath has 21 leaves: the left bough has 11 leaves and the right has 10 leaves. The leaves are counted by the order in which they are attached to the bough and are numbered L-1 to L-11 and R-1 to R-10. This numbering will aid in identification of the reverse varieties.

Left Bough **Right Bough**

WREATH WITH 22 LEAVES

Reverse Maple Leaf Wreath Design

The wreath has 22 leaves with both the left and right boughs having 11 leaves. The leaves are counted by the order in which they are attached to the bough and are numbered L-1 to L-11 and R-1 to R-10. The “22 Leaves” wreath design has a division in the sequencing of the order of the leaves.

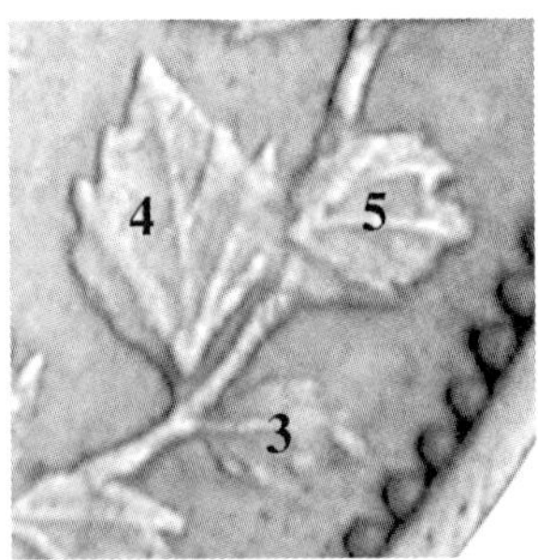

On coins dated 1882 Right Leaf 3 ®-3) appears on the right side of the bough and Right Leaf 4 ®-4) appears on the left side.

Left Bough **Right Bough**

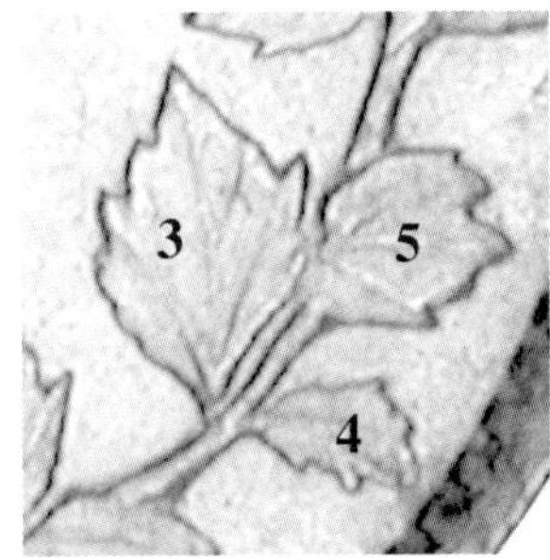

On coins dated 1883 to 1901 Right Leaf 3 ®-3) is on the left side of the bough and Right Leaf 4 ®-4) is on the right side of the bough.

Victoria Reverse Variety RT1

Left bough detail

Bough and ribbon detail

Right bough detail

RT1 **Left bough detail:** 11 leaves. The lower outline of L-1 is in the shape of an inverted "W". The bough supporting L-8, L-9 and L-10 is hidden. The stem of L-11 is not attached to the bough.
Bough and ribbon detail: The left bough end is long and thin with a square end.
Right bough detail: The right bough has 10 leaves.
Dates: Reverse RT1 is currently known on the following dates: 1858, 1870, 1871, 1871H, 1872H, 1874H, 1875H, 1881H and 1891.

Victoria Reverse Variety RT2

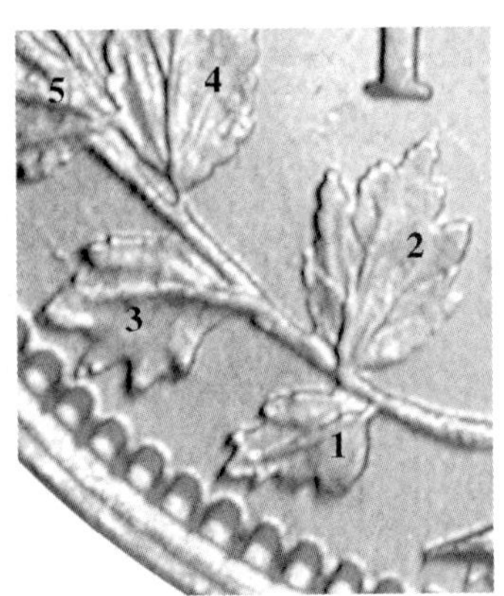

Left bough detail

Bough and ribbon detail

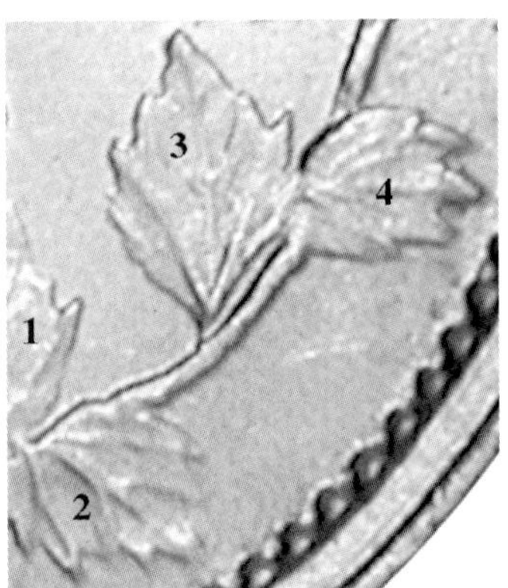

Right bough detail

RT2 Left bough detail: 11 leaves. L-1 is long and pointed. The bough supporting L-8, L- 9, and L-10 is complete. L-11 is attached to the bough.
Bough and ribbon detail: Both bough ends are long and flared.
Right bough detail: The right bough has 10 leaves.
Dates: Reverse RT2 is currently known on the following date: 1880H.

Victoria Reverse Variety RT3

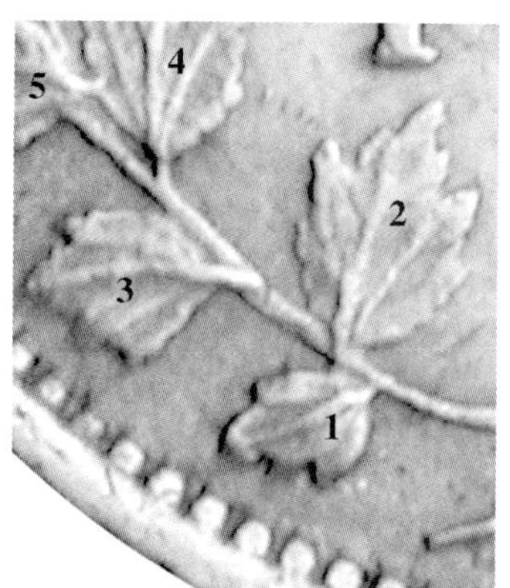

Left bough detail

Bough and ribbon detail

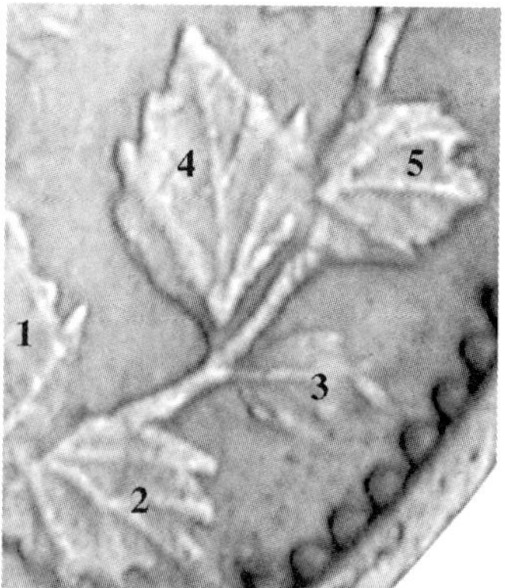

Right bough detail

RT3 Left bough detail: 11 leaves. L- 1 is small with an indistinct inverted "W" formation on the lower side. L-11 is attached to the bough.

Bough and ribbon detail: The left ribbon, instead of being behind the bough, is re-engraved on top of the bough.

Right bough detail: 11 leaves. The right bough has a new leaf in Position 3.

Dates: Reverse RT3 is currently known on the following date: 1882H.

Victoria Reverse Variety RT4

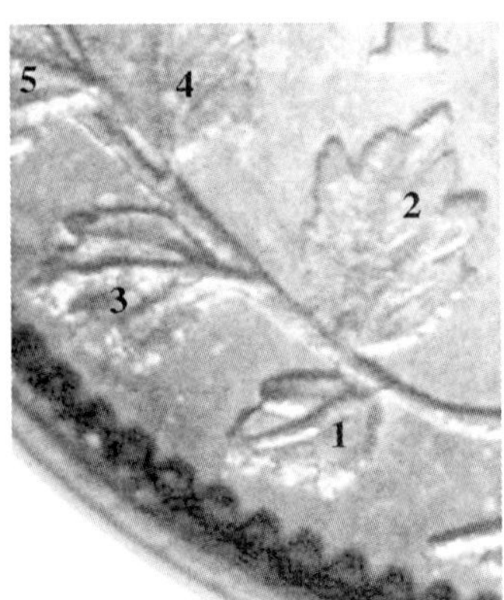

Left bough detail

Bough and ribbon detail

Right bough detail

RT4 **Left bough detail:** 11 leaves. L-1 is similar to RT3, but now has prominent veins. L-11 is attached to the bough.
Bough and ribbon detail: Thick boughs. The left bough has a plain end, and the left ribbon is behind the bough end.
Right bough detail: 11 leaves. The maple leaf wreath has been reworked, R-3 has a thick overlapping stem. R-9, R-10 and R-11 are attached to the bough.
Dates: Reverse RT4 is currently known on the following date: 1882H.

Victoria Reverse Variety RT5

Left bough detail | Bough and ribbon detail | Right bough detail

RT5 **Left bough detail:** 11 leaves. L-1 is wide with a small inverted "W" outline. L-11 is attached to the bough.
Bough and ribbon detail: The boughs have been strengthened, and the bough ends are thick.
Right ribbon detail: 11 leaves. The right bough is thick. Leaves L-9, L-10 and L-11 are attached to the bough.
Dates: Reverse RT5 is currently known on the following date: 1882H.

Victoria Reverse Variety RT6

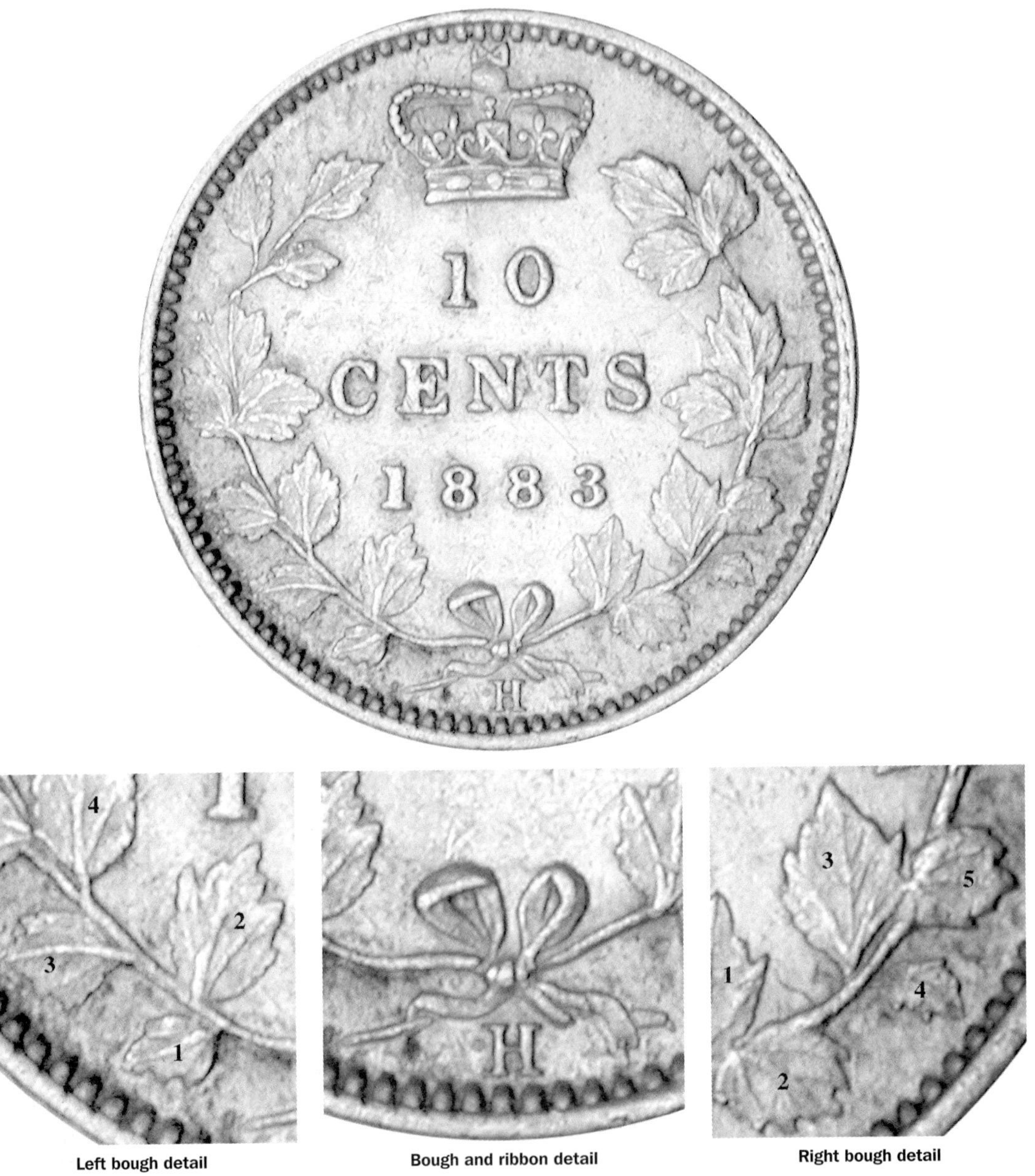

Left bough detail

Bough and ribbon detail

Right bough detail

RT6 **Left bough detail:** 11 leaves. L-1 is again small, with the inverted "W" a more prominent part of the leaf design. L-11 is detached from the bough.

Bough and ribbon detail: Thin boughs. The left bough end is long and thin. The right bough end is short and stumpy.

Right bough detail: 11 leaves. The positions of R-3 and R-4 are reversed. R-4 is pointing downward. The bough to R-9, R-10 and R-11 is very weak to non-existent.

Dates: Reverse RT6 is currently known on the following dates: 1883H, 1884, 1885, 1886, 1887, 1888, 1889, 1890H, 1891, 1892, 1893, 1894, 1896, 1898, 1899 and 1900.

Victoria Reverse Variety RT7

Left bough detail

Bough and ribbon detail

Right bough detail

RT7 Left bough detail: 11 leaves. L-1 is now a small pointed leaf with indistinct veining. L-11 is attached to the bough.
Bough and ribbon detail: Similar to RT6, but the ribbon folds are reinforced.
Right bough detail: 11 leaves. R-4 is narrow and pointing downward. Leaves R-9, R-10 and R-11 are attached to the bough.
Dates: Reverse RT7 is currently known on the following dates: 1900 and 1901.

TEN CENTS
VICTORIA 1870 - 1901

The initial designs for the Victoria 10-cent pieces issued by the Dominion of Canada were identical to those of the 1858 Province of Canada issue. During the reign, six obverse portraits were used. They differed primarily in the features of the Queen's face. Two major varieties of the reverse exist; only in 1891 were both used for the same year's coinage (see page 126).

Heaton Mint strikings of 1871-1883 and 1890 have an "H" mint mark on the reverse under the wreath. Royal Mint strikings have no mint mark.

"H" Mint Mark

Designer and Engraver: Leonard C. Wyon
Composition: .925 silver, .075 copper
Weight: 2.33 grams
Diameter: 18.03 mm
Edge: Reeded
Die Axes: ↑↓

LAUREATE PORTRAIT, 21 MAPLE LEAVES DESIGN, 1870-1881.

Through a clerical error part of the mintage of 1874H dated coins was assigned to the next year's production figures. Therefore, the mintage figures for the two years, 600,000 and 1,000,000, respectively, have been combined.

Two styles of "0" appear in the date of the 1870 issue. The Narrow 0 with sides of equal thickness is more common than the Wide 0, on which the right-hand side is thicker.

1870 Narrow 0 (N)

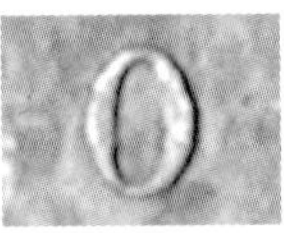

Narrow 0

1870 Wide 0 (W)

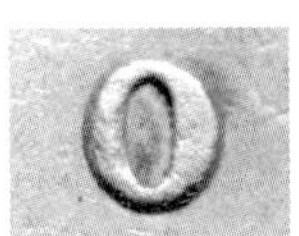

Wide 0

1870 Narrow 0/0 (N)

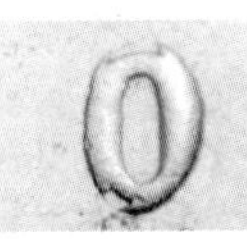

Narrow 0/0

1870 Wide 0/0 (W)

Wide 0/0

1870 Wide 0, 1/1, 8/8

1870 1/1

1871H 7/7

1871H 7/7

DATE / MINT PORTRAIT / VAR.	MINTAGE (thous.)	G-4	VG-8	F-12	VF-20	EF-40	AU-50	AU-55	MS-60	MS-63	MS-65	SP-63	SP-65
1870 T1 N (PE)	N/A	*	*	*	*	*	*	*	*	*	*	2,000.	5,000.
1870 T1 N	1,600	15.	30.	65.	110.	150.	225.	275.	500.	1,500.	5,000.	2,000.	5,000.
1870 T1 N 0/0	Incl.	20.	40.	85.	150.	225.	375.	500.	700.	—	—	*	*
1870 T1 W	Incl.	25.	50.	75.	175.	300.	475.	700.	900.	3,500.	—	2,000.	6,500.
1870 T1 W 1/1	Incl.	30.	60.	100.	200.	325.	550.	800.	1,200.	—	—	*	*
1870 T1 W 0/0	Incl.	30.	60.	125.	225.	375.	600.	800.	1,200.	—	—	*	*
1871 T1	800	25.	55.	100.	200.	275.	475.	600.	925.	4,500.	—	5,500.	8,000.
1871H T1	1,870	25.	55.	100.	225.	325.	500.	650.	900.	3,000.	—	5,500.	8,000.
1871H T1 7/7	Incl.	30.	60.	125.	250.	375.	600.	800.	1,200.	—	—	*	*
1872H T1	1,000	100.	200.	300.	500.	850.	1,500.	2,000.	2,500.	4,000.	—	4,000.	6,500.
1874H T1	1,600	20.	25.	45.	85.	200.	325.	400.	575.	1,800.	3,500.	*	*
1875H T1	Incl.	250.	475.	825.	1,400.	2,800.	4,000.	6,000.	—	—	—	12,000.	40,000.
1880H T1	1,500	20.	35.	45.	95.	175.	300.	425.	550.	1,800.	—	3,000.	9,500.
1880H T2	Incl.	20.	35.	60.	125.	275.	425.	750.	1,500.	—	—	4,000.	10,000.
1881H T1	950	75.	150.	250.	425.	700.	—	—	—	—	—	3,500.	12,000.
1881H T2	Incl.	20.	40.	65.	125.	250.	350.	475.	625.	1,800.	6,000.	*	*

LAUREATE PORTRAIT, 22 MAPLE LEAVES DESIGN, 1882-1901.

For the 1886 coinage three distinctly different styles of 6 were used on the reverse dies: a Small 6, a Large 6 with a point on its tail, and a large 6 with a large knob on its tail. All three are found with obverses T4 and T5.

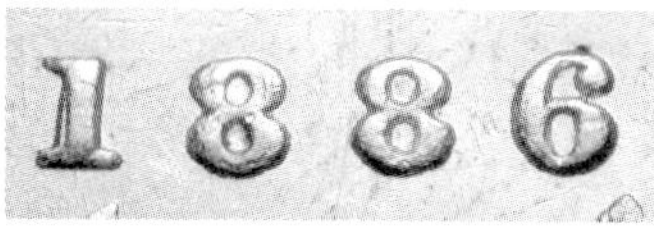

1886 T4 and T5, Large Knob 6 (L6)

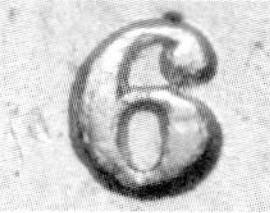

Large Knob 6

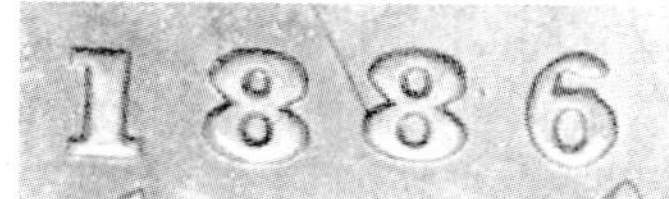

1886 T4 and T5, Pointed 6 (Pt6)

Pointed 6

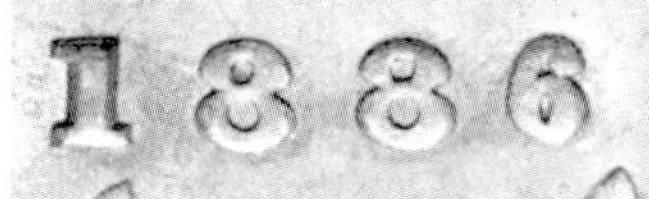

1886 T4 and T5, Small 6 (S6)

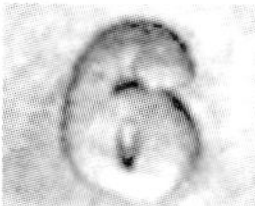

Small 6

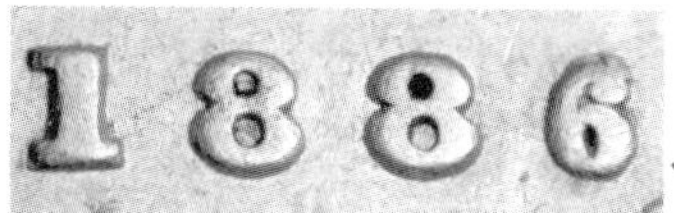

1886 T5, Small 6 / Small 6

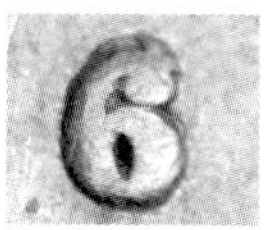

1886 6/6

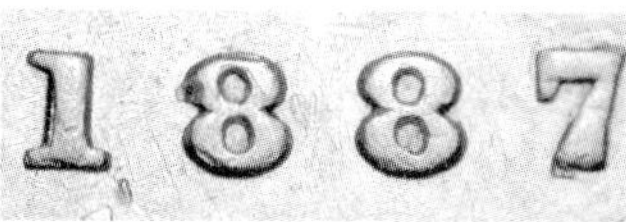

1887 7/7

1887 7/7

DATE / MINT/ PORTRAIT/VAR.	MINTAGE (thous.)	G-4	VG-8	F-12	VF-20	EF-40	AU-50	AU-55	MS-60	MS-63	MS-65	SP-63	SP-65
1882H T3	1,000	20.	40.	65.	120.	200.	300.	400.	725.	2,500.	5,000.	4,000.	10,000.
1883H T3	300	60.	125.	225.	375.	700.	1,000.	1,500.	2,000.	4,000.	—	*	*
1884 T4	150	200.	400.	700.	1,200.	2,500.	5,000.	6,000.	10,000.	25,000.	—	*	*
1885 T4	400	45.	90.	150.	350.	775.	1,500.	2,500.	—	—	—	10,000.	25,000.
1885 T5	Incl.	100.	200.	400.	800.	—	—	—	—	—	—	*	*
1886 T4 L6	800	45.	75.	175.	300.	650.	—	—	—	—	—	*	*
1886 T4 Pt6	Incl.	ONLY SIX CERTIFIED										*	*
1886 T4 S6	Incl.	75.	150.	300.	600.	—	—	—	—	—	—	*	*
1886 T5 L6	Incl.	35.	100.	175.	300.	575.	—	—	—	—	—	*	*
1886 T5 Pt6	Incl.	75.	175.	300.	600.	1,200.	—	—	—	—	—	*	*
1886 T5 S6	Incl.	30.	60.	150.	275.	600.	—	—	—	—	—	*	*
1886 T5 S6/6	Incl.	50.	100.	200.	325.	675.	—	—	—	—	—	*	*
1887 T5	350	50.	100.	150.	350.	750.	1,250.	1,800.	2,500.	5,500.	—	*	*
1887 T5 7/7	Incl.	75.	150.	250.	500.	1,000.	2,000.	—	—	—	—	*	*
1888 T5	500	15.	25.	50.	100.	200.	300.	400.	600.	1,250.	4,500.	7,000.	20,000.
1889 T5	600	600.	1,200.	2,000.	3,000.	5,000.	—	—	—	—	—	*	*
1890H T5	450	20.	40.	85.	150.	275.	450.	800.	1,200.	2,500.	6,000.	8,000.	15,000.

SYMBOLS USED IN PRICING TABLES

- **— No two coins have been assigned this grade by a Canadian grading company.**
- *** Not issued in that finish.**
- **BV Bullion value.**
- **C Circulating coins, coins which are purchased from banks, or found in change.**
- **FV Face value.**
- **NC Noncirculating coins identical in design to the circulating issue, but sold in sets or special packaging by the Royal Canadian Mint.**
- **N.I.I. Not issued individually, but included in a set of some nature.**
- **P.E. Plain edge**

VARIETIES OF 1891, 1892 and 1893.

One 1891 large date die was carried over into 1892 and the 1 was overdated with a 2. Aside from the overpunching, the 1892 over 1 differs from the non-overdate 1892s in the style of the 9. The overdate has the large 9 of the 22 leaves, 1891 variety, and the non-overdates have the small 9 of the 21 leaves, 1891 variety.

Dating varieties continued into 1893. In that year three different dies were used. The flat top 3 dies are found with a large and small 9, while the round top 3 is found only with a large 9.

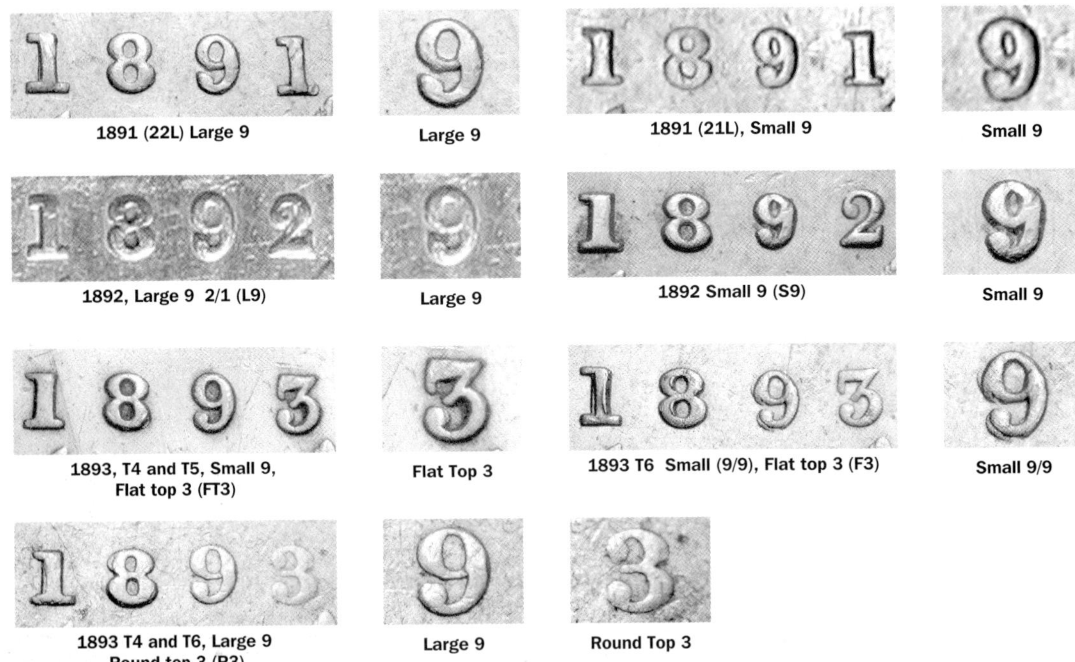

1891 (22L) Large 9 — Large 9 — 1891 (21L), Small 9 — Small 9

1892, Large 9 2/1 (L9) — Large 9 — 1892 Small 9 (S9) — Small 9

1893, T4 and T5, Small 9, Flat top 3 (FT3) — Flat Top 3 — 1893 T6 Small (9/9), Flat top 3 (F3) — Small 9/9

1893 T4 and T6, Large 9 Round top 3 (R3) — Large 9 — Round Top 3

DATE / MINT / PORTRAIT VAR.	MINTAGE (thous.)	G-4	VG-8	F-12	VF-20	EF-40	AU-50	AU-55	MS-60	MS-63	MS-65	SP-63	SP-65
1891 T5 21L	800	20.	45.	80.	150.	300.	400.	500.	700.	2,000.	5,000.	*	*
1891 T5 22L	Incl.	20.	40.	75.	175.	250.	400.	600.	850.	2,000.	—	*	*
1892 T5 2/1 L9	520	250.	500.	1,000.	2,000.	3,000.	4,000.	5,000.	—	—	—	6,500.	18,000.
1892 T5 S9	Incl.	20.	35.	60.	125.	225.	400.	650.	800.	2,100.	—	*	*
1892 T6 2/1 L9	Incl.	225.	450.	675.	1,200.	2,400.	—	—	—	—	—	*	*
1892 T6 S9	Incl.	35.	60.	125.	225.	375.	800.	—	—	—	—	*	*
1893 T5 R3	500						ONLY ONE CERTIFIED						
1893 T5 F3	Incl.	50.	75.	150.	300.	700.	—	—	—	—	—	*	*
1893 T6 R3	Incl.	800.	1,650.	2,500.	4,250.	8,000.	—	—	—	—	—	*	*
1893 T6 F3	Incl.	35.	75.	135.	250.	450.	800.	1,000.	1,800.	4,000.	—	*	*

VARIETIES OF 1894, 1899 and 1900.

During the production of the 1899 10-cent pieces, two styles of 9 were used for dating the dies: a small, narrow 9 and a large, wide 9. The upper centre of the wide 9 is almost round, compared with the tall, rectangular centre of the narrow 9.

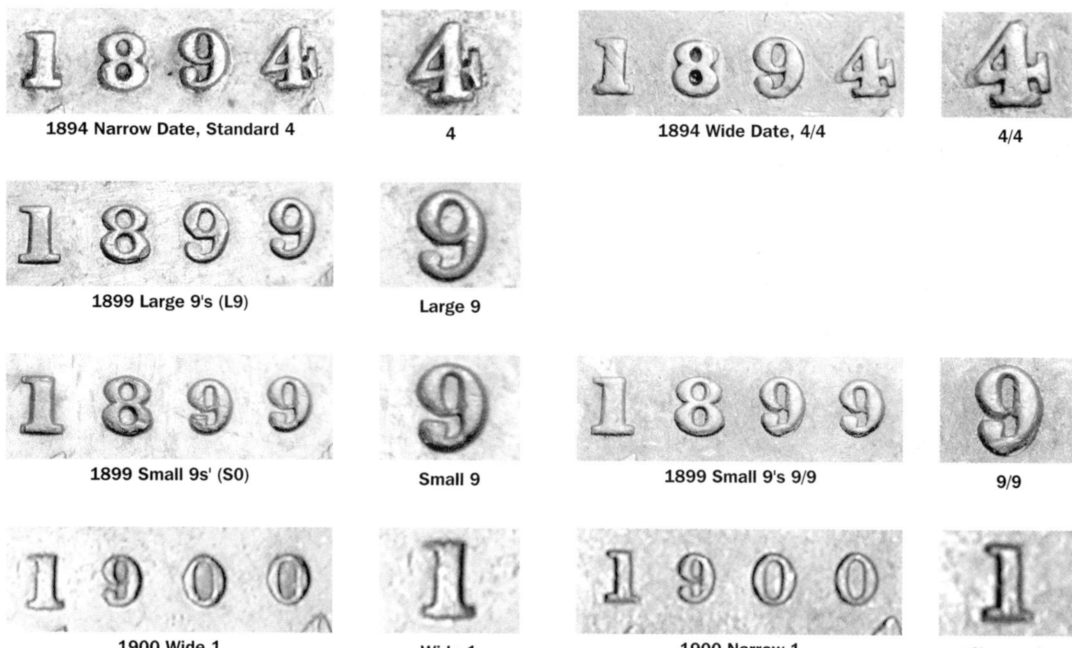

1894 Narrow Date, Standard 4 — 4 — 1894 Wide Date, 4/4 — 4/4

1899 Large 9's (L9) — Large 9

1899 Small 9s' (S0) — Small 9 — 1899 Small 9's 9/9 — 9/9

1900 Wide 1 — Wide 1 — 1900 Narrow 1 — Narrow 1

DATE / MINT / PORTRAIT VAR.	MINTAGE (thous.)	G-4	VG-8	F-12	VF-20	EF-40	AU-50	AU-55	MS-60	MS-63	MS-65	SP-63	SP-65
1894 T5	500	30.	60.	100.	175.	375.	725.	1,100.	—	—	—	6,000.	18,000.
1894 T6	Incl.	30.	60.	100.	175.	300.	475.	750.	1,200.	2,500.	—	*	*
1896 T5	650	50.	100.	150.	250.	—	—	—	—	—	—	*	*
1896 T6	Incl.	15.	30.	50.	85.	150.	275.	400.	550.	1,100.	4,000.	*	*
1898 T5	720	30.	65.	100.	250.	500.	—	—	—	—	—	*	*
1898 T6	Incl.	15.	25.	40.	75.	125.	250.	325.	525.	1,200.	5,500.	*	*
1899 T6 L9	1,200	25.	50.	70.	175.	250.	350.	450.	750.	1,200.	5,000.	*	*
1899 T6 S9	Incl.	15.	20.	40.	75.	150.	225.	300.	450.	1,000.	2,000.	*	*
1900 T6	1,100	15.	20.	35.	60.	125.	175.	275.	500.	850.	1,500.	*	*
1901 T6	1,200	12.	20.	35.	60.	125.	175.	250.	425.	900.	4,250.	*	*

PRICING

The Charlton Press pricing tables are based on market prices for **Canadian certified coins.** Currently there are two coin grading companies located in Canada. Our prices are gathered from prices realized at land auctions, internet auctions, and dealer fixed price lists and their internet listings. It is important to realize that coin certification incurs a cost, and on low value coins it will be a significant factor in their listed value. The cost for certification per coin averages between $7-$10 for standard service.

TEN CENTS
EDWARD VII 1902 - 1910

IMPERIAL STATE CROWNED PORTRAIT, MAPLE LEAVES DESIGN, 1902-1910.

The reverse first employed for the 10-cent pieces of this reign was adapted from the 22-leaf Victorian reverse. The Imperial State crown replaced the St. Edward's crown at the top and the word "CANADA" was transferred from the obverse legend.

The Mint Birmingham Ltd. strikings (1902-1903) have an "H" mint mark on the reverse under the wreath. Royal Mint issues have no mint mark.

"H" Mint Mark

Designer and Engraver:
Obv.: George W. DeSaulles
Rev.: Victorian Leaves
1902-09: G.W. DeSaulles
Broad Leaves
1909-1910: W. H. J. Blakemore

Composition: .925 silver, .075 copper

Weight:
1902-1910: 2.32 grams
1910: 2.33 grams

Diameter: 18.03 mm

Edge: Reeded

Die Axes:
1902-1907: ↑↓
1908-1910: ↑↑

VARIETIES OF 1908.

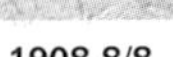

1908 8/8

1908 8/8

A 1908 With Die Deterioration

VARIETIES OF 1909.

In 1909 an entirely new model was prepared for this denomination. The variety thus created has been called the Broad Leaves variety because of its broad leaves with strong, detailed venation.

1909 Victorian Leaves

1909 Broad Leaves

DATE / MINT / VARIETY	MINTAGE	VG-8	F-12	VF-20	EF-40	AU-50	AU-55	MS-60	MS-63	MS-64	MS-65	SP-63	SP-65
1902	720,000	15.	25.	50.	95.	200.	300.	475.	1,250.	2,000.	3,000.	*	*
1902H	1,100,000	10.	15.	35.	65.	110.	135.	200.	375.	600.	1,400.	4,000.	15,000.
1903	500,000	20.	40.	110.	275.	675.	1,000.	1,500.	2,500.	3,500.	6,000.	*	*
1903H	1,320,000	15.	25.	55.	95.	175.	250.	500.	1,000.	1,600.	3,000.	7,500.	15,000.
1904	1,000,000	20.	35.	75.	150.	225.	325.	800.	1,200.	2,500.	—	*	*
1905	1,000,000	20.	40.	85.	175.	300.	500.	800.	1,500.	3,500.	—	*	*
1906	1,700,000	15.	20.	40.	95.	175.	250.	400.	1,100.	1,700.	3,500.	*	*
1907	2,620,000	15.	20.	30.	85.	110.	200.	300.	750.	1,200.	3,500.	*	*
1908	776,666	20.	40.	75.	200.	275.	375.	500.	850.	1,250.	2,000.	500.	900.
1908 8/8	Included	30.	75.	125.	250.	325.	450.	575.	—	—	—	*	*
1909 Victorian	1,697,200	15.	30.	65.	175.	275.	350.	650.	1,250.	2,800.	—	*	*
1909 Broad	Included	15.	30.	75.	150.	350.	500.	850.	2,250.	3,500.	—	*	*
1910	4,468,331	15.	20.	30.	65.	110.	125.	175.	450.	700.	1,500.	*	*

TEN CENTS GEORGE V 1911 - 1936

IMPERIAL STATE CROWNED PORTRAIT, MAPLE LEAVES DESIGN, 1911-1936.

The obverse combined with the 1911 reverse aroused criticism because it lacked reference to the King's ruling "by the grace of God." The coinage tools were modified during 1911 and a new legend containing the Latin abbreviation "DEI GRA." appeared on the 1912 and subsequent issues. The first reverse was a continuation of the Broad Leaves design introduced in 1909. It was replaced during 1913 (see below).

1911 Obverse "Godless"

1912-1936 Obverse "Dei Gra"

1911-1913 Broad Leaves

1913 Small Leaves

Designer and Engraver:
Obv.: Sir E. B. MacKennal
Rev.: W. H. J. Blakemore
(Small Leaves Reverse)

Composition:
1911-1919: .925 silver, .075 copper
1920-1936: .800 silver, .200 copper

Weight: 2.32 grams
Diameter: 18.03 mm
Edge: Reeded
Die Axes: ↑↑

VARIETIES OF 1913. The reverse that replaced the Broad Leaves design during 1913 has smaller leaves with less venation. It is from a completely new model.

1936 DOT VARIETY.

Early in 1937, while the Royal Canadian Mint was awaiting the arrival of the master tools for the new coinage for George VI, an emergency coinage of 10-cent pieces dated 1936 and from George V dies is said to have taken place. To mark the special nature of the coinage the dies bore a small raised dot on the reverse under the wreath.

Although the mintage of the 1936 dot variety is claimed to be 191,237, only five examples are known to survive today. All are specimen strikes, adding to the suspicion that circulation strikes were either never produced or were all melted. No genuine circulation strike has been confirmed.

1936 With Raised Dot Below Date, struck in 1937

The latest sale of the 1936 Dot 10 cent coin was in the Heritage Auction of Canadiana Collection, January 2010, in which a specimen (PCGS-SP68) realized $184,000.

DATE / VARIETY	MINTAGE	VG-8	F-12	VF-20	EF-40	AU-50	AU-55	MS-60	MS-63	MS-64	MS-65	SP-63	SP-65
1911 Broad	2,737,584	10.	20.	45.	60.	85.	110.	175.	350.	525.	675.	500.	1,250.
1912 Broad	2,234,557	10.	15.	20.	35.	150.	225.	325.	750.	1,200.	2,500.	*	*
1913 Broad	3,613,937	175.	275.	500.	1,200.	3,000.	4,5000.	9,000.	—	—	—	*	*
1913 Small	Included	10.	12.	15.	35.	65.	125.	225.	525.	950.	2,500.	5,000.	10,000.
1914	2,549,811	10.	12.	15.	35.	75.	125.	175.	625.	1,000.	2,000.	*	*
1915	688,057	15.	20.	65.	150.	250.	350.	550.	1,500.	2,000.	4,000.	*	*
1916	4,218,114	10.	12.	15.	25.	55.	75.	125.	275.	475.	1,500.	*	*
1917	5,011,988	10.	12.	15.	20.	40.	55.	75.	150.	250.	625.	*	*
1918	5,133,602	10.	12.	15.	20.	50.	60.	70.	125.	200.	500.	*	*
1919	7,877,722	8.	10.	12.	20.	50.	75.	100.	125.	225.	475.	*	*
1920	6,305,345	8.	10.	12.	20.	50.	75.	100.	175.	275.	1,250.	*	*
1921	2,469,562	8.	10.	12.	25.	55.	100.	150.	275.	575.	1,250.	3,000.	10,000.
1928	2,458,602	8.	10.	12.	25.	55.	75.	125.	225.	500.	1,250.	1,800.	6,000.
1929	3,253,888	8.	10.	12.	25.	50.	65.	100.	175.	300.	625.	2,000.	5,000.
1930	1,831,043	8.	10.	12.	25.	55.	60.	90.	200.	350.	1,500.	3,000.	8,000.
1931	2,067,421	8.	10.	12.	25.	40.	65.	100.	150.	250.	600.	3,000.	7,500.
1932	1,154,317	8.	10.	12.	50.	70.	85.	125.	250.	500.	1,000.	4,500.	10,000.
1933	672,368	8.	10.	20.	65.	125.	200.	250.	500.	925.	2,000.	*	*
1934	409,067	10.	15.	40.	125.	225.	300.	425.	725.	1,200.	2,500.	4,000.	7,000.
1935	384,056	10.	12.	40.	125.	225.	300.	425.	700.	1,250.	2,000.	*	*
1936	2,460,871	10.	12.	15.	20.	45.	55.	70.	125.	185.	500.	*	*
1936 Dot	Included	ONLY FIVE CERTIFIED. ALL SPECIMEN										150K	200K

TEN CENTS
GEORGE VI 1937 - 1952

COINAGE OF GEORGE VI 1937-1952.

The new reverse design introduced in 1937 was destined to become one of the most loved and most controversial of Canada's coinage designs. It features a "fishing schooner under sail," as the official proclamation states. Proud Nova Scotians, believing the ship represents the famous fishing and racing schooner "Bluenose," continually pressed for official acknowledgment. It was not until March 15th, 2002 that the design was officially recognized as the Bluenose. Available information indicates that the designer, Emanuel Hahn, used that ship as his primary model. The original master tools for the reverse were prepared at the Paris Mint. To improve the wearing qualities of the date, larger size digits were introduced in 1938.

UNCROWNED PORTRAIT, 'ET: IND: IMP:', BLUENOSE DESIGN, 1937-1947.

The initial obverse bore a legend containing the Latin abbreviation "ET IND: IMP:" to indicate that the King was the Emperor of India.

Designers and Engravers:
Obv.: T. H. Paget
Rev.: Emanuel Hahn
Composition: .800 silver, .200 copper

Weight: 2.33 grams
Diameter: 18.03 mm
Edge: Reeded
Die Axes: ↑↑

MAPLE LEAF ISSUE 1947.

The granting of independence to India posed a problem for the Royal Canadian Mint in the early part of 1948. The new obverse coinage tools (with the Latin phrase "ET IND: IMP:" omitted to indicate that the King was no longer the Emperor of India) would not arrive for several months, yet there was a need for all denominations of coins. The mint satisfied the demand by striking coins dated 1947 bearing the obverse with the outmoded titles. To differentiate this issue from the regular strikings of 1947, a tiny maple leaf was placed after the date.

1947 Maple Leaf Issue struck in 1948 (ML)

DATE / VARIETY	MINTAGE	EF-40	AU-50	AU-55	MS-60	MS-63	MS-64	MS-65	MS-66	SP-63	SP-65
1937	2,500,095	10	12.	15.	20.	35.	45.	175.	850.	75.	150.
1937 Matte	Included	*	*	*	*	*	*	*	*	75.	200.
1938	4,197,323	20.	35.	40.	65.	110.	225.	1,000.	3,000.	2,500.	5,000.
1939	5,501,748	15.	25.	30.	55.	150.	200.	625.	—	1,750.	4,000.
1940	16,526,470	10.	15.	25.	35.	50.	75.	225.	725.	*	*
1941	8,716,386	10.	20.	35.	55.	110.	175.	500.	—	*	*
1942	10,214,011	10.	20.	25.	45.	65.	100.	600.	1,500.	*	*
1943	21,143,229	10.	15.	20.	25.	35.	100.	225.	1,750.	*	*
1944	9,383,582	10.	15.	20.	40.	75.	110.	275.	1,500.	2,000.	4,000.
1945	10,979,570	8.	10.	15.	25.	45.	70.	225.	2,000.	200.	1,500.
1946	6,300,066	10.	20.	25.	35.	40.	70.	200.	1,750.	125.	500.
1947	4,431,926	10.	15.	25.	50.	60.	110.	450.	—	150.	450.
1947 ML	9,638,793	8.	10.	15.	25.	30.	65.	150.	1,200.	150.	300.

UNCROWNED PORTRAIT, 'DEI GRATIA', BLUENOSE DESIGN, 1948-1952.

Following the arrival of the master tools with the obverse legend omitting "ET IND: IMP:" production of the 1947 Maple Leaf coinage was terminated. For the remainder of the year coins were produced with the new obverse and the true date, 1948. This obverse was employed for the rest of the reign.

DATE / VARIETY	MINTAGE	EF-40	AU-50	AU-55	MS-60	MS-63	MS-64	MS-65	MS-66	SP-63	SP-65
1948	422,741	30.	45.	60.	80.	150.	225.	1,250.	—	200.	400.
1949	11,336,172	8.	10.	12.	20.	25.	40.	250.	—	150.	350.
1950	17,823,075	8.	10.	12.	20.	25.	45.	300.	—	100.	350.
1951	15,079,265	8.	10.	12.	20.	25.	35.	200.	—	100.	350.
1951 DD	Included	20.	25.	35.	50.	120.	225.	750.	—	*	*
1952	10,474,455	8.	10.	12.	15.	20.	25.	110.	750.	125.	400.

TEN CENTS
ELIZABETH II 1953 TO DATE

LAUREATE PORTRAIT; BLUENOSE DESIGN, 1953-1964.

Two obverse varieties, termed the No Shoulder Fold and the Shoulder Fold obverses, saw use during 1953 (see 1-cent Elizabeth II 1953 to date for full explanation). On heavily circulated 10-cent pieces these varieties are most easily distinguished by observing the lettering styles in the legend. The No Shoulder Fold obverse has thicker letters with more flared ends (note the difference in the I's). The use of the George VI reverse was continued.

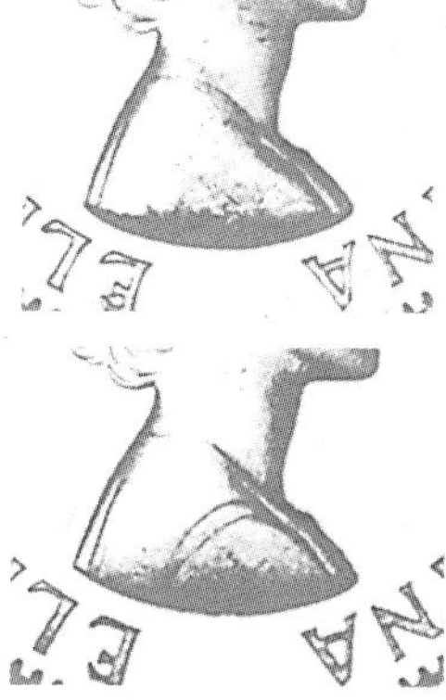

No Shoulder Fold Obverse 1953. Note the flared ends of the letters.

Shoulder Fold Obverse 1953-1954. The ends of the letters are not as flared.

Designers and Engravers:
Obv.: Mary Gillick, Thomas Shingles
Rev.: Emanuel Hahn
Composition: .800 silver, .200 copper
Weight: 2.33 grams
Diameter: 18.03 mm
Thickness: 1.16
Edge: Reeded
Die Axes: ↑↓, ↑↑

DATE / VARIETY	MINTAGE	AU-50	AU-55	MS-60	MS-63	MS-64	MS-65	MS-66	PL-65	PL-65 HC	SP-63	SP-65
1953 NSF	17,706,395	8.	10.	12.	15.	20.	60.	500.	—	—	250.	500.
1953 SF	Included	8.	10.	12.	20.	40.	200.	1,000.	250.	400.	250.	500.
1954	4,493,150	8.	10.	20.	30.	40.	150.	400.	50.	65.	*	*
1955	12,237,294	8.	10.	12.	20.	30.	70.	600.	35.	45.	*	*
1956	16,732,844	8.	10.	12.	15.	20.	70.	300.	25.	40.	*	*
1957	16,110,229	8.	10.	12.	15.	20.	30.	200.	20.	30.	*	*
1958	10,621,236	8.	10.	12.	15.	18.	40.	200.	15.	30.	*	*
1959	19,691,433	8.	10.	12.	15.	18.	40.	150.	15.	30.	*	*
1960	45,466,835	8.	10.	12.	15.	18.	50.	200.	10.	30.	*	*
1961	26,850,859	8.	10.	12.	15.	18.	50.	150.	10.	30.	*	*
1962	41,864,335	8.	10.	12.	15.	18.	25.	125.	10.	15.	*	*
1963	41,916,208	8.	10.	12.	15.	20.	25.	100.	10.	15.	*	*
1964	49,518,549	8.	10.	12.	15.	18.	25.	90.	10.	15.	400.	750.

TIARA PORTRAIT, BLUENOSE DESIGN, 1965-1966 and 1968; MACKEREL CENTENNIAL DESIGN, 1967.

A new obverse with the Queen showing more mature facial features and wearing a tiara was introduced on all denominations in 1965. A reverse design showing a mackerel was chosen as part of the group of commemorative designs for the centennial of Confederation. During the year, the rising price of silver forced a reduction in the silver content to .500 from .800. The two varieties are not distinguishable by appearance. The obverse is the same as on the 1965-1966 issues.

Bluenose design

Mackerel Centennial design

Designer and Engraver:
Obv.: Arnold Machin;
Rev.: 1965-1966: Emanuel Hahn;
1967: Alex Colville, Myron Cook
Composition:
1965-1967: .800 silver, .200 copper
1967-1968: .500 silver, .500 copper

DATE COMP. / AXIS	MINTAGE	MS-60	MS-63	MS-64	MS-65	MS-66	PL-65	PL-65 HC	SP-63	SP-65
1965	55,965,392	8.	10.	15.	20.	65.	10.	15.	50.	100.
1966	34,330,199	8.	10.	12.	20.	95.	10.	15.	*	*
1967 .800 silver	32,309,135	6.	8.	15.	25.	125.	10.	15.	20.	35.
1967 .500 silver	30,689,080	6.	8.	15.	25.	125.	*	*	*	*
1968 .500 ↑↑	70,460,000	6.	8.	10.	20.	75.	*	*	*	*
1968 .500 ↑↓	Included	ONLY SIX CERTIFIED							*	*

TIARA PORTRAIT, BLUENOSE DESIGN RESUMED, NICKEL, 1968.

During 1968 the use of silver in circulation coins was discontinued. Nickel was used in its place. The nickel coins are darker and are attracted to a magnet. About half of the 1968 nickel 10-cent pieces were coined at the Philadelphia Mint in the United States because of the pressure of other work at the Royal Canadian Mint. The Philadelphia and Ottawa issues differ only in the number and shape of the grooves in the edge of the coins; the grooves have square bottoms on the Philadelphia coins and V-shaped bottoms on the Ottawa strikings.

Philadelphia Mint Edge grooves have flat bottoms

Royal Canadian Mint Edge grooves have V-shaped bottoms

Designers and Engravers:
Obv.: Arnold Machin
Rev.: Emanuel Hahn
Composition: 1.00 nickel
Weight: 2.07 grams
Diameter: 18.03 mm
Thickness: 1.16 mm
Edge: Reeded
Die Axes: ↑↑

DATE	VARIETY	MINTAGE	MS-64 C	MS-65 C	MS-66 C	MS-65 NC	MS-66 NC	MS-67 NC	SP-66	SP-67	PR-67	PR-68
1968	US Mint	85,170,000	30.	125.	200.	*	*	*	*	*	*	*
1968	RC Mint	87,412,930	15.	20.	100.	10.	25.	40.	*	*	*	*

TIARA PORTRAIT, MODIFIED BLUENOSE DESIGN, NICKEL, 1969.

The 1969 Large Schooner-Large Date design is a rare variety. A small quantity was struck early in the year before it was discovered that the original design had deteriorated so much as to be unfit for further use. A completely new model with a noticeably smaller schooner and small date replaced the original master matrix in early 1969. The obverse is as on the 1965-1968 issues. As of April 2010, only sixteen examples of the rare large date variety have been certified.

1969 Large Date (LD) **1969 Small Date (SD)**

Designers and Engravers:
Obv.: Arnold Machin, Myron Cook
Rev.: Emanuel Hahn, Myron Cook
Composition: 1.00 nickel
Weight: 2.07 grams
Diameter: 18.03 mm
Thickness: 1.16 mm
Edge: Reeded
Die Axes: ↑↑

DATE / VARIETY	MINTAGE	VF-20	EF-40	AU-50	AU-55	MS-60 C	MS-63 C	MS-65 NC	MS-66 NC	MS-67 NC	SP-63	SP-65
1969 LD	55,833,929	12,000.	18,000.	25,000.	—	—	—	*	*	*	*	*
1969 SD	Included	—	—	—	—	4.	5.	10.	45.	75.	20.	125.

TIARA PORTRAIT, MODIFIED BLUENOSE DESIGN, NICKEL, 1970-1978.

DATE	MINTAGE	MS-64 C	MS-65 C	MS-66 C	MS-65 NC	MS-66 NC	MS-67 NC	SP-66	SP-67
1970	5,249,296	10.	15.	45.	5.	10.	30.	10.	20.
1971	41,016,968	10.	15.	35.	5.	10.	25.	10.	20.
1972	60,169,387	10.	20.	55.	5.	10.	25.	10.	20.
1973	167,715,435	10.	25.	55.	5.	10.	25.	10.	20.
1974	201,566,565	15.	35.	70.	5.	10.	25.	10.	20.
1975	207,680,000	15.	30.	150.	5.	10.	25.	10.	20.
1976	94,724,000	10.	45.	85.	5.	10.	25.	10.	20.
1977	128,056,000	10.	25.	60.	5.	10.	25.	10.	20.
1978	170,366,431	10.	30.	75.	5.	10.	30.	10.	15.

MODIFIED TIARA PORTRAIT, BLUENOSE DESIGN, NICKEL, 1979-1980.

With the 1979 issue a general standardization of the coinage was started. The portrait of the Queen was reduced to make it proportional to the diameter of the coin, regardless of the denomination.

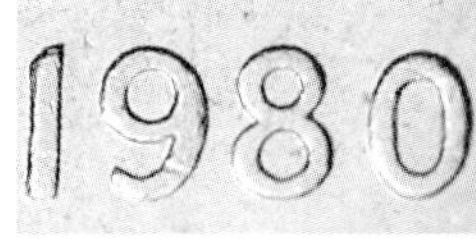

1980 Bold Type, Wide 0

1980 Fine Type, Narrow 0

Designers and Engravers:
Obv.: Arnold Machin, Walter Ott
Rev.: Emanuel Hahn, Myron Cook
Composition: 1.00 nickel
Weight: 2.07 grams
Diameter: 18.03 mm
Thickness: 1.16 mm
Edge: Reeded
Die Axes: ↑↑

VARIETIES OF 1980.

In the general make over, the type style came under review, with a finer style being selected.

DATE / VARIETY	MINTAGE	MS-64 C	MS-65 C	MS-66 C	MS-65 NC	MS-66 NC	MS-67 NC	SP-66	SP-67
1979	236,910,479	10.	25.	75.	5.	10.	25.	10.	15.
1980 W0	169,910,479	15.	50.	100.	*	*	*	*	*
1980 N0	Included	15.	30.	70.	5.	10.	25.	10.	15.

MODIFIED TIARA PORTRAIT, BLUENOSE DESIGN RESUMED, NICKEL, 1981-1989.

In 1981 the Royal Canadian Mint revised their product line, adding a proof finish to their offerings. The proof coins were struck on standard nickel planchets.

DATE / VARIETY	MINTAGE	MS-64 C	MS-65 C	MS-66 C	MS-65 NC	MS-66 NC	MS-67 NC	SP-66	SP-67	PR-67	PR-68
1981	123,912,900	15.	90.	150.	5.	10.	25.	10.	15.	15.	25.
1982	93,960,898	15.	70.	175.	5.	10.	25.	10.	15.	15.	25.
1983	111,501,710	15.	65.	100.	5.	10.	25.	10.	15.	15.	25.
1984	119,080,000	15.	50.	150.	5.	10.	25.	10.	15.	15.	25.
1985	142,800,000	10.	40.	100.	5.	10.	25.	10.	15.	15.	25.
1986	168,620,000	10.	30.	100.	5.	10.	25.	10.	15.	15.	25.
1987	147,309,000	10.	45.	100.	5.	10.	25.	10.	15.	15.	25.
1988	162,998,558	10.	40.	85.	5.	10.	25.	10.	15.	15.	25.
1989	198,693,414	10.	30.	65.	5.	10.	25.	10.	15.	15.	25.

DIADEMED PORTRAIT, MODIFIED BLUENOSE DESIGN, NICKEL, 1990-2000.

A new obverse portrait of the Queen wearing a diamond diadem and jewellery was introduced on all denominations in 1990.

In 1992 the reverse design was modified to include the bracket dates 1867-1992 for the 125th birthday of Canada.

In 1993 the practice of using a single date was resumed. The transition to beads from rim denticles which began in 1982 on the one-cent piece, was completed on the ten-cent piece in 1993. The Winnipeg Mint Mark (W) is found only on coins from the Brilliant Uncirculated, "Oh! Canada!" and "Tiny Treasures" sets issued by the Numismatic Department of the Mint.

1990 and 1991

Double dates
1867 1992

Designers and Engravers:
Obv.: Dora de Pédery-Hunt, Ago Aarand
Rev.: Emanuel Hahn
Composition: Nickel
Weight: 2.07 grams
Diameter: 18.03 mm
Thickness: 1.25 mm
Edge: Reeded
Die Axes: ↑↑

DATE	MINTAGE	MS-64 C	MS-65 C	MS-66 C	MS-65 NC	MS-66 NC	MS-67 NC	SP-66	SP-67	PR-67	PR-68
1990	65,023,000	10.	30.	150.	5.	10.	25.	10.	15.	15.	20.
1991	50,397,000	10.	45.	75.	5.	10.	25.	10.	15.	15.	20.
1992 (1867-)	174,476,000	10.	40.	50.	5.	10.	25.	10.	15.	15.	20.
1993	135,569,000	10.	45.	125.	5.	10.	20.	10.	15.	15.	20.

DIADEMED PORTRAIT, MODIFIED BLUENOSE DESIGN, NICKEL, 1990-2000 (cont.).

DATE	MINTAGE	MS-64 C	MS-65 C	MS-66 C	MS-65 NC	MS-66 NC	MS-67 NC	SP-66	SP-67	PR-67	PR-68
1994	145,800,000	10.	60.	125.	5.	10.	20.	10.	15.	15.	20.
1995	123,875,000	10.	25.	70.	5.	10.	20.	10.	15.	15.	20.
1996	51,814,000	10.	60.	150.	5.	10.	20.	10.	15.	15.	20.
1997	43,126,000	15.	30.	100.	5.	15.	20.	10.	15.	15.	20.
1998	203,514,000	15.	30.	125.	5.	15.	20.	10.	15.	15.	20.
1998W	N.I.I.	*	*	*	5.	20.	45.	*	*	*	*
1999	258,462,000	15.	25.	50.	5.	10.	20.	10.	15.	15.	20.
2000	160,798,000	15.	30.	50.	5.	10.	20.	10.	15.	15.	20.
2000W	N.I.I.	*	*	*	15.	25.	35.	*	*	*	*

DIADEMED PORTRAIT, BLUENOSE DESIGN, MULTI-PLY PLATED STEEL, 1999-2001.

In 2001 the Royal Canadian Mint began issuing 10 cent coins struck from their new multi-ply plated steel blanks. The process is acid based and electroplates a thin coating of nickel, then copper, then nickel again onto a steel core. Prior to 2001, "P" coinage was only issued to the vending industry for testing purposes. The 1999P and 2000P ten-cents originated from this source.

'P' Composition Mark

Designers and Engravers:
Obv.: Dora de Pédery-Hunt, Ago Aarand
Rev.: Emanuel Hahn
Composition: Multi-Ply Plated steel;
.920 steel, .055 copper, .025 nickel
Weight: 1.75 grams
Diameter: 18.03 mm
Thickness: 1.22 mm
Edge: Reeded
Die Axes: ↑↑

DATE / COMP. MARK	MINTAGE	MS-64 C	MS-65 C	MS-66 C	MS-65 NC	MS-66 NC	MS-67 NC	SP-66	SP-67
1999P	Issued for testing	*	*	*	15.	25.	40.	*	*
2000P	Issued for testing	1,350.	2,500.	3,000.	*	*	*	*	*
2001P	46,265,000	10.	20.	30.	5.	10.	20.	10.	15.

DIADEMED PORTRAIT, INTERNATIONAL YEAR OF THE VOLUNTEER DESIGN, MULTI-PLY PLATED STEEL, 2001.

This coin was issued for circulation in multi-ply plated steel to commemorate the 7.5 million Canadian volunteers who work towards making this country a better place for all. The Volunteer ten cents was also issued in sterling silver: see *Canadian Coin, Volume Two, Collector and Maple Leaf Issues*.

Designers and Engravers:
Obv.: Dora de Pédery-Hunt
Rev.: RCM Design, Stan Witten
Specifications:
Same as 1999P issue

DATE / COMP. MARK	MINTAGE	MS-64 C	MS-65 C	MS-66 C	MS-65 NC	MS-66 NC	MS-67 NC	SP-66	SP-67
2001P	224,714,000	15.	25.	40.	*	*	*	*	*

PRICING

The Charlton Press pricing tables are based on market prices for **Canadian certified coins**. Currently there are two coin grading companies located in Canada. Our prices are gathered from prices realized at land auctions, internet auctions, and dealer fixed price lists and their internet listings. It is important to realize that coin certification incurs a cost, and on low value coins it will be a significant factor in their listed value. The cost per certification coin averages between $7-$10 for standard service.

DIADEMED PORTRAIT, BLUENOSE DESIGN, MULTI-PLY PLATED STEEL, 2002-2003.

In 2002 all circulating coinage carried the double dates 1952-2002, to commemorate the 50th anniversary of the reign of Queen Elizabeth II. This was also the year the Royal Canadian Mint officially acknowledged the schooner that has graced the reverse of the Canadian ten cent coin since 1937 (except for 1967 and 2001) as the Bluenose.

Double dates 1952 2002P

Designers and Engravers:
Obv.: Dora de Pédery-Hunt
Rev.: Emanuel Hahn
Specifications:
Same as 1999P issue

DATE / COMP. MARK	MINTAGE	MS-64 C	MS-65 C	MS-66 C	MS-65 NC	MS-66 NC	MS-67 NC	SP-66	SP-67
2002P (1952)	252,563,000	10.	20.	30.	5.	10.	20.	10.	15.
2003P	163,684,000	10.	20.	45.	5.	10.	25.	10.	15.

UNCROWNED PORTRAIT, BLUENOSE DESIGN, MULTI-PLY PLATED STEEL, 2003-2006.

The 2003 ten cent coin which carried both the Winnipeg mint mark W and the composition mark P is found only in the Special Brilliant Uncirculated set of that year. It was not issued for circulation.

Designers and Engravers:
Obv.: Susanna Blunt, Susan Taylor
Rev.: Emanuel Hahn
Specifications:
Same as 1999P issue

DATE / COMP. MARK	DESCRIPTION	MINTAGE	MS-64 C	MS-65 C	MS-66 C	MS-65 NC	MS-66 NC	MS-67 NC	SP-66	SP-67
2003P		Included	10.	20.	45.	*	*	*	*	*
2003WP		N.I.I.	*	*	*	10.	20.	45.	*	*
2004P		214,143,000	10.	20.	30.	5.	10.	15.	10.	15.
2005P		212,175,000	10.	20.	30.	5.	10.	20.	10.	15.
2006P		312,122,000	10.	20.	30.	5.	10.	20.	10.	15.

UNCROWNED PORTRAIT, BLUENOSE DESIGN, MULTI-PLY PLATED STEEL, RCM LOGO, 2006-2010.

Designers and Engravers:
Obv.: Susanna Blunt, Susan Taylor
Rev.: Emanuel Hahn
Specifications:
Same as 1999P issue

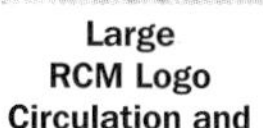

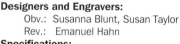

Large RCM Logo Circulation and Proof Issues

2007 St7

Small RCM Logo Brilliant Unc. and Specimen Sets

2007 Cr7

DATE / MINT LOGO	DESCRIPTION	MINTAGE	MS-64 C	MS-65 C	MS-66 C	MS-65 NC	MS-66 NC	MS-67 NC	SP-66	SP-67
2006		Included	10.	15.	35.	5.	15.	25.	*	*
2007 St7		304,110,000	10.	15.	20.	5.	10.	25.	*	*
2007 Cr7		N.I.I.	*	*	*	20.	40.	60.	10.	15.
2008		467,495,000	10.	15.	25.	5.	10.	25.	10.	15.
2009		370,700,000	10.	15.	25.	5.	10.	25.	10.	15.
2010		252,450,000	10.	15.	20.	5.	10.	25.	10.	15.

UNCROWNED PORTRAIT, BLUENOSE DESIGN, MULTI-PLY PLATED STEEL, RCM LOGO, 2011-2014.

With the cessation in 2011 of the brilliant uncirculated finish (MS-65-NC) on coins contained in the uncirculated sets, it was necessary to remove that block of grades from the pricing tables.

RCM Logo

Designers and Engravers:

Obv.: Susanna Blunt, Susan Taylor

Rev.: Emanuel Hahn

Specifications:

Same as 1999P issue

DATE / MINT LOGO	DESCRIPTION	MINTAGE	MS-64 C	MS-65 C	MS-66 C	MS-67 C	SP-66	SP-67
2011		292,325,000	10.	15.	20.	45.	10.	15.
2012		334,675,000	10.	15.	20.	50.	10.	15.
2013		104,775,000	10.	20.	30.	60.	10.	15.
2014		N/A	10.	20.	30.	60.	10.	15.

NOTES ON TEN CENT COINS

1. When the pricing table lists Specimen finishes (SP-66 and SP-67) the prices are for those coins which have been removed from Specimen Sets and certified by a Canadian grading company.
2. The MS-65 NC (non-circulating) and higher grades are listings for coins removed from Uncirculated Sets.
3. The 2000W, 2003WP and 2007 Cr7 ten cent coins are currently found only in Brilliant Uncirculated Sets and Specimen Sets for those years. They were not issued for circulation. See *Canadian Coins, Volume Two, Collector and Maple Leaf Issues*.
4. The 2010 Finish Mule is found in *Canadian Coins, Volume Two*, Fifth Edition (page 376).
5. Mintage numbers listed in the pricing tables are for circulation coinage (MS-64 to MS-66-C Business Strikes). The mintage figures for Brilliant Uncirculated (MS-65 to MS-67-NC), Specimen (SP-66 to SP-67), and Proof (PR-67 to PR-68) must be obtained from *Canadian Coins, Volume Two, Collector and Maple Leaf Issues*.

VICTORIA TWENTY-FIVE CENT MAJOR OBVERSE VARIETIES

Victoria Obverse Variety OQ1

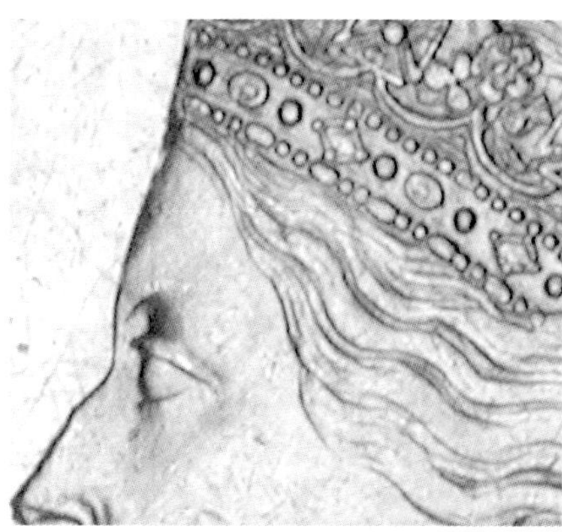

Crown, hair and eye detail | Lips and chin detail | Right ribbon end detail

OQ1 Crown, hair and eye detail: The hairline between the brow and crown is composed of one thick and one minor strand of hair. The upper eyelid is straight. The upper and lower eyelids do not meet at the corner of the eye.
Lips and chin detail: The upper lip has a slight curl and curves outward. The chin has a slight doubling.
Right ribbon end detail: The right ribbon end "V" is off centre, to the right.
Dates: Portrait OQ1 is currently known on the following dates: 1870, 1871, 1871H and 1872H.

Victoria Obverse Variety OQ2

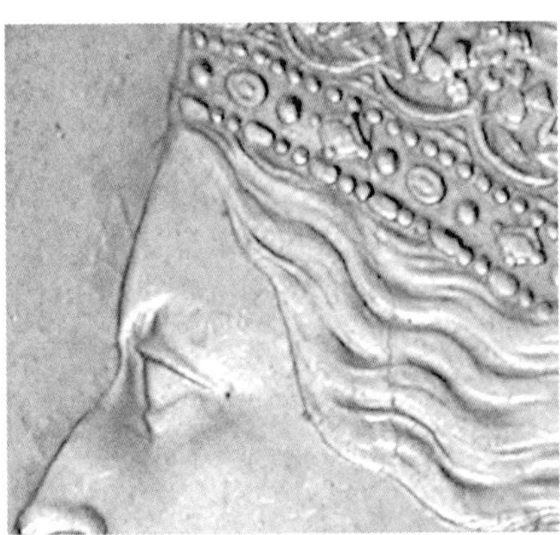

Crown, hair and eye detail

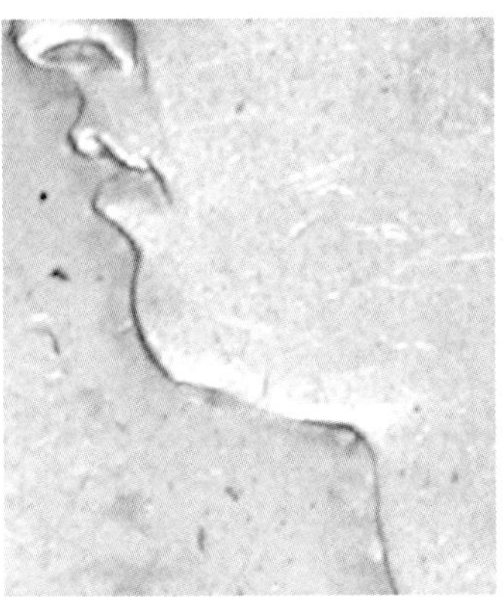

Lips and chin detail

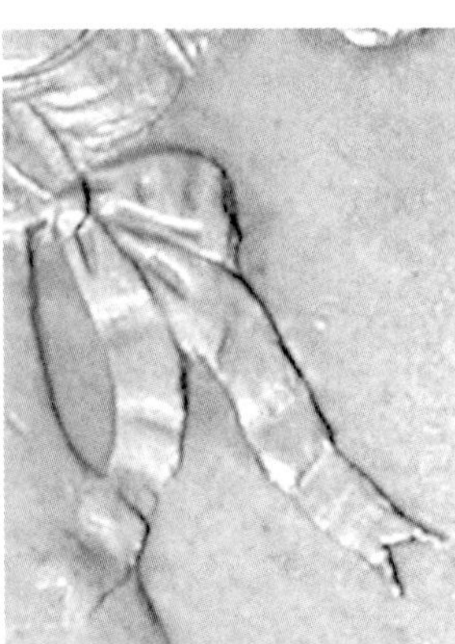

Right ribbon end detail

OQ2 Crown, hair and eye detail: The hairline between the brow and crown is composed of one thick strand of hair. The upper eyelid is straight and meets the lower lid at the corner of the eye.

Lips and chin detail: The upper lip has a prominent curl curving outward. The chin has a slight doubling.

Right ribbon end detail: The right ribbon end "V" is off centre, to the left.

Dates: Portrait OQ2 is currently known on the following dates: 1870, 1871, 1871H, 1872H, 1874H, 1875H, 1880H (all varieties), 1881H, 1885 (all varieties) and 1886.

Victoria Obverse Variety OQ3

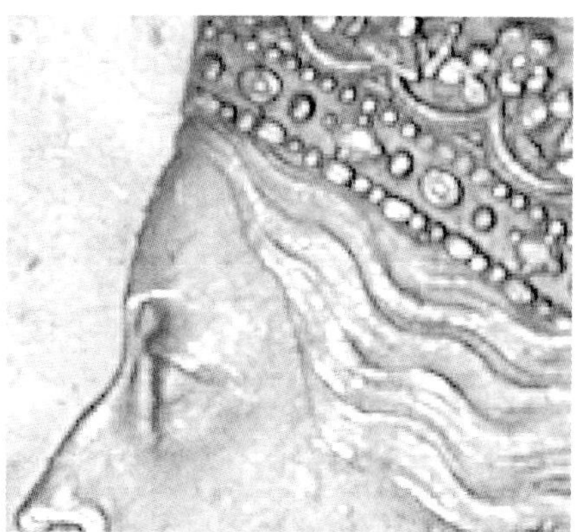

Crown, hair and eye detail

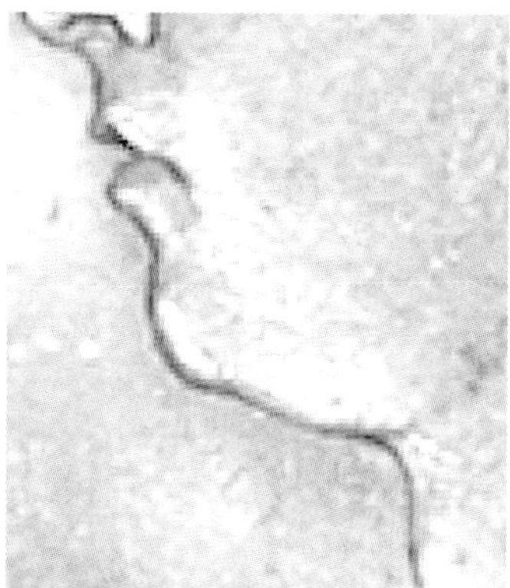
Lips and chin detail

Right ribbon end detail

OQ3 Crown, hair and eye detail: The hairline between the brow and crown is composed of two thick strands of hair. The upper eyelid is straight and thin, joining the lower lid at the corner of the eye.

Lips and chin detail: The upper lip falls straight down from the nostril with only a slight curl. The chin doubling is more pronounced.

Right ribbon end detail: The right ribbon end “V” is split equally between right and left points.

Dates: Portrait OQ3 is currently know on the following date: 1882H.

Victoria Obverse Variety OQ4

Crown, hair and eye detail

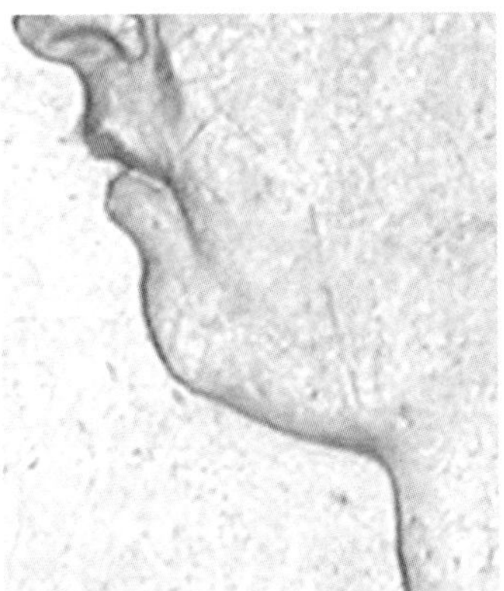
Lips and chin detail

Right ribbon end detail

OQ4 Crown, hair and eye detail: The hairline between the brow and crown is composed of one medium-sized strand. The upper eyelid is thick and straight. It does not join the lower lid at the corner of the eye.

Lips and chin detail: The upper lip falls straight down from the nose to a lip with a slight curl. There is a very slight doubling of a receding chin line.

Right ribbon end detail: The right ribbon end is in the form of a "U" with equal arms.

Dates: Portrait OQ4 is currently known on the following dates: 1883H and 1886.

Victoria Obverse Variety OQ5

Crown, hair and eye detail

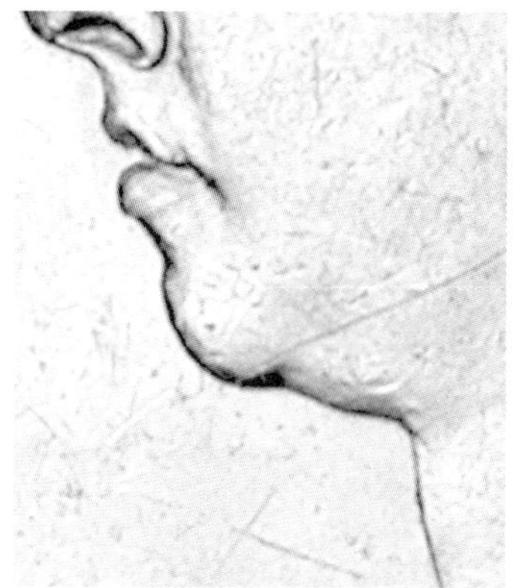
Lips and chin detail

Right ribbon end detail

OQ5 **Bust line:** The most dramatic diagnostic point for Variety Q5 is the location of the point of the bust line which falls to the serif of "C" of CANADA.

Crown, hair and eye detail: There is a very small strand of hair below the crown. The upper eyelid is thin and long. extending well back into the temple.

Lip and chin detail: The upper lip has a pronounced curl and falls with a slight curve out from the nostril. An aging chin shows definite doubling lines.

Right ribbon end detail: The right ribbon end has a lazy "U" shape with equal arms.

Dates: Portrait OQ5 is currently known on the following dates: 1886, 1887, 1888, 1889, 1890H, 1891, 1892, 1893, 1894, 1899, 1900 and 1901.

VICTORIA TWENTY-FIVE CENT MAJOR REVERSE VARIETIES

WREATH WITH SHORT BOUGH ENDS

The short bough ends reverse is found on the following dates:
1870, 1871, 1871H, 1872H, 1874H, 1875H, 1880H, 1881H, 1882H, 1883H, 1885 and 1886

Left Leaves **Right Leaves**

The left bough has 12 leaves while the right bough has 11 leaves.

The leaves are counted by the order in which they are attached to the bough and are numbered L-1 to L-12 and R-1 to R-11.

WREATH WITH LONG BOUGH ENDS

The long bough ends reverse is found on the following dates: 1886, 1887, 1888, 1889, 1890H, 1891, 1892, 1893, 1894, 1899, 1900 and 1901

Left Leaves **Right Leaves**

The left bough has 12 leaves while the right bough has 11 leaves.

The leaves are counted by the order in which they are attached to the bough and are numbered L-1 to L-12 and R-1 to R-11.

Victoria Reverse Variety RQ1

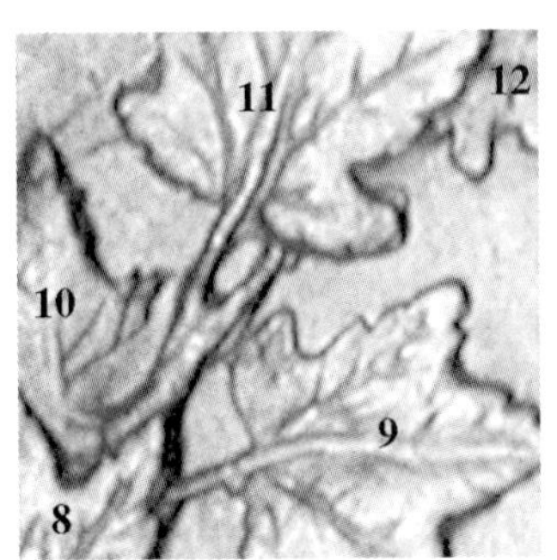

Top left bough detail

Ribbon and bough detail

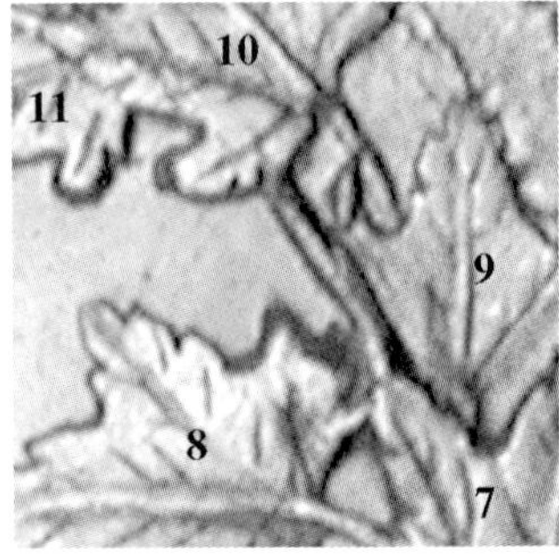

Top right bough detail

RQ1 Top left bough detail: The stem to L-11 and the stem to L-12 form a "Y" with arms of equal thickness.

Ribbon and bough detail: The left ribbon end is close to leaf L-1. The ribbon ends are U-shaped. The bough ends are short.

Top right bough detail: The stem to R-11 is thick. The stem to R-10 is to the right of the tip of R-9.

Dates: Reverse RQ1 is currently known on the following dates: 1870, 1871, 1871H, 1872H, 1874H, 1875H and 1880H.

Victoria Reverse Variety RQ2

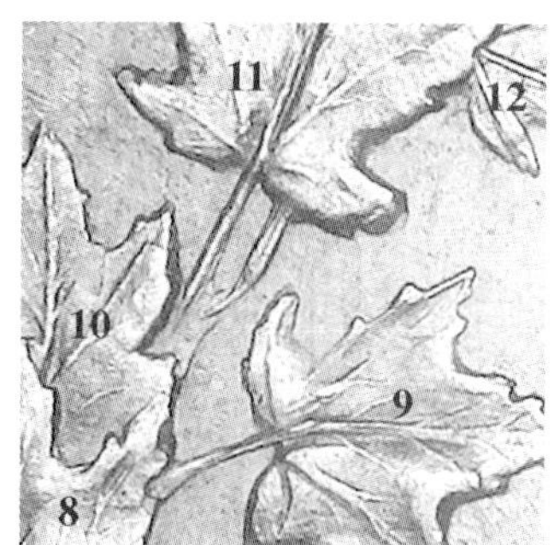

Top left bough detail

Ribbon and bough detail

Top right bough detail

RQ2 **Top left bough detail:** The stem to L-11 is straight. The stem to L-12 bends to the right before turning upward.
Ribbon and bough detail: The ribbon ends are re-engraved. The left ribbon end is far from leaf L-1. The bough ends are re-engraved.
Top right bough detail: The stem to R-11 is thin. The stem to R-10 has a slight curve. It rises from the left tip of R-9.
Dates: Reverse RQ2 is currently known only on the following date: 1881H

Victoria Reverse Variety RQ3

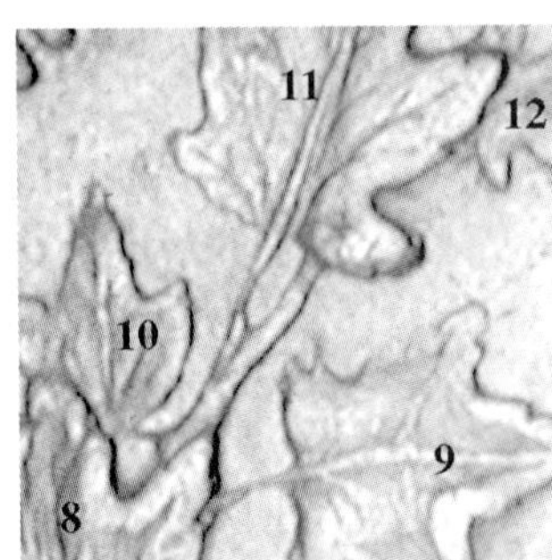

Top left bough detail

Ribbon and bough detail

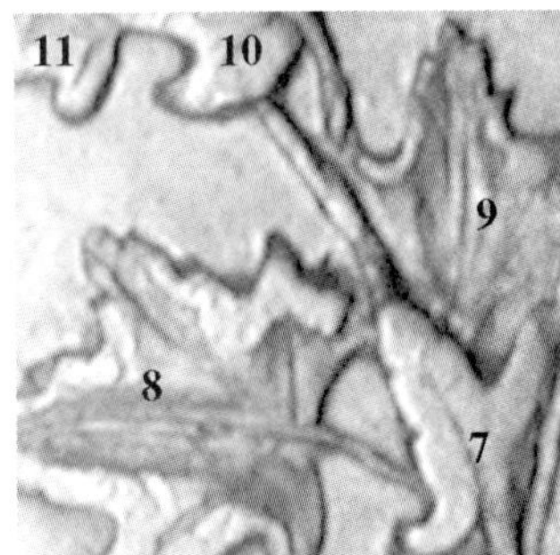

Top right bough detail

RQ3 Top left bough detail: The stem to L-11 is weak. The stem to L-12 is thick.

Ribbon and bough detail: The left ribbon end flairs upward toward leaf L-1. The left ribbon end is far from leaf L-1. The bough ends are short.

Top right bough detail: The stem to R-11 is thick. The stem to R-10 rises from the left tip of R-9.

Dates: Reverse RQ3 is currently known only on the following date: 1882H.

Victoria Reverse Variety RQ4

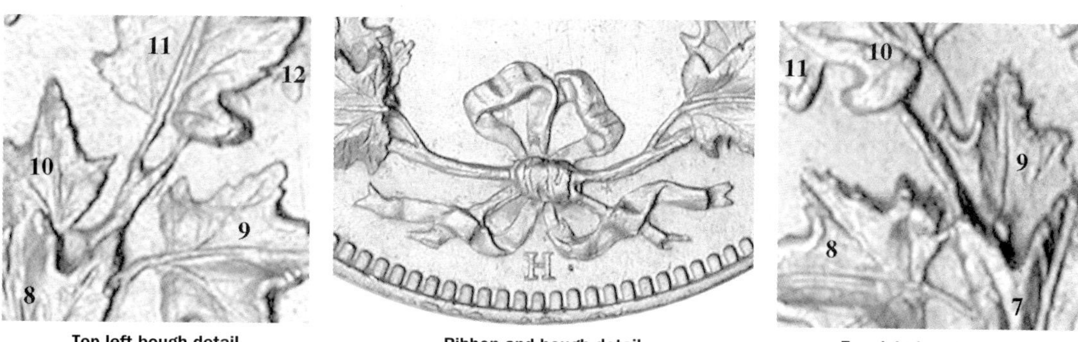

Top left bough detail

Ribbon and bough detail

Top right bough detail

RQ4 **Top left bough detail:** The stem to L-11 and the stem to L-12 form a "Y". The stems are of varying thickness.
Ribbon and bough detail: The ribbon ends are V-shaped. The left ribbon end is near leaf L-1. The bough ends are short.
Top right bough detail: The stem to R-11 is thick. The weak stem to R-10 is to the right of left tip of R-9.
Dates: Reverse RQ4 is currently know on the following dates: 1883H, 1885 and 1886.

Victoria Reverse Variety RQ5

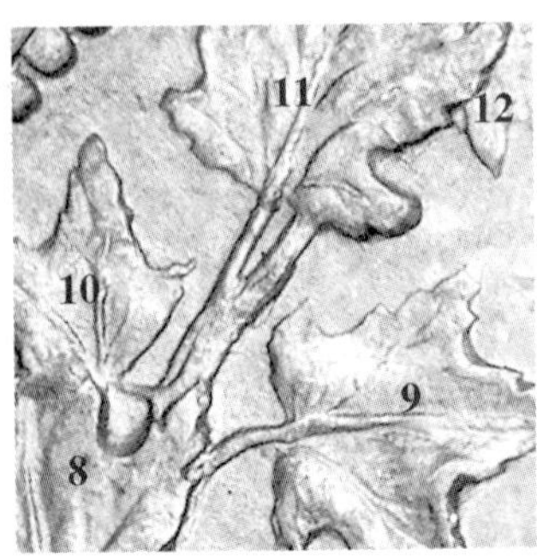

Top left bough detail

Ribbon and bough detail

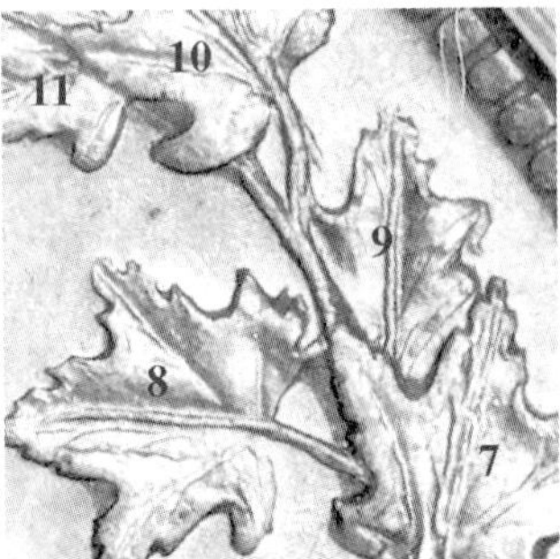

Top right bough detail

RQ5 Top left bough detail: The stem to L-11 is weak. The stem to L-12 is thick.

Ribbon and bough detail: The left ribbon end is in the form of a lazy "V". The ribbon end is close to leaf L-1. The bough ends are long.

Top right bough detail: The stems to R-10 and R-11 are of equal thickness. The stem to R-10 curves over the left tip of R-9.

Dates: Reverse RQ5 is currently known on the following dates: 1886, 1887, 1888, 1889, 1890H, 1892, 1893, 1894, 1899, 1900 and 1901.

Victoria Reverse Variety RQ6

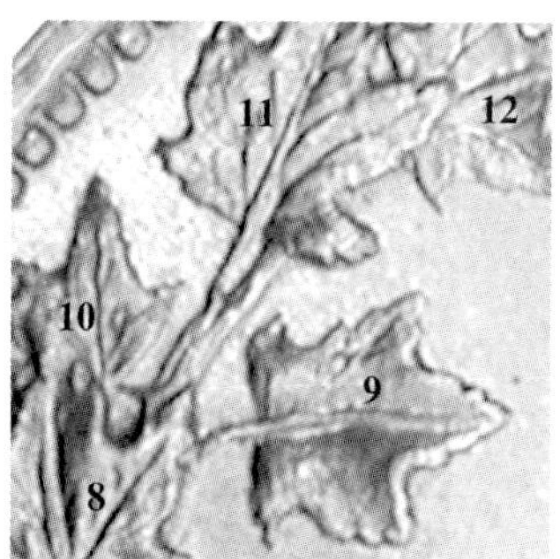

Top Left Bough Detail

Ribbon and Bough Detail

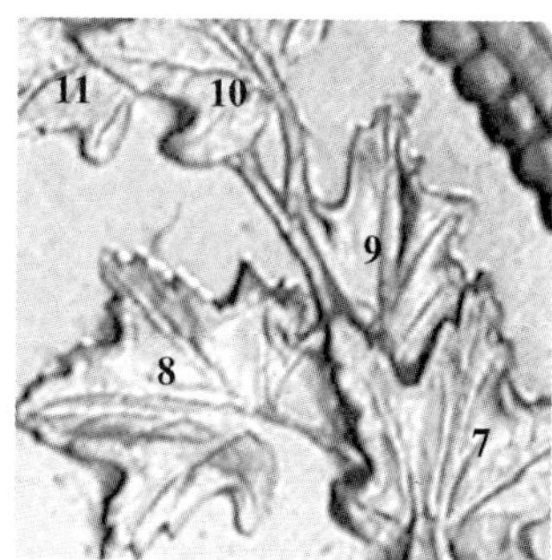

Top Right Bough Detail

RQ6 **Top Left Bough Detail:** A stem to L-11 and L-12 are parallel to each other. The stem to L-12 is thicker.
Ribbon and Bough Detail: The left ribbon end is in the form of a lazy "V". The ribbon end is far from leaf L-1. The bough ends are long.
Top Right Bough Detail: The stems to R-10 and R-11 are of equal thickness. The stem to R-10 curves upward below the left tip of R-9.
Dates: Reverse RQ6 is currently known on the following dates: 1886, 1887, 1888, 1889, 1890H, 1891, 1892, 1893, 1894, 1899, 1900 and 1901.

TWENTY-FIVE CENTS: Victoria 1870 - 1901

The Province of Canada did not issue this denomination so new coinage tools were required for the Dominion of Canada issue. During Victoria's reign, five obverse and two reverse device varieties were employed. Detailed descriptions of the obverses and corresponding date listings are show here. The basic design for the reverse is the same as all other silver denominations: crossed boughs of sweet maple, tied at the bottom by a ribbon and surmounted by St. Edward's crown.

Heaton Mint issues of 1871-1883 and 1890 have an "H" mint mark on the reverse under the wreath. Royal Mint strikings have no mint mark.

"H" Mint Mark

Designer and Engraver: Leonard C. Wyon
Composition: .925 silver, .075 copper
Weight: 5.81 grams
Diameter: 23.62 mm
Edge: Reeded
Die Axes: ↑↓

CROWNED PORTRAIT, 22 LEAVES, SHORT BOUGH ENDS, 1870-1880.

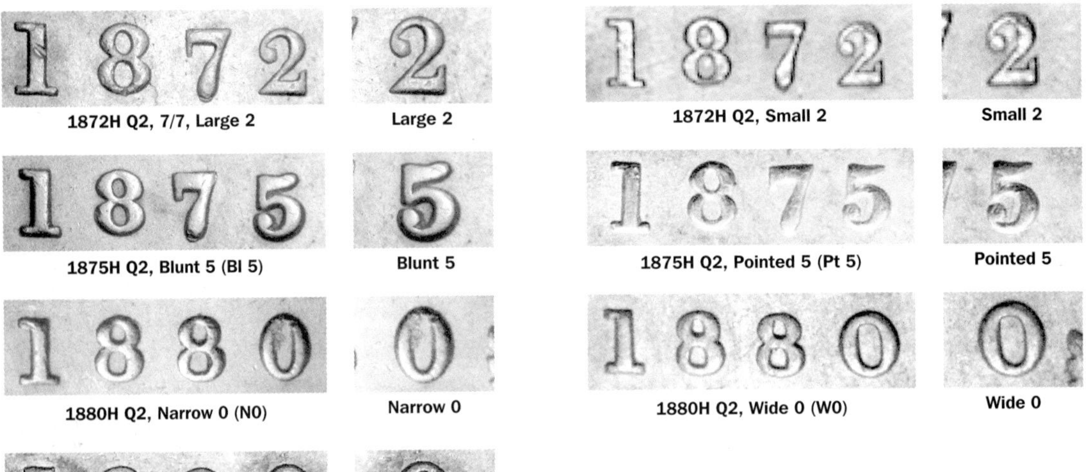

1872H Q2, 7/7, Large 2 — **Large 2** — **1872H Q2, Small 2** — **Small 2**

1875H Q2, Blunt 5 (Bl 5) — **Blunt 5** — **1875H Q2, Pointed 5 (Pt 5)** — **Pointed 5**

1880H Q2, Narrow 0 (N0) — **Narrow 0** — **1880H Q2, Wide 0 (W0)** — **Wide 0**

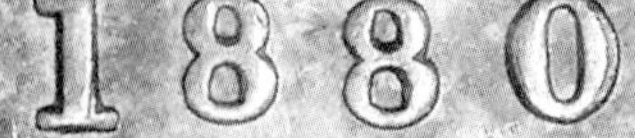

1880 Q2, Narrow 0 over Wide 0 (N/W)

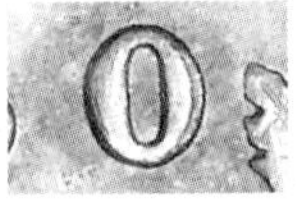

N/W 0

DATE / MINT / PORTRAIT/VAR.	MINTAGE (thous.)	G-4	VG-8	F-12	VF-20	EF-40	AU-50	AU-55	MS-60	MS-63	MS-65	SP-63	SP-65
1870 Q1	900	25.	40.	55.	150.	300.	550.	700.	1,350.	3,000.	—	4,000.	15,000.
1870 Q1 (PE)	Incl.	*	*	*	*	*	*	*	*	*	*	4,000.	15,000.
1870 Q2	Incl.	ONLY FOUR CERTIFIED										*	*
1871 Q1	400	75.	175.	350.	600.	1,200.	2,000.	—	—	—	—	8,000.	20,000.
1871 Q2	Incl.	35.	60.	100.	175.	425.	775.	1,000.	1,800.	5,000.	8,000.	—	—
1871H Q1	748	ONLY NINE CERTIFIED										*	*
1871H Q2	Incl.	25.	50.	100.	250.	500.	900.	1,100.	1,600.	3,000.	10,000.	9,000.	20,000.
1872H Q1	2,240	NONE KNOWN TO EXIST										*	*
1872H Q2 L2	Incl.	15.	25.	45.	75.	175.	350.	550.	1,000.	3,000.	6,000.	5,000.	15,000.
1872H Q2 S2	Incl.	15.	25.	45.	75.	175.	400.	575.	1,000.	2,500.	—	5,000.	15,000.
1872H Q2 L2 7/7	Incl.	20.	30.	65.	110.	250.	475.	—	—	—	—	*	*
1874H Q2	1,600	15.	25.	40.	70.	225.	375.	525.	725.	2,000.	—	*	*
1875H Q2 Bl 5	1,000	350.	750.	1,250.	2,500.	4,500.	9,000.	—	—	—	—	15,000.	30,000.
1875H Q2 Pt 5	Incl.	350.	750.	1,250.	2,500.	5,000.	9,000.	—	—	—	—	*	*
1880H Q2 N0	400	50.	100.	225.	425.	950.	1,500.	2,000.	3,000.	5,000.	—	7,000.	20,000.
1880H Q2 N/W	Incl.	100.	200.	400.	950.	—	—	—	—	—	—	*	*
1880H Q2 W0	Incl.	100.	200.	500.	800.	2,000.	3,000.	6,000.	—	—	—	7,000.	15,000.

CROWNED PORTRAIT, 22 LEAVES, LONG BOUGH ENDS, 1881.

Reverse: Re-engraved

The reverse is heavily re-engraved leading to the introduction of the long bough ends.

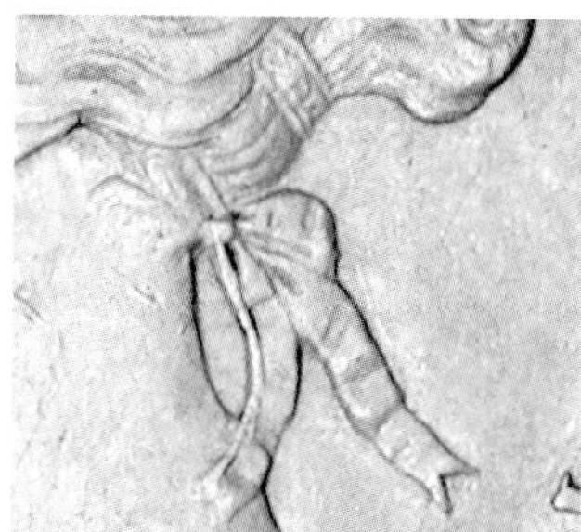

Obverse: Q2 Re-engraved (RE)

The left edge of the ribbon has been re-engraved for the full length

DATE / MINT / PORTRAIT/VAR.	MINTAGE (thous.)	G-4	VG-8	F-12	VF-20	EF-40	AU-50	AU-55	MS-60	MS-63	MS-65	SP-63	SP-65
1881H Q2	820	25.	50.	100.	150.	375.	625.	1,100.	2,250.	4,750.	—	7,500.	15,000.
1881H Q2 RE	Incl.	50.	100.	150.	250.	500.	1,000.	—	—	—	—	*	*

CROWNED PORTRAIT, 22 LEAVES, SHORT BOUGH ENDS, 1882-1886.

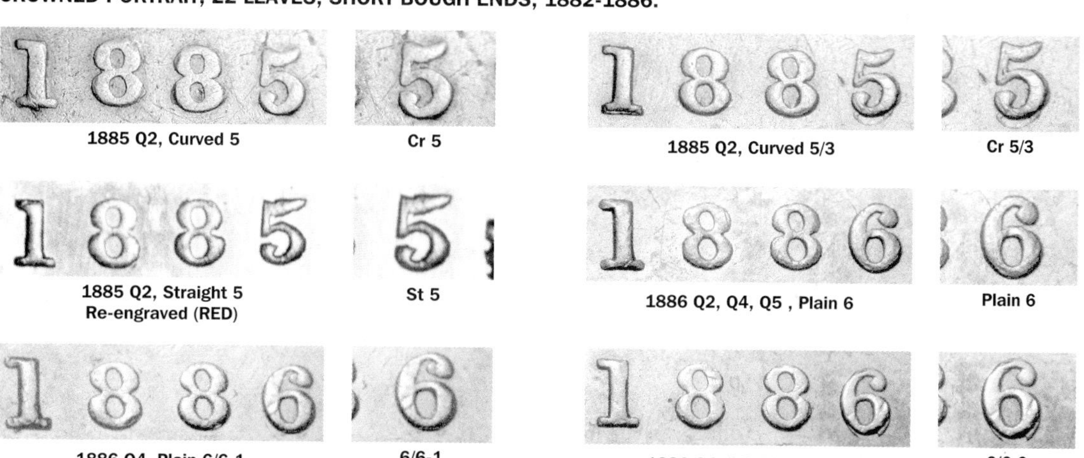

1885 Q2, Curved 5 — Cr 5 — 1885 Q2, Curved 5/3 — Cr 5/3

1885 Q2, Straight 5 Re-engraved (RED) — St 5 — 1886 Q2, Q4, Q5 , Plain 6 — Plain 6

1886 Q4, Plain 6/6-1 — 6/6-1 — 1886 Q4, Q5, Plain 6/6-2 — 6/6-2

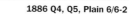

DATE / MINT / PORTRAIT/VAR.	MINTAGE (thous.)	G-4	VG-8	F-12	VF-20	EF-40	AU-50	AU-55	MS-60	MS-63	MS-65	SP-63	SP-65
1882H Q3	600	40.	55.	100.	200.	425.	675.	1,250.	2,000.	4,500.	—	7,500.	15,000.
1883H Q4	960	20.	35.	70.	125.	275.	450.	600.	900.	1,500.	—	5,000.	12,000.
1885 Q2 Cr 5	192	125.	300.	500.	900.	1,500.	3,000.	—	—	—	—	15,000.	30,000.
1885 Q2 Cr 5/3	Incl.	175.	400.	650.	1,250.	2,500.	—	—	—	—	—	*	*
1885 Q2 St 5	Incl.	150.	300.	600.	1,200.	2,000.	—	—	—	—	—	*	*
1886 Q2 P 6	540	60.	125.	250.	450.	800.	1,600.	—	—	—	—	*	*
1886 Q4 P 6	Incl.	60.	125.	175.	325.	750.	1,500.	—	—	—	—	*	*
1886 Q4 6/6-1	Incl.	75.	175.	350.	600.	1,250.	—	—	—	—	—	*	*
1886 Q4 6/6-2	Incl.	75.	175.	325.	700.	1,250.	—	—	—	—	—	*	*
1886 Q5	Incl.	40.	85.	175.	350.	900.	1,500.	2,000.	3,000.	6,000.	15,000.	*	*
1886 Q5 6/6-2	Incl.	175.	350.	550.	750.	1,250.	—	—	—	—	—	*	*

CROWNED PORTRAIT, 22 LEAVES, LONG BOUGH ENDS, 1886-1901.

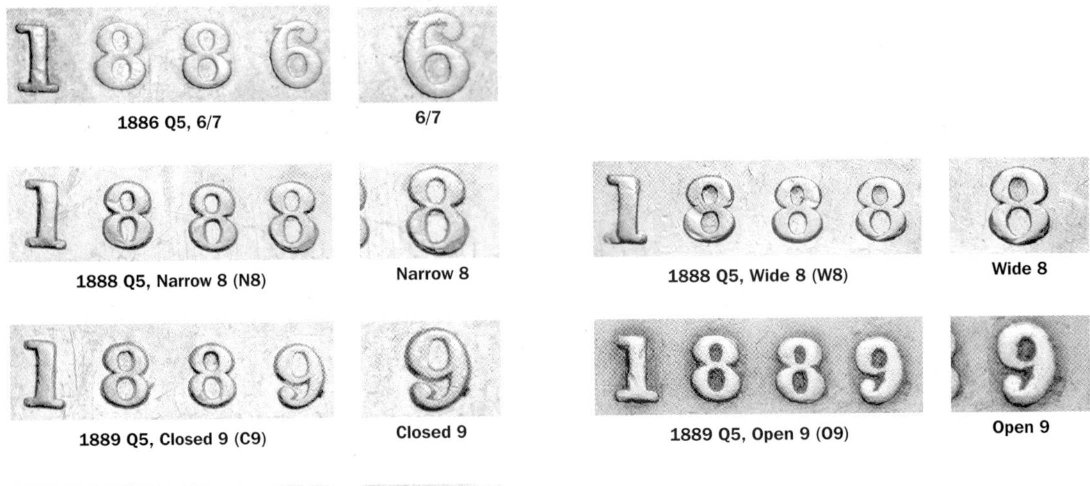

1886 Q5, 6/7 — 6/7

1888 Q5, Narrow 8 (N8) — Narrow 8

1888 Q5, Wide 8 (W8) — Wide 8

1889 Q5, Closed 9 (C9) — Closed 9

1889 Q5, Open 9 (O9) — Open 9

1901 Q5, 9/9 — 9/9

DATE / MINT / PORTRAIT/VAR.	MINTAGE	G-4	VG-8	F-12	VF-20	EF-40	AU-50	AU-55	MS-60	MS-63	MS-65	SP-63	SP-65
1886 Q5 6/7	Included	75.	175.	375.	650.	1,250.	2,000.	—	—	—	—	15,000.	30,000.
1887 Q5	100,000	150.	300.	500.	1,000.	2,000.	4,000.	6,500.	—	—	—	*	*
1888 Q5 N8	400,000	20.	50.	100.	175.	300.	525.	800.	1,250.	2,500.	15,000.	10,000.	25,000.
1888 Q5 W8	Included	30.	65.	125.	200.	325.	500.	750.	1,250.	2,500.	—	*	*
1889 Q5 C9	66,340	125.	275.	700.	1,500.	3,000.	4,000.	6,000.	8,500.	15,000.	—	20,000.	35,000.
1889 Q5 O9	Included	150.	350.	750.	1,500.	2,500.	3,500.	5,500.	—	—	—	*	*
1890H Q5	200,000	40.	60.	125.	250.	550.	900.	1,250.	1,750.	3,500.	—	*	*
1891 Q5	120,000	100.	200.	375.	625.	1,250.	1,750.	2,000.	3,000.	4,500.	10,000.	*	*
1892 Q5	510,000	20.	35.	75.	175.	350.	600.	850.	1,250.	3,000.	7,000.	15,000.	30,000.
1893 Q5	100,000	175.	275.	500.	800.	1,500.	2,000.	2,500.	3,000.	5,000.	10,000.	*	*
1894 Q5	220,000	30.	50.	125.	325.	425.	650.	875.	1,250.	2,500.	7,500.	*	*
1899 Q5	415,580	15.	25.	50.	125.	275.	475.	700.	900.	2,500.	7,500.	*	*
1900 Q5	1,320,000	10.	20.	35.	60.	200.	325.	400.	600.	1,500.	7,500.	9,000.	20,000.
1901 Q5	640,000	10.	20.	35.	85.	200.	400.	550.	850.	1,800.	5,000.	*	*
1901 Q5 9/9	Included	20.	45.	60.	150.	300.	500.	800.	—	—	—	*	*

NOTES ON VICTORIAN TWENTY-FIVE CENT COINS

New research is changing the way we look at the Victorian twenty-five cent series. An 1886 Q4, SBE 6/3 has not surfaced. Another variety which has not surfaced is the 1886 Q5, LBE, Plain 6. The 1886 Q5, LBE, 6/3 has been relisted as an 1886 Q5, LBE, 6/7.

TWENTY-FIVE CENTS
EDWARD VII 1902-1910

With the death of Queen Victoria and the coronation of Edward VII a new obverse design was required to strike the coinage of 1902. In keeping with the custom of rotating the bust with each new monarch, the bust of Edward VII faces right, the opposite direction to that of the Queen Victoria coinage. The obverse design depicts Edward VII wearing a newly designed Imperial crown. This crown appears also on the reverse separating the maple leaves at the top of the wreath. Another modification was moving "CANADA" from the obverse to the reverse.

IMPERIAL CROWNED PORTRAIT, MAPLE LEAF DESIGN, 1902-1910.

'H' Mint mark

Designers and Engravers:
Obv.: George W. DeSaulles
Rev.: 1902-1906 G. W. DeSaulles
1906-1910 W.H.J. Blakemore
Composition: .925 silver, .075 copper
Weight: 1902-1910: 5.81 grams
1910: 5.83 grams
Diameter: 23.62 mm
Edge: Reeded
Die Axes: 1902-1907: ↑↓
1908-1910: ↑↑

SMALL CROWN REVERSE VARIETY. 1902-1906.

The wreath of maple leaves reverse design was carried forward from the Victoria issues with the exception of the Imperial State Crown (St. Edward's Crown) which separates the leaves at the top of the wreath. This was replaced by a new Imperial crown designed by King Edward VII. The new crown does not fill the allotted space and is well clear of the maple leaves. The velvet below the jewelled arch conforms to the curvature of the arches. From the rarity of this variety it is possible that only one reverse die was carried forward from 1905 to 1906.

The striking of the 1902 issues was divided between the Royal Mint, London, and The Mint, Birmingham Ltd., with the latter marked with an "H".

Small crown (SC)
1902-1906

LARGE CROWN REVERSE VARIETY, 1906-1910.

The reverse design was modified in 1906 by W. H. J. Blakemore to improve die life and impart a balanced appearance to the reverse. The design modifications included enlarging and strengthening the Imperial Crown, notably the Maltese Cross on top of the crown.

An aid in identifying the large crown variety is the presence of a fold in the velvet lining inside the right side of the crown just below the jewelled arch. This fold is not present on the small crown variety.

Large crown (LC)
1906-1910

DATE/MINT VARIETY	MINTAGE	VG-8	F-12	VF-20	EF-40	AU-50	AU-55	MS-60	MS-63	MS-64	MS-65	SP-63	SP-65
1902	464,000	25.	50.	125.	325.	400.	650.	1,250.	2,500.	3,500.	12,500.	*	*
1902H	800,000	15.	30.	60.	125.	175.	250.	375.	625.	1,200.	3,000.	—	20,000.
1903	846,150	30.	60.	115.	300.	500.	650.	1,100.	2,500.	6,000.	10,000.	7,000.	15,000.
1904	400,000	50.	100.	300.	625.	1,200.	1,700.	2,800.	6,000.	7,500.	10,000.	*	*
1905	800,000	25.	50.	175.	300.	825.	1,500.	2,500.	5,000.	6,000.	8,000.	*	*
1906 SC.	Incl. below	3,500.	9,000.	—	—	—	—	—	—	—	—	*	*
1906 LC.	237,843	30.	45.	100.	325.	450.	725.	1,250.	2,500.	5,000.	—	*	*
1907	2,088,000	15.	30.	75.	200.	250.	450.	675.	1,250.	2,500.	5,000.	*	*
1908	495,016	30.	70.	125.	325.	475.	600.	750.	1,250.	1,750.	3,000.	900.	1,500.
1909	1,335,929	20.	50.	115.	275.	500.	725.	1,200.	2,250.	5,000.	—	*	*
1910	3,577,569	15.	30.	60.	125.	200.	300.	450.	1,000.	1,700.	5,000.	*	*

TWENTY - FIVE CENTS
GEORGE V 1911 - 1936

IMPERIAL STATE CROWNED PORTRAIT, 'GODLESS', MAPLE LEAF, LARGE CROWN DESIGN, 1911-1936.

The obverse issued on the 1911 coins provoked public outcry because it lacked reference to the King's ruling "by the grace of God." The coinage tools were modified during the year and a new legend including the Latin abbreviation "DEI GRA:" appeared on the 1912 and subsequent issues. The reverse was a continuation of the Large Crown variety of Edward VII.

51,494 25¢ pieces, .925 fine and presumably all dated 1919, were melted in 1920.

1911 Without DEI GRATIA

1912-1936 With DEI GRATIA

Designer and Engraver:
Obv.: Sir E. B. MacKennal
Rev.: W. H. J. Blakemore

Composition:
1912-1919: .925 silver, .075 copper
1920-1936: .800 silver, .200 copper

Weight: 5.83 grams
Diameter: 23.62 mm
Edge: Reeded
Die Axes: ↑↑

DATE	MINTAGE	VG-8	F-12	VF-20	EF-40	AU-50	AU-55	MS-60	MS-63	MS-64	MS-65	SP-63	SP-65
1911	1,721,341	15.	30.	75.	150.	225.	275.	400.	750.	1,100.	1,500.	750.	2,000.
1912	2,544,199	15.	25.	35.	100.	200.	300.	400.	1,500.	2,000.	5,000.	*	*
1913	2,213,595	15.	25.	50.	100.	175.	275.	500.	1,200.	2,000.	4,500.	*	*
1914	1,215,397	15.	25.	50.	100.	325.	400.	850.	2,000.	4,250.	—	*	*
1915	242,382	30.	70.	450.	775.	1,800.	3,000.	5,000.	10,000.	15,000.	—	*	*
1916	1,462,566	12.	15.	35.	60.	125.	200.	325.	950.	2,000.	5,000.	*	*
1917	3,365,644	12.	15.	25.	40.	100.	125.	175.	325.	650.	1,500.	*	*
1918	4,175,649	12.	15.	20.	45.	70.	125.	175.	250.	475.	1,100.	*	*
1919	5,852,262	12.	15.	20.	45.	70.	125.	200.	300.	550.	2,000.	*	*
1920	1,975,278	12.	15.	25.	60.	125.	175.	250.	650.	900.	3,750.	*	*
1921	597,337	25.	45.	150.	400.	925.	1,250.	2,000.	4,000.	8,000.	12,000.	7,500.	25,000.
1927	468,096	50.	95.	175.	375.	750.	1,500.	1,800.	2,750.	4,500.	6,000.	7,000.	25,000.
1928	2,114,178	12.	15.	25.	70.	125.	150.	225.	475.	1,000.	2,500.	2,500.	7,500.
1929	2,690,562	12.	15.	35.	60.	85.	125.	200.	400.	925.	2,250.	2,500.	7,500.
1930	968,748	12.	15.	35.	75.	125.	225.	325.	725.	1,325.	2,500.	2,500.	8,000.
1931	537,815	12.	15.	45.	90.	150.	225.	425.	900.	1,800.	3,500.	2,500.	8,000.
1932	537,994	12.	15.	45.	100.	150.	225.	425.	1,000.	1,500.	5,000.	*	*
1933	421,282	10.	15.	65.	125.	200.	275.	325.	500.	700.	1,350.	*	*
1934	384,350	10.	15.	45.	125.	175.	250.	450.	725.	1,600.	6,000.	7,000.	25,000.
1935	537,772	10.	15.	50.	90.	150.	200.	250.	450.	725.	1,500.	*	*
1936	1,125,779	10.	15.	25.	45.	70.	100.	150.	275.	450.	1,500.	*	*

THE DOT COINAGE OF 1936.

Early in 1937, while the Royal Canadian Mint was awaiting the arrival of the master tools for the new coinage for George VI, an emergency issue of 25-cent pieces occurred to satisfy urgent demands for this denomination. To mark the special nature of the coinage the dies bore a small raised dot on the reverse under the wreath. That such an emergency issue had even taken place was generally not known until 1940, when collectors began noticing that some of the 25-cent pieces dated 1936 had a dot under the wreath. It was learned that supposedly 1- and 10-cent pieces were issued also, but no circulated examples of the two latter denominations have been proved genuine.

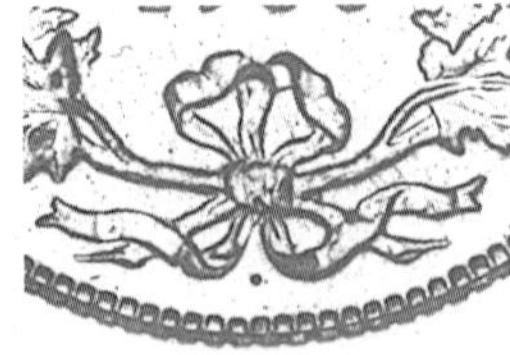

Physical specifications are as the 1911 issues Chemical specifications are as the 1920 issues. 1936 With raised dot below date struck in 1937.

DATE	MINTAGE	VG-8	F-12	VF-20	EF-40	AU-50	AU-55	MS-60	MS-63	MS-64	MS-65	SP-63	SP-65
1936 Dot	Included	50.	125.	275.	550.	800.	1,200.	1,500.	4,500.	6,000.	—	—	100K

TWENTY-FIVE CENTS
GEORGE VI 1937 - 1952

The design chosen for the reverse of the new George VI coinage in 1937 was Emanuel Hahn's caribou head. This design was part of the government's program of modernizing the coinage. The original master tools were prepared at the Paris Mint because of a heavy work load at the Royal Mint in London at that time.

UNCROWNED PORTRAIT, 'ET IND: IMP:', CARIBOU DESIGN, 1937-1947.

The initial obverse bore a legend containing an abbreviation for the Latin phrase, "ET INDIAE IMPERATOR"' meaning "and Emperor of India," referring to the fact that the monarch had held that position since Queen Victoria was made Empress of India in 1876.

1937 Double HP

Designer and Engraver:
Obv.: T. H. Paget
Rev.: Emanuel Hahn
Composition: .800 silver, .200 copper
Weight: 5.83 grams
Diameter: 23.62 mm
Edge: Reeded
Die Axes: ↑↑

DATE / VARIETY	MINTAGE	VF-20	EF-40	AU-50	AU-55	MS-60	MS-63	MS-64	MS-65	MS-66	SP-63	SP-65
1937	2,689,813	12.	15.	20.	30.	35.	50.	75.	275.	2,500.	150.	250.
1937 DHP	Included	20.	25.	30.	40.	55.	125.	—	—	—	*	*
1937 Matte	Included	*	*	*	*	*	*	*	*	*	100.	375.
1938	3,149,245	15.	25.	40.	50.	115.	200.	300.	1,200.	3,500.	2,500.	5,000.
1939	3,532,495	15.	25.	35.	50.	60.	125.	250.	450.	1,500.	2,500.	5,000.
1940	9,583,650	12.	15.	18.	20.	25.	50.	90.	300.	1,500.	*	*
1941	6,654,672	12.	15.	18.	25.	35.	55.	100.	300.	1,800.	*	*
1942	6,935,871	12.	15.	18.	25.	35.	60.	120.	400.	1,500.	*	*
1943	13,559,575	12.	15.	18.	25.	35.	60.	125.	375.	1,600.	*	*
1944	7,216,237	12.	15.	18.	35.	40.	80.	145.	500.	1,500.	2,500.	5,000.
1945	5,296,495	12.	15.	18.	30.	40.	75.	110.	450.	2,500.	400.	1,500.
1946	2,210,810	12.	25.	35.	55.	70.	115.	175.	575.	1.500.	300.	900.
1947	1,524,554	15.	20.	50.	60.	80.	110.	200.	1,000.	—	350.	1,500.

VARIETIES OF 1947.

The granting of independence to India posed a problem for the Royal Canadian Mint in the early part of 1948. The new obverse coinage tools (with the Latin phrase "ET IND: IMP:" omitted to indicate that the King was no longer the Emperor of India) would not arrive for several months, yet there was a need for all denominations of coins. The mint satisfied the demand by striking coins dated 1947 bearing the obverse with the outmoded titles. To differentiate this issue from the regular strikings of 1947, a tiny maple leaf was placed after the date.

1947 Dot Issue

1947 Maple Leaf Issue struck in 1948

DATE / VARIETY	MINTAGE	F-12	VF-20	EF-40	AU-50	AU-55	MS-60	MS-63	MS-64	MS-65	MS-66	SP-63	SP-65
1947 ML	4,393,938	10.	12.	15.	20.	35.	40.	50.	85.	300.	1,500.	200.	750.
1947 Dot	Included	125.	175.	310.	450.	600.	850.	1,300.	2,250.	5,000.	—	*	*

UNCROWNED PORTRAIT, 'DEI GRATIA', CARIBOU DESIGN, 1948-1952.

Following the arrival of the master tools with the new obverse legend lacking "ET IND: IMP:" in 1948, production of the 1947 Maple Leaf coinage was terminated. For the remainder of the year coins were produced with the new obverse and the true date, 1948. In an attempt to improve the appearance of the obverse of this denomination a fresh reduction was made to produce an obverse with a slightly larger, lower relief portrait. Both varieties were struck in 1951 and 1952. Aside from the difference in relief and the size of the portrait, the two varieties can be distinguished by the lettering. The High Relief variety has a plain lettering style in the legend, and both "A's" in "GRATIA" point to a large rim denticle. On the Low Relief variety the letters are more flared, and both "A's" in "GRATIA" point between small rim denticles.

Designers, Engravers and Specifications:
Same as 1937 issue

1951-1952
High Relief
Obverse (HR)
"A" Points at a
Denticle

1951-1952
Low Relief
Obverse (LR)
"A" Points
Between Denticles

DATE / VARIETY	MINTAGE	VF-20	EF-40	AU-50	AU-55	MS-60	MS-63	MS-64	MS-65	MS-66	SP-63	SP-65
1948	2,564,424	15.	25.	35.	60.	80.	150.	250.	800.	1,000.	300.	650.
1949	7,988,830	10.	12.	15.	18.	25.	45.	75.	725.	—	350.	550.
1950	9,673,335	10.	12.	15.	20.	25.	40.	65.	450.	1,500.	100.	425.
1951 HR	8,290,719	12.	14.	16.	18.	20.	30.	55.	475.	—	100.	425.
1951 LR	Included	250.	350.	500.	1,000.	1,500.	2,500.	—	—	—	300.	600.
1952 HR	8,859,642	12.	15.	20.	30.	50.	85.	125.	750.	—	*	*
1952 LR	Included	12.	15.	18.	20.	25.	30.	65.	550.	—	100.	400.

SYMBOLS USED IN PRICING TABLES

—	**No two coins have been assigned this grade by a Canadian grading company.**
*	**Not issued in that finish.**
BV	**Bullion value.**
C	**Circulating coins, coins which are purchased from banks, or found in change.**
FV	**Face value.**
NC	**Noncirculating coins identical in design to the circulating issue, but sold in sets or special packaging by the Royal Canadian Mint.**
N.I.I.	**Not issued individually, but included in a set of some nature.**
P.E.	**Plain edge**

TWENTY-FIVE CENTS
ELIZABETH II 1953 TO DATE

LAUREATE PORTRAIT, CARIBOU DESIGN, 1953-1964.

Two obverse varieties, called the No Shoulder Fold and Shoulder Fold obverses, saw use during 1953 (see 1-cent Elizabeth II, 1953 to date for full explanation). On the 25-cents these obverses are combined with reverses that are readily distinguishable. The No Shoulder Fold obverse comes with a Large Date reverse (carried over from George VI) and the Shoulder Fold was used with a Small Date reverse.

OBVERSE VARIETIES

1953 NSF Obverse

1953 SF Obverse

Designers and Engravers:
Obv.: Mary Gillick, Thomas Shingles
Rev.: Emanuel Hahn, Thomas Shingles
Composition: .800 silver, .200 copper
Weight: 5.83 grams
Diameter:
1953 Large date: 23.62 mm
1953 Small date-1964: 23.88 mm
Edge: Reeded
Die Axes: ↑↑

REVERSE VARIETIES

1953 Large Date Reverse

1953 Small Date Reverse

1955 Doubled Die Reverse

DATE / VARIETY	MINTAGE	AU-55	MS-60	MS-63	MS-64	MS-65	MS-66	PL-65	PL-65 HC	SP-65	SP-67
1953 NSF LD	10,456,769	10.	15.	20.	35.	125.	1,000.	—	—	300.	600.
1953 SF SD	Included	12.	20.	25.	65.	425.	—	275.	400.	300.	600.
1954	2,318,891	20.	25.	45.	130.	500.	—	100.	175.	*	*
1955	9,552,505	15.	20.	25.	55.	300.	—	50.	60.	*	*
1955 DD	Included	175.	250.	500.	1,000.	1,500.	—	*	*	*	*
1956	11,269,353	10.	15.	20.	50.	125.	475.	35.	60.	*	*
1957	12,770,190	10.	15.	20.	25.	85.	500.	30.	70.	*	*
1958	9,336,910	10.	12.	18.	20.	60.	300.	30.	45.	*	*
1959	13,503,461	10.	12.	18.	30.	175.	800.	25.	40.	*	*
1960	22,835,327	10.	12.	15.	20.	60.	—	15.	20.	*	*
1961	18,164,368	10.	12.	15.	20.	85.	—	15.	20.	*	*
1962	29,559,266	10.	12.	15.	20.	70.	—	15.	20.	*	*
1963	21,180,642	10.	12.	15.	20.	65.	—	15.	20.	*	*
1964	36,479,343	10.	12.	15.	20.	60.	350.	15.	20.	200.	400.

TIARA PORTRAIT, CARIBOU DESIGN, 1965, 1966 and 1968; CENTENNIAL DESIGN, SILVER, 1967.

A new obverse with the Queen showing more mature facial features and wearing a tiara was introduced on all denominations in 1965. A reverse design featuring a walking wildcat (bobcat) was selected as part of the commemorative set of coins for this year. During the year, the rising price of silver resulted in reduction of the silver content from .800 to .500. The two varieties are not distinguishable by appearance.

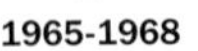
1965-1968

Caribou design
1965, 1966, 1968

Bobcat design
1967

Designers and Engravers:
Obv.: Arnold Machin, Walter Ott
Rev.: 1965, 1966, 1968 Emanuel Hahn, Thomas Shingles
1967 Alex Colville, Myron Cook
Composition:
1965-1967: .800 silver, .200 copper
1967-1968: .500 silver, .500 copper
Weight: 5.83 grams
Diameter: 23.88
Edge: Reeded
Die Axes: ↑↑, ↑↓

DATE / VARIETY	MINTAGE	MS-60	MS-63	MS-64	MS-65	MS-66	PL-65	PL-65 HC	SP-65	SP-67
1965 ↑↑	44,708,869	10.	12.	15.	35.	250.	10.	15.	150.	300.
1965 ↑↓	Included	ONLY ONE CERTIFIED							*	*
1966	25,388,892	10.	12.	15.	40.	125.	10.	15.	*	*
1967 .800 silver	48,855,500	10.	12.	15.	40.	150.	10.	15.	15.	25.
1967 .500 silver	Included	10.	12.	15.	30.	150.	*	*	*	*
1968 .500 silver	71,464,000	8.	10.	15.	30.	75.	*	*	*	*

TIARA PORTRAIT, CARIBOU DESIGN RESUMED, NICKEL, 1968-1972.

During 1968 it was necessary to discontinue the use of silver in favour of pure nickel. Nickel coins are darker in colour and are attracted to a magnet.

Designer and Engraver:
Obv.: Arnold Machin
Rev.: Emanuel Hahn
Composition: 1.00 nickel
Weight: 5.07 grams
Diameter: 23.88 mm
Thickness: 1.6 mm
Edge: Reeded
Die Axes: ↑↑

DATE	MINTAGE	MS-63 C	MS-64 C	MS-65 C	MS-66 C	MS-65 NC	MS-66 NC	MS-67 NC	SP-66	SP-67
1968	88,686,931	5.	10.	35.	100.	20.	45.	—	—	—
1969	133,037,929	5.	10.	40.	100.	10.	50.	100.	50.	100.
1970	10,302,010	5.	10.	30.	100.	25.	55.	100.	75.	150.
1971	48,170,428	5.	10.	30.	80.	5.	25.	—	25.	50.
1972	43,743,387	5.	10.	30.	80.	5.	25.	—	25.	50.

PRICING

The Charlton Press pricing tables are based on market prices for **Canadian certified coins**. Currently there are two coin grading companies located in Canada. Our prices are gathered from prices realized at land auctions, internet auctions, and dealer fixed price lists and their internet listings. It is important to realize that coin certification incurs a cost, and on low value coins it will be a significant factor in their listed value. The cost for certification per coin averages between $7- $10 for standard service.

TIARA PORTRAIT, COMMEMORATING THE CENTENNIAL OF THE FOUNDING OF THE R.C.M.P., NICKEL, 1973.

The special reverse on the 1973 25-cent piece commemorates the centennial of the founding of the North West Mounted Police, which later became the Royal Canadian Mounted Police.

A new obverse with a smaller, more detailed portrait and fewer rim beads placed farther from the rim was prepared for use with the commemorative reverse. However, a small quantity of coins was struck with the 1972 obverse, creating two varieties for the year. The quantity of the Large Bust variety struck for circulation is believed not to exceed 10,000.

1973 Large Bust

1973 Small Bust

Designers:
Obv.: Arnold Machin
Rev.: Paul Cedarberg

Engravers:
Large Bust Obv.: Arnold Machin
Small Bust Obv.: Patrick Brindley, modifying the existing Machin Portrait
Rev.: Walter Ott

Specifications:
Same as 1968 nickel issue

DATE / VARIETY	MINTAGE	EF-40	AU-50	MS-60 C	MS-63 C	MS-64 C	MS-65 C	MS-66 C	MS-65 NC	MS-66 NC	MS-67 NC	SP-66	SP-67
1973 LB	Included	225.	300.	400.	1,250.	2,000.	4,500.	—	350.	500.	—	575.	—
1973 SB	135,958,589	3.	3.	3.	5.	10.	25.	55.	5.	30.	75.	50.	75.

TIARA PORTRAIT, CARIBOU DESIGN RESUMED, NICKEL, 1974-1978.

With the return to the caribou reverse for the 25-cent piece in 1974, the use of the Large Bust obverse was resumed.

Specifications: Same as 1968 nickel issue

Canada far from rim

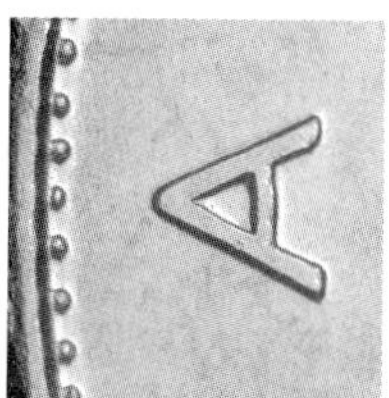
1978
148 Small Denticles

Canada near rim

1978
120 Large Denticles

DATE / VARIETY	MINTAGE	MS-63 C	MS-64 C	MS-65 C	MS-66 C	MS-65 NC	MS-66 NC	MS-67 NC	SP-66	SP-67
1974	192,360,598	5.	10.	15.	100.	5.	30.	75.	15.	30.
1975	252,259,000	5.	10.	30.	100.	5.	30.	75.	15.	30.
1976	86,898,261	5.	10.	30.	90.	5.	30.	75.	15.	30.
1977	99,634,555	5.	10.	20.	55.	5.	30.	75.	15.	30.
1978 L Dent.	174,475,408	5.	15.	45.	75.	5.	30.	65.	30.	75.
1978 S Dent.	Included	5.	15.	30.	100.	5.	30.	50.	15.	25.

MODIFIED TIARA PORTRAIT, CARIBOU DESIGN, NICKEL, 1979-1980.

Beginning with the 1979 issue and as part of a general standardization of the coinage, the portrait of the Queen was reduced. The intention was to make the size of the portrait proportional to the diameter of the coin, regardless of the denomination. This obverse is not the same as that employed in connection with the 1973 R.C.M.P. commemorative.

Designers, Engravers and Specifications:
Same as 1968 nickel issue.

MODIFIED OBVERSE DESIGN OF 1980.

As part of the design changes of the early 1980's, the position of the obverse beads was altered.

1980 Far Beads (FB)

1980 Near Beads (NB)

DATE	MINTAGE	MS-63 C	MS-64 C	MS-65 C	MS-66 C	MS-65 NC	MS-66 NC	MS-67 NC	SP-66	SP-67
1979	131,042,905	5.	10.	30.	75.	5.	20.	50.	15.	20.
1980 FB	76,178,000	5.	15.	85.	—	5.	15.	50.	15.	20.
1980 NB	Included	5.	45.	125.	—	5.	15.	50.	15.	20.

MODIFIED TIARA PORTRAIT, CARIBOU DESIGN RESUMED, NICKEL, 1981-1989

In 1981 the Royal Canadian Mint revised their product line, adding a proof finish to their offerings. The proof coins were struck on standard nickel planchets.

DATE	MINTAGE	MS-63 C	MS-64 C	MS-65 C	MS-66 C	MS-65 NC	MS-66 NC	MS-67 NC	SP-66	SP-67	PR-67	PR-68
1981	131,583,900	5.	15.	75.	—	5.	15.	50.	10.	20.	10.	25.
1982	171,926,000	5.	15.	60.	—	5.	15.	50.	10.	20.	10.	20.
1983	13,162,000	5.	15.	60.	125.	5.	15.	50.	10.	20.	10.	20.
1984	119,212,000	5.	15.	100.	—	5.	15.	40.	10.	20.	10.	20.
1985	158,734,000	5.	15.	125.	—	5.	15.	40.	10.	20.	10.	20.
1986	132,220,000	5.	15.	70.	200.	5.	15.	40.	10.	20.	10.	20.
1987	53,408,000	5.	15.	60.	150.	5.	15.	40.	10.	20.	10.	25.
1988	80,368,473	5.	15.	70.	200.	5.	15.	40.	10.	20.	10.	20.
1989	119,796,307	5.	15.	70.	—	5.	15.	40.	10.	20.	10.	20.

DIADEMED PORTRAIT, CARIBOU DESIGN, NICKEL, 1990-1992.

A new obverse portrait of the Queen wearing a diamond diadem and jewellery was introduced on all denominations in 1990.

Designers and Engravers:
Obv.: Dora de Pédery-Hunt, Ago Aarand
Rev.: Emanuel Hahn
Composition: 1.00 nickel
Weight: 5.05 grams
Diameter: 23.88 mm
Thickness: 1.6 mm
Edge: Reeded
Die Axes: ↑↑

DATE	MINTAGE	MS-64 C	MS-65 C	MS-66 C	MS-65 NC	MS-66 NC	MS-67 NC	SP-66	SP-67	PR-67	PR-68
1990	31,258,000	10.	40.	95.	5.	10.	40.	10.	20.	10.	20.
1991	459,000	30.	75.	250.	30.	50.	70.	45.	90.	35.	65.
1992 (1867-)	N.I.I	*	*	*	20.	40.	75.	15.	25.	15.	25.

Note: For the continuation of the 1993 to 1996 listing of twenty-five cent coins see page 164.

DIADEMED PORTRAIT, 125TH ANNIVERSARY OF CONFEDERATION DESIGNS, NICKEL 1867-1992.

During each month of 1992 the Royal Canadian Mint issued a twenty-five cent coin bearing a unique design to represent one of the twelve provinces and territories. Each coin was launched at a special event organized in the capital city of the province or territory commemorated by the design.

The designs for the thirteen coins issued to celebrate the 125th birthday (a one dollar coin was issued for Canada Day 1992) were chosen by a national contest.

Designers and Engravers:

Obv.: Dora de Pédery-Hunt, Ago Aarand

Rev.: See below

Specifications: Same as 1990 issue, however, die axes varieties exist.

The obverse and physical specifications are common to all twelve coins

New Brunswick
January 9, 1992
Ronald Lambert
Sheldon Beveridge

Northwest Territories
February 6, 1992
Beth McEachen
A. Aarand C. Saffioti

Newfoundland
March 5, 1992
Christopher Newhook
Sheldon Beveridge

Manitoba
April 7, 1992
Muriel Hope
Ago Aarand

Yukon
May 7, 1992
Libby Dulac
William Woodruff

Alberta
June 4, 1992
Mel Heath
William Woodruff

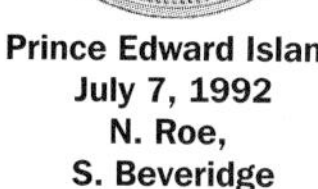

Prince Edward Island
July 7, 1992
N. Roe,
S. Beveridge

Ontario
August 6, 1992
Greg Salmela
Susan Taylor

Nova Scotia
September 9, 1992
Bruce Wood
Terry Smith

Quebec
October 1, 1992
R. Bukauskas
Stanley Witten

Saskatchewan
November 5, 1992
Brian Cobb
Terry Smith

British Columbia
November 9, 1992
Carla Egan
Sheldon Beveridge

DATE	DESCRIPTION	MINTAGE	MS-64 C	MS-65 C	MS-66 C	MS-65 NC	MS-66 NC	MS-67 NC	SP-66	SP-67
1992	NB (↑↑)	2,174,000	10.	30.	80.	5.	15.	50.	*	*
1992	NB (↑↓)	Included	75.	250.	—	*	*	*	*	*
1992	NB (↑→)	Included	150.	—	—	*	*	*	*	*
1992	NWT (↑↑)	12,580,000	15.	50.	75.	5.	15.	50.	*	*
1992	NWT (↑→)	Included	150.	—	—	*	*	*	*	*
1992	NL	11,405,000	15.	35.	—	5.	15.	50.	*	*
1992	MB	11,349,000	10.	35.	75.	5.	15.	50.	*	*
1992	YT	10,388,000	15.	45.	95.	5.	15.	50.	*	*
1992	AB	12,133,000	10.	30.	75.	5.	15.	50.	*	*
1992	PE	13,001,000	15.	55.	95.	5.	15.	50.	*	*
1992	ON	14,263,000	15.	50.	85.	5.	15.	50.	*	*
1992	NS	13,600,000	15.	55.	100.	5.	15.	50.	*	*
1992	QC	13,607,000	15.	55.	85.	5.	15.	50.	*	*
1992	SK (↑↑)	14,165,000	15.	55.	95.	5.	15.	50.	*	*
1992	SK (↑↓)	Included	ONLY THREE CERTIFIED			*	*	*	*	*
1992	BC	14,001,000	10.	65.	100.	5.	15.	50.	*	*

DIADEMED PORTRAIT, MILLENNIUM DESIGNS, NICKEL, 1999.

Struck to celebrate the millennium, the following series of coins reflect development, milestones, discoveries, inventions and achievements in the past millennium which helped shape today's Canada.

During production of this series of 25 cent coins, die deterioration appeared to be a major problem for the Mint. Design and font styles used on these coins played an important part in the life of the dies.

Designers and Engravers:
Obv.: Dora de Pédery-Hunt, Ago Aarand
Rev.: See below

Specifications: Same as 1990 issue.
The obverse and physical specifications are common to all twelve coins

January
A Country Unfolds
P. Ka-Kin Poon
Cosme Saffioti

February
Etched in Stone
L. Springer
José Osio

March
The Log Drive
M. Lavoie
Stanley Witten

April
Our Northern Heritage
Ken Ojnak Ashevac

May
The Voyageurs
S. Minenok
William Woodruff

June
From Coast to Coast
G. Ho
William Woodruff

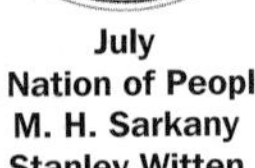

July
A Nation of People
M. H. Sarkany
Stanley Witten

August
The Pioneer Spirit
A. Botelho
Cosme Saffioti

September
Canada Through a Child's Eye
C. Bertrand
Stanley Witten

October
A Tribute to the First Nation
J. E. Read
Sheldon Beveridge

November
The Air Plane Opens the North
B. R. Bacon
Stanley Witten

December
This is Canada
J. L. P. Provencher
Stanley Witten

DATE	DESCRIPTION	MINTAGE	MS-64 C	MS-65 C	MS-66 C	MS-65 NC	MS-66 NC	MS-67 NC	SP-66	SP-67
1999	January	12,238,559	10.	45.	75.	5.	20.	50.	*	*
1999	February	13,985,195	10.	45.	75.	5.	20.	50.	*	*
1999	March	15,157,061	10.	35.	90.	5.	20.	50.	*	*
1999	April	15,214,397	10.	70.	120.	5.	20.	50.	*	*
1999	May	14,906,187	10.	50.	75.	5.	20.	50.	*	*
1999	June	19,821,722	10.	50.	90.	5.	20.	50.	*	*
1999	July	16,537,018	10.	45.	85.	5.	20.	50.	*	*
1999	August	17,621,561	10.	35.	100.	5.	20.	50.	*	*
1999	September	31,077,650	10.	35.	85.	5.	20.	50.	*	*
1999	October	31,964,487	10.	30.	100.	5.	20.	50.	*	*
1999	November	27,437,677	10.	35.	85.	5.	20.	50.	*	*
1999	December	42,927,482	10.	35.	70.	5.	20.	50.	*	*
1999	Total Mintage	258,888,000								

NOTES ON TWENTY-FIVE CENT LISTINGS

1. When the pricing table lists a Specimen finish, the prices are for those coins which have been removed from Specimen Sets and certified by a Canadian grading company.
2. The MS-65 NC (non-circulating) and higher grades are listings for coins removed from uncirculated sets.

DIADEMED PORTRAIT, MILLENNIUM DESIGNS, NICKEL, 2000.

The twelve-coin series for the year 2000 focussed on the hopes and dreams of the future: Canadians' vision of our culture, exploration, science and technology for the third millennium.

During the latter half of 2000 two coins, Creativity and Community, were struck using multi-ply plated steel planchets, and obverse dies with the "p" composition mark.

Designers and Engravers:

Obv.: Dora de Pédery-Hunt
Rev.: See below

Specifications: Same as 1990 issue
The obverse and physical specifications are common to all twelve coins

Pride (January) Donald F. Warkentin, José Osio

Ingenuity (February) John Jaciw, William Woodruff

Achievement (March) Daryl Dorosz, Stanley Witten

Health (April) Annie Wassef, Stanley Witten

Natural Legacy (May) Randy Trantau, José Osio

Harmony (June) Haver Demirer, José Osio

Celebration (July) Laura Paxton, Stanley Witten

Family (August) W. S. Baker, Susan Taylor

Wisdom (September) Cezar Serbanescu, Cosme Saffioti

Creativity (October) Jerik (Kong Tat) Hui, Susan Taylor

Freedom (November) Kathy Vinish, William Woodruff

Community (December) Michelle Thibodeau, José Osio

DATE	DESCRIPTION	MINTAGE	MS-64 C	MS-65 C	MS-66 C	MS-65 NC	MS-66 NC	MS-67 NC	SP-66	SP-67
2000	Pride (↑↑)	50,749,102	10.	30.	65.	5.	20.	50.	*	*
2000	Pride (↑→)	Included	125.	175.	—	*	*	*	*	*
2000	Ingenuity	35,812,988	10.	35.	70.	5.	20.	50.	*	*
2000	Achievement	35,135,154	10.	30.	125.	5.	20.	50.	*	*
2000	Health	34,663,619	10.	30.	70.	5.	20.	50.	*	*
2000	Natural Legacy	36,416,953	10.	30.	55.	5.	20.	50.	*	*
2000	Harmony (↑↑)	34,604,075	10.	30.	60.	5.	20.	50.	*	*
2000	Harmony (↑←)	Included	250.	500.	—	*	*	*	*	*
2000	Celebration	34,816,329	10.	45.	100.	5.	20.	50.	*	*
2000	Family	34,320,111	10.	35.	90.	5.	20.	50.	*	*
2000	Wisdom	33,993,016	10.	35.	95.	5.	20.	50.	*	*
2000	Creativity	35,102,206	10.	50.	100.	5.	20.	50.	*	*
2000P	Creativity	Included	ONLY TWO CERTIFIED			*	*	*	*	*
2000	Freedom	33,251,352	10.	30.	150.	5.	20.	50.	*	*
2000	Community	34,378,898	10.	50.	150.	5.	20.	50.	*	*
2000P	Community	Included	ONLY FIVE CERTIFIED			*	*	*	*	*
2000	Total Mintage	435,751,000								

DIADEMED PORTRAIT, CARIBOU DESIGN RESUMED, NICKEL, 1993-1995.

In 1993 the practice of using a single date was resumed. The transition to beads from rim denticles on the reverse, which began in 1982 on the one-cent piece, was completed in 1993 with the use of beads on the twenty-five cent coin. No circulating caribou reverse twenty-five cent coins were minted from 1997 to 2000. From 1997 through to 2000, the numismatic department minted caribou reverse twenty-five cent coins for use in the following numismatic sets: "Oh Canada!," "Tiny Treasures" and Specimen. The Winnipeg Mint 1998W twenty-five cent coins are only found in the "Oh Canada!" and "Tiny Treasures" sets, and were not issued for general circulation.

The last year for the use of pure nickel blanks in the production of 25-cent coins was 2001.

Designers, Engravers and Specifications:
Same as 1990 issue

DATE	MINTAGE	MS-64 C	MS-65 C	MS-66 C	MS-65 NC	MS-66 NC	MS-67 NC	SP-66	SP-67	PR-67	PR-68
1993	73,758,000	10.	80.	150.	5.	15.	50.	10.	20.	10.	20.
1994	77,670,000	10.	90.	150.	5.	15.	50.	10.	20.	10.	20.
1995	89,210,000	10.	30.	50.	5.	15.	50.	10.	20.	10.	20.

DIADEMED PORTRAIT, CARIBOU DESIGN RESUMED, NICKEL, 1996-2001.

Starting in 1996 the proof coins issued by the Royal Canadian Mint were struck on (non-standard) sterling silver planchets. For proof coins 1996 to 2011 see *Canadian Coins, Volume Two, Collector and Maple Leaf Issues.*

DATE	MINTAGE	MS-64 C	MS-65 C	MS-66 C	MS-65 NC	MS-66 NC	MS-67 NC	SP-66	SP-67
1996	28,106,000	10.	30.	75.	5.	15.	50.	10.	20.
1997	N.I.I.	*	*	*	5.	20.	50.	10.	20.
1998	N.I.I.	*	*	*	5.	15.	50.	10.	20.
1998W	N.I.I.	*	*	*	10.	20.	50.	*	*
1999	N.I.I.	*	*	*	5.	15.	50.	10.	20.
2000	N.I.I.	*	*	*	5.	20.	50.	10.	20.
2000W	N.I.I.	*	*	*	10.	20.	50.	*	*
2001	8,415,000	10.	50.	125.	*	*	*	*	*

DIADEMED PORTRAIT, CARIBOU DESIGN, MULTI-PLY PLATED STEEL, 1999-2003.

In 1999 the Royal Canadian Mint began issuing test and circulating coinage struck from their new Multi-Ply Plated steel blanks. The process is acid based and electroplates a thin coating of nickel, then copper, then nickel again onto a steel core. For the complete Multi-Ply Plated Test Coin Set (TTS-3), see page 284.

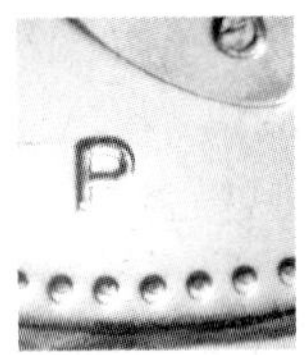

Composition Mark

Designers and Engravers:
Obv.: Dora de Pédery-Hunt, Ago Aarand
Rev.: Emanuel Hahn
Composition: .940 steel, .038 copper, .022 nickel
Weight: 4.4 grams
Diameter: 23.88 mm
Thickness: 1.58 mm
Edge: Reeded
Die Axes: ↑↑

DATE / COMP. MARK	MINTAGE	MS-64 C	MS-65 C	MS-66 C	MS-65 NC	MS-66 NC	MS-67 NC	SP-66	SP-67
1999P	Issued for testing	*	*	*	15.	25.	50.	*	*
2000P	Issued for testing	30,000.	—	—	*	*	*	*	*
2001P	55,773,000	10.	15.	35.	5.	20.	50.	10.	20.
2002P (1952-)	156,105,000	10.	15.	35.	5.	20.	50.	10.	20.
2003P	87,647,000	10.	15.	45.	5.	20.	40.	10.	20.

DIADEMED PORTRAIT, CANADA DAY DESIGN, MULTI-PLY PLATED STEEL, 2002.

The 2002 Canada Day twenty-five cents celebrates 135 years of National Pride. Presented to new Canadians at their citizenship ceremony during 'Celebrate Canada Day' week, this coin marks an important step for those who make Canada their home. The new 25 cent coins were issued for a three month period beginning July 2002 and ending September 2002.

Designers and Engravers:
Obv.: Dora de Pédery-Hunt, Ago Aarand
Rev.: Judith Chartier, Stan Witten
Specifications: Same as 1999P issue

DATE / COMP. MARK	MINTAGE	MS-64 C	MS-65 C	MS-66 C	MS-65 NC	MS-66 NC	MS-67 NC	SP-66	SP-67
2002P (1952-)	30,627,000	10.	15.	40.	*	*	*	*	*

UNCROWNED PORTRAIT, CARIBOU DESIGN, MULTI-PLY PLATED STEEL, 2003-2004.

In 2003 a new obverse design was introduced. An uncrowned portrait of Queen Elizabeth II was designed by Susanna Blunt.

Designers and Engravers:
Obv.: Susanna Blunt, Susan Taylor
Rev.: Emanuel Hahn
Specifications: Same as 1999P issue

DATE / COMP. MARK	MINTAGE	MS-64 C	MS-65 C	MS-66 C	MS-65 NC	MS-66 NC	MS-67 NC	SP-66	SP-67
2003P	Included	10.	15.	50.	*	*	*	*	*
2003WP	N.I.I.	*	*	*	10.	25.	50.	*	*
2004P	177,466,000	10.	15.	30.	5.	20.	40.	10.	20.

COMMEMORATIVE ISSUES OF 2004.

400th Anniversary of the First Settlement in North America. In 1603, Pierre Dugua, Sieur de Mons, was given the title of Lieutenant General of "La Cadie" (Acadie). The following year, he arrived in Acadie on the flagship Bonne-Renommée. The ship's company included Samuel de Champlain, a skilled map maker and chronicler. In search of a suitable site for settlement, the expedition arrived in the Passamaquoddy Bay in late June. De Mons named the Island Saint Croix and it was there that he tried to establish year-round French settlement in North America, an event that symbolizes the founding of Acadie.

The **Remembrance Day "Poppy"** coin was the first coloured circulating coin issued in Canada.

Common obverse

First Settlement

Remembrance Day "Poppy" 2004

Designers and Engravers:

400th Anniv. First Settlement
Obv.: Susanna Blunt, Susan Taylor
Rev.: Robert R. Carmichael, Stan Witten

Remembrance Day "Poppy"
Obv.: Susanna Blunt, Susan Taylor
Rev.: Cosme Saffioti, Stan Witten

Specifications: Same as 1999P issue except "Poppy" which is colourised (red).

DATE / COMP. MARK	DESCRIPTION	MINTAGE	MS-64 C	MS-65 C	MS-66 C	MS-65 NC	MS-66 NC	MS-67 NC	SP-66	SP-67
2004P	First Settlement	15,400,000	10.	15.	60.	*	*	*	*	*
2004P	Poppy	28,972,000	10.	15.	35.	35.	50.	100.	*	*

Note: See page 284 for the "Poppy" Test Set (TTS-4) of 2004 which contains a mint state coin.

UNCROWNED PORTRAIT, CARIBOU DESIGN, MULTI-PLY PLATED STEEL, 2005.

Designers and Engravers:
Obv.: Susanna Blunt, Susan Taylor
Rev.: Emanuel Hahn
Specifications: Same as 1999P issue

DATE / COMP. MARK	DESCRIPTION	MINTAGE	MS-64 C	MS-65 C	MS-66 C	MS-65 NC	MS-66 NC	MS-67 NC	SP-66	SP-67
2005P		206,346,000	10.	15.	35.	5.	20.	40.	10.	20.

UNCROWNED PORTRAIT, COMMEMORATIVE REVERSES, MULTI-PLY PLATED STEEL, 2005.

Common Obverse

100th Anniversary of Alberta

Designers/Engravers:
Obv.: S. Blunt, S. Taylor
Rev.: M. Grant, S. Witten

100th Anniversary of Saskatchewan

Designers/Engravers:
Obv.: S. Blunt, S. Taylor
Rev.: P. Sapergia, J. Osio

Year of the Veteran

Designers and Engravers:
Obv.: S. Blunt, S. Taylor
Rev.: Elaine Globe

Specifications: Same as 1999P issue

DATE / COMP. MARK	DESCRIPTION	MINTAGE	MS-64 C	MS-65 C	MS-66 C	MS-65 NC	MS-66 NC	MS-67 NC	SP-66	SP-67
2005P	Alberta	20,640,000	10.	15.	50.	5.	20.	50.	*	*
2005P	Saskatchewan	19,290,000	10.	15.	30.	5.	20.	50.	*	*
2005P	Year of the Veteran	29,390,000	10.	15.	40.	*	*	*	*	*

UNCROWNED PORTRAIT, CARIBOU DESIGN, MULTI-PLY PLATED STEEL, 2006.

Designers and Engravers:
Obv.: Susanna Blunt, Susan Taylor
Rev.: Emanuel Hahn

Specifications: Same as 1999P issue

DATE / COMP. MARK	DESCRIPTION	MINTAGE	MS-64 C	MS-65 C	MS-66 C	MS-65 NC	MS-66 NC	MS-67 NC	SP-66	SP-67
2006P		423,189,000	10.	15.	30.	5.	20.	50.	10.	20.

UNCROWNED PORTRAIT, BREAST CANCER AWARENESS DESIGN, MULTI-PLY PLATED STEEL, 2006.

Designers and Engravers:
Obv.: Susanna Blunt, Susan Taylor
Rev.: RCM Staff

Specifications: Same as 1999P issue; Colourised

DATE / COMP. MARK	DESCRIPTION	MINTAGE	MS-64 C	MS-65 C	MS-66 C	MS-65 NC	MS-66 NC	MS-67 NC	SP-66	SP-67
2006P		29,798,000	10.	15.	50.	5.	20.	50.	*	*

UNCROWNED PORTRAIT, MEDAL OF BRAVERY DESIGN, MULTI-PLY PLATED STEEL, RCM LOGO, 2006.

RCM Logo

Designers and Engravers:
Obv.: Susanna Blunt, Susan Taylor
Rev.: Cosme Saffioti

Specifications: Same as 1999P issue

DATE	DESCRIPTION	MINTAGE	MS-64 C	MS-65 C	MS-66 C	MS-65 NC	MS-66 NC	MS-67 NC	SP-66	SP-67
2006		20,040,000	10.	20.	70.	*	*	*	*	*

UNCROWNED PORTRAIT, CARIBOU DESIGN, MULTI-PLY PLATED STEEL, RCM LOGO, 2006-2008.

The mintage of 2006 is included in the mintage of 2006P.

Designers and Engravers:
Obv.: Susanna Blunt, Susan Taylor
Rev.: Emanuel Hahn

Specifications: Same as 1999P issue

DATE / MINT LOGO	DESCRIPTION	MINTAGE	MS-64 C	MS-65 C	MS-66 C	MS-65 NC	MS-66 NC	MS-67 NC	SP-66	SP-67
2006		Included	10.	15.	25.	5.	10.	40.	*	*
2007		274,763,000	10.	15.	25.	5.	20.	50.	10.	20.
2008		286,322,000	10.	15.	25.	5.	20.	50.	10.	20.

UNCROWNED PORTRAIT, REMEMBRANCE DAY POPPY, MULTI-PLY PLATED STEEL, 2008.

Designers and Engravers:
Obv.: Susanna Blunt, Susan Taylor
Rev.: Cosme Saffioti, Stan Witten

Specifications: Same as 1999P issue; Colourised

DATE / COMP. MARK	DESCRIPTION	MINTAGE	MS-64 C	MS-65 C	MS-66 C	MS-65 NC	MS-66 NC	MS-67 NC	SP-66	SP-67
2008	Remembrance Poppy	11,300,000	10.	20.	35.	*	*	*	*	*

COMMEMORATIVE ISSUES OF THE VANCOUVER 2010 OLYMPIC WINTER GAMES, OLYMPIC LOGO, 2007.

2007 Obv.
Olympic Games

2010 Olympic
Logo

Designers and Engravers:
Obv.: Susanna Blunt, Susan Taylor
Rev.: Glen Green
Specifications: Same as 1999P issue

Curling
February 23, 2007

Ice Hockey
April 3, 2007

Biathlon
Sept. 12, 2007

Alpine Skiing
October 24, 2007

DATE	DESCRIPTION	MINTAGE	MS-64 C	MS-65 C	MS-66 C	MS-65 NC	MS-66 NC	MS-67 NC	SP-66	SP-67
2007	Curling	22,400,000	10.	15.	25.	5.	20.	50.	*	*
2007	Ice Hockey	22,400,000	10.	15.	25.	5.	20.	50.	*	*
2007	Biathlon	22,400,000	10.	15.	25.	5.	20.	50.	*	*
2007	Alpine Skiing	22,400,000	10.	15.	25.	5.	20.	50.	*	*

COMMEMORATIVE ISSUES OF THE VANCOUVER 2010 OLYMPIC WINTER GAMES, OLYMPIC LOGO, 2008.

2008 Obv.
Olympic Games

2010 Olympic
Logo

Designers and Engravers:
Obv.: Susanna Blunt, Susan Taylor
Rev.: Glen Green
Specifications: Same as 1999P issue

Snowboarding
February 20, 2008

Freestyle Skiing
April 16, 2008

Figure Skating
June 23, 2008

Bobsleigh
November 8, 2008

DATE	DESCRIPTION	MINTAGE	MS-64 C	MS-65 C	MS-66 C	MS-65 NC	MS-66 NC	MS-67 NC	SP-66	SP-67
2008	Snowboarding	22,400,000	10.	15.	25.	5.	20.	50.	*	*
2008	Freestyle Skiing	22,400,000	10.	15.	25.	5.	20.	50.	*	*
2008	Figure Skating	22,400,000	10.	15.	25.	5.	20.	50.	*	*
2008	Bobsleigh	22,400,000	10.	15.	25.	5.	20.	50.	*	*

COMMEMORATIVE ISSUES OF THE VANCOUVER 2010 OLYMPIC WINTER GAMES, OLYMPIC LOGO, 2009.

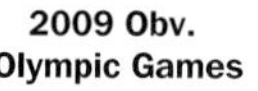

2009 Obv. Olympic Games

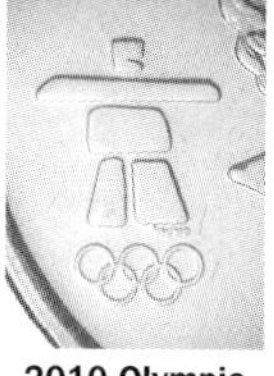

2010 Olympic Logo

Cross Country Skiing January 15, 2009

Speed Skating March 12, 2009

Designers and Engravers:
Obv.: S. Blunt, S. Taylor
Rev.: Glen Green
Specifications:
Same as 1999P issue

DATE	DESCRIPTION	MINTAGE	MS-64 C	MS-65 C	MS-66 C	MS-65 NC	MS-66 NC	MS-67 NC	SP-66	SP-67
2009	Speed Skating	22,400,000	10.	15.	25.	5.	20.	50.	*	*
2009	Cross Country Skiing	22,400,000	10.	15.	25.	5.	20.	50.	*	*

COMMEMORATIVE ISSUES OF THE VANCOUVER 2010 PARALYMPIC WINTER GAMES, PARALYMPIC LOGO, 2007 and 2009.

2007 Obv. Paralympic Games

Wheelchair Curling July 11, 2007

2010 Paralympic Logo

2009 Obv. Paralympic Games

Ice Sledge Hockey March 18, 2010

Designers and Engravers:
Obv.: Susanna Blunt, Susan Taylor
Rev.: Glen Green
Specifications: Same as 1999P issue

The Wheelchair Curling Mule

The Vancouver Olympic obverse was paired with the Paralympic Wheelchair Curling reverse to create a mule. This coin was not issued for circulation, but is found in the Vancouver 2010 Brilliant Uncirculated Sets of 2007, which were assembled in Ottawa. See *Canadian Coins: Volume Two*, Fifth Edition, page 38.

2007 Vancouver Logo

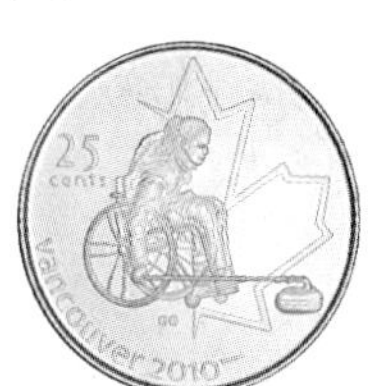

Wheelchair Curling

DATE	DESCRIPTION	MINTAGE	MS-64 C	MS-65 C	MS-66 C	MS-65 NC	MS-66 NC	MS-67 NC	SP-66	SP-67
2007	Wheelchair Curling	22,400,000	10.	15.	25.	5.	20.	50.	*	*
2009	Ice Sledge Hockey	22,400,000	10.	15.	25.	5.	20.	50.	*	*

2010 VANCOUVER WINTER OLYMPIC COINS

The Vancouver 2010 Winter Olympic Games twenty-five cent coins were issued for general circulation. However, they were also issued by the marketing department of the Royal Canadian Mint in many different types of packaging, in three different finishes (circulating, non-circulating and proof), and two different metal compositions (multi-ply plated steel and sterling silver). See *Canadian Coins, Volume Two*.

THE GOLDEN MOMENTS, VANCOUVER 2010 OLYMPIC WINTER GAMES, 2009.

The final three twenty-five cent Olympic coins celebrated Canada's two gold medals won in ice hockey in 2002 and Cindy Klassen's five medals (1 gold, 2 silver, 2 bronze) won in 2006. Currently four dies have been identified in striking the Men's Ice Hockey 25-cent coins. A fifth may exist, but it has yet to be identified (Men's Standard with an incused 2).

2009
Common Obverse

Designers and Engravers:
Obv.: Susanna Blunt, Susan Taylor
Rev.: Jason Bouwman, RCM Staff
Specifications: Same as 1999P issue, Coloured red

STANDARD CIRCULATION COINAGE REVERSES

Men's Ice Hockey Standard'

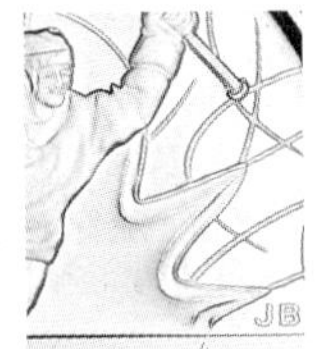

Leaf Standard'

Raised 2

Women's Ice Hockey Standard'

Cindy Klassen Standard'

COLOURISED CIRCULATION COINAGE REVERSES

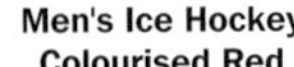

Men's Ice Hockey Colourised Red

Colourised Leaf

Raised 2

Incused 2

Women's Ice Hockey Colourised Red

Colourised Leaf

Cindy Klassen Colourised Red

Colourised Leaf

DATE	DESCRIPTION	MINTAGE (thous.)	MS-64 C	MS-65 C	MS-66 C	MS-65 NC	MS-66 NC	MS-67 NC	SP-66	SP-67
	Men's Ice Hockey, 2002									
2009	Standard, Raised 2	22,000	10.	15.	25.	*	*	*	*	*
2009	Colourised, Raised 2	Included	30.	70.	125.	*	*	*	*	*
2009	Colourised, Incused 2	Included	10.	30.	60.	*	*	*	*	*
	Women's Ice Hockey, 2002									
2009	Standard	22,000	10.	15.	30.	*	*	*	*	*
2009	Colourised	Included	10.	25.	55.	*	*	*	*	*
	Cindy Klassen, 2006									
2009	Standard	22,000	10.	15.	25.	*	*	*	*	*
2009	Colourised	Included	15.	40.	65.	*	*	*	*	*

UNCROWNED PORTRAIT, CARIBOU DESIGN, MULTI-PLY PLATED STEEL, RCM LOGO, 2009-2010.

Designers and Engravers:
Obv.: Susanna Blunt, Susan Taylor
Rev.: Emanuel Hahn

Specifications: Same as 1999P issue

DATE	DESCRIPTION	MINTAGE	MS-64 C	MS-65 C	MS-66 C	MS-65 NC	MS-66 NC	MS-67 NC	SP-66	SP-67
2009		20,446,000	10.	15.	25.	5.	20.	50.	10.	20.
2010		28,827,000	10.	15.	25.	5.	20.	50.	10.	25.

UNCROWNED PORTRAIT, REMEMBRANCE DAY POPPIES, MULTI-PLY PLATED STEEL, RCM LOGO, 2010.

Designers and Engravers:
Obv.: Susanna Blunt, Susan Taylor
Rev.: Cosme Saffioti, Stan Witten

Specifications: Same as 1999P issue; Colourised

DATE	DESCRIPTION	MINTAGE	MS-64 C	MS-65 C	MS-66 C	MS-65 NC	MS-66 NC	MS-67 NC	SP-66	SP-67
2010	Remembrance Day	10,978,000	10.	15.	25.	5.	20.	50.	10.	25.

UNCROWNED PORTRAIT, CARIBOU DESIGN, MULTI-PLY PLATED STEEL, RCM LOGO, 2011-2014.

With the cessation in 2011 of the brilliant uncirculated finish (MS-65-NC) on coins contained in the uncirculated sets, it was necessary to remove that block of grades from the pricing tables.

Designers and Engravers:
Obv.: Susanna Blunt, Susan Taylor
Rev.: Emanuel Hahn

Specifications: Same as 1999P issue

DATE	DESCRIPTION	MINTAGE	MS-64 C	MS-65 C	MS-66 C	MS-67 C	SP-66	SP-67
2011		187,520,000	10.	15.	20.	50.	10.	25.
2012		153,450,000	10.	20.	35.	75.	10.	25.
2013		68,480,000	10.	20.	35.	55.	10.	35.
2014		N/A	10.	20.	35.	60.	10.	35.

NOTES ON TWENTY-FIVE CENT COINS

When the pricing table lists Specimen finishes (SP-66 and SP-67) the prices are for those coins which have been removed from Specimen Sets and certified by a Canadian grading company.

UNCROWNED PORTRAIT, OUR LEGENDARY NATURE: CANADIAN CONSERVATION SUCCESSES, MULTI-PLY PLATED STEEL, 2011.

These coins were issued to commemorate three specie brought back from near extinction by Canadian Conservation methods.

Common Obv.

Wood Bison

Wood Bison Colourised

Designers and Engravers:
Obv.: Susanna Blunt, Susan Taylor
Rev.: RCM Staff

Specifications:
Same as 1999P issue, Colourised

Orca Whale

Orca Whale Colourised'

Peregrine Falcon

Peregrine Falcon Colourised

DATE	DESCRIPTION	MINTAGE	MS-64 C	MS-65 C	MS-66 C	MS-67 C	SP-66	SP-67
2011	Wood Bison	12,500,000	10.	20.	30.	—	*	*
2011	Wood Bison, Colourised	Included	10.	25.	50.	—	*	*
2011	Orca Whale	450,000	10.	20.	30.	—	*	*
2011	Orca Whale, Colourised	Included	10.	25.	50.	—	*	*
2011	Peregrine Falcon	12,500,000	10.	20.	30.	—	*	*
2011	Peregrine Falcon, Colourised	Included	10.	25.	50.	—	*	*

UNCROWNED PORTRAIT, THE HEROES OF 1812, MULTI-PLY PLATED STEEL, 2012-2013.

These twenty-five cent coins were issued to commemorate the heroes of the War of 1812: Tecumseh, Brock, de Salaberry and Secord

Common Obv.

Tecumseh

Tecumseh Colourised

Engraver: Nick Martin

Designers and Engravers:

Obv.: Susanna Blunt, Susan Taylor
Rev.: Bonnie Ross, See reverse image

Specifications:

Standard: Multi-ply plated steel as 1999 issue
Colourised: Red maple leaf

Sir Isaac Brock

Sir Isaac Brock Colourised

Engraver: Matt Bowen

Charles-Michel de Salaberry

Charles-Michel de Salaberry Colourised

Engraver: Steven Stewart

Laura Secord

Laura Secord Colourised

Engraver: Samantha Strath

DATE	DESCRIPTION	MINTAGE	MS-64 C	MS-65 C	MS-66 C	MS-67 C	SP-66	SP-67
2012	Tecumseh	12,500,000	10.	30.	35.	70.	*	*
2012	Tecumseh, Colourised	Included	10.	20.	40.	150.	*	*
2012	Sir Isaac Brock	12,500,000	10.	20.	35.	65.	*	*
2012	Sir Isaac Brock, Colourised	Included	10.	25.	35.	100.	*	*
2013	Charles-Michel de Salaberry	12,500,000	10.	20.	25.	70.	*	*
2013	Charles-Michel de Salaberry, Colourised	Included	10.	20.	25.	—	*	*
2013	Laura Secord	12,500,000	10.	25.	40.	—	*	*
2013	Laura Secord, Colourised	Included	10.	30.	40.	150.	*	*

UNCROWNED PORTRAIT, 100TH ANNIVERSARY OF THE FIRST ARCTIC EXPEDITION, 1913-2013.

In 1913 and international crew of scientists, sailors, guides and crewmen called the Canadian Arctic Expedition (CAE) set sail on a remarkable voyage of discovery in Canada's high Arctic.

Common Obv.

Finish A Clothes of Crew Frosted

Finish B Compass Ring Frosted

Designers and Engravers:
Obv.: Susanna Blunt, Susan Taylor
Rev.: Bonnie Ross, RCM Staff

Specifications: Same as 1999P issue, Colourised

Finish: A: Circulation, Clothes of crew frosted
B: Circulation, Compass ring frosted

DATE	DESCRIPTION	MINTAGE	MS-64 C	MS-65 C	MS-66 C	MS-67 C	SP-66	SP-67
2013	Can. Arctic Expedition, Finish A	6,250,000	10.	15.	20.	100.	*	*
2013	Can. Arctic Expedition, Finish B	6,250,000	10.	15.	20.	100.	*	*

UNCROWNED PORTRAIT, CELEBRATION OF LIFE IN THE NORTH THROUGH ARCTIC SYMBOLS, 2013.

This commemorative coin tells many stories of life in the Canadian north, from the beluga and bowhead whales, to kayaks and umiaks, and the pattern of an igloo's snow blocks.

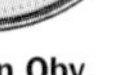
Common Obv.

Finish A Fin, Belly and Tail of Bowhead Whale Frosted

Finish B Two Beluga Whales Frosted

Designers and Engravers:
Obv.: Susanna Blunt, Susan Taylor
Rev.: Tim Pitsiulak, RCM Staff

Specifications:
Same as 1999P issue, Colourised

Finish: A: Circulation, Fin, belly and tail of bowhead whale frosted
B: Circulation, Two belugas whales frosted

DATE	DESCRIPTION	MINTAGE	MS-64 C	MS-65 C	MS-66 C	MS-67 C	SP-66	SP-67
2013	Arctic Symbols, Finish A	6,250,000	10.	15.	20.	100.	*	*
2013	Arctic Symbols, Finish B	6,250,000	10.	15.	20.	100.	*	*

VICTORIA FIFTY CENT MAJOR OBVERSE VARIETIES

Victoria Portrait Variety OH1

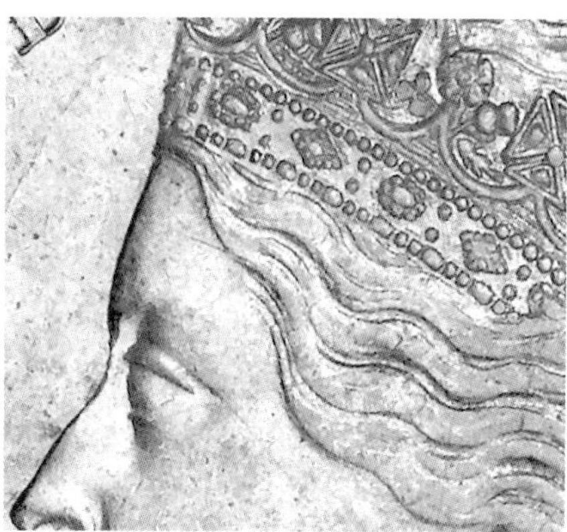

Crown, hair and eye detail

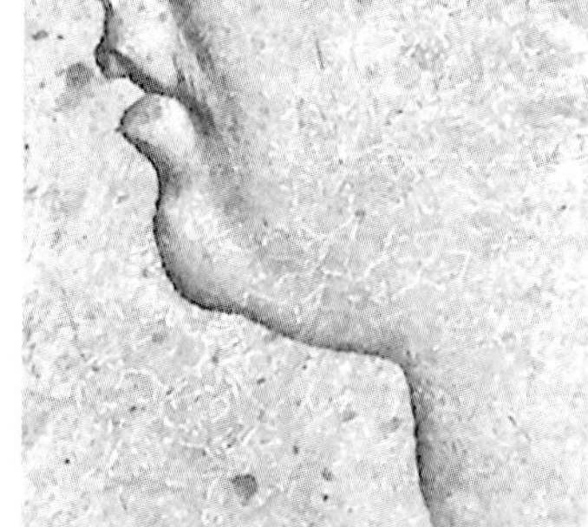

Lips and chin detail

Ribbon detail

OH1 **Crown, hair and eye detail:** The hair between the brow and crown is composed of one thick strand. The upper eyelid is straight. The upper and lower eyelids do not meet at the corner of the eye. There is no shamrock behind first jewel of crown.

Lips and chin detail: A thin upper lip has a slight curl and curves outward. A large crease line extends down from the corner of the mouth. The chin has slight doubling.

Ribbon detail: The right ribbon end "V" is off centre, to the left. The ribbon bow is well formed, with only a small space between it and the right ribbon

Dates: Portrait OH1 is currently known on the following date: 1870 No LCW.

Victoria Portrait Variety OH2

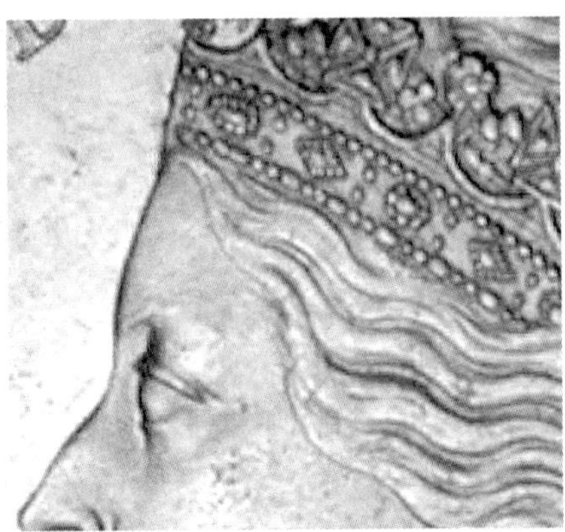

Crown, hair and eye detail

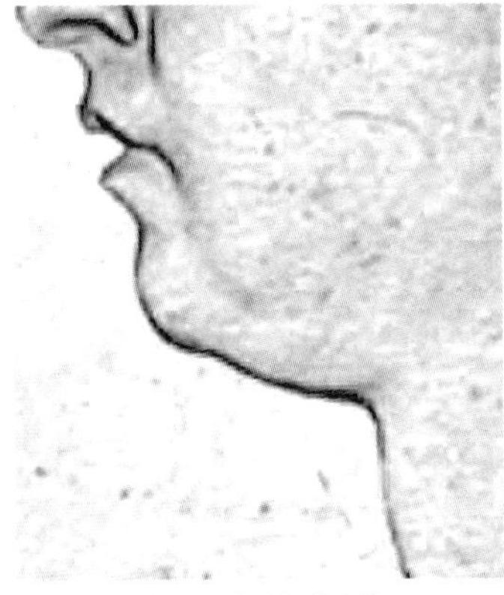

Lips and chin detail

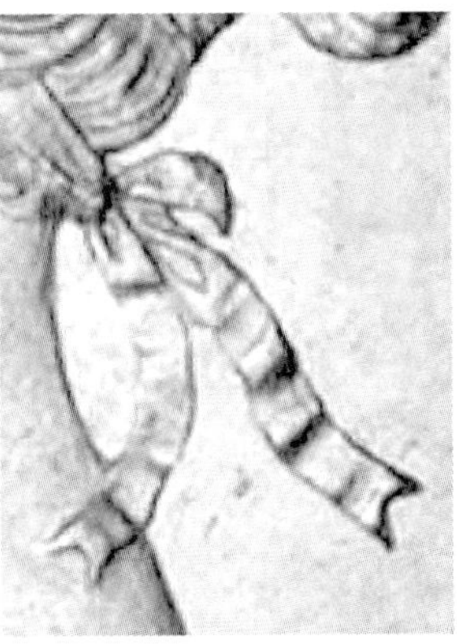

Ribbon detail

OH2 Crown, hair and eye detail: The hairline between the brow and crown is composed of one medium-sized strand. The upper eyelid is thin and straight. It does not join the lower lid at the corner of the eye. There is a shamrock behind the first jewel of the crown.

Lips and chin detail: The upper lip has a slight curl and curves outward. The crease line at the corner of the mouth is short. The chin has slight doubling.

Ribbon detail: The right ribbon end "V" is split in the middle with the left point being longer. The ribbon bow is poorly formed creating a gap between it and the right ribbon.

Dates: Portrait OH2 is currently known on the following dates: 1870 LCW, 1871, 1871H, 1872H and 1888.

Victoria Portrait Variety OH3

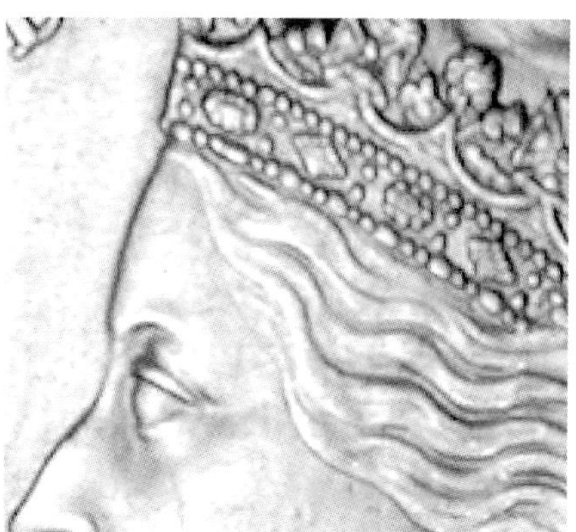
Crown, hair and eye detail

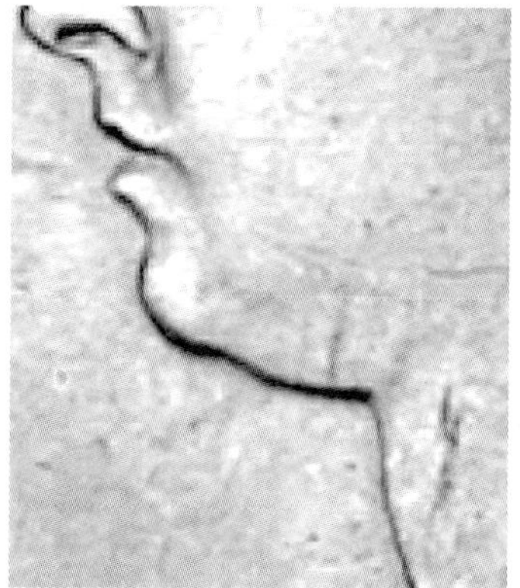
Lips and chin detail

Ribbon detail

OH3 **Crown, hair and eye detail:** The hairline between the brow and crown consists of one strand. There is a shamrock behind the first jewel of the crown. The upper eyelid is straight and thick, joining the lower lid at the corner of the eye.

Lips and chin detail: The upper lip falls straight down from the nostril to an ill-formed upper lip. There is no crease line at the corner of the mouth. There is slight doubling of the chin. There is a small space between a poorly formed bow and ribbon at the nape of the neck.

Ribbon detail: The coin illustrated is an 1881H with the left ribbon re-engraved variety. There is a slight gap between the poorly defined bow and the right ribbon. The right ribbon end has a lazy "U" shape with equal arms.

Dates: Portrait OH3 is currently known on the following dates: 1881H, 1888 and 1892.

Victoria Portrait Variety OH4

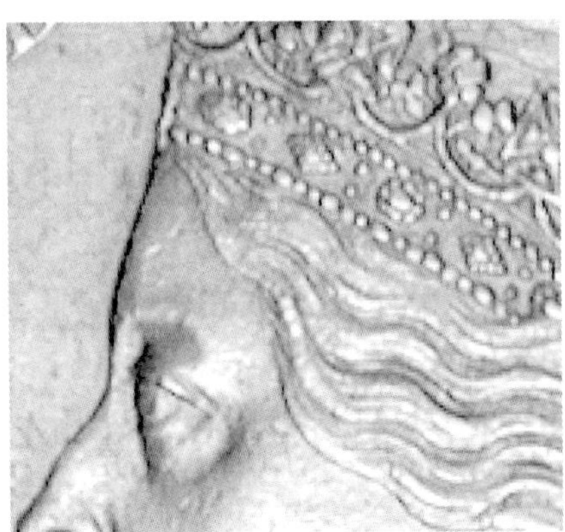

Crown, hair and eye detail

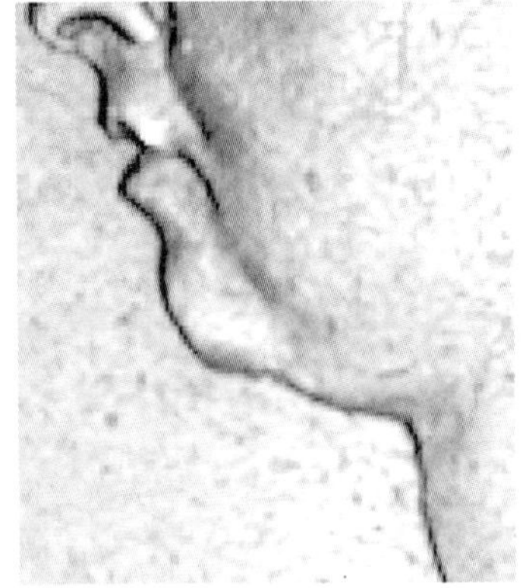

Lips and chin detail

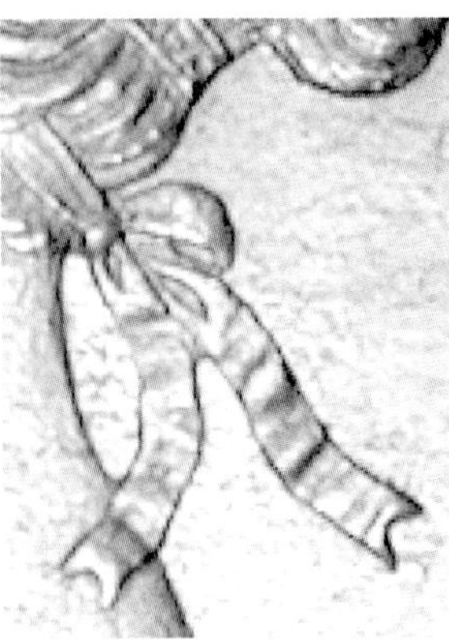

Ribbon detail

OH4 Crown, hair and eye detail: The hairline between the brow and crown is composed of one thin strand. The upper eyelid is straight and thin and joins the lower lid at the corner of the eye. There is a shamrock behind first jewel of crown.

Lips and chin detail: The upper lip has a slight curl and curves outward. There is a large crease line at the corner of the mouth that extends down to form a puffy cheek. There is a slight doubling of the chin.

Ribbon detail: The right ribbon end is in the shape of a "U" with the left side being longer. There is no space between a well defined bow and the right ribbon.

Dates: Portrait OH4 is currently known on the following dates: 1888, 1890H, 1892, 1894, 1898, 1899, 1900 and 1901.

VICTORIA FIFTY CENT MAJOR REVERSE VARIETIES

Victoria Reverse Varieties

Currently only one reverse matrix has been identified. In subsequent years modifications were made to the boughs and various leaves, but never sufficient change to merit a separate major variety classification. In the enlarged illustrations below are three different reverses (1870, 1892 and 1901) showing very little design change between the years. The bow, which is dimpled on the left side of the 1870 issue, carries through to the 1901 issue. The date digits vary resulting in spacing varieties.

It is estimated that a total of 30 working dies were needed to strike the 50-cent coins between 1870 and 1901.

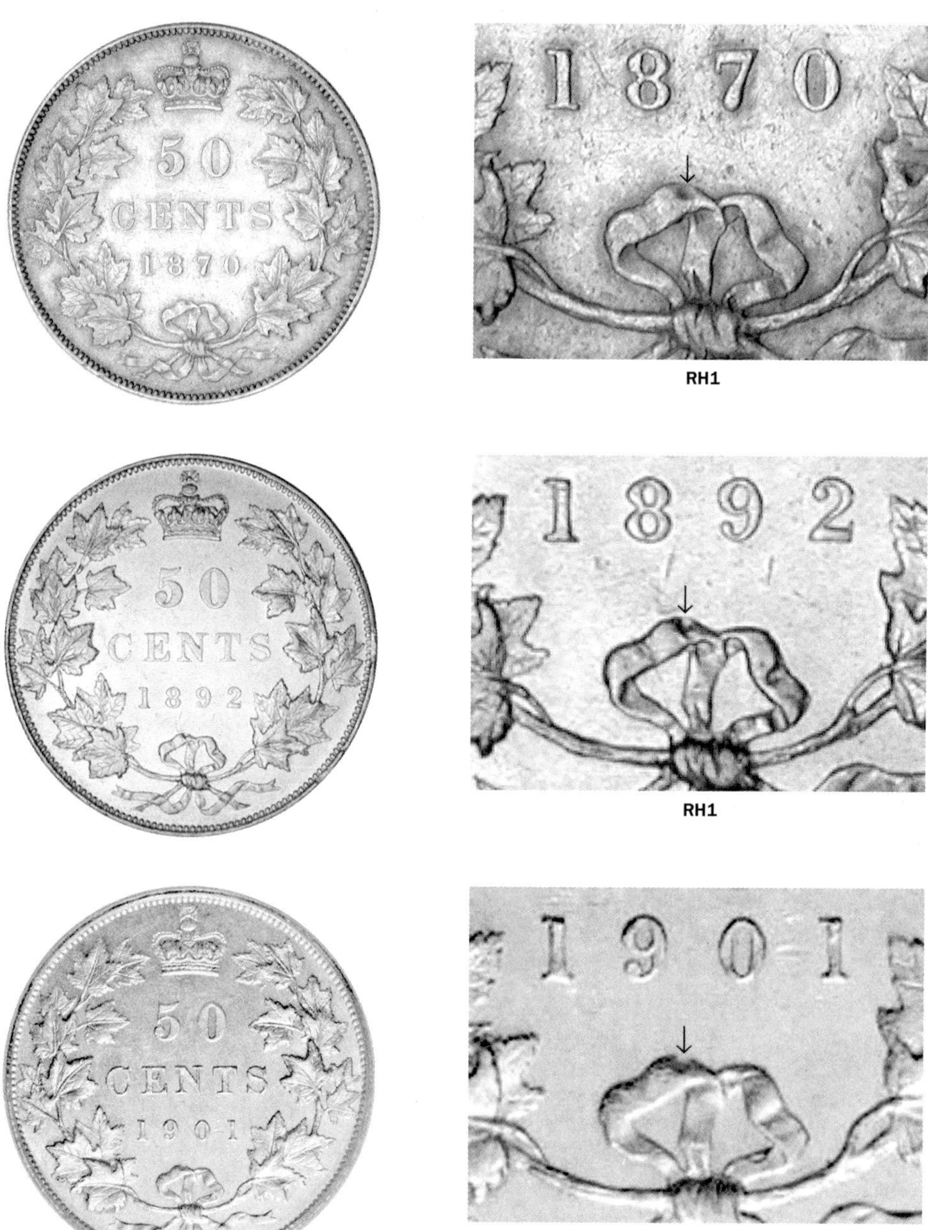

RH1

RH1

RH1

FIFTY CENTS
VICTORIA 1870 - 1901

Since the Province of Canada did not issue this denomination, new coinage tools had to be produced when the Dominion placed its first order for coins. For the obverse L.C. Wyon used the same portrait model as he did for the 25-cents: a crowned effigy of Victoria based on a model by William Theed. The reverse featured the St. Edward's crown atop crossed boughs of sweet maple, tied at the bottom by a ribbon.

Designer and Engraver: Leonard C. Wyon
Composition: .925 silver, .075 copper
Weight: 11.62 grams
Diameter: 29.72 mm
Edge: Reeded
Die Axes: ↑↓

DIADEMED PORTRAIT, MAPLE WREATH DESIGN, 1870.

DATE / PORTRAIT / VARIETY	MINTAGE (thous.)	G-4	VG-8	F-12	VF-20	EF-40	AU-50	AU-55	MS-60	MS-63	MS-65	SP-63	SP-65
1870 H1 No LCW	450	1,000.	1,750.	2,750.	3,800.	8,000.	13,500.	25,000.	40,000.	60,000.	—	*	*
1870 H1 No LCW (PE)	Incl.	*	*	*	*	*	*	*	*	*	*	25,000.	45,000.
1870 H2 LCW	Incl.	50.	90.	150.	250.	550.	1,100.	1,800.	5,000.	15,000.	—	15,000.	45,000.
1870 H2 LCW (PE)	Incl.	*	*	*	*	*	*	*	*	*	*	12,000.	40,000.

1871 Obverse Doubled Die DEI GRATIA

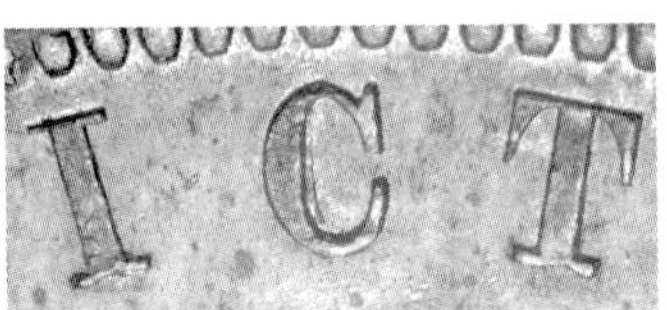

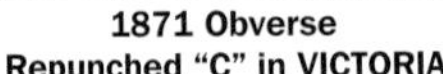

1871 Obverse
Repunched "C" in VICTORIA

Repunched "C"

DIADEMED PORTRAIT, MODIFIED MAPLE WREATH DESIGN, 1871.

DATE / PORTRAIT/VAR.	MINTAGE (thous.)	G-4	VG-8	F-12	VF-20	EF-40	AU-50	AU-55	MS-60	MS-63	MS-65	SP-63	SP-65
1871 H2	200,000	70.	150.	225.	600.	900.	2,250.	3,500.	7,500.	10,000.	—	20,000.	50,000.
1871 H2 DD	Included	65.	135.	300.	675.	1,500.	—	—	—	—	—	*	*
1871 H2 C/C	Included	65.	135.	300.	675.	1,500.	—	—	—	—	—	*	*
1871H H2	45,000	90.	175.	350.	700.	1,500.	3,000.	4,500.	—	—	—	20,000.	50,000.

DIADEMED PORTRAIT, MODIFIED MAPLE WREATH DESIGN, 1872.

1872H Cross bar V in VICTORIA

VICTORIA

Obverse Variety 1872H

Cross bar "V" in VICTORIA (see below)

CANADA

Obverse Variety 1872H

Repunched "N" and last "A" in CANADA [1]

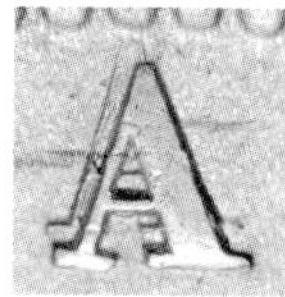

REGINA

Obverse Variety 1872H

Repunched "A" in REGINA [2]

1872

Reverse Variety 1872H

Repunched 2 (2/2)

The font style and size for the legends would have been selected by Wyon, with the letter punches ordered from a type foundry.

The sinking of the matrix was carried out in London under the supervision of Wyon. The subsequent punches and dies were also created in London, with the dies being shipped to Heaton & Sons Ltd, Birmingham for striking.

It is a matter of record that the Royal Mint, London, refurbished hundreds of worn dies during the 1870s. It is not unreasonable to assume that Heaton did the same. The refurbishing (softening, repair and hardening) of the dies would require letter punches identical to those used at the Royal Mint. However, the circumstances under which the punches were used was not identical. The punches at Heaton were required to repair work hardened steel dies, even after annealing. Maybe the letter V punch at Heaton required a small special type of reinforcing bar between the arms. The crossbar joining the arms of the "V" is narrow and sits beneath the level of the arms, while in the "A" the crossbar is much thicker and is level with the arms.

DATE / PORTRAIT/VAR.	MINTAGE (thous.)	G-4	VG-8	F-12	VF-20	EF-40	AU-50	AU-55	MS-60	MS-63	MS-65	SP-63	SP-65
1872H H2	80,000	35.	70.	125.	350.	700.	1,500.	2,500.	5,000.	15,000.	25,000.	12,500.	35,000.
1872H H2 Bar	Included	275.	500.	1,200.	1,700.	5,000.	10,000.	—	—	—	—	*	*
1872H H2 A/A-1	Included	75.	175.	250.	400.	800.	1,600.	—	—	—	—	*	*
1872H H2 A/A-2	Included	75.	175.	250.	400.	800.	1,600.	—	—	—	—	*	*
1872H H2 2/2	Included	80.	175.	275.	400.	800.	1,600.	—	—	—	—	*	*

DIADEMED PORTRAIT, MODIFIED MAPLE WREATH DESIGN, 1881-1901.

Reverse Variety

1899 Large 9 (L9)

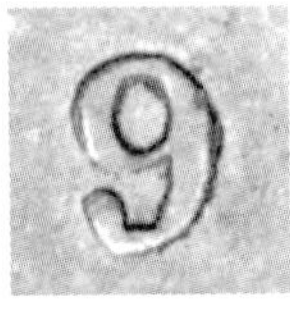

Reverse Variety

1899 Small 9 (S9)

DATE / PORTRAIT/VAR.	MINTAGE (thous.)	G-4	VG-8	F-12	VF-20	EF-40	AU-50	AU-55	MS-60	MS-63	MS-65	SP-63	SP-65
1881H H3	150,000	70.	100.	175.	400.	850.	2,000.	3,250.	7,500.	15,000.	30,000.	10,000.	25,000.
1888 H2	60,000	275.	650.	1,200.	1,800.	3,500.	6,000.	9,000.	—	—	—	20,000.	50,000.
1888 H3	Included	200.	450.	650.	1,400.	2,500.	4,000.	6,500.	12,500.	25,000.	—	*	*
1888 H4	Included	500.	1,000.	2,000.	—	—	—	—	—	—	—	*	*
1890H H3	20,000	NO CERTIFIED EXAMPLES KNOWN										*	*
1890H H4	Included	1,000.	2,400.	4,000.	6,000.	10,000.	15,000.	—	—	—	—	*	*
1892 H3	151,000	600.	1,200.	1,800.	—	—	—	—	—	—	—	*	*
1892 H4	Included	70.	125.	250.	525.	1,100.	3,000.	—	—	—	—	*	*
1894 H4	29,036	375.	650.	1,250.	2,250.	4,000.	8,000.	12,000.	18,000.	—	—	*	*
1898 H4	100,000	60.	150.	250.	500.	1,250.	3,250.	6,000.	—	—	—	*	*
1899 H4 L9	50,000	150.	350.	600.	1,200.	2,500.	5,000.	—	—	—	—	*	*
1899 H4 S9	Included	150.	350.	700.	1,300.	2,500.	5,000.	—	—	—	—	*	*
1900 H4	118,000	50.	90.	200.	375.	775.	2,000.	3,000.	6,000.	15,000.	—	*	*
1901 H4	80,000	70.	150.	250.	450.	1,000.	2,250.	3,500.	7,500.	—	—	*	*

FIFTY CENTS
EDWARD VII 1902 - 1910

A new obverse portrait design was engraved by DeSaulles and used from 1902-1910. The reverse of the Edward VII 50-cents followed the same design as the lower silver denominations: the word "CANADA" was made part of the legend, moved from it's former position at the bottom of the obverse, and the Imperial State crown replaced the St. Edward's crown. The first reverse used the Victorian maple wreath from 1902 to 1910, but the tools were modified by Blakemore in 1910 to accommodate the Royal Canadian Mint.

IMPERIAL CROWNED PORTRAIT, MAPLE WREATH DESIGN, 1902-1910.

Because the Victorian Leaves variety 50-cent pieces being coined at the Ottawa Mint had almost no rim, it was requested that the parent Royal Mint in London make new reverse tools. In addition to a wider rim the new variety (Edwardian Leaves reverse) had several altered leaves and a different cross atop the crown. The most noticeable difference affects two outside leaves at the right side of the date. On the Victorian Leaves reverse these leaves have long points which nearly touch the denticles, but on the Edwardian Leaves reverse these leaves have shorter, more curved points farther from the denticles.

The Birmingham Mint Ltd. issue of 1903 has an "H" mint mark on the reverse under the wreath. Royal Mint issues (1902-1907) and Royal Canadian Mint issues (1908-1910) have no mint mark.

"H" Mint Mark

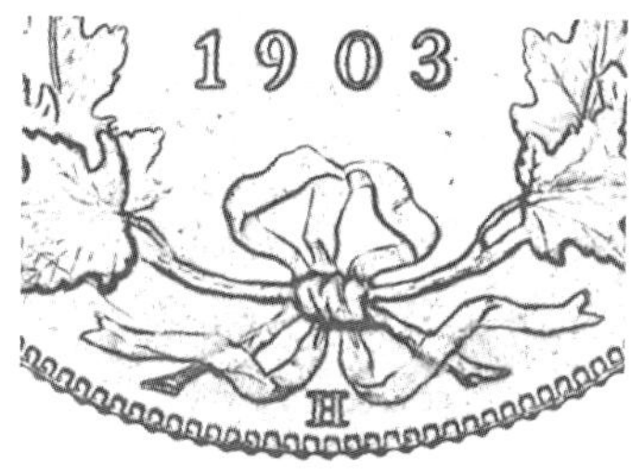

Designers and Engravers:
Obv.: G. W. DeSaulles
Rev.: L. C. Wyon

Engraver:
Victorian Leaves Reverse: G. W. DeSaulles
Edwardian Leaves Reverse: W. H. J. Blakemore

Composition: .925 silver, .075 copper

Weight:
Victorian Leaves, 1902-1910: 11.62 grams
Edwardian Leaves, 1910: 11.66 grams

Diameter: 29.72 mm

Thickness: 2.0 mm

Edge: Reeded

Die Axes:
1902-1907: ↑↓
1908-1910: ↑↑

REVERSE VARIETIES

1902-1910 Victorian Leaves (VL) Reverse

1910 Edwardian Leaves (EL) Reverse

DATE / VARIETY	MINTAGE	VG-8	F-12	VF-20	EF-40	AU-50	AU-55	MS-60	MS-63	MS-64	MS-65	SP-63	SP-65
1902	120,000	45.	85.	200.	475.	850.	1,250.	1,500.	3,000.	6,000.	8,000.	*	*
1903H	140,000	60.	125.	325.	675.	950.	1,200.	2,000.	6,500.	10,000.	—	*	*
1904	60,000	250.	500.	800.	1,500.	2,500.	3,500.	4,500.	15,000.	20,000.	30,000.	*	*
1905	40,000	300.	600.	1,200.	2,000.	4,000.	6,000.	9,000.	—	—	—	40,000.	60,000.
1906	350,000	40.	50.	175.	500.	850.	1,200.	1,800.	4,500.	8,000.	—	*	*
1907	300,000	40.	70.	150.	500.	700.	1,200.	2,000.	4,500.	7,000.	—	*	*
1908	128,119	60.	150.	325.	700.	1,200.	1,500.	1,800.	3,000.	4,000.	5,000.	1,000.	2,000.
1909	203,118	40.	125.	375.	750.	1,500.	2,250.	3,000.	7,000.	10,000.	—	*	*
1910 VL	649,521	55.	80.	175.	600.	1,200.	2,000.	2,500.	7,500.	—	—	*	*
1910 EL	Included	35.	40.	115.	450.	700.	1,200.	2,000.	6,000.	—	—	*	*

FIFTY CENTS
GEORGE V 1911 - 1936

IMPERIAL CROWNED PORTRAIT, MAPLE WREATH DESIGN, 1911-1936.

Public outcry greeted the new George V coins issued in 1911 because the obverse legend lacked reference to the King's ruling "by the grace of God."

The coinage tools were modified during the year and a new legend containing the Latin abbreviation "DEI GRA:" appeared on the 1912 and subsequent issues. The reverse was a continuation of the Edwardian Leaves variety of the previous reign. In 1920, 144,200 fifty-cent pieces of .925 silver were melted. It is believed they were all dated 1919.

1920 Narrow Date (NO)

1920 Wide Date (WO)

Designers and Engravers:
Obv,: Sir E. B. MacKennal
Rev.: L. C. Wyon, W. H. J. Blakemore
Composition:
1911-1919: .925 silver, .075 copper
1920-1936: .800 silver, .200 copper
Weight: 11.66 grams
Diameter: 29.72 mm
Thickness: 2.0 mm
Edge: Reeded
Die Axes: ↑↑

DATE VARIETY	MINTAGE	VG-8	F-12	VF-20	EF-40	AU-50	AU-55	MS-60	MS-63	MS-64	MS-65	SP-63	SP-65
1911	209,972	50.	150.	425.	825.	1,100.	1,800.	2,500.	4,000.	7,000.	12,000.	2,000.	5,000.
1912	285,867	30.	45.	175.	475.	850.	1,300.	1,800.	4,000.	8,000.	12,000.	*	*
1913	265,889	25.	40.	200.	375.	850.	1,250.	2,000.	6,000.	13,000.	—	*	*
1914	160,128	60.	115.	350.	800.	1,800.	2,500.	4,500.	9,000.	—	—	*	*
1916	459,070	30.	40.	100.	275.	500.	700.	1,100.	2,500.	5,500.	—	*	*
1917	752,213	30.	35.	60.	175.	350.	525.	800.	1,600.	3,200.	5,500.	*	*
1918	854,989	20.	30.	60.	150.	400.	500.	700.	1,750.	3,500.	5,500.	*	*
1919	1,113,429	25.	30.	50.	145.	250.	350.	600.	1,500.	3,250.	6,500.	*	*
1920 NO	584,429	25.	35.	70.	200.	400.	550.	800.	2,000.	3,250.	5,000.	*	*
1920 WO	Included	65.	85.	150.	450.	750.	1,000.	1,500.	—	—	—	*	*

FIFTY CENTS OF 1921.

During the early and mid-1920s the demand for 50-cent pieces was very light; only 28,000 pieces were issued between 1921 and 1929. These are assumed to have been almost entirely 1920s. When a greater demand for this denomination arose later in 1929, the Master of the Ottawa Mint decided to melt the stock of 1920 and 1921 coins (amounting to some 480,392 pieces) and recoin the silver into 1929 coins. He took this decision because he feared that the public would suspect they were receiving counterfeits if a large quantity of coins with "old" dates were issued. It is believed that the 75 or so 1921s that have survived came from specimen sets sold to collectors or from circulation strikes sold to Mint visitors.

DATE	MINTAGE	VG-8	F-12	VF-20	EF-40	AU-50	AU-55	MS-60	MS-63	MS-64	MS-65	SP-63	SP-65
1921	206,398	38,000.	45,000.	60,000.	70,000.	80,000.	90,000.	—	—	—	—	75,000.	150,000.
1929	228,328	25.	35.	60.	250.	400.	575.	800.	2,000.	3,250.	5,000.	5,000.	10,000.
1931	57,581	30.	50.	115.	450.	800.	975.	1,250.	2,500.	4,000.	5,500.	6,500.	15,000.
1932	19,213	200.	300.	525.	1,350.	3,500.	5,000.	7,500.	12,000.	20,000.	40,000.	7,000.	15,000.
1934	39,539	50.	65.	125.	450.	750.	1,000.	1,250.	2,000.	4,250.	5,000.	6,000.	15,000.
1936	38,550	50.	70.	150.	400.	575.	750.	1,000.	1,375.	3,000.	4,500.	8,000.	25,000.

Note: Only three 1921 fifty cent pieces in the Mint State grades are known to exist.

FIFTY CENTS
GEORGE VI 1937 - 1952

UNCROWNED PORTRAIT, 'ET IND:IMP:', COAT OF ARMS DESIGN, 1937-1947.

A stylized Canadian coat of arms designed by George Edward Kruger-Gray was selected for the George VI 50-cent piece, first issued in 1937. The initial obverse bore a legend containing an abbreviation for the Latin phrase, "ET INDIAE IMPERATOR," meaning "and Emperor of India," denoting that the King was emperor of that vast country.

Designer and Engraver:
Obv.: T.H. Paget
Rev.: G.E. Kruger-Gray
Composition: .800 silver, .200 copper
Weight: 11.66 grams
Diameter: 29.72 mm
Thickness: 2.00 mm
Edge: Reeded
Die Axes: ↑↑

DATE / VARIETY	MINTAGE	VF-20	EF-40	AU-50	AU-55	MS-60	MS-63	MS-64	MS-65	MS-66	SP-63	SP-65
1937	192,016	20.	30.	35.	55.	70.	100.	225.	1,800.	—	150.	300.
1937 Matte	Included	*	*	*	*	*	*	*	*	*	100.	225.
1938	192,018	30.	60.	90.	110.	200.	575.	1,600.	5,500.	—	3,500.	7,000.
1939	287,976	20.	45.	65.	100.	115.	300.	550.	2,100.	—	*	*
1940	1,996,566	15.	18.	25.	35.	50.	90.	175.	1,000.	2,500.	*	*

VARIETIES OF 1941 and 1942.

The matrices which arrived from the Royal Mint, London, carried the full date for the years 1937, 1938, 1939 and 1940. No spacing varieties have been found for these years. From 1941 on many hundreds of major and minor varieties exist. The easiest varieties to identify are the narrow and wide dates, and those are listed. Please be aware that within the narrow and wide date categories there are variations and that the example illustrated is just that, an example.

1941 Narrow date (ND)

1942 Narrow date (ND)

1941 Wide date (WD)

1942 Wide date (WD)

DATE / VARIETY	MINTAGE	VF-20	EF-40	AU-50	AU-55	MS-60	MS-63	MS-64	MS-65	MS-66	SP-63	SP-65
1941 ND	1,714,874	15.	18.	25.	40.	50.	95.	225.	2,000.	—	*	*
1941 WD	Included	20.	25.	30.	45.	60.	110.	250.	2,000.	—	*	*
1942 ND	1,974,165	15.	20.	30.	35.	45.	110.	225.	1,500.	—	3,000.	5,000.
1942 WD	Included	20.	25.	35.	40.	50.	120.	250.	1,600.	—	*	*

VARIETIES OF 1943, 1945 and 1946.

The previously listed and certified varieties of 1943 and 1944, the Near and Far 3, and the Near and Far 4, correspond to the new listings in the following manner: 1943 Near 3 is 1943 ND, 1943 Far 3 is 1943 WD, 1944 Near 4 is 1944 ND and 1944 Far 4 is 1944 WD.

1943 Narrow date (ND-Near 3)

1943 Wide date (WD-Far 3)

1943 Wide date (WD) 3/3 (Far 3)

1944 Narrow date (ND-Near 4)

1944 Wide date (WD-Far 4)

1944 Wide date (WD) Last 4/4/4 (Far 4)

1945 Narrow date (ND), Pointed 5/5

1945 Wide date (WD), Pointed 5/5

1945 Wide date (WD) Blunt 5

DATE / VARIETY	MINTAGE	VF-20	EF-40	AU-50	AU-55	MS-60	MS-63	MS-64	MS-65	MS-66	SP-63	SP-65
1943 ND	3,109,583	15.	20.	30.	40.	50.	100.	300.	1,500.	—	*	*
1943 WD	Included	15.	20.	30.	45.	60.	120.	325.	1,500.	—	*	*
1943 WD 3/3	Included	40.	50.	75.	125.	200.	300.	400.	—	—	*	*
1944 ND	2,460,205	15.	18.	30.	35.	45.	90.	250.	1,500.	—	3,000.	10,000.
1944 WD	Included	30.	35.	40.	45.	60.	100.	350.	1,250.	—	*	*
1944 WD 4/4/4	Included	35.	40.	45.	60.	75.	125.	—	—	—	*	*
1945 ND	1,959,528	15.	25.	30.	45.	70.	130.	275.	3,000.	—	1,000.	3,000.
1945 WD	Included	15.	25.	30.	40.	65.	125.	350.	3,000.	—	*	*
1945 WD BL5	Included	25.	35.	40.	50.	85.	150.	400.	—	—	*	*

NOTES ON GEORGE VI FIFTY CENT COINS

1941	In the narrow date the 1 is close to the 4. In the wide date the 1 is far from the 4.
1942	In the narrow date the 4 is very close to the 9. In the wide date there is separation between the 9 and 4.
1943	In the narrow date the 3 is very close to the 4. In the wide date the 3 is far from the 4.
1944	In the narrow date the two 4s touch. In the wide date the 4s are separate.
1945	In the narrow date the 5 is far from the ring. In the wide date the 5 is close to the ring.
1946	In the narrow date the 6 is far from the ring. In the wide date the 6 is very close to the ring.

1946 Narrow date (ND)

Hoof through 6

1946 Wide date (WD)

DATE / VARIETY	MINTAGE	VF-20	EF-40	AU-50	AU-55	MS-60	MS-63	MS-64	MS-65	MS-66	SP-63	SP-65
1946 ND	950,235	35.	45.	70.	80.	100.	175.	325.	4,000.	—	900.	4,000
1946 ND H6	Included	70.	150.	600.	1,100.	1,600.	3,500.	5,000.	—	—	*	*
1946 WD	Included	35.	45.	70.	80.	100.	175.	350.	3,500.	—	*	*

VARIETIES OF 1947.

There are two styles of 7 for the 1947 issue. The first is a tall figure with a tail curving to the left at the bottom (Straight 7), similar to that on the 1937 issue. The second (Curved 7) has a bottom that curves to the right.

With the granting of independence to India, the Royal Canadian Mint was faced with a dilemma in early 1948. The new obverse coinage tools with the Latin abbreviation "ET IND: IMP" omitted would not arrive for several months, yet there was a great need for all denominations of coins. The Mint satisfied the demand by striking coins dated 1947 and bearing an obverse with outmoded titles. To differentiate this issue from the regular strikings of 1947, a tiny maple leaf was placed after the date. Both styles of 7 (see below) were employed for the Maple Leaf coinage.

1947 Straight 7, Narrow date (S7 ND)

1947 Curved 7, Narrow date (C7 ND)

1947 Maple Leaf, Straight 7/7/7 (ML S7)

1947 Straight 7/7, Wide date (S7 WD)

1947 Curved 7, Wide date (C7 WD)

1947 Maple Leaf, Curved 7 (ML C7)

DATE / VARIETY	MINTAGE	VF-20	EF-40	AU-50	AU-55	MS-60	MS-63	MS-64	MS-65	MS-66	SP-63	SP-65
1947 S7 ND	424,885	25.	40.	60.	85.	125.	275.	700.	—	—	900.	4,000.
1947 S7 WD	Included	25.	45.	65.	90.	150.	350.	800.	—	—	*	*
1947 C7 ND	Included	25.	45.	85.	100.	125.	425.	1,300.	3,500.	—	*	*
1947 C7 WD	Included	30.	50.	100.	125.	150.	450.	1,400.	—	—	*	*
1947 ML S7/7/7	38,433	70.	125.	165.	225.	350.	500.	925.	5,000.	—	*	*
1947 ML C7	Included	3,000.	4,000.	5,000.	6,000.	10,000.	20,000.	—	—	—	4,000.	7,000.

NOTES ON GEORGE VI FIFTY CENT COINS

1947 S7	In the narrow date the 7 is close to the ring and rim denticles. In the wide date the 7 is very close to the ring, but far from the rim denticles.
1947 C7	In the narrow date the 7 is far from the ring. In the wide date the 7 is very close to the ring.
1947 ML S7	Only one die has been identified.
1947 ML C7	Only one die has been identified.

UNCROWNED PORTRAIT, 'DEI GRATIA', COAT OF ARMS DESIGN, 1948-1952.

In 1948, following the arrival of the master tools with the new obverse legend, production of the 1947 Maple Leaf coinage was terminated. For the remainder of the year coins were produced with the new obverse and reverse dies for 1948.

The 1948 concave (CV) specimen coinage is the result of a positive die radius. The 1948 convex (CX) specimen coinage is the result of a negative die radius.

Designers, Engravers and Specifications:
Same as 1937 issue

VARIETIES OF 1948 and 1949.

1948 Narrow date (ND) (Low 4/4)

1948 Wide date (WD) (High 4)

1949 Narrow date (ND)

1949 Wide date (WD) (9/9)

1949 Wide date Hoof over 9/9 (H/9)

1949 H/9/9 Wide date Hoof over 9/9 (H/9)

DATE / VARIETY	MINTAGE	VF-20	EF-40	AU-50	AU-55	MS-60	MS-63	MS-64	MS-65	MS-66	SP-63	SP-65
1948 ND	37,784	175.	225.	275.	325.	400.	550.	975.	2,000.	—	*	*
1948 WD	Included	200.	250.	300.	350.	450.	575.	1,200.	2,250.	—	*	*
1948 SP, CV	Included	*	*	*	*	*	*	*	*	*	1,000.	3,000.
1948 SP, CX	Included	*	*	*	*	*	*	*	*	*	1,000.	3,000.
1949 ND	858,991	20.	22.	25.	50.	80.	150.	300.	1,100.	3,000.	500.	1,000.
1949 WD	Included	20.	30.	35.	60.	95.	170.	325.	1,200.	—	*	*
1949 H/9/9	Included	60.	125.	275.	425.	600.	1,325.	2,500.	—	—	*	*

NOTES ON GEORGE VI FIFTY CENT COINS

1948 Only two varieties of business strikes are known, a wide and narrow date.

1949 In the narrow date the 9 does not touch the hoof. In the wide date the 9 touches the hoof. The hoof over 9/9 variety is a die break and grandfathered in to the listings.

VARIETIES OF 1950, 1951 and 1952.

1950 Full design

1950 Half design

1950 No design

1950 Full design

1950 Half design

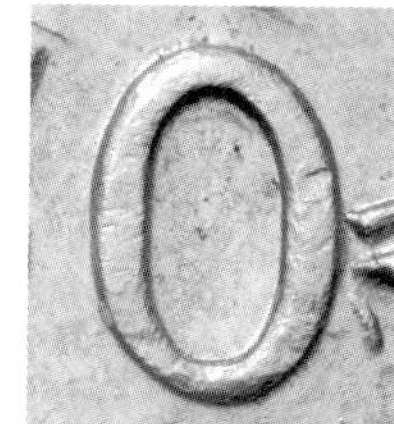

1950 No design

1951 Narrow date (ND)

1952 Narrow date (ND)

1951 Wide date (WD)

1952 Wide date (WD)

DATE / VARIETY	MINTAGE	VF-20	EF-40	AU-50	AU-55	MS-60	MS-63	MS-64	MS-65	MS-66	SP-63	SP-65
1950 F Des	2,384,179	15.	25.	30.	35.	40.	70.	150.	1,150.	—	200.	500.
1950 H Des	Included	20.	30.	35.	40.	50.	100.	200.	1,200.	—	*	*
1950 No Des	Included	35.	85.	150.	200.	275.	400.	825.	3,500.	—	*	*
1951 ND	2,421,730	20.	22.	25.	30.	35.	40.	70.	200.	—	250.	750.
1951 WD	Included	20.	22.	25.	30.	35.	40.	50.	200.	—	*	*
1952 ND	2,596,465	15.	18.	20.	22.	25.	35.	50.	150.	—	250.	750.
1952 WD	Included	15.	18.	20.	22.	30.	35.	50.	150.	—	*	*

NOTES ON GEORGE VI FIFTY CENT COINS

1950	The matrix carries the full date 1950. There are no spacing varieties, just polishing varieties.
1951 / 1952	The first three digits are fixed. The 1 or 2 digit is punched into the die. In the narrow date the 1 or 2 is close to the 5. In the wide date the 1 or 2 is far from the 5.

FIFTY CENTS
ELIZABETH II 1953 TO DATE

LAUREATE PORTRAIT, COAT OF ARMS DESIGN, 1953-1954.

During 1953 two obverse varieties were employed. Known as No Shoulder Fold and Shoulder Fold varieties (see 1-cent Elizabeth II, 1953 to date for full description), they were combined with two major reverse varieties. The No Shoulder Fold obverse was used with both Small and Large Date reverses, though only a modest quantity of the latter were struck. The Small Date reverse was carried over from George VI issues. The Shoulder Fold obverse appeared only with the Large Date reverse.

Designers and Engravers:
Obv.: Mary Gillick, Thomas Shingles
Rev.: Small Date: G. E. Kruger-Gray
Large Date: G. E. Kruger-Gray, Thomas Shingles

Composition: .800 silver, .200 copper
Weight: 11.66 grams
Diameter: 29.72 mm
Thickness: 2.00 mm
Edge: Reeded
Die Axes: ↑↑

OBVERSE VARIETIES

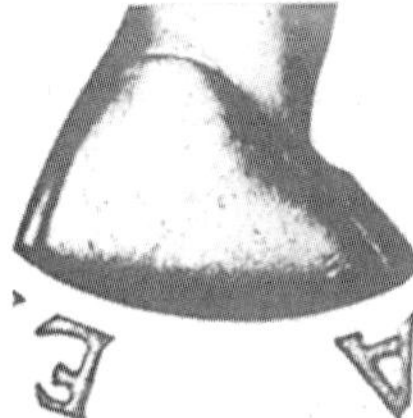

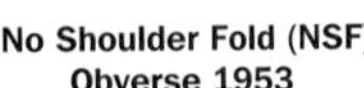

No Shoulder Fold (NSF) Obverse 1953

Letters have pronounced flaring

Shoulder Fold Obverse (SF) 1953-1964

Letters have subdued flaring

REVERSE VARIETIES

Small Date Reverse (SD) 1953

Large Date Reverse (LD) 1953-1964

DATE VARIETY	MINTAGE	EF-40	AU-50	AU-55	MS-60	MS-63	MS-64	MS-65	MS-66	PL-65	PL-65 HC	SP-65	SP-67
1953 NSF SD	1,630,429	15.	18.	20.	25.	35.	55.	250.	—	750.	850.	1,100.	2,000.
1953 NSF LD	Included	25.	45.	50.	110.	200.	625.	—	—	750.	1,000.	2,000.	3,500.
1953 SF LD	Included	15.	18.	20.	30.	75.	175.	800.	—	450.	550.	1,500.	3,000.
1954	506,305	18.	20.	25.	30.	60.	85.	325.	850.	100.	150.	*	*

NOTE ON LISTINGS

The listing sequence is obverse - reverse - edge. For example, in the classification of the 1953 fifty cents, we have obverse variety, No Shoulder Fold (NSF) first. The reverse variety follows, Small Date (SD) and, of course, there is no edge variety. The next listing is 1953 NSF, LD. Again, obverse first, reverse second, and again, no edge variety.

LAUREATE PORTRAIT, REVISED COAT OF ARMS DESIGN, 1955-1958.

Continuing difficulties with the coat of arms reverse design resulted in the introduction of a major modification in 1955. The problem was that the obverse portrait tended to draw away too much metal at the moment the coin was struck, leaving insufficient metal to bring up the design fully on the reverse. Thus, the coins sometimes showed a weakness in the design at and around the crown and top of the shield. This problem was largely solved by a new reverse with a smaller version of the coat of arms.

Designer and Engraver:
Obv.: Mary Gillick, Thomas Shingles
Rev.: Thomas Shingles
Specifications:
Same as 1953 issue

DATE VARIETY	MINTAGE	EF-40	AU-50	AU-55	MS-60	MS-63	MS-64	MS-65	MS-66	PL-65	PL-65 HC	SP-66	SP-67
1955	753,511	15.	18.	20.	25.	40.	65.	275.	—	60.	125.	*	*
1956	1,379,499	15.	18.	20.	22.	30.	55.	300.	—	45.	65.	*	*
1957	2,171,689	15.	18.	20.	22.	25.	35.	175.	—	40.	90.	*	*
1958	2,957,266	15.	18.	20.	22.	25.	35.	225.	—	40.	50.	*	*

LAUREATE PORTRAIT, MODIFIED COAT OF ARMS DESIGN, 1959-1964.

In 1959 the new Canadian coat of arms which had received government approval in 1957 was adopted for the 50-cent piece. One of the major changes compared to the previous design was the addition of a ribbon at the bottom bearing "A MARI USQUE AD MARE," meaning "from sea to sea" and making reference to the territorial extent of the country. The 1959 issue had horizontal lines in the bottom panel, indicating the colour incorrectly as blue. To indicate the correct colour, white, these lines were removed from the 1960 and subsequent issues. The obverse continued unchanged.

Designers and Engravers:
Obv.: Mary Gillick, Thomas Shingles
Rev.: Thomas Shingles
Composition: .800 silver, .200 copper
Weight: 11.66 grams
Diameter: 29.72 mm
Thickness: 2.00 mm
Edge: Reeded
Die Axes: ↑↑

DATE	MINTAGE	MS-60	MS-63	MS-64	MS-65	MS-66	PL-65	PL-65 HC	SP-66	SP-67
1959	3,095,535	20.	25.	35.	300.	750.	30.	55.	*	*
1960	3,488,897	15.	20.	25.	175.	—	20.	35.	*	*
1961	3,584,417	15.	20.	25.	150.	—	25.	35.	*	*
1962	5,208,030	15.	20.	25.	90.	350.	20.	25.	*	*
1963	8,348,871	15.	20.	25.	90.	—	20.	25.	*	*
1964	9,377,676	15.	20.	25.	100.	350.	20.	25.	150.	300.

NOTE ON FIFTY CENT COINS

The 1958 Dot, which is actually a die chip, was removed from the listing as it is not a non-progressive variety. It is a progressive variety which will change over time with continued use of the die.

TIARA PORTRAIT, MODIFIED COAT OF ARMS REVERSE, SILVER, 1965-1966.

A new obverse with the Queen showing more mature facial features and wearing a tiara was introduced in 1965.

Designers and Engravers:
Obv.: Arnold Machin, Thomas Shingles
Rev.: Thomas Shingles

Specifications:
Same as 1959 issue

DATE	MINTAGE	MS-60	MS-63	MS-64	MS-65	MS-66	PL-65	PL-65 HC	SP-65	SP-67
1965	12,629,974	15.	20.	25.	125.	—	20.	25.	400.	1,000.
1966	7,683,228	15.	20.	30.	100.	—	20.	30.	*	*

TIARA PORTRAIT, CENTENNIAL DESIGN, 1967.

A design for the reverse showing a howling wolf was chosen as part of the set of commemorative coins for this year. The obverse continued unchanged.

Designers and Engravers:
Obv.: Arnold Machin, Thomas Shingles
Rev.: Alex Colville, Myron Cook

Specifications:
Same as 1959 issue

DATE	MINTAGE	MS-60	MS-63	MS-64	MS-65	MS-66	PL-65	PL-65 HC	SP-65	SP-67
1967 ↑↑	4,211,395	15.	20.	30.	150.	—	20.	30.	30.	60.
1967 ↑↓	Included	ONLY ONE CERTIFIED								

TIARA PORTRAIT, MODIFIED COAT OF ARMS DESIGN RESUMED, REDUCED SIZE, NICKEL, 1968-1976.

When the coat of arms reverse design was resumed in 1968, the new nickel composition dictated a coin of reduced diameter for ease of striking.

Designers and Engravers:
Obv.: Arnold Machin, Walter Ott
Rev.: Thomas Shingles

Composition: 1.00 nickel
Weight: 8.10 grams
Diameter: 27.13 mm
Thickness: 1968-1979: 1.93 mm
1980-2000: 1.90 mm
Edge: Reeded
Die Axes: ↑↑

DATE	MINTAGE	MS-63 C	MS-64 C	MS-65 C	MS-66 C	MS-65 NC	MS-66 NC	MS-67 NC	SP-66	SP-67
1968	3,966,932	7.	10.	100.	—	10.	50.	—	*	*
1969	7,113,929	7.	10.	100.	300.	10.	50.	—	250.	500.
1970	2,429,516	7.	10.	55.	150.	10.	50.	75.	100.	300.
1971	2,166,144	7.	10.	55.	200.	10.	35.	75.	10.	20.
1972	2,515,632	7.	10.	60.	125.	10.	35.	60.	10.	20.
1973	2,546,096	7.	10.	75.	200.	10.	35.	60.	10.	25.
1974	3,436,650	7.	10.	50.	150.	10.	30.	60.	10.	20.
1975	3,710,000	7.	15.	125.	—	10.	30.	75.	10.	20.
1976	2,646,000	7.	15.	125.	150.	10.	30.	75.	10.	20.

TIARA PORTRAIT, MODIFIED COAT OF ARMS DESIGN, NICKEL, 1977-1980.

The 1977 coinage features pronounced changes on both sides. The obverse bears a smaller bust with increased hair detail, smaller lettering, and larger beads placed farther from the rim. The reverse shows a smaller coat of arms and, for the first time, beads instead of denticles around the rim.

In 1978 the Mint's attempts to settle upon standard designs continued. The beaded motif for the reverse was dropped and a design essentially the same as that for 1968-1976 was restored. Two minor varieties of the 1978 reverse are known. The 1978 obverse was a combination of the 1968-1976 and 1977 designs. The unmodified Machin portrait was restored, but the smaller lettering of 1977 was retained.

The modification to the Coat of Arms in 1977 was carried into 1978, with the reverse crown undergoing design changes.

Designers and Engravers:
Obv.: Arnold Machin, Patrick Brindley
Rev.: Thomas Shingles

Specifications:
Same as 1968 issue

1978 Square Jewels (SJ)

1978 Round Jewels (RJ)

DATE	MINTAGE	MS-63 C	MS-64 C	MS-65 C	MS-66 C	MS-65 NC	MS-66 NC	MS-67 NC	SP-66	SP-67	PR-67	PR-68
1977	709,939	7.	10.	75.	150.	10.	30.	60.	10.	20.	*	*
1978 SJ	3,341,892	20.	30.	100.	250.	10.	25.	40.	10.	20.	*	*
1978 RJ	Included	15.	25.	75.	150.	10.	30.	60.	20.	40.	*	*
1979	3,425,000	7.	15.	30.	75.	10.	15.	30.	10.	20.	*	*
1980	1,943,155	7.	15.	40.	50.	10.	15.	30.	10.	20.	*	*

TIARA PORTRAIT, MODIFIED COAT OF ARMS DESIGN, NICKEL, 1981.

DATE	MINTAGE	MS-63 C	MS-64 C	MS-65 C	MS-66 C	MS-65 NC	MS-66 NC	MS-67 NC	SP-66	SP-67	PR-67	PR-68
1981	2,588,900	7.	15.	55.	75.	10.	15.	25.	10.	20.	15.	20.

MODIFIED TIARA PORTRAIT VARIETIES OF 1982.

In the drive to increase die life in the striking of Canadian coins from nickel planchets, the design of the fifty cent coin was modified by decreasing the relief needed to create the Queen's image.

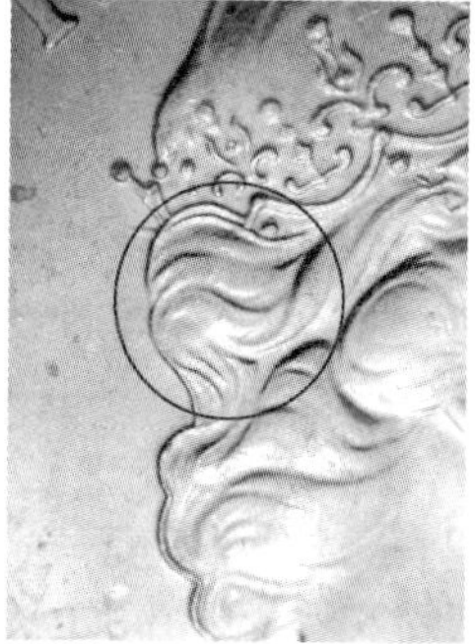
Large Beads, High Relief
Type 1

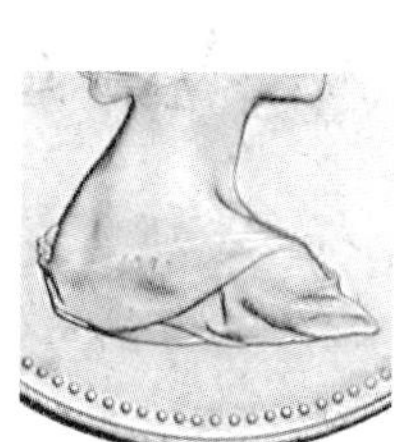
Large Beads (LB)

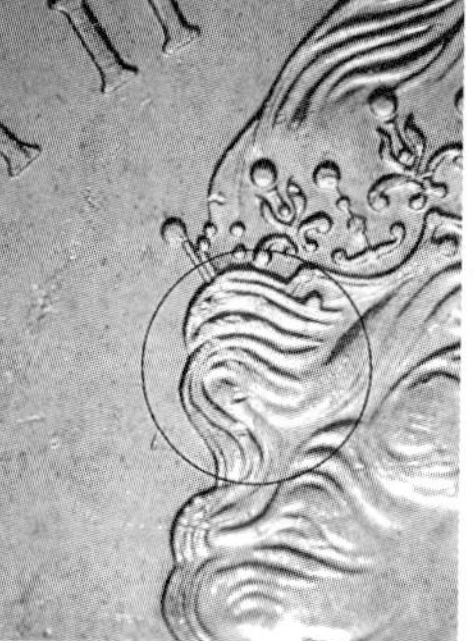
Small Beads, Low Relief
Type 2

Small Beads (SB)

TIARA PORTRAIT, MODIFIED COAT OF ARMS DESIGN, NICKEL, 1982-1989.

DATE / VARIETY	MINTAGE	MS-63 C	MS-64 C	MS-65 C	MS-66 C	MS-65 NC	MS-66 NC	MS-67 NC	SP-66	SP-67	PR-67	PR-68
1982 LB	2,884,572	7.	15.	30.	70.	10.	15.	30.	10.	20.	15.	20.
1982 SB	Included	35.	75.	200.	300.	*	*	*	*	*	*	*
1983	1,177,000	7.	15.	45.	75.	10.	15.	30.	10.	20.	15.	20.
1984	1,502,989	7.	15.	30.	75.	10.	15.	30.	10.	20.	15.	20.
1985	2,188,374	7.	20.	75.	—	10.	15.	25.	10.	20.	15.	20.
1986	781,400	7.	20.	30.	75.	10.	15.	25.	10.	20.	15.	20.
1987	373,000	7.	15.	25.	150.	10.	15.	25.	10.	20.	15.	20.
1988	220,000	7.	15.	25.	125.	10.	15.	25.	10.	20.	15.	20.
1989	266,419	7.	15.	35.	100.	10.	15.	25.	10.	15.	15.	20.

DIADEMED PORTRAIT, COAT OF ARMS DESIGN, NICKEL, 1990-1996.

A new obverse portrait of the Queen wearing a diamond diadem and jewellery was introduced on all denominations in 1990. In 1992 the reverse design was modified to include the dates 1867-1992, to celebrate the 125th birthday of Canada.

In 1993 the practice of using a single date was resumed. Also, the transition to beads from rim denticles, which began in 1982 on the one cent coin, was completed in 1993 on the fifty cent piece.

1990, 1991-1996

Common Obverse

Double date 1867 1992

Designer and Engraver:
Obv.: Dora de Pédery-Hunt, Ago Aarand
Rev. : Thomas Shingles
Specifications::
Same as 1968 issue

DATE	MINTAGE	MS-64 C	MS-65 C	MS-66 C	MS-65 NC	MS-66 NC	MS-67 NC	SP-66	SP-67	PR-67	PR-68
1990	207,000	15.	35.	65.	10.	15.	25.	10.	15.	15.	20.
1991	490,000	15.	30.	60.	10.	15.	25.	10.	15.	15.	20.
1992 (1867-)	248,000	15.	30.	100.	10.	15.	25.	10.	15.	15.	20.
1993	393,000	15.	30.	75.	10.	15.	25.	10.	15.	15.	20.
1994	987,000	15.	30.	50.	10.	15.	25.	10.	15.	15.	20.
1995	626,000	15.	30.	125.	10.	15.	25.	10.	15.	15.	20.
1996	458,000	15.	30.	75.	10.	15.	25.	10.	15.	15.	20.

DIADEMED PORTRAIT, REDESIGNED COAT OF ARMS, NICKEL, 1997-2000.

A new coat of arms appeared for the first time in 1997. The new coin incorporates the motto DESIDERANTES MELIOREM PATRIAM ("They desire a better country") on a ribbon behind the shield. The mantling depicts a series of overlapping stylized maple leaves. The arrangement of the English rose, Scottish thistle, Irish shamrock and the French fleur-de-lis has been modified and extends the width of the motto. The Winnipeg Mint Mark (W) is found only on coins from the "Oh Canada!" and "Tiny Treasures" sets issued by the Numismatic Department of the Mint.

Designers and Engravers:
Obv.: Dora de Pédery-Hunt, Ago Aarand
Rev.: C. Bursey-Sabourin, William Woodruff
Specifications:
Same as 1968 issue

DATE	MINTAGE	MS-64 C	MS-65 C	MS-66 C	MS-65 NC	MS-66 NC	MS-67 NC	SP-66	SP-67
1997	387,000	15.	30.	75.	10.	15.	25.	10.	15.
1998	308,000	15.	75.	—	10.	15.	25.	10.	15.
1998W	N.I.I.	*	*	*	10.	15.	30.	*	*
1999	496,000	15	30.	100.	10.	15.	25.	10.	15.
2000	573,000	15	50.	100.	10.	15.	25.	10.	15.
2000W	N.I.I.	*	*	*	10.	15.	30.	*	*

DIADEMED PORTRAIT, REDESIGNED COAT OF ARMS, MULTI-PLY PLATED STEEL, 1999-2003.

In 2001 the Royal Canadian Mint began issuing circulating coinage struck from their new Multi-Ply Plated steel blanks. The process is acid based and electroplates a thin coating of nickel, then copper, then nickel again to a steel core.

A 50-cent coin, dated 2000P, was incorporated into the cover of a desk clock and presented at the launch of the plating facilities in Winnipeg in 2000. It is believed that fewer than 276 clocks were produced. This coin is classed as NCLT.

In 2002 to commemorate the 50th anniversary of the reign of Queen Elizabeth II, all circulating coinage carried the double dates of her reign, 1952-2002, on the obverse.

1999P, 2000P, 2001P, and 2003P

Composition Mark 'P'

Designers and Engravers: As for the 1997 issue.
Composition: .9325 steel, .0475 copper, .0200 nickel
Weight: 6.9 grams
Diameter: 27.13 mm
Thickness: 1.95 mm
Edge: Reeded
Die Axes: ↑↑

1952-2002

DATE / COMP. MARK	MINTAGE	MS-64 C	MS-65 C	MS-66 C	MS-65 NC	MS-66 NC	MS-67 NC	SP-66	SP-67
1999P	Issued for testing	*	*	*	20.	30.	45.	*	*
2000P	Issued in clocks	*	*	*	6,000.	7,000.	8,000.	*	*
2001P	389,000	20.	40.	75.	10.	20.	30.	10.	15.
2002P (1952-)	N.I.I.	*	*	*	10.	15.	40.	10.	15.
2003P	N.I.I.	*	*	*	10.	20.	30.	10.	15.

IMPERIAL STATE CROWNED PORTRAIT, REDESIGNED COAT OF ARMS DESIGN, 2002.

Using the obverse design of the 1953 Canadian Coronation Medallion, a new 50-cent circulating coin was issued to commemorate the golden jubilee of Her Majesty Queen Elizabeth II. The reverse design features Canada's coat of arms struck with the dual dates 1952-2002.

Designers and Engravers:
Obv.: Susan Taylor
Rev.: C. Bursey-Sabourin
William Woodruff
Specifications:
Same as 1999P issue

DATE / COMP. MARK	MINTAGE	MS-64 C	MS-65 C	MS-66 C	MS-65 NC	MS-66 NC	MS-67 NC	SP-66	SP-67
2002P (1952-)	14,440,000	10.	30.	50.	10.	15.	40.	10.	15.

NOTE ON FIFTY CENT COINS

With the exception of the Coronation Commemorative issue of 1952-2002, no fifty cent coins were issued for circulation in the years 2002-2005. These dates will only be found in collector sets issued by the Royal Canadian Mint, see *Canadian Coins, Volume Two, Collector and Maple Leaf Issues*..

UNCROWNED PORTRAIT, REDESIGNED COAT OF ARMS, MULTI-PLY PLATED STEEL, 2003-2006.

Designers and Engravers:
Obv.: Susanna Blunt, Susan Taylor
Rev.: C. Bursey-Sabourin, William Woodruff

Specifications:
Same as 1999P issue

DATE / COMP. MARK	DESCRIPTION	MINTAGE	MS-64 C	MS-65 C	MS-66 C	MS-65 NC	MS-66 NC	MS-67 NC	SP-66	SP-67
2003WP	From sets only	N.I.I.	*	*	*	15.	30.	40.	*	*
2004P	From sets only	N.I.I.	*	*	*	15.	20.	25.	10.	15.
2005P	From Mint rolls	200,000	15.	20.	25.	10.	15.	25.	10.	15.
2006P	From Mint rolls	98,000	10.	15.	45.	10.	15.	25.	10.	15.

UNCROWNED PORTRAIT, REDESIGNED COAT OF ARMS, MULTI-PLY PLATED STEEL, RCM LOGO, 2006-2010.

Designers and Engravers:
Obv.: Susanna Blunt, Susan Taylor
Rev.: C. Bursey-Sabourin, William Woodruff

Specifications:
Same as 1999P issue

DATE / MINT LOGO	DESCRIPTION	MINTAGE	MS-64 C	MS-65 C	MS-66 C	MS-65 NC	MS-66 NC	MS-67 NC	SP-66	SP-67
2006	From sets only	N.I.I.	*	*	*	15.	20.	30.	*	*
2007	From Mint rolls	111,550	15.	20.	45.	10.	15.	30.	10.	15.
2008	From Mint rolls	150,000	10.	20.	45.	10.	15.	30.	10.	15.
2009	From Mint rolls	120,000	10.	20.	45.	10.	15.	30.	10.	15.
2010	From Mint rolls	150,000	10.	20.	40.	10.	15.	25.	10.	15.

UNCROWNED PORTRAIT, REDESIGNED COAT OF ARMS, MULTI-PLY PLATED STEEL, RCM LOGO, 2011-2014.

With the cessation in 2011 of the Brilliant Uncirculated finish (MS-65-NC) on coins contained in the Uncirculated Sets, it was necessary to remove that block of grades from future pricing tables.

Designers and Engravers:
Obv.: Susanna Blunt, Susan Taylor
Rev.: C. Bursey-Sabourin, William Woodruff

Specifications:
Same as 1999P issue

DATE / MINT LOGO	DESCRIPTION	MINTAGE	MS-64 C	MS-65 C	MS-66 C	MS-67 C	SP-66	SP-67
2011	From Mint rolls	175,000	10.	20.	40.	95.	10.	15.
2012	From Mint rolls	250,000	10.	20.	40.	85.	10.	15.
2013	From Mint rolls	375,000	10.	20.	40.	95.	10.	15.
2014	From Mint rolls	N/A	10.	20.	40.	95.	10.	15.

NOTES ON FIFTY CENT COINS

1. No fifty cent pieces were issued through the Banks for circulation in the years 2005 to 2014. They are available only from rolls or sets sold by the Numismatic Department of the Royal Canadian Mint.
2. Mintage numbers listed in the pricing tables are for circulation coinage (MS-64 to MS-66-C Business Strikes). The mintage figures for Brilliant Uncirculated (MS-65 to MS-67-NC), Specimen (SP-66 to SP-67), and Proof (PR-67 to PR-68) must be obtained from *Canadian Coins, Volume Two, Collector and Maple Leaf Issues*.

ONE DOLLAR - SILVER
GEORGE V 1935 - 1936

Canada's first silver dollar for circulation, also the first commemorative coin, marked the 25th anniversary of the accession of King George V. The Bank of Canada $25 bill also commemorated the special event. The reverse of the silver dollar was a modern design by sculptor Emanuel Hahn, showing an Indian and a voyageur (a travelling agent for a fur company) paddling a canoe by an islet on which there are two wind-swept trees. In the canoe are bundles of goods; the bundle at the right has HB, representing the Hudson's Bay Company. The vertical lines in the background represent the northern lights. This modern design began a trend which produced the beautiful reverses for 1937.

IMPERIAL CROWNED PORTRAIT, VOYAGEUR REVERSE, JUBILEE ISSUE, 1935.

The obverse was the commemorative side of the coin with the Latin legend indicating the King was in the 25th year of his reign. The portrait was by Percy Metcalfe and was never used for any other Canadian coinage, but had been used previously for the obverses of some New Zealand and Australian coinages.

Generally, the coins were issued in cardboard tubes of 20.

Designer and Engraver:
Obv.: Percy Metcalfe
Rev.: Emanuel Hahn
Composition: .800 silver, .200 copper
Weight: 23.33 grams
Diameter: 36.00 mm
Edge: Reeded
Die Axes:↑↑

DATE	MINTAGE	VF-20	EF-40	AU-50	MS-60	MS-62	MS-63	MS-64	MS-65	MS-66	SP-63	SP-65
1935	428,707	40.	50.	60.	65.	75.	95.	140.	375.	1,100.	2,000.	7,000.
1935 SWL	Included	50.	60.	75.	80.	125.	150.	275.	2,000.	—	*	*
1935 Matte	Included	*	*	*	*	*	*	*	*	*	—	—

IMPERIAL CROWNED PORTRAIT, VOYAGEUR REVERSE, 1936.

In 1936 the issue of silver dollars continued, with the new reverse remaining unchanged. The obverse was the regular MacKennal design used for 1- to 50-cent pieces of 1912-1936. The tools for this obverse had already been prepared in 1911 for use on the 1911 dollar (see DC-6 in the chapter on Patterns).

Designer and Engraver:
Obv.: Sir E. B. MacKennal
Rev.: Emanuel Hahn
Specifications:
Same as 1935 issue

DATE	MINTAGE	VF-20	EF-40	AU-50	MS-60	MS-62	MS-63	MS-64	MS-65	MS-66	SP-63	SP-65
1936	306,100	40.	50.	60.	65.	100.	130.	250.	900.	2,500.	2,500.	7,500.
1936 Matte	Included	*	*	*	*	*	*	*	*	*	—	—

NOTE ON SPECIMEN COINAGE

During the years 1935 to 1939 and then again in 1947, with the 1947 Blunt 7, two finishes were used on specimen coins, either Mirror or Matte. For an explanation of Finishes see page xxii of the introduction.

ONE DOLLAR - SILVER
GEORGE VI 1937 - 1952

UNCROWNED PORTRAIT, VOYAGEUR REVERSE, 1937-1938.

New reverse designs were under consideration for the 1937 issues; however, it was decided to retain the voyageur design, since it was already modern.

Designer and Engraver:
Obv.: T.H. Paget
Rev.: Emanuel Hahn
Composition: .800 silver, .200 copper
Weight: 23.33 grams
Diameter: 36.00 mm
Edge: Reeded
Die Axes: ↑↑

DATE	MINTAGE	VF-20	EF-40	AU-50	MS-60	MS-62	MS-63	MS-64	MS-65	MS-66	SP-63	SP-65
1937	241,002	35.	45.	55.	60.	75.	110.	275.	4,000.	—	750.	1,500.
1937 DHP	Included	45.	50.	60.	65.	70.	150.	400.	4,500.	—	*	*
1937 Matte	Included	*	*	*	*	*	*	*	*	*	250.	750.
1938	90,304	65.	80.	110.	140.	200.	300.	650.	5,000.	10,000.	6,000.	10,000.
1938 DHP	Included	75.	100.	125.	175.	225.	350.	725.	—	—	*	*

UNCROWNED PORTRAIT, PARLIAMENT BUILDINGS REVERSE, ROYAL VISIT ISSUE, 1939.

Canada's second commemorative coin was created when the reverse of the 1939 silver dollar was used to mark the visit of George VI and Queen Elizabeth to Canada. The design consists of the centre block of the Parliament Buildings in Ottawa and the Latin phrase, "FIDE SVORVM REGNAT," meaning "He reigns by the faith of his people."

The usual means of issuing coins was through the Bank of Canada, but for this special coinage it was decided to make them available through the Post Office as well. Consequently, 369,500 of the original mintage of nearly 1.4 million were issued directly to the Post Office. This mintage proved to be larger than public demand and between 1939 and 1945, 158,084 pieces were returned to the Mint and melted.

Designer and Engraver:
Obv.: T. H. Paget
Rev.: Emanuel Hahn
Specifications:
Same as 1937 issue

DATE	MINTAGE	VF-20	EF-40	AU-50	MS-60	MS-62	MS-63	MS-64	MS-65	MS-66	SP-63	SP-65
1939	1,363,816	30.	32.	35.	38.	40.	45.	95.	625.	—	750.	1,500.
1939 QHP	Included	40.	42.	45.	50.	60.	70.	150.	800.	—	*	*
1939 Matte	Included	*	*	*	*	*	*	*	*	*	500.	1,000.

NOTE FOR COLLECTORS

The grade SP-67 was removed from the listings due to the low population of George V and George VI silver dollars in that grade. The total population is only nine coins spread over 13 dates. The price, therefore, is between the buyer and the seller.

UNCROWNED PORTRAIT, VOYAGEUR REVERSE, 1945-1946.

Beginning with the 1945 silver dollar a more brilliant appearance was achieved. This resulted from the use of chromium-plated coinage dies. For previous issues unplated dies with a rougher surface had been used.

Designer and Engraver:
Obv.: T. H. Paget
Rev.: Emanuel Hahn
Composition: .800 silver, .200 copper
Weight: 23.33 grams
Diameter: 36.00 mm
Edge: Reeded
Die Axes: ↑↑

1945 5 over 5

1945 5/5

1945 Doubled HP

1946 Quadrupled HP

DATE / VARIETY	MINTAGE	VF-20	EF-40	AU-50	MS-60	MS-62	MS-63	MS-64	MS-65	MS-66	SP-63	SP-65
1945	38,391	250.	300.	350.	475.	700.	1,100.	1,750.	8,000.	—	1,500.	5,500.
1945 5/5	Included	275.	325.	375.	500.	700.	1,200.	—	—	—	*	*
1945 DHP	Included	275.	325.	375.	500.	700.	1,200.	—	—	—	1,500.	6,000.
1946 FWL	93,055	55.	80.	100.	150.	225.	500.	1,500.	7,000.	10,000.	1,500.	5,000.
1946 FWL, QHP	Included	60.	85.	110.	175.	300.	600.	2,000.	—	—	*	*
1946 SWL	Included	60.	90.	140.	200.	300.	600.	3,000.	—	—	*	*

VARIETIES OF 1947.

Two styles of 7 were used to date the 1947 dies; a tall figure with the lower tail pointing back to the right (Pointed 7); and a shorter 7 with the lower tail pointing almost straight down (Blunt 7).

The 'dot' after the seven variety is the result of a specimen die being put in service as a working die for business strikes. The dot is the result of an accidental pit on the die.

1947 Pointed 7 (Pt 7)

1947 Pointed 7 Repunched 4

1947 Pointed 7 Dot (Pt7 Dot)

Pointed 7 Doubled (DHP)

Pointed 7 Quadrupled (QHP)

DATE / VARIETY	MINTAGE	VF-20	EF-40	AU-50	MS-60	MS-62	MS-63	MS-64	MS-65	MS-66	SP-63	SP-65
1947 Pt 7	65,595	175.	250.	300.	400.	750.	1,800.	4,500.	—	—	3,000.	6,000.
1947 Pt 7 Dot	Included	275.	400.	550.	1,250.	1,500.	2,000.	5,000.	—	—	3,000.	6,000.
1947 Pt 7 Dot DHP	Included	300.	400.	550.	1,500.	2,000.	6,250.	—	—	—	3,000.	6,000.
1947 Pt 7 RP4	Included	300.	400.	550.	850.	1,350.	3,000.	5,500.	—	—	*	*
1947 Pt 7 DHP	Included	175.	225.	375.	475.	1,000.	1,900.	7,000.	—	—	—	—
1947 Pt 7 THP	Included	175.	300.	425.	600.	1,000.	2,750.	7,500.	—	—	3,000.	6,000.
1947 Pt 7 QHP	Included	175.	300.	425.	600.	1,100.	2,750.	7,500.	—	—	*	*

1947 Blunt 7 (Bl 7)

1947
Bl 7/7

Blunt 7
Doubled HP
(DHP)

Blunt 7
Tripled HP
(THP)

DATE / VARIETY	MINTAGE	VF-20	EF-40	AU-50	MS-60	MS-62	MS-63	MS-64	MS-65	MS-66	SP-63	SP-65
1947 Bl 7	Included	115.	165.	200.	275.	325.	600.	1,100.	7,500.	—	3,000.	6,000.
1947 Bl 7 Matte	Included	*	*	*	*	*	*	*	*	*	—	—
1947 Bl 7 7/7	Included	150.	175.	225.	300.	350.	625.	1,250.	—	—	*	*
1947 Bl 7 DHP	Included	150.	200.	250.	300.	350.	650.	1,650.	—	—	*	*
1947 Bl 7 THP	Included	150.	200.	250.	300.	350.	650.	1,650.	—	—	*	*

VARIETIES OF THE 1947 MAPLE LEAF ISSUE.

In early 1948 the Royal Canadian Mint was faced with a problem. New obverse coinage tools with the Latin abbreviation "ET IND: IMP:" omitted to indicate that the King's titles had been changed to concur with India's recently granted independence would not arrive for several months. Yet, there was a great need for all denominations of coins. The Mint satisfied the demand by striking coins dated 1947 and bearing an obverse with outmoded titles. To differentiate this issue from the regular strikings of 1947, a tiny maple leaf was placed after the date. Only the Blunt 7 was employed for dating this issue.

Designer and Engraver:
Obv.: T. H. Paget
Rev.: Emanuel Hahn
Composition: .800 silver, .200 copper
Weight: 23.33 grams
Diameter: 36.00 mm
Edge: Reeded
Die Axes: ↑↑

1947 Maple Leaf Issue, struck in 1948 (ML)

1947 ML Doubled HP (ML DHP)

DATE / VARIETY	MINTAGE	VF-20	EF-40	AU-50	MS-60	MS-62	MS-63	MS-64	MS-65	MS-66	SP-63	SP-65
1947 ML	21,135	250.	300.	400.	500.	725.	1,000.	1,800.	7,500.	10,000.	2,500.	7,000.
1947 ML DHP	Included	300.	375.	425.	475.	800.	1,150.	2,000.	9,000.	15,000.	*	*

UNCROWNED PORTRAIT, "DEI GRATIA", VOYAGEUR REVERSE, 1948.

Following the arrival in 1948 of the master tools with the new obverse legend, production of the 1947 Maple Leaf coinage was terminated. For the remainder of the year coins were produced with the new obverse and the true date, 1948.

Designers, Engravers and Specifications:
Same as 1937 issue

DATE	MINTAGE	VF-20	EF-40	AU-50	MS-60	MS-62	MS-63	MS-64	MS-65	MS-66	SP-63	SP-65
1948	18,780	1,100.	1,400.	1,600.	1,900.	2,100.	3,000.	5,000.	15,000.	—	5,000.	10,000.

UNCROWNED PORTRAIT, "DEI GRATIA", NEWFOUNDLAND COMMEMORATIVE REVERSE DESIGN, 1949.

On March 31, 1949 Newfoundland became the tenth province of the Dominion of Canada. This historic event was recognized on the Canadian coinage with a special reverse for the 1949 silver dollar. The design shows the ship *"Matthew"* in which it is thought John Cabot discovered Newfoundland in 1497. Below it is the Latin phrase, "FLOREAT TERRA NOVA," meaning "May the new found land flourish." The reverse design was taken from a photograph of a model of the "Matthew" provided by Ernest Maunder of St. John's, Newfoundland. The obverse continued unchanged from that of 1948.

The 1949 dollars were struck more carefully than those of previous years and were issued in plastic or cardboard tubes of 20 to protect them. Many of these coins remain in proof-like condition today. Thomas Shingles was the engraver, doing his work entirely by hand, without the aid of a "reducing" machine.

It was decided to strike these coins, dated 1949, as long as there was a demand for them. In 1950 some 40,718 pieces were coined. The 1949 and 1950 strikings have been combined to give the total production for the type.

Designers and Engravers:
Obv.: T. H. Paget
Rev.: Ernest Maunder, Thomas Shingles
Specifications:
Same as 1937 issue

DATE	MINTAGE	VF-20	EF-40	AU-50	MS-60	MS-62	MS-63	MS-64	MS-65	MS-66	SP-63	SP-65
1949	672,218	30.	35.	40.	45.	50.	55.	65.	115.	275.	800.	2,000.

UNCROWNED PORTRAIT, "DEI GRATIA", VOYAGEUR REVERSE RESUMED, 1950-1952.

During the year 1950 a technical problem arose that was to plague the Mint throughout the 1950's. At each end of the canoe are four (not three as is so often claimed) shallow water lines. In the process of polishing or repolishing the dies, parts of these lines tended to disappear, creating differences within a given year's coinage. Collectors have decided arbitrarily that a certain pattern of partial water lines at the right-hand end of the canoe should be collected separately and command a premium over dollars with perfect water lines or other partial lines configurations.

The original design in front of the canoe is made up of four lines, three water lines and a horizon line. The horizon line is just up from the island tip, and naturally above the three waterlines. When polishing takes place the horizon line is removed.

The so-called Arnprior configuration (see One Dollar, Queen Elizabeth II 1955 for more details) consists of 1 ½ water lines at the right. Any trace of the bottom water line disqualifies a coin from being an Arnprior. One should also beware of coins that have had part of the water line fraudulently removed.

See page 202 for an explanation of the origin of the term Arnprior.

Designers, Engravers and Specifications:
Same as 1937 issue

VARIETIES OF 1950 AND 1951.

1950-1951 Normal (FWL)
4 full water lines at right

1950-1951 Three or four
short water lines (SWL)

1950-1951 Arnprior (ARN)
1½ water lines at right

DATE / VARIETY	MINTAGE	VF-20	EF-40	AU-50	MS-60	MS-62	MS-63	MS-64	MS-65	MS-66	SP-63	SP-65
1950 FWL	261,002	30.	32.	35.	40.	55.	80.	115.	275.	550.	1,200.	2,000.
1950 SWL	Included	35.	38.	40.	50.	70.	100.	150.	800.	—	1,500.	2,500.
1950 ARN	Included	30.	35.	45.	70.	100.	150.	425.	2,500.	—	1,500.	3,500.
1950 ARN DHP	Included	40.	45.	55.	85.	125.	200.	475.	2,600.	—	*	*
1950 Matte	Included	*	*	*	*	*	*	*	*	*	—	20,000.
1951 FWL	416,395	30.	35.	40.	45.	50.	60.	125.	850.	—	850.	1,500.
1951 FWL DHP	Included	35.	40.	45.	50.	55.	100.	200.	1,000.	—	*	*
1951 SWL	Included	35.	40.	50.	60.	70.	95.	250.	4,000.	—	—	—
1951 ARN	Included	65.	125.	175.	225.	350.	525.	950.	6,000.	—	1,500.	4,000.

VARIETIES OF 1952.

In 1952 a modified reverse, with no water lines at all, was put into use. In addition to removing the water lines, this reverse differs from the Water Lines variety in having a remodelled (larger) islet tip at the right end of the canoe. This variety is fundamentally different from the Arnpriors in that it is was deliberately, not accidentally created. The Water Lines variety was also used in 1952.

1952 Short Water Lines (SWL)

1952 No Water Lines (NWL)

WATERLINE DEFINITIONS

FWL: At least one of the three or four lines touches the canoe.

SWL: No lines touch the canoe, but three or four lines are present.

ARN: No lines touch the canoe, but one and a half lines are present.

NWL: No waterlines

DATE / VARIETY	MINTAGE	VF-20	EF-40	AU-50	MS-60	MS-62	MS-63	MS-64	MS-65	MS-66	SP-63	SP-65
1952 FWL	406,148	30.	35.	40.	50.	60.	70.	100.	650.	—	750.	2,000.
1952 FWL DHP	Included	35.	40.	45.	60.	65.	125.	150.	—	—	*	*
1952 SWL	Included	35.	40.	45.	65.	80.	175.	250.	1,500.	—	750.	2,000.
1952 ARN	Included	45.	80.	125.	200.	275.	400.	1,000.	—	—	*	*
1952 NWL	Included	30.	35.	40.	45.	55.	70.	150.	800.	—	750.	2,000.

ONE DOLLAR - SILVER
ELIZABETH II 1953 - 1967

LAUREATE PORTRAIT; VOYAGEUR REVERSE, 1953-1957.

As on all the lower denominations, the 1953 silver dollars occur with two obverses, called the No Shoulder Fold and Shoulder Fold varieties (see one cent, Queen Elizabeth II, 1953 to date for full explanation). On this denomination these obverses are combined with different reverses. The No Shoulder Fold variety appears with the Wire Edge reverse, the Water Lines reverse of 1950-1952, and the Shoulder Fold obverse with the Wide Border reverse.

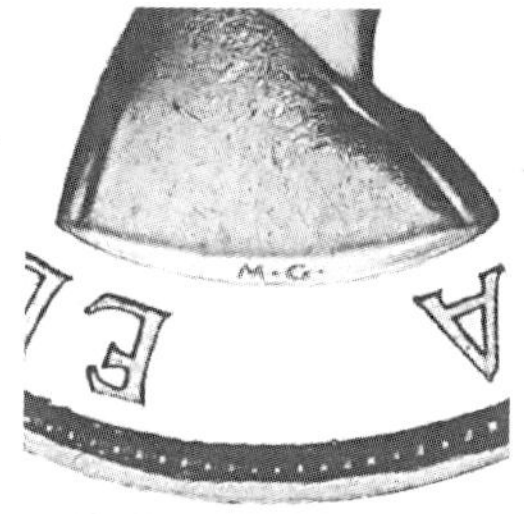

No Shoulder Fold (NSF) Obverse 1953 Letters have pronounced flaring

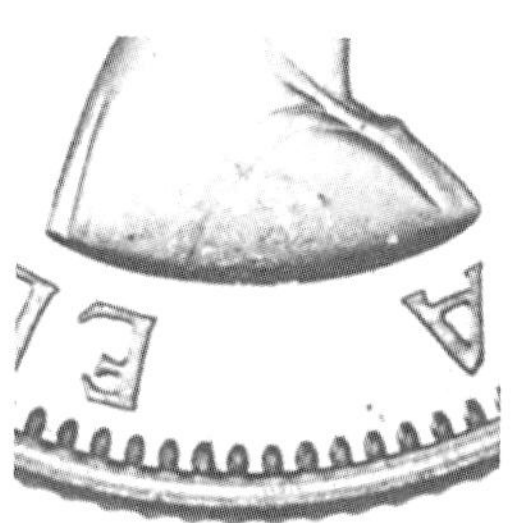

Shoulder Fold Obverse (SF) 1953-1964 Letters have subdued flaring

Designers and Engravers:
Obv.: Mary Gillick, Thomas Shingles
Rev.: Emanuel Hahn
Composition: .800 silver, .200 copper

Weight: 23.33 grams
Diameter: 36.00 mm
Edge: Reeded
Die Axes: ↑↑

DATE / VARIETY	MINTAGE	EF-40	AU-50	AU-55	MS-60	MS-63	MS-64	MS-65	MS-66	PL-65	PL-65 HC	SP-63	SP-65
1953 NSF, FWL	1,074,578	30.	32.	35.	40.	50.	85.	550.	—	1,100.	1,500.	900.	2,500.
1953 NSF, SWL	Included	30.	32.	35.	45.	75.	125.	900.	—	*	*	*	*
1953 SF, FWL	Included	30.	32.	35.	40.	55.	100.	850.	—	925.	1,250.	1,000.	2,500.
1953 SF, SWL	Included	30.	32.	35.	40.	95.	135.	1,000.	—	*	*	*	*
1954 FWL	246,606	30.	35.	40.	50.	65.	150.	1,600.	—	275.	400.	*	*
1954 SWL	Included	40.	50.	55.	60.	100.	300.	1,600.	—	*	*	*	*

ARNPRIOR VARIETY OF 1955.

In December, 1955 the Mint made up an order of 2,000 silver dollars for a firm in Arnprior, Ontario. These coins had 2 ½ water lines at the right of the canoe, similar to the configuration which occurred on some of the 1950 - 1951 dollars. It was the 1955 dollars that first attracted the attention of collectors, but the term Arnprior has been applied to any dollar with a similar configuration of defective water lines. Confirmation of the 1955 Arnprior is given by the die break on the obverse legend, the joining of the "T"and "I" of GRATIA. Arnprior dollars without this die break will command a slightly lower price. See the 1950-1951 silver dollars issues for additional comments.

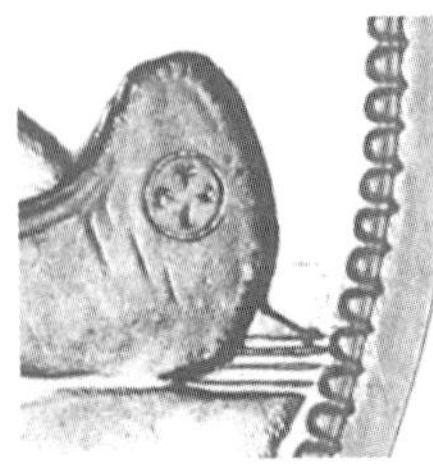

1955 Normal 4 Water Lines

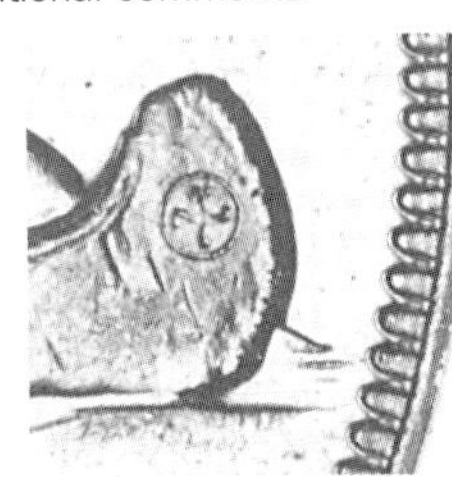

1955 Arnprior (ARN) 2½ Water Lines

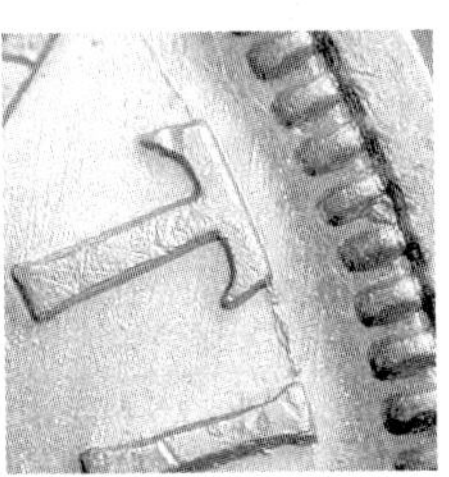

Obverse die break between "T" and "I" of GRATIA

DATE / VARIETY	MINTAGE	EF-40	AU-50	AU-55	MS-60	MS-63	MS-64	MS-65	MS-66	PL-65	PL-65 HC	SP-63	SP-65
1955	268,105	30.	35.	40.	45.	75.	125.	1,350.	—	200.	250.	*	*
1955 ARN.	Included	60.	80.	90.	110.	225.	500.	2,500.	—	300.	350.	*	*
1955 ARN. w/DB	Included	100.	150.	175.	200.	375.	725.	3,500.	—	*	*	*	*
1956	209,092	30.	35.	40.	50.	95.	475.	3,500.	—	175.	225.	*	*

VARIETIES OF 1957.

Another Arnprior 'type' variety was created by the polishing of the 1957 reverse dies, resulting in a die with only one water line to the right of the canoe.

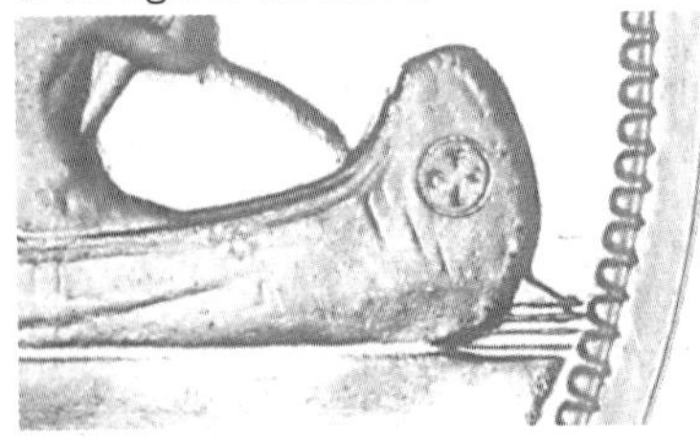

1957 Full (4) Water (FWL) Lines at Right

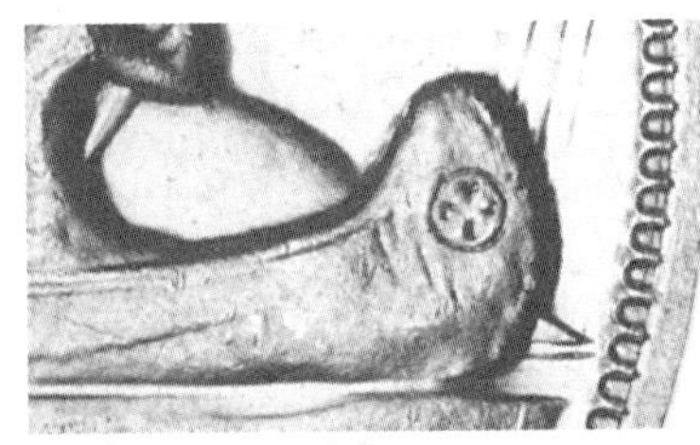

1957 One Water Line (One WL) at Right

DATE / VARIETY	MINTAGE	MS-60	MS-63	MS-64	MS-65	MS-66	PL-65	PL-65 HC	SP-63	SP-65
1957 FWL	496,389	35.	50.	125.	1,800.	—	85.	125.	*	*
1957 One WL	Included	50.	75.	500.	4,500.	—	200.	250.	*	*

LAUREATE PORTRAIT, BRITISH COLUMBIA COMMEMORATIVE, 1958.

The reverse of the 1958 dollar commemorates the centenary of the Caribou gold rush and the establishment of British Columbia as a crown colony. The design shows a totem pole section with mountains in the background. The top element in the totem is a raven, used by some Indians to symbolize death. As a result, it was rumoured that those Indians disliked the dollars, causing them to be called "death dollars." The obverse was the same as that on the 1954-1957 issues.

Designers and Engravers:
Obv.: Mary Gillick, Thomas Shingles
Rev.: Stephan Trenka, Thomas Shingles
Specifications: Same as 1953 issue

DATE	MINTAGE	MS-60	MS-63	MS-64	MS-65	MS-66	PL-65	PL-65 HC	SP-63	SP-65
1958	3,039,630	35.	40.	65.	400.	675.	45.	65.	*	*

LAUREATE PORTRAIT, VOYAGEUR REVERSE RESUMED, 1959-1963.

By 1959 the master dies utilizing the Emanuel Hahn reverse design had been in use for nearly twenty-five years. The 'Northern Lights' and 'water line' details were weakening. In 1960, Thomas Shingles re-engraved the matrix, strengthening the weak design elements.

Designers and Engravers:
Obv.: Mary Gillick, Thomas Shingles
Rev.: Emanuel Hahn, Thomas Shingles
Specifications:
Same as 1953 issue

DATE	MINTAGE	MS-60	MS-63	MS-64	MS-65	MS-66	PL-65	PL-65 HC	SP-63	SP-65
1959	1,443,502	30.	40.	100.	2,000.	—	45.	65.	*	*
1960	1,420,486	30.	40.	110.	1,500.	5,000.	30.	60.	*	*
1961	1,262,231	30.	40.	115.	1,500.	4,500.	30.	45.	*	*
1962	1,884,789	30.	40.	85.	1,000.	—	30.	45.	*	*
1963	4,179,981	30.	35.	80.	1,125.	—	30.	45.	*	*

LAUREATE PORTRAIT, CONFEDERATION MEETINGS COMMEMORATIVE REVERSE, 1964.

The reverse of the 1964 silver dollar carried a special design marking the centennial of the 1864 meetings in Charlottetown, P.E.I. and Quebec City, Quebec which prepared the way for Confederation in 1867. The design depicts, conjoined within a circle, the French fleur-de-lis, the Irish shamrock, the Scottish thistle and the English rose. The obverse coupled with the commemorative reverse was a reworking of the Shoulder Fold variety.

Designers and Engravers:
Obv.: Mary Gillick, Myron Cook
Rev.: Dinko Vodanovic, Thomas Shingles
Specifications:
Same as 1953 issue

DATE	MINTAGE	MS-60	MS-63	MS-64	MS-65	MS-66	PL-65	PL-65 HC	SP-63	SP-65
1964	7,296,832	30.	35.	80.	1,300.	—	30.	40.	250.	625.

TIARA PORTRAIT, VOYAGEUR REVERSE RESUMED, 1965.

A new obverse with the Queen showing more mature facial features and wearing a tiara was introduced on all denominations in 1965. The first new obverse for the dollar had to be replaced because it gave such poor die life. The difficulty was caused by a flat field (Small Beads variety). A single trial die (Medium Beads variety) established that an obverse with the field sloping up at the edge was preferable, so new master tools were prepared (Large Beads variety) and those dies became the standard. In addition two reverses, bearing slightly different 5s were employed, creating five varieties in all for 1965.

An anomaly was generated with the 1965 varieties. When the silver dollars for 1965 were released the varieties were discovered in the order they are classified: Type 1 through Type 5, not in the order they were struck at the Mint. which is as follows: Type 1, then 2, then 5, then 3 and finally, Type 4. The Type 5 variety was an internal test coin, to investigate whether a sloping field improved die life. The test worked and the dish was extended producing Types 3 and 4.

Designers and Engravers:
Obv.: Arnold Machin, Walter Ott
Rev.: Emanuel Hahn, Thomas Shingles

Specifications:
As for the 1953 issue

VARIETY 1 and 2: SMALL BEADS

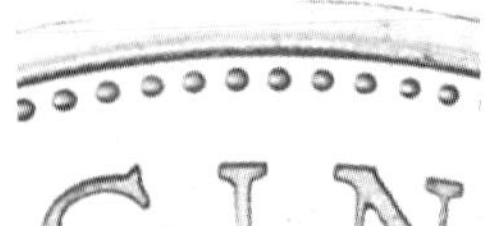

Small Beads Obverse (SB) 1965-1966, rear jewel in tiara is well attached

POINTED and BLUNT FIVE

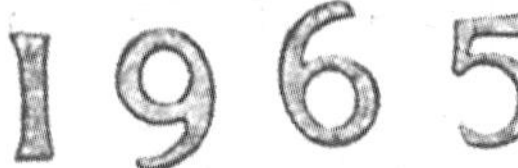

1965 Pointed 5 (at bottom)

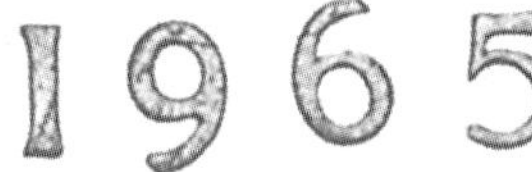

1965 Blunt 5 (at bottom)

REAR JEWEL

VARIETY 5: MEDIUM BEADS

Medium Beads Obverse (MB) Rear jewel in tiara is nearly detached

POINTED FIVE

1965 Pointed 5 (at bottom)

REAR JEWEL

VARIETY 3 and 4: LARGE BEADS

Large Beads Obverse (LB) Rear jewel in tiara is well attached

BLUNT and POINTED FIVE

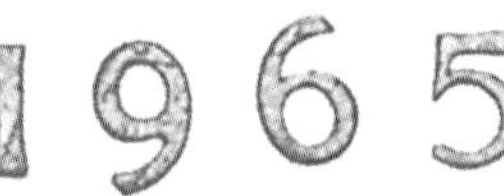

1965 Blunt 5 (at bottom)

1965 Pointed 5 (at bottom)

REAR JEWEL

DATE / VARIETY	MINTAGE	MS-60	MS-63	MS-64	MS-65	MS-66	PL-65	PL-65 HC	SP-63	SP-65
1965 SB P5 T-1	10,768,569	30.	35.	75.	900.	—	30.	35.	300.	1,000.
1965 SB B5 T-2 ↑↑	Included	30.	40.	95.	2,000.	—	30.	40.	300.	750.
1965 SB B5 T-2 ↑↓	Included	ONLY FIVE CERTIFIED								
1965 LB B5 T-3	Included	30.	40.	65.	600.	2,000.	200.	225.	250.	600.
1965 LB P5 T-4	Included	30.	50.	100.	675.	4,500.	125.	150.	500.	1,000.
1965 MB P5 T-5	Included	45.	55.	175.	1,500.	5,000.	*	*	*	*

TIARA PORTRAIT, VOYAGEUR REVERSE, 1966

In 1966 at the Hull Mint, which was established to relieve the strain at the Ottawa Mint for the production of numismatic products, a 1965 small bead obverse die was paired with a 1966 reverse die which was intended for use in the production of the 1966 brilliant uncirculated sets (proof-like sets). The question still remains as to whether or not this was an official or unauthorized striking. The final result was that dollars that were struck with "proof-like" quality dies were rejected and in turn shipped to Ottawa for melting and reprocessing. They did not make it, but instead, they were bagged and shipped to a branch bank. The finish on the 1966 small bead dollars is mixed between mint state and proof-like because of the route they took from rejection to final shipment.

Large Beads (LB) (normal)

Small Beads (SB)

DATE / VARIETY	MINTAGE	MS-60	MS-63	MS-64	MS-65	MS-66	PL-65	PL-65 HC	SP-63	SP-65
1966 LB	9,912,178	30.	35.	50.	600.	2,500.	30.	35.	300.	1,000.
1966 SB	Included	3,500.	5,000.	6,000.	9,000.	—	—	—	*	*

TIARA PORTRAIT, CENTENNIAL OF CONFEDERATION COMMEMORATIVE REVERSE, 1967.

A design for the reverse showing a Canada goose in flight was chosen as part of the set of commemorative coins for this year. The obverse is the Large Beads variety of 1965-1966. As a matter of interest beads replaced denticles on the reverse of the dollar coins for the first time.

In 1967 141,741 pieces were melted.

Designers and Engravers:
Obv.: Arnold Machin, Walter Ott
Rev.: Alex Colville, Myron Cook
Composition: .800 silver, .200 copper
Weight: 23.33 grams
Diameter: 36.00 mm
Edge: Reeded
Die Axes: ↑↑, ↑↓

DATE / VARIETY	MINTAGE	MS-60	MS-63	MS-64	MS-65	MS-66	PL-65	PL-65 HC	SP-63	SP-65
1967 ↑↑	6,767,496	30.	40.	50.	400.	2,500.	40.	90.	35.	45.
1967 ↑↓	Included	5,000.	8,000.	12,000.	16,000.	—	12,000.	—	*	*

SYMBOLS USED IN PRICING TABLES

— No two coins have been assigned this grade by a Canadian grading company.
***** Not issued in that finish.
BV Bullion value.
C Circulating coins, coins which are purchased from banks, or found in change.
FV Face value.
NC Noncirculating coins identical in design to the circulating issue, but sold in sets or special packaging by the Royal Canadian Mint.
N.I.I. Not issued individually, but included in a set of some nature.
P.E. Plain edge

ONE DOLLAR - NICKEL
ELIZABETH II 1968 - 1987

TIARA PORTRAIT, VOYAGEUR REVERSE RESUMED; REDUCED SIZE COINAGE, NICKEL, 1968-1969.

When the voyageur reverse design was resumed in 1968, the composition had changed to nickel. In order to make coining easier in the harder metal the diameter was reduced considerably.

Designers and Engravers:
Obv.: Arnold Machin, Myron Cook
Rev.: Emanuel Hahn, T. Shingles
Composition: 1.00 nickel
Weight: 15.62 grams
Diameter: 32.13 mm
Edge: Reeded
Die Axes: ↑↑

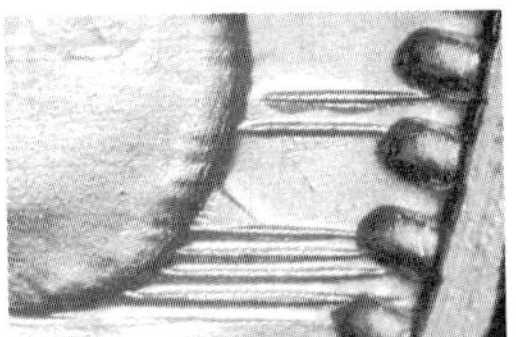

Normal Island

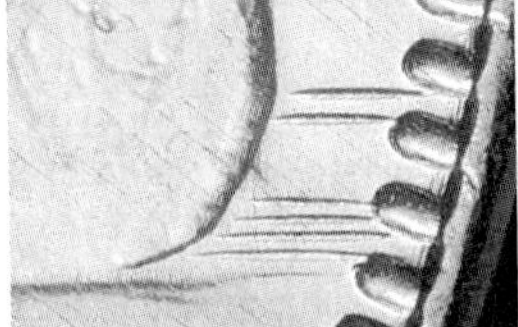

Small Island (S Is)

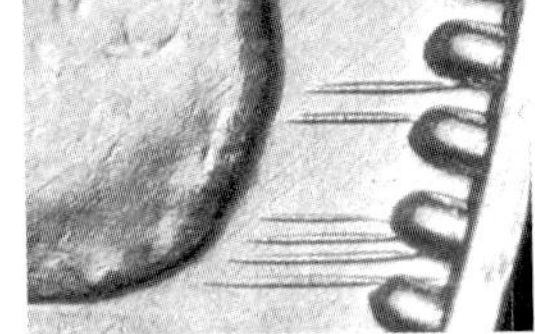

No Island (N Is)

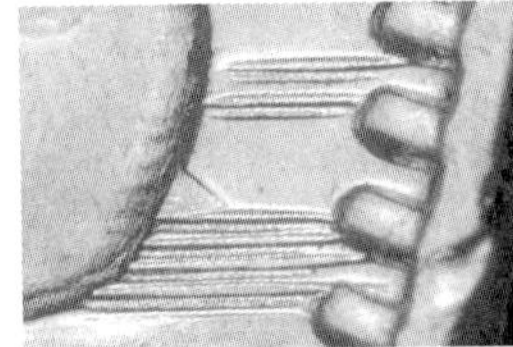

Doubled horizon line (DHL)

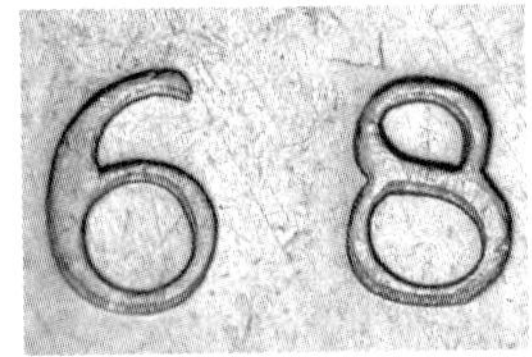

Doubled Die Reverse
Doubled 68 (DD)

DATE / VARIETY	MINTAGE	MS-63 C	MS-64 C	MS-65 C	MS-66 C	MS-65 NC	MS-66 NC	MS-67 NC	SP-66	SP-67
1968	5,579,714	8.	15.	75.	150.	15.	20.	30.	*	*
1968 S Is	Included	20.	35.	125.	—	10.	20.	30.	*	*
1968 N Is	Included	15.	30.	70.	150.	25.	35.	60.	*	*
1968 DHL	Included	15.	30.	95.	250.	45.	65.	100.	*	*
1968 DD	Included	15.	25.	60.	—	*	*	*	*	*
1969	4,809,313	10.	20.	200.	—	10.	15.	30.	750.	1,500.

TIARA PORTRAIT, MANITOBA CENTENNIAL COMMEMORATIVE REVERSE, NICKEL, 1970.

The year 1970 saw Canada's first commemorative nickel dollar, with a special reverse featuring a prairie crocus in recognition of the centenary of Manitoba's entry into Confederation. The obverse continued unchanged from the 1968-1969 issues.

Designers and Engravers:
Obv.: Arnold Machin, Walter Ott
Rev.: Raymond Taylor, Walter Ott
Specifications:
Same as 1968-69 issues

DATE	MINTAGE	MS-63 C	MS-64 C	MS-65 C	MS-66 C	MS-65 NC	MS-66 NC	MS-67 NC	SP-66	SP-67
1970	4,140,058	10.	20.	125.	—	15.	85.	150.	50.	75.

TIARA PORTRAIT, BRITISH COLUMBIA CENTENNIAL COMMEMORATIVE REVERSE, NICKEL, 1971.

The nickel dollar for 1971 commemorates the entry of British Columbia into Confederation in 1871. Its design is based on the arms of the province, with a shield at the bottom and dogwood blossoms at the top. The obverse is the same as on previous nickel issues.

Designers and Engravers:
Obv.: Arnold Machin, Walter Ott
Rev.: Thomas Shingles
Specifications: Same as 1968 issue

DATE	MINTAGE	MS-63 C	MS-64 C	MS-65 C	MS-66 C	MS-65 NC	MS-66 NC	MS-67 NC	SP-66	SP-67
1971	4,260,781	10.	20.	200.	—	15.	75.	125.	50.	75.

VOYAGEUR REVERSE RESUMED, 1972.

In 1972 the standard voyageur reverse was resumed. The obverse and reverse are the same as for the 1968-1969 issues. The physical and chemical specifications are as for the 1968-1969 issues.

DATE	MINTAGE	MS-63 C	MS-64 C	MS-65 C	MS-66 C	MS-65 NC	MS-66 NC	MS-67 NC	SP-66	SP-67
1972	2,193,000	8.	15.	350.	—	10.	35.	150.	45.	75.

TIARA PORTRAIT, PRINCE EDWARD ISLAND CENTENNIAL COMMEMORATIVE REVERSE, NICKEL, 1973.

The special reverse on the nickel dollar of 1973 marks the 100th anniversary of the entry of Prince Edward Island into Confederation. The design depicts the provincial legislature building. A new obverse with a smaller, more detailed portrait, and fewer rim beads placed farther from the rim, is brought into use with this reverse.

Designers and Engravers:
Obv.: Arnold Machin, Patrick Brindley
Rev.: Terry Manning, Walter Ott
Specifications: Same as 1968 issue

DATE	MINTAGE	MS-63 C	MS-64 C	MS-65 C	MS-66 C	MS-65 NC	MS-66 NC	MS-67 NC	SP-66	SP-67
1973	3,196,452	8.	10.	100.	175.	15.	50.	100.	45.	75.

PRICING

The Charlton Press pricing tables are based on market prices for **Canadian certified coins**. Currently there are two coin grading companies located in Canada. Our prices are gathered from prices realized at land auctions, internet auctions, and dealer fixed price lists and their internet listings. It is important to realize that coin certification incurs a cost, and on low priced coins it will be a significant factor in their listed value. The cost per coin averages between $7 and $10 for standard certification service.

TIARA PORTRAIT, WINNIPEG CENTENNIAL COMMEMORATIVE REVERSE, NICKEL, 1974.

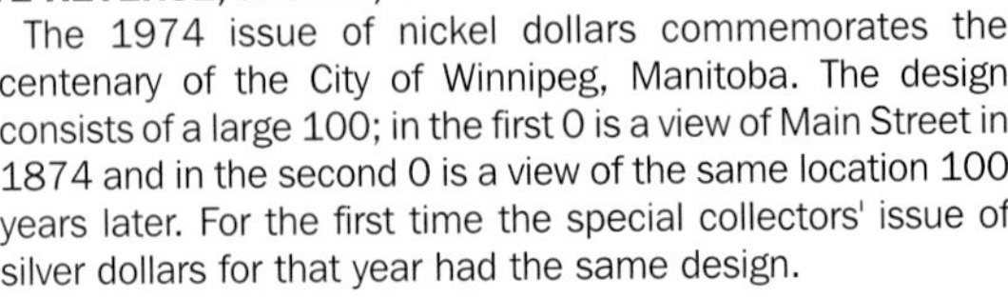

The 1974 issue of nickel dollars commemorates the centenary of the City of Winnipeg, Manitoba. The design consists of a large 100; in the first 0 is a view of Main Street in 1874 and in the second 0 is a view of the same location 100 years later. For the first time the special collectors' issue of silver dollars for that year had the same design.

Designers and Engravers:
Obv.: Arnold Machin, Patrick Brindley
Rev.: Paul Pederson, Patrick Brindley
Specifications: Same as 1968 issue

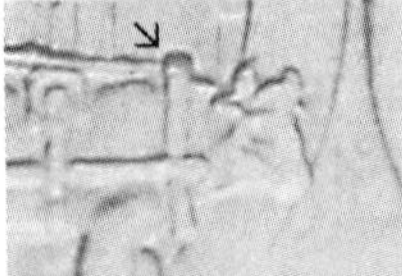

1974 Single Yoke (SY)

1974 Doubled Yoke Variety 1 (DY V1)

1974 Doubled Yoke Variety 2 (DY V2)

1974 Doubled Yoke Variety 3 (DY V3)

DATE / VARIETY	MINTAGE	MS-63 C	MS-64 C	MS-65 C	MS-66 C	MS-65 NC	MS-66 NC	MS-67 NC	SP-66	SP-67
1974 SY	2,799,363	10.	20.	100.	—	10.	50.	75.	20.	40.
1974 DY V1	Included	*	*	*	*	900.	1,500.	2,500.	1,500.	—
1974 DY V2	Included	125.	175.	300.	—	—	—	—	—	—
1974 DY V3	Included	*	*	*	*	800.	2,500.	—	2,200.	—

TIARA PORTRAIT, VOYAGEUR REVERSE RESUMED, NICKEL, 1975-1976.

The designs employed for the voyageur dollars of 1975-1976 were essentially continuations of previous designs, except for some minor variations on the obverse. The physical and chemical specifications are as for the 1974 issues.

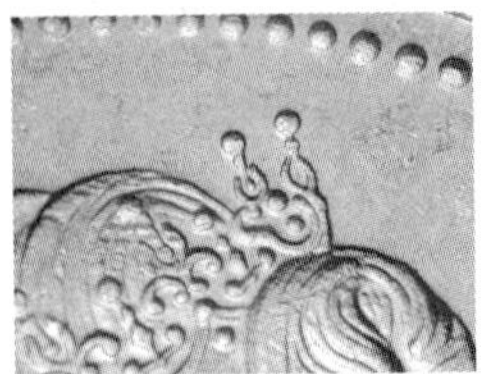

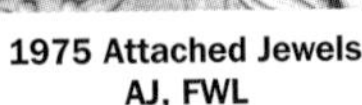

1975 Attached Jewels
AJ, FWL

1975 Detached Jewels
DJ, FWL

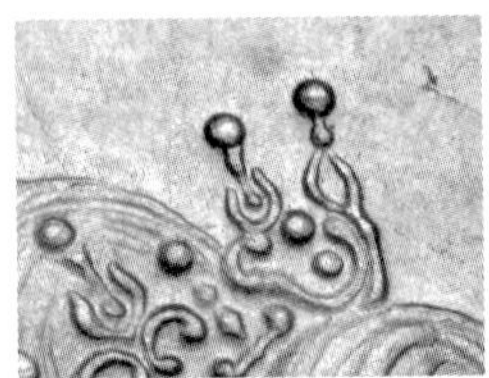

1976 Attached Jewels
AJ, FWL

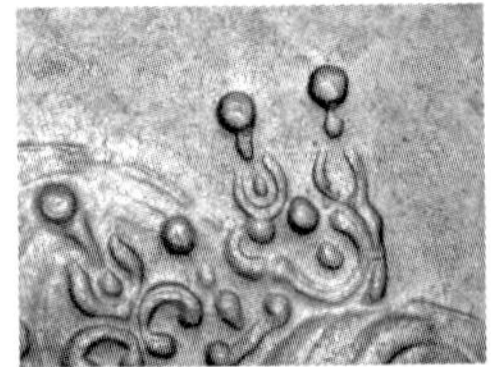

1976 Detached Jewels
DJ, FWL

DATE/ VARIETY	MINTAGE	MS-63 C	MS-64 C	MS-65 C	MS-66 C	MS-65 NC	MS-66 NC	MS-67 NC	SP-66	SP-67
1975 AJ, FWL	3,256,000	10.	20.	50.	—	15.	60.	100.	45.	75.
1975 DJ, FWL	Included	30.	50.	100.	—	20.	40.	100.	20.	75.
1976 AJ, FWL	2,101,000	30.	60.	325.	—	35.	75.	350.	20.	75.
1976 DJ, FWL	Included	10.	30.	125.	—	10.	25.	65.	30.	75.

A Note on Catalogue Listings

1. A dash in place of a value in the pricing table simply means that no Canadian grading company has certified a coin in that date and grade.
2. Mintage numbers listed in the pricing tables are for circulation coinage (MS-64 to MS-66-C Business Strikes). The mintage figures for Brilliant Uncirculated (MS-65 to MS-67-NC), Specimen (SP-66 to SP-67), and Proof (PR-67 to PR-68) must be obtained from *Canadian Coins, Volume Two, Collector and Maple Leaf Issues*.

TIARA PORTRAIT, VOYAGEUR REVERSE, MODIFIED DESIGN, NICKEL, 1977.

A major alteration was made on the reverse of the 1977 dollar. A new model was prepared on which the size of the device was reduced and the legend was in small lettering, much farther from the rim. The rim denticles were replaced with beads.

Designers and Engravers:
Obv.: Arnold Machin, Patrick Brindley
Rev.: Emanuel Hahn, Terry Smith
Specifications: Same as 1968 issue

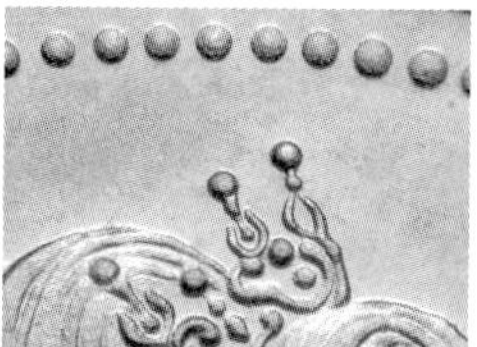
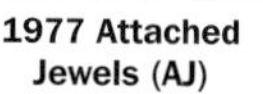

1977 Attached Jewels (AJ)

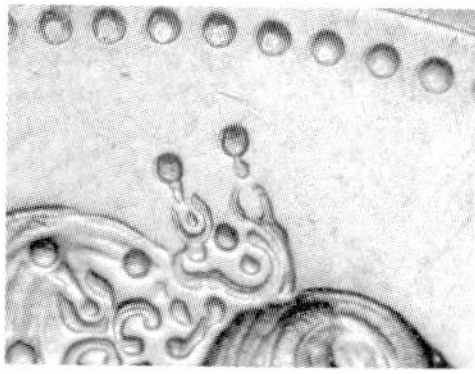

1977 Detached Jewels (DJ)

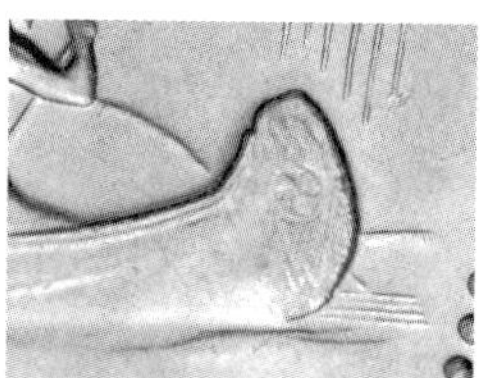

1977 Full Water Line (FWL)

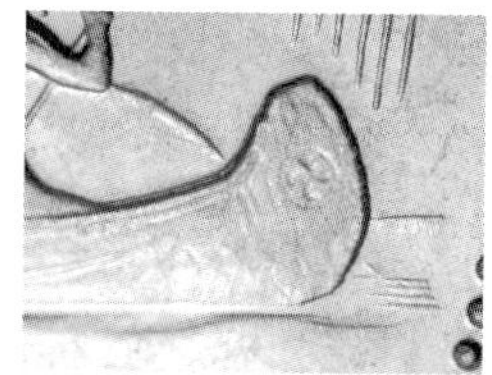

1977 Short Water Line (SWL)

DATE	MINTAGE	MS-63 C	MS-64 C	MS-65 C	MS-66 C	MS-65 NC	MS-66 NC	MS-67 NC	SP-66	SP-67
1977 AJ, SWL	1,393,745	15.	20.	150.	—	20.	50.	100.	25.	75.
1977 DJ, FWL	Included	10.	15.	100.	150.	20.	40.	60.	30.	75.
1977 DJ, SWL	Included	10.	20.	125.	—	20.	40.	65.	15.	25.

Note: Currently, a 1977 Attached Jewel Obverse / Full Water Line Reverse variety has not been found.

TIARA PORTRAIT, VOYAGEUR REVERSE, MODIFIED DESIGN, NICKEL, 1978-1980.

Continued major changes occurred in the nickel dollar coinage in 1978. In a reversal of design policy, the Mint returned to designs more like those used prior to 1977. On the obverse the unmodified Machin portrait was restored, but the beads were farther from the rim than on the 1968-1972 issues. The reverse had a design similar to that of 1975-1976, complete with rim denticles instead of beads, but the northern lights were rendered as raised lines, as they were for the 1977 issue.

Designer and Engraver:
Obv.: Arnold Machin
Rev.: Emanuel Hahn
Specifications: Same as 1968 issue

DATE	MINTAGE	MS-63 C	MS-64 C	MS-65 C	MS-66 C	MS-65 NC	MS-66 NC	MS-67 NC	SP-66	SP-67
1978	2,948,488	10.	20.	150.	—	10.	20.	50.	15.	25.
1979	1,884,789	10.	15.	175.	—	10.	20.	40.	15.	25.
1980	2,544,000	10.	15.	75.	425.	10.	20.	50.	15.	25.

TIARA PORTRAIT, VOYAGEUR REVERSE, MODIFIED DESIGN, NICKEL, 1981.

In 1981 the Royal Canadian Mint revised their product line, adding a proof finish to their offerings. The proof coins were struck on standard nickel planchets.

DATE	MINTAGE	MS-63 C	MS-64 C	MS-65 C	MS-66 C	MS-65 NC	MS-66 NC	MS-67 NC	SP-66	SP-67	PR-67	PR-68
1981	2,778,900	10.	20.	150.	250.	10.	20.	40.	15.	25.	15.	30.

TIARA PORTRAIT, CONSTITUTION COMMEMORATIVE REVERSE, NICKEL, 1982.

On June 10,1982, a one dollar pure nickel circulating coin was struck to commemorate the new Canadian Constitution. The obverse of the coin depicts the effigy of Queen Elizabeth II and the year 1982. The reverse features a faithful reproduction of the celebrated painting of the Fathers of Confederation. It commemorates the Constitution with the inscription "1867 CONFEDERATION" above the painting and "CONSTITUTION 1982" beneath it. This was the first time a commemorative and a voyageur dollar were issued in the same year for circulation. For the collector's edition of this dollar see *Volume Two Collector Issues*.

Two varieties from the regular 1982 Constitution dollar are known: one with a coinage die axis, the other where the coin was struck on an underweight planchet. The thin planchet variety is the result of purchases of blanks from a private producer. Most of the latter were recovered by the Mint's quality control staff.

Designers and Engravers:
Composition:
Obv.: Arnold Machin, RCM Staff
Rev.: Ago Aarand, RCM Staff
Specifications: Same as 1968 issue

DATE / VARIETY	MINTAGE	MS-63 C	MS-64 C	MS-65 C	MS-66 C	MS-65 NC	MS-66 NC	MS-67 NC	SP-66	SP-67
1982 ↑↑	11,812,000	10.	15.	40.	150.	*	*	*	15.	20.
1982 ↑↓	Included	6,000.	8,000.	—	—	*	*	*	*	*
1982 ↑↑ Thin planchet	Included	5,000.	—	—	—	*	*	*	*	*
1982 ↑↓ Thin planchet	Included	6,000.	—	—	—	*	*	*	*	*

TIARA PORTRAIT, VOYAGEUR REVERSE, MODIFIED DESIGN, NICKEL, 1982-1983.

The modified designs of 1978 were continued for 1982 and 1983.

DATE	MINTAGE	MS-63 C	MS-64 C	MS-65 C	MS-66 C	MS-65 NC	MS-66 NC	MS-67 NC	SP-66	SP-67	PR-67	PR-68
1982	1,544,398	10.	20.	75.	—	10.	15.	60.	15.	20.	10.	15.
1983	2,267,525	10.	15.	100.	—	10.	15.	50.	15.	20.	10.	15.

TIARA PORTRAIT, JACQUES CARTIER COMMEMORATIVE REVERSE, NICKEL, 1984.

The four hundred and fiftieth anniversary of Jacques Cartier's landing at Gaspé, Quebec was honoured on July 24, 1984 by the issuing of a commemorative nickel dollar. Again, as in 1982, a commemorative and a voyageur design were issued for circulation in the same year.

Designers and Engravers:
Obv.: Arnold Machin, RCM Staff
Rev.: Hector Greville, Victor Cote
Specifications:
Same as 1968 issue

DATE	MINTAGE	MS-63 C	MS-64 C	MS-65 C	MS-66 C	MS-65 NC	MS-66 NC	MS-67 NC	SP-66	SP-67	PR-67	PR-68
1984	6,141,503	10.	20.	50.	200.	*	*	*	*	*	10.	15.

TIARA PORTRAIT, VOYAGEUR REVERSE, MODIFIED DESIGN, NICKEL, 1984-1987.

The modified designs of 1978 were continued between 1984 and 1987. The 1987 issue of the nickel dollar appeared only in Uncirculated Sets sold by the Numismatic Department of the Mint.

DATE	MINTAGE	MS-63 C	MS-64 C	MS-65 C	MS-66 C	MS-65 NC	MS-66 NC	MS-67 NC	SP-66	SP-67	PR-67	PR-68
1984	1,223,486	10.	20.	75.	—	10.	15.	50.	15.	20.	10.	15.
1985	3,104,592	25.	50.	200.	—	10.	20.	45.	10.	15.	10.	15.
1986	3,089,225	10.	25.	75.	—	10.	25.	50.	10.	15.	10.	15.
1987	N.I.I.	*	*	*	*	15.	20.	40.	10.	20.	15.	20.

ONE DOLLAR - NICKEL/BRONZE
ELIZABETH II 1987 TO DATE

TIARA PORTRAIT, LOON REVERSE, 1987-1989.

The increased costs associated with the production of the one dollar bank note led the Bank of Canada to request from the Mint a high denomination coin that would circulate, eventually replacing the paper note. The new loon reverse is of reduced size, eleven-sided and new composition allowing the coin to be easily distinguishable from other circulating denominations. Of course, being lighter in weight facilitated its use in pocket change. In 1987 two different sizes of dollar coins were issued, the Voyageur and the Loon. See *Volume Two: Collector and Maple Leaf Issues* for the proof Loon dollar.

Designers and Engravers:
Obv.: Arnold Machin, R.C.M. Staff
Rev.: Robert R. Carmichael, Terrence Smith
Composition: .915 nickel, .085 bronze
Weight: 7.00 grams
11-sided: 1987: 26.72 mm, 1988-2013: 26.50 mm
Thickness: 1987: 1.95 mm, 1988-2013: 1.75 mm
Edge: Plain **Die Axes:** ↑↑

DATE	MINTAGE	MS-64 C	MS-65 C	MS-66 C	MS-65 NC	MS-66 NC	MS-67 NC	SP-66	SP-67	PR-67	PR-68
1987	205,405,000	10.	40.	50.	*	*	*	*	*	15.	20.
1988	138,893,539	15.	40.	95.	10.	20.	40.	10.	20.	20.	40.
1989	184,773,902	20.	60.	150.	10.	20.	45.	10.	20.	20.	40.

DIADEMED PORTRAIT, LOON REVERSE, 1990-1992.

Common obverse

1990 and 1991

Double dates 1867-1992

A new obverse portrait of the Queen wearing a diamond diadem and jewellery was introduced on all denominations in 1990. In 1992 the reverse design was modified to include the dates 1867-1992 to commemorate the 125th birthday of Canada.

Designers and Engravers:
Obv.: Dora de Pédery-Hunt, Ago Aarand
Rev.: Robert R. Carmichael, Terrence Smith
Specifications:
Same as 1988 issue

DATE	MINTAGE	MS-64 C	MS-65 C	MS-66 C	MS-65 NC	MS-66 NC	MS-67 NC	SP-66	SP-67	PR-67	PR-68
1990	68,402,000	15.	50.	150.	10.	20.	45.	10.	20.	20.	30.
1991	23,156,000	15.	40.	85.	10.	15.	35.	10.	20.	20.	30.
1992 (1867-)	4,242,085	15.	40.	100.	10.	15.	35.	10.	20.	20.	30.

DIADEMED PORTRAIT, 125TH ANNIVERSARY OF CONFEDERATION REVERSE, 1867-1992.

This commemorative dollar was issued as part of the "Canada 125" coin program celebrating Canada's 125th birthday. The design features the centre block of the Parliament Buildings and three children seated on the ground. One child holds a Canadian flag while another points to the Peace Tower clock which reads 1:25. For the collector's issue see *Volume Two: Collector Issues*.

Designers and Engravers:
Obv.: Dora de Pédery-Hunt, Ago Aarand
Rev.: Rita Swanson, Ago Aarand
Specifications: Same as 1988 issue

DATE	MINTAGE	MS-64 C	MS-65 C	MS-66 C	MS-65 NC	MS-66 NC	MS-67 NC	SP-66	SP-67	PR-67	PR-68
1992 (1867-)	23,010,915	10.	35.	50.	*	*	*	*	*	15.	20.

DIADEMED PORTRAIT, LOON REVERSE DESIGN RESUMED, 1993-1994.

In 1993 the practice of using a single date was resumed. Between the years 1997 and 2001, no one dollar nickel-bronze coins were issued for circulation. The year 2002 saw the first dollar coins issued to commemorate the 50th anniversary of the reign of Queen Elizabeth II, and like all circulating coinage, the dollars carried the double dates of her reign, 1952-2002.

Designers, Engravers and Specifications:
Same as 1988 issue

DATE	MINTAGE	MS-64 C	MS-65 C	MS-66 C	MS-65 NC	MS-66 NC	MS-67 NC	SP-66	SP-67	PR-67	PR-68
1993	33,662,000	15.	55.	75.	10.	15.	30.	10.	20.	20.	30.
1994	40,406,000	15.	30.	75.	10.	20.	40.	10.	20.	20.	30.

DIADEMED PORTRAIT, REMEMBRANCE REVERSE, 1994.

The National War Memorial in Ottawa, unveiled by King George VI in May of 1939, commemorates Canadians who died in WWI. The National War Memorial was rededicated in 1982 to include veterans from WWII and the Korean War. For the collector's issue see *Volume Two: Collector and Maple Leaf Issues*.

Designers and Engravers:
Obv.: Dora de Pédery-Hunt, Ago Aarand
Rev.: RCM Staff

Specifications: Same as 1988 issue

DATE	MINTAGE	MS-64 C	MS-65 C	MS-66 C	MS-65 NC	MS-66 NC	MS-67 NC	SP-66	SP-67	PR-67	PR-68
1994	15,000,000	15.	45.	100.	*	*	*	*	*	15.	20.

DIADEMED PORTRAIT, PEACEKEEPING REVERSE, 1995.

This coin commemorates Canada's commitment to world peace, and the 50th anniversary of the founding of the United Nations. The reverse depicts the Peacekeeping Monument in Ottawa, unveiled in 1992. For the collector's issue see *Volume Two: Collector and Maple Leaf Issues*.

Designers and Engravers:
Obv.: Dora de Pédery-Hunt, Ago Aarand
Rev.: J. K. Harman, R. G. Enriquez
C. H. Oberlander, Susan Taylor

Specifications:
Same as 1988 issue

DATE	MINTAGE	MS-64 C	MS-65 C	MS-66 C	MS-65 NC	MS-66 NC	MSP-67 NC	SP-66	SP-67	PR-67	PR-68
1995	Incl. in 1995 Loon mintage	15.	35.	100.	*	*	*	*	*	15.	20.

N.I.I. – NOT ISSUED INDIVIDUALLY

N.I.I. appearing in the mintage column signifies the coin was not issued for circulation but will be found in sets issued by the Numismatic Department of the Royal Canadian Mint. Pricing is for certified coins taken from those sets.

DIADEMED PORTRAIT, LOON REVERSE CONTINUED, 1995-2003.

From 1997 to 2001 the One Dollar Loon coins were not issued for general circulation. They are found in the collectors' sets for these years.

1995, 1996, and 2003

Double dates 1952 2002

Designers, Engravers and Specifications:
Same as 1988 issue

DATE	MINTAGE	MS-64 C	MS-65 C	MS-66 C	MS-65 NC	MS-66 NC	MS-67 NC	SP-66	SP-67	PR-67	PR-68
1995	41,813,100	15.	35.	125.	10.	15.	35.	10.	20.	15.	25.
1996	17,101,000	15.	35.	75.	10.	20.	40.	10.	30.	15.	25.
1997	N.I.I.	*	*	*	10.	20.	40.	10.	30.	15.	25.
1998	N.I.I.	*	*	*	10.	25.	40.	10.	20.	15.	25.
1998W	N.I.I.	*	*	*	10.	30.	50.	*	*	*	*
1999	N.I.I.	*	*	*	10.	20.	60.	10.	20.	15.	25.
2000	N.I.I.	*	*	*	10.	20.	60.	10.	20.	15.	25.
2000W	N.I.I.	*	*	*	15.	25.	50.	*	*	*	*
2001	N.I.I.	*	*	*	15.	25.	50.	10.	20.	15.	25.
2002 (1952-)	2,302,000	10.	25.	100.	10.	30.	40.	10.	20.	15.	25.
2003	5,101,000	10.	25.	125.	10.	30.	40.	10.	20.	15.	25.

UNCROWNED PORTRAIT, LOON REVERSE, 2003-2004.

Designer and Engravers:
Obv.: Susanna Blunt, Susan Taylor
Rev.: Robert R. Carmichael, Terrence Smith

Specifications: Same as 1988 issue

DATE	DESCRIPTION	MINTAGE	MS-64 C	MS-65 C	MS-66 C	MS-65 NC	MS-66 NC	MSP-67 NC	SP-66	SP-67	PR-67	PR-68
2003	Loon	Included	20.	35.	100.	*	*	*	*	*	*	*
2003W	Loon	Included	*	*	*	15.	25.	50.	*	*	*	*
2004	Loon	3,408,000	15.	25.	75.	10.	15.	40.	*	*	15.	25.

UNCROWNED PORTRAIT, LOON AND OLYMPIC FLAMES REVERSE, 2004.

Carrying on the spirit established in the Winter Olympic Games of 2002, the Royal Canadian Mint issued a Lucky Loon as a good luck symbol for the 2004 Summer Olympic Games held in Athens, Greece.

Designer and Engravers:
Obv.: Susanna Blunt, Susan Taylor
Rev.: R. R. Carmichael, Susan Taylor, RCM Staff

Specifications: Same as 1988 issue

DATE	DESCRIPTION	MINTAGE	MS-64 C	MS-65 C	MS-66 C	MS-65 NC	MS-66 NC	MSP-67 NC	SP-66	SP-67	PR-67	PR-68
2004	Olympic Flames	6,526,000	15.	25.	45.	*	*	*	*	*	*	*

UNCROWNED PORTRAIT, LOON REVERSE, 2005.

Designer and Engravers:
Obv.: Susanna Blunt, Susan Taylor
Rev.: Robert R. Carmichael, Terrence Smith

Specifications: Same as 1988 issue

DATE	DESCRIPTION	MINTAGE	MS-64 C	MS-65 C	MS-66 C	MS-65 NC	MS-66 NC	MS-67 NC	SP-66	SP-67	PR-67	PR-68
2005	Loon	32,336,000	15.	20.	55.	10.	20.	40.	*	*	15.	25.

UNCROWNED PORTRAIT, 25TH ANNIVERSARY OF THE MARATHON OF HOPE REVERSE, 2005.

On April 12th, 1980, Terry Fox began his Marathon of Hope in St. John's, Newfoundland. He was not to finish, but his marathon continues. The Terry Fox dollar is the first circulating commemorative to feature a Canadian hero.

A variety of the Terry Fox dollar has been created by die polishing. Polishing variations exist.

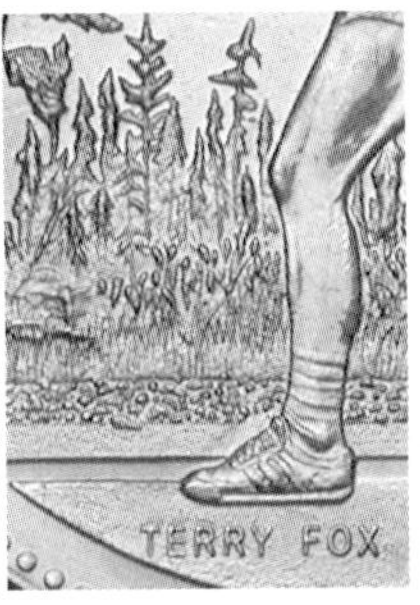

Grass

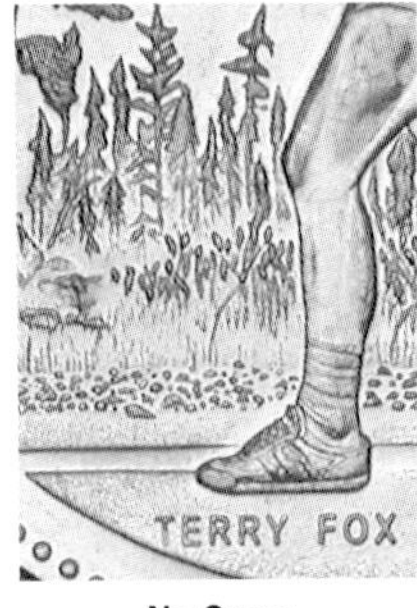

No Grass

Designer and Engravers:
Obv.: Susanna Blunt, Susan Taylor
Rev.: Stan Witten, R.C.M. Staff

Specifications: Same as 1988 issue

DATE	DESCRIPTION	MINTAGE	MS-64 C	MS-65 C	MS-66 C	MS-65 NC	MS-66 NC	MS-67 NC	SP-66	SP-67	PR-67	PR-68
2005	Grass	12,909,00	15.	20.	35.	*	*	*	*	*	*	*
2005	No Grass	Included	35.	60.	225.	*	*	*	*	*	*	*

UNCROWNED PORTRAIT, LOON SETTLING, CANADIAN OLYMPIC SYMBOLS REVERSE, 2006.

Designer and Engravers:
Obv.: Susanna Blunt, Susan Taylor
Rev.: Unknown

Specifications: Same as 1988 issue

DATE	DESCRIPTION	MINTAGE	MS-64 C	MS-65 C	MS-66 C	MS-65 NC	MS-66 NC	MS-67 NC	SP-66	SP-67	PR-67	PR-68
2006	Loon Settling	10,495,000	15.	20.	35.	*	*	*	*	*	*	*

UNCROWNED PORTRAIT, LOON REVERSE, 2006.

Designer and Engravers:
Obv.: Susanna Blunt, Susan Taylor
Rev.: Robert R. Carmichael, Terrence Smith

Specifications: Same as 1988 issue

DATE	DESCRIPTION	MINTAGE	MS-64 C	MS-65 C	MS-66 C	MS-65 NC	MS-66 NC	MS-67 NC	SP-66	SP-67	PR-67	PR-68
2006	Loon	37,085,000	15.	25.	40.	10.	15.	40.	*	*	15.	25.

UNCROWNED PORTRAIT, RCM LOGO, LOON REVERSE, 2006-2008.

Designer and Engravers:
Obv.: Susanna Blunt, Susan Taylor
Rev.: Robert R. Carmichael, Terrence Smith

Specifications: Same as 1988 issue

DATE	DESCRIPTION	MINTAGE	MS-64 C	MS-65 C	MS-66 C	MS-65 NC	MS-66 NC	MS-67 NC	SP-66	SP-67	PR-67	PR-68
2006	Loon	Included	15.	25.	50.	10.	15.	35.	*	*	*	*
2007	Loon	38,045,000	15.	20.	35.	15.	20.	35.	*	*	15.	25.
2008	Loon	18,710,000	10.	20.	40.	10.	15.	35.	*	*	15.	25.

UNCROWNED PORTRAIT, RCM LOGO, LOON DANCE, CANADIAN OLYMPIC SYMBOLS REVERSE, 2008.

Designer and Engravers:
Obv.: Susanna Blunt, Susan Taylor
Rev.: Jean-Luc Grondin, RCM Staff

Specifications: Same as 1988 issue

DATE	DESCRIPTION	MINTAGE	MS-64 C	MS-65 C	MS-66 C	MS-65 NC	MS-66 NC	MS-67 NC	SP-66	SP-67	PR-67	PR-68
2008	Loon Dance	10,851,000	10.	20.	35.	10.	15.	35.	*	*	*	*

UNCROWNED PORTRAIT, RCM LOGO, MONTREAL CANADIENS REVERSE, 2009.

Designer and Engravers:
Obv.: Susanna Blunt, Susan Taylor
Rev.: RCM Staff

Specifications: Same as 1988 issue

DATE	DESCRIPTION	MINTAGE	MS-64 C	MS-65 C	MS-66 C	MS-65 NC	MS-66 NC	MS-67 NC	SP-66	SP-67	PR-67	PR-68
2009	Loon	10,250,000	10.	20.	40.	*	*	*	*	*	*	*

UNCROWNED PORTRAIT, RCM LOGO, LOON REVERSE, 2009-2010.

Designer and Engravers:
Obv.: Susanna Blunt, Susan Taylor
Rev.: Robert R. Carmichael, Terrence Smith

Specifications: Same as 1988 issue

DATE	DESCRIPTION	MINTAGE	MS-64 C	MS-65 C	MS-66 C	MS-65 NC	MS-66 NC	MS-67 NC	SP-66	SP-67	PR-67	PR-68
2009	Loon	29,351,000	10.	25.	50.	10.	15.	40.	*	*	15.	25.
2010	Loon	4,110,000	10.	25.	45.	10.	25.	35.	*	*	15.	25.

UNCROWNED PORTRAIT, VANCOUVER WINTER OLYMPIC GAMES REVERSE, 2010.

Designer and Engravers:
Obv.: Susanna Blunt, Susan Taylor
Rev.: RCM Staff

Specifications: Same as 1988 issue

DATE	DESCRIPTION	MINTAGE	MS-64 C	MS-65 C	MS-66 C	MS-65 NC	MS-66 NC	MS-67 NC	SP-66	SP-67	PR-67	PR-68
2010	Vancouver 2010	10,250,000	10.	20.	40.	10.	15.	35.	*	*	*	*

UNCROWNED PORTRAIT, 100TH ANNIVERSARY OF THE CANADIAN NAVY REVERSE, 1910-2010.

Designer and Engravers:
Obv.: Susanna Blunt, Susan Taylor
Rev.: Bonnie Ross, Stan Witten

Specifications: Same as 1988 issue

DATE	DESCRIPTION	MINTAGE	MS-64 C	MS-65 C	MS-66 C	MS-65 NC	MS-66 NC	MS-67 NC	SP-66	SP-67	PR-67	PR-68
2010	Canadian Navy	7,000,000	10.	20.	30.	*	*	*	*	*	*	*

UNCROWNED PORTRAIT, 100TH ANNIVERSARY OF THE SASKATCHEWAN ROUGHRIDERS REVERSE, 1910-2010.

Designer and Engravers:
Obv.: Susanna Blunt, Susan Taylor
Rev.: Saskatchewan Roughriders Football Club, RCM Staff

Specifications: Same as 1988 issue

DATE	DESCRIPTION	MINTAGE	MS-64 C	MS-65 C	MS-66 C	MS-65 NC	MS-66 NC	MS-67 NC	SP-66	SP-67	PR-67	PR-68
2010	Sask. Roughriders	3,100,000	10.	15.	40.	*	*	*	*	*	*	*

UNCROWNED PORTRAIT, RCM LOGO, LOON REVERSE, 2011-2012.

With the cessation in 2011 of the Brilliant Uncirculated finish (MS-65-NC) on coins contained in the Uncirculated Sets, it was necessary to remove that block of grades from the pricing tables.

Designer and Engravers:
Obv.: Susanna Blunt, Susan Taylor
Rev.: Robert R. Carmichael, Terrence Smith

Specifications: Same as 1988 issue

DATE	DESCRIPTION	MINTAGE	MS-64 C	MS-65 C	MS-66 C	MS-67 C	SP-66	SP-67	PR-67	PR-68
2011	Loon	20,410,000	10.	20.	50.	—	*	*	15.	25.
2012	Loon	2,414,000	15.	25.	40.	100.	*	*	15.	25.

UNCROWNED PORTRAIT, RCM LOGO, PARKS CANADA REVERSE, 2011.

The Dominion Parks Branch, known today as Parks Canada, was founded in 1911. Its mandate is to conserve Canada's unrivalled wilderness for Canadians to explore.

Designer and Engravers:
Obv.: Susanna Blunt, Susan Taylor
Rev.: Nolin DDBO Montreal, William Woodruff

Specifications: Same as 1988 issue

DATE	DESCRIPTION	MINTAGE	MS-64 C	MS-65 C	MS-66 C	MS-67 C	SP-66	SP-67	PR-67	PR-68
2011	Parks Canada	*5,000,000*	10.	15.	40.	100.	*	*	*	*

UNCROWNED PORTRAIT, 100 YEARS OF THE GREY CUP, REVERSE WITH SECURITY CIRCLE, 2012.

This coin was issued to commemorate the 100th anniversary of the Grey Cup. Commissioned in 1909 by Earl Grey, then Canada's Governor-General, the cup was awarded as the national championship of the Canadian Football League (CFL).

Designer and Engravers:
Obv.: Susanna Blunt, Susan Taylor
Rev.: RCM Engravers

Composition: Multi-ply brass plated steel
Weight: 6.27 g
11-sided: 26.5 mm
Thickness: 1.95 mm
Edge: Plain
Die Axis: ↑↑

DATE	DESCRIPTION	MINTAGE	MS-64 C	MS-65 C	MS-66 C	MS-67 C	SP-66	SP-67	PR-67	PR-68
2012	Grey Cup	5,000,000	15.	20.	45.	—	*	*	*	*

UNCROWNED PORTRAIT, LUCKY LOONIE, REVERSE WITH SECURITY CIRCLE, 2012.

The 2012 Lucky Loonie was issued to support the Canadian athletes who competed in the London 2012 Olympic and Paralympic Games.

Security Device

Designer and Engravers:
Obv.: Susanna Blunt, Susan Taylor
Rev.: Emily Damstra, RCM Staff

Composition: Multi-ply brass plated steel
Weight: 6.27 g
11-sided: 26.5 mm
Thickness: 1.95 mm
Edge: Plain
Die Axis: ↑↑

DATE	DESCRIPTION	MINTAGE	MS-64 C	MS-65 C	MS-66 C	MS-67 C	SP-66	SP-67	PR-67	PR-68
2012	Lucky Loonie	5,000,000	15.	30.	50.	—	*	*	*	*
2014	Lucky Loonie	N/A	15.	30.	50.	—	*	*	*	*

UNCROWNED PORTRAIT, LOON REVERSE WITH SECURITY CIRCLE, 2012-2014.

Besides a change in composition to multi-ply brass plated steel, the one-dollar loon now carries a security device on the reverse of the coin. The micro-laser security mark is produced on the ridges of the maple leaf contained in the circle above the loon. This laser security mark is produced during the striking of the coins using contrasting pattern micro-engraved on the coin die itself.

Security Device

Designer and Engravers:
Obv.: Susanna Blunt, Susan Taylor
Rev.: Robert R. Carmichael, T. Smith

Composition: Multi-ply brass plated steel
Weight: 6.27 g
11-sided: 26.5 mm
Thickness: 1.95 mm
Edge: Plain
Die Axis: ↑↑

DATE	DESCRIPTION	MINTAGE	MS-64 C	MS-65 C	MS-66 C	MS-67 C	SP-66	SP-67	PR-67	PR-68
2012	Rev. Security Stamp	107,105,000	15.	30.	50.	125.	*	*	*	*
2013		120,330,000	15.	30.	60.	150.	*	*	*	*
2014		N/A	15.	30.	60.	150.	*	*	*	*

TWO DOLLAR CIRCULATING COINS

TWO DOLLAR BIMETALLIC
ELIZABETH II 1996 TO DATE

DIADEMED PORTRAIT, MAPLE LEAF LOGO OBVERSE, POLAR BEAR REVERSE, 1996.

Canada's official launch of the bimetallic two dollar coin took place on February 19, 1996. In the months leading up to the launch date concern was mounting whether the new striking process being developed by The Mint would be ready in time. The Mint had guaranteed the Government of Canada that 60 million coins would be ready for launch date, as the sequence was such that production of the $2 bank note would stop on the same day as what was later to be called the "toonie" was launched.

The process under development by The Mint envisioned that the assembly and striking of the two metal parts would take place in the striking chamber of the coin press. Upon striking, the core and ring would expand into each other forming an interlocking fit as a result of the hardness differential of the ring and core.

As time drew near, and to ensure that the guarantee would be met, 10 million preassembled planchets with the same specifications were purchased from a German supplier, Deutsche Nickel. The planchets were used and no more orders placed. The Mint process was operating successfully.

Identification of the two planchet varieties is difficult at best and may be accomplished only with practise. The identification of planchet varieties in circulated coins is even more difficult.

The two dollar coin stuck from a Canadian planchet has a shiny, polished finish that some collectors describe as "oily". The two dollar coin struck from a German planchet has a dull, matte-like finish, with lines similar to the bullion finish across the ring.

Designers and Engravers:
Obv.: Dora de Pédery-Hunt, Ago Aarand
Rev.: Brent Townsend, Ago Aarand

Composition:
Ring: .99+ nickel
Core: .92 copper, .06 aluminum, .02 nickel

Weight: 7.3 grams
Diameter: Ring: 28.0 mm; Core: 16.8 mm
Thickness: 1.80 mm
Edge: Interrupted serration
Die Axes: ↑↑

1996 Obverse: Die Clash

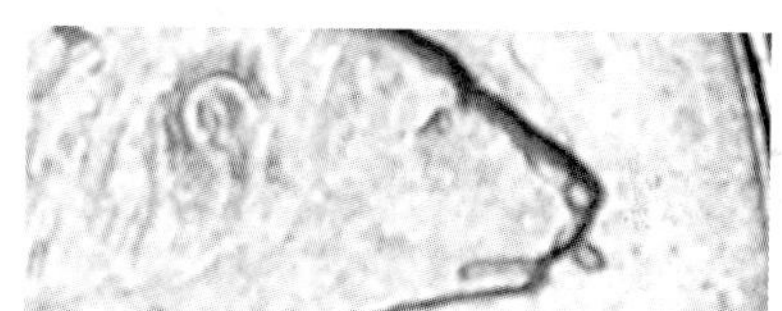
1996 Reverse: Die Chip "Cigar"

1996 Reverse: Die Chip "Horn"

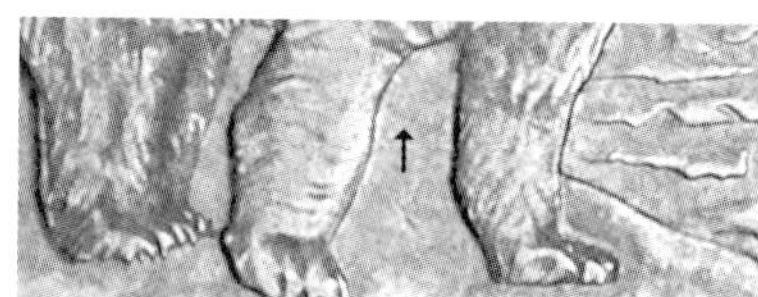
1996 Reverse: Die Polishing "No Ice"

DATE	MINTAGE	MS-64 C	MS-65 C	MS-66 C	MS-65 NC	MS-66 NC	MS-67 NC	SP-66	SP-67	PR-67	PR-68
1996 Canadian	315,483,000	15.	50.	120.	*	*	*	15.	20.	15.	20.
1996 German	10,000,000	200.	250.	—	*	*	*	*	*	*	*
1996 Die Clash	Included	20.	70.	135.	*	*	*	*	*	*	*
1996 Cigar	Included	20.	70.	135.	*	*	*	*	*	*	*
1996 Horn	Included	20.	70.	150.	*	*	*	*	*	*	*
1996 No Ice	Included	30.	75.	150.	*	*	*	*	*	*	*

Note: Normally clashes, die chips, etc. are not listed in this catalogue. We made an exception for the two dollar coins due to their short life span. You will find clashes and chips throughout the date range.

DIADEMED PORTRAIT, MAPLE LEAF LOGO OBVERSE, POLAR BEAR REVERSE, 1997-1999.

Starting in 1997 the proof two dollar coins issued by the Royal Canadian Mint were struck on (non-standard) sterling silver planchets. For the two dollar proof coins 1997 to 2011 see *Canadian Coins, Volume Two, Collector and Maple Leaf Issues*.

DATE	MINTAGE	MS-64 C	MS-65 C	MS-66 C	MS-65 NC	MS-66 NC	MS-67 NC	SP-66	SP-67	PR-67	PR-68
1997	16,942,000	10.	25.	95.	10.	20.	60.	15.	20.	15.	20.
1998	5,309,000	15.	45.	60.	10.	20.	30.	15.	20.	20.	25.
1998W	N.I.I.	*	*	*	20.	40.	50.	*	*	*	*
1999	N.I.I.	*	*	*	10.	20.	45.	15.	20.	15.	20.

DIADEMED PORTRAIT, MAPLE LEAF OBVERSE; NUNAVUT REVERSE, 1999.

This two dollar coin was issued on May 27, 1999, to commemorate the creation of a third territory in Canada, Nunavut.

Designers and Engravers:
Obv.: Dora de Pédery-Hunt
Rev.: G. Arnaktavyok, José Osio

Specifications: Same as 1996 issue

DATE	MINTAGE	MS-64 C	MS-65 C	MS-66 C	MS-65 NC	MS-66 NC	MS-67 NC	SP-66	SP-67
1999	25,130,000	15.	30.	50.	10.	20.	50.	15.	30.

DIADEMED PORTRAIT, MAPLE LEAF OBVERSE; PATH OF KNOWLEDGE REVERSE, 2000.

Issued to commemorate the 2000 Millennium, the Path of Knowledge $2.00 coin was launched July 1, 2000 at a citizenship ceremony at Downsview, Toronto. The coin is inscribed with Knowledge - Le Savoir reflecting the experience, wisdom and knowledge that is passed down from generation to generation.

Designer and Engraver:
Obv.: Dora de Pédery-Hunt
Rev.: Cosme Saffioti

Specifications: Same as 1996 issue

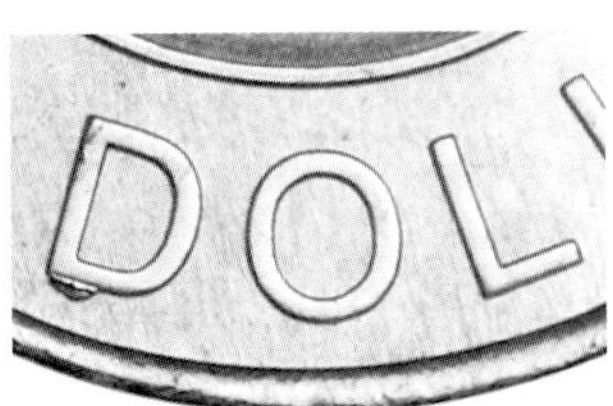

Obverse: Pedestal "D"

Obverse: Pedestal "S"

DATE	MINTAGE	MS-64 C	MS-65 C	MS-66 C	MS-65 NC	MS-66 NC	MS-67 NC	SP-66	SP-67
2000	29,880,000	10.	30.	40.	10.	30.	70.	15.	20.
2000 D	Included	15.	35.	50.	*	*	*	*	*
2000 S	Included	15.	25.	50.	*	*	*	*	*

DIADEMED PORTRAIT, MAPLE LEAF OBVERSE; POLAR BEAR REVERSE RESUMED, 2000-2003.

The 2000 Polar Bear reverse is only found in numismatic sets of that year, it was not issued for circulation.

The 2002 Jubilee issue commemorates the 50th anniversary of the reign of Queen Elizabeth II. All circulating coinage carries the dual dates of her reign, 1952-2002.

2000 and 2003

1952-2002
Double dates

Designers, Engravers, and Specifications:
Same as 1996 issue

2000 Reverse:
Pedestal "O" (PED)

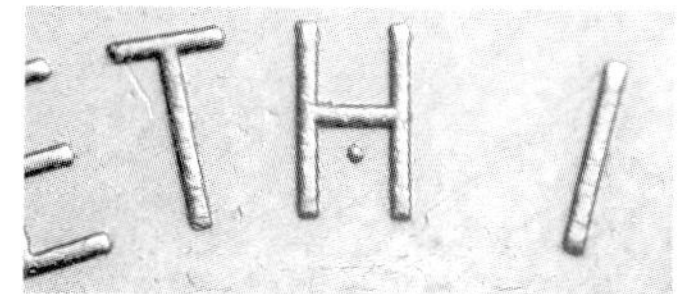

2002 Obverse:
Dot in "H" of ELIZABETH

DATE	MINTAGE	MS-64 C	MS-65 C	MS-66 C	MS-65 NC	MS-66 NC	MS-67 NC	SP-66	SP-67
2000	N.I.I.	*	*	*	10.	25.	50.	20.	25.
2000 PED O	N.I.I.	*	*	*	15.	25.	50.	*	*
2000W	N.I.I.	*	*	*	10.	20.	30.	*	*
2001	11,910,000	15.	30.	150.	10.	20.	35.	15.	20.
2002 (1952-)	27,020,000	10.	20.	70.	10.	20.	50.	15.	20.
2002 Dot	Included	20.	30.	60.	*	*	*	*	*
2003	7,123,697	10.	40.	70.	10.	20.	50.	15.	20.

UNCROWNED PORTRAIT, MAPLE LEAF OBVERSE; POLAR BEAR REVERSE, 2003-2006.

Mid-year 2006 the maple leaf which appeared above the Queen's portrait was discontinued. The date now appeared above the Queen's portrait, and the Royal Canadian Mint logo appeared below. The mintage shown in the table below is a combination of both varieties (see also page 225).

Designers and Engravers:
Obv.: Susanna Blunt, Susan Taylor
Rev.: Brent Townsend, Ago Aarand

Specifications: Same as 1996 issue

DATE	MINTAGE	MS-64 C	MS-65 C	MS-66 C	MS-65 NC	MS-66 NC	MS-67 NC	SP-66	SP-67
2003	4,120,104	15.	50.	150.	*	*	*	*	*
2003W	71,142	*	*	*	15.	30.	45.	*	*
2004	12,907,000	10.	25.	70.	15.	20.	35.	15.	20.
2005	38,318,000	10.	20.	35.	10.	15.	50.	15.	25.
2006	25,274,000	10.	20.	50.	10.	15.	50.	*	*

Note: The mintage figure for 2006 (25,274,000) is divided between the 2006 Uncrowned Portrait, Maple Leaf Obverse, and the Uncrowned Portrait, RCM Logo Obverse (see page 225).

UNCROWNED PORTRAIT, MAPLE LEAF AND DOUBLE DATE OBVERSE; POLAR BEAR REVERSE, 1996-2006.

The year 2006 was the 10th anniversary of the "Toonie" Canada's two dollar coin. This design is found in the Proof, Specimen and Brilliant Uncirculated sets dated 2006.

Designers, Engravers and Specifications:
Same as 1996 issue

DATE	MINTAGE	MS-64 C	MS-65 C	MS-66 C	MS-65 NC	MS-66 NC	MS-67 NC	SP-66	SP-67
2006 (1996-)	N.I.I.	*	*	*	15.	25.	50.	15.	20.

UNCROWNED PORTRAIT, RCM LOGO, DOUBLE DATE OBVERSE; "CHURCHILL" REVERSE, 1996-2006.

In 2006 a contest was held to name the new polar bear design to appear on the 10th anniversary two dollar coin. The name "Churchill" was the winner. The 10th anniversary coin has the double dates above the Queen's portrait and the Royal Mint logo below.

The two dollar "Churchill" coin was struck at both the Winnipeg and Ottawa Mints. The coins from the Winnipeg Mint, which are the circulation issue, have the "Pixie" ear. The coins from the Ottawa Mint have the normal polar bear ear, and were issued in the 2006 Special Edition Uncirculated Set (see *Canadian Coins, Volume Two*, 5th edition, page 353) and the 2006 Concept Test Token Set (see Concept Token Set, page 290).

Designers and Engravers:
Obv.: Susanna Blunt, Susan Taylor
Rev.: Tony Bianco, Stan Witten

Specifications: Same as 1996 issue

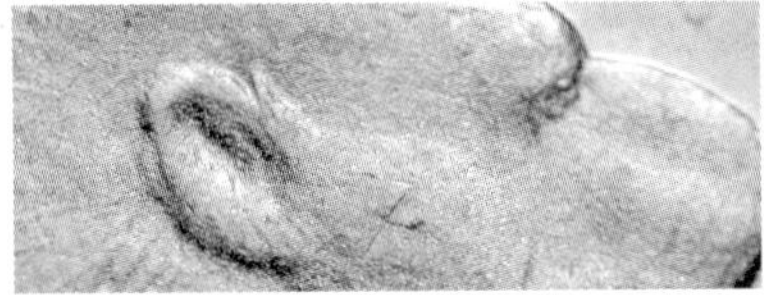

Reverse: Pixie Ear "Churchill"

DATE/ MINT LOGO	DESCRIPTION	MINTAGE	MS-64 C	MS-65 C	MS-66 C	MS-65 NC	MS-66 NC	MS-67 NC	SP-66	SP-67
2006 (1996-)	Pixie Ear	5,005,000	15.	35.	75.	*	*	*	*	*
2006 (1996-)	Normal Ear	31,636	*	*	*	15.	25.	50.	*	*

NOTES ON TWO DOLLAR LISTINGS

1. When the pricing table list Specimen (SP-66 and SP-67) varieties the prices are for those coins which have been removed from Specimen Sets and certified by a Canadian grading company.
2. The MS-65 NC (non-circulating) and higher grades are listings for coins removed from Brilliant Uncirculated sets.
3. Mintage numbers listed in the pricing tables are for circulation coinage (MS-64 to MS-66-C Business Strikes). The mintage figures for Brilliant Uncirculated (MS-65 to MS-67-NC), Specimen (SP-66 to SP-67), and Proof (PR-67 to PR-68) must be obtained from Volume two, Collector and Maple Leaf Issues.

UNCROWNED PORTRAIT, RCM LOGO OBVERSE, POLAR BEAR REVERSE, 2006-2008.

Designers and Engravers:
Obv.: Susanna Blunt, Susan Taylor
Rev.: Brent Townsend, Ago Aarand

Specifications: Same as 1996 issue

DATE/ MINT LOGO	DESCRIPTION	MINTAGE	MS-64 C	MS-65 C	MS-66 C	MS-65 NC	MS-66 NC	MS-67 NC	SP-66	SP-67
2006		Included	15.	35.	75.	*	*	*	*	*
2007		38,957,000	10.	15.	40.	10.	15.	50.	15.	40.
2008		12,390,000	10.	20.	70.	10.	15.	50.	15.	40.

UNCROWNED PORTRAIT, QUEBEC CITY REVERSE, 1608-2008.

This coin was issued to commemorate the 400th anniversary of Quebec City.

Designers and Engravers:
Obv.: Susanna Blunt, Susan Taylor
Rev.: Genevieve Bertrand, William Woodruff

Specifications:
Same as 1996 issues

DATE	DESCRIPTION	MINTAGE	MS-64 C	MS-65 C	MS-66 C	MS-65 NC	MS-66 NC	MS-67 NC	SP-66	SP-67
2008 (1608-)	Quebec City	6,010,000	10.	20.	45.	*	*	*	*	*

UNCROWNED PORTRAIT, RCM LOGO OBVERSE; POLAR BEAR REVERSE, 2009-2010.

The 2010 two dollar coin can be found with two edge variations: the standard 16-serrations in use since 1996, and the 14-serration edge now in use on the 2012 issue. A quick visual identification of the two edge varieties is by the length of the serrations.

Designers and Engravers:
Obv.: Susanna Blunt, Susan Taylor
Rev.: Brent Townsend, Ago Aarand

Specifications: Same as 1996 issue except for Edge Interrupted Serration varieties on 2010 coins

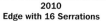

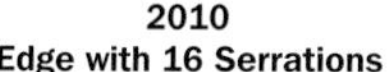
2010
Edge with 16 Serrations

2010
Edge with 14 Serrations

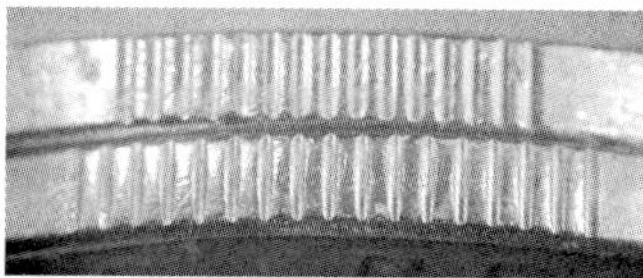
Serration comparison

DATE/ MINT LOGO	DESCRIPTION	MINTAGE	MS-64 C	MS-65 C	MS-66 C	MS-65 NC	MS-66 NC	MS-67 NC	SP-66	SP-67
2009		38,430,000	10.	20.	60.	10.	15.	50.	15.	40.
2010	16 Serrations	8,220,000	10.	30.	45.	10.	20.	50.	15.	40.
2010	14 Serrations	Included	20.	80.	250.	*	*	*	*	*

UNCROWNED PORTRAIT, RCM LOGO OBVERSE; POLAR BEAR REVERSE, 2011-2012.

Designers and Engravers:
Obv.: Susanna Blunt, Susan Taylor
Rev.: Brent Townsend, Ago Aarand

Specifications: Same as 1996 issue

DATE	DESCRIPTION	MINTAGE	MS-64 C	MS-65 C	MS-66 C	MS-67 C	SP-66	SP-67
2011		22,488,000	10.	15.	50.	—	15.	40.
2012		1,531,000	10.	15.	50.	—	15.	40.

UNCROWNED PORTRAIT, BOREAL FOREST REVERSE, 2011.

Designers and Engravers:
Obv.: Susanna Blunt, Susan Taylor
Rev.: Nolin BBDO Montreal, Christie Paquet

Specifications: Same as 1996 issue

DATE	DESCRIPTION	MINTAGE	MS-64 C	MS-65 C	MS-66 C	MS-67 C	SP-66	SP-67
2011	Boreal Forest	5,000,000	15.	25.	30.	100.	*	*

UNCROWNED PORTRAIT, POLAR BEAR WITH SECURITY FEATURE REVERSE, 2012-2014.

There are three visible changes to the new two-dollar coin. There are two laser marks of maple leaves, each within a circle, at the bottom of the coin's reverse. A virtual image of two maple leaves will appear at the top of the reverse. A different image is produced as the coin is turned from side to side. The virtual image is produced by engraving different patterns on each side of the two-sided grooves on the reverse window of the coin.

The edge lettering may be upright in relation to the obverse, or upset in relation to obverse, depending on which way the coin passed through the edge lettering die. The frequency is 50/50, therefore of equal value.

Designers and Engravers:
Obv.: Susanna Blunt, Susan Taylor
Rev.: Brent Townsend, Ago Aarand

Composition:
Ring: Multi-ply nickel plated steel
Core: Multi-ply brass plated aluminum bronze

Weight: 6.92 grams
Diameter: Ring: 28.0 mm
Thickness: 1.75 mm
Edge: Interrupted serration
Edge lettering: CANADA 2 DOLLARS
Die Axes: ↑↑

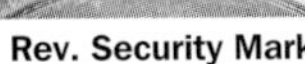
Rev. Security Mark

Rev. Security Mark

Edge Serrations and Lettering

DATE	DESCRIPTION	MINTAGE	MS-64 C	MS-65 C	MS-66 C	MS-67 C	SP-66	SP-67
2012	Security Marks	82,862,000	15.	40.	50.	—	*	*
2013		12,390,000	15.	35.	75.	—	30.	45.
2014		N/A	15.	35.	75.	—	30.	45.

UNCROWNED PORTRAIT, HMS SHANNON, WAR OF 1812, SECURITY FEATURE REVERSE, 2012.

This two-dollar coin which features *HMS Shannon*, a Leda-class frigate, commemorates the historic eleven-minute battle with the *USS Chesapeake* off the coast of Boston.

Designers and Engravers:
Obv.: Susanna Blunt, Susan Taylor
Rev.: Brent Townsend, Ago Aarand
Specifications: Same as 1996 issue

DATE	DESCRIPTION	MINTAGE	MS-64 C	MS-65 C	MS-66 C	MS-67 C	SP-66	SP-67
2012	HMS Shannon	5,000,000	10.	30.	—	—	*	*

FIVE AND TEN DOLLAR SILVER COINS

Montreal was chosen as the site for the XXI Olympiad, the summer Olympics of 1976. Taking the lead from the Munich Olympics in 1972, it was proposed that Canada Post issue Olympic coins to assist in the financing of the Montreal games. The Olympic Coin Program, a marketing arm of Canada Post, was established to assume overall control, with the Royal Canadian Mint being assigned the role of manufacturer for the 28-coin series. The first four coins of the series were issued in two parts: a monetizing issue through the banking system at face value, where **no packaging** was involved; the second, a more complicated issue, offering two types of finishes and many different varieties of packaging. Only the four coins placed into circulation are listed here. The complete set of collector issues are listed in *Canadian Coins, Volume Two*, pages 162 to 170.

Obverse $5

Map of North America

Kingston and Sailboats

Obverse $10

Map of the World

Montreal Skyline

Designers: Obv.: Arnold Machin
Rev.: Georges Huel, worked by invitation

Engravers:
1. ($10 Map of the World): design was photochemically etched
2. ($5 Map of North America): design was photochemically etched
3. ($10 Montreal Skyline): Ago Aarand
4. ($5 Kingston and Sailboats): Terrance Smith

$5 Coin
Composition: .925 silver, .075 copper
Weight: 24.30 grams
Edge: Reeded
Diameter: 38.00 mm
Thickness: 2.35 mm
Die Axes: ↑↑

$10 Coin
Composition: .925 silver, .075 copper
Weight: 48.60 grams
Edge: Reeded
Diameter: 45.00 mm
Thickness: 3.15 mm
Die Axes: ↑↑

DATE	DENOM.	DESCRIPTION	MINTAGE	FINISH	MS-65	MS-66	MS-67
1973	$5	Map of North America		Circulation	20.	40.	75.
1973	$5	Kingston and Sailboats	Not	Circulation	20.	40.	75.
1973	$10	Map of the World	Known	Circulation	40.	75.	150.
1973	$10	Montreal Skyline		Circulation	40.	75.	150.

OTTAWA MINT SOVEREIGNS

The British £1 pieces (sovereigns) coined at the Ottawa Mint between 1908 and 1919 occupy a controversial position in Canadian numismatics. Some argue that these pieces are Canadian and must be collected as part of the Canadian series, while others claim that they are British and are separate from the decimal series of the Dominion of Canada.

From the time of the opening of the Ottawa Mint it was the intention of the Dominion government to mint decimal gold coins; however, the fact that the Ottawa Mint was a branch of the Royal Mint in London meant it was obligated to mint sovereigns on request. And while sovereigns were legal tender in Canada, so were gold coins of the United States. Neither type of gold circulated to any significant degree in Canada in the 20th century. Most companies who requested the Ottawa Mint to strike sovereigns did so because they wanted the coins for export purposes. Finally, the fact that some sovereigns were coined at the Ottawa Mint does not automatically make them Canadian, any more than other coinages (e.g. Newfoundland or Jamaica) produced there.

ONE POUND (SOVEREIGNS)
EDWARD VII 1908-1910

As with all other branch mint sovereigns of the period, the Edward VII Canadian sovereigns are identical to the corresponding London mint issues except for the branch mint mark. The 1908 strikes were Specimen coins only and the tiny mintage was struck merely to establish the series. The "C" mint mark (for Canada) is on the ground line above the centre of the date.

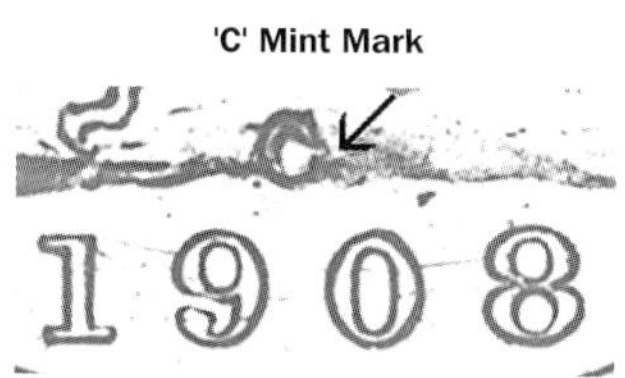

Designer and Engraver:
Obv.: George W. DeSaulles
Rev.: Benedetto Pistrucci
Composition: .917 gold, .083 copper
Weight: 7.99 grams
Diameter: 22.05 mm
Edge: Reeded
Die Axes: ↑↑

DATE / MINT MARK	MINTAGE	FINISH	GRADE 20	40	50	55	60	63	64	65	66
1908C	636	Specimen	2,500.	3,500.	4,000.	4,500.	5,000.	6,000.	10,000.	14,000.	—
1909C	16,273	Circulation	425.	450.	475.	525.	725.	2,000.	3,500.	15,000.	—
1910C	28,012	Circulation	425.	450.	475.	750.	1,000.	2,500.	6,000.	—	—

ONE POUND (SOVEREIGNS)
GEORGE V 1911 - 1919

The mintages for the Ottawa mint sovereigns of George V continued the modest trend set in the previous reign. The total of all sovereigns from Ottawa barely equalled the yearly mintage at London or one of the Australian branch mints.

The 1916C issue is rare, with about fifty or so pieces known. Most of the small mintage may have been melted, accounting for the rarity, although this is by no means an established fact. Until the last few years the 1916 London issue was also rare, but thousands of them were released from a British bank.

Another tale told about the 1916C sovereign is that the mintage was lost at sea on its way to England during World War I, as part of an international settlement. This is not established fact, only rumour. If there was to be a gold exchange between Canada and England in 1916, the gold needed only to be deposited with the New York Federal Reserve for the account of Great Britain, and not subjected to a perilous sea voyage during a time of war.

The reverse of the George V sovereigns is the same as that for Edward VII.

Designer and Engraver:
Obv.: E. B. Mackennal
Rev.: Benedetto Pistrucci
Composition: .917 gold, .083 copper
Weight: 7.99 grams
Diameter: 22.05 mm
Edge: Reeded
Die Axes: ↑↑

DATE / MINT	MINTAGE	VF-20	EF-40	AU-50	AU-55	MS-60	MS-62	MS-63	MS-64	MS-65	MS-66	SP-63	SP-65
1911C	256,946	400.	425.	450.	475.	500.	525.	550.	600.	3,000.	—	3,500.	9,000.
1913C	3,715	900.	1,200.	1,500.	2,000.	2,500.	3,000.	3,750.	5,000.	—	—	*	*
1914C	14,891	450.	475.	500.	550.	600.	750.	1,200.	2,000.	—	—	*	*
1916C	6,111	20,000.	22,000.	27,000.	29,000.	35,000.	37,500.	40,000.	60,000.	—	—	*	*
1917C	58,845	400.	425.	450.	475.	500.	525.	775.	1,500.	—	—	*	*
1918C	106,516	400.	425.	450.	500.	550.	650.	1,000.	—	—	—	*	*
1919C	135,889	400.	425.	450.	500.	550.	700.	900.	1,500.	—	—	*	*

FIVE DOLLARS — GOLD
George V 1912 - 1914

From the first year of operation of the Ottawa Mint it was planned that gold should be coined in dollar denominations as well as British sovereigns. The preparations proceeded slowly, however, and it was not until 1911 that final designs were decided upon (see DC-7 and DC-8 in the chapter on patterns) for the $5 and $10 coins. Originally it had been planned to strike denominations of $2.50, $5, $10 and $20, but some time in 1911 these plans were modified to include only the two middle denominations.

Coins for circulation were first issued in 1912. Their production was halted in 1914, when Canada adopted new wartime legislation to restrict the flow of gold. At that time notes issued by the Dominion government ceased to be redeemable in gold. This redeemability was not restored until 1926.

The design for the reverse features the then current Canadian coat of arms superimposed upon two boughs of maple.

Designer:
Obv.: Sir E. B. Mackennal
Rev.: W. H. J. Blakemore
Composition: .900 gold, .100 copper
Weight: 8.36 grams
Diameter: 21.59 mm
Edge: Reeded
Die Axes: ↑↑

DATE	MINTAGE	VF-20	EF-40	AU-50	AU-55	MS-60	MS-62	MS-63	MS-64	MS-65	MS-66	SP-63	SP-65
1912	165,680	450.	475.	500.	525.	575.	625.	825.	1,200.	3,000.	—	6,000.	15,000.
1913	98,832	450.	475.	500.	525.	575.	625.	825.	1,400.	3,000.	—	*	*
1914	31,122	500.	550.	725.	825.	1,100.	1,400.	3,000.	—	—	—	*	*

TEN DOLLARS — GOLD
GEORGE V 1912 - 1914

The designs of this denomination are the same as those of the $5 except for the change in size and value.

Designers:
Obv.: Sir E. B. Mackennal
Rev.: W. H. J. Blakemore
Composition: .900 gold, .100 copper
Weight: 16.72 grams
Diameter: 26.92 mm
Edge: Reeded
Die Axes: ↑↑

DATE	MINTAGE	VF-20	EF-40	AU-50	AU-55	MS-60	MS-62	MS-63	MS-64	MS-65	MS-66	SP-63	SP-65
1912	74,759	750.	850.	950.	1,050.	1,200.	1,400.	2,500.	3,500.	5,500.	10,000.	8,000.	15,000.
1913	149,232	750.	850.	950.	1,050.	1,200.	1,400.	2,500.	—	—	—	*	*
1914	140,068	750.	850.	950.	1,100.	1,300.	1,500.	3,000.	7,500.	—	—	*	*

SPECIMEN SETS 1858-1967

PROVINCE OF CANADA and CANADA

DATE	MINT	VARIETY	FINISH	DESCRIPTION	GRADE	PRICE
1858	Royal Mint	Plain edge	Mirror	4 coins, 1¢ to 20¢	SP-65	20,000.
1858	Royal Mint	Plain edge	Mirror	8 coins, 2 x 1¢ to 20¢	SP-65	40,000.
1858	Royal Mint	Reeded edge	Mirror	4 coins, 1¢ to 20¢	SP-65	25,000.
1858	Royal Mint	Reeded edge	Mirror	8 coins, 2 x 1¢ to 20¢	SP-65	50,000.
1870	Royal Mint	Plain	Mirror	4 coins, 1¢ to 20¢	SP-65	68,500.
1870	Royal Mint	Reeded	Mirror	4 coins, 1¢ to 20¢	SP-65	72,500.
1875H	Ralph Heaton and Sons	Reeded	Mirror	3 coins, 5¢ to 25¢	SP-65	100,000.
1880H	Ralph Heaton and Sons	25¢, Wide 0	Mirror	3 coins, 5¢ to 25¢	SP-65	35,000.
1880H	Ralph Heaton and Sons	25¢, Narrow 0	Mirror	3 coins, 5¢ to 25¢	SP-65	40,000.
1881H	Ralph Heaton and Sons	Reeded	Mirror	5 coins, 1¢ to 50¢	SP-65	65,000.
1902H	The Mint Birmingham Ltd.	Reeded	Matte	3 coins, 5¢ to 25¢	SP-65	85,000.
1908	Ottawa Branch Mint	5¢ Large 8	Matte	5 coins, 1¢ to 50¢	SP-65	5,500.
1908	Ottawa Branch Mint	5¢ Small 8	Matte	5 coins, 5¢ to 50¢	SP-65	5,500.
1911	Ottawa Branch Mint		Matte	5 coins, 1¢ to 50¢	SP-65	10,000.
1911/12	Ottawa Branch Mint		Matte	8 coins, 1¢ to 50¢ £1, $5, $10	SP-65	50,000.
1921	Ottawa Branch Mint		Matte	5 coins, 1¢ to 50¢	SP-65	275,000.
1929	Ottawa Branch Mint		Matte	5 coins, 1¢ to 50¢	SP-65	30,000.
1930	Ottawa Branch Mint		Matte	4 coins, 1¢ to 25¢	SP-65	30,000.
1931	Ottawa Branch Mint		Matte	5 coins, 1¢ to 50¢	SP-66	42,500.
1933	Royal Canadian Mint		Matte	4 coins, 1¢ to 25¢	SP-65	40,000.
1934	Royal Canadian Mint		Matte	5 coins, 1¢ to 50¢	SP-65	50,000.
1936	Royal Canadian Mint	Dot coinage	Matte	3 coins, 1¢, 10¢, 25¢	SP-65	675,000.
1937	Royal Canadian Mint		Mirror	6 coins, 1¢ to $1	SP-65	3,500.
1937	Royal Canadian Mint		Mirror	12 coins, 2 x 1¢ to $1	SP-65	6,000.
1937	Royal Canadian Mint		Matte	6 coins, 1¢ to $1	SP-65	1,750.
1938	Royal Canadian Mint		Matte	6 coins, 1¢ to $1	SP-65	55,000.
1939	Royal Canadian Mint		Mirror	3 coins, 10¢, 25¢, $1	SP-65	11,000.
1944	Royal Canadian Mint		Mirror	5 coins, 1¢ to 50¢	SP-65	23,000.
1945	Royal Canadian Mint		Mirror	6 coins, 1¢ to $1	SP-65	18,000.
1946	Royal Canadian Mint		Mirror	6 coins, 1¢ to $1	SP-65	13,000.
1947	Royal Canadian Mint	$1 Pointed 7	Mirror	6 coins, 1¢ to $1	SP-65	14,000.
1947	Royal Canadian Mint	$1 Blunt 7	Mirror	6 coins, 1¢ to $1	SP-65	14,000.
1947	Royal Canadian Mint	50¢ ML, St 7	Mirror	6 coins, 1¢ to $1	SP-65	13,000.
1947	Royal Canadian Mint	50¢ ML, C7	Mirror	6 coins, 1¢ to $1	SP-65	13,000.
1948	Royal Canadian Mint	50¢ Concave	Mirror	6 coins, 1¢ to $1	SP-65	15,000.
1948	Royal Canadian Mint	50¢ Convex	Mirror	6 coins, 1¢ to $1	SP-65	15,000.
1949	Royal Canadian Mint		Mirror	6 coins, 1¢ to $1	SP-65	5,000.
1950	Royal Canadian Mint	$1 SWL	Mirror	6 coins, 1¢ to $1	SP-65	7,000.
1950	Royal Canadian Mint	$1 Arnprior	Mirror	6 coins, 1¢ to $1	SP-65	5,500.
1951	Royal Canadian Mint	5¢ High relief	Mirror	7 coins, 1¢ to $1 (2 x 5¢)	SP-65	12,000.
1951	Royal Canadian Mint	5¢ Low relief	Mirror	7 coins, 1¢ to $1 (2 x 5¢)	SP-65	9,500.
1952	Royal Canadian Mint	$1 Waterline	Mirror	6 coins, 1¢ to $1	SP-65	4,850.
1952	Royal Canadian Mint	$1 No waterline	Mirror	6 coins, 1¢ to $1	SP-65	4,850.
1953	Royal Canadian Mint	Shoulder fold	Mirror	6 coins, 1¢ to $1	SP-65	8,000.
1953	Royal Canadian Mint	No shoulder fold	Mirror	6 coins, 1¢ to $1	SP-65	8,250.
1964	Royal Canadian Mint		Mirror	6 coins, 1¢ to $1	SP-65	2,750.
1965	Royal Canadian Mint		Mirror	6 coins, 1¢ to $1	SP-65	3,250.
1967	Royal Canadian Mint		Mirror	7 coins, 1¢ to $20	SP-65	800.

Note: Condition plays a very important part in pricing Specimen coins.. A SP-63 (Specimen-63) coin will be sold at a third of the price of a SP-65 (Specimen-65) coin.

PROOF-LIKE SETS 1954-1967

SIX COIN SILVER PROOF-LIKE SETS, 1954-1960.

1953 saw the first use of the white cardboard six-coin holder that in 1954 became the package for public sale of brilliant uncirculated sets. The holder with the coins included was wrapped in a cellophane jacket. The finish on the coins offered acquired the name proof-like.

In 1960 the white cardboard holders appeared with a Royal Canadian Mint domicile. Three varieties of stamps exist. A sealed wooden box containing 250 proof-like sets was available directly from the Mint in 1960.

1954-1959

1960 with Stamp One

ROYAL CANADIAN MINT
OTTAWA CANADA

Stamp Two

ROYAL CANADIAN MINT
OTTAWA CANADA

Stamp Three

DATE	MINTAGE	ISSUE PRICE	FINISH	SET PRICE
1954 NSF Cent	3,000	2.50	Proof-like (PL)	2,500.
1954 SF	Included	2.50	Proof-like (PL)	750.
1955	6,300	2.50	Proof-like (PL)	500.
1955 ARN	Included	2.50	Proof-like (PL)	600.
1956	6,500	2.50	Proof-like (PL)	300.
1957	11,862	2.50	Proof-like (PL)	200.
1957 1WL	Included	2.50	Proof-like (PL)	225.
1958	18,259	2.50	Proof-like (PL)	150.
1959	31,577	3.00	Proof-like (PL)	85.
1960	64,097	3.00	Proof-like (PL)	70.

SIX COIN SILVER PROOF-LIKE SETS, 1961-1967.

This is a continuation of the set offered previously. It contains one of each denomination (for a total of six coins) packaged in a flat pliofilm pouch, inserted in a brown kraft envelope.

1961-1967

DATE	MINTAGE	ISSUE PRICE	FINISH	SET PRICE
1961	98,373	3.00	Proof-like (PL)	65.
1962	200,950	3.00	Proof-like (PL)	50.
1963	673,006	3.00	Proof-like (PL)	30.
1964	1,653,162	3.00	Proof-like (PL)	30.
1965 Type 1	2,904,352	4.00	Proof-like (PL)	30.
1965 Type 2	Included	4.00	Proof-like (PL)	30.
1966 LB	672,514	4.00	Proof-like (PL)	35.
1967	963,714	4.00	Proof-like (PL)	40.

NOTES ON 1954 TO 1967 PROOF-LIKE SETS

1. The 1954 No Shoulder Fold designation applies only to the one cent coin; the balance of the coins (5) are of the Shoulder Fold variety.
2. The prices for proof-like sets are for sets in PL-65 condition and in their original packaging.
3. The single denomination proof-like coin prices have now been incorporated into the pricing tables in the circulating coinage section.
4. The 1961 set, which of course was the first set packaged under the pliofilm system, did not come without problems. The one cent coin was prone to discolouring, making a brilliant, red PL-65 cent a scarcity.
5. Types Three, Four and Five of the 1965 silver dollar were not packaged by the Mint for issue in proof-like sets.
6. The following variety combinations will be found in the 1965 proof-like sets.
   - **A.** Type 1 dollar with Type 1 cent
   - **B.** Type 1 dollar with Type 3 cent
   - **C.** Type 2 dollar with Type 1 cent
   - **D.** Type 2 dollar with Type 3 cent

   For clarification of the types of 1965 silver dollars and cents see page 206 for dollars and 63 for cents.
7. Since they were not officially released, no 1966 small bead dollars were issued in proof-like sets.
8. For listings of nickel and multi-ply plated sets see *Canadian Coins, Volume Two*.

CASES FOR SPECIMEN COINAGE

CASE ONE

CHARLTON NUMBER	INTENDED CONTENTS	EXTERIOR COLOUR AND DIMENSIONS	INTERIOR COLOURS	PRICE FOR EMPTY CASE
1	1858 1¢, 5¢, 10¢, 20¢ 1¢, 5¢, 10¢, 20¢	Red or black Gilt frame 7.5 x 11.5 cm	u: white satin l: dark blue velvet	$5,000.

CASE TWO

CHARLTON NUMBER	INTENDED CONTENTS	EXTERIOR COLOUR AND DIMENSIONS	INTERIOR COLOURS	PRICE FOR EMPTY CASE
2	New Brunswick, Double Set 1862, 1¢, 5¢, 10¢, 20¢ (2)	Details unknown.	Details unknown	$5,000.

CASE THREE

Image not available

CHARLTON NUMBER	INTENDED CONTENTS	EXTERIOR COLOUR AND DIMENSIONS	INTERIOR COLOURS	PRICE FOR EMPTY CASE
3	New Brunswick, Single Set 1862, 1¢, 5¢, 10¢, 20¢	Details unknown	Details unknown	$2,500.

CASE FOUR

Image not available

CHARLTON NUMBER	INTENDED CONTENTS	EXTERIOR COLOUR AND DIMENSIONS	INTERIOR COLOURS	PRICE FOR EMPTY CASE
4	Newfoundland, Double Set 1864 (1¢); 1865 (others) 1¢, 5¢, 10¢, 20¢, $2 1¢, 5¢, 10¢, 20¢, $2	Details unknown	Details unknown	$5,000.

CASE FIVE

Image not available

CHARLTON NUMBER	INTENDED CONTENTS	EXTERIOR COLOUR AND DIMENSIONS	INTERIOR COLOURS	PRICE FOR EMPTY CASE
5	1870 5¢, 10¢, 25¢, 50¢	Dark brown 6.5 x 10.5 cm	u: white satin l: dark blue velvet	$5,000.

CASE SIX

Struck to commemorate the opening of the Royal Canadian Mint in Ottawa in 1908, this is the first set of specimen coins offered to the general public. The issue price was $2.00. Coins had a matte finish. Impressed red leather strips were mailed separately to customers who possibly were initially sent sets housed in box 6a.

Case 6

Case 6b

CHARLTON NUMBER	INTENDED CONTENTS	EXTERIOR COLOUR AND DIMENSIONS	INTERIOR COLOURS	PRICE FOR EMPTY CASE
6	1908 1¢, 5¢, 10¢, 25¢, 50¢	Maroon 5.3 x 15.5 cm	u: blue satin, impressed in gold lettering: SOUVENIR FIRST COINS MADE AT / THE ROYAL MINT / OTTAWA, O. 2ND JANUARY 1908. l: purple velvet, 5 holes	$1,000.
6a	1908 1¢, 5¢, 10¢, 25¢, 50¢	Red 5.3 x 15.5 cm no inscription	u: blue satin l: blue velvet, 5 holes, no inscription	$250.
6b	1908 1¢, 5¢, 10¢, 25¢, 50¢	Red 5.3 x 15.5 cm top impressed in gold lettering FIRST COINAGE OF CANADIAN MINT / OTTAWA / 1908	u: purple satin l: purple velvet, 5 holes, no inscription	$350.
6c	1908 1¢, 5¢, 10¢, 25¢, 50¢	Red 5.3 X 15.5 cm no inscription	u: blue satin with affixed red leather strip impressed in gold lettering FIRST COINAGE OF CANADIAN MINT / OTTAWA / 1908 l: blue velvet, 5 holes	$250.

CASE SEVEN

As in 1908, the George V Coronation of 1911 prompted the Mint again to offer sets to the general public.

Case No. 7, which can hold 9 coins, one cent to ten dollars, was never issued.

Case 7a, which can hold 6 coins, one cent to one dollar, was never issued.

Case 7b or 7c
1911 Set 5 coins all dated 1911
1¢, 5¢, 10¢, 25¢, 50¢
Issue Price: $2.00

CASE SEVEN (cont.)

Case 7d
1911-12 Set
6 coins dated 1911 — 1¢, 5¢, 10¢, 25¢, 50¢, Sovereign
2 coins dated 1912 — $$5, $10,
Issue Price: $24.00

CHARLTON NUMBER	INTENDED CONTENTS	EXTERIOR COLOUR AND DIMENSIONS	INTERIOR COLOURS	PRICE FOR EMPTY CASE
7	1911 1¢, 5¢, 10¢, 25¢, 50¢, $1, £1, $5, $10	Red, 8.9 x 19.7 cm top impressed in gold lettering SPECIMEN COINS / OTTAWA MINT / 1911	u: blue satin l: blue velvet, 9 holes no inscription	$5,000.
7a	1911 1¢, 5¢, 10¢, 25¢, 50¢, $1	Red, 5.3 x 19.7 cm top impressed in gold lettering SPECIMEN COINS / SILVER AND BRONZE / OTTAWA MINT / 1911	u: blue satin, l: blue velvet, 6 holes no inscription	$750.
7b	1911 1¢, 5¢, 10¢, 25¢, 50¢	Red, 5.3 x 19.7 cm top impressed in gold lettering SPECIMEN COINS / SILVER AND BRONZE / OTTAWA MINT / 1911	u: blue satin l: blue velvet, 5 holes no inscription	$500.
7c	1911 1¢, 5¢, 10¢, 25¢, 50¢	Red, 5.3 x 19.7 cm top impressed in gold lettering SPECIMEN COINS / OTTAWA MINT / 1911	u: Blue satin l: blue velvet, 5 holes no inscription	$500.
7d	1911 1¢, 5¢, 10¢, 25¢, 50¢ £1 and 1912 $5, $10	Red, 8.9 x 19.7 cm top impressed in gold lettering SPECIMEN COINS / OTTAWA MINT / 1911-12	u: Blue satin l: blue velvet, 8 holes no inscription	$1,000.

CASE EIGHT

This five-hole case is similar to Cases 7b and 7c, but fitted to hold the small one cent and five cent nickel coins.

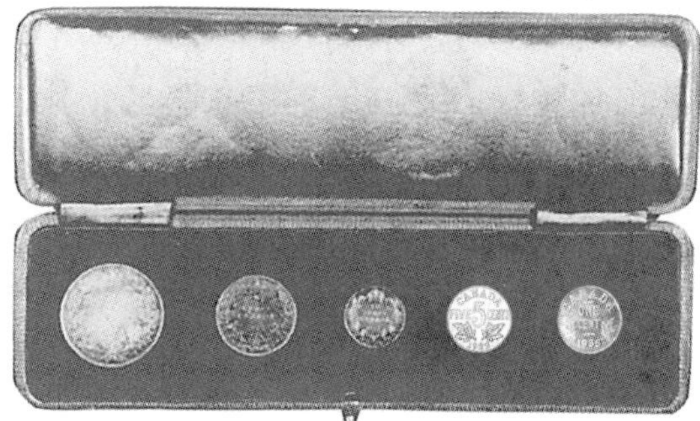

CHARLTON NUMBER	INTENDED CONTENTS	EXTERIOR COLOUR AND DIMENSIONS	INTERIOR COLOURS	PRICE FOR EMPTY CASE
8	1931 1¢ (small), 5¢ (nickel), 10¢, 25¢, 50¢	Red, 5.3 x 19.7 cm top impressed in gold lettering: SPECIMEN COINS / SILVER AND BRONZE / OTTAWA MINT	u: blue satin l: blue velvet 5 holes	$750.

CASE NINE

This six-hole, red cardboard case was used for the issue of 1937 matte specimen sets. This case is usually found in poor condition, and the price listed is for a mint condition case.

Case #9 1937

CHARLTON NUMBER	INTENDED CONTENTS	EXTERIOR COLOUR AND DIMENSIONS	INTERIOR COLOURS	PRICE FOR EMPTY CASE
9	1937 1¢, 5¢, 10¢, 25¢, 50¢, $1	Red cardboard, 10.2 x 15.3 cm with horizontal ridges, crowns and sceptres and in black lettering: ROYAL CANADIAN MINT / 1937 / OTTAWA, CANADA	u: coarse white cloth 6 holes	$75.

CASE NINE (cont.)

Case 9a or 9b Lid

Interior of Case 9a

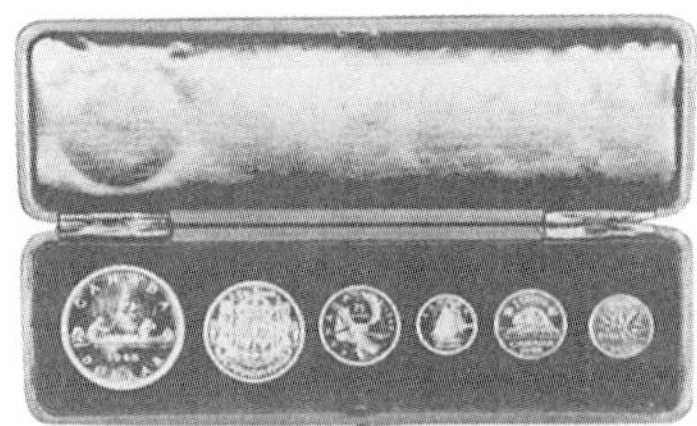

Interior of Case 9b

CHARLTON NUMBER	INTENDED CONTENTS	EXTERIOR COLOUR AND DIMENSIONS	INTERIOR COLOURS	PRICE FOR EMPTY CASE
9a	1937 1¢, 5¢, 10¢, 25¢	As case #7a except date covered by paper Union Jack.	u: blue satin l: blue velvet, 4 holes	$750.
9b	1937 1¢, 5¢, 10¢, 25¢, 50¢, $1	As case #7a, except the inscription is covered by a blue leather strip upon which is impressed in gold a view of the centre section of the Royal Canadian Mint surrounded on the sides and bottom by a ribbon;"1937" is below. On the ribbon is ROYAL CANADIAN MINT	u: blue satin l: blue velvet, 6 holes	$275.
9c	1937, Double Set 1¢, 5¢, 10¢, 25¢, 50¢, $1	Red, 8.9 x 19.7 cm top impressed in gold on a blue label ROYAL CANADIAN MINT / 1937 / OTTAWA / CANADA	u: blue satin l: blue velvet, 12 holes	$1,500.
9d	1937, Single Set 1¢, 5¢, 10¢, 25¢, 50¢, $1	Red, 5.3 x 19.7 cm top impressed in gold on a blue label ROYAL CANADIAN MINT / 1937 / OTTAWA / CANADA	u: blue satin l: blue velvet, 6 holes	$500.

Note: Case 9d (with the blue sticker on the case) is sometimes found with the label removed exposing the 1911 markings. This results in the case being neither a 1911 case (holes do not match), or a 1937 case (the label for the 1937 is now missing), and thus becomes an unofficial case.

CASE TEN

CHARLTON NUMBER	INTENDED CONTENTS	EXTERIOR COLOUR AND DIMENSIONS	INTERIOR COLOURS	PRICE FOR EMPTY CASE
10	1938-1953 1¢, 5¢, 10¢, 25¢, 50¢, $1	As case #9b, except for the absence of "1937"	As case #9b	$300.

CASE ELEVEN

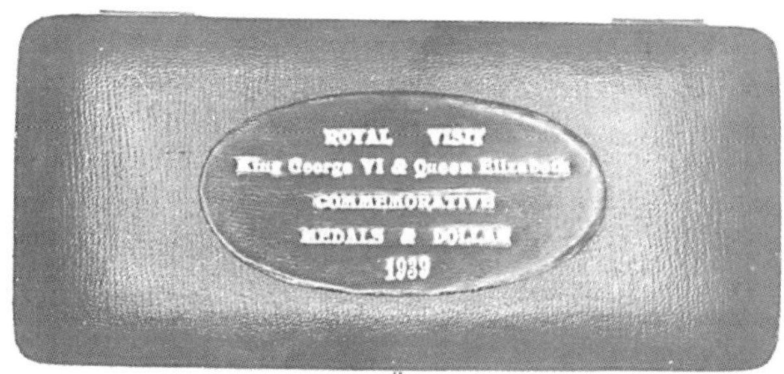

CHARLTON NUMBER	INTENDED CONTENTS	EXTERIOR COLOUR AND DIMENSIONS	INTERIOR COLOURS	PRICE FOR EMPTY CASE
11	1939 54mm medal, $1 54mm medal	As case #7, except the inscription is covered by an oval blue patch impressed in gold lettering: ROYAL VISIT / KING GEORGE VI & QUEEN ELIZABETH / COMMEMORATIVE / MEDALS & DOLLAR / 1939	As case #9a	$1,500.

CASE TWELVE

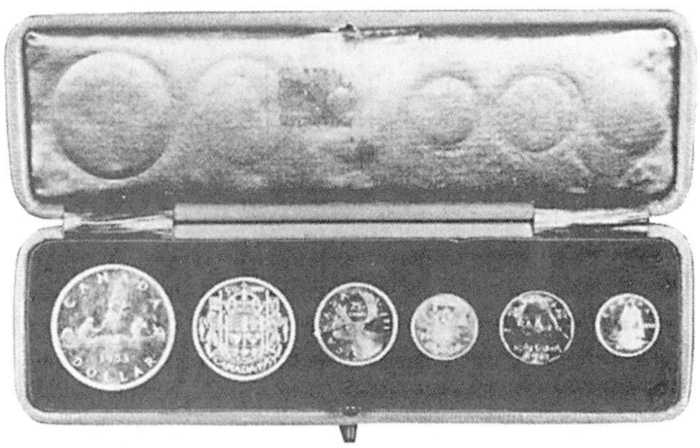

CHARLTON NUMBER	INTENDED CONTENTS	EXTERIOR COLOUR AND DIMENSIONS	INTERIOR COLOURS	PRICE FOR EMPTY CASE
12	1953 1¢, 5¢, 10¢, 25¢, 50¢, $1	Red, top impressed in gold with a view of the centre section of the Royal Canadian Mint surrounded on the sides and bottom by a ribbon bearing ROYAL CANADIAN MINT	u: blue satin l: blue velvet 6 holes	$300.

CASE THIRTEEN

CHARLTON NUMBER	INTENDED CONTENTS	EXTERIOR COLOUR AND DIMENSIONS	INTERIOR COLOURS	PRICE FOR EMPTY CASE
13	1953 1¢, 5¢, 10¢, 25¢, 50¢, $1	Large size, Red, top impressed in gold with a view of the centre section of the Royal Canadian Mint surrounded on the sides and bottom by a ribbon bearing ROYAL CANADIAN MINT	u: blue satin l: blue velvet 6 holes	$1,000.

CASE FOURTEEN

CHARLTON NUMBER	INTENDED CONTENTS	EXTERIOR COLOUR AND DIMENSIONS	INTERIOR COLOURS	PRICE FOR EMPTY CASE
14	1967 1¢, 5¢, 10¢, 25¢ 50¢, $1, $20	Black leather, impressed with gold Coat of Arms with 1867 to the left, and 1967 to the right; CANADA below Two varieties, based on method of closure, clasp or flap	u: white satin l: black plush 7 holes	$10.
14a	As above	Brown leather, as above	As above	$50.
14b	As above	Maroon leather, black highlights, as above	As above	$50.

CASE FIFTEEN

CHARLTON NUMBER	INTENDED CONTENTS	EXTERIOR COLOUR AND DIMENSIONS	INTERIOR COLOURS	PRICE FOR EMPTY CASE
15	1967 Sterling silver medallion	Black leather, impressed with gold Coat of Arms "1867 1967" either side of arms with CANADA below	u: white satin l: black plush 1 hole	$50.

PATTERNS, TRIAL PIECES AND OFFICIAL FABRICATIONS

A **PATTERN** is a piece submitted as a design sample by engravers when a new coinage is contemplated. If the design is adopted for regular coinage with the same date, the piece ceases to be a pattern. If the design is adopted with a later date, the piece remains a pattern. Patterns are usually struck as proofs.

A **TRIAL PIECE** is from dies already accepted for regular coinage. It may bear a date or mint mark other than on the coins issued for circulation or it may be in a different metal.

An **OFFICIAL FABRICATION** is a piece that was created for some special purpose unconnected with design proposals or experiments on coinage design or metals. For example, the New Brunswick pieces bearing the dates 1870, 1871 and 1875 were obviously not connected with an attempt to revive a separate coinage for that province after Confederation.

For many years the best listing of patterns, trial pieces and official fabrications was that published by Fred Bowman in his book *Canadian Patterns*. The present listing is greatly expanded compared to Bowman's and new numbers were necessary. However, Bowmans original numbers are also included for cross referencing.

An **ESSAY PIECE** is piece with a design submitted for approval purposes. Usually uniface, but at times may be joined by an approved obverse.

PROVINCE OF NOVA SCOTIA

PATTERNS

HALF CENT 1860.

Reverse – crown surrounded by wreath of roses; date below wreath. (The illustration is from a matrix. It is uncertain whether patterns bearing this date were actually produced.)

CHARLTON No.	BOWMAN No.	SP-63 to 65
NS-1	—	Unknown.

ONE CENT 1860.

Reverse – crown surrounded by wreath of roses; date below wreath. (The illustration is from a matrix. It is uncertain whether patterns bearing this date were actually produced.)

CHARLTON No.	BOWMAN No.	SP-63 to 65
NS-2	—	Unknown.

HALF CENT 1861.

Bronze. Specimen; dies ↑↓; wt. 2.85g; diam. 20.65 mm. Obverse - large bust of Victoria by James Wyon. Reverse - pattern design as on NS-1. (National Currency Collection).

CHARLTON No.	BOWMAN No.	SP-63 to 65
NS-3	B-11	$3,000. - $7,000.

ONE CENT 1861

Bronze. Specimen; dies ↑↑; wt. 4.69g; diam. 25.4 mm. Obverse - large bust of Victoria by James Wyon. Reverse - pattern design as on NS-2. (National Currency Collection). An electrotype copy on a double thick planchet exists from the British Museum

CHARLTON No.	BOWMAN No.	SP-63 to 65
NS-4	B-7	$3,000. - $7,000.

HALF CENT 1861

Bronze. Specimen; dies ↑↓. Obverse - adopted (small bust) design by L.C. Wyon. Reverse - pattern design as NS-3. (National Currency Collection).

Photo not available at press time

CHARLTON No.	BOWMAN No.	SP-63 to 65
NS-5	B-13	$3,000. - $7,000.

ONE CENT 1861.

Bronze. Not a specimen; dies ↑↑; wt. 5.59g;; diam. 25.4mm. Obverse - adopted (small bust) design by L.C. Wyon. Reverse - pattern design as NS-4. (National Currency Collection).

CHARLTON No.	BOWMAN No.	MS-63 to 65
NS-6	B-8	$3,000. - $7,000.

HALF CENT 1861.

Bronze. Specimen; dies ↑↑; wt. 2.78g; diam. 20.65mm. Obverse - pattern design as on NS-3. Reverse - adopted design (crown and date surrounded by a wreath of mayflowers and roses). (New Netherlands Coin Sale 1960).

CHARLTON No.	BOWMAN No.	SP-63 to 65
NS-7	B-12	$3,000. - $7,000.

ONE CENT 1861.

Bronze. Specimen; dies ↑↑; wt. 5.65g; diam. 25.4mm; and dies ↑↓; wt. 5.74g; diam. 25.4mm. Obverse - pattern design as on NS-4. Reverse - adopted design (1861), large rose bud variety. (National Currency Collection).

CHARLTON No.	BOWMAN No.	SP-63 to 65
NS-8	B-10	$3,000. - $5,000.

ONE CENT 1861.

Bronze. Specimen; dies ↑↑; wt. 5.80g; diam. 25.4mm. As NS-8, except the reverse is the small rose bud variety (adopted design for 1861-1864).

CHARLTON No.	BOWMAN No.	SP-63 to 65
NS-8a	B-10	$3,000. - $6,000.

HALF CENT 186-.

Bronze. Specimen. As NS-5, except for the incomplete date.

CHARLTON No.	BOWMAN No.	SP-63 to 65
NS-9	B-14	$3,500. - $7,500.

ONE CENT 186–.

Bronze. Specimen; dies ↑↑; wt. 5.78g; diam. 25.4mm. As NS-6, except for the incomplete date.

CHARLTON No.	BOWMAN No.	SP-63 to 65
NS-10	B-9	$3,500. - $7,500.

PROVINCE OF NEW BRUNSWICK

PATTERNS

ONE CENT 1861.

Bronze; proof; dies ↑↑; wt. 5.64g; diam. 25.4mm; obverse - large bust design by James Wyon as on NS-6, etc. reverse - adopted design. (National Currency Collection)

CHARLTON No.	BOWMAN No.	PR-63 to 65
NB-1	B-15	$4,000. - $8,000.

TEN CENTS 1862.

Silver; reeded edge; proof; dies ↑↑; wt. 2.34g; diam. 18.0mm; obverse - adopted design; reverse - legend and date surrounded by arabesque design somewhat similar to that used for Newfoundland. The arabesque reverse on this piece was also used for a pattern 10-cent piece for Hong Kong. (National Currency Collection)

CHARLTON No.	BOWMAN No.	PR-63 to 65
NB-2	B-20	$30,000. - $50,000.

TRIAL PIECES

ONE CENT 1862.

Bronze, proof. As adopted design, except for the date. Struck to make the date uniform for the 1862 proof sets.

Photograph not available
at press time

CHARLTON No.	BOWMAN No.	PR-63 to 65
NB-3	—	$5,000. - $10,000.

OFFICIAL FABRICATIONS

Twenty cents 1862.

Silver; plain edge; proof; dies ↑↑; wt. 5.6g; diam. 22.0mm; obverse - plain, except for the legend G.W. WYON/OBIT/MARCH 27TH 1862/AETAT/26YEARS. Reverse - adopted design. This is an obituary medalet for George W. Wyon, who was resident engraver at the Royal Mint. The fact that this reverse was chosen for the piece suggests that it was engraved by George Wyon. (National Currency Collection).

CHARLTON No.	BOWMAN No.	PR-63 to 65
NB-4	B-23	$10,000. - $15,000.

The following six pieces (NB-5 to NB-10) obviously have nothing to do with contemplated designs for New Brunswick, since they bear dates after Confederation. It is believed they were struck for exhibition purposes where only the type was considered important.

The rumour has it that Sir Charles Fremantle, Deputy Master of the Royal Mint 1868-1894, arranged for proof specimens of Canadian coins to be struck for the Royal Mint Museum Collection.

FIVE CENTS 1870.

Silver; plain edge; specimen; dies ↑↑; wt. 1.7g; diam. 15.5mm; obverse - adopted design; reverse - adopted design for the Dominion of Canada (wire rim variety). (National Currency Collection)

Photo not available
at press time

CHARLTON No.	BOWMAN No.	SP-63 to 65
NB-5	B-18	$25,000. - $40,000.

TEN CENTS 1870.

Silver; reeded edge; specimen; dies ↑↑; wt. 2.3g; diam. 18.03mm; plain edge; proof; dies ↑↑; wt. 2.32g; diam. 18.03mm; obverse - adopted design; reverse - adopted design for the Dominion of Canada and New Brunswick. (National Currency Collection, reeded edge; Norweb Collection, plain edge)

CHARLTON No.	BOWMAN No.	SP-63 to 65
NB-6a Reeded edge	B-21	$25,000. - $50,000.
NB-6b Plain edge		$25,000. - $50,000.

TEN CENTS 1871

Silver; reeded edge; specimen; dies ↑↑; wt. 2.32g; diam. 18.03mm; plain edge; wt. 2.3g; diam. 18.03mm. As NB-6, except for the date. (National Currency Collection).

Photo not available at press time

CHARLTON No.	BOWMAN No.	SP-63 to 65
NB-7	B-22	$35,000. - $55,000.

TWENTY CENTS 1871.

Silver; reeded edge; specimen; dies ↑↑; wt. 5.90g; diam. 22.5mm; plain edge; proof; wt. 4.7g; diam. 23.27 mm. As the adopted design, except for the date. (National Currency Collection)

CHARLTON No.	BOWMAN No.	SP-63 to 65
NB-8	B-24	$20,000. - $50,000.

FIVE CENTS 1875.

Silver; reeded edge; specimen; dies ↑↑, wt. 1.16g; diam. 15.5mm; obverse - adopted design; reverse - adopted design for the Dominion of Canada. (National Currency Collection)

CHARLTON No.	BOWMAN No.	SP-63 to 65
NB-9	B-19	$35,000. - $55,000.

FIVE CENTS 1875H.

Silver; reeded edge; specimen; dies ↑↑. As NB9, except for the H mint mark.

Photo not available at press time

CHARLTON No.	BOWMAN No.	SP-63 to 65
NB-10	—	$35,000. - $55,000.

PROVINCE OF NEWFOUNDLAND

PATTERNS

The following five patterns (NF-1 to NF-5) are the result of a directive given by the master of the Royal Mint, Thomas Graham, in which he stated that the designs for the reverses of the Newfoundland coins should be those of New Brunswick. This was later altered.

ONE CENT 1864.

Bronze; plain edge; specimen; dies ↑↓; Obverse: Adopted design; Reverse: Design from the New Brunswick cent.

CHARLTON No.	BOWMAN No.	SP-63 to 65
NF-1	—	$3,000. - $8,000.

FIVE CENTS 1864.

Bronze; plain edge; specimen; dies ↑↓; wt. 1.40g; diam. 15.5mm; obverse - adopted design; reverse - crown and wreath design adopted for New Brunswick. (W.W.C. Wilson Sale 1925).

Photo not available at press time

CHARLTON No.	BOWMAN No.	SP-63 to 65
NF-2	B-28	$15,000. - —

TEN CENTS 1864.

Bronze; plain edge; specimen; obverse - adopted design; reverse - crown and wreath design adopted for New Brunswick. (British Museum).

Photo not available at press time

CHARLTON No.	BOWMAN No.	SP-63 to 65
NF-3	B-29	$30,000. - $50,000.

TWENTY CENTS 1864.

Bronze; indented corded edge; specimen; dies ↑↓; wt. 6.2g; diam. 22.95mm; obverse - adopted design; reverse - crown and wreath design adopted for New Brunswick. (National Currency Collection).

CHARLTON No.	BOWMAN No.	SP-63 to 65
NF-4	B-32	$30,000. - $50,000.

TWO DOLLARS 1864.

Bronze; plain edge; specimen; dies ↑↓; wt. 2.4g; diam. 17.1mm; obverse - adopted design; reverse - crown and wreath for New Brunswick. 10 cents with the legend "TWO/DOLLARS/1864" in the centre. (National Currency Collection).

CHARLTON No.	BOWMAN No.	SP-63 to 65
NF-5	B-31	$125,000. - $150,000.

ONE CENT 1864.

Bronze; business strike; dies ↑↑; wt. 5.69g; diam. 25.4mm; obverse - similar to adopted design, except the legend reads VICTORIA QUEEN. Reverse - similar to adopted design, except one leaf is missing from the top of each side of the wreath. (National Currency Collection)

CHARLTON No.	BOWMAN No.	SP-63 to 65
NF-6	B-25	$3,500. - $10,000.

ONE CENT 1865.

Bronze; specimen; dies ↑↓; wt. 5.45g; diam. 25.4mm; obverse - adopted design for Nova Scotia and New Brunswick. Reverse - pattern design as for NF-6, except for the date. (National Currency Collection)

CHARLTON No.	BOWMAN No.	SP-63 to 65
NF-7	B-27	$2,500. - $5,000.

FIVE CENTS 1865.

Silver; plain edge; specimen; dies ↑↓; wt. 0.9g; diam. 15.5mm; obverse - adopted design; reverse - similar to the adopted design, except the arches are thinner. (National Currency Collection)

CHARLTON No.	BOWMAN No.	SP-63 to 65
NF-8	—	$4,000. - $8,000.

TEN CENTS 1865.

Silver; plain edge; specimen; dies ↑↓; obverse - adopted design; reverse - similar to the adopted design, except the arches are much thinner. (National Currency Collection)

CHARLTON No.	BOWMAN No.	SP-63 to 65
NF-9	—	$5,000. - $12,500.

TWENTY CENTS 1865.

Silver; plain edge; specimen; dies ↑↓; wt. 4.6g; diam. 23.19mm; obverse - adopted design; reverse - similar to the adopted design, except the arches are much thinner. (National Currency Collection)

CHARLTON No.	BOWMAN No.	SP-63 to 65
NF-10	—	$6,000. - $15,000.

FIVE CENTS 1865

Silver; plain edge; specimen; dies ↑↓; wt. 1.10g; diam. 15.5mm; obverse - adopted design; reverse - as the adopted design, except the arches and dots have raised edges. (National Currency Collection)

CHARLTON No.	BOWMAN No.	SP-63 to 65
NF-11	—	$4,000. - $8,000.

TEN CENTS 1865.

Silver; plain edge; specimen; dies ↑↓; wt. 2.3g; diam. 18.03mm; obverse - adopted design; reverse - as the adopted design, except the arches and dots have raised edges. (National Currency Collection)

CHARLTON No.	BOWMAN No.	SP-63 to 65
NF-12	—	$5,000. - $10,000.

TWENTY CENTS 1865.

Silver; plain edge; specimen; dies ↑↓; wt. 4.5g; diam. 23.19mm; obverse - adopted design; reverse - similar to the adopted design, except for some details of the arches and the presence of a raised line just inside the rim denticles. (National Currency Collection).

CHARLTON No.	BOWMAN No.	SP-63 to 65
NF-13	—	$5,000. - $15,000.

TWO DOLLARS 1865.

Gold; plain edge; specimen; dies ↑↑; wt. 3.3g; diam. 17.6mm; obverse - adopted design; reverse - similar to the adopted design, except the legend and date are in block type. (National Currency Collection)

CHARLTON No.	BOWMAN No.	SP-63 to 65
NF-14	B-33	$125,000. - $150,000.

TWO DOLLARS 1865.

Gold; plain edge; specimen; dies ↑↓; wt. 3.36g; diam. 17.98mm; obverse - small bust of Victoria (from the 5 cents) in beaded circle with the legend VICTORIA D:G REG:/NEWFOUNDLAND. Reverse - pattern design as on NF-14.

CHARLTON No.	BOWMAN No.	SP-63 to 65
NF-15	B-34	$125,000. - $150,000.

FIFTY CENTS 1870.

Bronze; plain edge; specimen; dies ↑↑; wt. 9.4g; diam. 29.6mm; obverse - adopted design; reverse - as the adopted design, except the denticles are longer and touch the device. (National Currency Collection)

CHARLTON No.	BOWMAN No.	SP-63 to 65
NF-16	B-35e	$100,000. - $125,000.

TWO DOLLARS 1870.

Gold; plain edge; specimen; obverse - pattern design as on NF-15; reverse - adopted design.

CHARLTON No.	BOWMAN No.	SP-63 to 65
NF-17	—	$125,000. - $150,000.

TRIAL PIECES

ONE CENT 1864.

Bronze; specimen; dies ↑↑; wt. 5.6g; diam. 25.4mm. As the adopted design, except for the date. This is the piece that is believed to have been included in the specimen sets of 1864-1865. Proofs of the adopted design of the cent dated 1865 seem not to have been produced. (National Currency Collection).

CHARLTON No.	BOWMAN No.	SP-63 to 65
NF-18	B-26	$3,500. - $7,500.

FIVE CENTS 1894.

Lead; trial impression of Reverse die.

CHARLTON No.	BOWMAN No.	SP-63 to 65
NF-19	—	$2,500. - —

TEN CENTS 1882H.

Lead; trial impression of Reverse die.

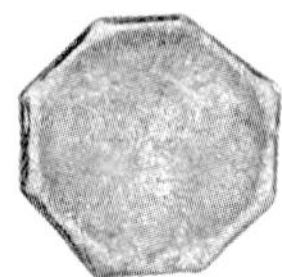

CHARLTON No.	BOWMAN No.	SP-63 to 65
NF-20	—	$2,500. - —

TEN CENTS 1903.

Lead; trial impression of Reverse die.

CHARLTON No.	BOWMAN No.	SP-63 to 65
NF-21	—	$2,500. - —

TEN CENTS 1945C.

Nickel. Struck on a thin blank; not a proof. This piece is rather weakly struck because of the thinness of the blank, suggesting that it is nothing more than a mint error. (National Currency Collection).

Photograph not available
at press time

CHARLTON No.	BOWMAN No.	MS-63 to 65
NF-22	—	Mint Error

TWENTY CENTS 1865.

Bronze; plain edge; specimen; dies ↑↑; wt. 5.16g, diam. 23.1mm as adopted design. (Norweb Collection).

Photograph not available at press time

CHARLTON No.	BOWMAN No.	SP-63 to 65
NF-23	—	$25,000. - $40,000.

FIFTY CENTS 1882.

Silver; reeded edge; specimen. As the adopted design, except for the absence of the H mint mark. (British Museum)

CHARLTON No.	BOWMAN No.	SP-63 to 65
NF-24	—	$60,000. - $100,000.

PROVINCE OF BRITISH COLUMBIA

PATTERNS

TEN DOLLARS 1862.

Silver; specimen; dies ↑↓; wt. 11.2g; diam. 27.0mm; obverse - crown and legend; reverse - wreath, denomination and date. (National Currency Collection)

CHARLTON No.	BOWMAN No.	SP-60 to 63
BC-1a	B-37	$75,000. - —.

TEN DOLLARS 1862.

Silver; reeded edge; specimen; dies ↑↑. Design as above. (Brand Sale 1983).

Photograph: See BC-1a

CHARLTON No.	BOWMAN No.	SP-60 to 63
BC-1b1	B-37	$75,000. - —

TEN DOLLARS 1862.

Gilt; reeded edge; specimen; dies ↑↑. Design as above.

Photograph: See BC-1a

CHARLTON No.	BOWMAN No.	SP-60 to 63
BC-1b2	—	$100,000 - —

TWENTY DOLLARS 1862.

Silver; specimen; dies ↑↓; obverse - crown and legend; reverse - wreath, denomination and date. (Brand Sale 1983).

CHARLTON No.	BOWMAN No.	SP-60 to 63
BC-2a1	B-36	$75,000. - —

TWENTY DOLLARS 1862.

Gilt; specimen; dies ↑↓; obverse - crown and legend; reverse - wreath, denomination and date.

Photograph: See BC 2a1

CHARLTON No.	BOWMAN No.	SP-60 to 63
BC-2a2	—	$100,000. - —

TWENTY DOLLARS 1862.

Silver; reeded edge; specimen; dies ↑↑; wt. 23.6g; diam. 34.0mm. Design as above. (National Currency Collection)

Photograph: See BC 2a1

CHARLTON No.	BOWMAN No.	SP-60 to 63
BC-2b	B-36	$75,000. - —

TEN DOLLARS 1862.

Gold. Design and specifications as BC-1. (B.C. Provincial Archives).

Photograph: See BC-1a

CHARLTON No.	BOWMAN No.	SP-60 to 63
BC-3	B-37	$750,000. - —

TWENTY DOLLARS 1862.

Gold. Design and specifications as BC-2. (B.C. Provincial Archives)

Photograph: See BC-1a

CHARLTON No.	BOWMAN No.	SP-60 to 63
BC-4	B-36	$750,000. - —

Note: The ten and twenty dollar gold patterns of British Columbia were designed by George Albert Ferdinand Kuner (1819-1906)

PROVINCE OF CANADA

ESSAY PIECES

ONE CENT 1858.

Bronze; specimen; wt. 5.7g; diam. 23.7mm; uniface - obverse blank; reverse - wreath of maple leaves and seed pods with beaded circle containing ONE/CENT/1858. (National Currency Collection).

CHARLTON No.	BOWMAN No.	SP-63 to 65
PC-1	B-4	$20,000. - $30,000.

ONE CENT 1858.

Bronze; specimen; wt. 4.0 - 5.4g; diam. 23.7mm; uniface - obverse blank; reverse - similar to PC-1 except the date is more closely spaced and the device is farther from the inner beaded circle. (National Currency Collection)

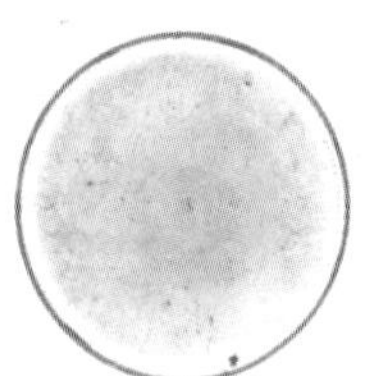

CHARLTON No.	BOWMAN No.	SP-63 to 65
PC-2	B-4	$15,000. - $20,000.

ONE CENT 1858.

Bronze; specimen; dies ↑↓; wt. 3.88g; diam. 23.7mm; obverse - adopted legend with diademed bust of Victoria. Reverse - pattern design as on PC-2. (Wayte Raymond Sale 1928)

CHARLTON No.	BOWMAN No.	SP-63 to 65
PC-3	B-3	$40,000. - $50,000.

TRIAL PIECES

TWENTY CENTS 1858.

Silver; plain edge; specimen; dies ↑↑; wt. 4.50g; diam. 23.7mm; dies ↑↓; wt. 4.03g; diam. 23.27mm; obverse - adopted design; reverse - adopted design for New Brunswick. (National Currency Collection).

CHARLTON No.	BOWMAN No.	SP-63 to 65
PC-4	B-6	$15,000. - $35,000.

ONE CENT 1858.

Cupro-nickel; specimen; dies ↑↑; wt. 9.11g; diam. 25.4mm. Adopted design; struck from proof dies on an unpolished blank of double thickness. (National Currency Collection)

Photograph not available at press time

CHARLTON No.	BOWMAN No.	SP-63 to 65
PC-6	—	$15,000. - $25,000.

ONE CENT 1858.

Cupro-nickel; specimen; dies ↑↑; wt. 4.42g; diam. 25.4mm. Adopted design; normal thickness. (National Currency Collection)

Photograph not available at press time

CHARLTON No.	BOWMAN No.	SP-63 to 65
PC-7	—	$8,000. - $15,000.

PATTERNS

ONE CENT 1859 (IN ROMAN NUMERALS).

Bronze; specimen; obverse - adopted design; reverse - Britannia reverse for a pattern British halfpenny. (Parsons Collection 1936. The Norweb Collection contained an example struck in copper-nickel; wt. 5.63g; diam. 25.4mm.)

CHARLTON No.	BOWMAN No.	SP-63 to 65
PC-5	B-5	$35,000. - $50,000.

CANADA

ONE CENT 1876H.

Bronze; specimen; dies ↑↑; diam. 25.45mm; obverse - adopted laureate head design for the Province of Canada. Reverse - adopted design. The existence of this pattern suggests that the government of the Dominion of Canada initially considered using the Province of Canada laureate obverse for its new cent. (National Currency Collection)

CHARLTON No.	BOWMAN No.	SP-63 to 65
DC-1	B-38	$40,000. - $50,000.

TEN CENTS (NO DATE)

Bronze; reeded edge; specimen; wt. 2.1g; diam. 17.85mm; obverse - adopted design (Charlton OT6); reverse - plain, except for a B engraved on the piece after it was struck. Probably unique. (National Currency Collection)

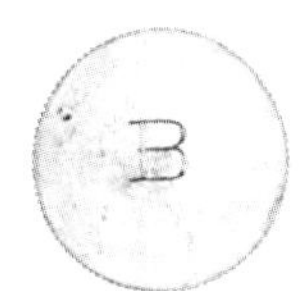

CHARLTON No.	BOWMAN No.	SP-63 to 65
DC-2	—	— - $50,000.

FIFTY CENTS 1870.

Bronze; plain edge; specimen; dies ↑↑; wt. 9.2g; diam. 29.72mm; obverse - no L.C.W. on the truncation, but otherwise very similar to Obv. P-2. Reverse - slight differences in some leaves compared to the adopted design. (National Currency Collection)

CHARLTON No.	BOWMAN No.	SP-63 to 65
DC-3	—	— - $175,000.

FIFTY CENTS 1870.

As DC-3, but silver. Specimen; dies ↑↓; wt. 11.2g; diam. 29.72mm. For an illustration see: See DC-3

CHARLTON No.	BOWMAN No.	SP-63 to 65
DC-4	—	— - $200,000.

ONE CENT 1911.

Bronze; specimen; dies ↑↑; wt. 5.6g; diam. 25.4mm. As the adopted design for 1912-1920, except for the date; i.e. the obverse legend has DEI GRA:. (Royal Mint Collection)

CHARLTON No.	BOWMAN No.	SP-63 to 65
DC-5	—	—. - $75,000.

ONE DOLLAR 1911.

Silver; reeded edge; specimen; dies ↑↑; obverse - the standard MacKennal design later adopted for the 1936 dollar. Reverse - crown, wreath, legend and date.

In the Dominion of Canada Currency Act of 1910, which received royal assent on May 4, 1910, provision was made for the striking of a Canadian silver dollar. The schedule appended to the act specified a coin of 360 grains weight and a standard fineness of .925 silver. The Dominion Government, having decided to add a silver dollar to the coinage, purchased a new coining press from Taylor and Challen of Birmingham, England, for the express purpose of striking coins of this size. A pair of dies for the new coin was prepared by the Die and Medal Department of the Royal Mint, London, and at least two specimens were struck. When cases were prepared for the specimen sets of the first Canadian coinage of George V, a space was left for the dollar. Later, however, the Dominion authorities decided against the issue of a silver dollar at that time, although no reason was given for this decision.

Only two specimens of the 1911 silver dollar are known to exist; one is in the National Currency Collection and the other was sold at auction in 2003 for $690,000 U.S. funds, at the Heritage Belzberg Sale.

CHARLTON No.	BOWMAN No.	SP-63 to 65
DC-6	B-40	$2,000,000.

PATTERNS

ONE DOLLAR 1911.

Lead. As DC-6, except for the metal. Probably unique. This piece was only recently discovered by the numismatic world, having been in storage in Ottawa since 1911. It is believed to be a sample piece struck at the Ottawa mint to be used for gaining approval to proceed with the production of coins for circulation. (National Currency Collection)

CHARLTON No.	BOWMAN No.	SP-63 to 65
DC-6a	—	$500,000.

FIVE DOLLARS 1911.

Gold; reeded edge specimen; dies ↑↑; diam. 21.6mm. As the adopted design for 1912-1914, except for the date. (Royal Mint Collection)

CHARLTON No.	BOWMAN No.	SP-63 to 65
DC-7	B-41	$100,000. - $150,000.

TEN DOLLARS, 1911.

Gold; reeded edge specimen; dies ↑↑; diam. 26.9mm. As the adopted design for 1912-1914, except for the date. (Royal Mint Collection

CHARLTON No.	BOWMAN No.	SP-63 to 65
DC-8	B-42	$100,000. - $150,000.

In 1926 Dominion notes (the treasury notes issued by the Government of the Dominion of Canada) were made redeemable in gold for the first time since 1914. Since the time of the production of the gold $5 and $10 of 1912-1914, it had been concluded that the coat of arms borne on their reverses was incorrect. Therefore, new reverses were engraved in the event that a gold coinage should again be struck. Bronze patterns were produced to provide samples of the designs. A few of these, probably made for the designer, G.E. Kruger-Gray, have the obverse design machined off, SPECIMEN punched in instead, and the entire piece acid-etched.

FIVE DOLLARS 1928.

Bronze; reeded edge; specimen; dies ↑↑; wt. 4.2 grams; diam. 21.6mm; obverse - as the adopted design for the 1912-1914 issues. Reverse - modified Canadian arms by G.E. Kruger-Gray. (National Currency Collection)

CHARLTON No.	BOWMAN No.	SP-63 to 65
DC-9	—	$50,000. - $75,000.

TEN DOLLARS 1928.

Bronze; reeded edge; specimen; dies ↑↑; wt. 8.49g; diam. 26.92mm; obverse - as the adopted design for the 1912-1914 issues. Reverse - modified Canadian arms by G.E. Kruger-Gray. (National Currency Collection)

CHARLTON No.	BOWMAN No.	SP-63 to 65
DC-10	—	$50,000. - $85,000.

FIVE DOLLARS 1928.

Bronze; reeded edge; wt. 3.7g; diam. 21.6mm; obverse - planed off flat just inside the denticles after striking; SPECIMEN has been punched in by hand. Reverse - pattern design as on DC-9. The entire piece has been acid-etched (officially) giving it a light brown colour. (National Currency Collection)

CHARLTON No.	BOWMAN No.	SP-63 to 65
DC-11	—	$60,000.

TEN DOLLARS 1928.

Bronze; reeded edge; wt. 7.2g; diam. 26.92mm; obverse - planed off flat just inside denticles after striking; SPECIMEN has been punched in by hand. Reverse - pattern design as on DC-10. The entire piece has been etched as for DC-11. (National Currency Collection)

CHARLTON No.	BOWMAN No.	SP-63 to 65
DC-12	—	$70,000.

TRIAL PIECES

ONE DOLLAR 1964.

Tin; plain edge, struck on a thick planchet; not a proof; wt. 26.9g; diam. 35.5mm; obverse - blank, except for small symbol ·Ꞁ·. Reverse - similar to the adopted design, except for being higher in relief and having thin rounded rim denticles instead of wide square ones. Unique. This unusual piece is a matrix trial. (National Currency Collection)

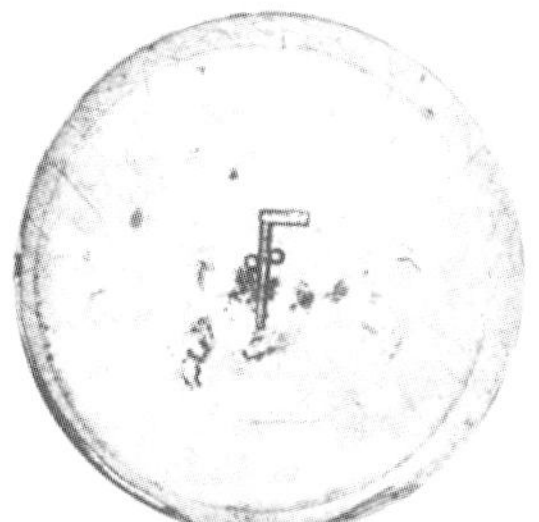

CHARLTON No.	BOWMAN No.	MS-63 to 65
DC-13	—	$50,000.

ONE DOLLAR 1967.

Silver; reeded edge; not a specimen. Similar to the adopted design, except the fields on both sides are flat instead of concave and the rim beads differ slightly in size and position.

CHARLTON No.	BOWMAN No.	MS-63 to 65
DC-14	—	$17,500. - $22,500.

FIFTY CENTS.

White metal. Trial impression of portrait of Victoria only; as on Obv. H2, 1870-1888. (National Currency Collection)

CHARLTON No.	BOWMAN No.	SP-63 to 65
DC-15	—	$5,000. - $7,500.

FIVE CENTS 1875.

Silver; reeded edge; specimen; dies ↑↓; wt. 1.20g; diam. 15.45mm. As the adopted design, except for the absence of the H mint mark. (National Currency Collection)

CHARLTON No.	BOWMAN No.	SP-63 to 65
DC-16	—	$40,000. - $60,000.

ONE CENT 1876H.

Cupro-nickel; specimen; dies ↑↓; wt. 5.81g; diam. 25.4mm. As the adopted design. These pieces are believed to have been struck for exhibition purposes, without regard to the fact that there was no currency issue corresponding exactly to them. (American Numismatic Society)

CHARLTON No.	BOWMAN No.	SP-63 to 65
DC-17	—	$3,500. - $7,500.

ONE CENT 1876.

Bronze; specimen; dies ↑↑; wt. 5.6g; diam. 25.4mm. As the adopted design, except for the absence of the H mint mark. (National Currency Collection)

CHARLTON No.	BOWMAN No.	SP-63 to 65
DC-18	—	$5,000. - $8,000.

The five brass pieces listed below (DC-19 to DC-23) were produced at the Paris mint. It is there that the original matrices for these denominations were engraved as the Royal Mint was too busy producing coins for Great Britain.

ONE CENT 1937.

Brass; specimen; dies ↑↓; wt. 3.1g; diam. 19.1mm. As the adopted design. Slightly thicker than normal. (National Currency Collection)

CHARLTON No.	BOWMAN No.	SP-63 to 65
DC-19	—	$7,500. - $10,000.

FIVE CENTS 1937.

Brass; specimen; dies ↑↓; wt. 4.98g; diam. 21.5mm. As the adopted design. Slightly thicker than normal. (National Currency Collection)

CHARLTON No.	BOWMAN No.	SP-63 to 65
DC-20	—	$7,500. - $10,000.

TEN CENTS 1937.

Brass; reeded edge; specimen; dies ↑↓; wt. 2.46g; diam. 18.3mm. As the adopted design. Slightly thicker than normal. (National Currency Collection)

CHARLTON No.	BOWMAN No.	SP-63 to 65
DC-21	—	$5,000. - $10,000.

TWENTY-FIVE CENTS 1937.

Brass; reeded edge; specimen; dies ↑↓; wt. 6.1g; diam. 23.9mm. As the adopted design. Slightly thicker than normal. (National Currency Collection)

CHARLTON No.	BOWMAN No.	SP-63 to 65
DC-22	—	$5,000. - $10,000.

FIFTY CENTS 1937.

Brass; reeded edge; specimen; dies ↑↓; wt. 14.9g; diam. 30.0mm. As the adopted design. Thicker than normal. (National Currency Collection)

CHARLTON No.	BOWMAN No.	SP-63 to 65
DC-23	—	$40,000. - $50,000.

TWENTY-FIVE CENTS 1937.

Bronze; reeded edge; specimen; dies ↑↑; wt. 5.5g; diam. 23.62mm. As the adopted design. Normal thickness. (National Currency Collection)

CHARLTON No.	BOWMAN No.	SP-63 to 65
DC-24	—	$6,500. - $10,000.

FIVE CENTS 1942.

Nickel; not a specimen; dies ↑↑; wt. 5.5g; diam. 23.62mm. As the 12-sided design adopted for the tombac pieces. (National Currency Collection)

CHARLTON No.	BOWMAN No.	MP-63 to 65
DC-25	—	$7,500. - $10,000.

ONE CENT 1943.

Copper-plated steel; not a specimen; dies ↑↑; wt. 3.0g; diam. 19.05mm. As the adopted design. (National Currency Collection)

CHARLTON No.	BOWMAN No.	MS-63 to 65
DC-26	—	—

ONE CENT 1943.

Steel; not a specimen; dies ↑↑; wt 3.1g; diam. 19.05mm. As the adopted design. (National Currency Collection)

CHARLTON No.	BOWMAN No.	MS-63 to 65
DC-26a	—	—

FIVE CENTS 1943.

Steel; specimen. As the design adopted for the tombac pieces. (Piece seen, but composition not confirmed.)

CHARLTON No.	BOWMAN No.	SP-63 to 65
DC-27	—	—

FIVE CENTS 1944.

Tombac. See page 98.

CHARLTON No.	BOWMAN No.	MS-63 to 65
DC-28	—	—

Note: Where the only known examples are in institutional collections the prices are not shown

FIVE CENTS 1951.

Chrome-plated nickel; specimen; dies ↑↑; wt. 4.6g; diam. 21.3mm. As the commemorative design struck in nickel. (National Currency Collection)

CHARLTON No.	BOWMAN No.	SP-63 to 65
DC-29	—	$8,000. - $10,000.

FIVE CENTS 1952.

Composition unknown; specimen; dies ↑↑; wt. 3.80g; diam. 21.3mm. As the adopted designs. (National Currency Collection)

CHARLTON No.	BOWMAN No.	SP-63 to 65
DC-30	—	$2,500. - $5,000.

FIFTY CENTS 1959.

Tin; uniface on thick, oversize blank; obverse - blank except for the engraved inscription (added after the piece was struck) FIRST TRIAL/Oct 27th/1958. Reverse - as the adopted design, except lacks rim denticles. Unique. (National Currency Collection)

CHARLTON No.	BOWMAN No.	MS-63 to 65
DC-31A Engraved Obv.	—	— - $35,000.
DC-31b Plain Obv.	—	— - $30,000.

ONE CENT 1966.

Nickel; dies ↑↑; wt. 3.50g; diam. 19.05mm. As the adopted designs.

CHARLTON No.	BOWMAN No.	MS-63 to 65
DC-32	—	$1,500. - $2,500.

TEN CENTS 1967.

Nickel; dies ↑↑; wt. 2.07g; diam. 18.03mm. As the adopted designs.

CHARLTON No.	BOWMAN No.	MS-63 to 65
DC-33	—	$3,000. - $5,000.

TWENTY-FIVE CENTS 1967.

Nickel; dies ↑↑; wt. 5.07g; diam. 23.62mm. As the adopted designs.

CHARLTON No.	BOWMAN No.	MS-63 to 65
DC-34	—	$3,000. - $5,000.

FIFTY CENTS 1881H.

Copper; reeded edge; circulation strike; dies ↑↑; wt. 9.74g; diam. 29.72mm. As the adopted design.

Photograph not available at press time

CHARLTON No.	BOWMAN No.	VF to EF
DC-35	—	$60,000.

OFFICIAL FABRICATION

TWENTY CENTS 1871.

Silver; reeded edge; specimen; dies ↑↓; wt. 4.62g; diam. 23.3mm. As the adopted design, see below. As the adopted design for the Province of Canada, except for the date. This piece does not represent a proposed 20 cents for the Dominion of Canada. It is believed to have been struck for exhibition to show the Province of Canada 20 cents. Only the type was important; no concern was given to using a date corresponding to the coins actually issued for circulation. (National Currency Collection)

CHARLTON No.	BOWMAN No.	SP-63 to 65
DC-50	—	$12,500. - $30,000.

TWENTY CENTS 1871.

Silver; plain edge; specimen; dies ↑↑; wt. 4.70g; diam. 23.3mm.

CHARLTON No.	BOWMAN No.	SP-63 to 65
DC-51	—	$12,500. - $30,000.

CANADA — TEST TOKENS

As far back as 1907, test tokens have been used during the various stages of design to ensure a flawless product. Test tokens are utilized for die and die coating testing, for plating process modifications, for dimensional testing, for metal tolerance, for the edge profile process, for coin collars, for the conformity of the electromagnetic signature in coins, as well as for other uses.

During 2011 two important test token collections became available for comparison with the "Standard" listing. This comparison resulted in additions and adjustments to the test token listings. So much so that the decision was reached to renumber the complete test token section. Realising the problems this would cause for collectors we have included a cross-referencing chart equating the old numbers to the new. Hopefully this will help lessen the confusion that may develop.

LISTING CRITERIA

1. Composition and shape are assigned a whole number.
2. All the rest, legends, weight, diameter, thickness, edge, and die axis are assigned a variety letter.
3. Brackets around the date indicate the token is undated. The date assigned to the token has not been confirmed by the Royal Canadian Mint but follows chronologically the order of the circulating coinage.

CROSS-REFERENCING TABLES OLD TO NEW NUMBERS

ONE CENT TEST TOKENS

Cat. Nos. to 2011	Revised Cat. Nos. 2012	Remarks
TT-1.1	TT.1.1	
TT-1.2	TT-1.2	
TT-1.3A	TT-1.3A	
TT-1.3B	TT-1.3B	
TT-1.3C	TT-1.3C	
TT-1.4A	TT.1-4A	
TT-1.4B	TT-1.4B	
TT-1.4C	TT-1.4C	
TT-1.5A	TT-1.6A	
TT-1.5B	TT-1.6B	
TT-1.6	TT-1.9	
TT-1.7A	TT-1.10A	
TT-1.7B	TT-1.10B	
TT-1.7C	TT-1.10C	
TT-1.8A	TT-1.11A	
TT-1.8B	TT-1.11B	
TT-1.8C	TT-1.11C	
TT-1.9	TT-1.13	
TT-1.10	TT-1.14	
TT-1.11	TT-1.15	

FIVE CENT TEST TOKENS

Cat. Nos. to 2011	Revised Cat. Nos. 2012	Remarks
TT-5.1A	TT-5.1A	
TT-5.1B	TT-5.1B	
TT-5.1C	TT-5.1C	
TT-5.2	TT-5.2	
TT-5.3	TT-5.3	
TT-5.4	TT-5.4	
TT-5.5	TT-5.5	
TT-5.6	TT-5.6	
TT-5.7	TT-5.7	
TT-5.8	TT-5.8	
TT-5.9	TT-5.9	
TT-5.10	TT-5.12	

TEN CENT TEST TOKENS

Cat. Nos. to 2011	Revised Cat. Nos. 2012	Remarks
TT-10.0	TT-10.1	
TT-10.1A	TT-10.2A	
TT-10.1B	TT-10.2B	
TT-10.2	TT-10.3B	
TT-10.3	TT-10.4	
TT-10.4	TT-10.5	
TT-10.5	TT-10.6	
TT-10.6	TT-10.7	
TT-10.7	TT-10.8A	
TT-10.8	TT-10.9	
TT-10.9	TT-10.10	
TT-10.10	TT-10.13	

CROSS-REFERENCING TABLES OLD TO NEW NUMBERS

TWENTY-FIVE CENT TEST TOKENS

Cat. Nos. to 2011	Revised Cat. Nos. 2012	Remarks
TT-25.1A	TT-25.1A	
TT-25.1B	TT-25.6	
TT-25.1C	TT-8	
TT-25.2A	TT-25.4	
TT-25.2B	TT-25.3	
TT-25.2C	TT-25.2A	
TT-25.2D	TT-25.6A	
TT-25.3A	TT-25.10A	
TT-25.3B	TT-25.10B	
TT-25.3C	TT-25.11A	
TT-25.3D	TT-25.11B	
TT.25.4	TT-25.12	
TT-25.5	TT-25.13A	
TT-25.6A	TT-25.14	
TT-25.7	TT-25.15A	
TT-25.8	TT-25.15B	
TT-25.9	TT-25.16A	
TT-25.10	TT-25.16B	
TT-25.11	TT-25.17A	
TT-25.12	TT-25.17D	
TT-25.13	TT-25.18A	
TT-25.14	TT-25.18B	
TT-25.15	TT-25.19A	
TT-25.16	TT-25.19B	
TT-25.17	TT-25.20	
TT-25.18	TT-25.21	
TT-25.19	TT-25.23	
TT-25.20	TT-25.25	
TT-25.21	TT-25.26	
TT-25.22	TT-25.24	

FIFTY CENT TEST TOKENS

Cat. Nos. to 2011	Revised Cat. Nos. 2012	Remarks
TT-50.1	TT-50.1	
TT-50.2	TT-50.2	
TT-50.3	TT-50.3	
TT-50.4	TT-50.4	Composition change
TT-50.5	TT-50.5	

ONE DOLLAR TEST TOKENS

Cat. Nos. to 2011	Revised Cat. Nos. 2012	Remarks
TT-100.1	TT-100.9	
TT-100.2	TT-100.12	
TT-100.3	TT-100.5	
TT-100.4	TT-100.13	
TT-100.5	TT-100.4	
TT-100.6	TT-100.8	
TT-100.7	TT-100.11	
TT-100.8	TT-100.7	
TT-100.9	TT-100.6	
TT-100.10	TT-100.3	
TT-100.11	TT-100.23	
TT-100.12	TT-100.21	
TT-100.13	TT-100.22	
TT-100.14	TT-100.19	
TT-100.15	TT-100.17	
TT-100.16	TT-100.15	
TT-100.17	TT-100.16	
TT-100.18	TT-100.18	
TT-100.19	TT-100.14	

TWO DOLLAR TEST TOKENS

Cat. Nos. to 2011	Revised Cat. Nos. 2012	Remarks
TT-200.17	TT-200.3	

CONCEPT TOKENS

Cat. Nos. to 2011	Revised Cat. Nos. 2012	Remarks
TT-200.1	TT-C1	
TT-200.2	TT-C2	
TT-200.3	TT-C3	
TT-200.4	TT-C4	
TT-200.5	TT-C6	
TT-200.6	TT-C7	
TT-200.7	TT-C8	
TT-200.8	TT-C5	Bimetallic
TT-200.9	TT-C9	
TT-200.10	TT-C9B	
TT-200.11	—	Not known to exist
TT-200.12	TT-C10	
TT-200.13	TT-C11	
TT-200.14	TT-C12	
TT-200.15	TT-C13	
TT-200.16	TT-C14	

ONE CENT TEST TOKENS

ROUND, THREE MAPLE LEAVES, WITH BEADS (1976).

Legend: TT-1.1 Obv. / Rev.: TEST TOKEN / ROYAL CANADIAN MINT

CAT. No.	COMPOSITION MARKS	WEIGHT GRAMS	DIAMETER MM	THICKNESS MM	EDGE	DIE AXIS	MAGNETIC	PRICE RANGE
TT-1.1	**Copper**	3.2	19.0	1.4	Plain	↑↓	No	150.-200.

ROUND REDUCED SIZE, NO BEADS (1977).

The Royal Canadian Mint tested a one-cent test token on December 15, 1977; however, because it was almost identical in diameter to tokens used by the Toronto Transit Commission, it was withdrawn, with very few escaping.

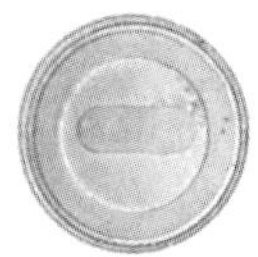
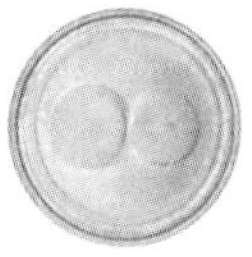

Legend: TT-1.2 Obv. / Rev.: None

CAT. No.	COMPOSITION MARKS	WEIGHT GRAMS	DIAMETER MM	THICKNESS MM	EDGE	DIE AXIS	MAGNETIC	PRICE RANGE
TT-1.2	**Copper**	1.9	16.0	1.4	Plain	↑↑	No	500.-750.

ROUND, THREE MAPLE LEAVES, WITH BEADS (1979).

In August 1979 another test token was introduced. This time the weight of the copper planchet was reduced.

English Legend TT-1.3A

French Legend TT-1.3B

English/French Legend TT-1.3C

Legend: TT-1.3A Obv. / Rev.: TEST TOKEN / ROYAL CANADIAN MINT
TT-1.3B Obv. / Rev.: EPREUVE / MONNAIE ROYALE CANADIENNE
TT-1.3C Obv.: TEST TOKEN / ROYAL CANADIAN MINT
Rev.: EPREUVE / MONNAIE ROYALE CANADIENNE"

CAT. No.	COMPOSITION MARKS	WEIGHT GRAMS	DIAMETER MM	THICKNESS MM	EDGE	DIE AXIS	MAGNETIC	PRICE RANGE
TT-1.3A	**Copper**, English legend	2.5	19.0	1.4	Plain	↑→	No	150.-200.
TT-1.3B	**Copper**, French legend	2.5	19.0	1.4	Plain	↑→	No	150.-200.
TT-1.3C	**Copper**, English/French legend	2.8	19.0	1.4	Plain	↑↑	No	30.-50.

ROUND, THREE MAPLE LEAVES, WITHOUT BEADS (1979).

English Legend TT-1.4A

French Legend TT-1.4B

English/French Legend TT-1.4C

English/French Legend TT-1.5

Legend:		
	TT-1.4A	Obv. / Rev.: TEST TOKEN / ROYAL CANADIAN MINT
	TT-1.4B	Obv. / Rev.: EPREUVE / MONNAIE ROYALE CANADIENNE
	TT-1.4C and TT-1.5	Obv.: TEST TOKEN / ROYAL CANADIAN MINT Rev.: EPREUVE / MONNAIE ROYALE CANADIENNE

CAT. No.	COMPOSITION MARKS	WEIGHT GRAMS	DIAMETER MM	THICKNESS MM	EDGE	DIE AXIS	MAGNETIC	PRICE RANGE
TT-1.4A	**Copper**, English legend	2.5	19.0	1.4	Plain	↑↑	No	750.-850.
TT-1.4B	**Copper**, French legend	2.5	19.0	1.4	Plain	↑↑	No	750.-850.
TT-1.4C	**Copper**, English/French legend	2.5	19.0	1.4	Plain	↑↑	No	750.-850.
TT-1.5	**Nickel silver** (Cu/Ni/Zn) English/French legend	2.5	19.0	1.4	Plain	↑↑	Yes	750.-850.

ROUND, THREE MAPLE LEAVES, WITH BEADS (1979).

English Legend TT-1.6A

French Legend TT-1.6B

TT-1-7 Obv. English Legend

TT-1-7 Rev. French Legend

Legend:		
	TT-1.6A	Obv. / Rev.: TEST TOKEN / ROYAL CANADIAN MINT
	TT-1.6B	Obv. / Rev.: EPREUVE / MONNAIE ROYALE CANADIENNE
	TT-1.7 and TT-1.8	Obv.: TEST TOKEN / ROYAL CANADIAN MINT Rev.: EPREUVE / MONNAIE ROYALE CANADIENNE

CAT. No.	COMPOSITION MARKS	WEIGHT GRAMS	DIAMETER MM	THICKNESS MM	EDGE	DIE AXIS	MAGNETIC	PRICE RANGE
TT-1.6A	**Copper zinc**, English legend	2.7	19.0	1.3	Plain	↑↑	No	150.-200.
TT-1.6B	**Copper zinc**, French legend	2.7	19.0	1.9	Plain	↑↑	No	150.-200.
TT-1.7	**Copper**, Obv. and Rev.: "X" raised, English/French legend	2.7	19.0	1.8	Plain	↑↑	No	200.-300.
TT-1.8	**Copper nickel**, English/French legend	2.7	19.0	1.2	Reeded	↑↑	No	750.-1,000.

7-SIDED, THREE MAPLE LEAVES, WITH BEADS (1980).

Legend: TT-1.9 Obv.: TEST TOKEN / ROYAL CANADIAN MINT
Rev.: EPREUVE / MONNAIE ROYALE CANADIENNE

CAT. No.	COMPOSITION MARKS	WEIGHT GRAMS	DIAMETER MM	THICKNESS MM	EDGE	DIE AXIS	MAGNETIC	PRICE RANGE
TT-1.9	**Copper**	2.3	Corners 19.0 Flat 18.5	1.3	Plain	↑↑	No	175.-225.

11-SIDED, THREE MAPLE LEAVES, SHARP CORNERS, WITH BEADS (1981).

The 11-sided Mark I test token was tested on July 12, 1981, but because of its sharp corners it was rejected.

English Legend TT-1.10A

French Legend TT-1.10B

English/French Legend TT-1.10C

Legend: TT-1.10A Obv. / Rev.: TEST TOKEN / ROYAL CANADIAN MINT
TT-1.10B Obv. / Rev.: EPREUVE / MONNAIE ROYALE CANADIENNE
TT-1.10C Obv.: TEST TOKEN / ROYAL CANADIAN MINT
Rev.: EPREUVE / MONNAIE ROYALE CANADIENNE

CAT. No.	COMPOSITION MARKS	WEIGHT GRAMS	DIAMETER MM	THICKNESS MM	EDGE	DIE AXIS	MAGNETIC	PRICE RANGE
TT-1.10A	**Copper**, English legend	2.4	Corners 19.0 Flat 18.4	1.5	Plain	↑↑	No	175.-225.
TT-1.10B	**Copper**, French legend	2.4	Corners 19.0 Flat 18.4	1.5	Plain	↑↑	No	175.-225.
TT-1.10C	**Copper**, English/French legend	2.6	Corners 19.0 Flat 18.4	1.5	Plain	↑↑	No	75.-125.

12-SIDED, THREE MAPLE LEAVES, ROUNDED CORNERS, WITH BEADS, (1981).

This 12-sided test token (Mark II) was a success, and a new one cent coin went into production spring 1982.

English Legend TT-1.11A

French Legend TT-1.11B

English/French Legend TT-1.11C

Legend: TT-1.11A Obv. / Rev.: TEST TOKEN / ROYAL CANADIAN MINT
TT-1.11B Obv. / Rev.: EPREUVE / MONNAIE ROYALE CANADIENNE
TT-1.11C Obv.: TEST TOKEN / ROYAL CANADIAN MINT
Rev.: EPREUVE / MONNAIE ROYALE CANADIENNE

CAT. No.	COMPOSITION MARKS	WEIGHT GRAMS	DIAMETER MM	THICKNESS MM	EDGE	DIE AXIS	MAGNETIC	PRICE RANGE
TT-1.11A	**Copper**, English legend	2.5	Corners 19.1 Flat 18.5	1.5	Plain	↑↑	No	300.-350.
TT-1.11B	**Copper**, French legend	2.5	Corners 19.1 Flat 18.5	1.5	Plain	↑↑	No	300.-350.
TT-1.11C	**Copper**, English/French legend	2.5	Corners 19.1 Flat 18.5	1.5	Plain	↑↑	No	300.-350.

COPPER PLATED STEEL TEST COINAGE OF 1999 and 2000.

For a brief outline of the 1999-2000 test coinage see page 69. See also page 284 for the test token set TTS-3.

CAT. No.	DATE	COMPOSITION MARKS	WEIGHT GRAMS	DIAMETER MM	THICKNESS MM	EDGE	DIE AXIS	MAGNETIC	PRICE RANGE
TT-1.12A	1999P	**Copper plated steel**	2.35	19.0	1.45	Plain	↑↑	Yes	20.-40.
TT-1.12B	2000P	**Copper plated steel**	2.35	19.0	1.45	Plain	↑↑	Yes	10,000.

ROUND, THREE MAPLE LEAVES, WITH BEADS, (2004 and 2006).

This test token was issued as part of the "Poppy Test Token" set TTS-4, and the "Breast Cancer Token" set TTS-5.

Legend: TT-1.13 Obv.: TEST TOKEN / ROYAL CANADIAN MINT
Rev.: EPREUVE / MONNAIE ROYALE CANADIENNE

CAT. No.	COMPOSITION MARKS	WEIGHT GRAMS	DIAMETER MM	THICKNESS MM	EDGE	DIE AXIS	MAGNETIC	PRICE RANGE
TT-1.13	**Multi-ply plated steel**	2.4	19.0	1.4	Plain	↑↑	Yes	15.-20.

BALL, ROUND, THREE MAPLE LEAVES, NO BEADS (2005).

This test planchet was supplied by Ball Metal Corporation of Toronto. Currently, it is believed only three copper and fifty brass tokens are known to exist.

Legend: TT-1.14 and TT-1.15 Obv.: TEST TOKEN / BALL / ROYAL CANADIAN MINT
Rev.: EPREUVE / BALL / MONNAIE ROYALE CANADIENNE

CAT. No.	COMPOSITION MARKS	WEIGHT GRAMS	DIAMETER MM	THICKNESS MM	EDGE	DIE AXIS	MAGNETIC	PRICE RANGE
TT-1.14	**Copper**	2.5	19.2	1.4	Plain	↑↓	No	500.-750.
TT-1.15	**Brass**	3.0	19.2	1.4	Plain	↑↓	No	100.-150.

FIVE CENT TEST TOKENS

ROUND, THREE MAPLE LEAVES, WITH BEADS (1976).

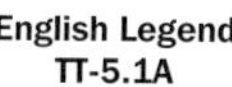

English Legend
TT-5.1A

French Legend
TT-5.1B

English/French Legend TT-5.1C

Legend: **TT-5.1A** Obv. / Rev.: TEST TOKEN / ROYAL CANADIAN MINT
TT-5.1B Obv. / Rev. EPREUVE / MONNAIE ROYALE CANADIENNE
TT-5.1C Obv.: TEST TOKEN / ROYAL CANADIAN MINT
Rev.: EPREUVE / MONNAIE ROYALE CANADIENNE

CAT. No.	COMPOSITION MARKS	WEIGHT GRAMS	DIAMETER MM	THICKNESS MM	EDGE	DIE AXIS	MAGNETIC	PRICE RANGE
TT-5.1A	**Nickel**, English legend	4.3	21.9	1.7	Plain	↑↑	Yes	75.-125.
TT-5.1B	**Nickel**, French legend	4.3	21.9	1.7	Plain	↑↑	Yes	75.-125.
TT-5.1C	**Nickel**, English/French legend	4.3	21.9	1.7	Plain	↑↑	Yes	75.-125.

ROUND, THREE MAPLE LEAVES (1983).

This series of tokens has either a letter, number, both a letter and number, or no markings. The letters and numbers can be either raised or incused.

TT-5.2

Raised "430"

TT-5.5

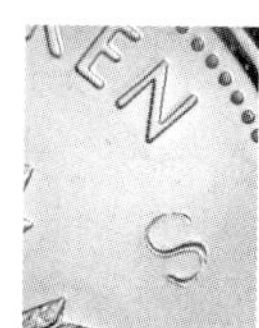

Incused "S"

Legend: **TT-5-2 to TT-5.10** Obv.: TEST TOKEN / ROYAL CANADIAN MINT
Rev.: EPREUVE / MONNAIE ROYALE CANADIENNE

CAT. No.	COMPOSITION MARKS	WEIGHT GRAMS	DIAMETER MM	THICKNESS MM	EDGE	DIE AXIS	MAGNETIC	PRICE RANGE
TT-5.2	**Stainless steel**, Obv.: "430" raised	3.5	21.2	1.8	Plain	↑↑	Yes	200.-300.
TT-5.3	**Nickel silver**, Obv./Rev.: "Ni Ag" raised	4.7	21.2	1.8	Plain	↑↑	No	200.-300.
TT-5.4	**Nickel bonded steel**, Obv.: "6.2" raised, Rev.: "NBS" raised	4.1	21.2	1.8	Plain	↑↑	Yes	200.-300.
TT-5.5	**Steel**, Obv.: "S" incused	4.0	21.2	1.8	Plain	↑↑	Yes	200.-300.
TT-5.6	**Nickel**, Obv.: "=T" raised	4.0	21.2	1.8	Plain	↑↑	Yes	200.-300.
TT-5.7	**Stainless steel**, Obv.: "304" raised	4.0	21.2	1.8	Plain	↑↑	Yes	200.-300.
TT-5.8	**Unknown**, Obv.: "A" incused	4.1	21.2	1.8	Plain	↑↑	Yes	200.-300.
TT-5.9	**Unknown**	4.1	21.2	1.8	Plain	↑↑	Yes	200.-300.
TT-5.10	(**Chrome plated steel**)	4.4	21.8	1.8	Plain	↑↑	Yes	200.-300.

Note: TT-5.10 has the composition shown in brackets. This simply means it is a best guess situation. The colour of the token is that of chrome plate.

MULTI-PLY PLATED STEEL TEST COINAGE OF 1999.

For a brief outline of the 1999 test coinage see page 107. See also page 284 for the test token set TTS-3.

CAT. No.	DATE	COMPOSITION MARKS	WEIGHT GRAMS	DIAMETER MM	THICKNESS MM	EDGE	DIE AXIS	MAGNETIC	PRICE RANGE
TT-5.11	1999P	**Multi-ply plated steel**	3.95	21.1	1.76	Plain	↑↑	Yes	20.-30.

ROUND, THREE MAPLE LEAVES, WITH BEADS, (2004 and 2006).

This test token was issued as part of the "Poppy Test Token" set TTS-4, and the "Breast Cancer Test Token" set TTS-5.

Legend: **TT-5.12** Obv.: TEST TOKEN / ROYAL CANADIAN MINT
Rev.: EPREUVE / MONNAIE ROYALE CANADIENNE

CAT. No.	COMPOSITION MARKS	WEIGHT GRAMS	DIAMETER MM	THICKNESS MM	EDGE	DIE AXIS	MAGNETIC	PRICE RANGE
TT-5.12	**Multi-ply plated steel**	4.0	21.2	1.8	Plain	↑↑	Yes	15.-20.

TEN CENT TEST TOKENS

ROUND, BOUQUET OF FLOWERS, 1965.

A 'ten tokens' struck on a one cent copper planchet.

Legend: TT-10.1 Obv. / Rev.: R.C.M. TEN TOKENS 1965

CAT. No.	COMPOSITION MARKS	WEIGHT GRAMS	DIAMETER MM	THICKNESS MM	EDGE	DIE AXIS	MAGNETIC	PRICE RANGE
TT-10.1	**Copper**	3.3	19.0	1.6	Plain	↑↑	No	750.-850.

ROUND, BOUQUET OF FLOWERS AND FLEUR-DE-LIS, 1965.

TT-10-2A

TT-10-2B

Legend: TT-10.2A Obv. / Rev.: R.C.M. TEN TOKENS 1965
TT-10.2B Obv. / Rev.: TEN TOKENS 1965

CAT. No.	COMPOSITION MARKS	WEIGHT GRAMS	DIAMETER MM	THICKNESS MM	EDGE	DIE AXIS	MAGNETIC	PRICE RANGE
TT-10.2A	**Nickel**, With R.C.M.	2.1	17.8	1.2	Reeded	↑↑	Yes	40.-60.
TT-10.2B	**Nickel**, Without R.C.M.	2.1	17.8	1.2	Reeded	↑↑	Yes	40.-60.

ROUND, THREE MAPLE LEAVES, WITH BEADS (1976).

English Legend TT-10-3A

English/French Legend TT-10-3B

Legend: TT-10.3A Obv. / Rev.: TEST TOKEN / ROYAL CANADIAN MINT
TT-10.3B Obv.: TEST TOKEN / ROYAL CANADIAN MINT
Rev.: EPREUVE / MONNAIE ROYAL CANADIENNE

CAT. No.	COMPOSITION MARKS	WEIGHT GRAMS	DIAMETER MM	THICKNESS MM	EDGE	DIE AXIS	MAGNETIC	PRICE RANGE
TT-10.3A	**Nickel**, English legend	2.1	17.8	1.2	Reeded	↑→	Yes	150.-200.
TT-10.3B	**Nickel**, English/French legend	1.8	18.0	1.2	Reeded	↑↑	Yes	75.-125.

ROUND, THREE MAPLE LEAVES, WITH BEADS, (1983).

The letters or numbers given in quotation marks, for example "S", are either raised or incused on the test token, indicating the composition of that token.

TT-10.4

Raised "430"

TT-10.8

Incused "T"

Legend: TT-10.4 to 10.10 Obv.: TEST TOKEN / ROYAL CANADIAN MINT
Rev.: EPREUVE / MONNAIE ROYALE CANADIENNE

CAT. No.	COMPOSITION MARKS	WEIGHT GRAMS	DIAMETER MM	THICKNESS MM	EDGE	DIE AXIS	MAGNETIC	PRICE RANGE
TT-10.4	**Stainless steel**, Obv.: "430" raised	2.0	18.0	1.1	Reeded	↑↑	Yes	200.-300.
TT-10.5	**Stainless steel**, Obv.: "304" raised	2.0	17.8	1.1	Reeded	↑↑	Yes	200.-300.
TT-10.6	**Nickel bonded steel**, Obv.: "NBS 6.3" raised, SHERRITT	1.8	17.9	1.1	Reeded	↑↑	Yes	200.-300.
TT-10.7	**Steel**, Obv.: "S" raised	2.0	17.9	1.2	Reeded	↑↑	Yes	200.-300.
TT-10.8A	**Nickel**, Obv.: "T" incused	2.0	18.0	1.2	Reeded	↑↑	Yes	200.-300.
TT-10.8B	**Nickel**, Obv.: "=T" incused	2.0	18.0	1.2	Reeded	↑↑	Yes	200.-300.
TT-10.9	**Unknown**	2.0	17.9	1.2	Reeded	↑↑	Yes	200.-300.
TT-10.10	**Copper**	2.0	17.9	1.2	Reeded	↑↑	No	200.-300.

MULTI-PLY PLATED STEEL TEST COINAGE OF 1999 and 2000.

For a brief outline of the 1999-2000 test coinage see page 134. See also page 284 for the test token set TTS-3.

CAT. No.	DATE	COMPOSITION MARKS	WEIGHT GRAMS	DIAMETER MM	THICKNESS MM	EDGE	DIE AXIS	MAGNETIC	PRICE RANGE
TT-10.11A	1999P	**Multi-ply plated steel**	1.75	18.0	1.22	Reeded	↑↑	Yes	30.-50.
TT-10.11B	2000P	**Multi-ply plated steel**	1.75	18.0	1.22	Reeded	↑↑	Yes	1,500.-3,000.

ROUND, THREE MAPLE LEAVES, WITH BEADS (DATE UNKNOWN).

This test token has a raised "I" on the obverse (English) of the token.

Legend: TT-10.12 Obv.: TEST TOKEN / ROYAL CANADIAN MINT
Rev.: EPREUVE / MONNAIE ROYAL CANADIENNE

CAT. No.	COMPOSITION MARKS	WEIGHT GRAMS	DIAMETER MM	THICKNESS MM	EDGE	DIE AXIS	MAGNETIC	PRICE RANGE
TT-10.12	**Multi-ply plated steel**, Obv.: "I" raised	1.8	18.1	1.2	Reeded	↑↑	Yes	15.-20.

ROUND, THREE MAPLE LEAVES, WITH BEADS, (2004 and 2006).

This test token was issued as part of the "Poppy Test Token" set TTS-4, and the "Breast Cancer Token" set TTS-5.

Legend: **TT-10.13** Obv.: TEST TOKEN / ROYAL CANADIAN MINT
Rev.: EPREUVE/MONNAIE ROYAL CANADIENNE

CAT. No.	COMPOSITION MARKS	WEIGHT GRAMS	DIAMETER MM	THICKNESS MM	EDGE	DIE AXIS	MAGNETIC	PRICE RANGE
TT-10.13	**Multi-ply plated steel**	1.8	18.1	1.2	Reeded	↑↑	Yes	15.-20.

TWENTY-FIVE CENT TEST TOKENS

ROUND, THREE CANADA GEESE, R.C.M./R.C.M., 1965.

These test tokens were struck to provide an example of the quality of coins produced by the Royal Canadian Mint and to provide a piece for adjusting vending machines for nickel coins.

Obverse

Reverse

Legend: TT-25.1 Obv. / Rev.: TWENTY FIVE TOKENS / 1965 / R.C.M.

CAT. No.	COMPOSITION MARKS	WEIGHT GRAMS	DIAMETER MM	THICKNESS MM	EDGE	DIE AXIS	MAGNETIC	PRICE RANGE
TT-25.1A	**Nickel**, Medal Axis	5.1	23.8	1.7	Reeded	↑↑	Yes	300.-400.
TT-25.1B	**Nickel**, Coinage Axis	5.9	23.9	1.9	Reeded	↑↓	Yes	300.-400.

ROUND, THREE CANADA GEESE, 1965.

Legend: TT-25.2 to TT-25.6 Obv. / Rev.: TWENTY FIVE TOKENS / 1965

CAT. No.	COMPOSITION MARKS	WEIGHT GRAMS	DIAMETER MM	THICKNESS MM	EDGE	DIE AXIS	MAGNETIC	PRICE RANGE
TT-25.2A	**Aluminum**	2.0	23.6	2.0	Plain	↑↑	No	400.-450.
TT-25.2B	**Aluminum**	1.8	23.9	1.9	Plain	↑↑	No	400.-450.
TT-25.2C	**Aluminum**	1.4	23.6	1.6	Plain	↑↑	No	400.-450.
TT-25.3	**Brass**	4.9	23.6	1.7	Plain	↑↑	No	400.-450.
TT-25.4	**Copper**	5.1	23.6	1.7	Plain	↑↑	No	400.-450.
TT-25-5	**Copper nickel**	4.8	23.6	1.6	Plain	↑↑	No	400.-450.
TT-25.6A	**Nickel**	5.1	23.6	1.7	Plain	↑↑	Yes	400.-450.
TT-25.6B	**Nickel**	5.1	23.6	1.7	Reeded	↑↑	Yes	750.-1,000.

ROUND, THREE CANADA GEESE, R.C.M. ON OBVERSE ONLY, 1965.

Obverse

Reverse

Legend: TT-25.7 to TT-25.9 Obv.: TWENTY FIVE TOKENS / 1965 / R.C.M.
Rev.: TWENTY FIVE TOKENS / 1965

CAT. No.	COMPOSITION MARKS	WEIGHT GRAMS	DIAMETER MM	THICKNESS MM	EDGE	DIE AXIS	MAGNETIC	PRICE RANGE
TT-25.7	**Brass**	4.7	23.5	1.8	Plain	↑↑	No	750.-1,000.
TT-25.8	**Copper nickel**	5.6	23.6	1.9	Plain	↑↑	No	750.-1,000.
TT-25.9	**Nickel silver** (Cu/Ni/Zn)	4.6	23.7	1.5	Reeded	↑↑	Yes	750.-1,000.

ROUND, CONJOINED BUSTS OF KING GEORGE VI AND QUEEN ELIZABETH / THREE CANADA GEESE, 1965.

The obverse design of this token is taken from the 1939 Royal Visit medal.

Legend: TT-25.10A to TT-25.11B Obv.: None
Rev.: TWENTY FIVE TOKENS / 1965 / CANADA

CAT. No.	COMPOSITION MARKS	WEIGHT GRAMS	DIAMETER MM	THICKNESS MM	EDGE	DIE AXIS	MAGNETIC	PRICE RANGE
TT-25.10A	**Copper nickel**	5.1	24.0	1.4	Reeded	↑↑	No	400.-600.
TT-25.10B	**Copper nickel**	5.1	24.0	1.4	Reeded	↑↓	No	400.-600.
TT-25.11A	**Nickel silver** (Cu/Ni/Zn)	4.8	24.0	1.4	Reeded	↑↑	Yes	1,200.-1,500.
TT-25.11B	**Nickel silver** (Cu/Ni/Zn)	4.8	24.0	1.4	Reeded	↑↓	Yes	1,200.-1,000.

ROUND, THREE CANADA GEESE, R.C.M. ON OBVERSE, 1965.

In 1977 these test tokens were struck to support a tender to supply circulating coinage to the Government of Bangladesh.

Legend: TT-25.12 Obv.: TWENTY FIVE TOKENS / 1965 / R.C.M.
Rev.: TWENTY FIVE TOKENS / 1965 / CANADA

CAT. No.	COMPOSITION MARKS	WEIGHT GRAMS	DIAMETER MM	THICKNESS MM	EDGE	DIE AXIS	MAGNETIC	PRICE RANGE
TT-25.12	**Stainless steel**, "304"	5.8	23.6	1.7	Plain	↑↑	Yes	800.-1,200.

ROUND, THREE MAPLE LEAVES, (1983).

The letters used to identify the test tokens' alloy are either raised or incused.

Raised "T"

TT-25.13A

Raised "T"

TT-25.17A

Incused "T"

Legend: TT-25.13A to TT-25.20 Obv.: TEST TOKEN / ROYAL CANADIAN MINT
Rev.: EPREUVE / MONNAIE ROYALE CANADIENNE

CAT. No.	COMPOSITION MARKS	WEIGHT GRAMS	DIAMETER MM	THICKNESS MM	EDGE	DIE AXIS	MAGNETIC	PRICE RANGE
TT-25.13A	**Aluminum**, Obv./Rev.: "T" raised	1.5	23.9	1.9	Reeded	↑↑	No	300.-350.
TT-25.13B	**Aluminum**, Obv./Rev.: "M" raised	1.8	24.0	1.9	Reeded	↑↑	No	300.-350.
TT-25.14	**Brass**, Obv./Rev.: "H" raised	5.9	24.0	1.9	Reeded	↑↑	No	300.-350.
TT-25.15A	**Copper**, Obv./Rev.: "O" raised	5.0	23.8	1.7	Reeded	↑↑	No	300.-350.
TT-25.15B	**Copper**, Obv./Rev.: "V" raised	4.7	23.8	1.6	Reeded	↑↑	No	300.-350.
TT-25.16A	**Copper nickel**, Obv./Rev.: "I" raised	5.1	23.8	1.7	Reeded	↑↑	No	300.-350.
TT-25-16B	**Copper nickel**, Obv./Rev.: "U" raised	5.1	23.8	1.7	Reeded	↑↑	No	300.-350.
TT-25.17A	**Nickel**, Rev.: "T" incused	4.6	23.8	1.4	Reeded	↑↑	Yes	300.-350.
TT-25.17B	**Nickel**, Obv.: "=T" raised	4.5	23.8	1.5	Reeded	↑↑	Yes	300.-350.
TT-25.17C	**Nickel**, Obv.: "=T=" raised	4.5	23.8	1.5	Reeded	↑↑	Yes	300.-350.
TT-25.17D	**Nickel**, Obv./Rev.: "W" raised	5.2	23.9	1.7	Reeded	↑↑	Yes	300.-350.
TT-25.18A	**Nickel bonded steel**, Obv./Rev.: "NBS 6.0" raised	4.5	23.9	1.1	Reeded	↑↑	Yes	300.-350.
TT-25.18B	**Nickel bonded steel**, Obv./Rev.: "NBS 6.3" raised	4.8	23.9	1.4	Reeded	↑↑	Yes	300.-350.
TT-25.19A	**Stainless steel**, Obv.: "304" raised	4.1	23.6	1.3	Reeded	↑↑	Yes	300.-350.
TT-25.19B	**Stainless steel**, Obv.: "430" raised	4.2	23.6	1.4	Reeded	↑↑	Yes	300.-350.
TT-25.20	**Steel**, Obv.: "S" raised	4.6	23.7	1.6	Reeded	↑↑	Yes	300.-350.

12-SIDED, THREE MAPLE LEAVES (1983).

Photograph not available at press time

Legend: **TT-25.21** Obv.: TEST TOKEN / ROYAL CANADIAN MINT
Rev.: EPREUVE / MONNAIE ROYALE CANADIENNE

CAT. No.	COMPOSITION MARKS	WEIGHT GRAMS	DIAMETER MM	THICKNESS MM	EDGE	DIE AXIS	MAGNETIC	PRICE RANGE
TT-25.21	**Aluminum**, "M" raised	1.8	24.0	1.3	Plain	↑↑	No	300.-350.

MULTI-PLY PLATED STEEL TEST COINAGE, 1999 and 2000.

For a brief outline of the 1999-2000 test coinage see page 164. See also page 284 for the test token set TTS-3.

CAT. No.	DATE	COMPOSITION MARKS	WEIGHT GRAMS	DIAMETER MM	THICKNESS MM	EDGE	DIE AXIS	MAGNETIC	PRICE RANGE
TT-25.22A	1999P	**Multi-ply plated steel**	4.4	23.88	1.58	Reeded	↑↑	Yes	30.-50.
TT-25.22B	2000P	**Multi-ply plated steel**	4.4	23.88	1.58	Reeded	↑↑	Yes	30,000.

ROUND, THREE MAPLE LEAVES, DATE UNKNOWN.

Legend: **TT-25.23 to TT-25.24** Obv.: TEST TOKEN / ROYAL CANADIAN MINT
Rev.: EPREUVE / MONNAIE ROYALE CANADIENNE

CAT. No.	COMPOSITION MARKS	WEIGHT GRAMS	DIAMETER MM	THICKNESS MM	EDGE	DIE AXIS	MAGNETIC	PRICE RANGE
TT-25.23	**Multi-ply plated steel**	4.7	23.7	1.6	Reeded	↑↑	Yes	300.-350.
TT-25.24	**Multi-ply plated zinc**	4.8	23.7	1.6	Reeded	↑↑	No	400.-450.

ROUND, RCM LOGO, UNCOLOURED POPPY REVERSE, (2004).

This test token was issued as part of the "Poppy Test Token" set, (TTS-4). The token does not carry the red colour of the "Poppy" circulating coin.

Legend: **TT-25.25** Obv.: TEST TOKEN / EPREUVE
Rev.: CANADA 2004 / REMEMBER / SOUVENIR

CAT. No.	COMPOSITION MARKS	WEIGHT GRAMS	DIAMETER MM	THICKNESS MM	EDGE	DIE AXIS	MAGNETIC	PRICE RANGE
TT-25.25	**Multi-ply plated steel**	4.4	23.8	1.6	Reeded	↑↑	Yes	15.-20.

ROUND, RCM LOGO, UNCOLOURED BREAST CANCER, 2006.

This test token was issued as part of the "Breast Cancer Token" set (TTS-5). The token does not carry the pink coloured ribbon of the "Breast Cancer" circulating coin.

Legend: **TT-25.26** Obv.: TEST TOKEN / EPREUVE
Rev.: CANADA CANADA CANADA / 25 CENTS 25 CENTS 25 CENTS

CAT. No.	COMPOSITION MARKS	WEIGHT GRAMS	DIAMETER MM	THICKNESS MM	EDGE	DIE AXIS	MAGNETIC	PRICE RANGE
TT-25.26	**Multi-ply plated steel**	4.4	23.8	1.6	Reeded	↑↑	Yes	15.-25.

FIFTY CENT TEST TOKENS

ROUND, LEGEND ONLY, 1907.

This piece was struck to adjust the coining presses prior to the first production of Canadian coins at the new Ottawa branch of the Royal Mint.

Legend: **TT-50.1** Obv.: OTTAWA MINT / TRIAL RUN
Rev.: NOVEMBER / 1907

CAT. No.	COMPOSITION MARKS	WEIGHT GRAMS	DIAMETER MM	THICKNESS MM	EDGE	DIE AXIS	MAGNETIC	PRICE RANGE
TT-50.1	**Bronze**	10.2 - 10.4	29.6-30.1	2.0	Reeded	↑↑	No	15,000.

ROUND, BIG HORN SHEEP, 1965.

This test token provides an example of the quality of coins produced at the Royal Canadian Mint.

Legend: **TT-50.2 to TT-50.5** Obv. / Rev.: 50 TOKENS / R. C. MINT / 1965

CAT. No.	COMPOSITION MARKS	WEIGHT GRAMS	DIAMETER MM	THICKNESS MM	EDGE	DIE AXIS	MAGNETIC	PRICE RANGE
TT-50.2	**Brass**	8.6	29.8	2.0	Reeded	↑↑	No	6,000.-7,500.
TT-50.3	**Bronze**	9.9	29.8	2.0	Reeded	↑↑	No	4,000.-5,000.
TT-50.4	**Cupro nickel**	12.0	29.6	2.3	Plain	↑↑	No	6,000.-7,500.
TT-50.5	**Nickel**	11.7	29.7	2.3	Reeded	↑↑	Yes	4,000.-5,000.

MULTI-PLY PLATED STEEL TEST COINAGE OF 1999 and 2000.

The 50-cent test coinage dated 1999P and 2000P was struck at the Winnipeg Mint. Only 300 of the 2000P tokens were issued, of which 250 were housed in watches, and 50 pieces issued singly.

For a brief outline of the 1999-2000 test coinage see page 195. See also page 284 for the test token set TTS-3.

CAT. No.	DATE	COMPOSITION MARKS	WEIGHT GRAMS	DIAMETER MM	THICKNESS MM	EDGE	DIE AXIS	MAGNETIC	PRICE RANGE
TT-50.6A	1999P	**Multi-ply plated steel**	6.9	27.13	1.95	Reeded	↑↑	Yes	30.-50.
TT-50-6B	2000P	**Multi-ply plated steel**	6.9	27.13	1.95	Reeded	↑↑	Yes	6,000.-7,000.

ONE DOLLAR TEST TOKENS

LARGE ROUND, THREE MAPLE LEAVES (DATE UNKNOWN).

Legend: TT-100.1 Obv.: TEST TOKEN / ROYAL CANADIAN MINT
Rev.: EPREUVE / MONNAIE ROYAL CANADIENNE

CAT. No.	COMPOSITION MARKS	WEIGHT GRAMS	DIAMETER MM	THICKNESS MM	EDGE	DIE AXIS	MAGNETIC	PRICE RANGE
TT-100.1	**Copper nickel**	17.8	36.8	2.4	Plain	↑↑	No	3,000.-5,000.

10-SIDED, THREE MAPLE LEAVES (DATE UNKNOWN).

Legend: TT-100.2 Obv.: TEST TOKEN / ROYAL CANADIAN MINT
Rev.: EPREUVE / MONNAIE ROYAL CANADIENNE

CAT. No.	COMPOSITION MARKS	WEIGHT GRAMS	DIAMETER MM	THICKNESS MM	EDGE	DIE AXIS	MAGNETIC	PRICE RANGE
TT-100.2	**Nickel**	13.4	Corners 33.3 Flat 32.3	2.0	Reeded	↑↑	Yes	3,000.-5,000.

ROUND, THREE MAPLE LEAVES, WITH BEADS (1983).

When the decision was made to retire the one dollar bank note the search began for a suitable replacement. The first test was to find a composition that the vending industry could use in their machinery. The following 10 tokens, which are divided into two groups (with beads and without beads) are all marked with their composition in raised letters. These tokens were sent from the Royal Canadian Mint packaged in pliofilm strips. There is an avenue of thought that these tokens may be concept tokens, however, with a low visual differential between the types, it is doubtful.

Raised "N.B.S."

Raised "N.B.S."

TT-100.9 Nickel Bonded Steel (with beads)

Legend: TT-100.3 to TT-100.10 Obv.: TEST TOKEN / ROYAL CANADIAN MINT
Rev.: EPREUVE / MONNAIE ROYALE CANADIENNE

CAT. No.	COMPOSITION MARKS	WEIGHT GRAMS	DIAMETER MM	THICKNESS MM	EDGE	DIE AXIS	MAGNETIC	PRICE RANGE
TT-100.3	**Aluminum**, Obv. / Rev.: "AL. 5454" raised	4.1	32.8	2.1	Plain	↑↑	No	200.-250.
TT-100.4	**Bronze**, Obv. / Rev.: "BR." raised	12.7	32.7	2.1	Plain	↑↑	No	200.-250.
TT-100.5	**Coloured bronze**, Obv. / Rev.: "C.Br." raised	12.5	32.7	2.1	Plain	↑↑	No	200.-250.
TT-100.6	**Copper aluminum**, Obv. / Rev.: "92/8" raised	12.8	32.7	2.1	Plain	↑↑	No	200.-250.
TT-100.7	**Copper nickel**, Obv. / Rev.: "CU.NI" raised	12.4	32.7	2.0	Plain	↑↑	No	200.-250.
TT-100.8	**Nickel**, Obv. / Rev.: "NI." raised	13.9	32.7	2.2	Plain	↑↑	Yes	200.-250.
TT-100.9	**Nickel bonded steel**, Obv. / Rev. "N.B.S." raised	13.0	32.8	2.3	Plain	↑↑	Yes	200.-250.

ROUND, THREE MAPLE LEAVES, WITHOUT BEADS (1983).

TT-100.12 Obverse

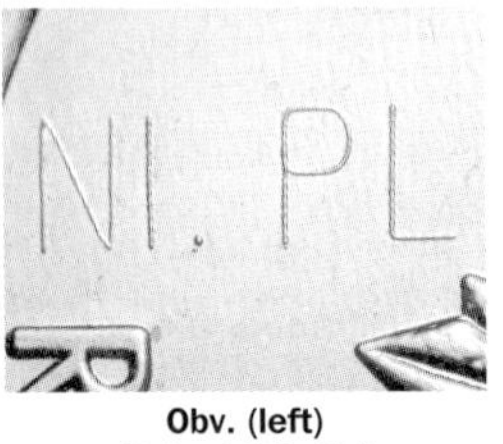

Obv. (left)
Raised "NI. PL"

TT-100.12 Reverse

Rev. (right)
Raised "NI.PL."

Obv. (left)
Raised "ZN."

Rev. (right)
Raised "ZN."

TT-100.12 Nickel Plated Zinc (without beads)

Legend: TT-100.11 to TT-100.13 Obv.: TEST TOKEN / ROYAL CANADIAN MINT
Rev.: EPREUVE / MONNAIE ROYALE CANADIENNE

CAT. No.	COMPOSITION MARKS	WEIGHT GRAMS	DIAMETER MM	THICKNESS MM	EDGE	DIE AXIS	MAGNETIC	PRICE RANGE
TT-100.11	**Gold plated nickel**, Obv. / Rev.: "AV.PL.NI" raised	14.1	32.8	2.3	Plain	↑↑	Yes	200.-250.
TT-100.12	**Nickel plated zinc**, Obv. / Rev.: "NI.PL.ZN" raised	10.2	32.8	2.2	Plain	↑↑	No	200.-250.
TT-100.13	**Stainless steel**, Obv. / Rev.: "S.S." raised	10.2	32.7	1.9	Plain	↑↑	Yes	200.-250.

ROUND, THREE MAPLE LEAVES (c.1983).

These test tokens, unlike the TT-100.3 to TT-100.13 series, do not carry the composition initials. The pliofilm packages in which these tokens were shipped from the Royal Canadian Mint were stickered with the composition.

Legend: TT-100.14 to TT-100.18 Obv.: TEST TOKEN / ROYAL CANADIAN MINT
Rev.: EPREUVE / MONNAIE ROYALE CANADIENNE

CAT. No.	COMPOSITION MARKS	WEIGHT GRAMS	DIAMETER MM	THICKNESS MM	EDGE	DIE AXIS	MAGNETIC	PRICE RANGE
TT-100.14	**Aluminum**	2.2	27.5	1.8	Reeded	↑↑	No	750.-1,000.
TT-100.15	**Copper nickel**	7.4	27.5	1.8	Reeded	↑↑	No	750.-1,000.
TT-100.16	**Nickel**	7.8	27.5	1.7	Reeded	↑↑	Yes	750.-1,000.
TT-100.17	**Nickel bonded steel**	8.2	27.9	1.8	Reeded	↑↑	Yes	750.-1,000.
TT-100.18	**Stainless steel**	5.8	27.4	1.5	Reeded	↑↑	Yes	750.-1,000.

11-SIDED, THREE MAPLE LEAVES, 120 BEADS, (c.1984).

These test tokens have wide rims and 120 beads in a circular pattern.

Legend: TT-100.19 Obv.: TEST TOKEN / ROYAL CANADIAN MINT
Rev.: EPREUVE / MONNAIE ROYALE CANADIENNE

CAT. No.	COMPOSITION MARKS	WEIGHT GRAMS	DIAMETER MM	THICKNESS MM	EDGE	DIE AXIS	MAGNETIC	PRICE RANGE
TT-100.19	**Bronze plated nickel**	7.1	26.5	1.8	Plain	↑↑	Yes	15.-20.
TT-100.20	**Nickel**	7.5	26.4	1.9	Plain	↑↑	Yes	400.-600.

11-SIDED, THREE MAPLE LEAVES, 121 BEADS, (c.1984).

The beads on these one dollar test tokens are arranged in an 11-sided pattern.

International Nickel

"S" Sherritt

Raised "S"

Legend: TT-100-21 to TT-100.22 Obv.: TEST / ROYAL CANADIAN MINT
Rev.: EPREUVE / MONNAIE ROYALE CANADIENNE

CAT. No.	COMPOSITION MARKS	WEIGHT GRAMS	DIAMETER MM	THICKNESS MM	EDGE	DIE AXIS	MAGNETIC	PRICE RANGE
TT-100.21	**Gold plated nickel** (International Nickel)	7.1	26.5	1.9	Plain	↑↑	Yes	250.-300.
TT-100.22	**Nickel bronze**, Obv.: "S" raised, (Sherritt)	7.1	26.5	1.8	Plain	↑↑	Yes	250.-300.

11-SIDED, THREE MAPLE LEAVES, 121 BEADS, (c.1986).

This test token has been tumbled and the edge rounded slightly from the original11-sides to mirror circulation wear. The question arises, who simulated the wear, the Royal Canadian Mint or Industry?.

Legend: TT-100.23 Obv.: TEST / ROYAL CANADIAN MINT
Rev.: EPREUVE / MONNAIE ROYALE CANADIENNE

CAT. No.	COMPOSITION MARKS	WEIGHT GRAMS	DIAMETER MM	THICKNESS MM	EDGE	DIE AXIS	MAGNETIC	PRICE RANGE
TT-100.23	**Nickel**	7.0	26.3	2.0	Plain	↑↑	Yes	100.-200.

11-SIDED, THREE MAPLE LEAVES, 121 BEADS, 2004 and 2006.

This test token was issued as part of the Poppy (TTS-4) and Breast Cancer (TTS-5) test token sets. It has narrow rims with beads in an 11-sided pattern. As these test tokens were issued in sets the finish on the tokens is brilliant uncirculated (MS-65-NC).

Legend: TT-100.24 Obv.: TEST TOKEN / ROYAL CANADIAN MINT
Rev.: EPREUVE / MONNAIE ROYALE CANADIENNE

CAT. No.	COMPOSITION MARKS	WEIGHT GRAMS	DIAMETER MM	THICKNESS MM	EDGE	DIE AXIS	MAGNETIC	PRICE RANGE
TT-100.24	**Bronze plated nickel**	7.1	26.5	1.8	Plain	↑↑	Yes	15.-20.

11-SIDED, UNCROWNED PORTRAIT, LOON REVERSE, TWO SECURITY MARKS, 2011.

This test token was issued to the vending industry in 2011. It was also part of the Circulation Coin and Test Token Set (TTS-6).

"T" left security mark

"É" right security mark

Legend: TT-100.25 Obv.: ELIZABETH II D G REGINA
Rev.: CANADA 2011 / DOLLAR / Maple Leaf at left contains letter "T", maple leaf at right contains letter "É"

CAT. No.	COMPOSITION MARKS	WEIGHT GRAMS	DIAMETER MM	THICKNESS MM	EDGE	DIE AXIS	MAGNETIC	PRICE RANGE
TT-100.25	**Three-ply plated brass steel,** Two security marks	6.3	26.5	1.8	Plain	↑↑	Yes	25.-30.

TWO DOLLAR TEST TOKENS

With the decision in the early 1990s to replace the two dollar bank note with a two dollar coin the selection process began on tokens of various alloys, shapes and sizes. The Mint explored two avenues, one of public acceptance, and then the preference of the vending industry. Concept tokens for testing public preferences are listed on the pages 286 to 290, while the test tokens for industry are listed below.

Since TT-200.1 and TT-200.2 are not counterstamped with a "C" it is assumed they were not part of the Canadian Coin Study, but belong in the industry testing group.

Token TT-200.3 (old TT-200.17) closely resembles TT-C9B of the concept tokens. Besides being used in industry testing, TT-200.3 was made available to collectors in singles, sets, and as souvenirs at the Mint Store. It is found in two finishes, Circulation and Brilliant Uncirculated (PL).

ROUND, COPPER ZINC, THREE MAPLE LEAVES, (1994-1995).

TT-200.1

ROUND, BIMETALLIC, THREE MAPLE LEAVES, (1994-1995).

TT-200.2

TT-200.3

Legend: TT-200.1 to 3 Obv.: TEST TOKEN / ROYAL CANADIAN MINT
Rev.: EPREUVE / MONNAIE ROYALE CANADIENNE

CAT. No.	COMPOSITION MARKS	WEIGHT GRAMS	DIAMETER MM	THICKNESS MM	EDGE	DIE AXIS	MAGNETIC	PRICE RANGE
TT-200.1	Round, **Copper zinc**	9.3	24.5	2.4	Reeded	↑↑	No	20.-25.
TT-200.2	Round, **Bi-metallic**	5.8	23.7	1.7	Reeded	↑↑	No	300.-400.
TT-200.3	Round, **Nickel ring; copper aluminum nickel centre**	7.3	28.0	1.7	Interrupted serration	↑↑	Yes	20.-25.

ROUND, BIMETALLIC, UNCROWNED PORTRAIT, POLAR BEAR REVERSE, TWO SECURITY MARKS, 2011.

This test token was issued to the vending industry in 2011. It was also issued as part of the Circulation Coin and Test Token Set (TTS-6).

"T" left security mark

"É" right security mark

Legend: **TT-200.4** Obv.: ELIZABETH II D G REGINA
Rev.: CANADA (maple leaf contains letter "T") 2 (maple leaf contains letter "É") DOLLARS

CAT. No.	COMPOSITION MARKS	WEIGHT GRAMS	DIAMETER MM	THICKNESS MM	EDGE	DIE AXIS	MAGNETIC	PRICE RANGE
TT-200-4	Round, **Three-ply nickel finish plated steel outer ring, three-ply brass finish plated aluminum bronze core**, Two security marks	6.9	28.0	1.8	Interrupted serrations, edge lettering	↑↑	Yes	25.-30.

TEST TOKEN SETS

TTS-1 1984: CIRCULATING COINS AND DOLLAR TEST TOKEN SET

SET No.	DATE	CATALOGUE No.	DESCRIPTION	PRICE RANGE
TTS-1	1973	One cent, Circulation	Round one cent,	500.-600.
	1984	One cent, Circulation	12-sided one cent	
	1984	One dollar, Circulation	Voyageur dollar	
	Undated	TT-100.19	11-sided test token	

TTS-2 1985: CIRCULATING COIN AND DOLLAR TEST TOKENS SET

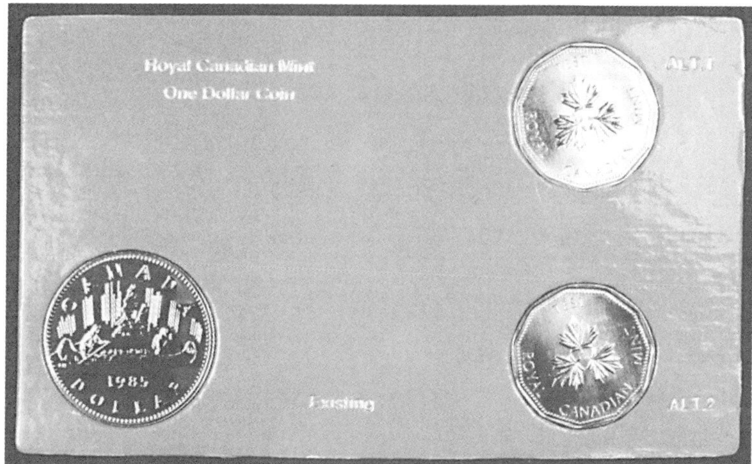

1985 Test Token Set

The sleeve for this set is found with a variety of inscriptions depending on the event for which it was intended.

1. Blue-grey with black pint: European distributors' meeting, Luxembourg, May 12, 13 and 14, 1986
2. White with black: With the compliments of / Avec les hommages de / the Honorable / l'honorable/ Harvie Andre Minister of Supply and Services and Minister responsible for the Royal Canadian Mint
3. White with gold print: With the compliments of / Avec les hommages de / the Honorable / l'honorable/ Stewart McInnes Minister of Supply and Services and Minister responsible for the Royal Canadian Min

SET No.	DATE	CATALOGUE No.	DESCRIPTION	PRICE RANGE
TTS-2	1985	One dollar, Circulation	Voyageur dollar	250.-300.
		TT-100.21	Gold plate on nickel test token	
		TT-100.22	Bronze plate on nickel test token	

TTS-3 1999: FIVE COIN MULTI-PLY PLATED STEEL COINAGE TEST SET

Multi-ply plated coinage was issued to the vending industry for test purposes in 1999. The industry's request was for "actual coins" that would be used in circulation, not "test" tokens that may or may not be issued. Five denominations, one cent through to the fifty cents, were issued to the industry on a deposit basis. Naturally not all were returned, for some found their way into the numismatic market. Finding superior demand for the legal tender "test coinage," the Mint issued a six-piece set containing five multi-ply plated steel coins and a medallion for sale to the numismatic market. The finish is brilliant relief on a brilliant background. Since the coins in this set are actual circulation issue and not test tokens. No test token numbers have been assigned.

Case of Issue: Pliofilm pouch, black envelope, COA

CAT. No.	DATE	DESCRIPTION	COMPOSITION
TT-1.12A	1999P	One Cent	Copper plated steel
TT-5.11	1999P	Five Cents	Multi-ply plated steel
TT-10.11A	1999P	Ten Cents	Multi-ply plated steel
TT-25.22A	1999P	Twenty-five Cents	Multi-ply plated steel
TT-50.6A	1999P	Fifty Cents	Multi-ply plated steel
—	—	RCM Medallion	Multi-ply plated steel

CAT No.	DESCRIPTION	MINTAGE	ISSUE PRICE	CATALOGUE PRICE
TTS-3	1999P Set of five Multi-ply Plated coins plus RCM Medallion	20,000	99.95	55.00

TTS-4 2004: TEST TOKEN "POPPY" SET

This set is a manufacturing tribute to Canada's first coloured circulating coins. The set contains one coin, a twenty-five cent Poppy commemorative, a Poppy test token and five other test tokens. All except the one and two dollar test tokens are made of multi-ply plated steel. The finish is brilliant relief on a brilliant background.

Case of Issue: Pliofilm pouch, black envelope, COA

CAT. No.	DESCRIPTION	COMPOSITION
TT-1.13	One cent test token	Copper plated steel
TT-5.12	Five cent test token	Multi-ply plated steel
TT-10.13	Ten cent test token	Multi-ply plated steel
TT-25.25	"Poppy" twenty-five cent test token	Multi-ply plated steel
—	2004 twenty-five cent Poppy commemorative coin	Multi-ply plated steel
TT-100.24	One dollar test token	Nickel plated bronze
TT-200.3	Two dollar test token	Nickel ring; copper/aluminum/nickel centre

CAT. No.	DESCRIPTION	MINTAGE	ISSUE PRICE	CATALOGUE PRICE
TTS-4	Six multi-ply plated test tokens, one 2004 twenty-five cent "Poppy" commemorative coin	9,534	49.95	50.00

TTS-5 2006: TEST TOKEN "BREAST CANCER" SET

This set contains one coin, a Breast Cancer twenty-five cents, a Breast Cancer test token and five other test tokens identical to those issued in the TTS-4 Poppy 2004 Test Token set. The finish is brilliant relief on a brilliant background.

Case of Issue: Pliofilm pouch, black envelope, COA

CATALOGUE No.	DESCRIPTION	COMPOSITION
TT-1.13	One cent test token	Copper plated steel
TT-5.12	Five cent test token	Multi-ply plated steel
TT-10.13	Ten cent test token	Multi-ply plated steel
TT-25-26	"Breast Cancer" twenty-five cent test token	Multi-ply plated steel, RCM Logo/Breast Cancer reverse (TTS-5)
—	2006 twenty-five cent Breast Cancer commemorative coin	Multi-ply plated steel
TT-100.24	One dollar test token	Nickel plated bronze
TT-200.3	Two dollar test token	Nickel ring; copper/aluminum/nickel centre

CAT. No.	DESCRIPTION	MINTAGE	ISSUE PRICE	CATALOGUE PRICE
TTS-5	Six multi-ply plated test tokens, one 2006 twenty-five cent "Breast Cancer" commemorative coin	10,061	49.95	50.00

TTS-6 2011-2012: CIRCULATION COIN and TEST TOKEN SET

This set contains a 2011 Loon circulating coin, a 2011 Test Loon with two security marks on the reverse, and a 2012 Loon circulating coin with a central security mark on the reverse. The set also contains three two-dollar coins: a 2011 circulating coin, a 2011 test token with two security marks on the reverse, and a 2012 circulating coin with two security marks on the reverse. The finish on the coins is circulation.

Case of Issue: Pliofilm pouch, white graphic envelope, COA

CATALOGUE No.	DESCRIPTION	COMPOSITION
—	2011 Circulating $1 Loon coin	Brass plated steel
TT-100.25	2011 $1 Loon coin with two security marks	Three-ply brass plated steel
—	2012 Circulating $1 Loon coin with one security mark	Three-ply brass plated steel
—	2011 Circulating $2 Polar Bear coin	Nickel ring, copper aluminum, nickel core
TT-200.4	2011 $2 Polar Bear coin with two security marks	Three-ply nickel finish plated steel ring, three-ply brass finish plated aluminum core
	2012 $2 Polar Bear coin with two security marks	Three-ply nickel finish plated steel ring, three-ply brass finish plated aluminum core

CAT. No.	DESCRIPTION	MINTAGE	ISSUE PRICE	CATALOGUE PRICE
TTS-6	Four circulation coins and two test tokens	50,000	49.95	50.00

CONCEPT TEST TOKENS

In 1994-1995 the Royal Canadian Mint organised a Canadian Coin Study group to sample public opinion on their prefer for a new two dollar coin. Fifteen tokens were designed and struck in many different alloys, shapes, size and thickness for the project leader to present to the focus groups. In this series of fifteen, concept tokens TT-9 and TT-9B seems to be the favoured design as it resembles TT-200.3.

For discussion purposes and control, each token was counterstamped with a letter and number: C1, C2, C3, etc. The tokens were numbered at the Mint, not numerical in order, but based on composition. Token TT-C5 is a bimetallic token and is thus listed with that group.

An article in *Canadian Coin News*, February 14th, 1995, stated that the Canadian Coin Study comprised of 24 samples of test tokens which were presented to the focus groups. This has not been confirmed.

SINGLE ALLOY CONCEPT TEST TOKENS, (1994-1995).

TT-C6 Round, Copper zinc

Legend: TT-C1 to TT-C8 Obv.: TEST TOKEN / ROYAL CANADIAN MINT
Rev.: EPREUVE / MONNAIE ROYALE CANADIENNE

CAT. No.	COMPOSITION MARKS	WEIGHT GRAMS	DIAMETER MM	THICKNESS MM	EDGE	DIE AXIS	MAGNETIC	PRICE RANGE
TT-C1	12-sided, **Copper-zinc**	4.0	22.5	1.4	Scalloped, plain	↑↑	No	500.-550.
TT-C2	6-sided, **Copper-zinc**	4.0	22.5	1.4	Scalloped, plain	↑↑	No	500.-550.
TT-C3	12-sided, **Stainless steel**	4.0	22.5	1.4	Scalloped, plain	↑↑	Yes	500.-550.
TT-C4	6-sided, **Copper-nickel**	4.0	22.5	1.4	Scalloped, plain	↑↑	No	500.-550.
TT-C6	Round, **Copper-zinc**	7.5	22.5	2.5	Reeded	↑↑	No	500.-550.
TT-C7	Round, **Copper-zinc**	10.0	24.5	3.3	Reeded	↑↑	No	500.-550.
TT-C8	7-sided, **Copper-zinc**	5.8	22.5	2.2	Plain	↑↑	No	500.-550.

BIMETALLIC CONCEPT TEST TOKENS, (1994-1995).

Round TT-C5

C-5

Round TT-C9B

7-sided TT-C10

C-10

8-sided TT-C11

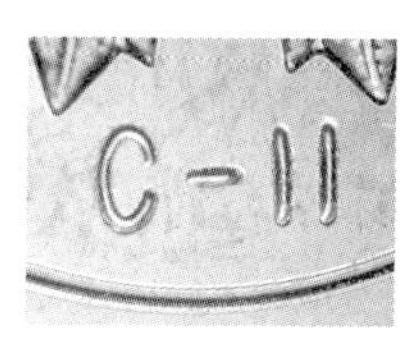

C-11

9-sided TT-C12

C-12

Legend: **TT-C5 and TT-C9 to TT-C12**
Obv.: TEST TOKEN / ROYAL CANADIAN MINT
Rev.: EPREUVE / MONNAIE ROYALE CANADIENNE

CAT. No.	COMPOSITION MARKS	WEIGHT GRAMS	DIAMETER MM	THICKNESS MM	EDGE	DIE AXIS	MAGNETIC	PRICE RANGE
TT-C5	Round, **Aluminum-bronze ring, Nickel centre**	5.0	22.5	1.8	Interrupted serration	↑↑	No	500.-550.
TT-C9	Round, **Copper zinc ring, Nickel centre**	6.2	25.3	1.9	Interrupted serration	↑↑	Yes	500.-550.
TT-C9B	Round, **Nickel ring, Aluminum-bronze centre**	6.2	25.3	1.9	Interrupted serration	↑↑	Yes	500.-550.
TT-C10	7-sided, **Copper nickel ring, Aluminum-bronze centre**	7.4	27.4	1.7	Plain	↑↑	No	500.-550.
TT-C11	8-sided, **Copper-nickel ring, Aluminum-bronze centre**	8.4	27.2	2.1	Plain	↑↑	No	500.-550.
TT-C12	9-sided, **Copper-nickel ring, Aluminum-bronze centre**	8.5	27.5	2.0	Plain	↑↑	No	500.-550.

TRIMETALLIC CONCEPT TEST TOKENS, (1994-1995).

Photograph not available at press time

Legend: TT-C13 and TT-C14 Obv.: TEST TOKEN / ROYAL CANADIAN MINT
Rev.: EPREUVE / MONNAIE ROYALE CANADIENNE

CAT. No.	COMPOSITION MARKS	WEIGHT GRAMS	DIAMETER MM	THICKNESS MM	EDGE	DIE AXIS	MAGNETIC	PRICE RANGE
TT-C13	11-sided, **Aluminum-bronze outer ring, Copper-nickel inner ring, Aluminum-bronze centre**	9.5	29.0	2.5	N/A	↑↑	No	500.-550.
TT-C14	11-sided, **Copper-nickel outer ring, Aluminum-bronze inner ring, Copper-nickel centre.**	9.6	29.0	2.5	N/A	↑↑	No	500.-550.

These concept test tokens were issued in the 2006 Tenth Anniversary Two Dollar Test Token Set (TTS-06). They were assigned numbers by the Royal Canadian Mint, with no apparent regard to previously issued numbers in the Canadian Coin Study. They are not counterstamped and have been renumbered for clarity purposes.

12-SIDED, NICKEL, CONCEPT TEST TOKEN.

The scalloped shape and size of TT-C15 (C3) has been utilized on the $150 gold coin Blessing Series which was first issued in 2009.

TT-C15 (C3)
Composition: 100% Nickel
Legend: Obv.: TEST TOKEN / ROYAL CANADIAN MINT
Rev.: EPREUVE / MONNAIE ROYALE CANADIENNE

ROUND, COPPER ZINC, CONCEPT TEST TOKEN

TT-C16 (C7)
Composition: 60% copper, 40% zinc
Legend: Obv.: TEST TOKEN / ROYAL CANADIAN MINT
Rev.: EPREUVE / MONNAIE ROYALE CANADIENNE

7-SIDED, BIMETALLIC CONCEPT TEST TOKEN.

TT-C17 (C7)
Composition: Outer ring: 99% nickel
Centre: 92% copper, 6% aluminum, 2% nickel
Legend: Obv.: TEST TOKEN / ROYAL CANADIAN MINT
Rev.: EPREUVE / MONNAIE ROYALE CANADIENNE

CAT. No.	DESCRIPTION	WEIGHT GRAMS	DIAMETER MM	THICKNESS MM	DIE AXIS	EDGE	PRICE RANGE
TT-C15 (C3)	12-sided, **Nickel**	4.5	22.5	1.7	↑↑	Plain	15.-25.
TT-C16 (C7)	Round, **Copper zinc**	8.4	22.5	2.8	↑↑	Reeded	15.-25.
TT-C17 (C10)	7-sided, **Nickel ring, copper aluminun nickel centre**	6.9	28.0	1.6	↑↑	Plain	15.-25.

CONCEPT SET-1 2006: 10TH ANNIVERSARY OF THE TWO DOLLAR COIN CONCEPT TOKEN SET

The finish is brilliant relief on a brilliant background (circulation).

Case of Issue: Maroon clamshell case, black flock insert, 5-coin plastic holder, COA

CATALOGUE No.	DESCRIPTION	COMPOSITION
TT-C15 (C3)	Concept Token, Scalloped	Nickel
TT-C16 (C7)	Concept Token, Round, Piedford	60% copper, 40% zinc
TT-C17 (C10)	Concept Token, 7-sided Bimetallic	Nickel ring; copper/nickel centre
2006	Two Dollar Polar Bear Coin	Nickel ring; copper/aluminum/nickel centre
10th Anniversary	Two Dollar Churchill Coin	Nickel ring; copper/aluminum/nickel centre

CATALOGUE No.	DESCRIPTION	MINTAGE	ISSUE PRICE	CATALOGUE PRICE
Concept Set -1	Three concept test tokens, two $2 coins	10,204	69.95	50.00

ROYAL CANADIAN MINT SALESMAN SAMPLES AND SOUVENIRS

The Royal Canadian Mint over the past fifteen years has produced numerous different tokens designed to serve many functions such as:

- Salesman samples
- Convention tokens for the RCNA, ANA and various numismatic functions
- Mint visit souvenir tokens struck at the Mint boutiques in Ottawa and Winnipeg
- Lunar Year souvenir tokens

These tokens are highly specialised and are beyond the scope of this catalogue. Salesman samples are listed here because they are working tokens, similar to the test tokens.

ROYAL CANADIAN MINT SALESMAN SAMPLES:

This set of samples, if it is complete, is similar to those on 292. They are round with an eight-sided rim design. The central design of three maple leaves appears on both the obverse and reverse. These sample tokens may have been made for potential foreign customers.

ROUND, THREE MAPLE LEAVES

Composition: Currently unknown
Legend: SS-10 to 12 None

CAT. No.	DESCRIPTION	COLOUR	WEIGHT GRAMS	DIAMETER MM	THICKNESS MM	EDGE	DIE AXIS	MAGNETIC	PRICE RANGE
SS-10	**Three maple leaves**	(Nickel)	7.5	21.5	2.8	Plain	↑↑	Yes	400.-600.
SS-11	**Three maple leaves**	(Brass)	9.5	25.0	2.5	Reeded	↑↑	No	400.-600.
SS-12	**Three maple leaves**	(Nickel)	8.4	28.5	1.9	Reeded	↑↑	Yes	400.-600.

ROYAL CANADIAN MINT SALESMAN SAMPLES, 1999-2000:

Sales personnel employed by the Royal Canadian Mint offer their customers, or potential customers, a brochure explaining the Mint's services. Accompanying the brochure are three different tokens in three sizes and compositions.

ROUND, SMALL SIZE, CANADA/MAPLE LEAVES

Composition: See below
Legend: SS-1 to 3 Obv.: CANADA / CANADA / CANADA / CANADA / CANADA / CANADA / CANADA / CANADA
Rev.: ROYAL CANADIAN MINT / MONNAIE ROYALE CANADIENNE

ROUND, MEDIUM SIZE, CANADA/MAPLE LEAVES

Composition: See below
Legend: SS-4 to 6 Obv.: CANADA / CANADA / CANADA / CANADA / CANADA / CANADA / CANADA / CANADA
Rev.: ROYAL CANADIAN MINT / MONNAIE ROYALE CANADIENNE

ROUND, LARGE SIZE, CANADA/MAPLE LEAVES

Composition: See below
Legend: SS-7 to 9 Obv.: CANADA / CANADA / CANADA / CANADA / CANADA / CANADA / CANADA / CANADA
Rev.: ROYAL CANADIAN MINT / MONNAIE ROYALE CANADIENNE

CAT. No.	DESCRIPTION	COLOUR	WEIGHT GRAMS	DIAMETER MM	THICKNESS MM	EDGE	DIE AXIS	MAGNETIC	PRICE RANGE
SS-1	**Two-ply copper-plated steel**	Bronze	6.3	25.0	1.9	Plain	↑↑	Yes	200.-300.
SS-2	**Two-ply copper-plated steel**	Bronze	8.9	30.0	2.0	Plain	↑↑	Yes	200.-300.
SS-3	**Two-ply copper-plated steel**	Bronze	12.5	35.0	2.1	Plain	↑↑	Yes	200.-300.
SS-4	**Multi-ply nickel-plated steel**	Silver	6.3	25.0	1.9	Plain	↑↑	Yes	200.-300.
SS-5	**Multi-ply nickel-plated steel**	Silver	9.1	30.0	2.0	Plain	↑↑	Yes	200.-300.
SS-6	**Multi-ply nickel-plated steel**	Silver	12.6	35.0	2.1	Plain	↑↑	Yes	200.-300.
SS-7	**Brass-plated steel**	Gold	6.3	25.0	1.9	Plain	↑↑	Yes	200.-300.
SS-8	**Brass-plated steel**	Gold	9.1	30.0	2.0	Plain	↑↑	Yes	200.-300.
SS-9	**Brass-plated steel**	Gold	12.6	35.0	2.1	Plain	↑↑	Yes	200.-300.

CANADIAN COUNTERFEITS

FOREWORD

The numismatic industry has been faced with counterfeiting for decades as scarce and rare collector coins have fraudulently been duplicated. Earlier counterfeit coins, while extremely annoying, were usually singular endeavours made by skilled craftsmen working in very small groups, if not alone, on producing one rare copy. The point being, it was really one-at-a-time, and not a production line.

In the mid-1950s a firm in Italy began striking British gold sovereigns in quantities. The sovereign at that time was no longer legal tender in the United Kingdom and the Italian government was not interested in prosecuting the counterfeiters. The British government did prosecute, however the case was thrown out because the Italian counterfeit sovereign contained more gold than the original sovereign. The court could not find the "counterfeiter's" quality a fraud. In 1957 the British Mint began again to strike sovereigns reestablishing their legal tender status.

Realizing the success of the Italian firm, a company in Lebanon began producing counterfeit US gold coins, from the one dollar through the $20 double eagle. In 1972 a gentleman who worked in Toronto wandered into our store on Queen Street and offered me a 1908 St. Gaudens high relief twenty dollar coin at double gold, which at that time was approximately $200. The workmanship on the coin was superb.

At that time Ingrid Smith and myself set up counterfeit detection seminars at the Charlton store on Queen Street West in Toronto to help the collector to identify counterfeit coins.

Now we have the Chinese and their tremendous flood of counterfeit coins and Mike Marshall spearheading the counterfeit detection drive of today.

W. K. Cross

CHINESE COUNTERFEIT CANADIAN 25 AND 50 CENT COINS

There are dozens of small factories throughout China producing counterfeit coins from many different countries of the world, Canada being just one of them. Two of the main producing factories are HK Replika Coins Co. and Big Tree Coin Co. These are striking factories, that is they operate coin presses and sell their finished product to wholesalers who in turn sell them on to small individual internet dealers.

It appears the production chain is divided into several sections: die production, planchet production, striking, and sales, with HK Replika and Big Tree at the end of the chain. We arrived at this possible conclusion by ordering and examining coins from each of the two companies. We concluded that the dies used by the HK Replika and Big Tree companies are very similar. It is extremely difficult to differentiate when two similar dated coins are placed side-by-side leading us to believe that the same die production company was used to produce dies for both the HK Replika and Big Tree companies.

Die Production:

There are four major methods of producing copies: casting, electrotypes, transfer dies and spark-erosion dies. The counterfeit coins produced by HK Replika Coins Co and Big Tree Coin Co. are struck with spark-erosion dies.

"Spark-erosion counterfeits are quite easy to detect because of the way in which they are manufactured.

In the spark-erosion process, a model coin (usually genuine) is submersed in an electrolytic bath where the coin faces the counterfeiter's die steel. An electrical current is charged through the coin so that a spark jumps across the shortest gap between the coin and the die, thus etching the coin's design onto the steel die.

After both the obverse and reverse have undergone the electrical current process, the dies are highly polished. This is necessary because once the dies have been etched, they remain somewhat pitted. The polishing generally will clean up the fields, but often the design will retain the pitting, since counterfeiters tend not to polish the main devices. Either they are unable to get down into the design, or for time's sake they choose to leave the design elements alone. In either case, these counterfeits are easy to detect, since their surfaces are glassy smooth-resembling a Proof finish-yet their devices are lumpy (remember, the pitting on the dies becomes raised lumps on the finished product). Because the excessive polishing makes the dies sharp, these counterfeits appear to be extremely well-struck, with knifelike edges and rims."

Reprint from PCGS's Coin Grading and Counterfeit Detection.

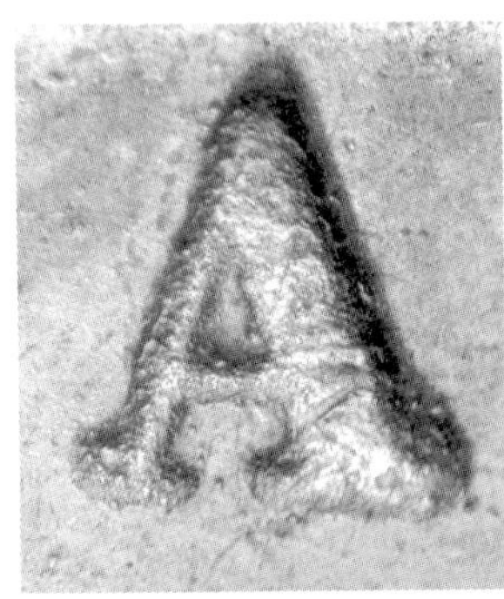

Obverse of an 1872H fifty cent coin illustrating the pitting of the last "A" in VICTORIA from a spark-erosion die. This roughness is not present on punched dies created by the Royal Mint, Heaton Mint, or Royal Canadian Mint.

Dates produced by HK Replica Coin Co.:

These dates are listed and illustrated on the following pages showing pickup points for identification.

Dates produced by Big Tree Coin Co.:

Victoria 25 cents: 1875H, 1880H, 1889, 1893
Victoria 50 cents: 1870, 1872H, 1888, 1890H, 1894
George V 50 cents: 1921, 1932

It is interesting to note that the Big Tree Victoria 1872H fifty cents counterfeit die is also the reverse 'Repunched "S" in Cents' variety as used by HK Replica.

Planchet characteristics and specifications: Currently counterfeit coins are available in three different compositions.

1. Silver plated base metal blanks. The blank is made from a mixture of elements, e.g., zinc (Zn), cobalt (Co), copper (Cu), nickel (Ni), and iron (Fe). It seems like and end-of-day mixture and certainly keeps costs low.
2. Forty percent silver blanks. The only difference from the silver plated blank is that now 44-49% silver is added to the base metal mix. The additional element is in the 44-49% range.
3. Ninety percent silver blanks. Now the blank is 98.9-99.9% silver with traces of the above elements.

The other specifications are listed on pages 295, 313, 323 and 337 in the sections dealing with 25 and 50 cent descriptions of pickup points for counterfeit identification. As you will see weights and measurements are similar to the original coins and therefore not an accurate means for identifying the counterfeits. The only good specification for Victoria coins is the die axis. HK Replika Coin used the wrong axis, an upright (↑↑), or medal axis, While the Royal Mint and the Heaton Mint used an upset (↑↓), or coinage axis. This is an extremely quick pickup point to identifying counterfeit Victoria coins produced by HK Replica Coins Co. and Big Tree Coin Co. However, caution should be taken for as time passes counterfeiters will realize and correct their errors.

While we have listed on these pages only counterfeit coins produced by HK Relika Co., please remember that Big Tree Coins Co. employs the same dies, thus the same pickup points apply.

The counterfeit of Canadian coins is an ongoing problem please "pay attention" and have a good look at all coins before you buy.

Mike Marshall

Acknowledgment

Some of the original images have been taken from the Heritage Auction Archives for which a thank you is in order.

Victoria Twenty-Five Cents

H K Replica, China, 1870, 1871H, 1872H, 1875H, 1881H, 1882H, 1883H, 1885, 1887, 1888, 1889, 1890H, 1891, 1892, 1893, and 1894.

Specifications	Original	Counterfeit
Composition:	92.5% Ag, 7.5% Cu	98.46 to 99.76% Ag
Weight:	5.81 grams	5.7 to 5.8 grams
Diameter	23.62 mm	23.5 to 23.6 mm
Thickness	1.58 mm	1.6 TO 1.7 mm
Die Axis	↑↓	↑↑

VICTORIA TWENTY-FIVE CENT MARKERS, H K REPLICA COUNTERFEIT COINS

OBVERSE MARKERS or PICKUP POINTS - ORIGINAL

1. Correct obverse portrait.
2. Strong portrait, full hair design above and below crown.
3. Full serifs on bottom of “T” in VICTORIA.

OBVERSE MARKERS or PICKUP POINTS - COUNTERFEIT

1. Correct or incorrect obverse portrait.
2. Weak portrait, missing hair design above and below crown.
3. “T” in VICTORIA truncated bottom left serif.

REVERSE MARKERS or PICKUP POINTS - ORIGINAL

1. Correct reverse design.
2. Full stem to Leaf L-1.
3. Open “C” in CENTS.
4. Fine date digits.

REVERSE MARKERS or PICKUP POINTS - COUNTERFEIT

1. Correct or incorrect reverse design.
2. Missing stem to Leaf L-1.
3. Closed “C” in CENTS.
4. Thick date digits.

Note: The 1 to 2% difference in the composition of the silver counterfeit coins is composed of a variety of elements: Zinc (Zn), Cobalt (Co), Copper (Cu), Nickel (Ni) and Iron (Fe).

Victoria Twenty-Five Cents

1870 OBVERSE

1870 Obverse, Original
Marker 1: Portrait OQ2

1870 Obverse, Counterfeit
Marker 1: Portrait OQ2

ORIGINAL Obverse Markers	COUNTERFEIT Obverse Markers
 Obv. Marker 2 (Original) Strong portrait, full hair design above and below crown	 Obv. Marker 2 (Counterfeit) Weak portrait, missing hair design above and below crown
 Obv. Marker 3 (Original) Full serifs on bottom of "T" in VICTORIA	 Obv. Marker 3 (Counterfeit) "T" in VICTORIA truncated bottom left serif

Victoria Twenty-Five Cents

1870 REVERSE

1870 Reverse, Original
Marker 1: Reverse RQ1 with short bough ends

1870 Reverse, Counterfeit
Marker 1: Reverse RQ4 with short bough ends

ORIGINAL Reverse Markers

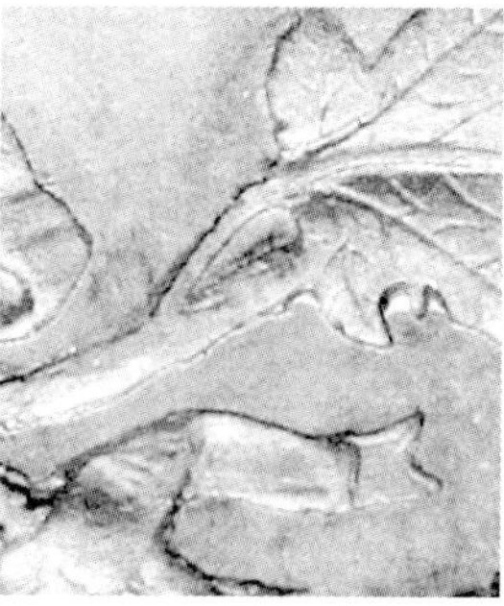

Rev. Marker 2 (Original)
Full stem to Leaf L-1

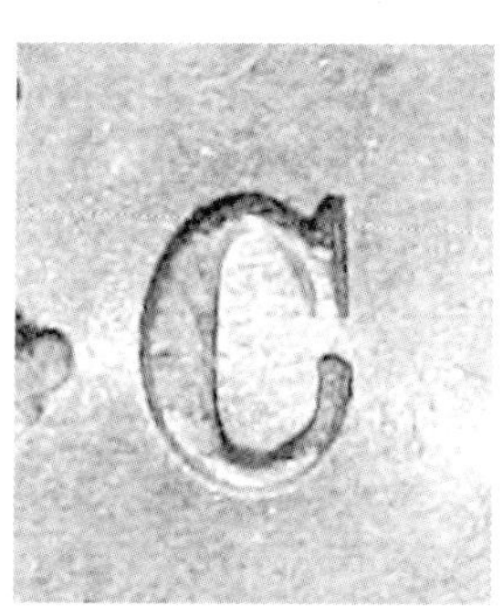

Rev. Marker 3 (Original)
Open "C" in CENTS

COUNTERFEIT Reverse Markers

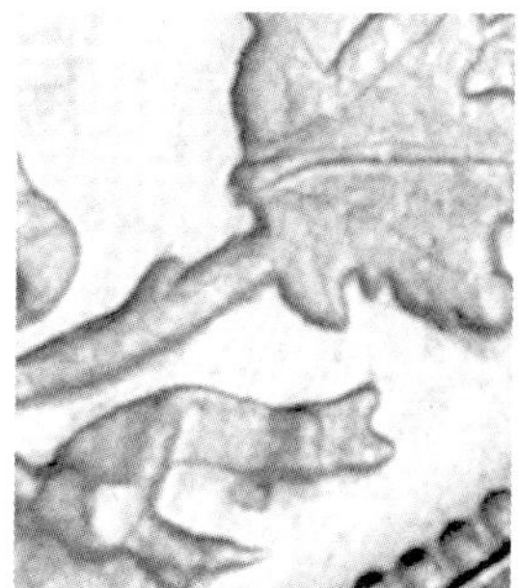

Rev. Marker 2 (Counterfeit)
Missing stem to Leaf L-1

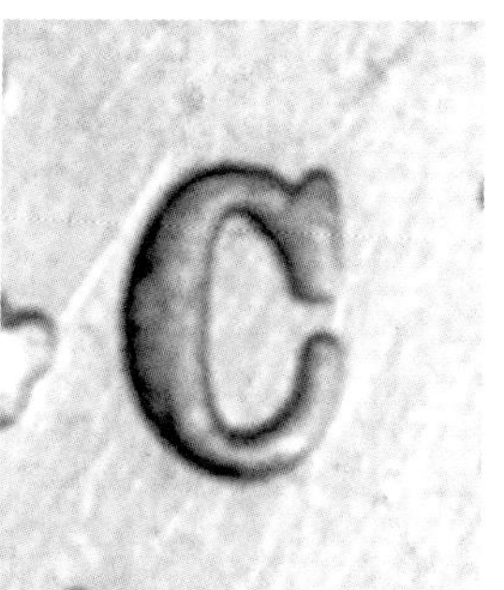

Rev. Marker 3 (Counterfeit)
Closed "C" in CENTS

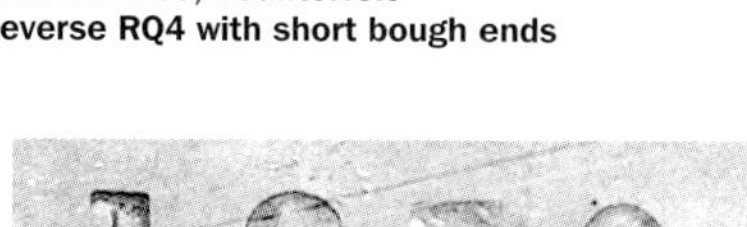

Rev. Marker 4 (Original)
1870 Date, Fine date digits
Oval "0"

Rev. Marker 4 (Counterfeit)
1870 Date, Thick date digits
Large round "0"

Victoria Twenty-Five Cents

1871H REVERSE

1871H Reverse, Original
Marker 1: Reverse RQ1 with short bough ends

1871H Reverse, Counterfeit
Marker 1: Reverse RQ4 with short bough ends

ORIGINAL
Reverse Markers

Rev. Marker 2 (Original)
Full stem to Leaf L-1

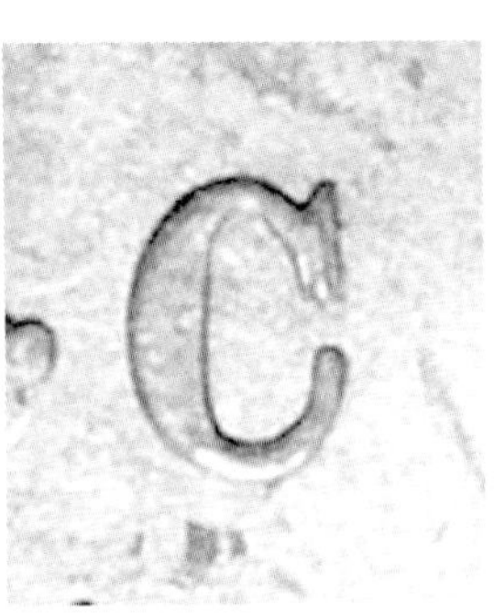

Rev. Marker 3 (Original)
Open "C" in CENTS

COUNTERFEIT
Reverse Markers

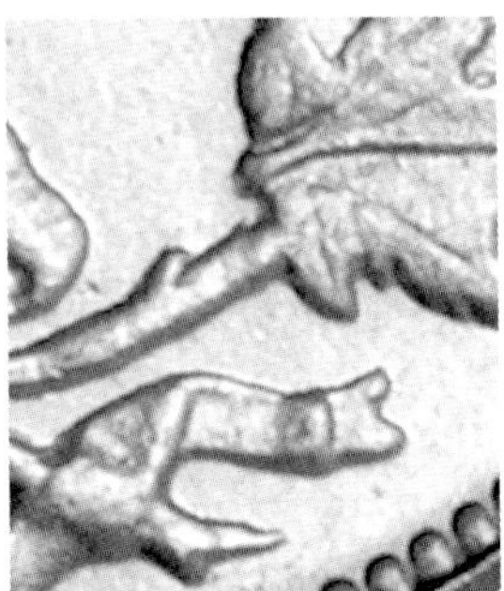

Rev. Marker 2 (Counterfeit)
Missing stem to Leaf L-1

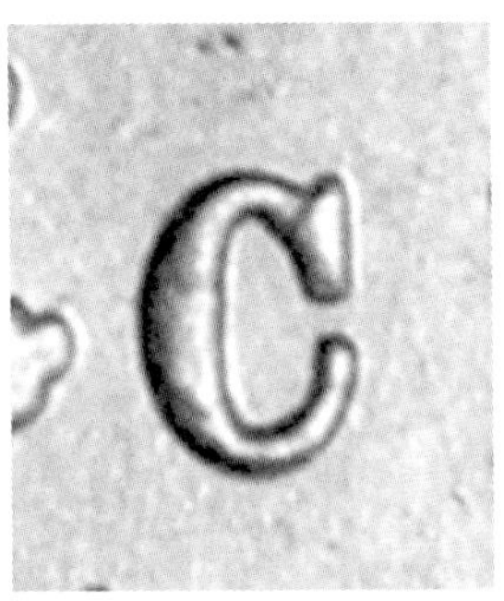

Rev. Marker 3 (Counterfeit)
Closed "C" in CENTS

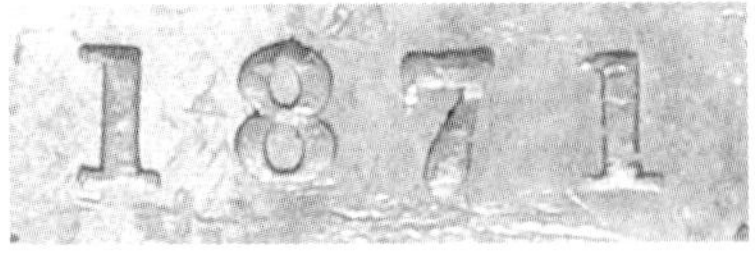

Rev. Marker 4 (Original)
1871H Date, Fine date digits
Small last "1"

Rev. Marker 4 (Counterfeit)
1871H Date, Thick date digits
Large last "1"

Victoria Twenty-Five Cents

1872H REVERSE

1872H Reverse, Original
Marker 1: Reverse RQ1 with short bough ends

1872H Reverse, Counterfeit
Marker 1: Reverse RQ4 with short bough ends

ORIGINAL Reverse Markers	COUNTERFEIT Reverse Markers
 Rev. Marker 2 (Original) Full stem to Leaf L-1	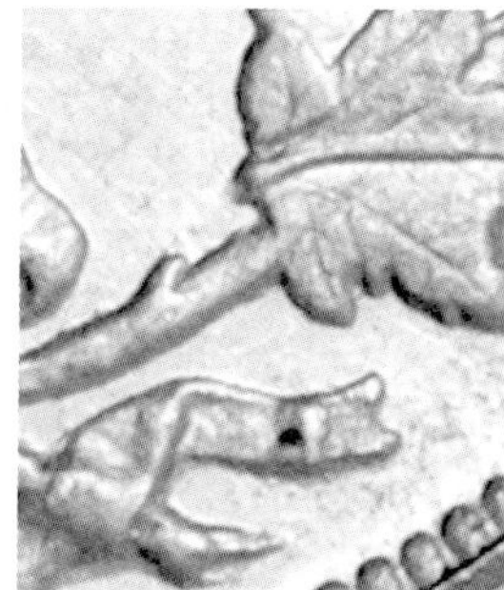 Rev. Marker 2 (Counterfeit) Missing stem to Leaf L-1
 Rev. Marker 3 (Original) Open "C" in CENTS	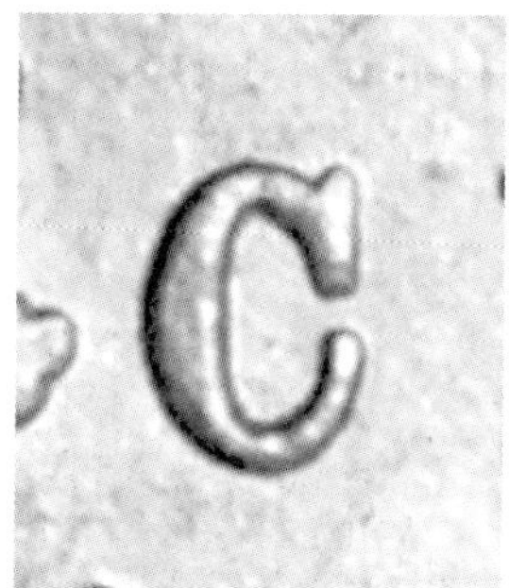 Rev. Marker 3 (Counterfeit) Closed "C" in CENTS

Rev. Marker 4 (Original)
1872H Date, Fine date digits
Even small "2"

Rev. Marker 4 (Counterfeit)
1872H Date, Thick date digits
Low large "2"

Victoria Twenty-Five Cents

1875H REVERSE

1875H Reverse, Original
Marker 1: Reverse RQ1 with short bough ends

1875H Reverse, Counterfeit
Marker 1: Reverse RQ4 with short bough ends

ORIGINAL
Reverse Markers

Rev. Marker 2 (Original)
Full stem to Leaf L-1

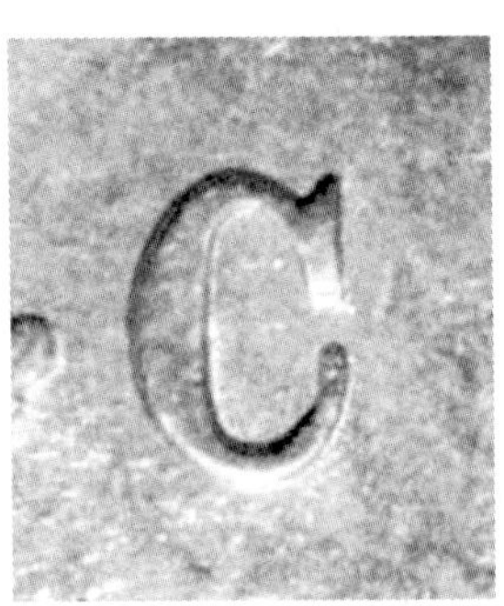

Rev. Marker 3 (Original)
Open "C" in CENTS

COUNTERFEIT
Reverse Markers

Rev. Marker 2 (Counterfeit)
Missing stem to Leaf L-1

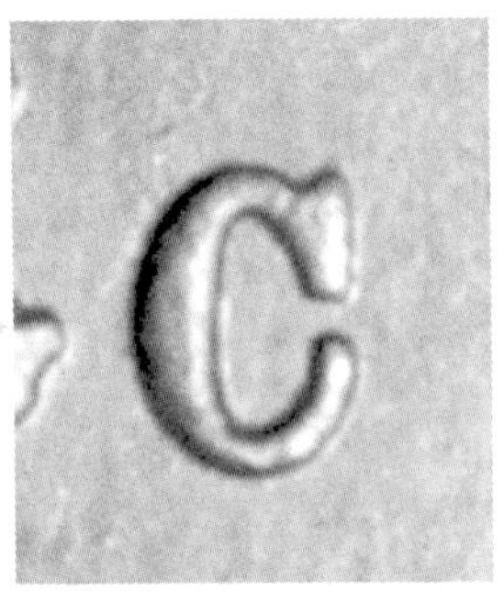

Rev. Marker 3 (Counterfeit)
Closed "C" in CENTS

Rev. Marker 4 (Original)
1875H Date, Fine date digits
Straight pointed "5"

Rev. Marker 4 (Counterfeit)
1875H Date, Thick date digits,
Large curved "5"

Victoria Twenty-Five Cents

1881H REVERSE

ORIGINAL Reverse Markers

COUNTERFEIT Reverse Markers

1881H Reverse, Original
Marker 1: Reverse RQ2 with short bough ends

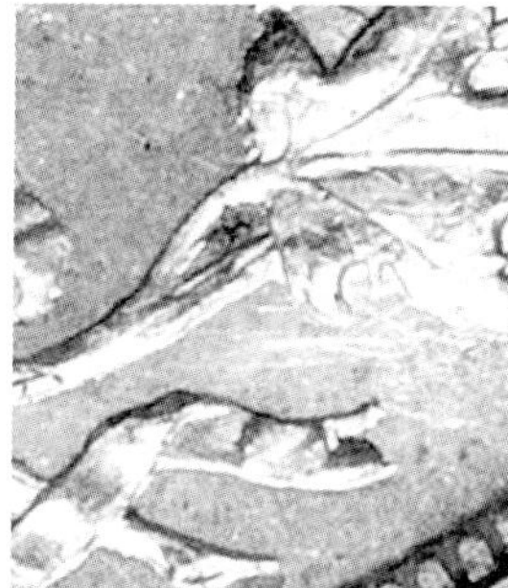

Rev. Marker 2 (Original)
Full stem to Leaf L-1

Rev. Marker 2 (Counterfeit)
Missing stem to Leaf L-1

Rev. Marker 3 (Original)
Open "C" in CENTS

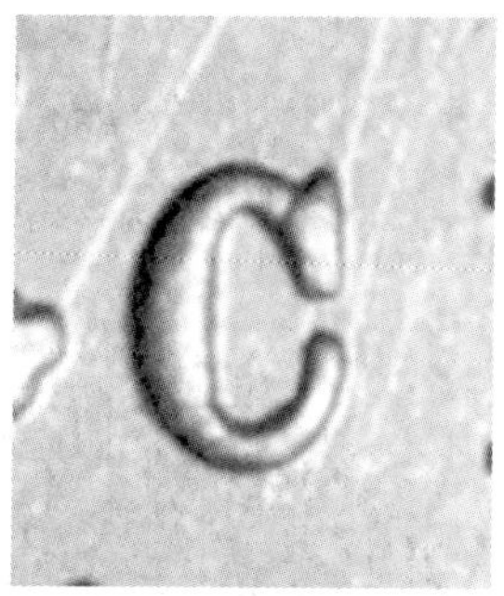

Rev. Marker 3 (Counterfeit)
Closed "C" in CENTS

1881H Reverse, Counterfeit
Marker 1: Reverse RQ4 with short bough ends

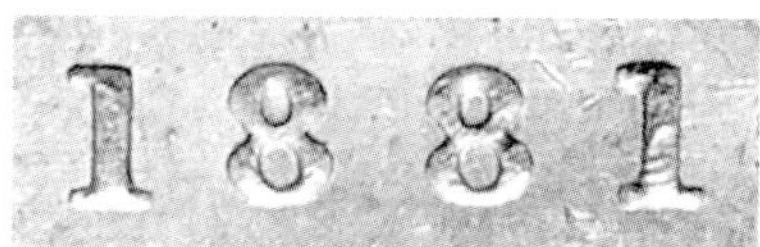

Rev. Marker 4 (Original)
1881H Date, Fine date digits

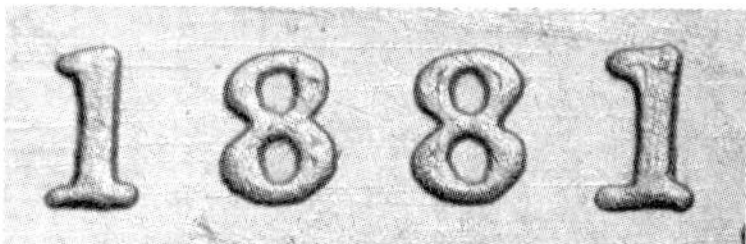

Rev. Marker 4 (Counterfeit)
1881H Date, Thick date digits
Large last "1"

Victoria Twenty-Five Cents

1882H REVERSE

1882H Reverse, Original
Marker 1: Reverse RQ3 with short bough ends

1882H Reverse, Counterfeit
Marker 1: Reverse RQ4 with short bough ends

ORIGINAL
Reverse Markers

COUNTERFEIT
Reverse Markers

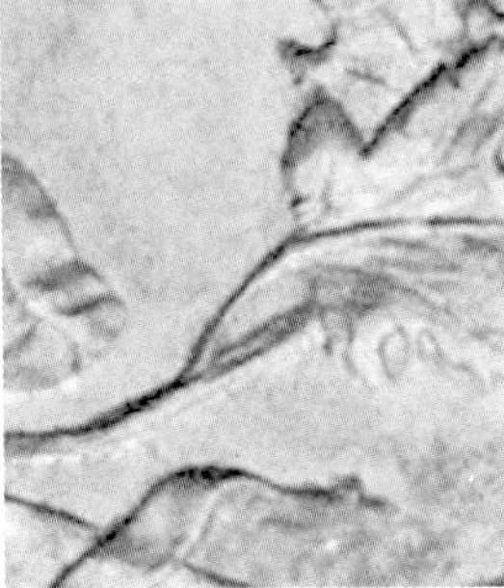

Rev. Marker 2 (Original)
Full stem to Leaf L-1

Rev. Marker 2 (Counterfeit)
Missing stem to Leaf L-1

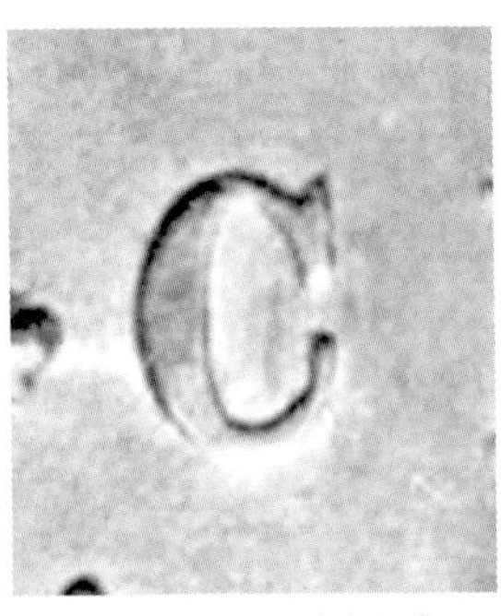

Rev. Marker 3 (Original)
Open "C" in CENTS

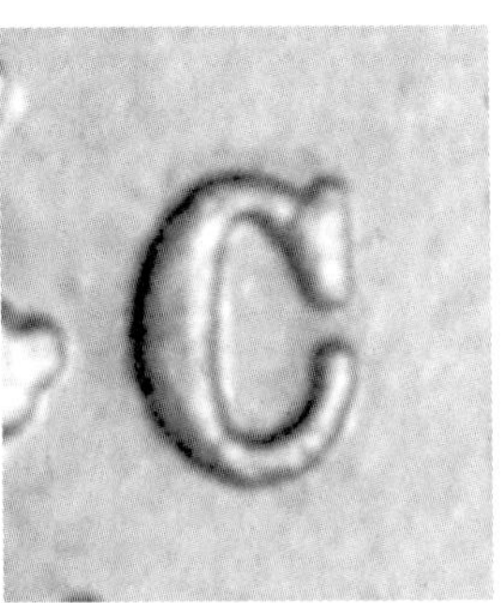

Rev. Marker 3 (Counterfeit)
Closed "C" in CENTS

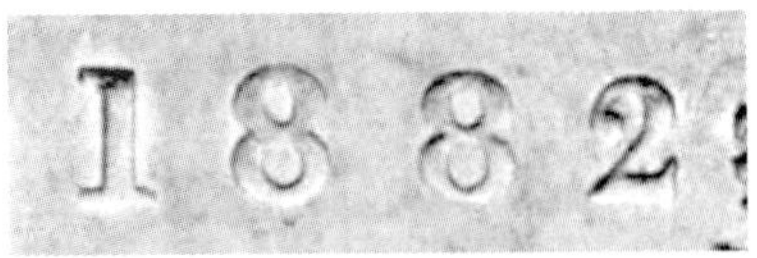

Rev. Marker 4 (Original)
1882H Date, Fine date digits

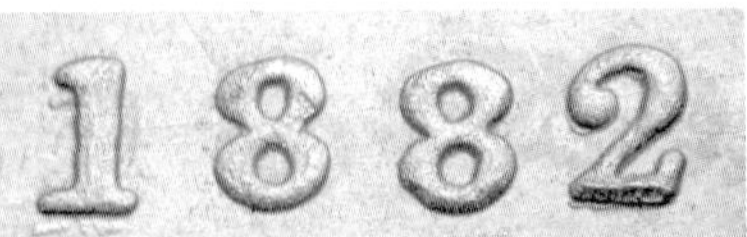

Rev. Marker 4 (Counterfeit)
1882H Date, Thick date digits
Large "2"

Victoria Twenty-Five Cents

1883H REVERSE

1883H Reverse, Original
Marker 1: Reverse RQ4 with short bough ends

1883H Reverse, Counterfeit
Marker 1: Reverse RQ4 with short bough ends

ORIGINAL
Reverse Markers

Rev. Marker 2 (Original)
Full stem to Leaf L-1

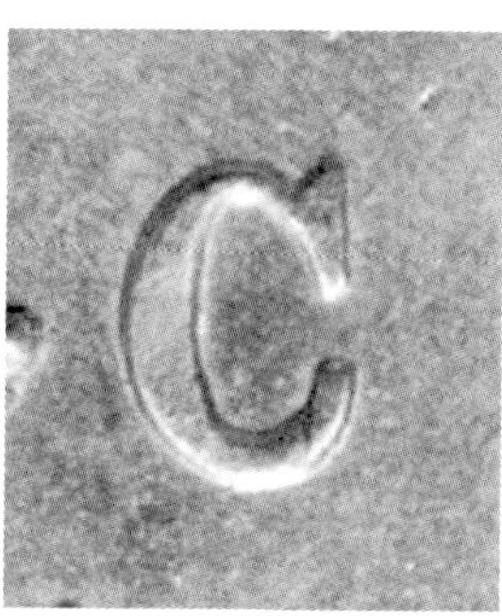

Rev. Marker 3 (Original)
Open "C" in CENTS

COUNTERFEIT
Reverse Markers

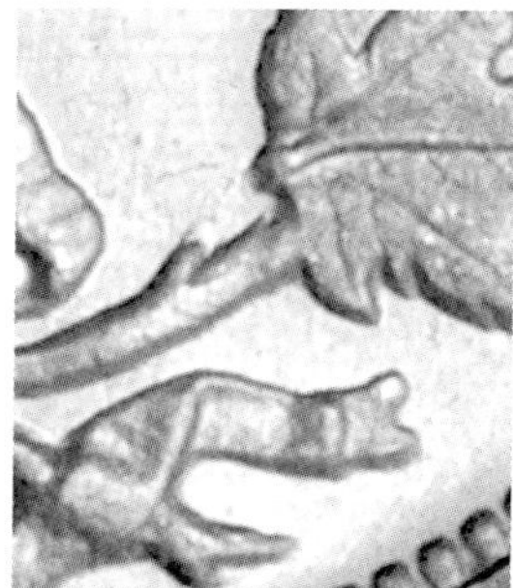

Rev. Marker 2 (Counterfeit)
Missing stem to Leaf L-1

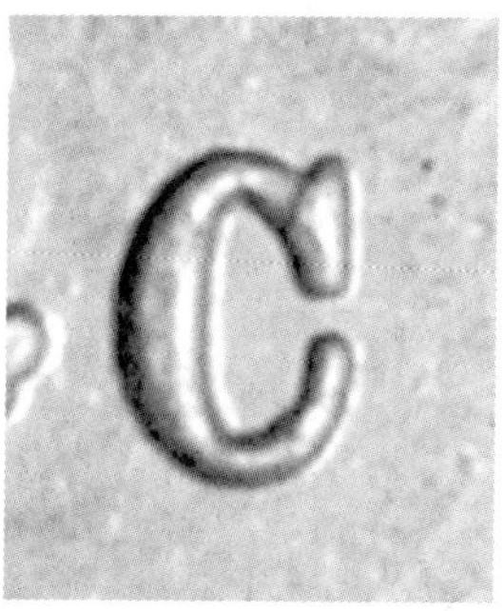

Rev. Marker 3 (Counterfeit)
Closed "C" in CENTS

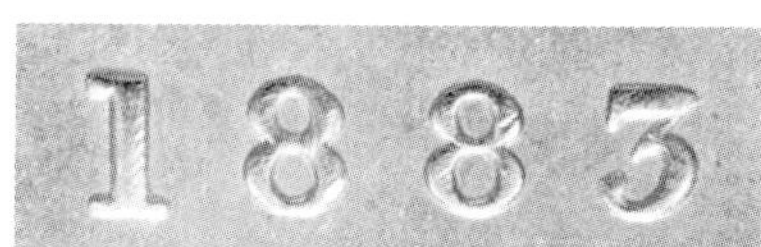

Rev. Marker 4 (Original)
1883H Date, Fine date digits
Flat top "3"

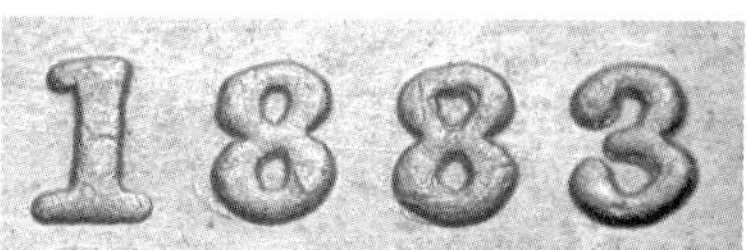

Rev. Marker 4 (Counterfeit)
1883H Date, Thick date digits
Large round top "3"

Victoria Twenty-Five Cents

1885 REVERSE

1885 Reverse, Original
Marker 1: Reverse RQ4 with short bough ends

1885 Reverse, Counterfeit
Marker 1: Reverse RQ4 with short bough ends

ORIGINAL Reverse Markers	COUNTERFEIT Reverse Markers
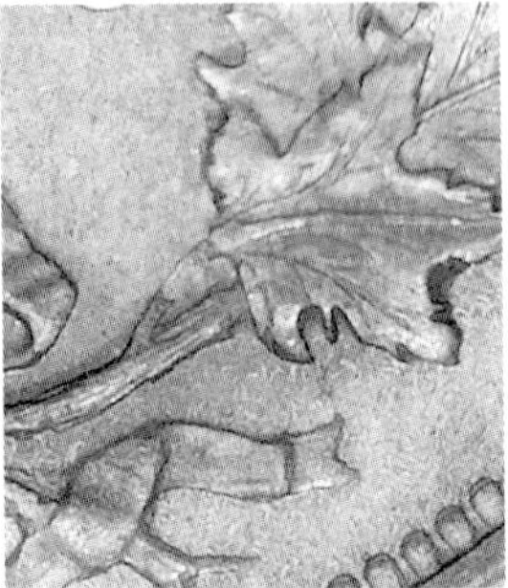 Rev. Marker 2 (Original) Missing partial stem to Leaf L-1	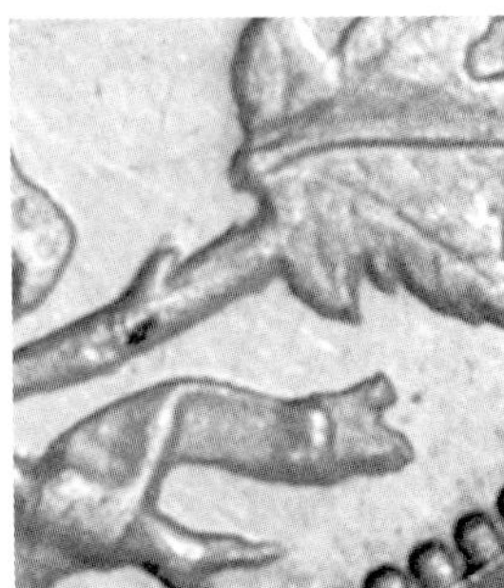 Rev. Marker 2 (Counterfeit) Missing stem to Leaf L-1
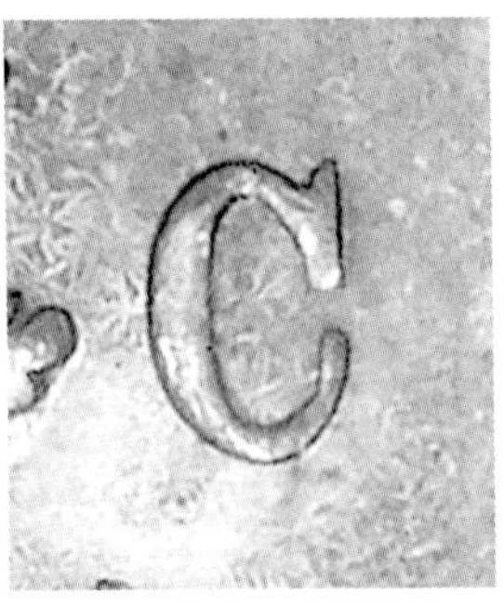 Rev. Marker 3 (Original) Open "C" in CENTS	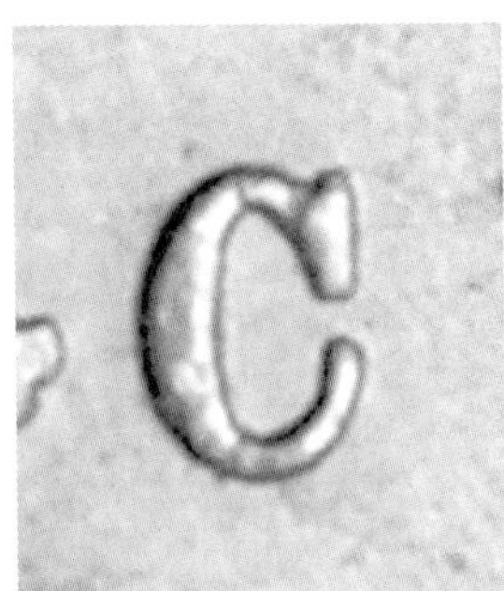 Rev. Marker 3 (Counterfeit) Closed "C" in CENTS

Note: An 1885 original coin was used as the model for producing the Victoria twenty-five cents series of counterfeits.

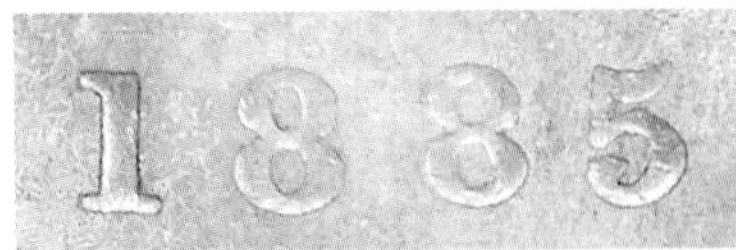

Rev. Marker 4 (Original)
1885 Date, Fine date digits
Curved top "5"

Rev. Marker 4 (Counterfeit)
1885 Date, Thick date digits
Large curved top "5"

Victoria Twenty-Five Cents

1887 REVERSE

1887 Reverse, Original
Marker 1: Reverse RQ6 with long bough ends

1887 Reverse, Counterfeit
Marker 1: Reverse RQ4 with short bough ends

ORIGINAL
Reverse Markers

Rev. Marker 2 (Original):
Full stem to Leaf L-1

Rev. Marker 3 (Original)
Open "C" in CENTS

COUNTERFEIT
Reverse Markers

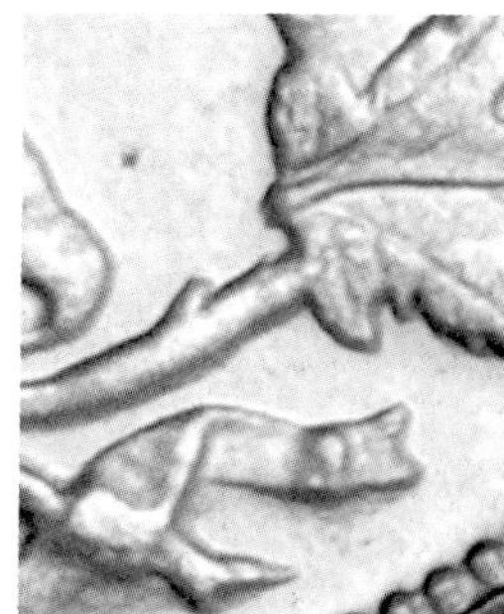

Rev. Marker 2 (Counterfeit)
Missing stem to Leaf L-1

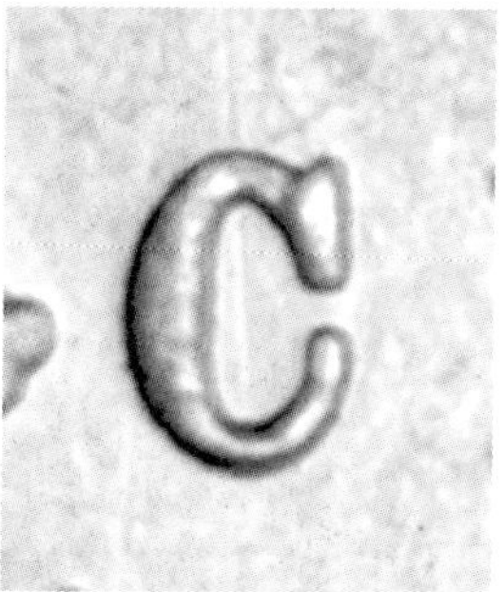

Rev. Marker 3 (Counterfeit)
Closed "C" in CENTS

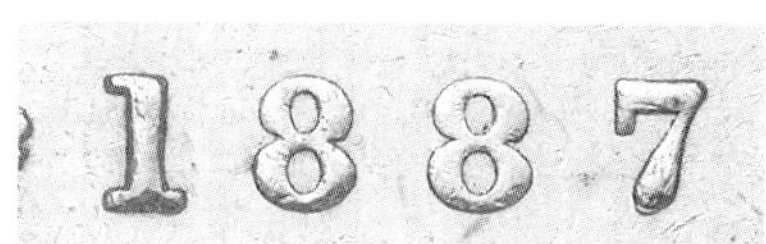

Rev. Marker 4 (Original)
1887 Date, Fine date digits

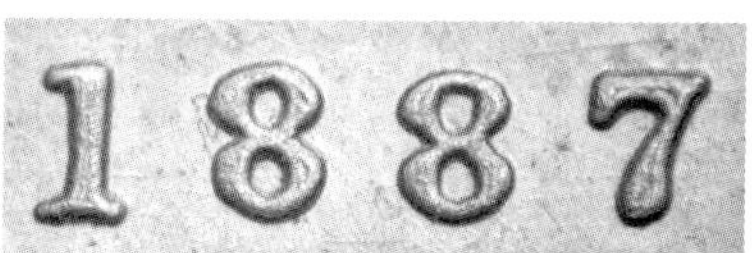

Rev. Marker 4 (Counterfeit)
1887 Date, Thick date digits
Large "7"

Victoria Twenty-Five Cents

1888 REVERSE

1888 Reverse, Original
Marker 1: Reverse RQ5 with long bough ends

1888 Reverse, Counterfeit
Marker 1: Reverse RQ4 with short bough ends

ORIGINAL Reverse Markers	COUNTERFEIT Reverse Markers
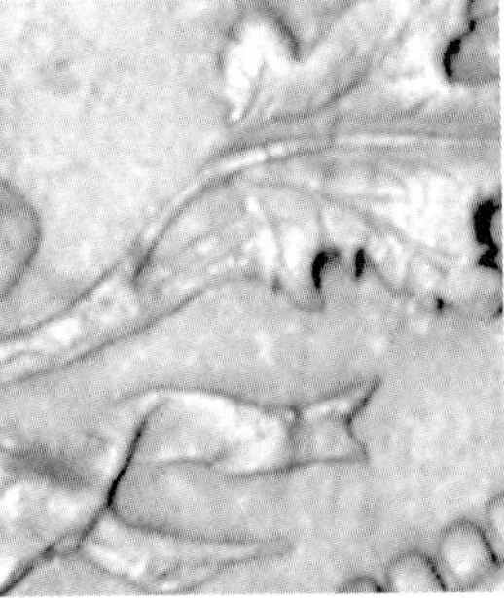 Rev. Marker 2 (Original) Full stem to Leaf L-1	 Rev. Marker 2 (Counterfeit) Missing stem to Leaf L-1
 Rev. Marker 3 (Original) Open "C" in CENTS	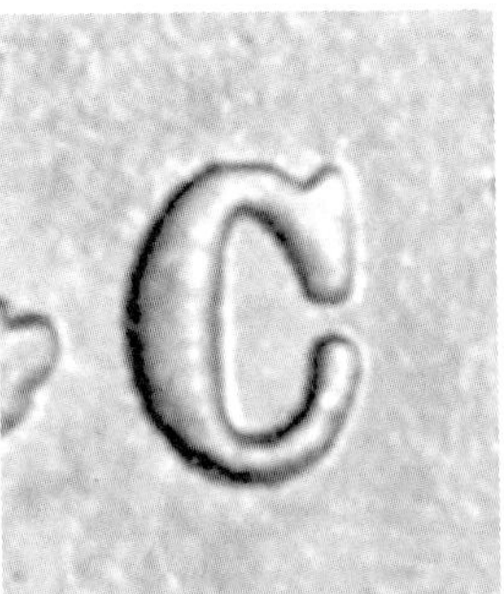 Rev. Marker 3 (Counterfeit) Closed "C" in CENTS

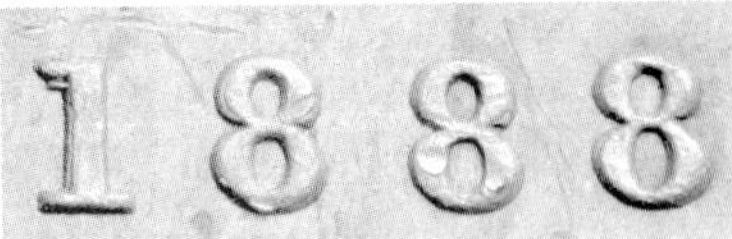

Rev. Marker 4 (Original)
1888 Date, Fine date digits
Wide "8's"

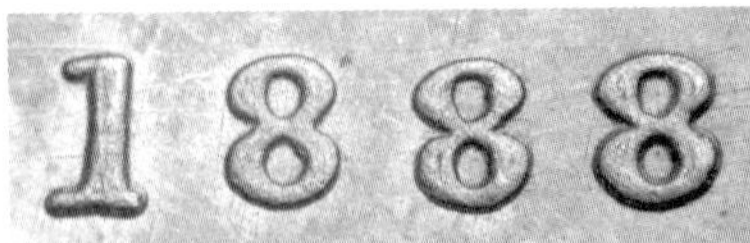

Rev. Marker 4 (Counterfeit)
1888 Date, Thick date digits
Large wide last "8"

Victoria Twenty-Five Cents

1889 REVERSE

1889 Reverse, Original
Marker 1: Reverse RQ5 with long bough ends

1889 Reverse, Counterfeit
Marker 1: Reverse RQ4 with short bough ends

ORIGINAL Reverse Markers

COUNTERFEIT Reverse Markers

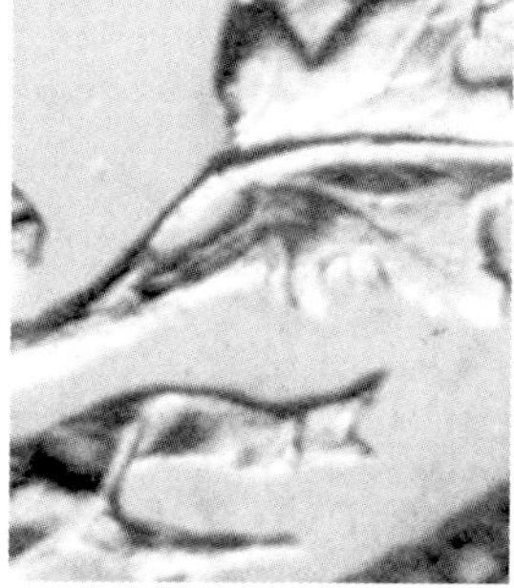

Rev. Marker 2 (Original)
Full stem to Leaf L-1

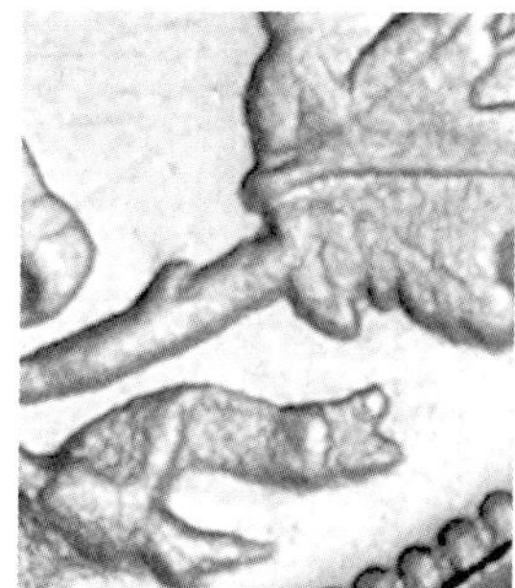

Rev. Marker 2 (Counterfeit)
Missing stem to Leaf L-1

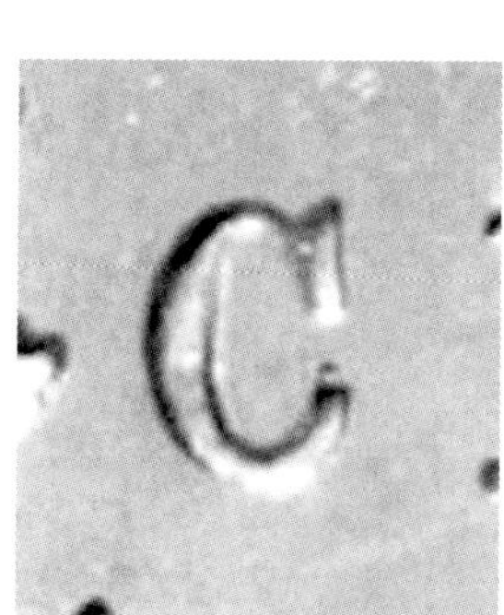

Rev. Marker 3 (Original)
Open "C" in CENTS

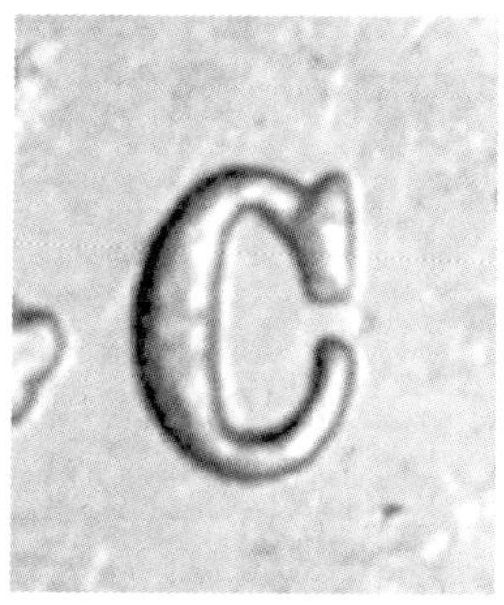

Rev. Marker 3 (Counterfeit)
Closed "C" in CENTS

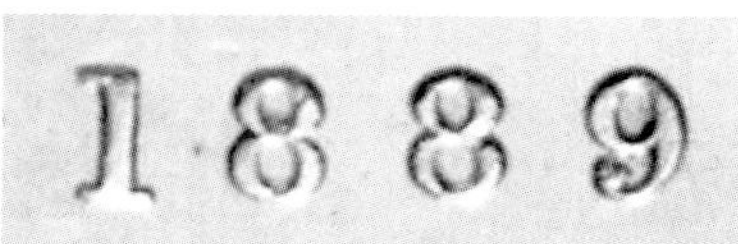

Rev. Marker 4 (Original)
1889 Date, Fine date digits

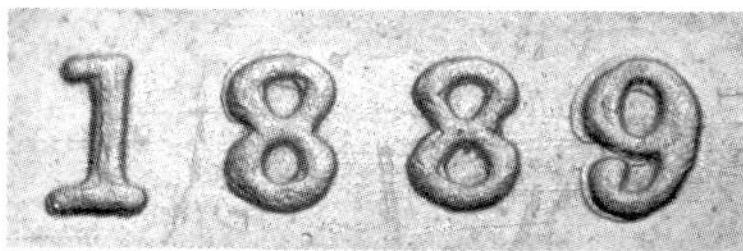

Rev. Marker 4 (Counterfeit)
1889 Date, Thick date digits
Large "9"

Victoria Twenty-Five Cents

1890H REVERSE

ORIGINAL Reverse Markers

COUNTERFEIT Reverse Markers

1890H Reverse, Original
Marker 1: Reverse RQ5 with long bough ends

Rev. Marker 2 (Original)
Full stem to Leaf L-1

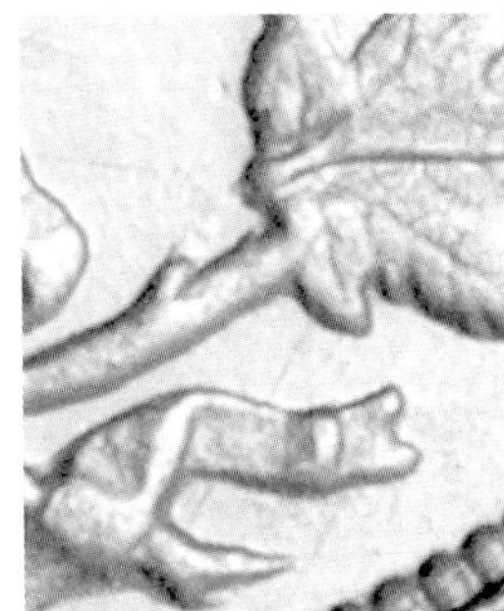

Rev. Marker 2 (Counterfeit)
Missing stem to Leaf L-1

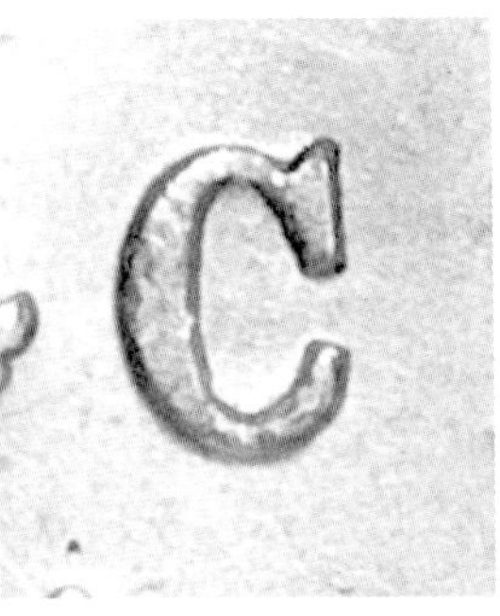

Rev. Marker 3 (Original)
Open "C" in CENTS

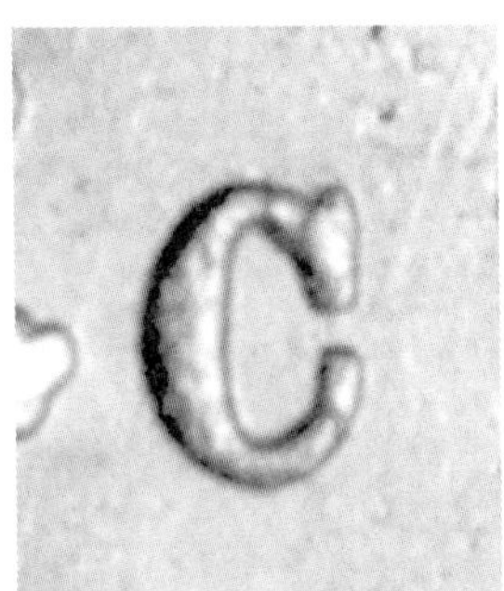

Rev. Marker 3 (Counterfeit)
Closed "C" in CENTS

1890H Reverse, Counterfeit
Marker 1: Reverse RQ4 with short bough ends

Rev. Marker 4 (Original)
1890H Date, Fine date digits

Rev. Marker 4 (Counterfeit)
1890H Date, Thick date digits
Large "0"

Victoria Twenty-Five Cents

1891 REVERSE

1891 Reverse, Original
Marker 1: Reverse RQ5 with long bough ends

1891 Reverse, Counterfeit
Marker 1: RQ4 with short bough ends

ORIGINAL Reverse Markers	COUNTERFEIT Reverse Markers
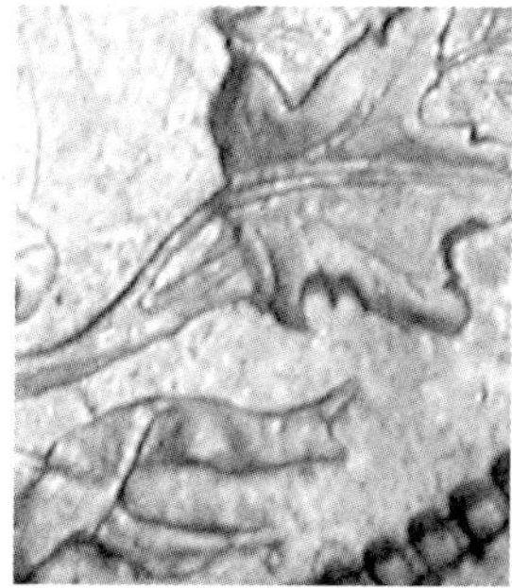 Rev. Marker 2 (Original) Full stem to Leaf L-1	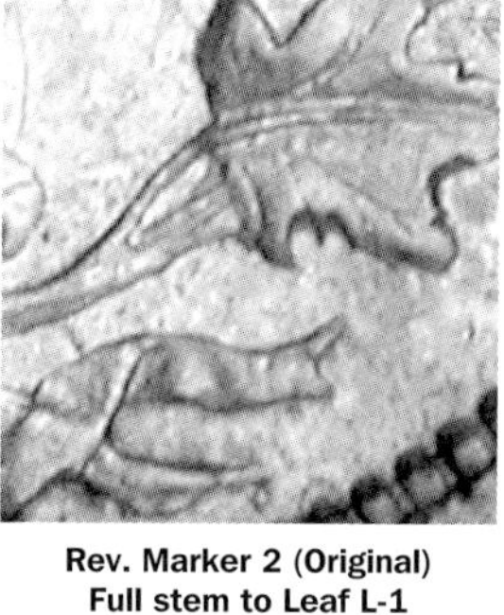 Rev. Marker 2 (Counterfeit) Missing stem to Leaf L-1
 Rev. Marker 3 (Original) Open "C" in CENTS	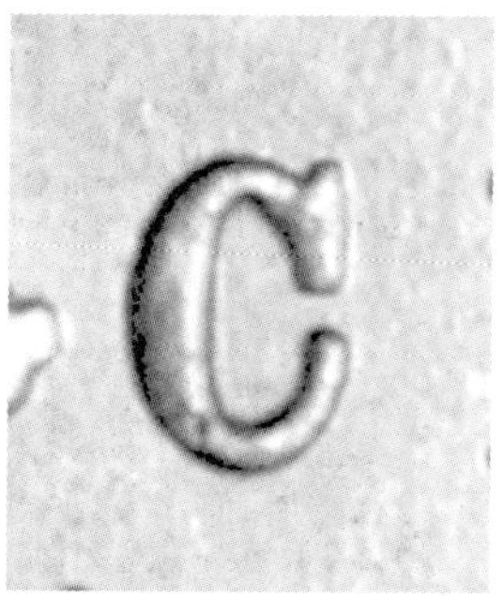 Rev. Marker 3 (Counterfeit) Closed "C" in CENTS

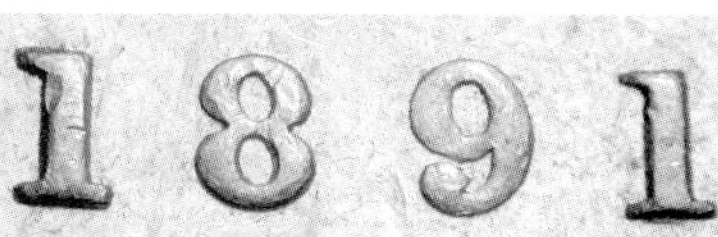

Rev. Marker 4 (Original)
1891 Date, Fine date digits

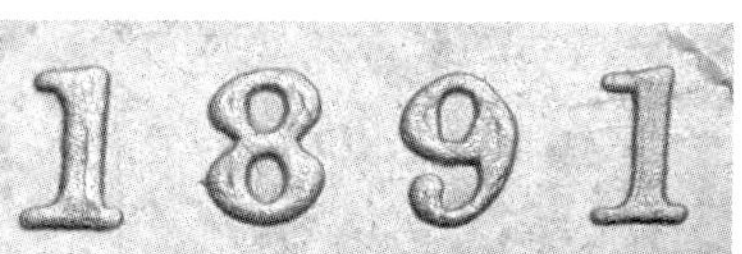

Rev. Marker 4 (Counterfeit)
1891 Date, Thick date digits,
except thin last "1"

Victoria Twenty-Five Cents

1892 REVERSE

1892 Reverse, Original
Marker 1: Reverse RQ5 with long bough ends

1892 Reverse, Counterfeit
Marker 1: Reverse RQ4 with short bough ends

ORIGINAL Reverse Markers	COUNTERFEIT Reverse Markers
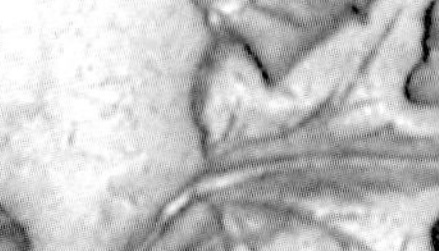 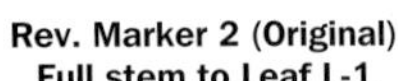 Rev. Marker 2 (Original) Full stem to Leaf L-1	 Rev. Marker 2 (Counterfeit) Missing stem to Leaf L-1
 Rev. Marker 3 (Original) Open "C" in CENTS	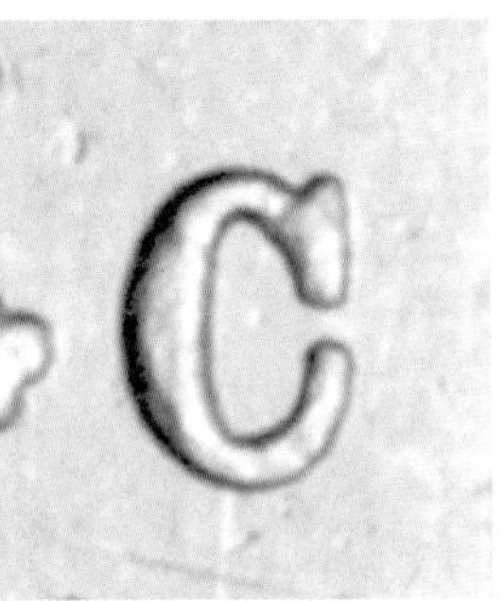 Rev. Marker 3 (Counterfeit) Closed "C" in CENTS

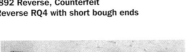

Rev. Marker 4 (Original)
1892 Date, Fine date digits

Rev. Marker 4 (Counterfeit)
1892 Date, Thick date digits
Large thin "2"

Victoria Twenty-Five Cents

1893 REVERSE

1893 Reverse, Original
Marker 1: Reverse RQ5 with long bough ends

1893 Reverse, Counterfeit
Marker 1: Reverse RQ4 with short bough ends

ORIGINAL Reverse Markers

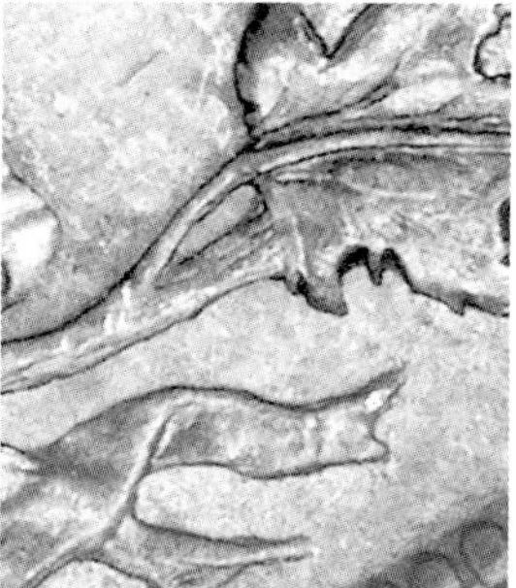

Rev. Marker 2 (Original)
Full stem to Leaf L-1

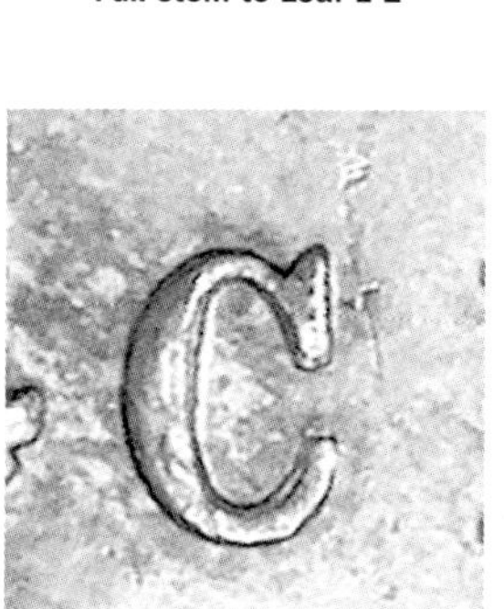

Rev. Marker 3 (Original)
Open "C" in CENTS

COUNTERFEIT Reverse Markers

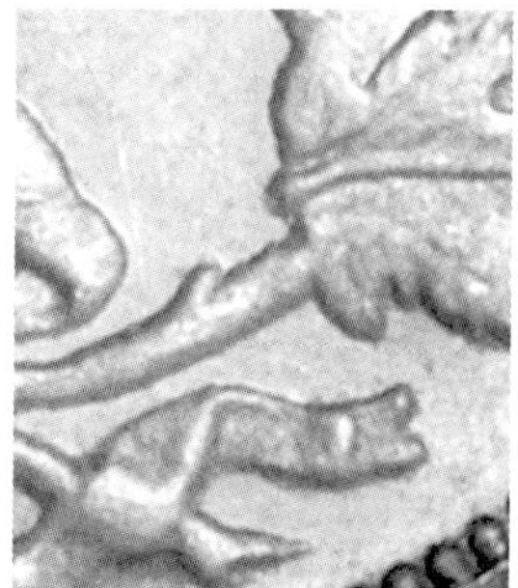

Rev. Marker 2 (Counterfeit)
Missing stem to Leaf L-1

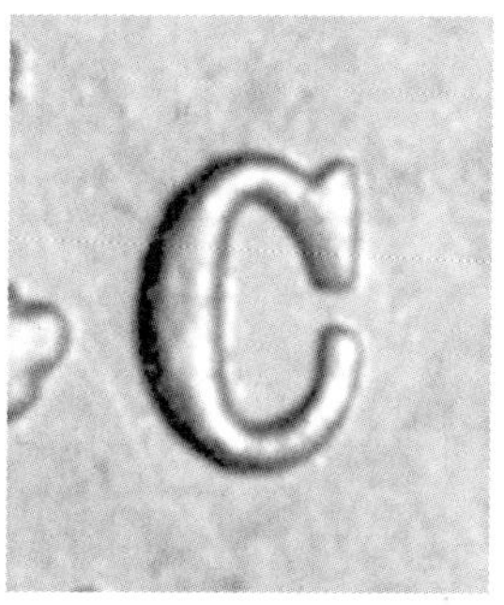

Rev. Marker 3 (Counterfeit)
Closed "C" in CENTS

Rev. Marker 4 (Original)
1893 Date, Fine date digits
Flat top "3"

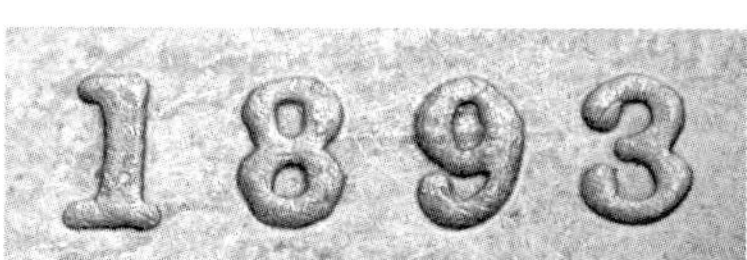

Rev. Marker 4 (Counterfeit)
1893 Date, Thick date digits
Round top "3"

Victoria Twenty-Five Cents

1894 REVERSE

1894 Reverse, Original
Marker 1: Reverse RQ5 with long bough ends

1894 Reverse, Counterfeit
Marker 1: Reverse RQ4 with short bough ends

ORIGINAL
Reverse Markers

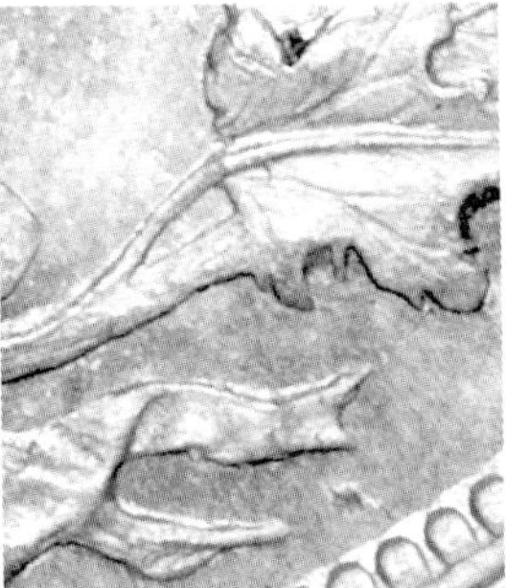

Rev. Marker 2 (Original)
Full stem to Leaf L-1

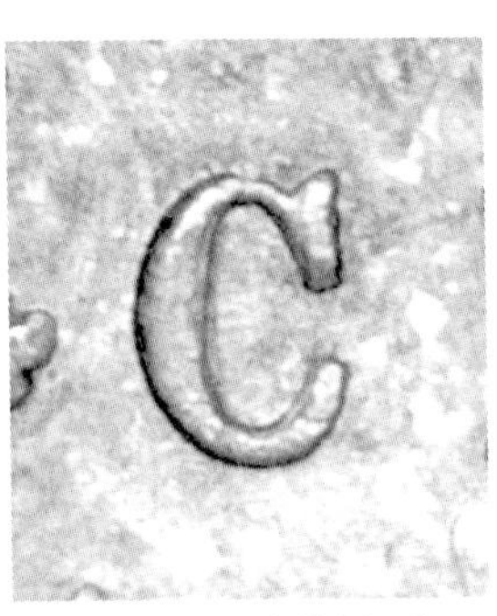

Rev. Marker 3 (Original)
Open "C" in CENTS

COUNTERFEIT
Reverse Markers

Rev. Marker 2 (Counterfeit)
Missing stem to Leaf L-1

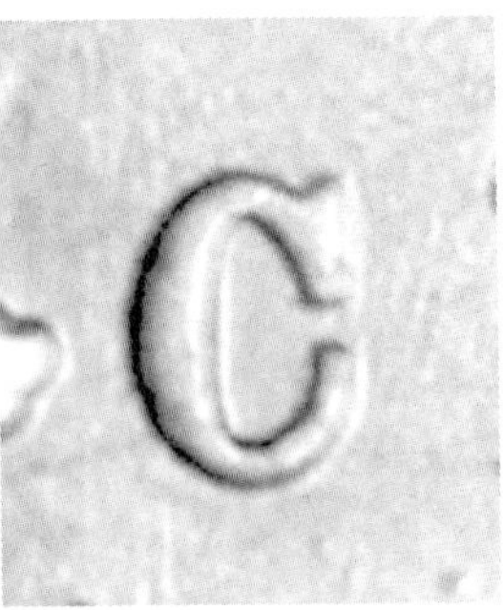

Rev. Marker 3 (Counterfeit)
Closed "C" in CENTS

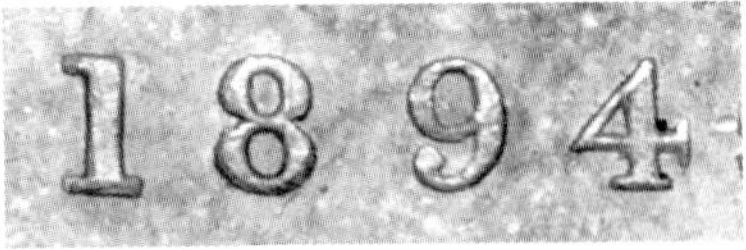

Rev. Marker 4 (Original)
1894 Date, Fine date digits
Crosslet "4"

Rev. Marker 4 (Counterfeit)
1894 Date, Thick date digits
Thick Crosslet "4"

George V Twenty-Five Cents

H K Replica, China, 1911, 1914, 1915, 1921, 1927, and 1928.

Specifications	Original	Counterfeit
Composition:		
1912-1919	92.5% Ag, 7.5% Cu	98.46 to 99.76 Ag
1920-1936	80.0% Ag, 20.0% Cu	98.46 to 99.76 Ag
Weight:	5.83 grams	5.7 to 5.8 grams
Diameter	23.62 mm	23.5 to 23.6 mm
Thickness	1.58 mm	1.6 to 1.7 mm
Die Axis	↑↓	↑↑

GEORGE V TWENTY-FIVE CENT MARKERS, H K REPLICA COUNTERFEIT COINS

OBVERSE MARKERS or PICKUP POINTS - ORIGINAL

1. Correct legend without "DEI GRA" (for 1911 only).
2. Strong portrait with clear facial details, bridge of nose rising from the field.
3. Coronation robes, decorations, chains and ribbons are sharp and distinct.

OBVERSE MARKERS or PICKUP POINTS - COUNTERFEIT

1. Incorrect legend with "DEI GRA" (for 1911 only).
2. Weak portrait, large eyebrow, bridge of nose disappears into field.
3. Coronation robes, decorations, chains and ribbons are very weakly reproduced.

REVERSE MARKERS or PICKUP POINTS - ORIGINAL

1. Original design with fine leaves and boughs.
2. Leaf R-1, full leaf definition.
3. Leaf L-3, full leaf definition.
4. Fine date digits.
5. Branch between Leaf L-3 and L-4 is fully formed.

REVERSE MARKERS or PICKUP POINTS - COUNTERFEIT

1. Design is soft with large leaves and boughs.
2. Leaf L-1, missing detail and definition of leaf.
3. Leaf L-3, weak leaf definition, without veins. Leaf not fully formed.
4. Branch between Leaf L-3 and L-4 is broken (1928).
5. Thick date digits.

George V Twenty-Five Cents

1911 OBVERSE

1911 Obverse, Original
Marker 1: Correct legend without "DEI GRA"

1911 Obverse, Counterfeit
Marker 1: Incorrect legend with "DEI GRA" (for 1911 only)

ORIGINAL Reverse Markers	COUNTERFEIT Reverse Markers
	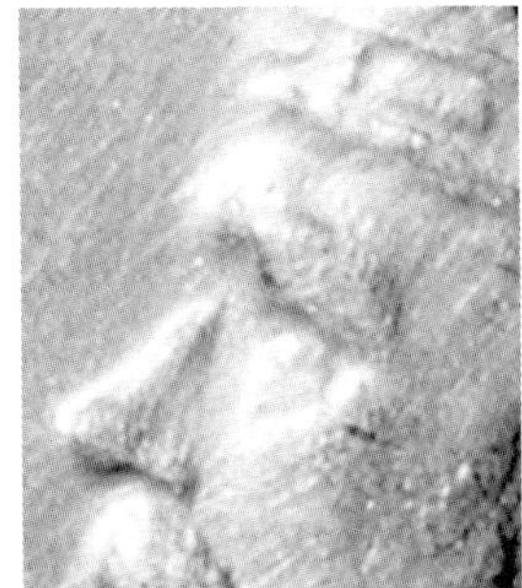
Obv. Marker 2 (Original) Strong portrait with clear facial details, bridge of nose rising from the field	**Obv. Marker 2 (Counterfeit)** Weak portrait, large eyebrow, bridge of nose disappears into field

Obv. Marker 3 (Original) Coronation robes, decorations, chains and ribbons are sharp and distinct	**Obv. Marker 3 (Counterfeit)** Coronation robes, decorations, chains and ribbons are very weakly reproduced

George V Twenty-Five Cents

1911 REVERSE

ORIGINAL
Reverse Markers

COUNTERFEIT
Reverse Markers

1911 Reverse, Original
Marker 1: Original design, fine leaves and boughs

Rev. Marker 2 (Original)
Leaf R-1
Full leaf definition

Rev. Marker 2 (Counterfeit)
Leaf R-1
Missing detail and definition of leaf

Rev. Marker 3 (Original)
Leaf L-3
Full leaf definition

Rev. Marker 3 (Counterfeit)
Leaf L-3
Weak leaf definition, without veins. Leaf not fully formed

1911 Reverse, Counterfeit
Marker 1: Design is soft with large leaves and boughs

Rev. Marker 5 (Original)
1911 Date, Fine date digits

Rev. Marker 5 (Counterfeit)
1911 Date, Thick date digits

George V Twenty-Five Cents

1912 REVERSE

1912 Reverse, Original
Original design with fine leaves and boughs

1912 Reverse, Counterfeit
Design is soft with large leaves and boughs

ORIGINAL
Reverse Markers

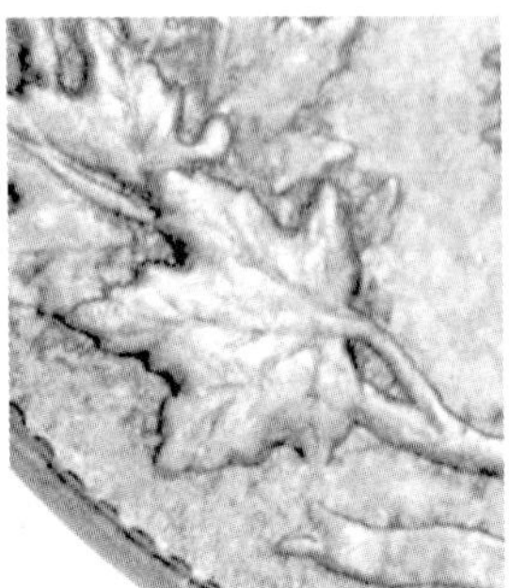

Rev. Marker 2 (Original)
Leaf R-1
Full leaf definition

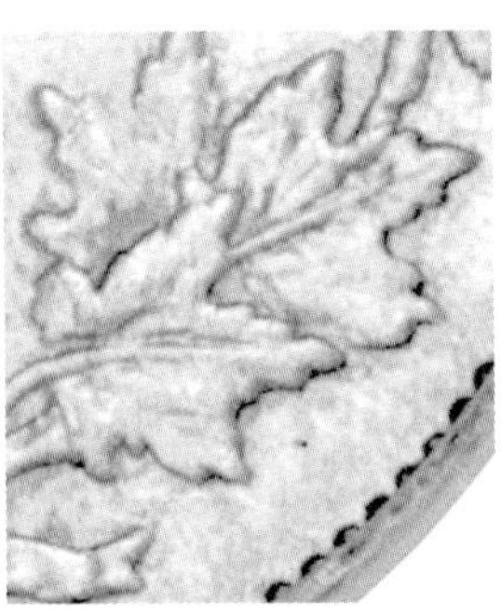

Rev. Marker 3 (Original)
Leaf L-3
Full leaf definition

COUNTERFEIT
Reverse Markers

Rev. Marker 2 (Counterfeit)
Missing detail and definition of leaf

Rev. Marker 3 (Counterfeit)
Leaf L-3
Weak leaf definition, without veins. Leaf not fully formed

Rev. Marker 5 (Original)
1912 Date, Fine date digits

Rev. Marker 5 (Counterfeit)
Thick date digits

George V Twenty-Five Cents

1914 REVERSE

1914 Reverse, Original
Marker 1: Original design, fine leaves and boughs

1914 Reverse, Counterfeit
Marker 1: Design is soft with large leaves and boughs

ORIGINAL
Reverse Markers

COUNTERFEIT
Reverse Markers

Rev. Marker 2 (Original)
Leaf R-1
Full leaf definition

Rev. Marker 2 (Counterfeit)
Leaf R-1
Missing detail and definition of leaf

Rev. Marker 3 (Original)
Leaf L-3
Full leaf definition

Rev. Marker 3 (Counterfeit)
Leaf L-3
Weak leaf definition, without veins. Leaf not fully formed

Rev. Marker 5 (Original)
1914 Date, Fine date digits
Flared “4”

Rev. Marker 5 (Counterfeit)
1914 Date, Thick date digits
Plain “4”

George V Twenty-Five Cents

1915 REVERSE

1915 Reverse, Original
Marker 1: Original design, fine leaves and boughs

1915 Reverse, Counterfeit
Marker 1: Design is soft with large leaves and boughs

ORIGINAL Reverse Markers

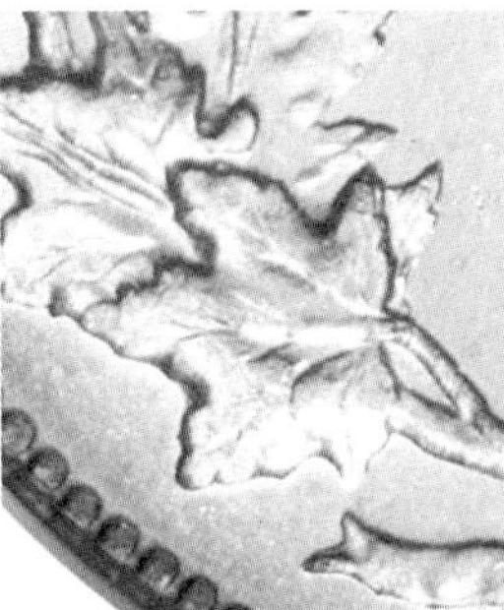

Rev. Marker 2 (Original)
Leaf R-1
Full leaf definition

Rev. Marker 3 (Original)
Leaf L-3
Full leaf definition

COUNTERFEIT Reverse Markers

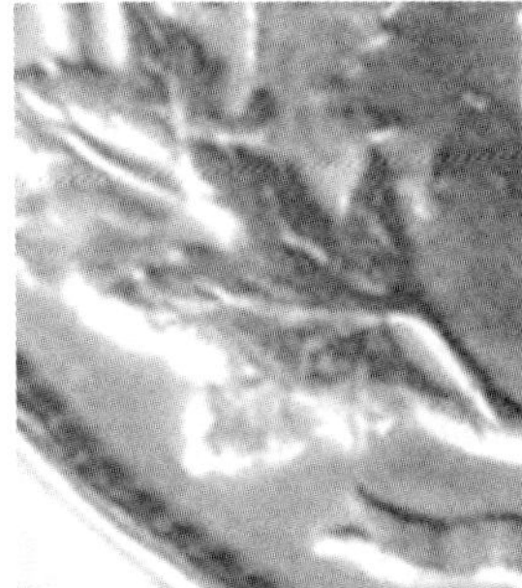

Rev. Marker 2 (Counterfeit)
Missing detail and
definition of leaf

Rev. Marker 3 (Counterfeit)
Leaf L-3
Weak leaf definition, without
veins. Leaf not fully formed

Rev. Marker 5 (Original)
1915 Date, Fine date digits
Small open "5"

Rev. Marker 5 (Counterfeit)
1915 Date, Thick date digits
Large closed "5"

George V Twenty-Five Cents

1921 REVERSE

1921 Reverse, Original
Marker 1: Original design, fine leaves and boughs

1921 Reverse, Counterfeit
Marker 1: Design is soft with large leaves and boughs

ORIGINAL Reverse Markers	COUNTERFEIT Reverse Markers
 Rev. Marker 2 (Original) Leaf R-1 Full leaf definition	 Rev. Marker 2 (Counterfeit) Leaf R-1 Missing detail and definition of leaf
 Rev. Marker 3 (Original) Leaf L-3 Full leaf definition	 Rev. Marker 3 (Counterfeit) Leaf L-3 Weak leaf definition, without veins. Leaf not fully formed

Rev. Marker 5 (Original)
1921 Date, Fine date digits
Small first and last “1”

Rev. Marker 5 (Counterfeit)
1921 Date, Thick date digits
Large first and last “1”

George V Twenty-Five Cents

1927 REVERSE

1927 Reverse, Original
Marker 1: Original design, fine leaves and boughs

1927 Reverse, Counterfeit
Marker 1: Design is soft with large leaves and boughs

ORIGINAL Reverse Markers	COUNTERFEIT Reverse Markers
	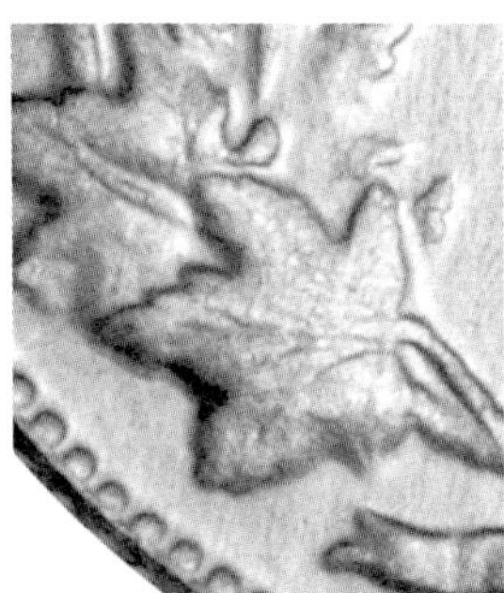
Rev. Marker 2 (Original) Leaf R-1 Full leaf definition	Rev. Marker 2 (Counterfeit) Missing detail and definition of leaf

Rev. Marker 3 (Original) Leaf L-3 Full leaf definition	Rev. Marker 3 (Counterfeit) Leaf L-3 Weak leaf definition, without veins. Leaf not fully formed

Rev. Marker 5 (Original)
1927 Date, Fine date digits
Small thin "7"

Rev. Marker 5 (Counterfeit)
1927 Date, Thick date digits
Large thick "7"

George V Twenty-Five Cents

1928 REVERSE

1928 Reverse, Original
Marker 1: Original design, fine leaves and boughs

1928 Reverse, Counterfeit
Marker 1: Design is soft with large leaves and boughs

ORIGINAL
Reverse Markers

Rev. Marker 2 (Original)
Leaf R-1
Full leaf definition

Rev. Marker 4 (Original)
Branch between Leaf L-3
and L-4 is fully formed

COUNTERFEIT
Reverse Markers

Rev. Marker 2 (Counterfeit)
Leaf R-1
Missing detail and
definition of leaf

Rev. Marker 4 (Counterfeit)
Branch between Leaf L-3
and L-4 is broken

Rev. Marker 5 (Original)
1928 Date, Fine date digits
Small "8"

Rev. Marker 5 (Counterfeit)
1928 Date, Thick date digits
Large "8"

An original 1885 Victoria twenty-five cents, similar to the model used by the counterfeiters in the manufacture of their dies for the production of the Victoria 25-cents counterfeit series. Note the missing stem to Leaf L-1, which is found on all Victoria counterfeit dates.

Victoria Fifty Cents

H K Replica, China, 1870 LCW, 1871H, 1881H, 1888, 1890H, 1892, 1894, 1898, 1899, 1900 and 1901

Specifications	Original	Counterfeit
Composition:	92.5% Ag, 7.5% Cu	98.9 to 99.9% Ag
Weight:	11.62 grams	11.4 - 11.7
Diameter	29.72 mm	29.68 to 29.74 mm
Thickness	1.93 mm	1.8 - 2.2
Axis:	↑↓	↑↑

VICTORIA FIFTY CENT MARKERS, H K REPLICA, CHINA, COUNTERFEIT COINS

OBVERSE MARKERS or PICKUP POINTS - ORIGINAL

1. Portrait OH2 with full detail.
2. Strong portrait, full hair design above crown.
3. Without gouge across neck of Victoria.

OBVERSE MARKERS or PICKUP POINTS - COUNTERFEIT

1. Portrait OH2, bridge of nose disappearing into field.
2. Weak portrait, missing hair design above crown.
3. Weak Portrait. Has a gouge running southeast across the neck of Victoria.

REVERSE MARKERS or PICKUP POINTS - ORIGINAL

1. Leaf R-5 is attached to the bough. Leaf has good detail.
2. Boughs are thin. Leaf L-1 has good detail.
3. The “S” in CENTS is not repunched.
4. Fine date digits.

REVERSE MARKERS or PICKUP POINTS - COUNTERFEIT

1. Leaf R-5 is not attached to the bough. Leaf has lost detail.
2. Boughs are thick. Leaf L-1 has little or no detail.
3. Repunched “S” in CENTS (beginning in 1871 and going forward to 1901).
4. Thick date digits.

Victoria Fifty Cents

1870 LCW OBVERSE

1870 LCW Obverse, Original
Portrait OH2 Variety

1870 LCW Obverse, Counterfeit
Portrait OH2 Variety

ORIGINAL Reverse Markers	COUNTERFEIT Reverse Markers
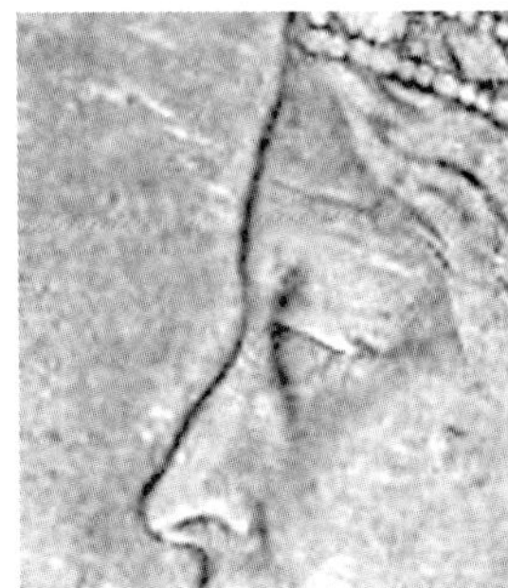 Obv. Marker 1 (Original) Portrait OH2 with full detail	 Obv. Marker 1 (Counterfeit) Weak Portrait OH-2, bridge of nose disappearing into field
 Obv. Marker 2 (Original) Strong portrait, full hair design above crown	 Obv. Marker 2 (Counterfeit) Weak Portrait OH2 missing hair design above crown
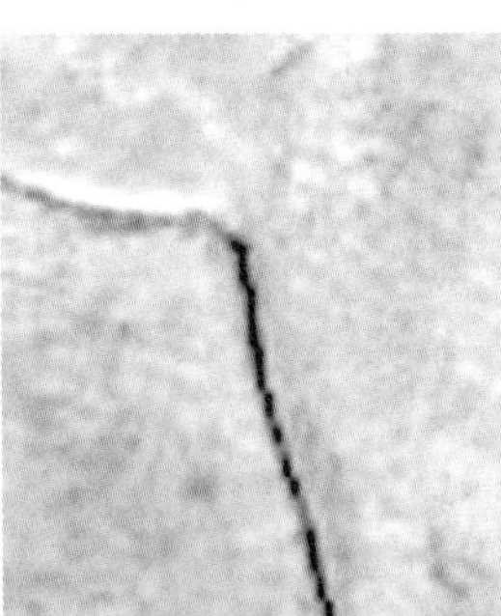 Obv. Marker 3 (Original) Without gouge across neck of Victoria	 Obv. Marker 3 (Counterfeit) Weak Portrait. Has a gouge running southeast across the neck of Victoria

Victoria Fifty Cents

1870 REVERSE

1870 Reverse, Original

1870 Reverse, Counterfeit

ORIGINAL
Reverse Markers

Rev. Marker 1 (Original)
Leaf R-5 is attached to the bough. Leaf has good detail.

Rev. Marker 2 (Original)
Boughs are thin. Leaf L-1 has good detail.

COUNTERFEIT
Reverse Markers

Rev. Marker 1 (Counterfeit)
Leaf R-5 is not attached to the bough. Leaf has lost detail.

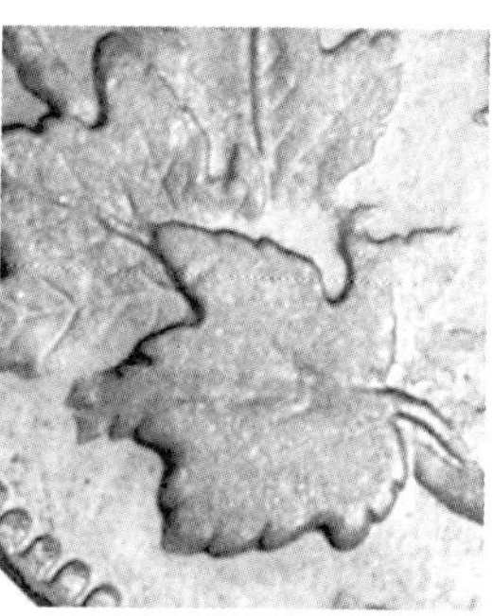

Rev. Marker 2 (Counterfeit)
Boughs are thick. Leaf L-1 has little or no detail.

Rev. Marker 4 (Original)
1870 LCW Date, Fine date digits

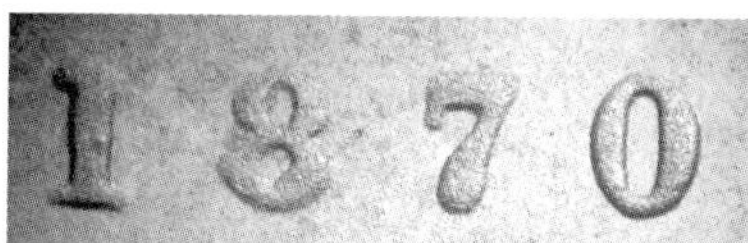

Rev. Marker 4 (Counterfeit)
1870 LCW Date, Thick date digits

Victoria Fifty Cents

1871H REVERSE

1871H Reverse, Original

1871H Reverse, Counterfeit

ORIGINAL
Reverse Markers

COUNTERFEIT
Reverse Markers

Rev. Marker 1 (Original)
Leaf R-5 is attached to the bough. Leaf has good detail.

Rev. Marker 1 (Counterfeit)
Leaf R-5 is not attached to the bough. Leaf has lost detail.

Rev. Marker 2 (Original)
Boughs are thin. Leaf L-1 has good detail.

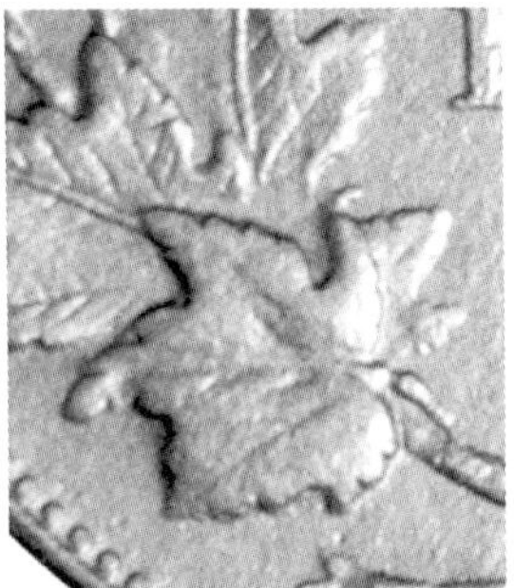

Rev. Marker 2 (Counterfeit)
Boughs are thick. Leaf L-1 has little or no detail.

Rev. Marker 3 (Original)
The "S" in CENTS is not repunched

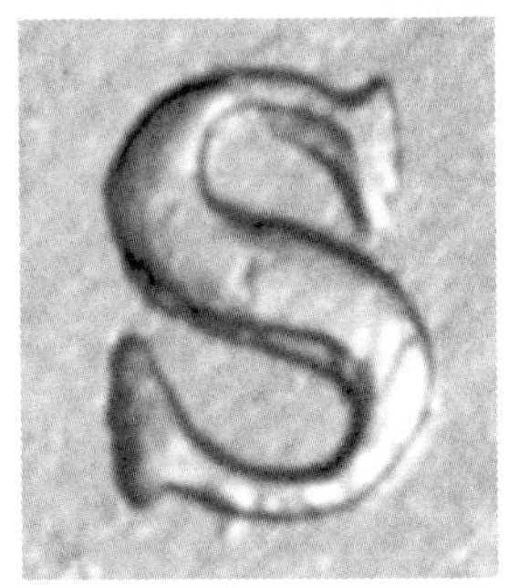

Rev. Marker 3 (Counterfeit)
Repunched "S" in CENTS

Rev. Marker 4 (Original)
1871H Date, Fine date digits

Rev. Marker 4 (Counterfeit)
1871H Date, Thick date Digits

Victoria Fifty Cents

1881H REVERSE

ORIGINAL
Reverse Markers

COUNTERFEIT
Reverse Markers

1881H Reverse, Original

Rev. Marker 1 (Original)
Leaf R-5 is attached to the bough. Leaf has good detail.

Rev. Marker 1 (Counterfeit)
Leaf R-5 is not attached to the bough. Leaf has lost detail.

1881H Reverse, Counterfeit

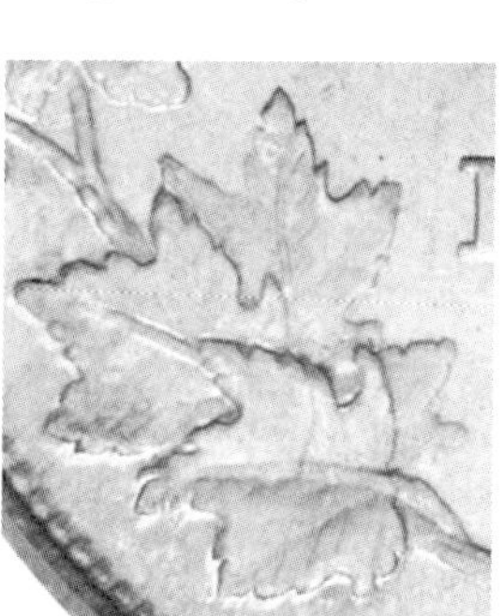

Rev. Marker 2 (Original)
Boughs are thin. Leaf L-1 has good detail.

Rev. Marker 2 (Counterfeit)
Boughs are thick. Leaf L-1 has little or no detail.

Rev. Marker 3 (Original)
The “S” in CENTS is not repunched

Rev. Marker 3 (Counterfeit)
Repunched “S” in CENTS

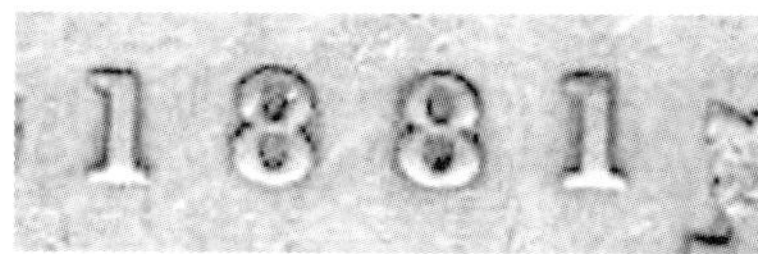

Rev. Marker 4 (Original)
1881H Date, Fine date digits

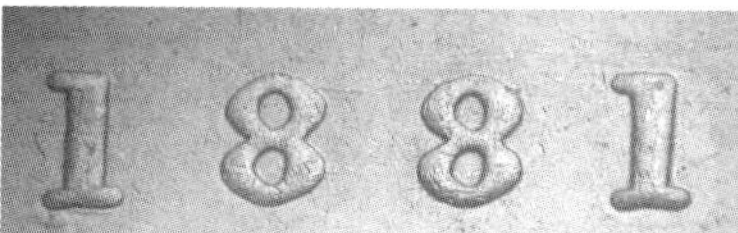

Rev. Marker 4 (Counterfeit)
1881H Date, Thick date dlgits

Victoria Fifty Cents

1888 REVERSE

1888 Reverse, Original

1888 Reverse, Counterfeit

ORIGINAL
Reverse Markers

COUNTERFEIT
Reverse Markers

Rev. Marker 1 (Original)
Leaf R-5 is attached to the bough. Leaf has good detail.

Rev. Marker 1 (Counterfeit)
Leaf R-5 is not attached to the bough. Leaf has lost detail.

Rev. Marker 2 (Original)
Boughs are thin. Leaf L-1 has good detail.

Rev. Marker 2 (Counterfeit)
Boughs are thick. Leaf L-1 has little or no detail.

Rev. Marker 3 (Original)
The "S" in CENTS is not repunched

Rev. Marker 3 (Counterfeit)
Repunched "S" in CENTS

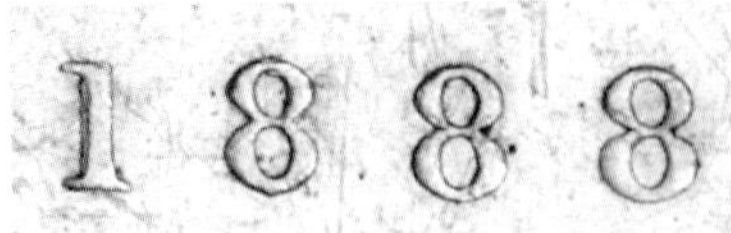

Rev. Marker 4 (Original)
1888 Date, Fine date digits

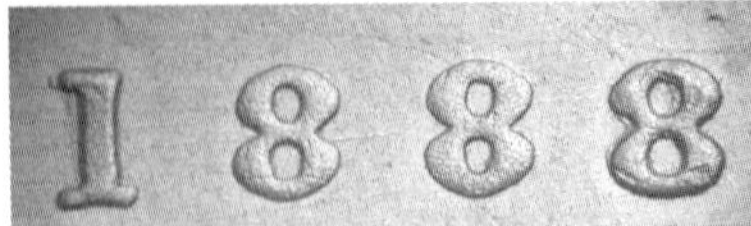

Rev. Marker 4 (Counterfeit)
1888 Date, Thick date digits
Various size fonts

Victoria Fifty Cents

1890H REVERSE

1890H Reverse, Original

1890H Reverse, Counterfeit

ORIGINAL Reverse Markers	COUNTERFEIT Reverse Markers
 Rev. Marker 1 (Original) Leaf R-5 is attached to the bough. Leaf has good detail.	  Rev. Marker 1 (Counterfeit) Leaf R-5 is not attached to the bough. Leaf has lost detail.
 Rev. Marker 2 (Original) Boughs are thin. Leaf L-1 has good detail.	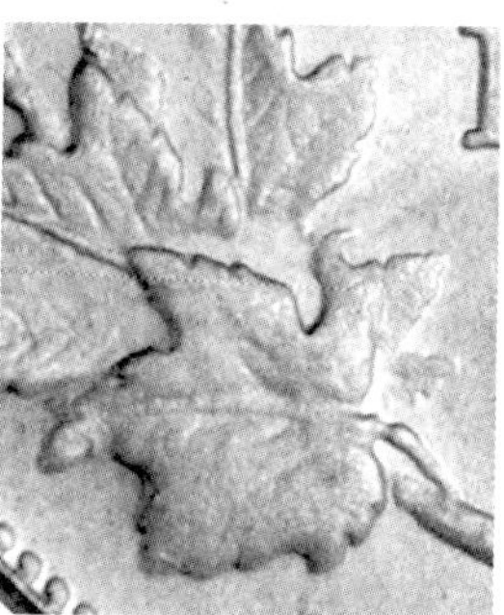 Rev. Marker 2 (Counterfeit) Boughs are thick. Leaf L-1 has little or no detail.
 Rev. Marker 3 (Original) The "S" in CENTS is not repunched	 Rev. Marker 3 (Counterfeit) Repunched "S" in CENTS
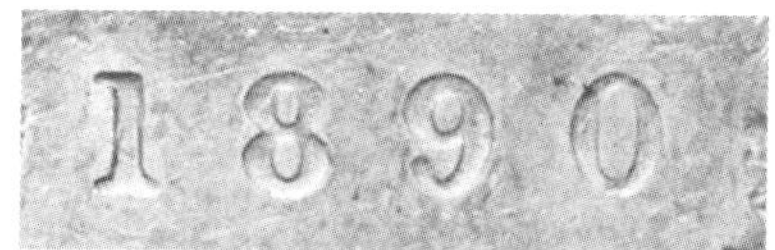 Rev. Marker 4 (Original) 1890H Date, Fine date digits Straight tail "9"	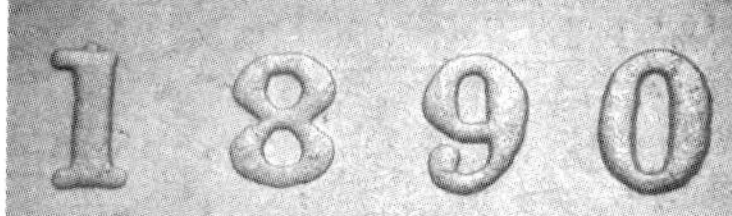 Rev. Marker 4 (Counterfeit) 1890H Date, Thick date digits Knob tail "9"

Victoria Fifty Cents

1892 REVERSE

ORIGINAL
Reverse Markers

COUNTERFEIT
Reverse Markers

1892 Reverse, Original

1892 Reverse, Counterfeit

Rev. Marker 1 (Original)
Leaf R-5 is attached to the bough. Leaf has good detail.

Rev. Marker 1 (Counterfeit)
Leaf R-5 is not attached to the bough. Leaf has lost detail.

Rev. Marker 2 (Original)
Boughs are thin. Leaf L-1 has good detail.

Rev. Marker 2 (Counterfeit)
Boughs are thick. Leaf L-1 has little or no detail.

Rev. Marker 3 (Original)
The "S" in CENTS is not repunched

Rev. Marker 3 (Counterfeit)
Repunched "S" in CENTS

Rev. Marker 4 (Original)
1892 Date, Fine date digits
Straight tail "9", Small "2"

Rev. Marker 4 (Counterfeit)
1892 Date, Thick date digits
Knob-tail "9", Large "2"

Victoria Fifty Cents

1894 REVERSE

1894 Reverse, Original

1894 Reverse, Counterfeit

ORIGINAL Reverse Markers	COUNTERFEIT Reverse Markers

Rev. Marker 1 (Original)
Leaf R-5 is attached to the bough. Leaf has good detail.

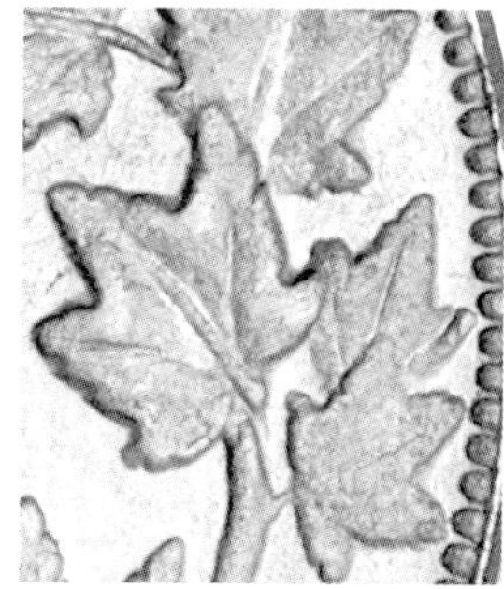

Rev. Marker 1 (Counterfeit)
Leaf R-5 is not attached to the bough. Leaf has lost detail.

Rev. Marker 2 (Original)
Boughs are thin. Leaf L-1 has good detail.

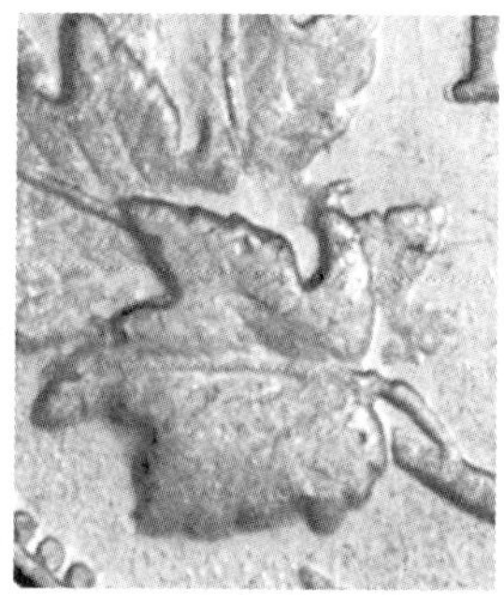

Rev. Marker 2 (Counterfeit)
Boughs are thick. Leaf L-1 has little or no detail.

Rev. Marker 3 (Original)
The "S" in CENTS is not repunched

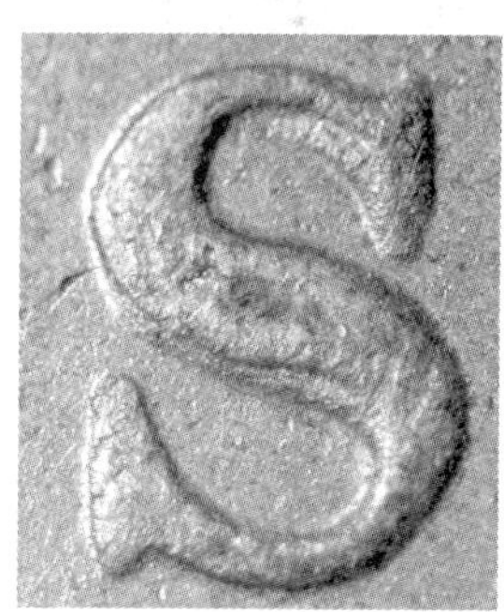

Rev. Marker 3 (Counterfeit)
Repunched "S" in CENTS

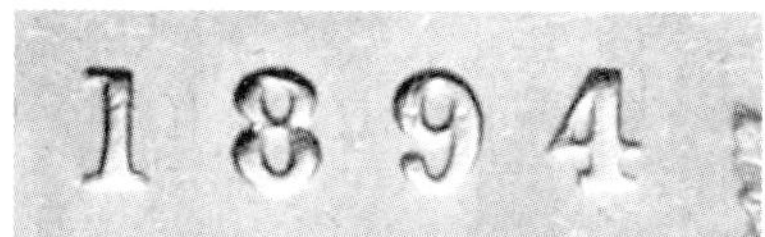

Rev. Marker 4 (Original)
1894 Date, Fine date digits
Plain "4"

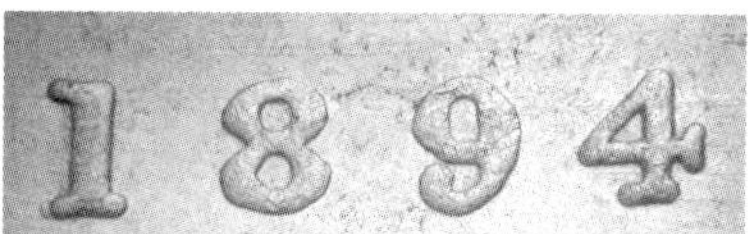

Rev. Marker 4 (Counterfeit)
1894 Date, Thick date digits
Crosslet "4"

Victoria Fifty Cents

1898 REVERSE

1898 Reverse, Original

1898 Reverse, Counterfeit

ORIGINAL Reverse Markers	COUNTERFEIT Reverse Markers
 Rev. Marker 1 (Original) Leaf R-5 is attached to the bough. Leaf has good detail.	 Rev. Marker 1 (Counterfeit) Leaf R-5 is not attached to the bough. Leaf has lost detail.
 Rev. Marker 2 (Original) Boughs are thin. Leaf L-1 has good detail.	 Rev. Marker 2 (Counterfeit) Boughs are thick. Leaf L-1 has little or no detail.
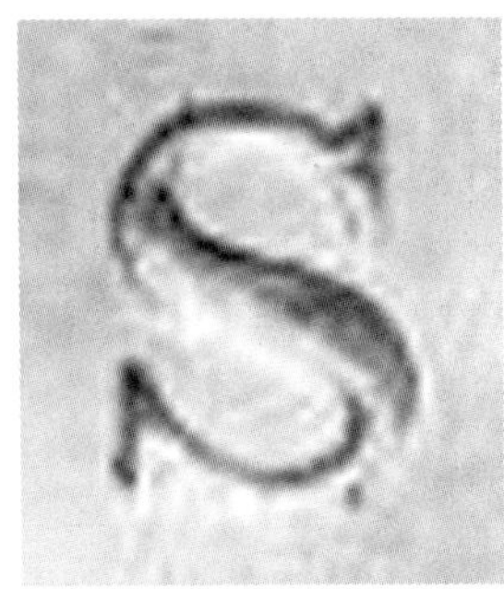 Rev. Marker 3 (Original) The "S" in CENTS is not repunched	 Rev. Marker 3 (Counterfeit) Repunched "S" in CENTS

Rev. Marker 4 (Original)
1898 Date, Fine date digits
Straight tail "9"

Rev. Marker 4 (Counterfeit)
1898 Date, , Thick date digits
Knob tail "9"

Victoria Fifty Cents

1899 REVERSE

1899 Reverse, Original

1899 Reverse, Counterfeit

ORIGINAL
Reverse Markers

COUNTERFEIT
Reverse Markers

Rev. Marker 1 (Original)
Leaf R-5 is attached to the bough. Leaf has good detail.

Rev. Marker 1 (Counterfeit)
Leaf R-5 is not attached to the bough. Leaf has lost detail.

Rev. Marker 2 (Original)
Boughs are thin. Leaf L-1 has good detail.

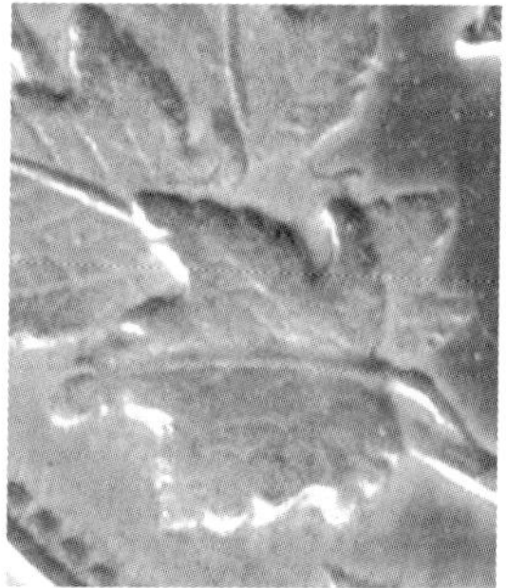

Rev. Marker 2 (Counterfeit)
Boughs are thick. Leaf L-1 has little or no detail.

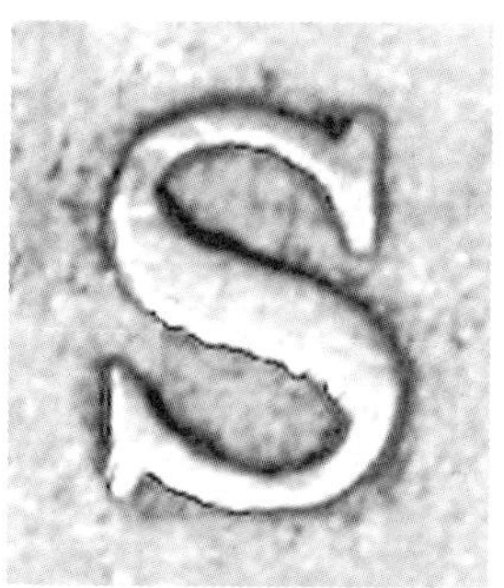

Rev. Marker 3 (Original)
The “S” in CENTS is not repunched

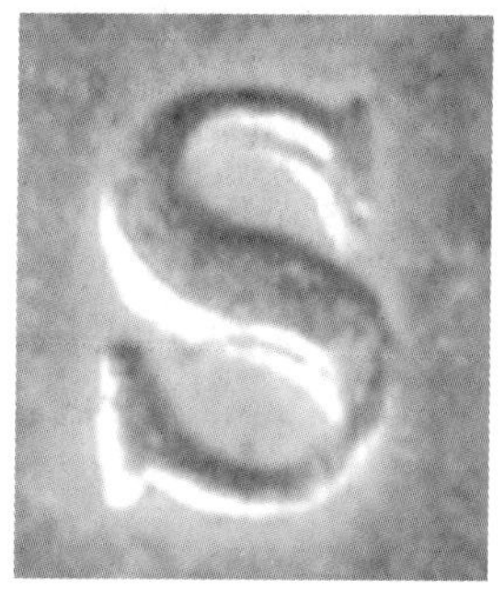

Rev. Marker 3 (Counterfeit)
Repunched “S” in CENTS

Rev. Marker 4 (Original)
1899 Date, Fine date digits
Straight tail “9's”

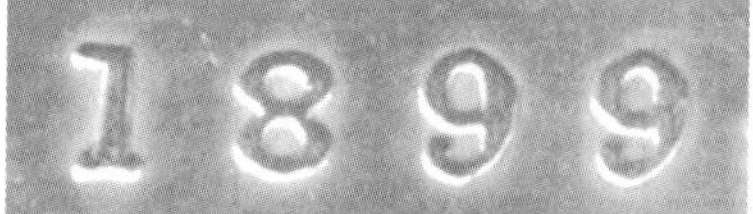

Rev. Marker 4 (Counterfeit)
1899 Date, Thick date digits
Knob tail “9's”

Victoria Fifty Cents

1900 REVERSE

1900 Reverse, Original

1900 Reverse, Counterfeit

ORIGINAL Reverse Markers

Rev. Marker 1 (Original) Leaf R-5 is attached to the bough. Leaf has good detail.

Rev. Marker 2 (Original) Boughs are thin. Leaf L-1 has good detail.

Rev. Marker 3 (Original) The "S" in CENTS is not repunched

COUNTERFEIT Reverse Markers

Rev. Marker 1 (Counterfeit) Leaf R-5 is not attached to the bough. Leaf has lost detail.

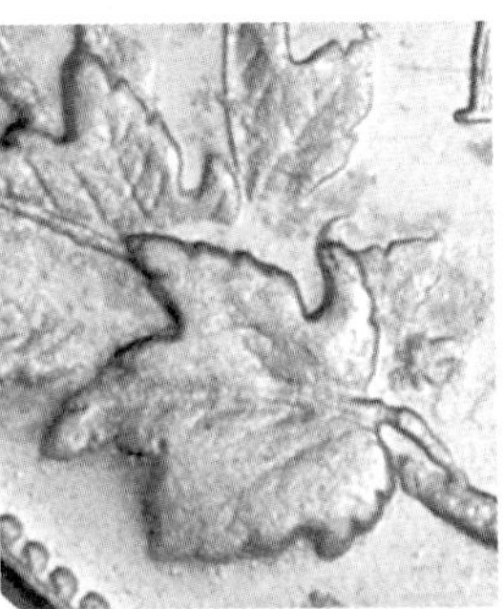

Rev. Marker 2 (Counterfeit) Boughs are thick. Leaf L-1 has little or no detail.

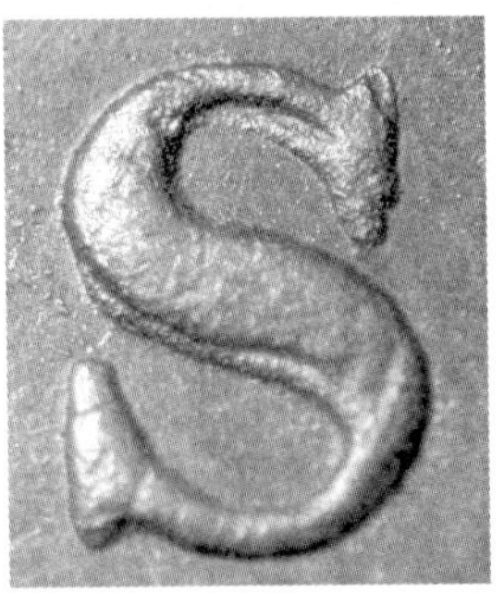

Rev. Marker 3 (Counterfeit) Repunched "S" in CENTS

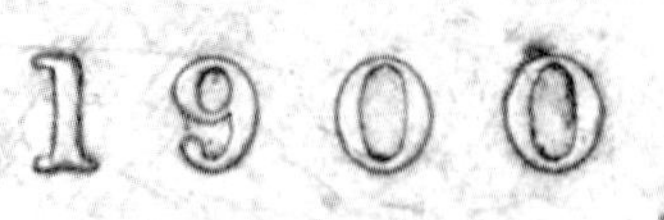

Rev. Marker 4 (Original) 1900 Date, Fine date digits Oval "9"

Rev. Marker 4 (Counterfeit) 1900 Date, Thick date digits Round "9"

Victoria Fifty Cents

1901 REVERSE

ORIGINAL
Reverse Markers

COUNTERFEIT
Reverse Markers

1901 Reverse, Original

1901 Reverse, Counterfeit

Rev. Marker 1 (Original)
Leaf R-5 is attached to the bough. Leaf has good detail.

Rev. Marker 1 (Counterfeit)
Leaf R-5 is not attached to the bough. Leaf has lost detail.

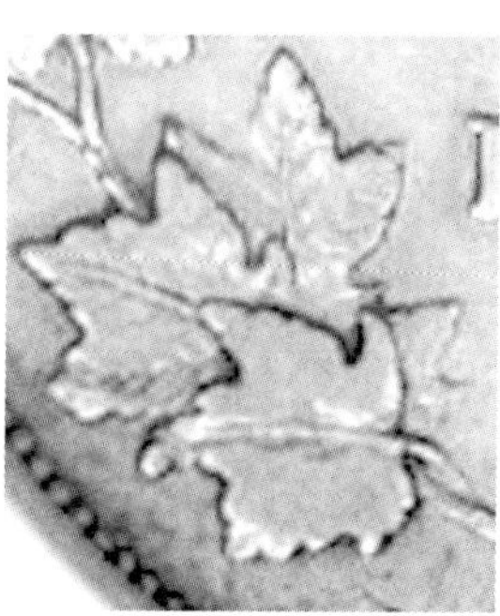

Rev. Marker 2 (Original)
Boughs are thin. Leaf L-1 has good detail.

Rev. Marker 2 (Counterfeit)
Boughs are thick. Leaf L-1 has little or no detail.

Rev. Marker 3 (Original)
The "S" in CENTS is not repunched

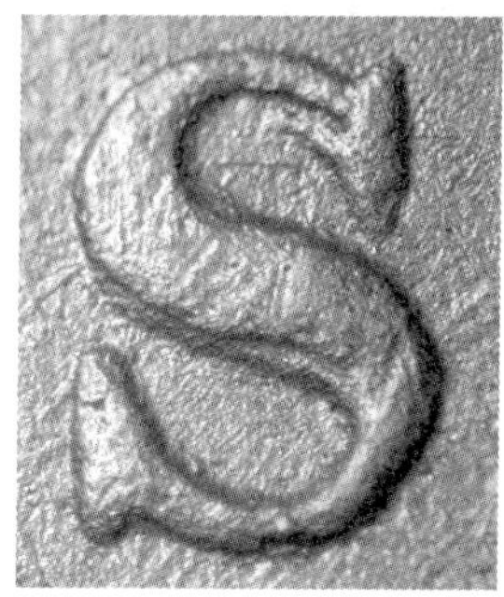

Rev. Marker 3 (Counterfeit)
Repunched "S" in CENTS

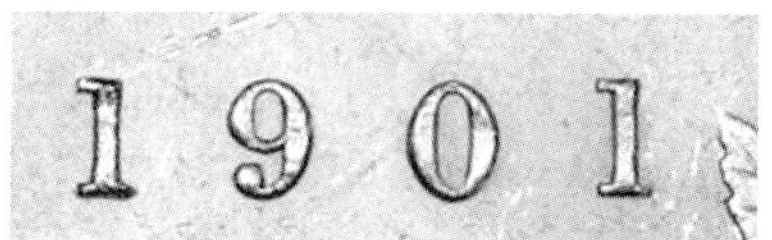

Rev. Marker 4 (Original)
1901 Date, Fine date digits
Open "9"

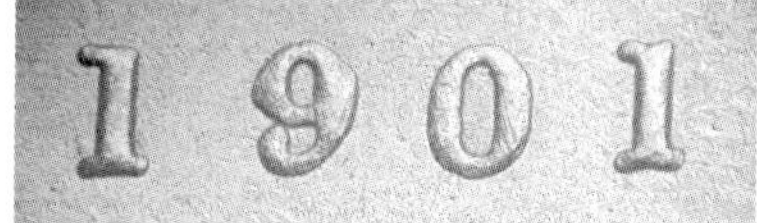

Rev. Marker 4 (Counterfeit)
1901 Date, Thick date digits
Closed "9"

Original 1872H fifty cent coin with repunched "S" used by counterfeiters as a model to produce counterfeit dies

As above, original 1872H fifty cent coin with repunched "S"

George V Fifty Cents

H K Replica, China, 1911, 1912, 1913, 1914, 1916, 1917, 1918, 1919, 1921, 1929, 1931, 1932, 1934, and 1936.

H K Replika issued an extensive list of counterfeit dates for George V coinage, even to the extent of using the wrong obverse and the incorrect legend on their 1911 copy.

The copying process always results in the loss of detail between the original and the copy which helps in identification. Also, the counterfeit designs are slightly larger than the original, which is smaller and more detailed.

Dates 1911 to 1936 have a common obverse punch, therefore a common obverse die. The coin copied by HK Replica was an EF-40 to AU-50 example, thus the counterfeits they produced are of that grade.

The reverse counterfeit punch was copied from a date in the 1911 to 1919 range. The last number was ground off and the resulting die had the final digit punched in. For 1921 and 1929 the last two digits were removed. It appears for 1931, 1932, 1934 and 1936, a new coin, this time AU to UNC, served to generate a new punch, and thus a new series of reverse dies.

Specifications	Original	Counterfeit
Composition:		
1911-1919	92.5% Ag, 7.5% Cu	98.9 to 99.9% Ag
1920-1936	80.0% Ag, 20.0% Cu	98.9 to 99.9% Ag
Weight:	11.66 grams	11.4 to 11.7 grams
Diameter	29.72 mm	29.68 to 29.74 mm
Thickness	2.0 mm	1.8 to 2.2 mm
Axis	↑↑	↑↑

GEORGE V FIFTY-CENT MARKERS, H K REPLICA, CHINA

OBVERSE MARKERS or PICKUP POINTS - ORIGINAL

1. Legend without "DEI GRA" (for 1911 only).
2. Strong portrait with clear detail of the bridge of nose and eyebrow.
3. Strong detail of the coronation robes, chains, decorations and ribbon.

OBVERSE MARKERS or PICKUP POINTS - COUNTERFEIT

1. Legend with "DEI GRA" (a new die with the correct legend was not cut for 1911).
2. Weak portrait with the bridge of the nose disappearing into the field, overly large eyebrow.
3. Weak detail of the coronation robes, chains, decoration, and ribbon.

REVERSE MARKERS or PICKUP POINTS - ORIGINAL

1. Leaves L-1 and L-2 have detail and separation.
2. Leaf R-7 has full detail across leaf.
3. Fine date digits.

REVERSE MARKERS or PICKUP POINTS - COUNTERFEIT

1. Leaves L-1 and L-2 are combined and have no definition.
2. Leaf R-7 has a flat centre with no detail.
3. Thick date digits.

George V Fifty Cents

1911 OBVERSE

1911 Obverse, Original
Obv. Marker 1: Without DIE GRA in legend

1911 Obverse, Counterfeit
Obv. Marker 1: Legend with DEI GRA
(a new die with the correct legend was not cut for 1911)

ORIGINAL Obverse Markers	COUNTERFEIT Obverse Markers

Obv. Marker 2 (Original) Strong portrait with clear detail of the bridge of nose and eyebrow	Obv. Marker 2 (Counterfeit) Weak portrait with the bridge of the nose disappearing into the field, overly large eyebrow

Obv. Marker 3 (Original) Strong detail of the coronation robes, chains, decorations and ribbon	Obv. Marker 3 (Counterfeit) Weak detail of the coronation robes, chains, decorations, and ribbon

George V Fifty Cents

1911 REVERSE

ORIGINAL Reverse Markers

COUNTERFEIT Reverse Markers

1911 Reverse, Original

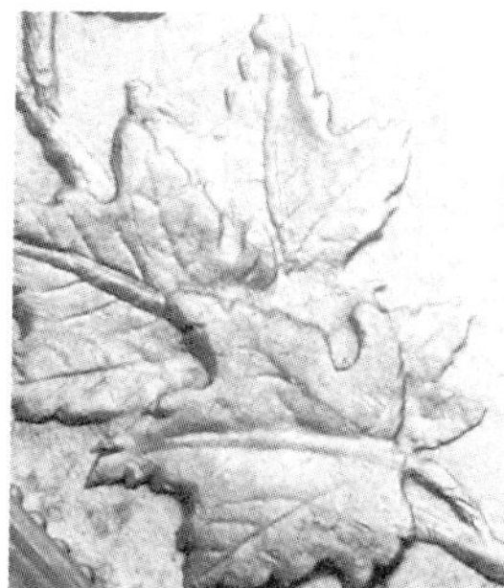

Rev. Marker 1 (Original)
Leaves L-1 and L-2 have detail and separation

Rev. Marker 1 (Counterfeit)
Leaves L-1 and L-2 are combined and have no definition

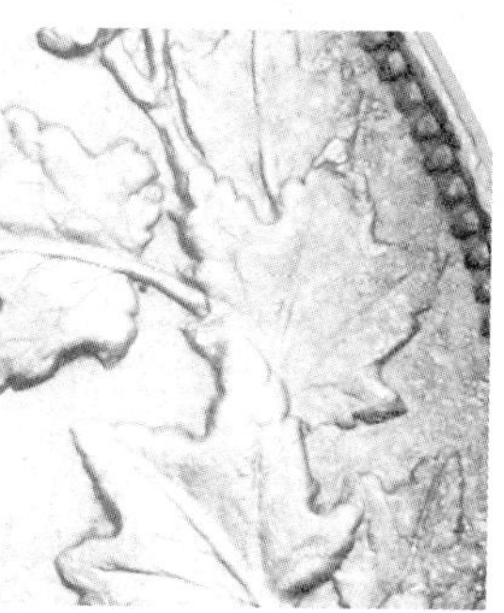

Rev. Marker 2 (Original)
Leaf R-7 has full detail across leaf

Rev. Marker 2 (Counterfeit)
Leaf R-7 has a flat centre with no detail

1911 Reverse, Counterfeit

Rev. Marker 3 (Original)
1911 Date, Fine date digits
Closed "9", Small "1's"

Rev. Marker 3 (Counterfeit)
1911 Date, Thick date digits
Open "9", Large "1's"

George V Fifty Cents

1912 REVERSE

1912 Reverse, Original

1912 Reverse, Counterfeit

ORIGINAL Reverse Markers	COUNTERFEIT Reverse Markers
 Rev. Marker 1 (Original) Leaves L-1 and L-2 have detail and separation	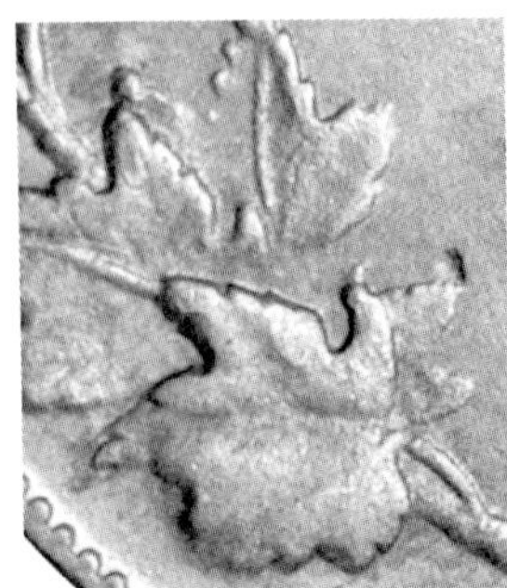 Rev. Marker 1 (Counterfeit) Leaves L-1 and L-2 are combined and have no definition
 Rev. Marker 2 (Original) Leaf R-7 has full detail across leaf	 Rev. Marker 2 (Counterfeit) Leaf R-7 has a flat centre with no detail

Rev. Marker 3 (Original)
1912 Date, Fine date digits

Rev. Marker 3 (Counterfeit)
1912 Date, Thick date digits
Large "2"

George V Fifty Cents

1913 REVERSE

ORIGINAL
Reverse Markers

COUNTERFEIT
Reverse Markers

1913 Reverse, Original

Rev. Marker 1 (Original)
Leaves L-1 and L-2 have detail and separation

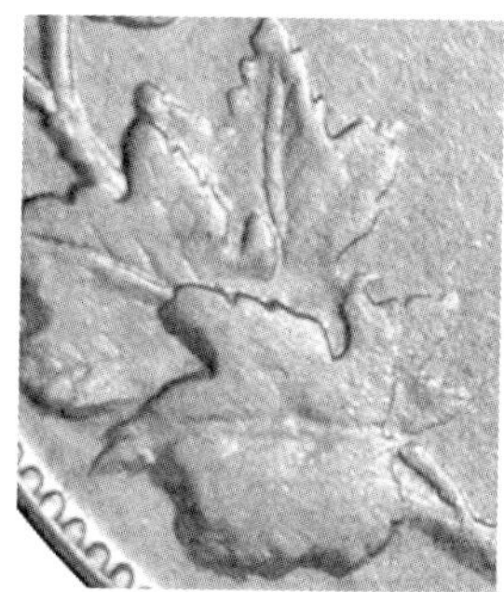

Rev. Marker 1 (Counterfeit)
Leaves L-1 and L-2 are combined and have no definition

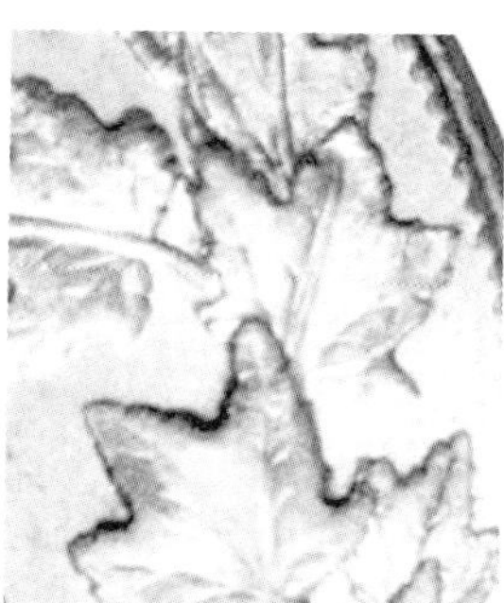

Rev. Marker 2 (Original)
Leaf R-7 has full detail across leaf

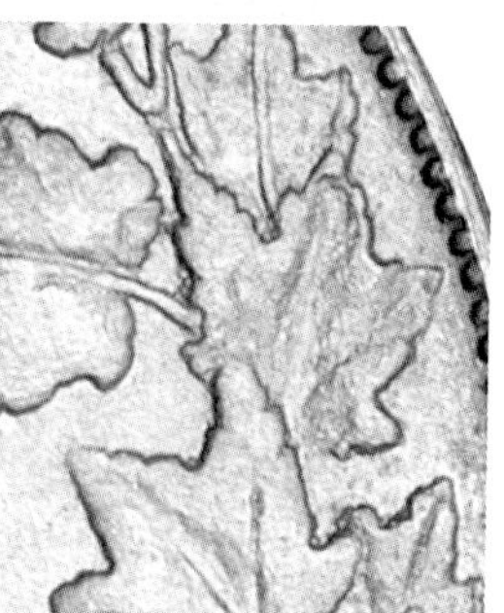

Rev. Marker 2 (Counterfeit)
Leaf R-7 has a flat centre with no detail

1913 Reverse, Counterfeit

Rev. Marker 3 (Original)
1913 Date, Fine date digits
Open "3"

Rev. Marker 3 (Counterfeit)
1913 Date, Thick date digits
Closed "3"

George V Fifty Cents

1914 REVERSE

1914 Reverse, Original

1914 Reverse, Counterfeit

ORIGINAL Reverse Markers

Rev. Marker 1 (Original)
Leaves L-1 and L-2 have detail and separation

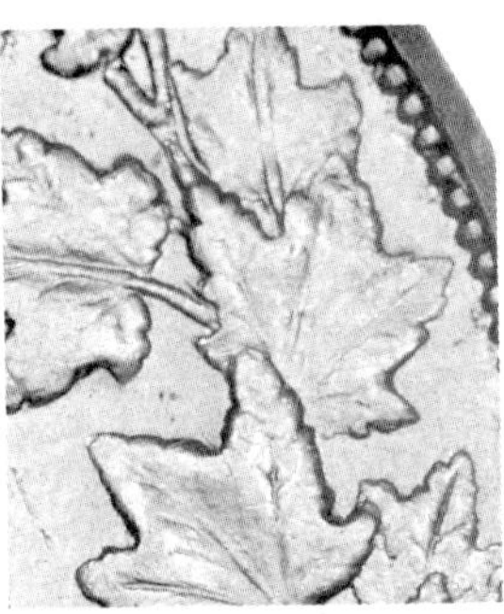

Rev. Marker 2 (Original)
Leaf R-7 has full detail across leaf

COUNTERFEIT Reverse Markers

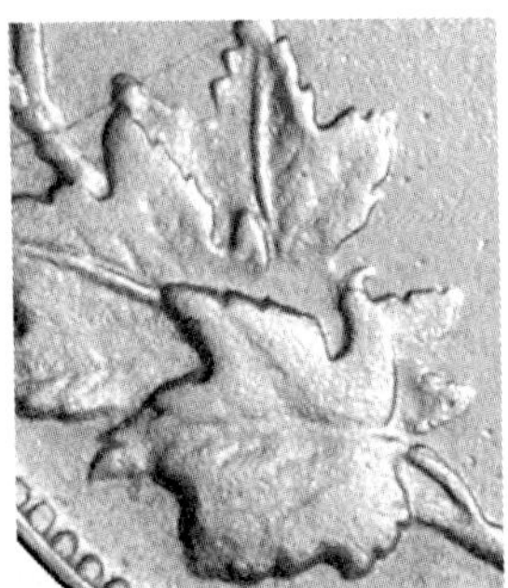

Rev. Marker 1 (Counterfeit)
Leaves L-1 and L-2 are combined and have no definition

Rev. Marker 2 (Counterfeit)
Leaf R-7 has a flat centre with no detail

Rev. Marker 3 (Original)
1914 Date, Fine date digits
Flared "4"

Rev. Marker 3 (Counterfeit)
1914 Date, Thick date digits
Large plain "4"

George V Fifty Cents

1916 REVERSE

1916 Reverse, Original

1916 Reverse, Counterfeit

ORIGINAL Reverse Markers

Rev. Marker 1 (Original)
Leaves L-1 and L-2 have detail and separation

Rev. Marker 2 (Original)
Leaf R-7 has full detail across leaf

COUNTERFEIT Reverse Markers

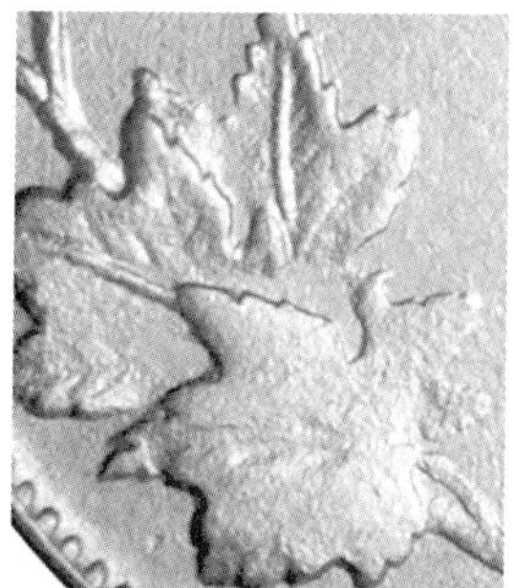

Rev. Marker 1 (Counterfeit)
Leaves L-1 and L-2 are combined and have no definition

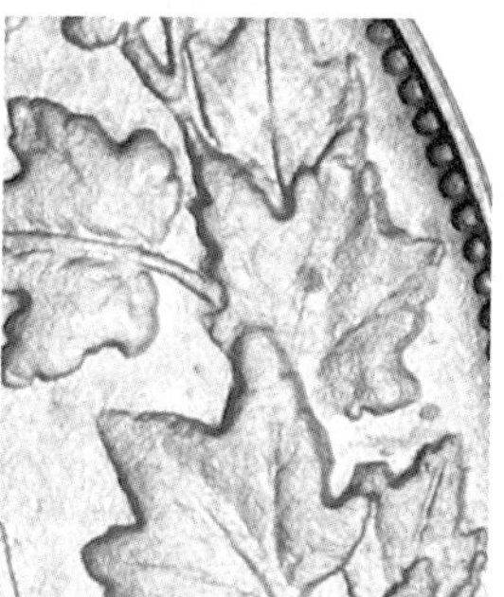

Rev. Marker 2 (Counterfeit)
Leaf R-7 has a flat centre with no detail

Rev. Marker 3 (Original)
1916 Date, Fine date digits
Small even "6"

Rev. Marker 3 (Counterfeit)
1916 Date, Thick date digits
Large high "6"

George V Fifty Cents

1917 REVERSE

1917 Reverse, Original

1917 Reverse, Counterfeit

ORIGINAL Reverse Markers	COUNTERFEIT Reverse Markers
 Rev. Marker 1 (Original) Leaves L-1 and L-2 have detail and separation	 Rev. Marker 1 (Counterfeit) Leaves L-1 and L-2 are combined and have no definition
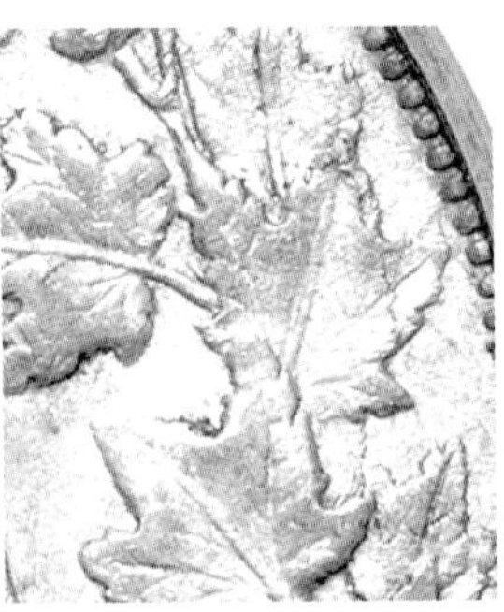 Rev. Marker 2 (Original) Leaf R-7 has full detail across leaf	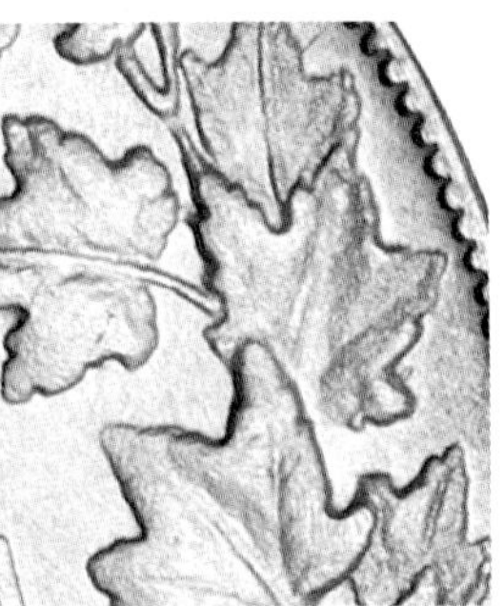 Rev. Marker 2 (Counterfeit) Leaf R-7 has a flat centre with no detail

Rev. Marker 3 (Original)
1917 Date, Fine date digits

Rev. Marker 3 (Counterfeit)
1917 Date, Thick date digits
Large high "7"

George V Fifty Cents

1918 REVERSE

1918 Reverse, Original

1918 Reverse, Counterfeit

ORIGINAL Reverse Markers	COUNTERFEIT Reverse Markers

Rev. Marker 1 (Original) Leaves L-1 and L-2 have detail and separation	Rev. Marker 1 (Counterfeit) Leaves L-1 and L-2 are combined and have no definition
	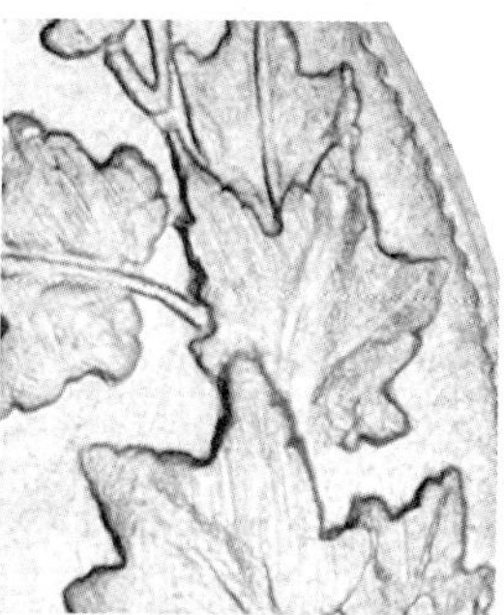
Rev. Marker 2 (Original) Leaf R-7 has full detail across leaf	Rev. Marker 2 (Counterfeit) Leaf R-7 has a flat centre with no detail

Rev. Marker 3 (Original)
1918 Date, Fine date digits

Rev. Marker 3 (Counterfeit)
1918 Date, Thick date digits
Large low "8"

George V Fifty Cents

1919 REVERSE

1919 Reverse, Original

1919 Reverse, Counterfeit

ORIGINAL Reverse Markers

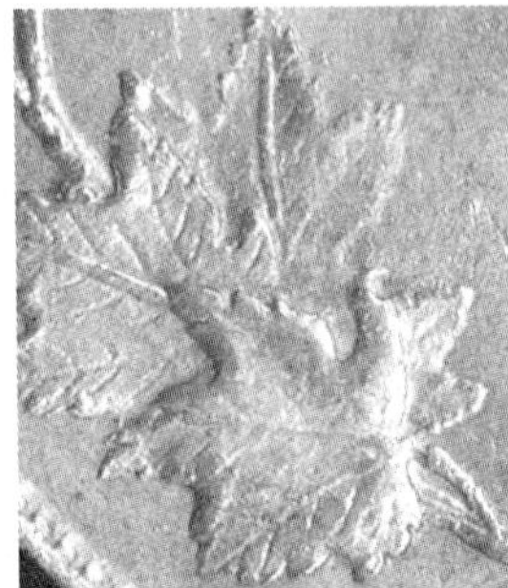

Rev. Marker 1 (Original)
Leaves L-1 and L-2 have detail and separation

Rev. Marker 2 (Original)
Leaf R-7 has full detail across leaf

COUNTERFEIT Reverse Markers

Rev. Marker 1 (Counterfeit)
Leaves L-1 and L-2 are combined and have no definition

Rev. Marker 2 (Counterfeit)
Leaf R-7 has a flat centre with no detail

Rev. Marker 3 (Original)
1919 Date, Fine date digits

Rev. Marker 3 (Counterfeit)
1919 Date, Thick ate digits
Open last "9"

George V Fifty Cents

1921 REVERSE

ORIGINAL
Reverse Markers

COUNTERFEIT
Reverse Markers

1921 Reverse, Original

Rev. Marker 1 (Original)
Leaves L-1 and L-2 have detail and separation

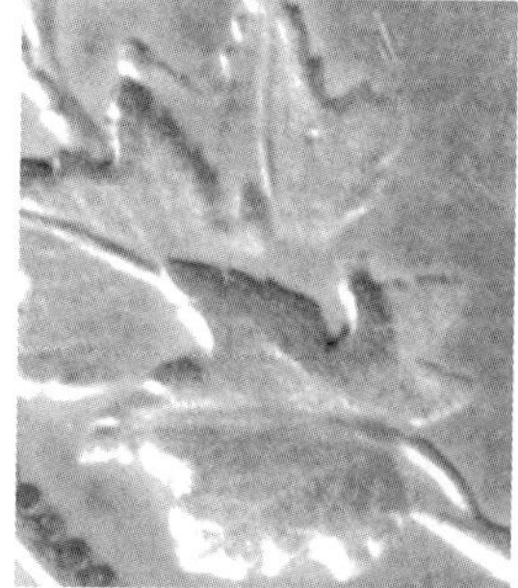

Rev. Marker 1 (Counterfeit)
Leaves L-1 and L-2 are combined and have no definition

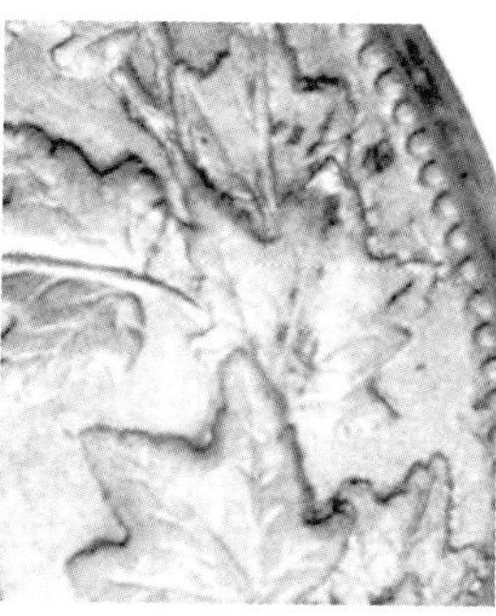

Rev. Marker 2 (Original)
Leaf R-7 has full detail across leaf

Rev. Marker 2 (Counterfeit)
Leaf R-7 has a flat centre with no detail

1921 Reverse, Counterfeit

Rev. Marker 3 (Original)
1921 Date, Fine date digits
Slanting last "1"

Rev. Marker 3 (Counterfeit)
1921 Date, Thick date digits
Large "2", Upright last "1"

George V Fifty Cents

1929 REVERSE

1929 Reverse, Original

1929 Reverse, Counterfeit

ORIGINAL Reverse Markers	COUNTERFEIT Reverse Markers

Rev. Marker 1 (Original) Leaves L-1 and L-2 have detail and separation	Rev. Marker 1 (Counterfeit) Leaves L-1 and L-2 are combined and have no definition
	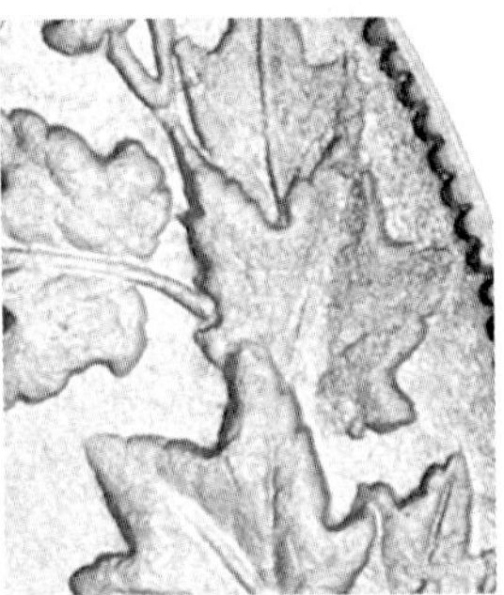
Rev. Marker 2 (Original) Leaf R-7 has full detail across leaf	Rev. Marker 2 (Counterfeit) Leaf R-7 has a flat centre with no detail

Rev. Marker 3 (Original)
1929 Date, Fine date digits

Rev. Marker 3 (Counterfeit)
1929 Date, Thick date digits
Large "2"

George V Fifty Cents

1931 REVERSE

1931 Reverse, Original

1931 Reverse, Counterfeit

ORIGINAL Reverse Markers	COUNTERFEIT Reverse Markers
 Rev. Marker 1 (Original) Leaves L-1 and L-2 have detail and separation	 Rev. Marker 1 (Counterfeit) Leaves L-1 and L-2 are combined and have no definition
 Rev. Marker 2 (Original) Leaf R-7 has full detail across leaf	 Rev. Marker 2 (Counterfeit) Leaf R-7 has a flat centre with no detail

Rev. Marker 3 (Original)
1931 Date, Fine date digits

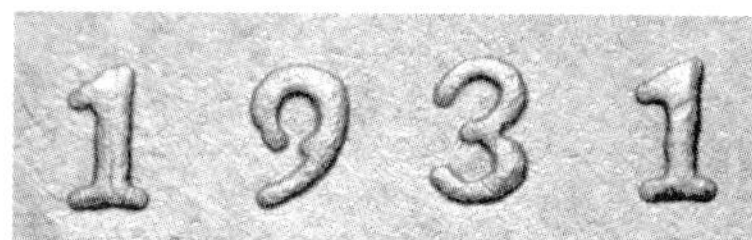

Rev. Marker 3 (Counterfeit)
1931 Date, Thick date digits
High "3"

George V Fifty Cents

1932 REVERSE

1932 Reverse, Original

1932 Reverse, Counterfeit

ORIGINAL Reverse Markers	COUNTERFEIT Reverse Markers

Rev. Marker 1 (Original)
Leaves L-1 and L-2 have detail and separation

Rev. Marker 1 (Counterfeit)
Leaves L-1 and L-2 are combined and have no definition

Rev. Marker 2 (Original)
Leaf R-7 has full detail across leaf

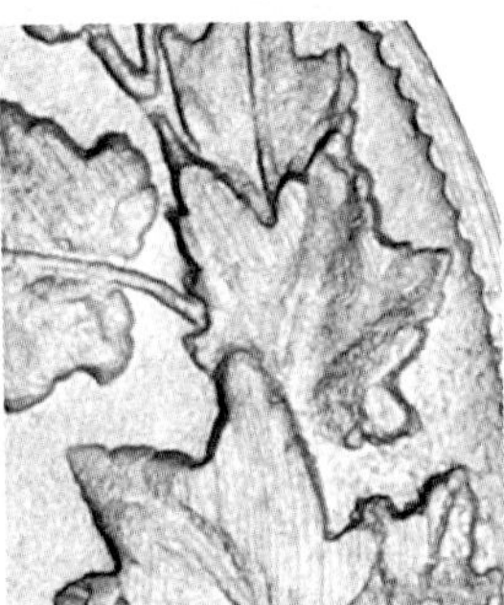

Rev. Marker 2 (Counterfeit)
Leaf R-7 has a flat centre with no detail

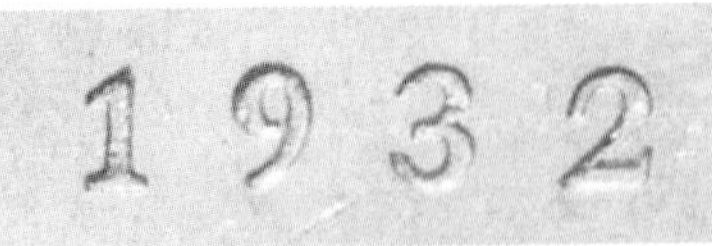

Rev. Marker 3 (Original)
1932 Date, Fine date digits
Open "3", Small "2"

Rev. Marker (Counterfeit)
1932 Date, Thick date digits
Large closed "3", Large "2"

George V Fifty Cents

1934 REVERSE

ORIGINAL
Reverse Markers

COUNTERFEIT
Reverse Markers

1934 Reverse, Original

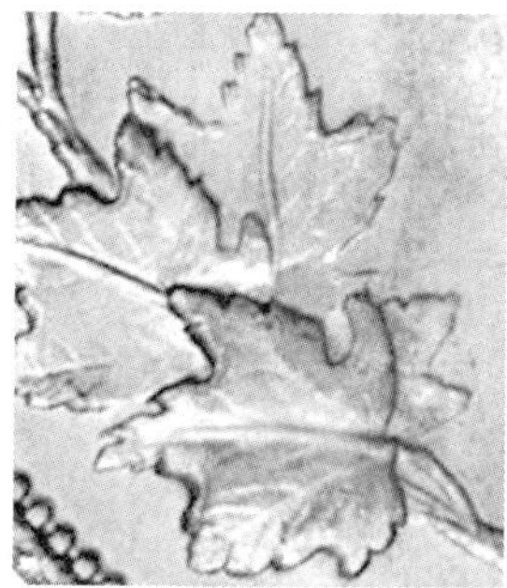

Rev. Marker 1 (Original)
Leaves L-1 and L-2 have detail and separation

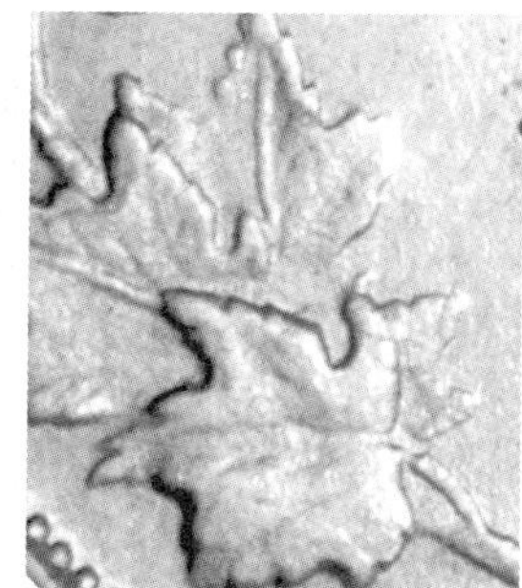

Rev. Marker 1 (Counterfeit)
Leaves L-1 and L-2 are combined and have no definition

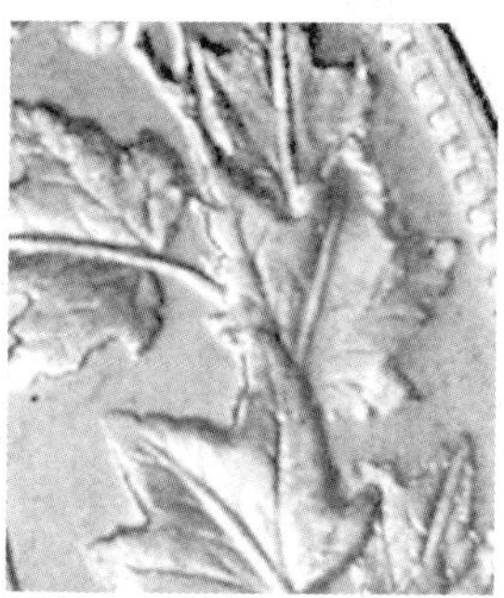

Rev. Marker 2 (Original)
Leaf R-7 has full detail across leaf

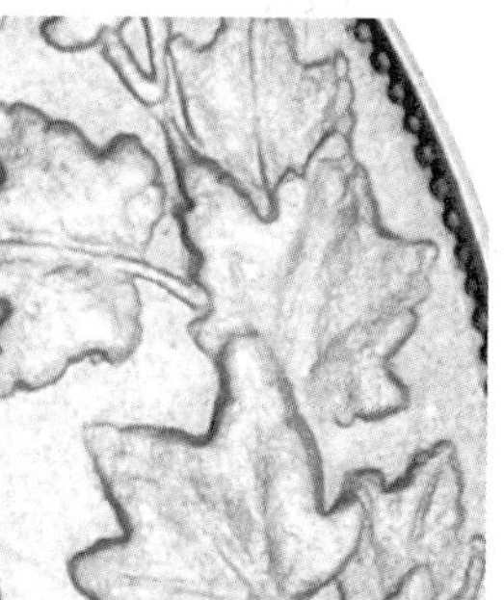

Rev. Marker 2 (Counterfeit)
Leaf R-7 has a flat centre with no detail

1934 Reverse, Counterfeit

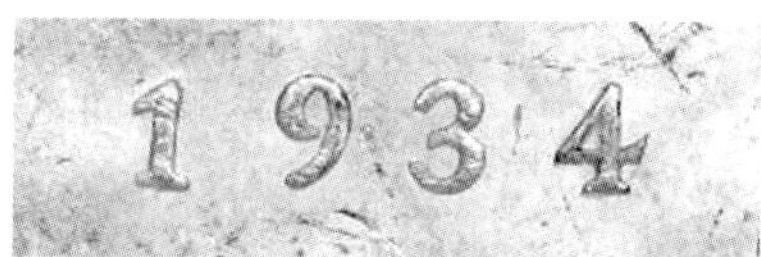

Rev. Marker 3 (Original)
1934 Date, Fine date digits
Open "3", Flared "4"

Rev. Marker 3 (Counterfeit)
1934 Date, Thick date digits
Closed "3", Plain "4"

George V Fifty Cents

1936 REVERSE

1936 Reverse, Original

1936 Reverse, Counterfeit

ORIGINAL Reverse Markers

Rev. Marker 1 (Original)
Leaves L-1 and L-2 have detail and separation

Rev. Marker 2 (Original)
Leaf R-7 has full detail across leaf

COUNTERFEIT Reverse Markers

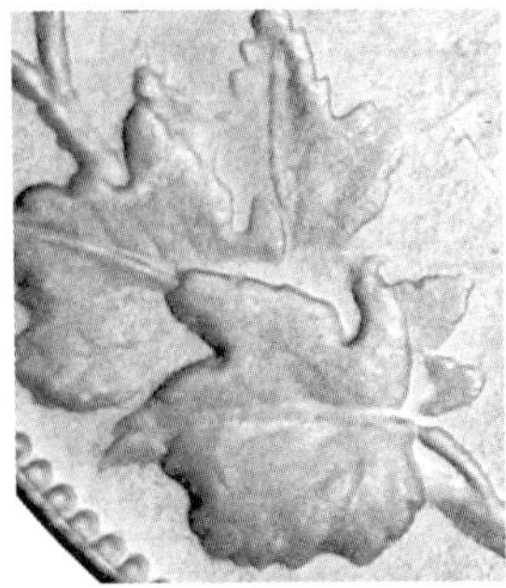

Rev. Marker 1 (Counterfeit)
Leaves L-1 and L-2 are combined and have no definition

Rev. Marker 2 (Counterfeit)
Leaf R-7 has a flat centre with no detail

Rev. Marker 3 (Original)
1936 Date, Fine date digits
Open "3", Small "6"

Rev. Marker 3 (Counterfeit)
1936 Date, Thick date digits
Closed "3", Large "6"

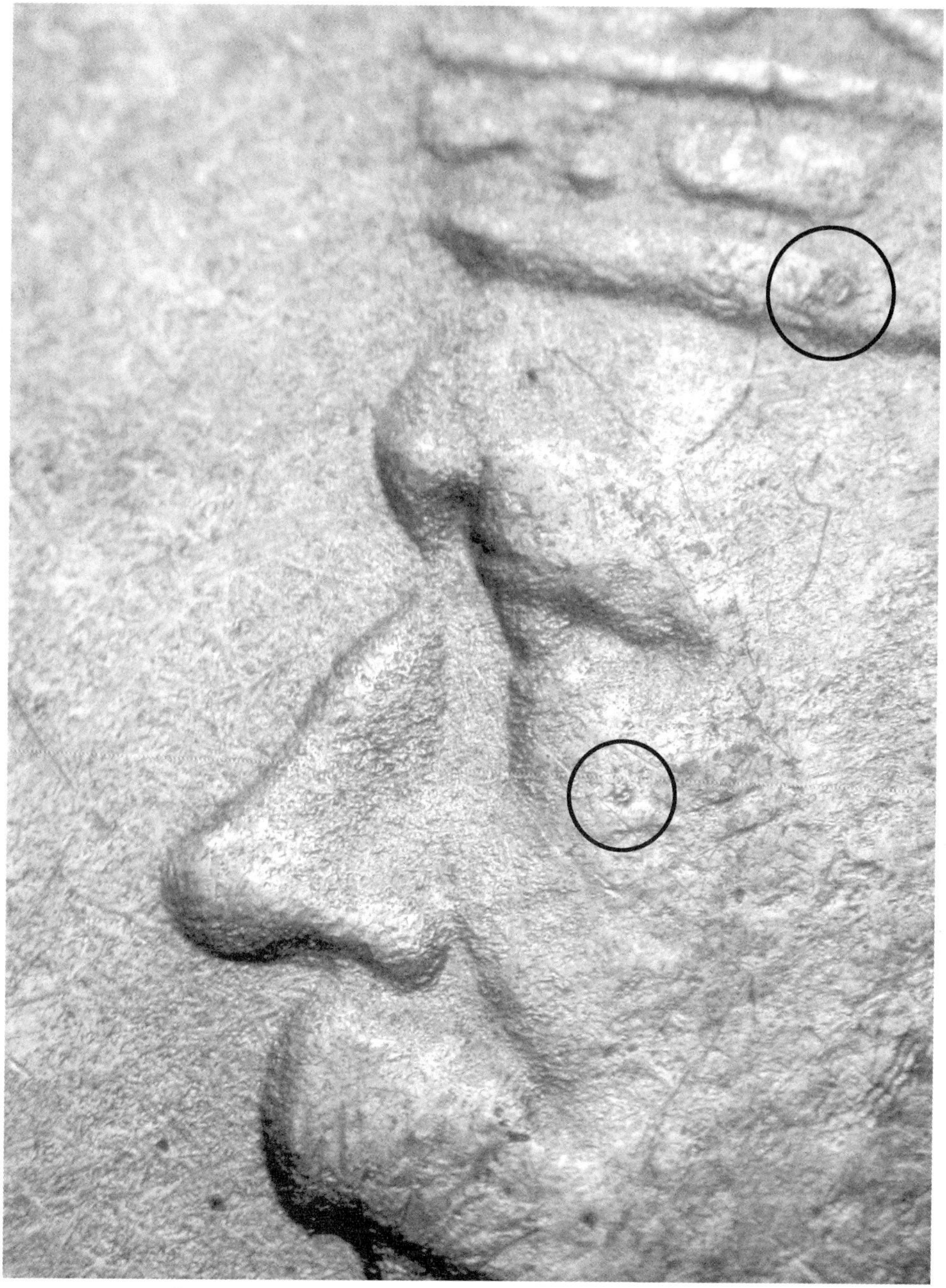

This image illustrates the rough surface a spark-erosion die leaves behind after striking.

APPENDICES

BULLION VALUES

Silver and gold coins and other numismatic items are often bought by dealers for their bullion value, which is the value of the pure precious metals which they contain. The weight of the precious metals is expressed in grams or troy ounces, not in avoirdupois ounces. A troy ounce is greater that an avoirdupois ounce.

1 Troy Ounce = 31.1035 grams
1 Avoirdupois ounce = 28.349 grams

GOLD

The quantity of pure gold in gold coins is calculated by multiplying the gold fineness or purity of the coin by its weight in troy ounces or grams. Gold purity can also be expressed in karats, a 24-part system with 24 karats equalling pure gold, 22 karats equalling 22 parts gold to two parts base metal, 18 karats equalling 18 parts gold to six parts base metal, etc.

KARATS	FINENESS	PURITY
24	.999	99.9%
22	.916	91.6%
18	.750	75.0%
14	.585	58.5%
10	.417	41.7%
9	.375	37.5%

One 14-karat or .583 fine gold coin weighing one troy ounce contains one ounce x .585 = .585 troy ounces of pure gold. If gold is worth $1,500 per troy ounce, then this coin is worth $1,500 x .585 = $877.50. (See extended charts on the following page.)

SILVER

The quantity of pure silver in silver coins is calculated by multiplying the silver fineness or purity of the coin by its weight in troy ounces.

DESCRIPTION	FINENESS	PURITY
Pure	.9999	99.99%
Fine	.999	99.90%
Sterling	.925	92.50%
Coin	.800	80.00%
Coin	.500	50.00%

An .800 fine silver coin weighing one troy ounce contains 1 x .800 = .800 troy ounces of pure silver. If silver is worth $30 an ounce, then this coin is worth $30 x .800 = $24. (See extended charts on the following page.)

CONTENT TABLES

The following tables are comprised of classic and modern coins. The classic coins of Volume One are listed, but only a partial listing for the modern coins contained in Volume Two, For a full listing of the modern coin series 1967 to 2014 please refer to *Canadian Coins, Volume Two*, 5th edition.

GOLD CONTENT OF CANADIAN GOLD COINS

Date and Denom.	Mint Mark	Gross Weight Grams	Fineness	Pure Gold Content Grams	Troy Oz.
25 cents	2010-2011, 2014	0.50	.9999	0.50	.016
50 cents	2011-2014	1.27	.9999	1.27	.040
£1 (Sovereign)	1908C-1910C	7.99	.917	7.32	.236
£1 (Sovereign)	1911C-1919C	7.99	.917	7.32	.236
$2 Newfoundland	1865-1888	3.33	.917	3.05	.100
$5	1912-1914	8.36	.900	7.52	.242
$5 Maple Leaf	1982 to date	3.11	.9999	3.11	.100
$10	1912-1914	16.72	.900	15.05	.484
$10 Maple Leaf	1982 to date	7.78	.9999	7.78	.250
$20	1967	18.27	.900	16.45	.529
$20 Maple Leaf	1986 to date	15.57	.9999	15.57	.500
$50 Maple Leaf	1979 to date	31.10	.9999	31.10	1.000
$100	1976 (Unc.)	13.33	.583	7.78	.250
$100	1976 (Proof)	16.96	.917	15.55	.500
$100	1977-1986	16.96	.917	15.55	.500
$100	1987-2003	13.33	.583	7.78	.250
$100	2004 to date	12.00	.583	7.00	.225
$150 Hologram, Lunar	2000-2003	13.61	.750	10.20	.328
$150 Hologram, Lunar	2004-2011	11.84	.750	8.88	.285
$150 Blessings	2009-2014	10.40	.99999	10.40	.334
$175	1992	16.97	.916	15.556	.500
$200	1990-2003	17.13	.916	15.703	.500
$200	2004 to date	16.00	.916	14.67	.471
$300 (50 mm diameter)	2002-2009	60.00	.5833	35.00	1.125
$300 (40 mm diameter)	2005-2008	45.00	.5833	26.25	.844
$350 Thick	1998-2003	38.05	.99999	38.05	1.222
$350 Thin	2004-2013	35.00	.99999	35.00	1.125
$500	2007-2013	155.76	.9999	155.76	5.010
$2,500	2007-2014	1000.00	.9999	1000.00	32.150

SILVER CONTENT OF CANADIAN SILVER COINS

Denom.	Date	Gross Weight Grams	Fineness	Silver Content Grams	Troy Oz.
5¢	1858-1919, 1998	1.16	.925	1.08	.035
5¢	1920-1921	1.16	.800	.933	.030
10¢	1858-1919	2.33	.925	2.146	.069
10¢	1920-1967	2.33	.800	1.866	.060
10¢	1967-1968	2.33	.500	1.170	.038
10¢	1997-2004	2.40	.925	2.22	.071
25¢	1870-1919	5.81	.925	5.370	.173
25¢	1920-1967	5.83	.800	4.665	.150
25¢	1967-1968	5.83	.500	2.923	.094
25¢	1992 -2009	5.90	.925	5.458	.175
50¢	1870-1919	11.66	.925	10.792	.347
50¢	1920-1967	11.66	.800	9.330	.300
50¢	1995-2005	9.30	.925	8.603	.277
$1	1935-1967	23.30	.800	18.661	.600
$1	1971-1991	23.30	.500	11.65	.375
$1	1992-2002	25.18	.925	23.29	.750
$5 Montreal Olympics	1973-1976	24.30	.925	22.48	.720
$5 Maple Leaf	1988 to date	31.04	.9999	31.1035	1.000
$10 Montreal Olympics	1973-1976	48.60	.925	44.95	1.440
$10	2005-2006	25.175	.9999	25.175	.810
$10 Blue Whale	2010	27.78	.925	25.70	.826
$10	2010-2014	15.90	.9999	15.90	.511
$15 Lunar	1998-2009	33.63	.925	31.108	1.000
$15 Vignettes	2008-2009	30.00	.925	27.75	.890
$20 Calgary Olympics	1985-1987	34.07	.925	31.51	1.010
$20 Transportation	1990-2003	31.10	.925	28.77	.925
$20	2003-2014	31.39	.9999	31.39	1.010
$25 Vancouver Olympics	2007-2009	27.78	.925	25.70	.826
$30	2005-2008	31.50	.925	29.137	.937
$50	2006-2014	156.36	.9999	156.34	5.026
$250	2007-2014	1000.00	.9999	1000.00	32.151

APPLICATION FOR RCNA MEMBERSHIP / DEMANDE D'ADHÉSION À L' ARNC

Application for membership in **The Royal Canadian Numismatic Association** may be made by any reputable party upon payment of the required dues.
Les demandes d'adhésion à **l'Association royale de numismatique du Canada** peuvent être faites par une partie de bonne réputation sur paiement des frais exigés.

The Royal Canadian Numismatic Association · L'Association royale de numismatique du Canada · Established · Fondée 1950

❑ Mr. / M. ❑ Mrs. / Mme ❑ Ms. / Mlle
❑ Renewal / Renouvèlement ❑ Reinstatement / Réintégration *previous #*______

Full Name / Nom *for family membership include name of spouse / pour une adhésion familiale, inclure le nom du conjoint*

Mailing Address / Adresse postale complète

City / Ville Province / State / État Country / Pays Postal Code/Zip

Phone / N^o^ de téléphone Email / Courriel

Signature of Applicant / Signature du demandeur *W.K. Cross & Randy Ash* Sponsored By / Commandité par

Junior applicants (under age 18), state birth date / pour une adhésion junior (moins de 18 ans), inclure la date de naissance: ________

My numismatic speciality / spécialité numismatique (*optional/optionnel*): ________

❑ *I would like to be contacted by a mentor who also has my speciality.*
J'aimerais être mis en contact avec un mentor qui partage mes intérêt numismatiques.

Membership Types: *Check only one* **Types d'adhésion**: *cochez une seule option*	Standard		Digital*	
	1 year	2 year	1 year	2 year
Regular: Canada and USA residents, age 18+ **Régulier:** adresses Canadiennes et aux États-unis (18 ans et plus)	❑ $42.00	❑ $82.00	❑ $32.00	❑ $62.00
Regular: Foreign (non-USA) **Régulier:** étranger (autre que les États-unis)	❑ $78.00	❑ $154.00	❑ $32.00	❑ $62.00
Junior: Applicants under age 18 *must be sponsored by a parent or guardian* *Les membres de moins de 18 ans doivent être commandités par un parent ou un gardien*	❑ $25.50	❑ $49.00	❑ $18.50	❑ $35.00
Family: Canada and USA residents. Member, spouse & children under age 18, (one printed and mailed *CN Journal* only) **Familial**: membre, époux (se) et enfants de moins de 18 ans. Un seul Journal	❑ $44.00	❑ $92.00	❑ $32.00	❑ $62.00
Corporate / Entreprises: Clubs, Societies / Sociétés, Libraries / Librairies & non-profit organizations / et autres organisations sans but lucratif	❑ $42.00	❑ $82.00	N.A.	N.A.
Life Membership / Adhésion à Vie:**	❑ $1,195.00		❑ $895.00	
Life Membership Senior: (65+) **Adhésion à Vie Aîné:**** (65 ans et plus)	❑ $895.00		❑ $695.00	
Life Membership Foreign: Adhésion à Vie Etranger:	❑ $2,195.00		❑ $895.00	

Dues shown below are in Canadian$ to Canadian addresses and US$ to all other addresses and are exempt from Canadian sales taxes.

* (A Digital Membership includes all of the benefits of membership except a printed copy of *The CN Journal*.)

** (After one year of regular membership. Details of payment plan available on request.) Mail completed application with dues to:

Les cotisations sont indiquées en dollars canadiens à des adresses canadiennes, ou en dollars américains à toutes les autres adresses. Les cotisations sont exonérées de taxes sur les ventes domestiques.

* (Adhésions numériques comprennent tous les avantages de l'adhésion, sauf une copie imprimée de *Le Journal canadien de numismatique*.)

** (Après un an comme membre régulier. Détails du plan de paiement disponibles sur demande.) Envoyez la demande d'adhésion dûment complétée et le paiement à :

The Royal Canadian Numismatic Association
l'Association royale de numismatique du Canada
5694 Highway #7 East, Suite 432, Markham ON Canada L3P 1B4
Phone / Tel: 647–401–4014 Fax / Télécopie: 905–472–9645 Email / Courriel: *info@rcna.ca*
Apply online at: www.rcna.ca/paydues.php